T0369759

Apocalypticism
IN THE
Bible and Its World

Apocalypticism

IN THE

Bible and Its World

A COMPREHENSIVE INTRODUCTION

Frederick J. Murphy

Baker Academic
a division of Baker Publishing Group
Grand Rapids, Michigan

© 2012 by Frederick J. Murphy

Published by Baker Academic
a division of Baker Publishing Group
P.O. Box 6287, Grand Rapids, MI 49516-6287
www.bakeracademic.com

Printed in the United States of America

All rights reserved. No part of this publication may be reproduced, stored in
a retrieval system, or transmitted in any form or by any means—for example,
electronic, photocopy, recording—without the prior written permission of the
publisher. The only exception is brief quotations in printed reviews.

Library of Congress Cataloging-in-Publication Data
Murphy, Frederick James.
    Apocalypticism in the Bible and its world : a comprehensive intro-
duction / Frederick J. Murphy.
        p.   cm.
    Includes bibliographical references (p.   ) and indexes.
    ISBN 978-0-8010-3978-2 (pbk.)
    1. Apocalyptic literature—History and criticism. 2. Eschatology—
Biblical teaching. 3. Bible—Criticism, interpretation, etc. I. Title.
    BS646.M87 2012
    220′.046—dc23   2012007216

12   13   14   15   16   17   18   7   6   5   4   3   2   1

In keeping with biblical principles of
creation stewardship, Baker Publishing Group advocates the responsible
use of our natural resources. As a
member of the Green Press Initiative, our company uses recycled
paper when possible. The text paper
of this book is composed in part of
post-consumer waste.

With deep gratitude

I dedicate this book
to the many medical professionals
who have generously given me their time,
compassion, and expertise
over the past five years.
They spend their lives in helping others.

"No one has greater love than this,
to lay down one's life for one's friends."
(John 15:13)

Contents

Illustrations

Foreword

On September 13, 2011, our esteemed colleague and friend Dr. Frederick J. Murphy succumbed to complications of multiple myeloma, a devastating disease he had fought heroically and with dignity since his diagnosis five years before. As this book, written entirely during his illness, attests, Rick's death is a true loss not only to his family and friends but also to all who esteem learning and the advancement of knowledge.

Rick was a singular person. As a husband and father, colleague and scholar, teacher and mentor, he embodied qualities of honesty, fidelity, good humor, and compassion that drew people to him and made them glad to count him their friend. The psalmist may have asked, "What is man, O God, that you should be mindful of him? A human being, that you should pay him heed?" Yet we know there are people who embody characteristics that, by even the toughest standards, earn our deepest respect and merit God's attention as well. Rick was just such a person.

Rick was born and raised in the College Hill neighborhood of Worcester, Massachusetts, just a few streets away from the College of the Holy Cross, where he ultimately would spend twenty-eight years teaching. After graduating as a mathematics major from Harvard University in 1971, Rick joined the Society of Jesus and spent seven years as a Jesuit, learning about the Society's educational vision and becoming formed by its spirituality. He graduated again from Harvard in 1984, now with a doctorate in New Testament and Christian Origins.

No longer a Jesuit, Rick joined the Department of Religious Studies at Holy Cross in 1983. During his tenure at the College, he exemplified what it means to teach, to do research, to mentor, and to serve wholeheartedly at a liberal arts school that is both Catholic and Jesuit. Alongside his research, he became a significant though unassuming presence on campus, motivated always by his commitment to fairness and justice. In recognition of his scholarly and campus accomplishments, in 2007 Rick was appointed the College's first Class of 1956 Professor of New Testament.

Rick Murphy was the author of numerous scholarly articles and seven books, including *The Religious World of Jesus: An Introduction to Second Temple Palestinian Judaism*, which received the Alpha Sigma Nu Book Award in 1991, and *Early Judaism: The Exile to the Time of Jesus*. But as much as his scholarship meant to him, Rick also knew and loved politics, and (in good Jesuit fashion!) he was passionate about a faith that does justice. His next book, after the present one, would have been about the contemporary political landscape in the United States. For him, no study of history or ancient texts could be complete without thoroughly thinking about what events and ideas mean, how they change the lives of those who live them, and what they teach us about how we might better live our own lives.

Scripture in particular captured Rick's mind and imagination. Scripture: texts to be studied and treasured; not artifacts of a bygone age but life-giving pages that guide and sustain communities of faith, generation after generation. Rick was fascinated by the way ancient texts and ideas shaped human horizons, and he relished the chance to think and talk about how the world gets to be the way that it is. This, his last book, shows how much politics and religion were of enduring interest to him.

It is not surprising that some thirteen years ago Rick published a commentary on the Book of Revelation. The reality of empire and the scars it left made an ancient writer—a seer—wonder about the world and its history. If the "new heavens and the new earth" of which Revelation speaks, as Isaiah spoke centuries earlier—if that vision were to vanish like a pool in the desert, then the dragon wins. But the seer saw a different ending to the human story. And so did Rick.

William Reiser, SJ
Alan Avery-Peck
Alice L. Laffey
Department of Religious Studies
College of the Holy Cross

Acknowledgments

Many people helped me during the writing of this book. The project was initially to cover the entire period from the ancient Near East to American life today. That project was unwieldy, and, following the wise advice of the editors at Baker Academic, I wrote just about the ancient period. I did, however, do extensive research and writing on the later period, which I hope will eventually be published. In that work I was helped substantially by two colleagues at Holy Cross, Prof. Mathew N. Schmalz and Prof. Anthony J. Kuzniewski. They read and critiqued several chapters, and I was fortunate to benefit from their wide knowledge, sharp analysis, and personal encouragement.

My reliance on many who study apocalypticism today will be obvious both from my citations and from the centrality of their ideas to this presentation. I am especially indebted to the work of John Joseph Collins and Adela Yarbro Collins. I did not consult them during the writing, but I resorted to their vast array of studies constantly. Other scholars who have especially influenced my work are George W. E. Nickelsburg, James C. VanderKam, Richard J. Clifford, and Richard A. Horsley. Many other wonderful scholars are also due thanks, and there is no way I could possibly list them all here. I refer the reader to my long list of works cited.

Holy Cross has been my professional home for almost thirty years. It continues to be an extraordinary place to work. It combines in an exemplary way focus on the students and excellent teaching with generous support for faculty research. I am especially grateful for the support of the Dean, Timothy R. Austin, PhD, and the president, Rev. Michael C. McFarland, SJ, for their support. The Department of Religious Studies is made up of accomplished, dedicated scholars. Their support has been invaluable and is deeply appreciated.

The Holy Cross class of 1956 did me the honor, on the occasion of their fiftieth anniversary, of awarding me an endowed chair: the Class of 1956

Professor of New Testament. Their financial and moral support has helped me tremendously over the past five years.

I feel privileged to teach the students of Holy Cross. They are an impressive group of people, to whom I dedicated my previous book. Relating to them has been fulfilling to me in countless ways, and they are the real reason that I do what I do.

I dedicate this book to those in the medical profession who have given tirelessly of themselves to help me not only survive, but live a happy and productive life, despite having been diagnosed with multiple myeloma in August, 2006. I am especially grateful to my primary care physician, Dr. Putcha Murthy, my oncologist in Worcester, Dr. Tony Samaha, my nurse in Worcester, Yen Araquel, as well as Dawn Cosby and Diane Blanchard. At Dana Farber, I thank Dr. Paul Richardson, a world-renowned researcher in multiple myeloma, as well as my nurses: Mary McKenney, Deborah Doss, Kathy Colson, Culleen Murphy, Kathy Finn, Kelley Bisset, and so many others. I also owe a debt of gratitude to Danny Johnson and Yelena Zakon. Finally, I thank my dentist, Dr. William Pollack, as well as Gail Morton and Beth Clark.

My family is my rock. My wife, Leslie, supports me as do all spouses in good marriages, but with the added burden of my health. I don't know how she manages it all, but she does. I could not carry on without her. My children, Rebecca and Jeremy, each read portions of the manuscript. Rebecca graduated with a major in Religious Studies from Holy Cross in 2006. Jeremy graduated in 2009 from NYU with a student-designed major including a large component of creative writing. Both made substantive, constructive critiques. It is a real turning point in life when your children become two of your main intellectual conversation partners.

Finally, I thank my friend and editor James Ernest. Without his interest and professional knowledge, this book would never have appeared. He is unfailingly helpful, responsive, knowledgeable, and a sure guide to scholarship and publishing. It is a pleasure for me to work with him again.

Introduction

Few phenomena in the history of Western religious traditions have been so important, or so controversial, as apocalyptic eschatology.

Bernard McGinn

We are about to enter the strange world of apocalypses and apocalypticism. It abounds in weird creatures; columns of fire tumbling in bottomless abysses; angels and demons; visions of heaven, hell, and distant cosmic regions; fierce battles between awe-inspiring forces; odd mathematical calculations that disclose the end of the world; and countless other features bound to confuse the modern mind. How can citizens of the twenty-first century begin to understand such a world? Even more, how can we encounter it so that it actually means something to us and perhaps even tells us something about ourselves?

Most readers of this book probably do not subscribe to an apocalyptic worldview, but there are many millions of people around the globe who do, especially in the United States. How can apocalyptic believers and those who do not share their beliefs communicate? How can they understand one another? Study of the ancient roots of Jewish and Christian apocalypticism can provide both information for self-understanding and common ground for mutual understanding, as every Jew and Christian to some degree has an apocalyptic heritage. For those who are nonbelievers but are intellectually curious and engaged in the world around them, this study can bring some order into what might seem to them like the chaos of apocalyptic thought. The aim of this book is to provide such a study.

If apocalypticism and the questions it raises do not make sense to us, then we do not belong to the millions of Americans who are what Paul Boyer calls "prophecy believers" (Boyer 1992). They include fundamentalists, but they also include conservative evangelicals, and they have advocates in less likely groups, such as Catholics, as well. Such beliefs have influenced American culture in general throughout its history. Understanding American culture and history requires knowledge of apocalypticism. Even today, apocalyptic convictions about biblical inerrancy, the imminent second coming of Jesus Christ, and the fate of the universe are accepted well beyond the boundaries of apocalyptic sects and churches. For the more fundamentalistic, the apocalyptic worldview is relevant to their everyday lives. It influences their religion, political judgment, social attitudes, and relationships with others. It shapes how they encounter and interpret the world as a whole. But members of much less apocalyptic religious groups are also heir to beliefs that ultimately spring from apocalypticism, beliefs such as the end of the world, resurrection, afterlife, last judgment, and rewards and punishments after death.

This book examines apocalypticism in ancient Judaism and Christianity. The two religions are both very similar and very different today. In the ancient world, they were not always clearly distinguishable. A nexus between the two religions is the collection of sacred texts that Jews call the Tanak, or Bible, and that Christians call the Old Testament, or the Hebrew Bible. The books contained in the Tanak and in the Protestant Old Testament are the same. Roman Catholics include an additional seven books in their Old Testament and have additions to some other books, such as Daniel. Those additional works are called the Apocrypha, or, acknowledging their place in Catholicism, deuterocanonical.

We can grasp the main difference in the way Jews and Christians read the Bible simply by noting that Christians traditionally refer to the Hebrew Bible as the Old Testament. For there to be an "old" there must be a "new." The word "testament" is more helpfully translated "covenant," which means an agreement between two parties, in this case between God and God's people. For Christians, there is a new covenant, that is, a new agreement between God and humanity. For Jews, there is no need for a new covenant because the Sinai covenant is divinely ordained and completely adequate. Although Christianity began as an apocalyptic movement within Judaism, it evolved into a separate religion (Dunn 1991). But that was a long and complex process. Some New Testament texts, such as the book of Hebrews, see the two religions as separate and incompatible. Others, like Matthew, are far less clear on this point.

Another important difference between how Jews and Christians read their shared Hebrew Bible is that they order the books differently. The Jewish Bible, the Tanak, ends with the ideal situation—the temple operating in Jerusalem, surrounded by worshipers, a Jewish community serving the God of Israel and of all creation, and a Davidic monarchy whose main purpose is to support worship in the sanctuary. This is depicted in Ezra–Nehemiah, and 1–2 Chronicles. In contrast, the Christian order of Old Testament books ends with the prophet Malachi, who predicts the coming of Elijah to warn of God's coming in judgment. This orients the reader to the future, to eschatological events—those having to do with the end of the world's present state—events that will change the world as we know it forever. It emphasizes the apocalyptic strand in Second Temple Judaism. It was an aspect of Jewish religion at the time of Jesus through which Jesus himself, his followers, and the early church experienced life and interpreted their own situation. The first three Gospels held that John the Baptist was Elijah returned, so there is a firm connection between the end of the Old Testament and the beginning of the New. For the most part, rabbinic Judaism downplayed the apocalyptic strand in Judaism (Saldarini 1975, 1977, 1979). In Christianity it remained crucial.

One cannot study Second Temple Judaism and the beginnings of Christianity without giving full consideration to the prevalence of apocalypticism in both religions during this period. There are only two apocalypses in the Bible—Daniel in the Hebrew Bible and Revelation in the New Testament—but the New Testament is heavily influenced by apocalypticism throughout, and the Hebrew Bible ends just as apocalypticism is becoming an important aspect of Jewish thought. For late Second Temple Jewish belief, we must go beyond the Bible to works like *1 Enoch*, a collection of at least five apocalypses, two of which date to the third century BCE and another contemporary with Daniel (around 165 BCE). Much of Jewish literature from this time is either in the form of an apocalypse or has substantial apocalyptic elements. It is often said that one must know the Old Testament to understand the New. But there is a gap between the last written Hebrew Bible document, Daniel, and the first written New Testament text, 1 Thessalonians, one of Paul's letters. That has sometimes been called the intertestamental period. Judaism was not static between the last books of the Hebrew Bible and the beginnings of Christianity; it was a living culture and religion that continued to develop. In that development, apocalypticism played an important role.

In teaching at Holy Cross and elsewhere, I have found it necessary in almost every class to provide a description of apocalypticism. Whether one studies the Hebrew Bible, the New Testament, the historical Jesus, Second Temple Judaism, or related subjects, one cannot ignore the topic. A very large number of Jewish and Christian literary works from 300 BCE to 200 CE are in the form of apocalypses or have apocalyptic elements. Jesus thought in apocalyptic terms. So did Paul. The Gospels are loaded with apocalyptic features. Early Christianity and contemporary Judaism continued to produce apocalypses after the time of Jesus and the fall of Jerusalem, at least up until the end of the second century BCE.

Until recent decades, scholars have been ambivalent toward apocalypticism. A measure of this is the role apocalypticism has played in the study of the historical Jesus. During the first flowering of study of apocalypticism (beginning with the work of F. Lücke in 1832), writers tended to denigrate apocalypticism and to separate Jesus from it (Lücke 1832). In 1892, Johannes Weiss argued that Jesus's concept of the kingdom was apocalyptic and firmly grounded in contemporary Jewish ideas (Weiss 1971). In 1906, Albert Schweitzer made much the same point (Schweitzer 2000).

   Scholars are much more comfortable with apocalypticism today. Exciting work on apocalypticism has been done in recent decades, and it is the aim of this book to bring much of it to the fore in a form accessible to a wide audience.

Suggestions for Further Reading

Boyer, Paul. *When Time Shall Be No More: Prophecy Belief in Modern American Culture*. Cambridge: Harvard University Press, 1992.

Dunn, James D. G. *The Partings of the Ways: Between Christianity and Judaism and Their Significance for the Character of Christianity*. Philadelphia: Trinity Press, 1991.

1

Definitions and Origins

The Advent of Apocalypticism in Ancient Judaism

The history of ancient Israel, like that of all peoples, is marked by key events and periods that define or redefine its identity. Many of those watershed moments are so important to the people's self-conception that they become enshrined in a sacred story that changes over time, as does the people itself. History and legend intermingle and often become indistinguishable. This is especially true in the ancient world, when civic life and religious life were not separate realms. A change in the political or economic life of a people resulted in a change in its religion as well.

Israel's sacred story is embodied in the Hebrew Bible, roughly what Christians call the Old Testament. Since all Jews and Christians whom we will study in this book take for granted at least the main lines of this story, it is well for us to begin by briefly outlining a few aspects of it that affect our study.

Discouraged with trying to deal with humanity as a whole, God called Abraham and told him that he would make of him a great people and would give him a land (Gen. 12). Abraham traveled from Mesopotamia to Canaan, the land God chose to give to Abraham's posterity. Abraham and his descendants were to practice circumcision as a sign of their special relationship with God and their separateness from other nations (Gen. 17). Abraham's son Isaac had a son Jacob. Jacob and eleven of his twelve sons traveled with their families to Egypt, where the twelfth son, Joseph, had assumed political power and could protect them. After spending about four centuries there, they escaped the clutches of an oppressive Pharaoh (an Egyptian king). God split the Red Sea to allow them, under Moses's leadership, to cross and escape the Egyptians. God then brought the sea back onto their Egyptian pursuers, drowning them. This was the exodus, to which later generations would look back as the basis for their relationship with Yahweh, Israel's own God.

Moses and Israel traveled to Mount Sinai in the desert where they made a covenant (an agreement) with the God who had just saved them. God promised to be their God if they obeyed his commands. He gave them the Ten Commandments, along with many other statutes. Central to those commands was how God was to be worshiped in the cult (Israel's religion as it concerned temple, altar, sacrifice, priests, and priestly liturgy), as well as instructions for keeping the major feasts (weekly Sabbath, the Day of Atonement, Passover and Unleavened Bread, Weeks, Tabernacles, New Year). Other rules concerned food, ritual purity, sexual practices, and civil law. The totality was Torah, literally "instruction," but usually translated "law." It was Israel's road map to God's will. Although "Torah" can be used more widely, it comes to mean primarily the first five books of the Bible—Genesis, Exodus, Leviticus, Numbers, and Deuteronomy—also known as the books of Moses.

After wandering for forty years in the desert as punishment for not trusting God, the Israelites entered Canaan under Joshua's leadership and took possession of it. Joshua distributed the land among the twelve tribes. After several centuries of rule by tribal heroes called judges, a monarchy was established. The first king, Saul, failed to establish a lasting dynasty, so he was succeeded by David and then by David's son Solomon. After Solomon's death, the kingdom split into a northern kingdom called Israel and a southern realm called Judah (922 BCE).

In 721 BCE, the north was swallowed up by the expanding Assyrian Empire, and the northern tribes were not heard from again. Legend believes that the ten lost tribes still exist somewhere in the world. Ultimately, these tribes must be restored. This restoration plays a role in many "eschatological" scenarios—pictures of the end of history as we know it, involving a radical change in current conditions.

In 586 BCE, the southern kingdom, Judah, was destroyed by the Babylonians, and Jerusalem and its temple were torn down. The most important members of the Judahite community were exiled to Babylonia, so this period is called the Babylonian exile.

The Persian Cyrus the Great conquered the Babylonian Empire in 539 BCE; he allowed the Judahites to return to Jerusalem and rebuild their city and temple. This is the Restoration. The temple was rebuilt in 520–515 BCE, and it stood until the Romans destroyed it in 70 CE. This defines the Second Temple period. Differences in the historical situation and in Israel's religion before and after the exile have led to the use of the adjective "Israelite" for the preexilic period and "Jewish" for the postexilic period. Cyrus did not allow the reinstitution of the monarchy. Eschatological scenarios often anticipated a renewal of the monarchy. Since the king was anointed, he was a *māšîyaḥ*, a messiah, Hebrew for "anointed one."

In the next century, the Jewish Nehemiah was sent by the Persian crown to be governor of Judah, to rebuild Jerusalem's walls, and to institute certain reforms, especially ones that supported the temple's operations and the observance of the Sabbath (his initial trip occurred in 445 BCE). Around the same time (perhaps 458 BCE, perhaps later), Ezra, another Jew well trusted by the Persians, was sent to Judah to bring the written Torah, assembled and edited by the Babylonian Jewish community, to become the law of the land, along with applicable Persian law. The introduction of a written Torah helped make Judaism a religion of the book, as well as one centered on temple sacrifice and residence in a particular God-given land. Ezra was a Jewish priest of the line of Zadok (Solomon's high priest) and a scribe, one of the few in the ancient world who could read and write and who was therefore qualified to know Israel's traditions in depth (Hezser 2001; Harris 1989).

The conquests of Alexander the Great (333–323 BCE) initiated the Hellenistic period. "Hellenistic" comes from the Greek word *hellas*, meaning Greece. This was a long period of intense interaction between Greek culture and local culture, and it met with mixed reactions by the Jews. Some welcomed the changes, and some resisted. Conflict between parties in Jewish Palestine was ideological and sometimes violent.

At this time, Jewish apocalypticism makes its appearance. It is at least partly a reaction to momentous changes taking place in the world as a consequence of Alexander's conquests. Those changes were political, economic, religious, social, and cultural. Apocalypticism was one way to resist the inroads of empire in Israel (Horsley 2010b; Portier-Young 2011). Apocalyptic ideas and literature are attested in Persia, Israel's former overlord and still the residence of many Jews, and in Egypt, which had a considerable Jewish population. The earliest extant Jewish apocalypses are two sections of *1 Enoch*—the *Book of the Watchers* (*1 Enoch* 1–36) and the *Astronomical Book* (*1 Enoch* 72–82), both written sometime in the third century BCE, shortly after the imposition of Hellenistic imperial rule. The book of Daniel, the only apocalypse in the Jewish Bible, was written in the following century (165 BCE). It was written in response to the attempts of the Hellenistic king Antiochus IV to impose Hellenism and annihilate Judaism.

Apocalypticism changed Israel's view of the world and history. Information about God, history, Israel, and the world was now available through direct revelation to a seer (one who "sees" visions). History was viewed as a whole, from beginning to an inevitable end. Death was not the end for individuals; there were rewards and punishments after death. Corresponding beliefs in a last judgment, cosmic dissolution, resurrection, heaven and hell, and a restored Israel became common. The unseen world of angels and demons became a subject of intense interest and speculation.

Christianity began as an apocalyptic sect within Judaism. When the temple was destroyed by the Romans in 70 CE, Judaism redefined itself with the Torah at its core, and apocalyptic beliefs became less important for Jews. Christianity's identity was tied up with apocalypticism, so as it emerged as a religion separate from Judaism, it preserved its apocalyptic foundations and has done so to the present day.

The Problem of Definition

Scholars have spilled a lot of ink trying to define the terms that head this chapter. Why is it so hard to define apocalypses, apocalypticism, and millenarianism? One obstacle is the difference between scholarly and popular usage. Although there were many ancient Jewish and Christian apocalypses, the most popular has always been the book of Revelation. It is the only apocalypse included in the New Testament.

Revelation gives us only one version of an apocalyptic worldview. It describes divine direction of eschatological events; foresees a great battle at Armageddon in which God, Satan, and their allies wage the final battle; expects the defeat of Satan and his angelic and human supporters by Jesus and his angelic forces; and anticipates cosmic disaster, resurrection, last judgment, postmortem (after death) rewards and punishments, and a new heaven and a new earth. It culminates in the descent of the new Jerusalem onto earth, the dwelling place of God and Christ. Popular views of apocalypticism are heavily influenced by Revelation. Cosmic disaster is central, so that the very word "apocalypse," which literally means simply "revelation" and which scholars use to designate the literary genre, has come to mean that disaster itself. It can designate any such catastrophe or any situation that puts the existence of the world at risk. The movie *Apocalypse Now*, concerning the chaos and destruction of the Vietnam War, is typical in that regard.

There are problems with using our terms this way. One objection is that we cannot rest with Revelation as our sole source for determining what an apocalypse is or what an apocalyptic worldview entails. We must use all the evidence at our disposal, which means examining at least a healthy selection of extant apocalypses. We also will not use "apocalypse" to mean the end of the world or a situation that puts the world at risk. For that, we will use the word "eschaton," which comes from the Greek word *eschaton* meaning "end." "Eschatology," commonly used in this context, means knowledge about the end of things as we know them, often involving the sorts of events mentioned above with respect to Revelation, but sometimes involving things that differ from that book. In any case, eschatological events are end-time happenings. We reserve "apocalypse" to refer to a literary work of a particular genre.

Another issue in defining apocalypticism is that it has assumed many different forms and has played a variety of functions. It was once common to include all sorts of phenomena under the term "apocalyptic," including literary genres, social movements, religious ideas, and eschatological expectations. Daniel and Revelation have always been influential in such definitions, but each scholar decided what other texts and phenomena to use. This produced imprecise usage. Eventually, many grew uncomfortable with the vagueness of it all and tried to sharpen the definitions.

In this book we use the following terminology: "apocalypse" is a literary genre; "apocalypticism" is a worldview; the adjective "apocalyptic" designates imagery, concepts, worldview, themes, literary forms, and social manifestations associated with apocalypses (Koch 1972; Hanson 1976a, 1976b). When speaking of a social movement, we make that clear. We discuss the term "millenarianism" later in this chapter.

Apocalypse: The Apocalyptic Genre

A major contribution to defining apocalypses and apocalypticism came through a study group of the Society of Biblical Literature (SBL). They reasoned that genre was the place to begin the project of clarification, since everything posited about apocalypticism ultimately originates in literary texts deemed apocalyptic. Apocalypticism is the worldview shared by apocalypses.

In the first half of the nineteenth century, scholars began to attend closely to a collection of literary works from the ancient world, both Jewish and Christian, that resembled each other in form and content. Interest was originally spurred by the publication in 1821 of *1 Enoch*, which had been brought back to England from Ethiopia (Collins 1997, 2). The works that caught scholarly notice all bore some resemblance to the canonical texts of Daniel and Revelation. ("Canonical" means belonging to the Bible; the "canon," those books deemed authoritative by Judaism or Christianity.) At the same time, they manifested variety in form and content.

In 1832, Lücke used the apocalyptic texts then available to him (Daniel, *4 Ezra*, *1 Enoch*, the *Sibylline Oracles*) to illuminate Revelation (Lücke 1832). As the century progressed, more texts came to light that belonged to the same genre (*2 Baruch*; *3 Baruch*; *2 Enoch*; *Apocalypse of Abraham*) (Collins 1997, 2). Scholars began to call such texts "apocalypses," because they resembled Revelation, whose first words are "the revelation [*apocalypsis*] of Jesus Christ." The ancient texts predating Revelation did not explicitly call themselves apocalypses, but many written afterward did (Morton Smith 1983).

In 1979, the SBL group published its results. It had developed a definition for "apocalypse" and had classified ancient texts accordingly. The definition it produced is the following:

A genre of revelatory literature with a narrative framework, in which revelation is mediated by an otherworldly being to a human recipient, disclosing a transcendent reality which is both temporal, insofar as it envisages eschatological salvation, and spatial, insofar as it involves another, supernatural world. (Collins 1998)

The group judged that every apocalypse had these characteristics. In a later article, Collins characterized content of apocalypses in other words: "The mysteries they disclose involve a view of human affairs in which major importance is attached to the influence of the supernatural world and the expectation of eschatological judgment" (Collins 1991, 16).

Some advocate including social function in the definition of genre. Determining function is a slippery process, however. A given genre might serve a variety of functions. A novel should entertain, but it might also instruct. The instruction might be a moral lesson, or it might also give the reader a taste of a given historical period or a different culture. To determine function accurately, we would have to know a good deal about how a specific culture operates. Such knowledge is not always available. Despite these reservations, trying to determine the function of a genre can be informative. In the case of apocalypses, another study group of the SBL tackled the problem and produced the following statement:

[Apocalypses are] intended to interpret the present, earthly circumstances in light of the supernatural world and of the future, and to influence both the understanding and the behavior of the audience by means of divine authority. (Yarbro Collins 1986, 7)

What do modern readers expect when they pick up an apocalypse? One answer is "nothing." How would they know what to expect? Little in our modern literary experience prepares us to read one. Christians with an apocalyptic worldview do have such experience. But even they are likely to be familiar only with Daniel and Revelation, and not with noncanonical (nonbiblical) apocalypses such as *1 Enoch*.

The SBL group on genre found that apocalypses are of two main types, one containing a heavenly journey and the other a review of history. Those with a heavenly journey demonstrate greater interest in cosmological knowledge, and those with a review of history focus on history itself—its course, the cosmic forces behind it, and its goal. The distinction is not absolute. The *Apocalypse of Abraham*, written around the turn of the second century CE, has both a heavenly journey and a review of history. Nonetheless, the two types of apocalypses alert us to variety within the genre.

Apocalypses are usually pseudonymous, written under a false (*pseudos*) name (*onoma*). Exceptions to this rule are the book of Revelation and the second-century Christian *Shepherd of Hermas*. All Jewish apocalypses are pseudonymous. Apocalypses are attributed to ancient heroes, such as Moses, Abraham, Ezra, and Enoch, who play the role of seer (one who sees visions). The attribution of an apocalypse to an ancient hero lends legitimacy and status to the work. It is impressive when apocalypses show an ancient hero receiving revelation relevant to present times. When the apocalypse contains a "prediction" of events between the era of the fictional writer (Enoch, for example) and that of the real writer, those predictions will, of course, be accurate, to the degree that the author knows history. Therefore ancient readers will trust real predictions made by the writer. We can sometimes date a work by determining the point at which the review of history switches from being accurate to being inaccurate (Clifford 1975). "Prediction" after the fact is called by the technical term *vaticinium ex eventu*, a Latin phrase meaning "prophecy from the event."

To a modern mind, pseudonymity might seem like simple deception. It is less clear how to judge this issue in antiquity. Surely in their ordinary lives the authors of apocalypses would know that they were not the ancient seers in whose names they wrote, although if they received visions in a trance, they might not distinguish between themselves and their fictive seers. It is likely that readers would have taken attribution to an ancient seer seriously.

Ideas of authorship were different in the ancient world than in the modern one. The five books of Torah and all the historical books in the Bible are anonymous. Those who added oracles to the prophetic books did so anonymously, but they meant for them to be taken as part of the prophetic heritage of the original prophet whose name appears in the book. Perhaps these later prophets thought of themselves as being in the tradition of the named prophet or having his spirit. If we admit the possibility of spiritual possession into the discussion, we could imagine that prophets or apocalyptic seers actually went into trances and "became" the seer or prophet in question (Stone 1990, 119–25).

Both the prophets of Israel and the apocalyptic writers concerned themselves with eschatology. For Israel's prophets, the expected future remained this-worldly. For apocalypses, there is an element of postmortem rewards and punishments. This accounts for the most fundamental difference between prophetic and apocalyptic eschatology (Collins 1974a).

In 1982, Christopher Rowland argued that the eschatological element of apocalypses had been overplayed and that the focus should be on revelation itself as the essential element of apocalypses (1982). Apocalypses are as likely to be interested in cosmological knowledge as in eschatology. Rowland had been anticipated by Michael Stone, who wrote a seminal article entitled "Lists of Revealed Things in the Apocalyptic Literature" (1976). His lists demonstrate that eschatology is one of many things revealed in apocalypses. However, although apocalyptic literature demonstrates a wide range of interests, eschatology is always present in some form and is often central.

Collins (1997) recently offered a restatement of the definition of apocalypses that makes even clearer than the one in 1979 that eschatology and judgment are integral to apocalypses:

> They [both types of apocalypses—historical and cosmological] are presented as supernatural revelations, mediated by an angel or some heavenly being, and they invariably focus on the final end of life and history. This final end usually entails the transformation of this world (the new creation of the book of Revelation) but it also involves the judgment of the individual dead and their assignment to eternal bliss or damnation. (Collins 1997, 3)

Apocalypticism

It is more difficult to define apocalypticism than apocalypse. Most simply, it is the worldview contained in apocalypses. But apocalypses vary widely. Even traits widely attested in many apocalypses may not be present in every one of them. If we restrict ourselves to elements present in every apocalypse, we end up with a list too limited to do justice to the broader worldview. If we are too broad, the designation loses focus and meaning. Here we start with elements common to all apocalypses and then proceed to important elements that might not be universal.

The Unseen World

Every apocalypse assumes an unseen world. The unseen world affects and even determines the visible world. The unseen world is not accessible to humans by ordinary means. No matter how diligently a member of Israel studies Torah, for example, he or she cannot access the knowledge conveyed in apocalypses. Human reason cannot arrive at this knowledge, either. Revelation is necessary and comes through visions, auditions, and visits to normally inaccessible places like heaven, hell, and remote parts of the earth (Himmelfarb 1983; 1993). The seer sees and interacts with the inhabitants of that world—angels, demons, strange monsters, God, and gods. The interaction results in special, esoteric knowledge being given to the seer.

The word "supernatural" is not entirely appropriate here because modern conceptions of nature differ greatly from how the ancients thought of it (D. Martin 2004, 13–16). For the ancients, heaven and hell are part of a single, continuous universe, not "spiritual" places or places in another dimension. Earth and heaven together can come into or pass out of existence, or be renewed. A seer can travel to heaven and hell and come back, and hell is often localized at the ends of the earth or beneath it. Similarly, demons, angels, and gods are not really "supernatural," for they all part of nature. "Unseen" is not a perfect substitute for "supernatural," since that world is indeed seen by the seer, as granted by God. We are left with inadequate terminology.

The Future

Apocalypses reveal not just the unseen world but also the future. For some apocalypses, this aspect is dominant. For others, it is less prominent than other things, such as cosmological knowledge. Apocalypses often anticipate an end to the present order that is cosmic in scope. Radical change is always in sight. Sometimes this means the end of the world, but more frequently it means its transformation. A few texts are mainly interested in the fate of the individual. But in all cases, postmortem rewards and punishments are present. This can mean that resurrection is envisaged, but not necessarily. Another common form of survival of death has been termed "astral immortality," meaning immortality in company with the stars, who are heavenly beings.

Divine Sovereignty

God's sovereignty is at issue in apocalypticism, particularly that of the historical variety. God will eventually rule all, but presently divine sovereignty is challenged by figures opposed to God, human and superhuman, and the universe is therefore not as God intended. God's ultimate victory is certain, but conflict in the present is real and will intensify as the end approaches. Recent scholarship stresses the role of apocalypticism in resisting empire, first the Hellenistic empires and then Rome (Portier-Young 2011; Horsley 2010b). Political circumstances are closely associated with cosmic realities.

Dualism

Dualism is common in apocalypses. It sees things in terms of polar opposites. Socially, that means that humanity consists of the righteous and the wicked, with no middle group. Temporally, it means that there are two worlds, present and future. Cosmically, it means that there are forces arrayed on God's side and forces against him—angels against demons, or good angels against bad angels. In terms of belief, it means that the in-group has the truth, and no one else does. Behaviorally, it means strict regulation of behavior as either compatible or incompatible with community rules and norms. Apocalypses generally leave little or no middle ground in any of these categories (Gammie 1974).

Eschatological Timetables

Other features often appear in apocalypses, even if they are not present in all. One concerns the timing of the end, the eschaton. It is common for apocalypses to give some sort of indication of how close the end is, but it is almost always vague. The end is usually imminent. The book of Revelation, for example, repeatedly says that the end is coming "soon" (the word appears ten times in the book) but does not say exactly when. Daniel is unusual in that it tries to be more precise about when the end will come. It preserves two self-contradictory efforts to calculate the end down to the day: "From the time that the regular burnt-offering is taken away and the abomination that desolates is set up, there shall be one thousand two hundred ninety days. Happy are those who persevere and attain the thousand three hundred thirty-five days" (Dan. 12:11–12). These may have been added shortly after the failure of Daniel's prediction that the end would come in three and a half years.

The Eschaton

The eschaton is the end of the world as we know it. The eschaton is cosmic in scope in most apocalypses. It involves more than just humanity. It affects all of creation. Sun, moon, and stars are changed. Mountains melt, the earth trembles, and the heavens are ripped open. The eschaton comes in a great variety of versions, although many elements are frequently repeated across texts, times, and places.

The World to Come

Apocalypses consider the world to come as ideal. The wicked, human and superhuman, are eternally punished or go out of existence. Those who remain fully accept God's will. Sin is gone, so what sin brought—death, suffering, sickness, warfare, famine, and so on—also disappears. What follows varies from apocalypse to apocalypse. Most expect a renewed earth on which humans will live, but others see rather the translation of righteous humans to fellowship with the stars in the heavens.

Dissatisfaction with the Present

Apocalypses usually display dissatisfaction with the state of the world. That is why they envisage a better world to come. When that vision entails a renewal of this world, it is sometimes conceptualized in terms of a return to the original state of creation. The famous German dictum for this is that the *Endzeit* becomes the *Urzeit*. That is, the end time is a return to origins. Elements such as the conquest of death, which according to Genesis came into the world through sin, and almost limitless fertility of the earth, which according to Genesis became much less fertile because of sin, show that the end time reverses the changes effected by a primeval rebellion against God. Central to the changes are also what we think of as political and economic concerns. Power relations—political, economic, social, and even religious—in the present are perverted, with the wicked ruling and oppressing the righteous. This will be reversed. God is intimately concerned with the world's injustice.

End-Time Conflict and Tribulation

The end does not come without resistance. It is common to read of a final battle between God's forces and those of God's enemies. The final struggle sometimes entails the participation of humans and sometimes not. Earthly war can be part of the end time, but not necessarily. Humans may remain passive as God accomplishes the divine purpose, alone or with angelic aid. Although we might expect a messiah as part of the end time, he is not always present. Apocalypses may expect the end to be preceded by a period of unprecedented suffering, known in Revelation as the "tribulation" (*thlipsis*).

Periodization of History and Determinism

Periodization of history and determinism are widespread in historical apocalypses. History has a set course to which it must adhere. God plans and knows all in advance. It is fixed. While the prophets normally offer repentance as a way to avoid punishments to come, in apocalypses one cannot alter the course of history. People have free will to the extent that they can choose one side or another in the eschatological struggle. But one cannot prevent or forestall what is to come. Since the readers live in the last period or in a time just prior to that, the decision to live according to the views of the apocalyptic writer is pressing.

Angelology and Demonology

Apocalypses often contain developed angelology and demonology, especially the former. Angels and an occasional demon appear in the Hebrew Bible, but they are few, relatively undifferentiated, and function primarily as a substitute for God's presence. Through apocalypses, angels and demons enter the Jewish world in numbers and detail. Many receive names—some familiar, such as Michael, Raphael, and Gabriel; others not so familiar, such as Shemyaza, Azazel, and Uriel. Angels have various tasks to perform, helping God to govern the universe in all its complexity. Individual demons are not often named nor their functions specified, but their leader assumes a variety of names. Satan is the name most familiar to modern readers, but the demonic leader is also called other things, including Belial, Beliar, Beelzebul, and Mastema.

Apocalyptic Language

Apocalyptic language is a world unto itself, although it borrows heavily from many sources. "Language" here means the full array of rhetoric, imagery, motifs, metaphor, and narrative at work in apocalypses. Apocalypticism is heavily mythological and owes a debt to some of the great myths of the ancient Near East and the Hellenistic world. This language is simultaneously metaphorical and literal, even though these terms are usually thought to be mutually exclusive (Lincoln 1999). We commonly think of metaphor as ornamental and dispensable, and suggestive rather than literal. It differs from scientific thought and philosophical inquiry. It is "artsy" rather than metaphysical. But the case has been made persuasively that metaphor is at the core of human experience and intelligence (Lakoff and Johnson 1980). Through metaphor humans assimilate new knowledge and arrive at an understanding of the world. Metaphor even underlies science and philosophy. If we take this approach to metaphor, seeing it as to some extent literal is less surprising. This needs fuller explanation.

Apocalypses abound in strange creatures from an unseen world that interact with other superhuman creatures and with humans. They are both like and unlike creatures on earth. For example, they may have the characteristics of earthly beasts such as lions, bears, and leopards, but they combine features that are found together in no earthly animals. Apocalypses also tell of angels, demons, and other cosmic beings. Some represent the awesome power of earthly empires, and some form part of God's heavenly army. They fight one another, receive God's approval or endure God's wrath, and interfere in human history. Do apocalyptic writers and their ancient readers or hearers actually believe in such creatures? Are we to take apocalyptic scenarios of the end literally? Will mountains really melt? Will stars actually fall from the skies? How are we to construe this language?

Apocalyptic language is simultaneously literal and figurative. Apocalyptic metaphors do relate to real places, creatures, and events, but not always in a simple one-to-one, referential way. All apocalypses have allegorical features, some more than others. But to push every detail for its referent in the "real" world is to reduce the entirety to allegory. Similarly, an overly literalistic reading can push their referentiality too far. It can miss their mythological, even poetic nature. It is unhelpful to insist either that the seer of Revelation thinks that there is a literal beast with seven heads and ten horns that has arisen out of the sea (Rev. 13) or that this is a "mere" symbol. For this seer, the beast is real, but it also operates as a metaphor and can mean more than a single thing. Collins calls this "multivalence" (1984a, 51–52). This accords with the fact that many apocalypses use recapitulation; that is, they record or predict the same events in various ways, all of which are to some degree literal and to some degree not (Murphy 1998, 51–53). We cannot always restrict apocalyptic referents to one of two or more contrasting choices. One might say that apocalyptic language has more in common with poetry than prose, but that feeds into modern misconceptions of poetry, such that it is flowery, decorative, even sentimental, and not to be taken literally. Poetry, and truth, are far more complicated.

Apocalyptic language invites us to experience the world it creates, with all its fluidity and complexity and contradictions. It appeals to our deepest emotions, fears, and desires, much as do mythology and poetry. Truth here is not only a question of verisimilitude or historical accuracy. It has more to do with basic ways of experiencing the world. Do the writers believe in the unseen worlds they depict? They do. Do they believe that seers are granted visions into and tours of the unseen world? Yes. Do they believe that the specifics of that world are accurate as described? Yes and no. Remember that these are often visions that

Apocalyptic Language

- Draws heavily on mythology
- Is both literal and metaphorical
- Has allegorical features and concrete referents
- Evokes deep emotions
- Brings the reader into an unseen world
- Relates to social groups and movements

need interpretation. They symbolize things, such as empires and kings. At the same time, even if an empire can be symbolized by a beast, it can be symbolized in other ways as well. And both are true and revelatory. The superhuman power of empires, angels, and demons is real. How it is presented can change.

This is a version of the age-old problem of how to talk about God. Thomas Aquinas, the Dominican theologian of the thirteenth century, can help us, even though he himself had little use for apocalypticism as such. Much of his theology is strictly logical and sounds almost scientific. At the same time, he warns that we can speak of God only by analogy. God, ultimately unknowable, can be spoken of only in terms of things that we know and understand. This is the way of analogy, the *cognitio analogica*. A degree of anthropomorphism (portraying God in human terms) is unavoidable. Still, God is totally other, so everything we say about God must simultaneously be negated. This is known as the *via negativa*, the "negative way." God must at least be able to speak, for we speak, but God does not really speak as humans do. God must love, since humans love and God is greater than we, but God does not love as do humans. By combining analogy and the *via negativa* in his theology, Aquinas comes close to what we mean by saying that apocalyptic language is both metaphorical and literal. What can be taken to be "mere" analogies and figurative language is at the same time literal to some degree.

We leave this difficult but fascinating topic here, hoping that the experience of reading apocalyptic literature will do more to illuminate the nature of apocalyptic language than this abstract discussion can do.

Social Movements

It is difficult to determine whether a given ancient apocalypse is the product of a social movement. We usually do not have enough evidence to judge. But we are lucky to have two groups that were apocalyptic in their worldview—the

Elements of an Apocalyptic Worldview

- An unseen world affects or even determines this one.
- The unseen world is accessible only through revelation.
- After death, humans are judged and rewarded or punished.
- There is often a future world that entails a renewal of the present one or its replacement with a better one.
- God's sovereignty is at issue. Humans and/or angels have rebelled against God's rule, but divine rule will soon be reasserted. Resistance to the coming of God's rule is common. God sometimes accomplishes the reestablishment of divine rule alone, sometimes with angelic aid, and sometimes with human aid. God's sovereignty is contrary to earth's empires, especially those that oppress Israel or Christians.
- Dualism pervades apocalypses—humanity is divided into the righteous and the unrighteous; time is divided into the present world and the one to come; cosmic powers are seen to be either for or against God.
- There is dissatisfaction with the present world.
- The coming of the eschaton is often accompanied by cosmic disturbances, as well as by social upheaval.
- The coming of a messiah is not present in every apocalypse but is not uncommon.
- The apocalyptic worldview is deterministic. At least on the macro level, things happen according to God's plans, regardless of human action. Individuals and groups can affect their own fate by aligning with or against God.
- The apocalyptic worldview has a developed angelology and demonology.
- Apocalyptic language is used to communicate the apocalyptic worldview.

community of the Dead Sea Scrolls and early Christianity. We could go further and include the earliest Jesus movement, the group of people who followed Jesus, but we have less certitude in that case.

Origins of Apocalypses and Apocalypticism

Did this new way of looking at the world and this new literary genre evolve out of what had gone before within Israel's religion and culture, or was it imported from outside? Most take the position that apocalypticism developed in Israel under both external and internal influences. Exposure to other civilizations, particularly that of the Persians, was important, as was development of elements from within Israel, drawing on both prophecy and wisdom, all of which gained special impetus from the new Hellenistic world set in motion by the conquests of Alexander and a new situation determined by oppressive empires.

External Influences

The religion of ancient Israel was not a pure, self-contained, unchanging religion that at times was jeopardized by its contact with outsiders. No major religion has ever been a static, pure entity, immune from external influence and internal change. Preexilic Israelite religion and postexilic Judaism are no exceptions. Careful reading of the Bible discloses that before the Babylonian exile, it was more the rule than the exception that the Israelites were open to religious influences from their neighbors and that they worshiped multiple gods and goddesses. They were especially open to Canaanite influence (Collins 2004, 188–89; M. S. Smith 2002).

During the Babylonian exile, Israel experienced Mesopotamian influences. The Persian king Cyrus the Great conquered the Babylonian Empire in 539 BCE, thereby subjecting the Jews to Persian influence. Persian religion was Zoroastrianism, and it contained elements that fed into apocalypticism. These included dualism, periodization of history, heaven and hell, postmortem rewards and punishments, resurrection, angels and demons, the clash of superhuman forces of good and evil, eschatological battles with attendant suffering, and ascent of the soul. Apocalypses also have much in common with political prophecy from Mesopotamia (Babylonia, Sumeria, Akkadia), as well as with mantic wisdom from the same area, that is, wisdom that comes from decoding enigmatic visions.

Here we depend on the work of Richard Clifford, who provides the following list of elements and topics from ancient mythology that were influential on the apocalyptic genre:

> The divine assembly under the high god responding to a major threat, cosmic enemies portrayed as monsters, various heavenly beings, divine decrees or secret knowledge, and a sage-mediator of heavenly knowledge. Among the topics are explorations of the nature of evil and new creation or restoration of the original order. (Clifford 1998, 4–5)

Clifford also points to three Mesopotamian genres that helped shape the apocalyptic genre, which we will look at in detail: combat myths, *vaticinia ex eventu* (Latin for "prophecies after the fact"), and dream visions (visions seen by a seer while asleep), both from Akkadian sources.

Combat myths. In 1895, Hermann Gunkel showed that Gen. 1 and Rev. 12 were heavily influenced by an ancient Near Eastern narrative called the "combat myth" (Gunkel 2006). It depicts a battle between gods. At stake is the sovereignty of specific gods as well as the integrity of creation. The combat myth contains much that is central to apocalypticism: "the *Urzeit* ('primal time') *Endzeit* ('end-time') equation, creation and new creation, the monster symbolizing evil, and divine kingship" (Clifford 1998, 4). The combat myth is one of the most important influences of the ancient Near East on apocalypses.

The ancient world was generally polytheistic. This was true even of Israel before the Babylonian exile (M. S. Smith 2002). There were many gods and goddesses. Religions often pictured a divine assembly modeled on earthly royal courts. The divine assembly of the ancient Near East consisted of many gods, among whom were three prominent ones: Anu (god of the sky, head of an older generation of gods; his consort is Antu), Enlil (god of the inhabited earth, Anu's son, head of the younger generation of gods; his consort was Ninlil or Ninhursag), and Ea (god of water, wisdom, and incantations; his consort was Ninmah or Damkina). There were variations, depending on the nation involved. For Assyria, the head god was Asshur. For Babylon, he was Marduk. The interactions between these gods were modeled on human interactions. The head god was not all-powerful, there was a degree of democracy among the gods, and power shifts were possible. Interactions among the gods reflected political shifts between and within nations on earth. The divine assembly was also present in the Canaanite religion and has left its trace on biblical literature.

Knowledge of the divine assembly makes possible an understanding of the combat myth, whose basic plot Clifford summarizes as follows: a force (often depicted as a monster) threatens cosmic and political order, instilling fear and confusion in the assembly of the gods; the assembly or its president, unable to find a commander among the older gods, turns to a younger god to battle the hostile force; he successfully defeats the monster, creates the world (including human beings) or simply restores the pre-threat order, builds a palace, and receives acclamation of kingship from the other gods (Clifford 1998, 7).

Clifford finds three ancient Near Eastern instances of the combat myth that are complete enough to be analyzed. The first is *Lugal-e*, a myth originating in Sumeria in the late third millennium BCE. The monster Azag freezes the mountain water needed to fill the rivers of Mesopotamia, and the young god Ninurta fights and defeats Azag, thus restoring the flow of water and returning the earth to its pre-threat state. Ninurta is not successful at first. It takes two attempts to defeat Azag. Ninurta's father, Enlil, helps him through with advice. Upon his victory, Ninurta receives the acclamation of all the gods.

Clifford enumerates five features central to the combat myth found in *Lugal-e*. First is the relationship between Ninurta and his father Enlil. The younger god fights the battle and is acclaimed, while the older god is the supreme ruler. The second feature is that evil is defeated. The third is that the threat has overtones of a struggle against nature and political enemies. Fourth is that the defeated enemies are punished, and fifth is that the original order is restored.

The second myth is *Anzu*, dating from the second millennium BCE. The myth begins with a crisis caused by lack of water. The birth of Anzu, a strange, composite creature who is like a bird but of bizarre proportions, results in the restoration of water. Anu, the high god, recommends to Enlil to trust Anzu with the office of the gods' gatekeeper. Anzu betrays Anu and Enlil by stealing from Enlil the Tablet-of-Decrees, a tool that enables its possessor to control the destiny of all. Despite desperate pleas by Anu to the divine assembly and to three gods in particular to fight Anzu, all refuse. Then Ninurta, Enlil's son, takes up the challenge. As in *Lugal-e*, Ninurta at first fails, but he then takes advice from Ea and succeeds. The divine assembly honors Ninurta with many new names.

Clifford highlights four elements in *Anzu* important to later apocalypses. First, although the first crisis is solved by Anzu's birth, the more serious crisis, concerning the Tablets-of-Decrees, is solved only with Anzu's defeat by Ninurta. Second, this has political overtones, since the Tablets are needed to rule. It also has dynastic overtones because Ninurta's mother asks him to fight based on family considerations. Third, the basic issue is kingship. Finally, the plot involves a monster composed of elements from several creatures, and there are interactions among the divine assembly.

The final myth is *Enuma Elish*, a widely copied and read myth of the ancient Near East, dating to the second millennium BCE. This can be termed a cosmogony (a creation myth). The myth begins with a theogony (the emergence of the gods), resulting in two rival dynasties, that of Apsu and Tiamat (the primordial waters) and that of Anshar, Anu, Ea, and Marduk (Marduk is Babylonian). Nature and politics are intertwined. The rival dynasties clash and Ea defeats Apsu and then builds a palace to celebrate.

Tiamat seeks revenge and frightens the divine assembly. Tiamat is represented by a dragon or a seven-headed serpent. Marduk takes up Tiamat's challenge and is successful. Having slain Tiamat, Marduk makes the universe and his sanctuary from her body. The gods give Marduk sovereignty, and he responds that they will live in Babylon and that a new creature, humanity, will be their servant. Marduk fashions this new creature from the blood of Tiamat's general, Kingu. The gods build Marduk a city and temple and award him fifty honorable names.

Ancient accounts usually imagined creation on the model of human activity (molding clay, building a house, fighting a battle) or natural processes (life forms left by the ebbing Nile flood). What emerged from the process for the ancients was a *populated* universe, human society organized for the service of the gods with a king and a culture (Clifford 1998, 11–12).

Vaticinia ex eventu. Clifford lists similarities and differences between the "prophecies after the fact" and apocalypses (Clifford 1998, 14). Similarities include the following: fictional "predictions" bolster belief in real predictions; interest is in a sequence of kingdoms rather than of cities, shrines, or deities; persons are unnamed; portrayals of history are broad; knowledge contained in the prophecies is of divine origin; influence of "omen texts," texts that convey technology for divination (mantic wisdom), is present. The main difference between ancient Near Eastern *vaticinia ex eventu* and apocalyptic reviews of history is that the apocalypses place such predictions in a cosmic

Fig. 1. Ancient Near Eastern mythologies legitimated and supported political powers. Empires were political structures, but they were also closely associated with gods and cosmic powers. Here, the otherworldly sphinx guards a pyramid, tomb of an Egyptian Pharaoh. (Jim Yancey)

context including cosmic threat, combat, and divine sovereignty.

Dream visions. There is some doubt about whether the third Mesopotamian genre of dream visions actually influenced apocalypses. Nonetheless, Clifford sees this genre as a precedent for later tours of heaven and hell in apocalypses.

Recurrent elements. Clifford identifies several elements that recur in ancient texts and are found in apocalypses. First is the combat myth. Second is the divine assembly. The Tablet-of-Decrees is analogous to the secrets of the future discovered by apocalyptic seers as well as to cosmological secrets. Another element is the portrayal of the enemy as a monster. The monster can have overtones of natural forces as well as of political and military forces.

Themes. Two crucial ancient Near Eastern themes that Clifford identifies as important to apocalypticism are threat and new creation. Order is challenged by a god or gods, the threat is ended through the victory of another god, and creation is renewed. There are historical overtones, since they deal with order, divine sovereignty, kingship, and social control.

Canaanite myth. Canaan is the broad area later known as Palestine and Phoenicia. Canaanite influence on Israelite culture is undeniable. The two cultures are close geographically, linguistically, and culturally. A window into Canaanite myth was opened with the discovery in 1928 of the site of the ancient city of Ugarit, a coastal city in northern Syria. Canaanite tablets were found there containing stories about the god Baal. Unfortunately, the tablets are fragmentary, and the precise plot of the stories is unsure. Operating by analogy with the Mesopotamian combat myths, however, scholars have plausibly reconstructed major features of the Baal cycle.

The head god of the Canaanite pantheon is El, whose consort is Asherah. Like Anu in Mesopotamia, El is surrounded by a divine assembly, but the gods Enlil and Ea do not have corresponding figures in Canaan. Mesopotamian myths see Anu as the senior and supreme god, while Ninurta is a young god who faces the challenge to the order of the gods; similarly in Canaan, El is the senior and supreme god who interacts with a younger god, Baal. Baal faces two enemies—Yamm (Sea) and Mot (Death). These are portrayed as personal, not simply natural forces. Baal conquers both, establishes his kingship, and builds a palace. The names of Baal's enemies suggest that they threaten cosmic order. Yamm recalls Tiamat from Babylonia, who is also connected with destructive waters. Just as Tiamat is associated with monsters—a dragon and a seven-headed serpent—so Mot has an ally, Lotan—a seven-headed, serpent-like monster who has his counterpart in the biblical Leviathan, the sea-monster.

Conclusions from the ancient Near East. Clifford presents Forsyth's outline of the ideal plot of the combat myth (Forsyth 1987, 448–51), cautioning that not every instance of the myth fits the ideal (Clifford 1998, 28–29). Forsyth's work, in turn, depends on that of Vladimir Propp, who analyzed the form of folktale (Propp 1968). The ideal plot of the combat myth involves the following elements:

1. Lack/villainy
2. Hero emerges/prepares to act
3. Donor/Consolation
4. Journey
5. Battle
6. Defeat
7. Enemy ascendant
8. Hero recovers/new hero
9. Victory
10. Enemy punished
11. Triumph

Kingship and cosmic order are intertwined; cosmic order depends on the supreme kingship of a single god in the heavenly realm. The political implications are clear. History and "nature" are not clearly distinguished, so that historical forces can be described in terms of nature and cosmic forces. Although people might hope for a permanent order, the possibility of it being disturbed is always present, since the threat to it is never fully eradicated.

Internal Development

Outside influence does not exclude internal development. Prophecy and wisdom are characteristically Jewish traditions that fed into apocalypticism. We look at wisdom first, since it is probably less familiar than prophecy. Scholarship has discredited the view that apocalypticism grew solely out of wisdom, but there was interaction between the two kinds of tradition.

The wisdom tradition. Three books in the Hebrew Bible belong to the wisdom tradition—Proverbs, Job, and Ecclesiastes (the last called Qoheleth in Hebrew). Two other wisdom works are accepted as part of the Bible by Catholics, but not by Protestants and Jews—Sirach and the Wisdom of Solomon.

The wisdom tradition (also called the "sapiential" tradition, from the Latin for "wisdom," *sapientia*) is most clearly exemplified in the five wisdom books mentioned above, but wisdom's influence is wider. At the heart of the sapiential tradition is the operation of reason on human experience. Its most characteristic form is the proverb. Proverbs were originally oral and then were collected into books like Proverbs and Sirach. Proverbs do not have the authority today they once did, but they still occur in daily speech, and we take them seriously. For example, in a discussion on the wisdom of eating healthy, one might say, "An apple a day keeps the doctor away." No one thinks that proverbs contain absolute truth, but they do somehow embody the accumulated wisdom of the ages. That is why they are anonymous.

Some proverbs contain folk wisdom, the wisdom of the common person, and some embody the sophisticated wisdom of the royal court. Proverbs range from insight on wise farming to how to get ahead in society. Ancient intellectuals, called the "wise" or the "sages," compiled and availed themselves of written proverb collections. They also learned the wisdom of foreign nations; ancient wisdom was international. Solomon is often associated with wisdom, probably because he assembled wise men to staff his bureaucracy and run his empire. By collecting and analyzing human wisdom, the ancients thought that they could make incisive statements about the universe and even about God (Sirach, prologue).

Eventually, wisdom developed into speculative and theological wisdom. Speculative wisdom goes beyond the workings of the farm or the court to ask broader questions about the universe and even metaphysical questions. Qoheleth does this from a skeptical point of view. Job sharply critiques conventional wisdom but is itself a product of the wisdom tradition. Theological wisdom combines the wisdom tradition with Israel's sacred laws and traditions. An example is Sir. 24, which says that wisdom is identifiable with the Torah. Finally, we speak of personified wisdom. The word "wisdom" is feminine in both Hebrew (ḥokmâ) and Greek (sophia), so it was easy for ancient Jewish writers to picture wisdom as a goddess, companion to God, agent of or present at the creation. Whether this is meant literally is debated (Yarbro Collins and Collins 2008).

Gerhard von Rad, a prominent twentieth-century scholar of the Hebrew Bible, considered apocalypticism a natural outgrowth of the wisdom tradition, since it both consisted of insight into the cosmos and posited that correct action followed right knowledge (von Rad and Hanson 2005). Another similarity is that both phenomena are scribal. To be well versed in the wisdom tradition, it was necessary to be a scribe (J. Smith 1975; Horsley 2010b). Their authors were writers, and writing was a rare skill in the ancient world. Apocalyptic authors knew a lot about other books and about national and international traditions.

Despite these similarities, apocalyptic and sapiential wisdom are very different. The former is based on revelation, while the latter comes from human reason and is empirical. Their interests are often quite different as well, although this distinction is not absolute. While apocalypticism focuses on eschatology and cosmological knowledge, wisdom more frequently concerns itself with the everyday life of an ordinary person or of a member of the upper class.

The prophetic tradition. Most scholars find stronger similarities between prophecy and apocalypses than between wisdom and apocalypses (Grabbe and Haak 2003). Indeed, the author of Revelation calls his book a prophecy. Prophetic books and apocalypses both speak of future events; they do so to shed light on the present; each is deeply rooted in Israel's traditions; each intends to influence the opinions and behavior of its audiences; apocalypses draw on prophetic images and motifs; and both prophets and apocalyptic seers claim that their words are divine revelation.

The clearest difference between prophecy and apocalypticism is their eschatology. The apocalypses contain belief in postmortem rewards and punishments. The idea of the afterlife in the Hebrew Bible is quite different from what we find in apocalypticism. The Bible speaks of people being gathered to their ancestors, but dying is going to Sheol, often translated "the Pit." There are no rewards or punishments. The fate of all is the same. One cannot even pray to God there. It is a shadowy existence. Israel did not give much thought to the afterlife until the Hellenistic period.

Collins enumerates other differences between prophecy and apocalypticism (Collins 1997, 4–7). Both prophecy and apocalyptic revelations are precisely that—revelations. In both cases, information is given to a human to pass on to others. That information is available only through direct revelation. In apocalypses and related literature, however, the supernatural nature of the revelation is greater than in prophecy. It is more mysterious and sometimes "bewildering" (Collins 2000a, 4). A prophet may stand before God's heavenly throne, as do Micaiah ben Imlah (1 Kings 22) and Isaiah (Isa. 6), but apocalypses offer far more elaborate descriptions of the heavenly scenes and of their superhuman figures. Prophets can come into contact with angels, but in apocalypses angels are more numerous, are named, have specific jobs, belong to hierarchies, and are more active. The idea that angels and/or demons are organized under the control of one figure—Satan or Beliar or some other name—emerges with apocalypticism.

Both prophecy and apocalypticism expect divine intervention in history, but for prophets, that intervention deals with a specific historical situation and the resolution results in something not so different from what preceded it. Cosmic disruption is for the most part metaphorical, such as a new heaven and new earth (Isa. 65:17). The metaphors for the most part interpret earthly events, such as conquest by a foreign empire. When prophets speak of an "end," it is within history, not the end of history. "They do not attempt to survey the course of history as a whole or measure out the time from beginning to end" (Collins 1997, 5–6). Apocalypses do precisely this. They see history as a whole and make sense of all of it. This view of history provides a comprehensive explanation of how the seer's audience got to where it is, what is happening in the world and how it influences them, and where it is all going to end up. Generally, apocalypses locate their audiences at the end of time or close to it.

Apocalypses as Hellenistic. Although apocalypticism has deeper roots in prophecy than in wisdom, wisdom and apocalypticism interacted throughout the Hellenistic period. The Wisdom and Apocalypticism Group of the Society of Biblical Literature has studied that interaction and has delineated large areas where we still have much to learn (Wills and Wright 2005). The interaction between Nickelsburg and Tanzer in the group's publication lays out the issues clearly (Nickelsburg 2005a; 2005b; Tanzer 2005).

Jewish apocalypses emerged during the Hellenistic period. They show the influence of Persian and Greek forms and thought, characteristic of the mixing of cultures that defined Hellenism. They are products of factors both internal and external to Israel's culture.

Loew delineates a "cosmological conviction" in ancient Mesopotamia that holds that "the meaning of life is rooted in an encompassing cosmic order in which man, society and the gods all participate" (1967, 5). It assumes mythological form in ancient Mesopotamia, but in Greek thought of the sixth and fifth centuries BCE, it was more abstract. These thinkers made the intellectual discovery that "nature is an autonomous realm" (216–17). They explained reality in the abstract terms of science and philosophy. They spoke more of earth, air, fire, and water than of gods and goddesses. Human nature and even history was intimately connected with this cosmos, and salvation lay in understanding the cosmos and in living in harmony with it.

Collins notes that the Wisdom of Solomon, a Jewish work written in Greek in Egypt during the Hellenistic period, moves beyond conventional Jewish wisdom (Collins 1977a; 1977d). It speaks in general, abstract—even "scientific"—Greek terms, and it finds meaning in the cosmos itself. The cosmos mediates the divine to humans. Understanding cosmic order is the aim of life and such understanding makes righteousness possible. At the same time, more than any other sapiential book, Wisdom incorporates apocalyptic thought. Its first five chapters speak in terms that are both eschatological and cosmological. Right understanding reveals that the world was created by God for life-fostering purposes and that God's plan never included death. Death comes through the devil to those who do not have a right understanding of the world. They think that death is real and final and do not know that the righteous are justified after death. Eschatology and right understanding of the universe go together.

Collins points out that the book of Wisdom agrees with apocalypticism precisely in terms of the cosmological conviction. To understand the cosmos is to understand human nature and destiny. To align oneself with the cosmic structure is to live properly and to find salvation. Both the Wisdom of Solomon and apocalypticism call this "wisdom." In finding wisdom in the structure of the cosmos, both Wisdom and apocalypticism participate in the "Hellenistic mood" or *Zeitgeist* (spirit of the times). Collins finds it much more likely that each reached its cosmological conviction because of their place in the Hellenistic world than from direct mutual borrowing.

There are marked differences between the sapiential outlook, even as found in the Wisdom of Solomon, and the apocalyptic worldview. Wisdom is optimistic about the cosmos. Apocalypticism posits that the world has been ruined and is now controlled by forces hostile to the creator. For wisdom, God's will can still be found in the cosmos through the exercise of human reason. For apocalypticism, wisdom is accessible only through direct revelation by

> **Apocalyptic Origins**
>
> *External*
>   Mesopotamian political prophecy
>   Mesopotamian mantic prophecy
>   Persian religion
> *Internal*
>   Sapiential wisdom
>   Prophecy

a heavenly figure. If one has access to heaven and hell, parts of an integrated cosmos, then one can discover truth; but unaided human reason cannot do so. Wisdom sees divine wisdom as permeating the cosmos and available to humans.

Millennialism

Millennialism, also called millenarianism, is the hope that this imperfect world will pass away and that a new, perfect world will replace it. Millennialism is a subset of apocalypticism.

The word "millennium" comes from Rev. 20:1–21:5. The passage says that after Satan is bound, those beheaded will reign on earth with Christ for a thousand years (*chilia etē*). In the Latin translation of the Bible, that becomes *mille annis*. The Latin word for "thousand" is *mille* and for "year," *annos*. From that comes the noun "millennium," which means "a thousand years." And from that we derive "millenarianism" and "millennialism," which refer to literal belief in the thousand-year reign of Christ envisioned in Rev. 20. Another term for early Christian millennial expectations is "chiliasm." It derives from the Greek word for "thousand," *chilias*. "Millenarianism" is often used in the broad sense of an idyllic future, even when the thousand-year belief is not present. Belief in the literal thousand-year millennium is found nowhere in the New Testament except Rev. 20 (Porter 2001).

Norman Cohn's *The Pursuit of the Millennium* investigates utopian movements over the centuries. Following is how he delineates millennial salvation.

Millenarian sects or movements always picture salvation as

- collective, in the sense that it is to be enjoyed by the faithful as a collectivity;
- terrestrial, in the sense that it is to be realized on this earth and not in some otherworldly heaven;
- imminent, in the sense that it is to come both soon and suddenly;

- total, in the sense that it is to utterly transform life on earth, so that the new dispensation will be no mere improvement on the present but perfection itself;
- miraculous, in the sense that it is to be accomplished by, or with the help of, supernatural agencies. (Cohn 1970, 15)

Cohn's definition is more or less the same as is found in apocalypses, with a couple of qualifications. There are apocalypses in which salvation is less collective than individual. The best example is the *Apocalypse of Abraham*, from the late first century CE. Also, eschatological salvation does not always occur on earth. In Daniel, *2 Baruch*, and others, it takes place in the heavens with the angels. In Revelation, it happens on earth, when the new Jerusalem descends. The eschaton is often expected soon, but this is not always so clear either in apocalypses or among apocalyptic thinkers.

Apocalypticism and Jewish Mysticism

After the destruction of Jerusalem by the Romans in 70 CE, Judaism played down apocalypticism. Jewish apocalyptic texts were preserved primarily by Christians. However, apocalyptic ideas did survive in Jewish mysticism. At the center of much of this mysticism was a desire to behold God on his throne. This builds on the throne scenes we will study in the Hebrew Bible and in apocalyptic literature. God's throne is frequently seen as a chariot (Hebrew: *merkābâ*), so this mysticism is often called merkavah mysticism (Gruenwald 1980).

When Prophecy Fails

For those who do not think apocalyptically, it is puzzling that prophecies can fail repeatedly without dampening eschatological enthusiasm. All predictions of the end have failed. One might think that after more than two thousand years, apocalypticism would have been definitively discredited and would have lost its attraction.

Many do not realize that Christianity itself is the result of failed prophecy. Jesus apparently expected the kingdom of God to come soon, and this urgent expectation of an imminent end pervades the New Testament. The apostle Paul expected the end to come in his own lifetime. Yet although these expectations were not fulfilled when expected, Christianity overcame its disappointment and grew to become one of the world's largest religions. Even more, it retained its eschatological hopes, which have resurfaced repeatedly throughout history.

The most famous treatment of failed prophecy is that of Festinger, Riecken, and Schlachter (1964). (For another view, see Bader [1999].) They claim that failed prophecy results in increased proselytism designed to reduce "cognitive dissonance." "Cognitive dissonance" means the tension between what people think and what their actual experience is (Festinger 1989). Somehow people must reduce this tension. The hypothesis is that they do so first by believing even more strongly in their original conviction and second by converting more people so that they have more social support. As Festinger puts it,

> Suppose an individual believes something with his whole heart; suppose further that he has a commitment to his belief and that he has taken irrevocable actions because of it; finally, suppose that he is presented with evidence, unequivocal and undeniable evidence, that his belief is wrong: what will happen? The individual will frequently emerge, not only unshaken, but even more convinced of the truth of his beliefs than ever before. Indeed, he may even show a new fervor for convincing and converting other people to his view. (Festinger 1989, 259)

Festinger's theory has been influential. "Cognitive dissonance" is now a common notion in academia. Festinger does not claim that each and every instance of failed prophecy will result in stronger belief and engagement in missionary activity. It is only if believers are committed to the belief and have taken irrevocable measures in their own lives because of it, and if they are confronted with undeniable proof of the prophecy's failure, that things will go as Festinger suggests.

At the least, Festinger draws attention to the fact that failed prophecy does not necessarily bring a movement to an end, nor does it mean a lack of faith in the prophecy itself. It makes it less strange that failed prophecy is often not taken as simple failure by believers. But it does oversimplify possible reactions to failed prophecy. A common response is to reinterpret the prophecy, for example. If Jesus says that the end will come before the present generation passes away, then perhaps he meant something different by "generation" than is usual. He may have meant the present age in an apocalyptic sense, which could be quite a long time. Schmalz shows how the repeated failure of prophecy has been dealt with by the Jehovah's Witnesses (1994). Five times they expected the end to come in the twentieth century, and each time they were disappointed. On each occasion, their response was somewhat different and reshaped their theology and church structure.

Conclusion

We have now laid the foundations for our exploration of apocalypses and apocalypticism. We have working definitions of the literary form and world-view, and we have some idea about apocalyptic origins. Since ancient Hebrew prophecy was such an important source for apocalyptic forms and images, the next step will be to examine prophetic sections of the Hebrew Bible that fed into apocalypses.

Suggestions for Further Reading

Cohn, Norman. *The Pursuit of the Millennium: Revolutionary Millenarians and Mystical Anarchists of the Middle Ages*. New York: Oxford University Press, 1970.

Collins, John Joseph. *The Apocalyptic Imagination: An Introduction to Jewish Apocalyptic Literature*. 2nd ed. Grand Rapids: Eerdmans, 1998.

Cook, Stephen L. *Prophecy and Apocalypticism: The Postexilic Social Setting*. Minneapolis: Fortress, 1995.

Festinger, Leon, Henry W. Riecken, and Stanley Schlachter. *When Prophecy Fails: A Social and Psychological Study of a Modern Group That Predicted the Destruction of the World*. New York: Harper Torchbooks, 1964.

Forsyth, Neil. *The Old Enemy: Satan and the Combat Myth*. Princeton: Princeton University Press, 1987.

Horsley, Richard A. *Revolt of the Scribes: Resistance and Apocalyptic Origins*. Minneapolis: Fortress, 2010.

Koch, Klaus. *The Rediscovery of Apocalyptic: A Polemical Work on a Neglected Area of Biblical Studies and Its Damaging Effects on Theology and Philosophy*. London: SCM, 1972.

O'Leary, Stephen D. *Arguing the Apocalypse: A Theory of Millennial Rhetoric*. New York: Oxford University Press, 1994.

2

Proto-Apocalyptic Biblical Texts

Proto-apocalyptic biblical texts are passages from the Hebrew Bible that contain literary forms, images, mythological elements, and ideas that lay the groundwork for later apocalypses. Especially important are eschatological scenarios, as well as throne scenes and messianic passages. The works in which these passages are found are not apocalypses, and they lack some full-blown apocalyptic ideas, but they expose the deep roots in Israel's sacred traditions from which Jewish apocalypticism grew. The main Israelite and Jewish contributions to the Jewish apocalypses come from the prophets and the Psalms.

Our working definition of proto-apocalyptic is quite broad. Any elements that proved useful in apocalypses and in apocalyptic scenarios are included. The aim is to make available and familiar the rich store of biblical tradition available to apocalyptic thought. When we inventory "apocalyptic elements" at the end of documents, the phrase does not mean that these elements are necessary to apocalypses. Rather, it lists elements present elsewhere in Jewish tradition, but that found a congenial home in apocalypses as well. We do this in the interest of demonstrating how deeply apocalyptic thinkers dipped into Jewish traditions and equipping the reader with knowledge of such traditions. Perhaps this use of terminology is too loose for some stricter delineations of apocalypticism, and that is understandable. Nonetheless, they will suffice for the purpose of this book, which is to introduce readers to apocalyptic concepts.

The Combat Myth in the Bible

The combat myth is important to ancient Near Eastern mythology; allusions to it are present within the Hebrew Bible. Clifford delineates four stages in the biblical use of the combat myth (Clifford 1998, 29–35).

Stages of Biblical Use of the Combat Myth

Stage	Time	Characteristics	Examples
1	Early period	Hymns celebrating God's past victory that brought Israel into existence	Exod. 15
2	Monarchic period	Hymns similar to stage one; laments asking that God again assert himself to rescue Israel against its enemies who threaten it	Like stage one hymns: Pss. 93, 96, 114 Laments: Pss. 74, 77, 89
3	Postexilic period	Israel has lost land, city, temple, and it asks for a future intervention of God to rectify the situation	Isa. 43:18–21; 51:9–11
4	Late biblical and postbiblical period	Transformation of the combat myth in terms of monotheism; preservation of elements such as two related godlike figures; divine assembly	Dan. 7; Rev. 4–5; 12

Stage One

Exodus tells the story of Israel's escape from Egypt. After the splitting of the Red Sea, Moses sings a hymn to God (Exod. 15:1–18). In keeping with the Bible's tendency to historicize mythology, Yahweh, Israel's God, does not fight the sea directly; his victory over Pharaoh at the sea is celebrated. That occupies the first part of the hymn. In the second part, Yahweh leads the way to his sanctuary.

In Exod. 15:9, Israel's enemy declares his intention to destroy Israel (Forsyth 1987, 448–51). God responds by exhibiting his warlike qualities, epitomized in 15:3: "The LORD [Yahweh] is a warrior; the LORD [Yahweh] is his name." (The NRSV substitutes LORD in small capital letters for each occurrence of "Yahweh" in the text. This is out of respect for the sacredness of the divine name, which Jews avoid pronouncing.) Exodus 15 describes God throwing the Egyptian army into the sea, with all its riders, horsemen, and chariots. The splitting of the sea is described as follows: "At the blast of your nostrils the waters piled up, the floods stood up in a heap; the deeps congealed in the heart of the sea" (15:8). This is direct confrontation between God and the sea. Exodus 15:11 asks, "Who is like you, O LORD, among the gods? Who is like you, majestic in holiness, awesome in splendor, doing wonders?" God is the greatest of the gods, but the verse assumes polytheism.

God guides the people to his land, plants them on its mountain, and makes his abode there (15:13–15). These are allusions to the land of Israel, Jerusalem, and its temple. The new order is associated with a political arrangement, in this case, Israel's possession of the hill country of Canaan and the establishment of Jerusalem. The building of a temple after victory is typical of the combat myth. Acclamation of God's kingship concludes the hymn: "the LORD will reign forever and ever" (15:18).

Stage Two

Several laments among the psalms appeal to the combat myth because Israel needs God to fight for it as in the past (Pss. 74, 77, 89). Clifford analyzes Ps. 89. The psalm celebrates God's relationship with King David and laments the fact that his dynasty is in jeopardy. Remembering God's promises to David that his descendants would always rule, the hymn praises God for his supreme status within the divine assembly.

> Let the heavens praise your wonders, O LORD,
>   your faithfulness in the assembly of the holy ones.
> For who in the skies can be compared to the LORD?
>   Who among the heavenly beings [literally, "sons of gods"] is like the
>   LORD,
> a God feared in the council of the holy ones,
>   great and awesome above all that are around him? . . .
> You rule the raging of the sea;
>   when its waves rise, you still them.
> You crushed Rahab like a carcass;
>   you scattered your enemies with your mighty arm. (89:5–7, 9–10)

Rahab is a mythological monster (see Job 26:12; Ps. 87:4; Isa. 30:7; 51:9); God triumphed over Egypt when he "conquered" the Red Sea. In Job, the identity of sea and Rahab is clear: "By his power he stilled the Sea; by his understanding he struck down Rahab" (26:12). This recalls Marduk's victory over Tiamat (Babylonian) and Baal's victory over Yamm (Canaanite).

In the combat myth, the god's victory is followed by his assuming kingship and building a temple; this psalm now speaks of God's bringing David as king to God's temple (89:19–37). God promises to protect David, bring him prosperity, and make him victorious. But God has apparently deserted David, since his enemies prevail. The psalm urges God to act, lest God's past victory and his promises to David be in vain.

Stage Three

Toward the end of the Babylonian exile a prophet arose who prophesied the end of Israel's punishment. His oracles are preserved in Isa. 40–55, known as Second Isaiah. The following oracle begs God to repeat his past victory to restore Israel.

> Was it not you who cut Rahab in pieces,
>   who pierced the dragon?
> Was it not you who dried up the sea,
>   the waters of the great deep;
> who made the depths of the sea a way
>   for the redeemed to cross over? (Isa. 51:9–10)

New divine intervention is needed. Mythology, cutting Rahab in pieces, is juxtaposed with "history," the crossing of the Red Sea.

Stage Four

We treat Daniel and Revelation later in this book.

Messiah and Messianic Hopes

"Messiah" (*māšîyaḥ*) is Hebrew for "anointed." Anointing with oil in ancient Israel set individuals apart for special tasks. Kings were anointed, as were head priests. Anointing is occasionally done to others—patriarchs, prophets, and, in one case, a foreign king, the Persian Cyrus the Great. Messiahs in the Bible are human (Fitzmyer 2007, 8–25). The Greek equivalent of "messiah" is *christos*.

References to a messiah do not necessarily imply "messianic" hopes. The word "messianic" refers to an eschatological leader. Messianic texts originate when there is no king and an idealized one is expected. Even when the term "messiah" is not explicit, scholars sometimes use the adjective "messianic" in reference to hopes for an eschatological leader. Eschatological messiahs can be royal, priestly, prophetic, or none of these. For a full consideration of terminology, see Collins (1995, 11–14; Yarbro Collins and Collins 2008, 1–2).

Royal Ideology

Royal ideology is a set of idealistic assertions about kingship. Essential elements of Israelite kingship were that it was founded, maintained, and guaranteed by God, and that it promotes and enforces God's will on earth.

The Deuteronomistic History

The Deuteronomistic History consists of Joshua, Judges, 1–2 Samuel, and 1–2 Kings. It views Israel's history in the light of certain themes, some of which derive from the book of Deuteronomy. It is anti-idolatry, biased in favor of the southern kingdom of Judah as opposed to the northern kingdom of Israel, and considers the house of David as the legitimate bearer of God's authority on earth. Prophets play an important role in the history. They condemn idolatry and reveal God's intention to reward or punish Israel. They make predictions, but their main purpose is to critique their contemporaries.

When David had secured his hegemony over north and south, he wished to build a temple ("house") for God. Every dynasty in the Near East needed a protector god. The prophet Nathan told David that his son, Solomon, would build the temple, but that God would establish a dynasty ("house") for David. In the following passage, God tells Nathan what to tell David about Solomon, his son.

> **2 Samuel 7: Davidic Kingship**
>
> - Solomon builds God's temple.
> - God establishes the Davidic dynasty.
> - The Davidic dynasty is everlasting.
> - The son of David is the son of God.
> - God gives the king rest from his enemies.
> - Israel's king is comparable to the great ones of the earth.

> He shall build a house for my name, and I will establish the throne of his kingdom forever. I will be a father to him, and he shall be a son to me. . . . Your house and your kingdom shall be made sure forever before me; your throne shall be established forever. (2 Sam. 7:13–14, 16)

Important elements of the passage are the following: God creates for David an everlasting dynasty; the Davidic king is also God's son; enemies of the dynasty will be defeated; kingship is associated with Israel's occupation of the land. The promise that the dynasty will last forever raises messianic hopes when the monarchy goes out of existence. This passage brings together the notions of son of David, son of God, king of Israel, and messiah. It is religious and political; the two are inseparable.

Psalm 2

Several psalms express royal ideology. Psalm 2 may have been recited on the occasion of a royal coronation in Jerusalem.

Psalm 2 assumes that Jerusalem is the seat of an empire. One king has died and another is to take his place. Subject nations decide to revolt, since the empire is vulnerable. God laughs, because he has already set his king, his "anointed" (messiah), on the throne in Zion. In verse 7, the king says,

> I will tell of the decree of the LORD:
> He said to me, "You are my son;
> today I have begotten you." (Ps. 2:7)

Psalm 2: Proto-Apocalyptic Elements

- The nations wish to revolt against God and God's messiah.
- God crowns his messiah and sets him on Zion.
- God is the king's father.
- God gives the messiah victory over his enemies.
- Wishes for long life for the king are expressed.

Psalm 72: Proto-Apocalyptic Elements

- The king enforces God's justice.
- The king defends the weak and the needy and crushes the oppressor.
- The king rules over the whole earth.
- Foreign kings bring Israel's kings tribute.
- The king brings fertility and prosperity.
- Wishes for long life for the king are expressed.

"Today I have begotten you" is adoption language. The king may not be literally divine, but he is no mere mortal, either (the question is debated) (Yarbro Collins and Collins 2008, 1–24). God promises the messiah victory over his enemies and worldwide rulership.

Psalm 72

Psalm 72 adds other elements to royal ideology. The king enforces God's justice (72:1–2). He protects the weak and needy and crushes the oppressor (72:4). God grants the king rule over all the kings of the earth (72:8–11), and his rule is as beneficial as rain that brings fertility (72:6). The earth is fruitful and its people prosper (72:16).

Psalm 89

Psalm 89 is another royal psalm (see also Ps. 132; Laato 1992). God declares that he has made a covenant with David. A "covenant" is an agreement between two parties. The covenant between a great emperor and his vassal was one way ancient Israel conceived of its relationship with God. God's covenantal qualities are "steadfast love [ḥesed]" and "faithfulness [ʾĕmet]." Steadfast love is what God does for Israel concretely, and faithfulness is his complete reliability, truthfulness, and loyalty to Israel (Doob Sakenfeld 1992; Healy 1992). David is "chosen" by God to be king, and God promises that his dynasty will last forever.

God is the greatest god, dominant in the divine assembly. Other gods respect and fear him, and none can compare to him. Verses 9–10 recall the combat myth. God rules the raging sea and calms it, and he crushes Rahab, the sea monster, and destroys his enemies. God possesses the earth, and steadfast love and faithfulness, along with righteousness and justice, are the foundation of God's throne. Israelite kingship ought to reflect the qualities of God's kingship.

God chooses David, crowns him, and sets his hand on the sea and his right hand on the rivers, another allusion to the combat myth, symbolizing

David's power and the extent of his reign. God says that David will cry, "You are my Father" (89:26). His dynasty will last forever.

David's kingship is divinely conferred, makes him God's messiah, and is everlasting. God is the king's father. God brings him success and victory, and the Davidic line will never fail.

Prophet and King

The prophet's role is exemplified in the relationship between David and Nathan. God speaks to the prophet. This is direct revelation. A truly wise king will accept the prophet's word, God's word, for his success depends on God's favor.

Micaiah ben Imlah

Israel's notorious King Ahab persuades Judah's king Jehoshaphat to ally with him against Aram (Syria; 1 Kings 22). They summon prophets to determine God's will. Four hundred court prophets urge the kings on. Ahab finally summons his prophetic nemesis, Micaiah ben Imlah, who is independent of the court establishment.

Micaiah says, "I saw the LORD sitting on his throne, with all the host of heaven standing beside him to the right and to the left of him" (22:19). God asks for a volunteer to mislead Ahab so that the king will pursue his war plans, even though God will not support him. A spirit volunteers and becomes a "lying spirit." Micaiah's negative prophecy is vindicated by events.

Psalm 89: Proto-Apocalyptic Elements

- God makes a covenant with David.
- God chooses David as king.
- David is God's messiah.
- David's dynasty is everlasting.
- God brings David victory over his enemies.
- God dominates the heavenly council.
- God conquers the sea.
- God conquers the sea dragon, Rahab.
- God's throne is founded on steadfast love, faithfulness, righteousness, and justice.

The Role of Prophet

- Prophets receive God's revelation directly.
- Their revelation reveals God's will and plans.
- They often interact with kings.
- They interpret their own times.
- They are involved in politics.
- They deliver oracles (God's words) of doom and salvation.

Divine King and Warrior

In a world of multiple gods, demons, angels, and cosmic powers, divine sovereignty cannot be assumed. Cosmic figures opposed to God can usurp creation.

<table>
</table>

1 Kings 22: Proto-Apocalyptic Elements

- Micaiah ben Imlah is a prophet in the time of King Ahab of Israel.
- There is a throne scene.
- In the heavenly court (divine assembly), Micaiah hears God's plans to deceive Ahab.
- The unseen world determines the seen world.
- Micaiah prophesies against Israelite and Judahite war plans, and his prophecy comes true.

Issues of divine and cosmic sovereignty mirror those on earth, where the wrong powers often rule. Cosmic realities reflect political realities.

God's kingship is prominent in the Hebrew Bible, as illustrated by the following list of texts and commentary (Scullion 1992, 1047).

Pss. 93:1; 96:10; 97:1; 99:1; see 1 Chron. 16:31:

The LORD is king [*yhwh mālāk*]!

Ps. 74:12–14, 16–17:

Yet God my King is from of old,
  working salvation in the earth.
You divided the sea by your might;
  you broke the heads of the dragons in the waters.
You crushed the heads of Leviathan;
  you gave him as food for the creatures of the wilderness. . . .
Yours is the day, yours also the night;
  you established the luminaries and the sun.
You have fixed all the bounds of the earth;
  you made summer and winter.

In Ps. 74, God is the universal creator, king of all. The psalm draws on the combat myth. God's violent action introduces the theme of God as divine warrior.

Ps. 93:1, 4:

The LORD is king, he is robed in majesty;
  the LORD is robed, he is girded with strength.
He has established the world; it shall never be moved. . . .
More majestic than the thunders of mighty waters,
  more majestic than the waves of the sea,
  majestic on high is the LORD!

Psalm 93 also associates creation with God's kingship. It refers to God's conquest of the waters, alluding to the combat myth. As king, God makes decrees on which one may rely. God is holy.

Ps. 98:6–8:

With trumpets and the sound of the horn
  make a joyful noise before the King, the LORD.

> Let the sea roar, and all that fills it;
>> the world and those who live in it.
> Let the floods clap their hands;
>> let the hills sing together for joy.

Psalm 98 calls for creation to praise God the King. The waters are enjoined to praise God as is the dry land. A universe subject to God will keep these two elements in balance—water and earth.

Ps. 89:9–11, 14:

> You rule the raging of the sea;
>> when its waves rise, you still them.
> You crushed Rahab like a carcass;
>> you scattered your enemies with your mighty arm.
> The heavens are yours, the earth also is yours;
>> the world and all that is in it—you have founded them. . . .
> Righteousness and justice are the foundation of your throne;
>> steadfast love and faithfulness go before you.

Psalm 89 echoes the familiar themes of kingship and conquest of the waters. Rahab, the sea monster, is singled out for attention. As king, God is a warrior who crushes his enemies. Mounts Tabor and Hermon, sacred to Canaanite religion, praise Yahweh, proving his universal rule. Might is not all that defines God's reign. It is built on righteousness, justice, steadfast love, and faithfulness. God is in a covenantal relationship with Israel.

Ps. 29:10:

> The Lord sits enthroned over the flood;
>> the Lord sits enthroned as king forever.

Psalm 29:10 emphasizes that God's kingship relates to his conquest of the waters, as does Ps. 104:6, following:

Ps. 104:6:

> You cover it with the deep as with a garment;
>> the waters stood above the mountains.

Ps. 24:1–2, 7–8:

> The earth is the Lord's and all that is in it,
>> the world, and those who live in it;
> for he has founded it on the seas,
> and established it on the rivers. . . .

> Lift up your heads, O gates!
>> and be lifted up, O ancient doors!
>> that the King of glory may come in.
> Who is the King of glory?
>> The LORD, strong and mighty,
>> the LORD, mighty in battle.

Psalm 24 proclaims God's universal sovereignty, basing it on his role as creator, here associated with the conquest of the waters. The psalm associates divine kingship with Zion and the temple cult. Those who seek God wish to enter the temple. They must be worthy (have "clean hands and pure hearts"). They seek the face of the God of Jacob. "Jacob" is used here because he is the father of all Israel, all twelve tribes. Psalm 24 may well have been sung at a festival where the ark circled and entered the temple. The idea that the temple gates must be open to let God in suggests this. Since the psalm opens with God's conquest of the waters, it is appropriate that he is depicted as "mighty in battle" toward the end (v. 8).

1 Sam. 4:4:

> So the people sent to Shiloh, and brought from there the ark of the covenant of the LORD of hosts, who is enthroned on the cherubim.

First Samuel 4:4 ties God's kingship to the ark of the covenant. It is his throne, and it accompanies Israel into battle so that a battle becomes a holy war.

Ps. 102:12:

> But you, O LORD, are enthroned forever;
>> your name endures to all generations.

Psalm 102:12 proclaims that God's rule is everlasting.

The idea that Israel's God is a warrior is associated with his kingship. The technical term for God's appearance is theophany (*theos* is "god" and *phanō* is "appear"). When God appears, it is terrifying. Earthquakes, the melting of mountains, thunder, and lightning accompany his appearance. When he appears in anger, things are even more extreme. When God appears as a warrior, his enemies tremble.

God is seen as the divine warrior in numerous biblical passages (Scullion 1992, 47). We saw that when Israel escaped pursuing Egyptian forces at the exodus, God's splitting of the Red Sea and drowning of the Egyptians was portrayed as a military victory, and God was declared in Moses's song to be a mighty warrior (Exod. 15:1–12). In Num. 10:9 Israel is told to sound the trumpets as it engages in battle so as to rouse God to their aid. God gives Israel victory over the Canaanites at Gibeon by throwing them into panic before Joshua's forces (Josh. 10:10). God does the same to Sisera's forces when they face the Israelite Barak (Judg. 4:15).

Jeremiah uses the warrior God figuratively as he declares that his enemies cannot prevail because God accompanies him as a "dread warrior" (20:11). Zephaniah assures his listeners that God is among them as a warrior and will give them success (3:17). Isaiah is vivid in his description: "The LORD goes forth like a soldier, like a warrior he stirs up his fury; he cries out, he shouts aloud, he shows himself mighty against his foes" (42:13). In Isaiah 59, God is enraged that there is no justice in Jerusalem. He comes as a warrior, armed with righteousness, salvation, and vengeance to redeem those in Israel who repent (59:15–20). Isaiah remembers when God came down in the past, and the mountains quaked in his presence. He prays that this will happen again so that God's adversaries and the nations might tremble (64:1–3).

The wisdom tradition generally does not make direct reference to God's historical actions or present eschatological scenarios. However, the picture of God as warrior is present even there. The book of Wisdom provides an awe-inspiring view of God's word, which leaped down from heaven from the divine throne. God has a sword and fills the earth with death. He touches heaven while standing on earth. Sirach, another wisdom work, paints a similar picture. God is a warrior who will demolish the unmerciful and wreak retribution on the nations. Kings are unrighteous, and God will destroy their scepters. All the unrighteous will pay for their evil deeds, but ultimately God will have mercy on his people (Sir. 35:22–25).

God tells Israel whether or not to fight and what tactics to use (for example, Exod. 17:16; Num. 31:3; Deut. 23:14; 2 Sam. 5:19, 23; 1 Kings 22:5–8). It is often said that God does not need human strength, such as a large army, to conquer (1 Sam. 14:6; 17:47). This encourages Israel when it faces a superior enemy. Israel's leaders tell Israel that God has already given their enemies into their hand, so that they should fight with confidence (Judg. 3:28). The intercession of figures like Moses and Samuel brings God to Israel's aid (1 Sam. 7:8). These are the basics of holy war.

Preexilic Prophetic Books

Joel

Joel provided later prophets and seers with vivid images. The historical circumstances in which the book was written are vague. Two crises form its historical background—a plague of locusts and an invasion by a foreign power, but we cannot identify either.

Joel's locust plague is haunting. The swarming locusts have lion-like teeth to devour crops. Before them the land is like the Garden of Eden; behind

Joel: Proto-Apocalyptic Elements

- There is disruption of heavenly bodies, the failing of moon and sun, and the falling of stars (three times).
- Portents appear in heaven and earth.
- Trumpets call to a fast.
- A locust invasion destroys the earth and its crops—revealing God as divine warrior and general of a vast army.
- In a theophany, God roars from Zion.
- Divine judgment occurs.
- There is language of the day of the Lord in the valley of decision.
- Zion is protected because God dwells there.
- Holiness of Zion is spoken of.
- Trumpets call Israel to prayer.
- The Spirit is poured out on Israel.

them is devastation (2:3). They look like warhorses and sound like chariots. Their destructive force is like fire. They are disciplined warriors.

Joel commands that trumpets blow in Zion to proclaim a fast. In 2:1, the sound of the trumpet on God's holy mountain warns of the approach of the "day of the Lord." This day may have originally meant a joyous feast for God, so when Joel says it is a day of darkness, he reverses expectations (Collins 2004, 421).

The locusts are God's army, so God is the Divine Warrior: Their fearsomeness causes an earthquake. The heavens shake, and the sun, moon, and stars stop shining. The crisis is enormous. This is a punishing theophany. God leads a vast army in an invasion of his own land. The day of the Lord, the day of judgment, is "terrible indeed." The scene will inspire Revelation's author.

Despite all, God stands ready to forgive. Joel calls for repentance. God will restore the land's prosperity if Israel responds. Prosperity will be accompanied by something greater—an outpouring of God's prophetic Spirit:

> Then afterward
>   I will pour out my spirit on all flesh;
> your sons and your daughters shall prophesy,
>   your old men shall dream dreams,
>   and your young men shall see visions.
> Even on the male and female slaves,
>   in those days, I will pour out my spirit. (Joel 2:28–29)

Again God predicts heavenly and earthly portents—blood, fire, smoke, darkened sun, bloody moon. All will precede the "great and terrible day of the Lord" (2:31). The prophet uses celestial disruption yet a third time to accompany God's theophany in the "valley of decision" (3:14). Sun and moon darken, stars cease shining, and God roars from Jerusalem, causing heaven and earth to shake and making clear that God dwells there and protects his people (3:14–17). Henceforth, strangers cannot even pass through it.

Fig. 2. Megiddo was a fortress in the Jezreel Valley. It was located on a strategic road, and many important battles were fought there. Solomon fortified Megiddo. The book of Revelation expects the great eschatological battle to take place there (16:16). (Jim Yancey)

Amos

There is not a great deal in Amos that feeds directly into apocalypticism. However, several aspects of the book are worth mentioning in this context. Amos prophesied in the eighth century in the northern kingdom. He was outraged by the social injustices he witnessed—the blatant exploitation of the poor by the rich. He declares that the day of the Lord, expected to be a joyous cultic celebration, will in fact be a time of darkness and judgment (5:18–20). The book is unrelentingly negative and judgmental until the very end, which may be an addition to provide hope.

Amos claims that God does nothing without revealing it to his prophets (3:7). This becomes a principle in the community of the Dead Sea Scrolls, which searches the prophets for references to itself (1QpHab 7:1–5), as well as the book of Revelation (10:7).

First Isaiah (Isaiah 1–39)

First Isaiah consists of Isa. 1–39. Isaiah prophesied in Judah in the eighth and early seventh centuries (738–688 BCE). During this critical period, the northern kingdom, Israel, fell to the expanding Assyrian Empire (721 BCE), and Judah barely escaped the same fate.

Throne scene. First Isaiah contains a throne scene in which the prophet receives his prophetic commission:

> In the year that King Uzziah died, I saw the LORD sitting on a throne, high and lofty; and the hem of his robe filled the temple. Seraphs were in attendance above him; each had six wings: with two they covered their faces, and with two they covered their feet, and with two they flew. And one called to another and said:
>   "Holy, holy, holy is the LORD of hosts;
>   the whole earth is full of his glory." (Isa. 6:1–3)

The temple shakes at the sound and fills with smoke. Isaiah's vision legitimates his ministry. In the presence of God and his court, God sends Isaiah with special revelation and a specific task. Isaiah does not travel to heaven. God sits on an immense throne, while only the hem of his garment fills the temple. This is a way of saying that God is associated with the temple and that Isaiah encounters God in that sacred place, but that the temple cannot hold God (compare 1 Kings 8). Nevertheless, the prophet has access to the divine realm.

Isaiah beholds an imperial court. God has attendants, as would any great emperor. They are heavenly beings. Humans can be granted access to that realm at God's pleasure but cannot enter or see it without divine approval.

God's attendants are "seraphs." These are semidivine figures. They belong to the heavenly realm. They are God's servants. The text does not use the term "angel," but we use the term as one of convenience and convention, though the terminology is unsatisfactory since they are not called angels, nor do they fit the stereotype most moderns have of angels. The English word "angel" is in any case rather general, translating the Hebrew *mal'ak* and transliterating the Greek *angelos*, each meaning "messenger." The seraphs praise God, and one mediates between the prophet and God.

The seraphs are strange and fearsome. We do not hear what they look like, apart from the fact that they have six wings, along with faces and feet. The Hebrew *śāraph* means "to burn." References to seraphs (plural: *śĕrāphîm*) occur in Isa. 14:29 and 30:6. Taken together, these references describe a fiery creature in the shape of a flying serpent. The seraphs use two wings to cover their faces, an act of humility before God's majesty, and two to cover their feet. If feet is a biblical euphemism here for sexual organs, then the seraphs are modest before God. Modern readers might wonder whether heavenly beings were sexual. They sometimes were. Finally, the seraphs use two of their wings to fly. They are mobile and swift. Isaiah reacts with fear.

Judgment. Isaiah is disturbed that Israel is not socially just, and that it uses the cult (official temple worship) as if that could establish a good relationship with God without righteous behavior. Isaiah says, "For the LORD of hosts has a day against all that is proud and lofty, against all that is lifted up and high" (2:12). The "day" of the Lord came to mean the day on which God comes to judge. The day is against the lofty—the powerful, the rich, the arrogant, those who oppose the poor, and those who disrespect God's sovereignty. God's coming in judgment is terrifying (2:21).

Themes of judgment reappear throughout Isaiah. Isaiah 13:9–10 says that the coming of God's day will be filled with cruelty, wrath, and anger, and that it will desolate the earth. Stars, moon, and sun will fail, and the arrogant will be brought down.

Isaiah 14:12–21 preserves a fragment of mythology in which a lesser god assaults heaven. It is an oracle in which the king of Babylon is taunted for his defeat. The king's ambitions amount to an attack on the heavenly order. Heavenly events correspond to earthly, political ones. Ancient Near Eastern mythology envisaged rebellion in heaven—the attempt by a lesser god to usurp the place of the head of the pantheon (Hanson 1977), and the fragment draws on this tradition (as does Daniel in the case of Antiochus IV). The mythological mountain where the gods gathered in Canaanite mythology was Mount Zaphon in the far north (see Pss. 48:2; 89:12) (Clifford 1972). We know of an instance of heavenly rebellion in Canaanite mythology that informs Isa. 14. In that episode, "Day Star, son of Dawn" in Isa. 14:12 alludes to the Canaanite god Ashtar, the day star (first star of the morning, Venus), who aspires to become the head god. He seeks to establish his throne on the sacred mountain, in the divine assembly, and to make himself like the "most high" god. He challenges Baal and fails (Seow 2003, 122; Clifford 1972, 165).

In Isa. 14, the offender is cast down to the "pit," Sheol (14:9). Babylon's fall is both political and cosmic. Babylon is not only a city; it is a divine force opposed to God. Just as Ashtar challenges Baal in the Canaanite myth, the Babylonian king challenges God through his treatment of God's people, Israel.

Isaiah's prophecies of doom are interspersed with oracles of salvation. In 4:2–6 he speaks of the "branch" of the Lord which is beautiful and glorious, while the land is fruitful to the glory of Israel's remnant. The "remnant" is what is left of Israel after God's punishment. "Branch" is a royal term, coming ultimately from Isa. 11, where the stump of Jesse, David's father, sprouts a branch to renew the monarchy. The branch is in Jerusalem. When this passage is read in an eschatological context where there is no king, it becomes messianic. God cleanses Jerusalem from the pollution caused by Israel's sin, the "filth of the daughters of Zion." This is purity language. God cleanses "by a spirit of judgment and by a spirit of burning." Everyone in Jerusalem will be "holy."

God creates a cloud to protect Mount Zion by day, and it flames at night. This alludes to the pillar of cloud and fire that guided Israel in the wilderness after they escaped from Egypt (Exod. 13:21). It is a symbol of God's presence and of his benefits. God protects Mount Zion, even to the extent of surpassing the function of the sun and moon (Isa. 4:5–6).

Another passage of interest is Isa. 2 (see Mic. 4:1–3). It may be an eschatological scenario from after Isaiah's time. It portrays a time when "the mountain of the LORD's house," Zion, will be the highest of all mountains on earth (2:2). The nations will stream to it to learn God's ways. "For out of Zion shall go forth instruction (*tôrâ*), and the word of the LORD from Jerusalem" (2:3). God will judge between the nations, and warfare will end. The passage contains the famous words, "They shall beat their swords into plowshares, and their spears into pruning hooks; nation shall not lift up sword against nation, neither shall they learn war any more" (2:4).

Ideal king. Isaiah 9 and 11 portray the ideal king (Collins 2004, 314–16). In chapter 9, the birth of a royal child means the defeat of Israel's oppressors. The newborn receives exalted titles—"Wonderful Counselor, Mighty God, Everlasting Father, Prince of Peace" (9:6). Particularly noteworthy is the title "God." The chapter identifies the child as of the line of David, as the bringer of endless peace, and as establishing eternal justice.

Isaiah 11 pictures the resurgence of a glorious Davidic dynasty. The oracle stems from a time when Judah's dynasty was in eclipse. A new Judahite king will arise to destroy Judah's enemies, institute justice, and bring peace. The exiles will return to their homeland and there will be a reconciliation between Israel and Judah (11:10–16).

"Isaiah Apocalypse." A final text from First Isaiah almost certainly dates from later than the original prophet. It is often called the "Isaiah Apocalypse" (chaps. 24–27). It is not formally an apocalypse, but it does have apocalyptic elements. It begins with the announcement of divine judgment on the whole earth. God is about to come to "lay waste the earth and make it desolate" (24:1). Humans have "polluted" by transgressing God's laws and violating "the eternal covenant" (24:5). The effects of transgression are cosmic. The passage recalls the flood of Gen. 6. The order God imposed by restricting the waters at creation breaks down. In Isa. 24:18, the "windows of heaven" are opened (cf. Gen. 7:11). Waters pour in from above, and the very foundations of the earth tremble. The earth is in peril of reverting to its original chaotic state. It staggers like a drunken person. A close connection between human action and the universe typifies later prophecy and is integral to apocalypticism.

God's judgment affects all segments of society, low and high, and it uses the language of cosmic destruction. God's wrath is terrifying, and there is nowhere to escape it.

Isaiah 24:21–23 presents an apocalyptic scene.

> On that day the LORD will punish
>   the host [*sĕbā'*] of heaven in heaven,
>   and on earth the kings of the earth.
> They will be gathered together
>   like prisoners in a pit;
> they will be shut up in a prison,
>   and after many days they will be punished.

First Isaiah: Proto-Apocalyptic Elements

- There is a throne scene.
- God is on the throne.
- Seraphim (fiery, winged, serpent-like creatures) surround God.
- Isaiah reacts with fear.
- Isaiah is commissioned as a prophet.
- The unseen world determines the seen world.
- Rebellion occurs in heaven.
- The ideal king (messiah) is described.
- Jerusalem is central; all nations worship there; it is the source of divine instruction (*tôrâ*) for the nations.
- Cosmic transformation happens (Zion is the greatest of mountains).
- There are allusions to the mythological sea monster (Leviathan) of the combat myth.
- In the "Isaiah Apocalypse," the mighty and the angels are punished.
- Angels are temporarily imprisoned under the earth.
- The exiles return.
- God holds an end-time banquet.
- There is cosmic disruption: the stars, sun, and moon fail to give light.
- There is a theophany.
- Judgment occurs.
- God leads a heavenly host.
- The windows of heaven are opened.
- Earth staggers like a drunkard.
- There is universal peace.

> Then the moon will be abashed,
>   and the sun ashamed;
> for the LORD of hosts will reign
>   on Mount Zion and in Jerusalem,
> and before his elders he will manifest his glory.

"Hosts" means multitudes. Hosts is also a military term, so the hosts of heaven can mean God's army. God punishes heavenly beings and kings of the earth. Both are imprisoned in a "pit," a space under the earth, and stay there until their final punishment. God restores order, and the sun and moon are ashamed. God reigns on Mount Zion.

Isaiah 25 pictures a banquet given by God on Zion. Invited are all nations who recognize God's sovereignty. God's people, having once lived in shame, are properly honored. The scene foreshadows apocalyptic banquet scenes. When a messiah is present, it can properly be called a "messianic banquet" (D. Smith 1992).

Isaiah 26:19 speaks of corpses rising and dwellers in the dust awakening. If this refers to individual resurrection and if it predates Daniel, it would be the first extant Jewish reference to resurrection. Unfortunately, we cannot date the passage with certainty, and the reference to resurrection may be symbolic, representing restoration of the nation.

In Isa. 27:1 God takes a sword to punish "Leviathan the fleeing serpent, Leviathan the twisting serpent, and he will kill the dragon that is in the sea," an allusion to the combat myth.

God will bring the Israelite exiles back to their homeland (27:12–13). The exiles return from north and south (Egypt). The text is written from the point of view of the south, Judah, so all Israel gathers in Jerusalem to worship.

Prophecy during the Babylonian Exile

Ezekiel

Ezekiel prophesied from 593 to 571 BCE. When Nebuchadnezzar II deported some of Jerusalem's leading citizens to Babylonia in 597 BCE, Ezekiel was among them. He was still there when Nebuchadnezzar destroyed Jerusalem and its temple and exiled most of the rest of its important citizens in 586 BCE. So his entire prophetic career transpired in Babylon, part of it before 586 and part afterward. Chapters 1–24 address issues before the second deportation, and the rest of the book deals with what follows.

Ezekiel was a Zadokite priest, a descendant of Solomon's high priest (Hunt 2006). The Zadokite family was the most important priestly family in the Second Temple period (Hunt 2006).

Ezekiel was the recipient of direct visions from God. More than any other prophet, he furnished apocalypticism with forms, patterns, images, and concepts (Ruiz 1989).

The book of Ezekiel begins with a magnificent vision of God. The prophet is in Babylonia. He is beside the River Chebar, a canal near the city of Nippur which was just southeast of Babylon itself. Suddenly he experiences a theophany. He perceives a stormy wind coming from the north (site of the Canaanite holy mountains). A fiery cloud appears, and gleaming amber is in its midst, a feature of God's presence in 1:27.

In the middle of it [the cloud] was something like four living creatures. This was their appearance: they were of human form. Each had four faces, and each of them had four wings. . . . Under their wings on their four sides they had human hands. And the four had their faces and their wings thus: their wings touched one another; each of them moved straight ahead, without turning as they moved. As for the appearance of their faces: the four had the face of a human being, the face of a lion on the right side, the face of an ox on the left side, and the face of an eagle; such were their faces. Their wings were spread out above; each creature had two wings, each of which touched the wing of another, while two covered their bodies. Each moved straight ahead; wherever the spirit would go, they went, without turning as they went. . . .

Their rims were tall and awesome, for the rims of all four were full of eyes all around. . . . Wherever the spirit would go, they went, and the wheels rose along with them; for the spirit of the living creatures was in the wheels. (Ezek. 1:5–6, 8–12, 18, 20)

Fire and cloud are often associated with God's presence, as is strong wind. A god on clouds recalls Baal, rider of the clouds. The repetition of phrases such as "something like," as throughout this chapter, typically signals mystical language. Heavenly entities experienced by the visionary are both capable and incapable of being described. They are both like and unlike things of common experience.

Ezekiel describes within the cloud "something like four living creatures" (1:5). Although he does not call them angels, they seem to be such. Angels are frequently said to look like humans. The Hebrew for "living creatures" is *ḥayyôt*, and later Jewish tradition took them to be a class of angels. They are strange and composite, looking something like humans, but with wings and hooved feet, sparkling like burnished bronze, and with four faces on the four sides of their heads. The faces may have something to do with including different categories of creatures—of the air, of the ground and wild, of the ground and tame, and human. Faces pointing in four directions may convey watchfulness, on the lookout for God's enemies. They are a species of bodyguard and of transportation for God.

The creatures have four wings. Two cover their bodies in modesty and two stretch toward the nearest creatures, so that they form a foundation for the dome they carry, discussed below. Wings also indicate mobility.

Burning coals like torches are common in such scenes. God's altar always has a fire burning; a fire consumes sacrifices. Heaven and earth correspond.

Ezekiel sees a wheel beside each creature. The wheels have eyes all around. Again, the point is mobility and watchfulness. Wheels are found on chariots, and gods ride on heavenly chariots. Later tradition sees the wheels themselves as angels, and since the Hebrew word for "wheels" here is *'ôphanîm*, that becomes the name for another angelic category. The Hebrew for chariot is *merkābā*. Later Jewish mysticism gifted its practitioners with a vision of God's chariot and so is termed merkabah mysticism (Gruenwald 1980).

Ezekiel has described God's transportation and retinue. Now his focus moves upward. He sees a "dome" (*rāqîyaʾ*). This is the same Hebrew word that designates the dome ("firmament") of heaven in the creation narrative in Gen. 1. The dome here is like an upside-down bowl of transparent crystal.

The creatures' wings spread beneath the dome and carry it. Their wings make "the sound of mighty waters, like the thunder of the Almighty (*Šadday*), a sound of tumult like the sound of an army" (1:24). *Šadday* was an epithet for El, supreme god of the Canaanite pantheon, an epithet adopted for Yahweh. Ezekiel hears a voice from above the dome.

Finally Ezekiel sees God. Indirect language ("something like," and so on) grows abundant when Ezekiel describes the most transcendent one. Ezekiel sees a "dome" above the creatures, and above the dome, or firmament, there is a throne. God's form is humanlike. From the loins up, he is like gleaming amber. From the loins down, he is fire. His throne is like a precious jewel. There is brightness as of a rainbow, a reference to the rainbow in the clouds at the conclusion of the flood narrative (Gen. 9:13–16). The conclusion is: "This was the *appearance* of the *likeness* of the *glory* of the LORD" (1:28). The italicized (not in the original) words stress the impossibility of really describing God, yet Ezekiel has seen God and must describe the divinity. "Glory" is a circumlocution for God's presence beloved of priests. Ezekiel adds two other qualifiers—"appearance" and "likeness." The reader remains at three removes from seeing God directly yet has experienced God's presence vicariously.

Ezekiel's response is awe and fear. He falls to the ground and immediately hears someone speaking. It turns out to be God. We hear his words in the next chapter.

In chapters 8–11, Ezekiel is transported through a vision back to Judah to observe the sins of the people in Jerusalem and the temple. As an upper-class priest, he is especially upset by what he sees—idolatry in the temple (chap. 8). In the postexilic period, monotheism was the general rule, first for Jews and then for Christians, although this must be qualified; Second Temple Jews did believe in a multitude of invisible beings that were superhuman, even if they were not equal to God (Hurtado 1988; Yarbro Collins and Collins 2008). Earlier, Israel was to some extent polytheistic (M. S. Smith 2002).

Ezekiel was staunchly anti-idolatry. Not all establishment priests followed his lead. Ezekiel believed that idolatry, as well as other sins such as bloodshed and sexual sins, defiled the land. In his concern for the holiness of the whole land, and not just the temple and its precincts, Ezekiel was in accord with the Holiness Code, a particular strand of priestly thought represented by Lev. 17–27 and other texts (Klawans 2000; 2006; Milgrom 1991; 2000; 2001).

The first idolatrous image that Ezekiel encounters is the "image of jealousy, which provokes to jealousy. And the glory of the God of Israel was there, like the vision that I had seen in the valley" (8:3–4). God is still in the temple, despite its pollution by idols.

In Ezek. 9, God summons six executioners, which are angelic figures (9:1–2). Then he calls a seventh, this one clothed in linen (priestly garb) with a writing case. God commands the latter to go through the city and mark the foreheads of all who lament the idolatry. The six executioners then go through the city and slaughter all who lack the mark.

Just before the destruction takes place, God begins to exit from the temple. The stages of his departure punctuate chapters 9–11 and tie it together. We collect them to clarify the process.

> Now the glory of the God of Israel had gone up from the cherub on which it rested to the threshold of the house. (9:3)
>
> The cherubim were standing on the south side of the house when the man went in; and a cloud filled the inner court. Then the glory of the Lord rose up from the cherub to the threshold of the house; the house was filled with the cloud, and the court was full of the brightness of the glory of the Lord. The sound of the wings of the cherubim was heard as far as the outer court, like the voice of God Almighty when he speaks. (10:3–5)
>
> Then the glory of the Lord went out from the threshold of the house and stopped above the cherubim. The cherubim lifted up their wings and rose up from the earth in my sight as they went out with the wheels beside them. They stopped at the entrance of the east gate of the house of the Lord; and the glory of the God of Israel was above them. (10:18–19)
>
> Therefore say: Thus says the Lord God: Though I removed them far away among the nations, and though I scattered them among the countries, yet I have been a sanctuary to them for a little while in the countries where they have gone. (11:16)
>
> Then the cherubim lifted up their wings, with the wheels beside them; and the glory of the God of Israel was above them. And the glory of the Lord ascended from the middle of the city, and stopped on the mountain east of the city. The spirit lifted me up and brought me in a vision by the spirit of God into Chaldea, to the exiles. (11:22–24)

God's first movement brings him from the inner temple to the threshold of the house (9:3). God arises from the cherubim and travels alone. The cherubim are represented by carved angelic figures who overshadow the ark in a protective manner. The cherubim he sees are the same as the living creatures Ezekiel saw in his initial vision by the River Chebar (10:15, 20, 22; see 43:3).

In 10:3–5, God's movement repeats what occurred previously, but God's presence now fills the temple and inner court, and the noise of the cherubim's movements are audible in the outer court.

In 10:15–19, God and the cherubim move together to the eastern gate of the temple complex. The complex faced east, and the eastern gate was an architectural focus. As God moves to the gate, he leaves the temple behind and goes east to the Mount of Olives, from which he presumably continues eastward, all the way to the exilic community.

In 11:1, Ezekiel moves to the east gate. God explains that he will be a sanctuary to the exiles in Babylon (11:16–21). Then God will gather and bring the exiles back to Jerusalem. They will return to the land, remove its abominations, and God will renew his covenantal relationship with Israel. Even in the midst of this devastation, there is promise of restoration.

Finally, God leaves the city (11:23) and goes to the Mount of Olives. The Babylonians can now destroy it.

Chapter 34 roundly condemns Israel's shepherds, primarily its royal leaders. Israel's shepherds feed not the sheep but themselves; they do not strengthen the weak, heal the sick, bind the injured, bring back the strayed, or find the lost. They rule badly. God will take over the care of the sheep personally (34:15). He will seek them out and gather them from exile.

Chapter 36 presents restoration in priestly terms. Israel has defiled the holy land, and Israel defiles God's name even in the exile because its transgressions dishonor God. God will cleanse Israel and reinstate it in the land for the sake of the holiness of his name, not because Israel deserves it. Holiness means God's majesty, God's honor, and proper recognition of God by all peoples. God will act for his name, making it holy. This is the meaning of God's "sanctifying" his name in the chapter. The Hebrew word *qiddaš* means "to make holy." It could be translated "to hallow," an archaic English equivalent inscribed on Christian consciousness through frequent repetition of the Lord's Prayer. Indeed, Matthew's version of the Lord's Prayer preserves a version of what it means to hallow God's name—that his will be done on earth as it is in heaven (Matt. 6:9–10). This accords with Ezek. 36.

God promises that once Israel is cleansed and reinstated, the land will become like the "garden of Eden" (36:33–35). This follows the apocalyptic principle that the end is like the beginning. Origins are renewed.

Chapter 37 contains Ezekiel's vision of the valley of dry bones. As he preaches to the bones, they take on flesh and rise from the dead. This is not a literal resurrection of individuals but signifies renewal of the nation.

Ezekiel foresees that God again will make the kingdoms of Israel and Judah a single kingdom, ruled by a Davidic king (37:21–22). This is idealistic, since the northern kingdom is still "lost." Nonetheless, the restoration of Israel must involve all of Israel, not just the south. Israel's restoration convinces all nations that God sanctifies Israel (37:28).

Although Ezekiel expects restoration of the monarchy, he is wary of kingship. He indicts Israel's shepherds in chapter 34 and again in 43:7–9. In the latter, God accuses the kings of defiling the divine name and "whoring," a reference to idolatry. God does not want their tombs near him. Ezekiel 40–48 excludes the kings from the pure, restored priestly area.

Finally we arrive at the great eschatological vision in chapters 38–39. The chapters picture a huge battle preceding the establishment of peace in Jerusalem. This scene informs many apocalyptic final battles.

Ezekiel prophesies against Gog of the land of Magog. Gog is mythological as far as we can determine. Gog is "chief prince of Meshech and Tubal,"

Ezekiel: Proto-Apocalyptic Elements

- There is a throne scene.
- There is a chariot.
- Four "living creatures" are present.
- Ezekiel reacts with fear.
- God departs from the temple and goes to the exile.
- The exiles return.
- The end is like the beginning.
- Judgment occurs in Jerusalem, but those with a seal on their foreheads are spared; live coals are scattered over Jerusalem.
- God condemns the shepherds (leaders) and becomes shepherd of the sheep.
- The dead bones are raised.
- Final battle occurs between Israel and the nations (Gog of Magog) before Jerusalem.
- The ideal temple and city are described.

who in 32:26–28 are said to already be in the underworld. This adds to the mythological aspect of the passage. The Hebrew for "chief prince" is *rō'š*, literally, "head." Other members of the coalition against Jerusalem include Persia, Ethiopia, Put, Gomer, and Beth-togarmah (38:5–6), representative of the known world. The world rallies against Israel. God declares that he is against this coalition, but that Gog and his forces must muster at some time in the future. They will attack an Israel that has come back from exile and is living in peace in the promised land. The land of Israel is said to be the "center [navel] of the earth." The attack will seem overwhelming.

God declares that his coming victory over the nations will convince all nations of his supremacy and prove his holiness. The coalition members will die on Israel's mountains and be devoured by birds and wild animals. In 39:11–16, the land is cleansed as Israelites go through it burying the dead. Then birds and wild animals are invited to feast on kings, the mighty, and soldiers (39:17–20). God promises to pour his Spirit upon Israel (39:29).

The book of Ezekiel ends with nine chapters that detail what the restored Jerusalem and its temple will look like and what its practices will be (Tuell 1992). We do not lay out Ezekiel's details here but merely highlight a few key texts.

The great vision begins when Ezekiel is brought back to Judah by the "hand of the LORD." To the south, he spies a high mountain on which there is a city—clearly Jerusalem. An angelic figure is his guide to the city and temple. Ezekiel's tour shows that it is entirely dedicated to the temple.

Ezekiel is brought to the east gate and sees God coming from the east (43:1–5). God enters the temple in glory, and Ezekiel associates the vision with his original one in chapter 1. God's holiness is more protected in the new city than the old: "This is the law of the temple: the whole territory on top of the mountain all around shall be most holy. This is the law of the temple" (43:12). It is not just the temple complex that is holy, as before, but the whole of Mount Zion.

Chapter 44 has social and institutional implications. First, Israel is accused of idolatry, and Ezekiel blames this on admission of foreigners to the temple. That will cease in the new order (43:6–9). The Levites, whom Ezekiel holds responsible for idolatry, may not approach the altar. They fulfill lesser functions. Only the "levitical priests," the descendants of Zadok, will be full priests with unrestricted access to the altar. We know that this exclusive right of the Zadokites did not hold up in Second Temple Judaism, but the Zadokites were the most prominent priestly group. They are prominent in the apocalyptic sect of the Dead Sea Scrolls (second century BCE to first century CE). The name "Sadducees," familiar from the Gospels, may derive from "Zadok." The rest of the chapter enumerates strict rules by which this true priesthood must live.

Jeremiah

Jeremiah had a long prophetic career, stretching from 647 to 586 BCE. He was deeply involved in political events, supporting Josiah's reform, opposing rebellions against Babylon, and criticizing kings, prophets, and leaders. He saw the Babylonian exile as God's punishment of Israel for transgressions, particularly those of social injustice and idolatry, and he counseled Israel to accept the exile as punishment. He predicted that it would last for seventy years. That figure recurs often in apocalyptic thought, appearing, for example, in Dan. 9.

Jeremiah railed against Israel's complacency. In his famous temple sermon (chaps. 7 and 26, two versions of the same event), he warned Israel against relying on God's presence in the temple for protection. He declared that God would destroy the Jerusalem temple as he did the one at Shiloh unless the people followed God's will (7:14).

Jeremiah hopes for a new, better Davidic king. Chapter 25 contains such a vision. God criticizes the shepherds, Israel's kings, for neglecting the sheep. The scene inspired the author of John's Gospel (chap. 10). The shepherds have destroyed and scattered the sheep, God's people. God will recall the people from the lands to which they have been dispersed, and he will reinstitute the Davidic monarchy under a ruler who is called by the messianic title "Branch" (Isa. 11). Jeremiah makes the startling statement that Israel will no longer be known as the people whom God brought out of Egypt but rather the people God brought out of the Assyrian and Babylonian exiles. This is similar to the views of Second and Third Isaiah. They saw God's future action as similar to but even greater than his past actions. The future eclipses the past.

Jeremiah 33 is another vision of restoration. The nations will take note and fear. Israel's devastation and sorrow will be replaced by prosperity and joy. Jeremiah predicts a Davidic king, the Branch, who will be righteous and enforce justice. The Davidic dynasty will be everlasting. God's covenants with the Davidic dynasty and the priesthood will never fail.

Finally, we examine Jeremiah's famous prophecy concerning the "new covenant" in 31:31–37. It caught the attention of Jews and Christians alike. The apocalyptic sect of the Dead Sea Scrolls adopted its terminology and thought of themselves as the people of the new covenant. The idea also permeates Christianity, so much so that the second collection of texts in the Christian Bible is called the "New Testament" which is better translated "New Covenant." Jesus speaks of a new covenant at the Last Supper.

> The days are surely coming, says the LORD, when I will make a new covenant with the house of Israel and the house of Judah. It will not be like the covenant that I made with their ancestors when I took them by the hand to bring them out of the land of Egypt—a covenant that they broke, though I was their husband, says the LORD. But this is the covenant that I will make with the house of Israel after those days, says the LORD: I will put my law within them, and I will write it on their hearts; and I will be their God, and they shall be my people. . . .
> If this fixed order [of the universe] were ever to cease
> from my presence, says the LORD,
> then also the offspring of Israel would cease
> to be a nation before me forever. (Jer. 31:31–33, 36)

Jeremiah's oracle foresees repair of God's relationship with Israel. Israel disobeyed God and suffered justly. Now there will be a new covenant between God and Israel. What is different is not the Torah, but the fact that it is now within the heart. This results in God's promise that Israel will cease to exist only if the universe itself dissolves.

Second Isaiah (Isaiah 40–55)

Second Isaiah is a joyous cry of hope at the end of the Babylonian exile. The prophet declares Cyrus the Great's extensive conquests as God's doing, though even Cyrus does not know that. God even proclaims Cyrus to be a messiah, chosen to conquer the nations and thus clear the way for Israel to return to Judah and rebuild Jerusalem (44:28–45:7). God's action will catch the attention of the whole earth and cause all nations to worship God alone.

God proclaims, "I am the first and I am the last; besides me there is no god" (44:6; see 41:4; 48:12). This powerful proclamation of monotheism is relatively new in Israel. Second Isaiah is permeated with God's claims to be the only God. The proof is in history, in Israel's redemption from the Babylonian exile. This redemptive act is superior to anything God has ever done, as Jeremiah

Second Isaiah: Proto-Apocalyptic Elements

- Sovereignty is expressed through absolute monotheism.
- God's power works in new and powerful ways, surpassing former ways.
- There are allusions to the combat myth: creation, the old exodus, and the new exodus are all depicted as conquering of the sea (Rahab).
- God is the divine warrior.
- Zion is renewed.
- All nations recognize Israel's God as the absolute, only God; they come to Zion to worship.
- God's plans are hidden and then revealed to the prophets.
- The exiles return.

has said. Most striking are the parallels and contrasts that Second Isaiah draws with the exodus. God recites divine titles underscoring his relationship with Israel. God is creator, king, and warrior. God recalls his actions in the exodus, which grounded that relationship; then he tells Israel to forget that! What is to come surpasses it. Yet what is to come still follows the paradigm of the exodus. God makes a "way in the wilderness" and "rivers in the desert" for them. But the second exodus exceeds the first (Clifford 1984).

The exodus from Babylon to Judah compares even to creation itself. The three events—creation, first exodus, second exodus—are brought together within a mythological framework in chapter 51, a passage we discussed in chapter 1 and in the present chapter in our discussion of the combat myth in the Bible. Creation is a battle between God and the sea dragon, an evocation of the combat myth. The recollection of God's creation triumphing over the sea segues into God's drying up the sea for Israel to pass over as they flee from the Egyptians. At the same time, the mention of dry land alludes backward to the creation, where dry land was necessary. Finally, it all points forward to the future, when the exiles return joyously to Zion.

God tells the prophet about these momentous events before they happen: "See, the former things have come to pass, and new things I now declare; before they spring forth, I tell you of them" (42:9; see 43:19; 48:6). Until God tells the prophet about them, they are hidden (48:6).

Restoration: Haggai and Zechariah 1–8

Haggai

Cyrus was not being altruistic when he allowed Israel to return to Judah in 538 BCE. It served his purposes to have a loyal and stable province (called a satrapy in the Persian system) on his Egyptian border. Judah would be allowed to establish a temple-state, one administered by priests through the temple and by a governor on the civil side, but not a king.

The prophets Haggai and Zechariah urged Zerubbabel, the governor, and Joshua, the high priest, to rebuild Judah's temple. In Haggai's book there are four oracles delivered within a short span of time. The first excoriates the inhabitants of Jerusalem for not rebuilding the temple. They claim that this is not the time, for they need to concentrate on more "practical" matters like their own houses and their crops. Haggai counters that this is not really practical; they are not doing well because they have not rebuilt the temple. If they rebuild, God will dwell with them and bring them the usual blessings, especially good crops. This is a priestly view. Proper functioning of the cult ensures fertility of the land.

When work on the temple begins, many are discouraged at how pitiful it seems compared to Solomon's temple. Haggai assures them that the future holds something much more glorious:

> For thus says the LORD of hosts: Once again, in a little while, I will shake the heavens and the earth and the sea and the dry land; and I will shake all the nations, so that the treasure of all nations shall come, and I will fill this house with splendor, says the LORD of hosts. The silver is mine, and the gold is mine, says the LORD of hosts. The latter splendor of this house shall be greater than the former, says the LORD of hosts; and in this place I will give prosperity, says the LORD of hosts. (Hag. 2:6–9)

Silver and gold will flood into the temple from all nations, for the whole world belongs to God. Cosmic disturbance—heaven, sea, earth—marks the greatness of the recognition of Jerusalem's temple by all humanity.

Haggai's final oracle is addressed to Zerubbabel, the Davidic descendant.

> Speak to Zerubbabel, governor of Judah, saying, I am about to shake the heavens and the earth, and to overthrow the throne of kingdoms; I am about to destroy the strength of the kingdoms of the nations, and overthrow the chariots and their riders; and the horses and their riders shall fall, every one by the sword of a comrade. On that day, says the LORD of hosts, I will take you, O Zerubbabel my servant, son of Shealtiel, says the LORD, and make you like a signet ring; for I have chosen you, says the LORD of hosts. (Hag. 2:21–23)

Judah's restoration was carried out under the aegis of the Persian government. The Persians appointed Joshua and Zerubbabel. We know from 1 Chron. 3:19 that Zerubbabel belonged to the Davidic family. Yet his name incorporates the word "Babel," indicating his comfort with Babylonian society. He was a man of high standing and respect in the exilic Judahite community and assimilated to the Babylonian societal and political system, although still a

Haggai: Proto-Apocalyptic Elements

- Proper functioning of the Jerusalem temple ensures God's blessings—fertility of the land and recognition by the nations.
- The nations will recognize God's sovereignty and send riches to the temple.
- God will destroy the strength of the nations and will establish his messiah.
- God is the divine warrior.

Judahite leader. His status among the Judahites undoubtedly owed something to his Davidic lineage, but he was not distrusted by the Persians for that reason. Zerubbabel's position illuminates the complexity of the relationship between Persia and Judah, politics and religion, sovereignty and conquest, tradition and new historical circumstances.

Haggai's oracle exceeds what the Persian Empire would tolerate. God orders Haggai to inform Zerubbabel in particular that God is about to overthrow kingdoms and their armies (2:20–23). Then God will make Zerubbabel God's servant and signet ring. To the Persians, this would sound like sedition. Overthrow of kingdoms must surely mean the casting off of Persia's colonial rule.

Haggai delivers his oracles in the second year of King Darius of Persia, when Darius is consolidating his own rule (520 BCE). At a time when Darius is most vulnerable, Haggai's oracle encourages Zerubbabel to revolt. "Servant" is a word often associated with kings. A "signet ring" is the king's ring with which he seals letters and decrees. The metaphor means that Zerubbabel acts for God. He rules for God, as the Israelite and Judahite kings did before him. God has chosen Zerubbabel as he chose David.

We do not know what happened next. Zerubbabel disappears from history. We do not know whether he revolted and was defeated, or whether he paid no attention to Haggai and simply fulfilled his task for the Persians and passed on.

Zechariah 1–8

Zechariah 1–8 comes from a contemporary of Haggai. He prophesies in the second year of King Darius, as does Haggai (Zech. 1:1). The remaining six chapters of the book (9–14) date from later. Among Zechariah's interests are legitimacy of the priesthood and a renewed cult.

Zechariah marks a transition in form between prophecy and apocalypse (as did Ezekiel). Prophecy usually consists primarily of oracles introduced by a formula something like, "The word of the LORD came to the prophet X, saying." Occasionally the prophet has a vision, but that is relatively rare. More often the prophet simply hears what God says and passes it on.

The book of Zechariah contains conventional prophetic oracles, but it consists mostly of revelation in another form. Zechariah receives a cryptic vision, and an angel helps him to understand it. This form dominates apocalypses. The form may signal a shift in religious sensibility. God has become more mysterious and transcendent. No longer does God speak directly to the prophet or seer. Now revelation comes through a vision which itself is mysterious, and it must be explained by an angelic intermediary. The layers between God and humanity have multiplied and thickened.

Zechariah is not an apocalypse, but it comes close. It does not have a full narrative framework, but does contain visions interpreted by an angel, and the content of the revelation is temporal and spatial. It does not, however, contain transcendence of death.

In Zechariah's first vision, he sees four horses—two red, a sorrel, and a white—and he asks the angel what they are (1:7–11). They turn out to be God's agents sent to spy out the earth.

Chapter 3 is a throne scene, although the throne is not mentioned explicitly. The high priest Joshua stands before God's angel, and *haśśāṭān* ("the accuser" or "the adversary"; transliterated as "satan") stands to the angel's right. The distinction between God and God's angel is blurred. In verse 2, God speaks to Satan directly. The angel has become God.

This is the first time Satan appears in the Hebrew Bible. It is uncertain whether we should translate the word as a proper noun (Satan) here or leave it as a more general designation (the accuser). The latter is more likely. The title "Accuser" indicates a particular role in the heavenly court. He "accuses" or "acts as an adversary to" (*śāṭan*) Joshua. If we think of this in legal terms, Satan is the angelic prosecutor. He brings Israel's failings before God. This seed—a heavenly figure, yet Israel's adversary—grows over time into the Satan who leads superhuman (angelic or demonic) forces against God and humanity. The snake in Genesis is not called Satan, but later Jewish and Christian tradition will identify the two. Neither Genesis nor Zechariah make the connection.

God rebukes Satan for accusing Joshua. Joshua stands before God dressed in filthy clothes, symbolizing guilt. As Israel's ultimate representative, he bears its guilt. His presence before God in such a state is improper. Satan is correct, but God objects that Joshua is a "brand plucked from the fire." He embodies Israel's remnant, so God cannot reject him. He must be the foundation of a new community.

Joshua is a priest, and therefore needs access to God. His filthy clothes are removed, and he receives new, priestly raiment. God's angel lays out a basic agreement—a covenant, though the word is not used—that explains the grounds on which the priesthood is based:

> Thus says the LORD of hosts: If you will walk in my ways and keep my requirements, then you shall rule my house and have charge of my courts, and I will give you the right of access among those who are standing here. (Zech. 3:7)

"Here" is heaven. Charge of the temple courts means access to God in heaven. This legitimates the temple cult of the Second Temple period.

God promises to bring his servant, the Branch (3:8). Haggai uses the term "servant" in his fourth oracle messianically. Zechariah uses it the same way and adds the messianic term "Branch." He expects the reinstitution of the monarchy; a Persian loyalist would smell sedition.

Zechariah's fifth vision is jumbled, since there are several visions combined, and their interpretation is not entirely coherent (chap. 4). An intrusive oracle appears in 4:8–10a. Its import is that Zerubbabel will rebuild the temple. The connection between messiahship and temple building extends far back in Israel's traditions and through them to ancient Near Eastern mythology (Juel 1977).

Zechariah sees a vision of a lampstand with seven lamps, each having seven lips (chap. 4). There are two olive trees, one on the right and one on the left of the stand. This alludes to the seven-branched lampstand in the temple's holy place. Zechariah asks the angel what the vision means. His question incorporates an element to the vision that had not been narrated earlier—golden pipes running from each of the trees to the stand. The vision has been extensively rewritten.

The angel interprets the olive trees: "These are the two anointed ones who stand by the Lord of the whole earth" (4:14). The Hebrew does not use the word *māšîyaḥ*, "messiah," but rather speaks of two "sons of oil" (*bĕnê-hayyiṭhār*), but the allusion is clear. The cult, symbolized by the lampstand, is supported by two anointed figures—priest and king. The passage envisions a dyadic leadership for the restored community. This model of rulership becomes important in the late Second Temple period.

The oracle in 6:9–15 also shows evidence of rewriting (Collins 2003a). God tells Zechariah to collect gold from Judahites who have returned from Babylonia. They are to make "crowns" (the Hebrew has "crowns"; the NRSV emends that to the singular to make better sense of the text) and set it on the head of Joshua the high priest. This is an anomaly. Crowns are for kings; turbans are for priests. Should this not be a single crown, and for Zerubbabel, not Joshua?

Then God tells Joshua through Zechariah that he, Joshua, is the Branch and will rebuild the temple. We have seen Branch to be a royal title, and that it is Zerubbabel who will rebuild the temple (Zech. 3:8; 4:6–9). We suspect that this oracle was originally meant for Zerubbabel, not Joshua, and that it has been transferred to Joshua. Each of the two prophets, Haggai and Zechariah, may have prophesied a restored monarchy. This did not come to pass, and the predictions in Zechariah were transferred to Joshua. The high priest took on royal qualities and duties.

The rest of the oracle (6:13–15) confirms our suspicions. Joshua is said to bear royal honor and to have a priest by his throne. There is peace between them. They rule Israel together, each in his own sphere. This makes little sense, since Joshua himself is a priest. It would be more logical for a civil

Zechariah 1–8: Proto-Apocalyptic Elements

- There is a throne scene.
- The unseen world determines the seen world.
- The apocalyptic form is present: the prophet has a vision that is interpreted by an angel.
- In the vision four horses roam the earth.
- Satan appears.
- The temple provides access to God.
- Dyadic leadership: there are two messiahs.
- Zerubbabel is described as a messiah.
- The exiles return.
- There is peace in Jerusalem.
- The prophetic words are fulfilled.

figure, especially a Davidic one, to sit on the throne enjoying royal honors and relating well to the high priest. Again, Zerubbabel, not Joshua, fits the bill.

Chapter 8 contains many of the usual elements incorporated into most eschatological scenarios. God will return to Zion; it will be holy and be called the faithful city; it will be where the remnant of God's people come to dwell; it will enjoy prosperity and social peace; God will cause the exiles to return to Jerusalem; the covenant will be in effect; God's words to the prophets will be fulfilled.

After the Restoration

Third Isaiah (Isaiah 56–66)

The restoration was not a once-for-all event, but a gradual process with ample opportunity for disagreement and dissatisfaction. In the mid-fifth century BCE, the Persians sent Ezra, a Jewish priest of the Zadokite line and a scribe learned in Israel's sacred traditions, to Judah. He was to bring to Judah the newly edited version of Israel's traditions and laws completed in Babylonia. It was probably close to what we know as the Torah, the first five books of the Hebrew Bible. This written work was a huge step in the direction of the existence of our present Bible. Ezra was to promulgate it as law of the land, for those matters not mandated by Persian law. A few years later, the Persian emperor sent Nehemiah, another Jew trusted at court, the emperor's own cupbearer, to rebuild Jerusalem's walls (Murphy 2002, 61–91).

Segments of the community, particularly prophetic groups, disapproved of the emerging society. They authored oracles collected in Third Isaiah (Isa.

56–66) that are proto-apocalyptic. A seminal study of this topic is *The Dawn of Apocalyptic* by Paul Hanson, first published in 1975. Hanson's thesis builds on the work of Plöger in *Theocracy and Eschatology*, published in German in 1959 and translated into English in 1968. It proposes that once the restoration got under way, it took a route unacceptable to a visionary segment of the priesthood. Disagreements were not just between the rich and the poor or the powerful and the powerless, but they had to do with power struggles at the top as well. The literature we call proto-apocalyptic derives from those well-educated, probably priestly groups who were dissatisfied with the way things were going (Horsley 2010b; Cook 1995). Hanson suggests a growing disappointment by dating the oracles on the basis of content and form.

Isaiah 60–61 maintains the exultant hope found in Second Isaiah. Chapter 60 celebrates Zion, on whom God's light has shone. Selections from the chapter convey the tone and highlight key elements in Zion's triumph. The passage concentrates on foreign nations and their relation to Israel. The prophet longs for the day when all nations will recognize Zion as the true home of the one God. They will come to worship and will bring home Zion's children, exiled Israelites. They will bring their riches and offer them to God, including the riches of the sea. Foreigners build up Jerusalem's walls. Protective gates remain open, because these foreigners come with gifts. The descendants of those who conquered and oppressed Israel will bow down at Israel's feet, because Israel is itself "the city of the LORD." Israel will be righteous and will forever possess the land. Sun and moon will no longer be needed for light. Israel is God's "plant," a common image expressing Israel's rootedness in the land.

In chapter 61, the prophet describes his commission to bring God's "good news" to Jerusalem. He addresses the issue of Jerusalem's ruin. The prophet is "anointed" by God's Spirit, so he is a messiah, although not of the usual sort, being neither priest nor king. His message is "good news to the oppressed," binding up the "brokenhearted," "liberty to the captives," and "release to the prisoners" (61:1). The "year of the LORD's favor" in 61:2 may refer to the Jubilee Year of Lev. 25, in which Hebrew slaves go free and land returns to its original owners (C. Wright 1992). The prophet predicts the rebuilding of Jerusalem. Foreigners will feed Israel's flocks and cultivate its vines. Israel will be a priestly nation, a mediator between God and humanity, offering access to God.

All is as it ought to be, and the best is yet to come. But things soon turn bad. The next chapter (62) expresses doubt, as the prophet vows to post sentinels on Jerusalem's walls until God fulfills the divine promises.

Chapter 58 harshly critiques the cult (see also 66:3–6). The people pretend to seek God. They engage in cultic worship, but they oppress their workers. True worship is freeing the oppressed, feeding the hungry, housing the homeless, covering the naked, undoing injustice.

A split within Israel appears in 63:16: "For you are our father, though Abraham does not know us and Israel does not acknowledge us; you O LORD,

Third Isaiah: Proto-Apocalyptic Elements

- Nations come to Jerusalem to worship.
- The exiles return.
- Zion is the center of all; foreigners build its walls.
- The people are righteous.
- Judgment is threatened.
- New heavens and a new earth are promised.

are our father; our Redeemer from of old is your name." The speakers are a minority within Israel. "Your holy people took possession for a little while; but now our adversaries have trampled down your sanctuary" (63:18). God complains in chapter 65 that he appeals to Israel, but it does not listen. They commit idolatry and still claim holiness. He sarcastically quotes them as saying, "Keep to yourself, do not come near me, for I am too holy for you" (65:5). This may refer to priestly purity rules. The very observance of these rules antagonizes God. Meant to protect God's holiness, they now serve the interests of the ruling class.

Third Isaiah moves toward something entirely new. Its most extreme texts yearn to leave behind the present terrible situation and experience the birth of a new world. God proclaims, "I am about to create new heavens and a new earth; the former things shall not be remembered or come to mind" (65:17). This new order includes the return of the exiles (66:20) and the worship of God by all nations (66:23). The promise of a new heaven and a new earth seems figurative, only later to be taken literally in apocalyptic contexts. Nor is there any indication of the transcendence of death.

Zechariah 9–14

Dating Zech. 9–14 is problematic. Although the chapters have been appended to Zechariah's book, they do not fully fit. The sixth-century Zechariah, along with his contemporary Haggai, legitimated the priestly establishment through visions and oracles. Zechariah 9–14 criticizes the establishment and hopes for a restoration that will overcome its faults. They do not seem to have come from a single author or historical situation, except that they are all postexilic. They do not form a coherent whole. We choose certain passages to study, without claiming to capture all that these chapters have to offer.

The first passage we examine became the model for Christ's entrance into Jerusalem in the Gospels.

> Rejoice greatly, O daughter Zion!
> Shout aloud, O daughter Jerusalem!

Lo, your king comes to you;
    triumphant and victorious is he,
humble and riding on a donkey,
    on a colt, the foal of a donkey. (Zech. 9:9)

A peaceful and humble Israelite king comes and Jerusalem is exhorted to welcome him. He does away with the military establishment of both the northern and southern kingdoms as no longer necessary. The inclusion of the north (Ephraim) here is idealistic, for it no longer existed at this time. This peaceful king reigns from sea to sea and from the river to the earth's ends. His dominion is universal.

The text hopes for the liberation of Israel's exiles, "prisoners of hope." God declares that because of the "blood of my covenant with you" (9:11) he will set Israel's prisoners free. Judah and Ephraim are God's weapons: the sons of Zion will battle the sons of Greece (9:13). The historical situation is not clear, but the mention of Greece makes possible that we are now in the Hellenistic period, although eastern powers recognized Greek power before Alexander. The rising Greek empire is either already in existence or is on the horizon. The reference to the "blood of the covenant" is rare, occurring elsewhere in the Hebrew Bible only on Sinai, where Moses conducts a covenant-making ceremony (Exod. 24:8), and in the Gospels, where Jesus refers to his own death (Matt. 26:28; cf. Heb. 9:15–22).

Chapter 10 displays unhappiness with Israel's leaders. The priests do not speak the truth (10:2). The people wander, for their shepherds are false. Even the prophets, the "dreamers," are false. God will punish the shepherds but save Israel, here spoken of as the "house of Judah" (the south) and the "house of Joseph" (the north). The text foresees the ingathering of Israel's exiles from "among the nations," principal of whom are Assyria and Egypt.

In this same chapter, the prophet expresses disappointment. Things are not going as they should. God gives up. God had made the prophet tie two sticks together and name them "Favor," indicating God's favor on Israel, and "Unity," indicating the unity of north and south. The prophet now symbolically unties the sticks and breaks each. The hope of a new united kingdom vanishes. God again blames the shepherds, who are "worthless" (11:17).

The final three chapters are punctuated with the phrase "on that day." The day is the eschatological day. The Creator proclaims what he will do at the end. God will "make Jerusalem a cup of reeling for all the surrounding peoples" (12:2); Jerusalem will be his instrument of punishment. All nations attack Jerusalem. Acting as the divine warrior, God defends it, ultimately destroying Jerusalem's enemies.

Verse 10 is puzzling: "And I will pour out a spirit of compassion and supplication on the house of David and the inhabitants of Jerusalem, so that, when they look on the one whom they have pierced, they shall mourn for him,

Zechariah 9–14: Proto-Apocalyptic Elements

- A humble king comes.
- Peace is brought to Ephraim and Jerusalem.
- The king commands peace to the nations and has dominion over them.
- The exiles return, including those from the north.
- The north and south become a united kingdom.
- The nations fight Jerusalem and are destroyed.
- Idolatry is banished.
- All nations worship at Jerusalem.
- All Jerusalem is holy.
- All the people are righteous.
- Jerusalem and the Davidic dynasty are restored.
- The leaders (shepherds) are criticized.

as one mourns for an only child, and weep bitterly over him, as one weeps over a firstborn." We do not know the identity of the pierced one. Later Christian tradition identified him with Jesus. The pierced one may be the prophet. The prophet has suffered for his message, but he will be vindicated.

Zechariah 13 says that David and Jerusalem will be cleansed of anything separating them from God. They will be righteous. The rest of the chapter expresses disapproval of Israel's prophets and leaders (shepherds). Finally, God renews his covenantal relationship with the people.

A short oracle threatens punishment for leaders and people (13:7–9). Two-thirds of the people in the land will perish.

Chapter 14 contains a vivid eschatological scenario. It begins, "A day is coming for the LORD." The nations attack Jerusalem (14:1–2). God, the divine warrior, fights them (14:3). Next, God stands on the Mount of Olives, to the east of Jerusalem, and Israel flees the city (14:4–5). There are cosmic repercussions: there is no cold, and there is continuous day (14:6–7).

There follows an idyllic period. Jerusalem is a source of fertility (14:8). Fertile waters flow from the city east and west, in summer and winter. All seasons are growing seasons. The Lord rules the whole earth (14:9). There is a single God, the true God, over all. Jerusalem and Zion dominate the earth, for Zion remains a mountain while all else becomes a plain (14:10). It is invincible, invulnerable (14:11).

This is not the end. Just when it seems that all is well and Jerusalem is renewed, the nations renew their attack (see Ezek. 38–39). God defends Jerusalem, destroys the enemy, and collects their booty (14:12–15).

All surviving nations must come to Jerusalem to worship (14:16–19). They do so at Tabernacles, the feast beginning the rainy season. If they

Malachi: Proto-Apocalyptic Elements

- Theophany: God comes to the temple.
- God judges and purifies the priests.
- God punishes those who do not practice social justice.
- Elijah will come before the day of judgment to warn the people.

refuse, they receive no rain. The oracles end with a powerful statement of Jerusalem's holiness (14:20–21). It is proper that the temple vessels be holy, but now even the lowliest cooking vessel in the city is holy. The bells on the horses are holy.

The book's final verse says that "there shall no longer be traders in the house of the LORD of hosts on that day" (14:21). The Hebrew for "traders" may mean rather "Canaanites" (qĕna'ănî). If so, it may express the exclusivist strand we have noticed in our sources. No foreigners should be allowed in the temple. That is hard to reconcile with the earlier assertion that the nations must come up to Jerusalem to worship Israel's God. If it should be translated "traders," it may be a protest against the business side of the temple establishment.

Malachi

Malachi is a short, postexilic, prophetic book that criticizes the Jerusalem priestly establishment. It says that priests deliver faulty instruction (tôrâ), offer blemished sacrifices, and practice divorce. They pray for God's coming but will regret it when it happens:

> See, I am sending my messenger to prepare the way before me, and the LORD whom you seek will suddenly come to his temple. The messenger of the covenant in whom you delight—indeed, he is coming, says the LORD of hosts. But who can endure the day of his coming, and who can stand when he appears? (3:1–2)

The priests seek God's coming, but when he does come, they will be unpleasantly surprised. God will punish and "refine" them as in fire. God will punish adultery; sorcery; false witness; oppression of hired workers, widows, and orphans; and mistreatment of strangers (3:5). After God refines the priesthood, valid sacrifices can again be offered.

Malachi 3:16–18 speaks of a book, the "book of remembrance [sēper zikkārôn]" in which God records those who are faithful. They are God's special possession. Heavenly books are prominent in apocalypses.

Malachi ends by predicting Elijah's second coming. As judgment nears, society breaks down. Relations between the generations collapse. Malachi asserts that before God comes in judgment, Elijah will come to straighten

Genesis 6: Apocalyptic Elements

- The sons of God (heavenly beings; angels) take human wives.
- God limits the length of human life.
- The offspring of divine and human beings are giants.

things out (4:5–6). He will turn parents to their children and children to their parents to avert God's judgment.

Elijah did not die; God swept him up to heaven in a fiery chariot (2 Kings 2:11–12). The tradition surmised Elijah was preserved for a special task, one contained in Malachi (Allison 1984; Faierstein 1981; Malchow 1984; Fitzmyer 1985).

Foundations in Genesis

Genesis 6

A mythological fragment survives in Gen. 6 that proved fruitful for apocalypticism. After God creates humanity, "sons of God," divine beings, see that women are attractive and take them as wives. God responds by limiting human life to 120 years. He recognizes the risks in allowing this mixture of human and divine life to persist. One risk is that these semidivine figures will live forever or at least too long. The Nephilim, mythological creatures of gigantic proportions, may be the fruit of this sexual union. The *Book of the Watchers*, that is, *En.* 1–36, makes this the basis of a long narrative. The rest of Gen. 6 introduces the narrative of the great flood, a myth that Israel borrowed from its ancient Near Eastern environment.

Genesis 1–3

Genesis 1–3 contains two creation stories. The first is the story of creation in seven days (Gen. 1:1–2:3). Everything goes smoothly, and, were we left with this story alone as the introduction to history, we would expect all to be perfect. Scholars attribute this story to the priestly source. It stresses order and connects the Sabbath and creation.

The priestly version of creation posits a close relationship between God and humanity. The Hebrew for "humankind" is *'ādām*, which can be read either as the proper name Adam or as the word for "humankind." When the time comes for the creation of humanity, God says,

> "Let us make humankind ['*ādām*] in our image, according to our likeness; and let them have dominion over the fish of the sea, and over the birds of the air, and

Proto-Apocalyptic Elements in the Hebrew Bible

- Throne scenes
- God as divine warrior
- God as universal king
- God as creator
- Theophanies with cosmic disturbances
- Combat myth
- Prophet gets special revelation
- Concerns future events of judgment and salvation
- Concerns God's hidden plans
- Prophet sometimes fears
- Great final battle; God wins
- Future restoration
- Ideal kingship (messiahship)
  - Davidic
  - Everlasting
  - Kings are sons of God
  - Righteous and enforcing righteousness
  - Defending the needy
  - Crushing the oppressors
  - Promoting social justice
  - King's enemies are defeated
- Return of the exiles to the land of Israel

- Reunion of Israel and Judah
- Ideal temple
- Fertility and prosperity
- All Israel is righteous
- Nations worship God in Jerusalem.
- Centrality of Zion
- Angels and superhuman figures; Satan
- Politics and religion inseparable
- Cosmic disturbances
- New exodus
- New covenant
- End-time banquet
- Universal peace
- Condemnation of kings (shepherds)
- Apocalyptic revelatory form: vision and angelic interpretation
- New heavens and new earth
- Resurrection (figurative; later to be literal)
- Elijah comes before the judgment
- Sons of God take wives; produce the giants

over the cattle, and over all the wild animals of the earth, and over every creeping thing that creeps upon the earth." So God created humankind in his image, in the image of God he created them; male and female he created them. (1:26–27)

The image of God has to do with dominion over the animals; both God and humans rule over creation.

The second creation story is quite different. The story of Adam and Eve in Gen. 2–3 recounts their disobedience of God's command not to eat of the tree of the knowledge of good and evil and their ejection from the Garden of Eden. Humankind's situation changes drastically because of this event. Women now endure pain in childbirth, experience sexual attraction to men, and are subservient to their husbands; men cultivate the ground with difficulty;

humans and serpents are enemies. Most significantly, death enters the world. Such flaws characterize a world alienated from God.

Proto-Apocalyptic Elements in the Hebrew Bible

The list on the preceding page is a convenient way to refer back to this chapter as we later analyze apocalypses and apocalyptic texts, theologies, and prophecies. Again, we remind the reader that we have cast the net very widely. Most material from the Hebrew Bible that proved of use to apocalyptic writers is included. That does not mean that elements listed here are in themselves apocalyptic. Apocalypticism was not isolated. It drew from a rich store of traditions. These traditions remained available and were used by non-apocalyptic thinkers as well.

Conclusion

Ancient apocalyptic texts do not, for the most part, quote the biblical materials. They use them as paint from a pallet or as bricks with which to build, to use two different metaphors. The paint metaphor conveys the idea that biblical materials provide color and tone to apocalyptic writing, while the brick metaphor conveys the idea that the materials used already have a form in their original setting that carries over into their new use and that, seen as a whole, they comprise a certain structure or set of structures. One might add to the brick metaphor that of a foundation, connoting that larger literary or mythological structures in the Hebrew Bible supply the groundwork for larger structures in apocalyptic works. But there is no slavish imitation of biblical passages, nor is the act of receiving an apocalyptic vision and recording it in an apocalypse simply a decoding of past prophecies to discover present applications.

Given the richness of the proto-apocalyptic elements we have found in the Hebrew Bible, we can now see Jewish apocalypticism as an organic development of Israel's imaginative religious life and as a way of coming to terms with the new worlds that it must confront.

Suggestions for Further Reading

Batto, Bernard F. *Slaying the Dragon: Mythmaking in the Biblical Tradition.* Louisville: Westminster/John Knox, 1992.
Collins, John Joseph. *Introduction to the Hebrew Bible.* Minneapolis: Fortress, 2004.
Cook, Stephen L. *The Apocalyptic Literature: Interpreting Biblical Texts.* Nashville: Abingdon, 2003.

Cross, Frank Moore. *Canaanite Myth and Hebrew Epic: Essays in the History of the Religion of Israel*. Cambridge: Harvard University Press, 1973.

Hanson, Paul. *The Dawn of Apocalyptic*. Philadelphia: Fortress, 1979.

Von Rad, Gerhard. *Old Testament Theology*. 2 vols. Edinburgh: Oliver & Boyd, 1962.

Yarbro Collins, Adela, and John Joseph Collins. *King and Messiah as Son of God: Divine, Human, and Angelic Messianic Figures in Biblical and Related Literature*. Grand Rapids: Eerdmans, 2008.

3

Daniel and the *Animal Apocalypse*

D aniel is the only apocalypse in the Hebrew Bible. This chapter analyzes
Daniel and a contemporaneous apocalypse, the *Animal Apocalypse.*
The two apocalypses respond to the same historical situation—the vicious
persecution of Judaism by the Seleucid king Antiochus IV and the revolt of
the Maccabees against him (167–164 BCE).

Before we analyze the works, we must gain a better idea of what ancient
religion was like in the last few centuries of the Second Temple era, since that
was the cultural and religious milieu for ancient Jewish and Christian apocalypticism. Especially important is the relation between divinity and humanity
in the ancient world.

Aspects of Ancient Religion in the Hellenistic and Roman Periods

Mythology

In the previous chapter, we examined many texts where historical events were
interpreted in terms of ancient myths. Used in this way, a myth is much more
than simple embellishment of everyday affairs. Rather, mythology expressed
a worldview and provided a means of making sense of personal, cultural, and
political experience.

Aspects of Modern Religion that Do Not Apply

The Greco-Roman world is that vast area of the eastern Mediterranean and
beyond that had been under heavy Greek influence since Alexander's conquests

and the consequent annexation of the area by the Roman Empire. Ehrman (2008, 22–23) enumerates seven aspects of how moderns think about religion that do not apply generally to religions in the Greco-Roman world. Some of these aspects require qualification when applied to Judaism and Christianity. We shall make the necessary qualifications as we proceed. Still, the list alerts us to the nature of the ancient world in which Judaism and Christianity existed and of which they were a part. The list is as follows, with explanation of each item below:

Religious organization and hierarchy
Doctrinal statements
Ethical commitments
Sacred written authorities
Beliefs about the afterlife
Separation of church and state
Exclusive commitments

Religious organization and hierarchy. Greco-Roman religions did not have worldwide organizations and centralized control. No one spoke for a whole religion.

Doctrinal statements. Ancient religions did not produce creeds to which everyone had to subscribe. Belief in the gods and other superhuman beings was assumed. How to relate to such beings was key.

Ethical commitments; Sacred written authorities. Ethical commitments and sacred writings both found a place in ancient Judaism and Christianity. Both Judaism and Christianity reserved a key role for these aspects in their religions. But other Greco-Roman religions did not necessarily possess these commitments and writings.

Beliefs about the afterlife. Through most of the Hebrew Bible, there is no belief in the afterlife as we usually think of it. Where the continued existence of humans after death does come up, it is a shadowy existence in an underworld place called Sheol or the Pit, cut off from living humans and from God. There is no idea of rewards and punishments after death. The concept of postmortem rewards and punishments, with the attendant belief in resurrection or immortality of the soul, and of heaven and hell as places where humans go after death, all come into Judaism through apocalypticism. Ultimately, they may derive from traditional Persian religion, Zoroastrianism. The first clear canonical reference we have to belief in such an afterlife among Jews is in Dan. 12 in around 167 BCE. The earlier, noncanonical apocalypse the *Book of the Watchers*, a Jewish work from the third century BCE, also references such belief.

Outside Judaism, most did not believe in an afterlife. For those who did, mystery religions furnished a way of affecting one's status there. Others looked to what lay within the limits of this life for meaning. They looked for divine help for what the gods could give them in this life—health, prosperity, children, victory over enemies, rain, crop growth, love, and perhaps even justice.

Separation of church and state. In the ancient world, religion was fully enmeshed with all other aspects of society. The previous chapter attests to the large degree to which religion was enmeshed in politics, economics, kinship, culture, and society in general in ancient Israel. Our study of apocalypticism will show the same. Neither Judaism nor Christianity made clear distinctions between religion and other social domains.

Exclusive commitments. Greco-Roman religions, with the exception of Judaism and Christianity, did not require exclusive commitment. There were many gods and goddesses, and one did well to be on the good side of as many as were in a position to affect one's well-being. Since there was a close connection between some divine figures and politics, one was wise to be seen to fulfill obligations to them. Gentile converts to Judaism and Christianity struggled to determine how to relate to their former pluralistic world.

Jewish monotheism prevented Jews from worshiping other gods, but that did not mean all Jews were convinced that no other gods had power. They, like their fellows in the Hellenistic world, believed in a variety of superhuman figures occupying an ontological space between God and humans. There were certainly angels. There were also demons. There were also a species of superhuman figures called the *daimonia*, which were not demons in our sense but spirits that could affect human life and had to be dealt with. Many early Christians did not come from Jewish backgrounds, so they were accustomed to polytheism.

Aspects of Ancient Religion Different from Modern Religion

Having discussed the ways in which modern concepts of religion do not apply to the ancient world, Ehrman (2008, 23–29) goes on to look at aspects of ancient religion that distinguish it from modern religion:

Polytheism instead of monotheism
Present life instead of afterlife
Cultic acts rather than doctrine
Church and state together instead of separated
Tolerance instead of intolerance

To some degree, this is the mirror image of what we have just seen, which leaves us to look more closely at polytheism and at the ancient world's ways of thinking about superhuman beings.

There is certainly a difference between humans and gods in the ancient world, but to reduce that to a simple dichotomy between divinity and humanity is to misunderstand how the ancients saw the cosmos. Ehrman presents a "divine pyramid" that helps categorize the way an ancient person would think about and relate to various types of superhuman beings (Ehrman 2008, 24).

At the apex of the pyramid was one god, head god of a particular pantheon. For the Romans, it would be Jupiter. For the Greeks, it was Zeus. For the Jews, it was Yahweh.

On the second level were the great gods. These were the pantheon, the collection of gods of national import who figured largely in myths, such as Athena and Apollo for the Greeks, and Baal and Anat for the Canaanites. The great gods were associated with particular political powers—Hellenistic empires, for example, or the Roman Empire—and would demand attention from time to time, especially from those most indebted to them. Victory of one nation over another was interpreted as the victory of one god over another.

On the third level of Ehrman's pyramid are *daimonia*, local gods, and others. Local gods and goddesses abounded. They could protect from everyday problems faced by everyone—basic issues of food, shelter, clothing, childbirth, illness, and so on. Local gods went along with local loyalties. Gods had influence and authority over the geographical places with which they were associated. Daimonia were spirits of many sorts. They were not necessarily demons, nor were they necessarily hostile to humanity. They could be useful, depending on one's needs. There were also evil spirits, and "unclean spirits," whom we encounter in the Gospels.

The fourth level of the pyramid was occupied by divine beings. There was no impassable chasm between humans and superhumans with respect to sexual activity, so there was another class of figures who came from unions across such borders. Some ancient heroes were the children of one divine spouse and one human spouse. Heracles is an example, as is Dionysus. Jesus might be another, at least as viewed by outsiders.

Some nations looked at their monarchs as divine in some sense. In Isa. 14, the Babylonian emperor was portrayed as a god attacking the main god of the pantheon (see the previous chapter). The Hellenistic emperors who succeeded Alexander claimed divinity. When Rome shifted from republic to empire, their eastern subjects used emperor worship to profess their loyalty (Price 1984). For the vast majority of the empire's citizens, this was no problem. Polytheism ruled the day. Worship of the emperor did not exclude or threaten other gods.

Divine sexual activity might seem strange to modern Jews and Christians. The Jewish God, adopted to some extent by the Christians, was unusual. He was not married and had no consort. Most gods were not like that. Scrutiny of the Bible reveals that Israel was not unacquainted with divine sexuality. The mythological fragment at the beginning of Gen. 6 tells of "sons of God" who take human women as wives, have giants as children, and cause God to limit the length of human life. In one of the two earliest Jewish apocalypses, the *Book of the Watchers* (third century BCE), this mythological seed grows into a rich narrative about angels who descend from heaven, take human wives, and disrupt God's order.

Judaism, Hellenism, and the Maccabees

Judaism and Hellenism

Daniel was written around 165 BCE. Rarely can we assign an ancient book so specific a date. In this case, internal and external evidence converge to allow us to do so.

In 333–323 BCE, Alexander the Great conquered Greece and the Persian Empire. His conquests marked the beginning of the Hellenistic era, a watershed in world history. Greek language and culture spread throughout the eastern Mediterranean and all the way to the Indus River. After Alexander's death, his generals, called the *diadochi* ("successors"), divided up his empire. Successive wars determined who got what. A Hellenistic dynasty called the Ptolemies took over Egypt, and the Seleucids assumed power in Syria and lands east.

Judea first fell under the sway of the Ptolemies and remained there for over a century, despite repeated wars fought between the Ptolemies and Seleucids for control. There are few indications of resistance or rebellion on the part of Judea's population to the new order during the third century BCE. By this time, Judea was well habituated to living under foreign rule. Judeans had been part of the Persian Empire for two hundred years. Before that they were subject to Babylon, and before that they lived in the shadow of Assyria. Persia did not force its culture on Israel, although cultural influence was inevitable. During that time, Aramaic, the lingua franca of the Persian Empire, became Judea's main language. In chapter 1, we saw how Persian religious ideas seeped into Jewish religion and flowered in apocalypticism.

When the Ptolemies took over Judea, cultural influences shifted. Greek and local Judean culture interacted in subtle and not-so-subtle ways, transforming Jewish life in ways not fully clear until later. This was typical of Hellenism, which was an interaction between Greek and local cultures whose result was different in different places and with different peoples. The scholarly literature on this is immense. A basic work is by Peters (1971). The classic study of Judaism and Hellenism is by Hengel (1974). For a recent study focusing on Judea, see Collins and Sterling (2001). It is at this time that we encounter the first extant Jewish apocalypses—the *Book of the Watchers* and the *Astronomical Book*. Those works must be seen partly as reactions to Hellenization.

Hellenization seldom provoked a single, monolithic reaction from local populations. Some would have been open to it, perhaps seeing a chance to widen horizons, become part of a wider world, pursue profitable relationships with other Hellenized peoples, and give the intellect freer rein with respect to philosophy, religion, ethics, and politics. Others would see Hellenism as an attack on the very identity of one's people. Different attitudes could arise from different social locations—geographic, intellectual, and socioeconomic. As time moved on and Hellenism became more and more part of everyone's experience, some influences would have crept in without people even being aware of it. Questions of Hellenization would have become inextricably tied up with religious positions, power struggles, and ethnic self-identity. All of this would be seen not just in terms of cultural tension but also within the context of empire, war, conquest, and power struggles both within and between ethnic groups.

In 200 BCE, the Seleucids wrested Palestine from Ptolemaic control. At first, peaceful relations between emperor and subjects characteristic of the third century continued under the new rulers. That was not to last. In 175, Antiochus IV Epiphanes ascended the Seleucid throne. When Antiochus assumed power, Judea had been under Hellenistic influence for a long time. True to the urban nature of Hellenization, this was most evident in Jerusalem. Hellenization affected Jerusalem's ruling classes, particularly the priests, since Judea was a temple-state. Some in the priestly ruling class enthusiastically embraced Hellenism and began the Hellenistic Reform (Goldstein 1981; Gruen 1998).

The Hellenistic Reform is easily misunderstood because our best source for it, 2 Maccabees, opposes it. It is convinced that the reform was harmful to Judaism and offensive to God. Reading between the lines and exercising historical imagination, modern scholars can reconstruct a different attitude toward the reform on the part of other Jews. We begin by examining the key description of the reform (2 Macc. 4:7–17).

Jason, brother of the Jewish high priest Onias, saw Antiochus's accession to the throne as a chance to seize power. Jewish tradition would expect the high priesthood to be hereditary and lifelong. But Jason's behavior would be perfectly acceptable to the rest of the Hellenistic world. Paying for sacred status in cults was normal. Jason bore a Greek name; his brother bore a Hebrew name. This may hint at their differing attitudes toward Hellenization. It is likely that Jason's bid for power and his dedication to Hellenization went together.

Jason pledged Antiochus a large sum of money. In return, he obtained permission to transform Jerusalem into a Greek city, "to establish by his authority a gymnasium and a body of youth for it, and to enroll the people of Jerusalem as citizens of Antioch" (2 Macc. 4:9). The gymnasium was not just a sports arena; it was a political institution (Townsend 1992). It was the training ground for future citizens, and the "body of youth" associated with it, called in Greek the *ephēbeion*, was a school of higher education for future citizens. The gymnasium maintained the Greek nature of the city by being the center for political clubs and action, as well as for worship of the city's gods.

Jason received permission to make the citizens of Jerusalem citizens of Antioch (4:9). When emperors gave permission to found cities, the cities were usually named after themselves. There were lots of Antiochs and lots of

Fig. 3. Buildings like amphitheaters spread Greek culture in Palestine and elsewhere both through their architecture and the cultural influence of events held there. (Chris Miller)

Alexandrias. Jerusalem would now be renamed Antioch. The very renaming would indicate that Jerusalem was now a Greek city, with all the attendant perquisites.

What did Jerusalem's new status imply for Judaism? For 2 Maccabees, it meant that Judaism had been jettisoned in favor of "the Greek way of life." It is unlikely that this is how Jason saw things. He probably thought that he was bringing Jerusalem into the contemporary world, "modernizing" it. This suggestion receives support from a passage in 1 Maccabees. "In those days certain renegades came out from Israel and misled many, saying, 'Let us go and make a covenant with the Gentiles around us, for since we separated from them many disasters have come upon us'" (1 Macc. 1:11). Separation from the gentiles brought misfortune. Perhaps Jewish customs could be tailored to make it easier to interact with non-Jews.

Once Jason destabilized the political situation in Jerusalem with Antiochus's approval, the door was open for things to move rapidly. Menelaus, another Jewish priest with a Greek name (Rappaport 1992), did to Jason as Jason had done to his own brother—he got himself appointed high priest by the Hellenistic authorities. Jason was forced to flee from Jerusalem. Later, Antiochus was on a military campaign in Egypt. False rumor had it that he had been killed. Jason took the opportunity to attack Jerusalem to oust Menelaus and retake the high priesthood. Antiochus heard about what now amounted to civil war in Jerusalem, marched to the city, and put an end to it (2 Macc. 5:11–14).

In 167 BCE, Antiochus made the fateful decision to eradicate Judaism from Jerusalem and Judea. For moderns accustomed to two thousand years of religious persecution, this might not seem extraordinary. But it was odd in the ancient world. It is the first real example of religious persecution. Reasons for the crisis are debated among scholars. The classic study is by Tcherikover (1959). Important new contributions have been made by Portier-Young (2011). Antiochus's persecution was probably a logical reaction to what he saw as the course of events in Jerusalem. He saw what he considered to be a civil war in Judea, and he knew that part of the conflict was between Jews who opposed Hellenism and those who accepted it. Perhaps he saw outlawing Judaism as a solution.

Antiochus's steps to stamp out Judaism were cruel (1 Macc. 1:20–28; 2 Macc. 6:1–11). He forbade possession of Torah scrolls, circumcision, and Jewish sacrifices. He pitilessly tortured and killed resisters. He performed Greek sacrifices on the temple's altar and sent agents throughout the countryside to force Jews to participate in Greek sacrifices. Pork was a meat that the Greeks sacrificed and ate but Jews did not. Among other meats, it was declared unclean in Lev. 11, but there it received no special status as defining Judaism. Antiochus's persecutions involved eating sacrificial pork, so it was doubly problematic for Jews—it was pork, and it was from a foreign cult. It may have been at this time that abstinence from pork achieved its special significance as a marker of Jewish identity.

The Maccabees

Antiochus's persecution resulted in a Jewish revolution. A priestly family led by Mattathias and his five sons headed the opposition. They are nicknamed the "Maccabees," after one of the sons, Judah, who was called "the Hammer." In stages, the Maccabees won independence. As rulers, first as priests and then also as kings, the Maccabees soon took on the trappings and institutions of a Hellenistic dynasty (Bickerman 1979). Their dynastic name was the Hasmoneans, after an ancestor. Hellenism continued to transform Judaism under their rule. Jews in the wider Hellenistic world were even more open to Hellenism in places like Alexandria than in Jerusalem, with less resistance from within the Jewish community (Barclay 1996; Collins 2000d). But Judea was also influenced by Hellenism (Lieberman 1950).

The Book of Daniel

Antiochus's persecution of Judaism was one of the most disturbing events in Israel's history up till that point. Israel had faced many enemies and had lived under foreign domination for a long time, but never had anyone tried to obliterate its very identity. It is no wonder that the event provoked the first strong resistance to foreign rule since the beginning of the sixth century BCE, when the kings of Judah resisted Babylonia and paid for it with the destruction of their city and temple and with a couple of generations in exile.

Revolt was not the only Jewish response to the persecution. We have two others. They are both apocalypses—Daniel and the *Animal Apocalypse*. A literary work might seem a weak way to oppose tyranny, but Daniel's writer saw things differently (Portier-Young 2011). Remarkable as it may seem, there is no clear reference to the Maccabean revolt in the book of Daniel, even though it was written in the middle of the revolt (165 BCE) in Judea. The one possible reference to the Maccabees is 11:34, where the wise are given "a little help." If "a little help" refers to the Maccabees, it gives them scant credit. Those who allied with the Maccabees are said to have done so "insincerely." This is not to say that an apocalyptic solution would necessarily rule out military action. The *Animal Apocalypse* puts the Maccabees on center stage and sees their military campaign as God's work and as prologue to the eschaton.

Daniel is in two main parts—chapters 1–6 and chapters 7–12. Chapters 7–12 fit the definition of an apocalypse. Daniel, a human being, recounts visions he has received. The visions are interpreted by angels. They give Daniel knowledge of the unseen world and of what is soon to happen. Transcendence of death is evident in chapter 12, which speaks of resurrection as well as postmortem rewards and punishments.

Daniel 1–6 is different. Taken alone, these chapters are not an apocalypse. They are in the third person, not the first. Daniel receives no visions in these chapters; rather, he interprets the visions of others. Apocalyptic eschatology makes no appearance. There are no interpreting angels. These chapters are a collection of stories about prominent Jews living in the courts of foreign kings (Wills 1990). We have seen real historical examples of such Jews. The Persians trusted and worked through Jews like Joshua, Zerubbabel, Ezra, and Nehemiah. The stories in Dan. 1–6 describe a lifestyle in which there is a good relationship between the empire and Jewish subjects (Humphreys 1973). The following captures the stories' folkloric character: "They incorporate older, traditional material and exhibit many characteristics of folklore including stereotyped characters, stylized plots, marvelous interventions, and extensive repetition and elaboration. In chapters 2, 4, and 5 wise courtiers compete to interpret dreams and visions, while in chapters 3 and 6 Jewish courtiers are miraculously delivered from mortal danger after coming into conflict with foreign courtiers and their king" (Milne and Collins 2006, 1170). The joining of chapters 1–6 with chapters 7–12 is an instance of the composite nature of many apocalypses and of the genre's tendency to incorporate or be a part of other genres.

One of the major puzzles concerning Daniel is its language. It is written partly in Hebrew and partly in Aramaic. That would be understandable if the difference in language corresponded to the difference in literary form between chapters 1–6 and chapters 7–12, but that is not the case. Daniel 1:1–2:4a and chapters 8–12 are in Hebrew, while the rest is in Aramaic. No one has discovered a satisfactory solution to this enigma.

Pseudonymity characterizes almost every Jewish and Christian apocalypse. Daniel is no exception. It was written around 165 BCE, but its fictional setting is centuries earlier. Daniel was a legendary wise man. Ezekiel uses Daniel as a paragon of righteousness, associating him with Noah and Job (14:14), and as an embodiment of wisdom (28:3). The Daniel of Dan. 1–6 embodies both qualities—righteousness and wisdom—so the ancient sage was an appropriate choice as the hero for these stories.

Daniel 1–6 is an excellent preparation for Dan. 7–12 in a number of ways. First, Daniel is dedicated to the observance of Torah in a foreign setting. Second, he interprets dreams and visions with a political content; he does so not because he is skilled in the techniques of ancient wisdom but because God reveals to him their meaning. Third, God's sovereignty is a main theme of the chapters. Fourth, he can predict the future because God reveals it to him. Fifth, the stories contain apocalyptic elements that are taken up in the second part of the book, especially that of the four kingdoms and the mountain that fills the earth in chapter 2.

Daniel 1–6: Tales from the Diaspora

Chapter 1. The book begins with Nebuchadnezzar's taking of Jerusalem. He gives orders to bring to court some promising Jewish youths to learn the "literature and the language of the Chaldeans" (Babylonians) (1:4). Daniel and three Jewish companions enroll in the palace school and receive Babylonian names. The Chaldean wisdom they learn would have included the technology of dream and vision interpretation, for which the Chaldeans were famous. In 1:20 we learn that the kind of learning they get is, among other things, that of the *magoi* (Greek), from which the English word "magician" derives. They are not magicians in our sense but can interpret signs and dreams. The three "wise men" from the east in the infancy narrative of Matthew's Gospel are called the Magi, the same as *magoi*. In Matthew, their relevant skill is that they can interpret the stars. They are astrologers.

Daniel requests permission for his Jewish companions and himself to eat only food allowed by Torah. Their supervisor reluctantly agrees but fears they will not be as healthy as their fellow students. At the end of a trial period, the Jewish youths are healthier and wiser than anyone else. Adherence to Torah brings success. This is cultural competition, where Jewish culture proves superior to Babylonian. The superiority of the Jews is due not to their own talents. It is God-given (1:17).

Chapter 2. In chapter 2, Nebuchadnezzar has a dream. He summons his wise men to interpret it but refuses to tell them the dream. They must prove themselves first by knowing the dream without his disclosing it. The palace school did not prepare them for this. Nonetheless, the king threatens to execute them all. Daniel hears of this, prays, and receives a vision in the night where "the mystery was revealed" to him (2:19). "Mystery" translates *rāz*, originally a Persian word. This may indicate Persian roots for such dream interpretation. Greek texts of the Bible translate it as *mystērion*, an important word in apocalypticism, indicating the esoteric nature of apocalyptic wisdom (Brown 1958a, 1958b).

Before acceding to the king's request for interpretation, Daniel delivers a preface that insists that God and only God is the source of all mysterious knowledge (2:27–30). No professional interpreters in the king's court can tell the king what he wants to know. Daniel tells the king that the dream concerns the "end of days." He asserts that he, Daniel, gives the king the mysteries and their meaning because God has revealed it to him, not because of any personal talents or skills.

Nebuchadnezzar's dream and its interpretation anticipate Daniel's apocalyptic section. The king dreamed of a colossal statue in four parts—head of gold, chest and arms of silver, middle and thighs of bronze, and legs and feet a mixture of iron and clay. A huge stone is cut, "not by human hands" (2:34), that smashes the feet, and the whole statue disintegrates. The stone becomes a huge mountain that fills the earth.

Daniel explains that the dream concerns four successive kingdoms, of which Nebuchadnezzar's is the first, the golden head. As Daniel discloses this, he makes the point that the king gets his authority from God (2:37). The final kingdom is "divided," indicating political strife. This is an instance of the four-kingdom scheme, a commonplace in the ancient world (Swain 1940). The idea is that history consists of the reign of four kingdoms, each less worthy than the one preceding it. History is a story of decline. The fourth kingdom is soon to pass away. It will be replaced by an idyllic, utopian, everlasting order, divinely ordained. Jewish and Christian tradition would term the final kingdom the kingdom of God.

Since Dan. 2 once circulated independently of the apocalypse, its original historical situation is unknown. In its present context, the fourth kingdom refers to the Seleucid Empire. Applied to the Maccabean situation, the schema foretells the imminent fall of the Seleucid Empire and the coming of God's kingdom. The fall of the fourth empire happens not through human effort, but by God's action. This fits Daniel's disregard for the Maccabees as well as its apocalyptic worldview.

Nebuchadnezzar prostrates himself before Daniel and declares, "Truly, your God is God of gods and Lord of kings and a revealer of mysteries, for you have been able to reveal this mystery!" (2:47). The Babylonian king puts the Jewish God above his own.

Chapter 3. Nebuchadnezzar erects a gigantic golden statue of himself and decrees that anyone who will not worship it be thrown into a blazing furnace.

Daniel's three Jewish companions refuse to worship and so are cast into the fire. The emperor sees the three men unharmed in the fire, along with a fourth who seems divine, probably an angel. When the three emerge unscathed, Nebuchadnezzar proclaims that anyone who blasphemes against the Jewish God will be executed and their property confiscated. The story supplies another admission by a foreign emperor that Israel's God is sovereign. It also demonstrates that martyrdom is preferable to worship of foreign rulers.

Chapter 4. This chapter is a long confession of God's sovereignty. Nebuchadnezzar has a dream that Daniel interprets. The king is confident that Daniel has the "spirit of the holy gods" and "no mystery is too difficult for" him (4:9). The king has dreamt of a tree that was home to birds and that fed living beings. A "watcher" descends from heaven and orders the tree cut down. Watchers are a category of angel. He also orders that the mind of the tree (obviously representing a person at this point) be changed to the mind of an animal. This reflects a legend about a Babylonian ruler Nabonidus who allegedly spent time in the wilderness, having gone insane. The next verse calls this a "sentence" delivered by "the holy ones," that is, angels. It shows God's sovereignty over mortal kings (Dan. 4:17). The issue is divine sovereignty again. The king finally confesses God's supremacy.

Chapter 5. King Belshazzar of Babylonia hosts a feast and has the temerity to drink from the sacred vessels from Jerusalem's temple. A hand appears and writes on the wall. Terrified, Belshazzar summons his wise men, but they cannot read the writing. Daniel comes to the festal hall and interprets the words as judgment on Belshazzar for dishonoring God. Belshazzar dies that night. The episode is the origin of the saying "reading the writing on the wall," meaning deciphering the signs of what is to happen.

Chapter 6. We now meet Darius the Mede, probably not a historical figure. He appoints Daniel to a high position in his court, thereby arousing the jealousy of other courtiers. They plot against him, knowing that he is vulnerable only if he violates Torah. They induce the king to forbid worship of anyone but himself for thirty days. Daniel ignores the decree and worships God, and so he is thrown into the lions' den. The king, in distress because he honors and values Daniel, anxiously keeps vigil through the night. In the morning, Daniel is still alive, having been protected by God.

The group of stories in Dan. 1–6 could not have been a response to the crisis under Antiochus IV. A cruel persecution by the Seleucid king would not produce stories in which there is an ambivalent or even good relation between foreign emperors and their Jewish subjects. Nor is there any indication of a problem living within a different culture or being somewhat assimilated to it. Daniel and his companions have Babylonian names, they are trained in Chaldean schools, and they serve in the royal court. Even when they incur punishment, the foreign monarchs sympathize with them and end up acknowledging God's sovereignty.

Apocalyptic Elements in Daniel 1–6

- Royal figures receive dreams and visions.
- Daniel's wisdom consists of being able to interpret those dreams and visions.
- Dreams and visions reveal God's plans for the future.
- God gives Daniel the ability to interpret dreams and visions.
- God reveals mysteries (*rāz; mystērion*) to Daniel.
- God's sovereignty is at stake.
- Kings violate God's supremacy by not recognizing that their authority comes from God or by insisting on being worshiped.
- Kings acknowledge God's supremacy.

The stories in chapters 1–6 establish Daniel's credentials as a righteous man to whom God reveals mysteries; they portray him as superior to any Babylonian or Median wise man; they address the issue of God's sovereignty, repeatedly depicting foreign monarchs as threats to it and making those monarchs acknowledge God's supremacy.

Daniel 7–12

Daniel 7: First allegorical vision; Throne scene. Daniel 7 is of the utmost importance not just for this apocalypse, but for later Jewish and Christian apocalypticism. Chapter 7 switches to the first person. In previous chapters, Daniel interprets others' dreams. Now he relates his own night visions, which are interpreted by angels. Chapter 7 contains an allegorical vision (Collins 1992a, 31). The vision occupies verses 2–14 and its interpretation, the rest of the chapter.

The vision in Dan. 7 has four parts. Parts 1 and 3 take place on earth, while parts 2 and 4 happen in heaven. The whole is structured according to the pattern of the combat myth. The instance of the myth closest to Dan. 7 is the Canaanite exemplar (Collins 1977c, 95–106; Pritchard 1969, 129–42). In the Canaanite pantheon, El is the highest god, but Canaan's mythology followed the pattern of other ancient Near Eastern myths by having a younger god assume leadership. In Canaanite mythology, the younger god is Baal, son of Dagon. Yamm, the sea god, tries to usurp Baal's position, thus initiating combat, but Baal defeats him. Then Baal, a storm god, rides on the clouds to El who confirms his leadership.

In part one of Daniel's vision (7:2–8), he sees four fearsome beasts rise out of the sea. This is a threat to God's order. In part two (7:9–10), where the combat turns into a battle, there is a heavenly throne scene. At the throne scene, there is a trial, which replaces the battle. In Daniel, God's judgment, not the gods' combat, effects the empires' fall. In part three (7:11–12), the beasts on earth are defeated and the fourth burned. In part four (7:13–14), one like a human being comes on the clouds to the one on the throne and receives sovereignty.

The four parts of Dan. 7 are not joined by transitions. The text jumps from one section to the next. Ironically, this conveys the close connection between the sections. One needs no transition because the connection is so close. Action in the unseen world immediately affects the visible world. God's judgments produce the beasts' demise. No mediator need carry it out. No message need be delivered.

In part one, four strange and fearsome beasts rise out of the sea when it is stirred up by the four winds of heaven. Daniel will learn later in the chapter that each of the beasts is an empire that has oppressed Israel—the Babylonian, and Median, the Persian, and the Greek. Israel was never subject to the Medes, but Daniel's author was unclear about that (see Dan. 5:31). We have already seen this four-kingdom schema in Dan. 2 and decided that the author lives under the fourth kingdom, the kingdom of the Greeks (Seleucids). Each of the four beasts is hybrid and otherworldly but has familiar aspects. The first beast is basically a lion, the second a bear, the third a leopard with four heads, and the fourth undetermined. The fourth is especially fearsome, terrifying, and strong. It is extremely destructive. It devours with large iron teeth and stamps what is left with its feet. It has ten horns.

Taken together, the four beasts have seven heads and ten horns. In Canaanite mythology, Baal pursues a sea dragon with seven heads called Lothan. Animal horns are frequent symbols for strength in the Bible, often in a military context. In apocalyptic symbolism, they often represent kings or royal strength.

Daniel observes the ten horns on the fourth beast and sees another horn, a "little one." Three of the other horns are plucked up to make room for it. Later we learn that the little horn put down three kings (7:24; 11:21). This indicates dynastic struggle. The horn has eyes and a mouth and speaks arrogantly (7:8). The horn is human and a king. This is how Daniel's author sees Antiochus IV. He claims divinity (his throne name Epiphanes carries the idea of a god appearing); he takes over God's earthly dwelling, the temple, and seizes God's sacred space.

Daniel's throne scene is in 7:9–10. The divine figure is "an Ancient One." This may allude to the epithet of El, "Father of Years." His hair is like pure wool, which may allude to its color—white or gray—also indicating great age. His clothing is white, the pure color worthy of heaven. As in Ezekiel, God's throne is a chariot, so it has wheels. It is fiery. From it flows a stream of fire. Like any good emperor, God has countless attendants—a thousand thousands, and ten thousand times ten thousand. These are superhuman beings. The word "angel" does not appear, but moderns would think of them as angels.

Finally, the royal court enters into judgment and books are opened. The books' content is not specified. In the Bible and apocalyptic texts, heavenly books can play several roles. They may contain the names of those who enjoy

God's favor, they may record deeds, or they may lay out eschatological events. Here they probably contain the transgressions of the beasts—those acts by which they oppressed their subjects.

The scene shifts abruptly to earth. The opening of the books results in taking away power from the beasts and burning the fourth one. The cause-and-effect relationship between divine judgment and earthly punishment is implicit but clear.

The scene shifts to heaven once more and completes the combat myth pattern. The young god, having defeated the sea god, force of chaos, comes to the head of the pantheon and receives kingship: "As I watched in the night visions, I saw one like a human being coming with the clouds of heaven. And he came to the Ancient One and was presented before him. To him was given dominion and glory and kingship, that all peoples, nations, and languages should serve him. His dominion is an everlasting dominion that shall not pass away, and his kingship is one that shall never be destroyed" (Dan. 7:13–14).

Daniel's author adapts Canaanite myth to his own purposes. From the myth come El as the Ancient One, Baal riding on the clouds as a storm god, and Baal coming to El to receive dominion. Daniel adds that the one who comes to God is "one like a human being." The Aramaic reads literally "one like a son of man." This figure has been the object of much attention over the centuries (Collins 1993a, 306–9; Hartman and Di Lella 1978; Collins, Cross, and Yarbro Collins 1993, 304–10). "Messiah" is not used of this figure, but we have argued that the mere presence of the word is not definitive for whether a messianic figure is actually present (Murphy 1985, 11–14; Yarbro Collins and Collins 2008, 1–2). The figure does receive kingship and domination, so that counts in favor of messiahship. Nonetheless, Daniel shows no interest in earthly monarchy in general or the Davidic dynasty in particular. So the messianic interpretation is unlikely. The figure does have a close connection with Israel, as we shall see, but his representation of the people is of a sort different from corporate representation.

Collins offers the best solution to the problem (Collins 1977c; 1993a, 304–10). The one like a son of man in Dan. 7 is an angel. He is probably Michael, the angel who represents Israel in the heavenly court (first suggested by Schmidt in 1900).

We begin with the phrase "one like a human being." The Aramaic term, *bar ʿĕnoš*, found in Dan. 7:13, corresponds to the Hebrew *ben-ʾādām* (Dan. 8:17). The terms mean simply "human being." But their literal translation is "son of man."

It is common in apocalypses for angels to look like humans. In Daniel, when a figure is said to resemble a human, that is because it is not human and must be compared to humans for its appearance. (An exception is 8:17.) Elsewhere, angels are described in human terms. In 8:15, Daniel sees one "in the likeness of a man." He is the angel Gabriel. In 9:21, "the man Gabriel," identified as the one whom Daniel saw in a previous vision, appears to him. In 10:5, Daniel sees "a man clothed in linen" who is an angel. Two angelic figures appear in 12:5–7, one of whom is the "man clothed in linen," perhaps from chapter 10.

The angel, one like a human being, comes to God and receives dominion, glory, and kingship. All "peoples, nations, and languages" will serve him. His kingship is everlasting. So we have a royal angel. Like Baal in the Canaanite myth, he receives rulership from the highest God. Daniel approaches one of God's attendants and asks for an interpretation. The attendant explains that the four beasts are four kingdoms, "The holy ones of the Most High shall receive the kingdom and possess the kingdom forever—forever and ever" (Dan. 7:18). Collins finds that "holy ones" in the Hebrew Bible almost always means heavenly beings (Collins 1993a, 313–17). The same usage holds in the Dead Sea Scrolls, the Apocrypha and Pseudepigrapha, and Israel's linguistic environment. Daniel uses "holy ones" for superhuman beings in 4:10, 14, 20; 8:13; and 12:7. If "holy ones" means angels in Dan. 7:18, then the fall of the beasts in 7:11–12 is followed by dominion being conferred on the angels of heaven in 7:13–14. But the interpretation is still richer.

Daniel wants to know more about the beasts. His own description of them exceeds the night vision itself. In the vision, Daniel saw a little horn speaking arrogantly. This was Antiochus IV. His arrogance was toward God. But he went further. He suppressed God's cult. Daniel gives us more detail.

> As I looked, this horn made war with the holy ones and was prevailing over them, until the Ancient One came; then judgment was given for the holy ones of the Most High, and the time arrived when the holy ones gained possession of the kingdom. (Dan. 7:21–22)

The horn's arrogance is an attack on the holy ones, and he is prevailing. He will prevail only until God comes and gives judgment. This refers to the throne scene and the judgment of 7:9–10. God's judgment results in the angels' possessing the kingdom, which is equivalent to what happens in 7:13–14 where the one like a son of man receives kingship.

The angel identifies the fourth beast. The period of dominance of the four beasts culminates in the dominance of the fourth. It is worse than the others and tramples the whole earth. Most significant are the interpreter's last words about the fourth kingdom: He shall speak words against the Most High, shall wear out the holy ones of the Most High, and shall attempt to change the sacred seasons and the law; and they shall be given into his power for a time, two times, and half a time (Dan. 7:25). The little horn's arrogant words are against the Most High, against God. The horn's "words," which amount to all of his decrees and actions, attack God's heavenly host and prevail over it. Antiochus has changed Israel's sacred cultic feasts and the Torah.

Antiochus's prevailing over the angels, equivalent to outlawing the Jerusalem cult, will last a time, two times, and half a time. This means three and a half years. Each "time" is a year. This corresponds to about the same length of time as the persecution actually lasted. First Maccabees 4:54 says that it lasted exactly three years. The figures 1,290 days and 1,335 days in Dan. 12:11–12 seem to be attempts to reckon the time more closely. This is actual prediction. Our author knows of the onset of Antiochus's persecution of Judaism. He has not yet seen its end, unlike the books of the Maccabees, which describe the rededication of the temple and Antiochus's death. So he writes sometime between the desecration of the cult (167 BCE) and Judah Maccabee's restoration of it (164 BCE).

The heavenly courtroom scene results in the end of Antiochus's reign. Then the interpreting angel addresses the fourth part of Daniel's vision, the vision of the one like a son of man. But there is a twist in his interpretation. Rather than explaining what happens on the heavenly level, he explains its significance for what happens on earth:

> The kingship and dominion and the greatness of the kingdoms under the whole heaven shall be given to the people of the holy ones of the Most High; their kingdom shall be an everlasting kingdom, and all dominions shall serve and obey them. (Dan. 7:27)

Michael receives dominion in heaven. The "people of the holy ones of the Most High" receive kingship on earth. Such correspondence is essential in apocalypticism. The people of the angels must be Israel. Michael is their heavenly patron, as we learn in Dan. 10:21 and 12:1. Heaven corresponds to earth. The unseen corresponds to the seen. Michael's dominion corresponds to Israel's dominion.

Our analysis of the angel's interpretation is confirmed by Qumran's *War Scroll*, a document roughly contemporary with Daniel. In the eschatological war as presented in the *War Scroll*, angels and humans fight side by side. God's forces will win, which means that Michael and the good angels will defeat Belial (Qumran's name for Satan) and his forces. The victory is described as follows: "He [God] will raise up Michael in the midst of the gods, and the realm of Israel in the midst of all flesh" (1QM 17). The parallel with Dan. 7 is exact. The people of Qumran are an apocalyptic community, so it is not surprising that the apocalyptic worldview expressed in Dan. 7 and in the *War Scroll* is the same on this point. There is also a parallel between "people of the holy ones of the Most High" in Dan. 7:28 and "people of the holy ones of the covenant" in 1QM 10:10.

Daniel 8: Second allegorical vision. This chapter contains Daniel's second allegorical vision (8:1–14) and Gabriel's interpretation (8:15–26). It covers some of the same ground as Dan. 7 but supplies detail we have not yet encountered. Such repetition is called recapitulation and is common in apocalypses.

In this vision, humans again appear as animals. The Median and Persian Empires are represented by a ram with two horns. Alexander the Great is a male goat with a single horn. The horn is broken, symbolizing Alexander's death, and four grow up in its place, signifying the Hellenistic kingdoms. The vision goes straight from the four Hellenistic kingdoms to the little horn. The horn expands and includes in its power the "beautiful land," the land of Israel. The horn attacks the stars, trampling them and throwing some down to earth. Stars are heavenly beings. Here they are angels, and they are the same as the "holy ones" who are at first defeated in 7:21. The horn acts arrogantly "even to the prince of the host"; Antiochus ultimately attacks God. It takes away God's cult and sacrifices and takes over the sanctuary. It is victorious over God's host and even over truth itself. The attack corresponds to Antiochus's earthly persecution. The rest of the passage adds detail to the description of Antiochus's cultic offenses.

The abomination is to last 2,300 mornings and evenings, and the sanctuary and cult will be restored (8:14). Reference in this passage to the regular burnt offering—offered twice a day, morning and evening, and called the *tāmîd*—means that 2,300 mornings and evenings is 1,150 days (Collins 1993a, 336). That is the same order of magnitude as the three and a half times of Dan. 7:25.

Daniel cannot understand the vision (8:15). Gabriel says that the vision is for the end time (8:17). Gabriel speaks of this as the period of wrath and "the appointed time of the end" (8:19). The language here was fruitful for later apocalyptic thinkers. "Wrath" usually refers to God's wrath. It is unleashed on the wicked as the end approaches. The "end" is the end of history as we know it. The "period of wrath" suggests that there is an extended era during which God's wrath works in history. That time has an end preordained by God.

Daniel 9: Angelic discourse. The chapter opens with Daniel noticing "in the books," that is, in Israel's sacred writings, that Jeremiah predicted that the "devastation of Jerusalem" would last seventy years. Jeremiah's prediction caught the attention of many apocalyptic thinkers, because it supplied a concrete figure for the length of Israel's punishment.

Noticing Jeremiah's figure of seventy years, Daniel realizes that the end of the destruction must be near, and so he prays about it. Jeremiah spoke of the Babylonian exile. The fictional Daniel of the book of Daniel lived during that exile. Daniel sees the end of the exile approaching. The real author speaks not of the Babylonian exile but of the crisis under Antiochus IV, four centuries later.

Daniel offers a penitential prayer, confessing Israel's sins that led to the desolation of the sanctuary. God's wrath burns against Jerusalem and its temple, and Daniel prays for it to end. Gabriel comes to Daniel to give him "wisdom and understanding." Gabriel says, "Seventy weeks are decreed for your people and your holy city: to finish the transgression, to put an end to sin, and to atone for iniquity, to bring in everlasting righteousness, to seal both vision and prophet, and to anoint a most holy place" (Dan. 9:24). At their end, Israel will have paid for its sin and will be righteous, the predictions of traditional prophets like Jeremiah and seers like Daniel will have been accomplished, and the sanctuary in Jerusalem will have been restored.

Gabriel's explanation of the seventy weeks covers the Second Temple period up to the second century BCE. Seventy weeks must be allegorical, not literal. It cannot be literally about a year and a half; it must be much longer. Judging by what "weeks" means in other apocalyptic texts, it is most likely that a week here is really seven years. Seventy weeks would be 490 years. Gabriel starts the reckoning of the seventy weeks by saying there were seven weeks (forty-nine years) from the time when there was a decree to rebuild Jerusalem until an "anointed prince" would come. The decree to rebuild Jerusalem cannot be that of Cyrus (538 BCE), because the temple was rebuilt just eighteen years later. The most likely time is 586 BCE, when the destruction took place. The second temple was constructed from 520 to 515 BCE. Forty-nine years from 586 is 537 BCE. This is about the time of Cyrus's decree allowing the rebuilding of Jerusalem.

Gabriel says that there will be an "anointed prince" at the end of the first seven-week period. That is possibly Zerubbabel, but more likely the high priest Joshua. He is not an eschatological figure, so "anointed" here designates not a messianic figure but rather points to one of the usual meanings of the term in the Hebrew Bible, a high priest. Joshua and Zerubbabel date to around 520 BCE, the second major return of exiles to Judah.

In the next sixty-two "weeks," Jerusalem and its temple are rebuilt, "but in a troubled time" (9:25). The Second Temple period is frequently characterized as troubled or inadequate in texts from the era (Knibb 1976). Daniel's author does not consider the restoration after the exile complete. Things were still not as God wished. The sixty-two weeks are passed over quickly.

Our author's real interest is in his own time, under Antiochus. Gabriel says,

> After the sixty-two weeks, an anointed one shall be cut off and shall have nothing, and the troops of the prince who is to come shall destroy the city and the sanctuary. Its end shall come with a flood, and to the end there shall be war. Desolations are decreed. He shall make a strong covenant with many for one week, and for half of the week he shall make sacrifice and offering cease; and in their place shall be an abomination that desolates, until the decreed end is poured out upon the desolator. (Dan. 9:26–27)

There is another messiah here, but not an eschatological leader. This messiah is killed. He is probably Onias III, brother of the Hellenizer Jason. Then Antiochus destroys Jerusalem with his troops and destroys the sanctuary. The covenant Antiochus establishes is with unrighteous Jews, the Hellenizers. That lasts for a "week," during half of which (three and a half years) Antiochus prohibits God's cult. The three-and-a-half weeks matches the three-and-a-half times of Dan. 7. At that time, Antiochus will have established the foreign cult in the temple, here called the "abomination that desolates." After the time of the abomination is fulfilled, "the decreed end is poured out on the desolator." Antiochus's punishment is foreordained.

Daniel 10–11: Second angelic discourse. Daniel has a vision of a superhuman, frightening figure.

> I looked up and saw a man clothed in linen, with a belt of gold from Uphaz around his waist. His body was like beryl, his face like lightning, his eyes like flaming torches, his arms and legs like the gleam of burnished bronze, and the sound of his words like the roar of a multitude. (Dan. 10:5–6)

Twice this angel is said to be in human form (10:16, 18). Fear overcomes Daniel, and the angel touches him and tells him not to be afraid. The angel tells Daniel that he fought the prince of Persia for twenty-one days. Only Michael, "one of the chief princes" and Israel's patron, helped him (10:21). Gabriel left Michael there to visit Daniel. He tells Daniel that he will return to oppose the prince of Persia, and that then the prince of Greece will come. "Prince" in this passage refers to the superhuman patron of each nation. In Israel's polytheistic past, each nation was allotted its own god (see Pss. 58, 82, 86, 93, 96, 97). Yahweh received Israel. Deuteronomy 32:8–9 explains, "When the Most High apportioned the nations, when he divided humankind, he fixed the boundaries of the peoples according to the number of the gods; the LORD's own portion was his people, Jacob his allotted share."

The angel says that he will tell Daniel what is in the "book of truth." Since he proceeds in chapter 11 to "predict" the wars between the Hellenistic powers, the book contains what is to come. For Daniel's real author, these things are already past. They include the fall of Persia to Alexander, the founding of the Hellenistic kingdoms by Alexander's successors, and the kingdoms' wars against one another.

As usual, the real author's interest is in his own time. In returning from one of his campaigns against Egypt, Antiochus IV attacked Jerusalem. He had been thwarted in his campaign by the Romans, whose power was growing in the eastern Mediterranean. As the angel says, the "ships of Kittim shall come against him, and he shall lose heart and withdraw" (11:30). "Kittim," originally meaning those from Cyprus, is applied first to the Greeks and then to the Romans in Jewish texts. Here it means Romans. They turn Antiochus back. He is enraged and takes his anger out on "the holy covenant" (11:30). He listens to the unrighteous Jews, those who "forsake the holy covenant," the Hellenizers. His troops attack Jerusalem and "occupy and profane the temple and fortress. They shall abolish the regular burnt offering and set up the abomination that makes desolate" (11:31).

Those who "make wise" among the people, the people behind the book of Daniel, are the only ones in a position to know what is happening, for they have insight into the unseen world and know the future. Only apocalypticism furnishes answers. Antiochus receives his usual unflattering portrait here.

> The king shall act as he pleases. He shall exalt himself and consider himself greater than any god, and shall speak horrendous things against the God of gods. He shall prosper until the period of wrath is completed, for what is determined shall be done. He shall pay no respect to the gods of his ancestors, or to the one beloved by women; he shall pay no respect to any other god, for he shall consider himself greater than all. (Dan. 11:36–37)

Antiochus is not just a politician. He is a superhuman force.

The angelic interpreter tells of Antiochus's fall. It takes place "between the sea and the beautiful holy mountain" (11:45). In other words, he dies in the land of Israel. This is not accurate. He died in Persia. We can date the book through the error. It was written during the persecution, which began in 167 BCE, but before Antiochus's death in 164.

Daniel 12: Michael, suffering, resurrection, postmortem reward and punishment. This is a short chapter packed with significant information. Formally, it continues the previous chapter, so it is part of the second angelic discourse. After Antiochus's death, "Michael, the great prince, the protector of your people, shall arise" (12:1). When he arises, there comes a period of anguish such as the world has never experienced, but Israel is delivered—that is, everyone whose name is written in the heavenly book. The period of unprecedented anguish before the end becomes an apocalyptic commonplace. In Revelation, it is called the tribulation.

There follows a resurrection in which "many" rise, some to everlasting reward and others to everlasting punishment (12:2) (Nickelsburg 2006). It is the first clear mention of resurrection in Jewish literature. The punishment is unspecified. Reward is described: "Those who are wise shall shine like the brightness of the sky, and those who lead many to righteousness, like the stars forever and ever" (Dan. 12:3). "Those who are wise," more literally, "those who make [others] wise," stand behind the book of Daniel. The technical term for their future state of existence is "astral immortality." The stars are heavenly beings. The wise are in heaven with the angels.

It is not clear whether every dead person rises in Dan. 12. It may be only the very good and the very bad who rise. The righteous suffered and died for their loyalty to Torah and God. The wicked prospered. Now that is reversed.

The angel commands: "Keep the words secret and the book sealed until the time of the end" (12:4). This explains why Daniel's words were not known until the Maccabean crisis. They were sealed and hidden away. But the end is now. Daniel must be published.

Daniel: Apocalypse and Apocalypticism

- Daniel 1–6 collects legends from the Diaspora to prepare the way for the apocalypse.
- Kings have predictive dreams of political import.
- Daniel interprets those dreams, because God has given him their "mystery."
- The kings recognize God's sovereignty.
- Daniel 7–12 fits the definition of an apocalypse.
- Daniel has visions in the night.
- An angel interprets Daniel's dreams.
- The dreams concern Israel's historical circumstances.
- Antiochus's persecution of Judaism on the earthly level corresponds to his attack on heaven.
- Daniel 7 is a throne vision in which God gives dominion to one like a son of man, probably Israel's patron angel, Michael, and Israel receives dominion on earth.
- Daniel 8 is a second allegorical vision tracing historical events and telling of Antiochus IV's attack on heaven.
- Daniel 9 is an angelic discourse where Gabriel interprets Jeremiah's prediction of the exile lasting seventy years.
- Daniel 10–11 is another angelic discourse covering the same ground as Dan. 8.
- Daniel 12 portrays the end. Michael arises, there is a time of great suffering, and the good and bad are raised from the dead. The good live with the angels forever.

Two angels appear and take up once again the question of when the end will come. One answers that it will come after a time, two times, and half a time. Daniel is told to go his way, because what the book concerns is future.

Daniel ends with two adjustments to the eschatological timetable. The first is that the period between the taking away of the daily burnt offerings and the establishment of the "abomination that makes desolate" and the end is 1,290 days. The next verse sets it at 1,335 days. Someone, observing that the end did not arrive when scheduled, adjusted the schedule.

The *Animal Apocalypse* (*1 Enoch* 85–90)

The *Animal Apocalypse* is a second apocalypse written in response to the crisis under Antiochus IV (Tiller 1993). It is the second of two visions of the *Dream Visions*, chapters 85–90 of *1 Enoch*. At one point the *Animal Apocalypse* was an independent work. It recites the history of the world, from Adam's creation to the eschaton. Humans are portrayed as animals, while superhuman beings appear as humans or stars. The *Animal Apocalypse* gets its information from the Bible and from the *Book of the Watchers* (*1 Enoch* 1–36), a Jewish apocalypse from the third century BCE, so the better one knows the Bible and the earlier apocalypse, the more easily one can spot the writer's references.

Adam and His Descendants

Adam appears as a white bull (85:3). As such, he represents the perfect human. After a period of degradation, humanity returns at the end to being composed of white bulls, so this is the apocalypse's narrative arc. The end is like the beginning. Adam's first two children, Cain and Abel, are black and red bulls, respectively, so they are anomalies. The rest of Adam's children and their immediate descendants are white bulls. At first, things go as God intended.

Chapter 86 contains the myth of the watchers. In that myth, sin enters the world when angels descend from heaven and have intercourse with human women. This develops the mythic fragment we found in Gen. 6. In the *Book of the Watchers*, the angels sin by having intercourse with women, thus mixing the heavenly and the earthly, and by sharing with the women heavenly secrets they were not meant to know. They are imprisoned under the earth by good angels to await final judgment and punishment. Their offspring are giants who ravage the earth and ultimately kill one another. When the offspring die, evil spirits emerge from their bodies and plague humanity. The book looks forward to God's coming in judgment, a new Jerusalem, and the punishment of the wicked and the reward of the righteous.

Chapter 86 condenses all of this to a vision where stars descend from heaven and have intercourse with the oxen. Their offspring are black oxen, signifying that humanity is now changed definitively. They are no longer white bulls.

In chapter 87, Enoch is swept away by four "beings who were like white men," that is, angels, to a place from which he can observe all that is to happen.

In chapter 88, one of the four angels takes the erring stars, binds them hand and foot, and casts them into the abyss.

In chapter 89, Noah appears as a white bull. He retains the purity of God's original humans. Noah's sons are bulls, each a different color—white, red, and black. The Bible sees Noah's three sons as progenitors of the three segments of the human race—the Shemites (white) to whom belong Israel, those from around Greece (red), and those from Africa (black). The Shemites initially manage to maintain perfect humanity. Then humanity is depicted as all sorts of animals, but one remains a white bull. This is Abraham. His son Isaac is also a white bull, but Isaac's son Jacob is a sheep. This is a step down, but the depiction of Israel as sheep is common and has biblical roots (see Ezek. 34). Jacob's twelve sons are all sheep. Even Moses is a sheep.

Most of the rest of the *Animal Apocalypse* proceeds in predictable ways and follows the Bible closely, but the author adds features that reflect its apocalyptic worldview. After the destruction of the northern kingdom by the Assyrians and the southern by the Babylonians, God appoints seventy shepherds for the sheep (89:59). This alludes to Jeremiah's prediction that Israel's exile will last for seventy years. God appoints an angelic recorder to keep track of the shepherds' doings (89:61).

The apocalypse recounts the restoration of Jerusalem and its temple under the Persians, but he says that its bread was polluted and not pure (89:73). Jewish texts of the time frequently voice dissatisfaction with the temple or its establishment (Himmelfarb 2007). We have seen this in Third Isaiah, Haggai, Malachi, Ezra, Nehemiah, and Daniel.

The Maccabean Revolt

Chapter 90 tells of the Seleucid attack on Israel, the Maccabean revolt, and the final consummation of history. The birds of heaven attack the sheep. Lambs are born who cry out to the sheep, but are unheeded. The lambs wish to fight the birds (gentiles). They are the Maccabees and their allies. The lambs have open eyes. That is, they know what is truly happening. The rest of the sheep are blind. The lambs are like the wise of Daniel, although their policy is very different. Where the wise of Daniel are quietists, waiting for God's action and seeing little or no profit in the Maccabean revolt, those behind this apocalypse see the revolt as God's will. One of the sheep, Judah Maccabee, sprouts a horn, and all the rams rally to it. Most of the sheep remain docile. Battles ensue, and the birds are unable to subdue the horned ram. A "great sword" is given to the sheep, and they fight effectively against the other animals, that is, the nations.

The Last Judgment and Eschaton

The angelic recorder informs God that the shepherds have ruled his people poorly. God, "Lord of the sheep," comes to earth and smites it with the rod of his wrath, destroying the ravens, birds, and other animals. God sits on a throne in the "pleasant land," Israel, and the recorder brings sealed books and opens them. They are books of judgment, as in Dan. 7. God summons "those men the seven first white ones," his seven archangels. They bring before him the stars who sinned with the women. They are found guilty and cast into the fiery abyss. The seventy shepherds suffer the same fate, as do the blind sheep, so the punishment extends to part of Israel.

Enoch sees the second temple dismantled and put aside and a new one much grander than the former erected. All the beasts of the earth come to honor Israel. Enoch is transported to the midst of the sheep and observes that they are all white. They are all righteous. They seal up the sword in the

The *Animal Apocalypse*: Apocalypse and Apocalypticism

- The *Animal Apocalypse* is in the form of an apocalypse.
- Its consummation is a return to the beginning; humans become what they were originally created to be.
- It ends with a new Jerusalem and a new temple.
- The wicked are destroyed.
- Israel becomes completely righteous.
- God actively supports the Maccabean revolt.
- Angelic shepherds rule Israel.
- Sinful stars, erring shepherds, and sinful Jews suffer eternal punishment in the fiery abyss.

temple. There are so many of them that the house cannot hold them all, but the house is spacious.

The Restoration of Humanity

Now a white bull is born with large horns. Humanity is returning to its divinely intended state. The birds of the air petition him. Eventually all become white bulls. The "first among them" becomes a large lamb with black horns. God rejoices over it. It is probably a messianic figure. This ends the vision.

Daniel and the Animal Apocalypse Compared

It is a remarkable bit of luck that we have two extant apocalypses, Daniel and the *Animal Apocalypse*, written at precisely the same time to respond to the same set of circumstances (Davila 2005). Both claim to be based on visions from God. Both interpret earthly events in the light of heavenly ones. Both attribute earthly happenings to God's action. Both expect the resolution of earthly problems to happen through God's direct intervention.

They are also quite different. The *Animal Apocalypse* legitimizes the Maccabean revolt, while Daniel ignores it. The former advocates military action, while the latter does not. Daniel expects the eschaton to be the righteous living among the angelic stars and the wicked eternally punished. The *Animal Apocalypse* expects a new earthly Jerusalem, center of worship for a righteous Israel and recognized by the nations. It also expects the transformation of humanity into what God intended at the beginning. This idea has been compared to that of Paul, who sees the original Adam as having changed the human condition and the nature of humanity by his disobedience and Christ as the New Adam, who represents a new beginning for the human race, one where Christ is the perfect human (Murphy-O'Connor 2009).

Conclusion

The way that the ancients conceived of time, space, history, humanity, and the unseen world is bound to be strange to the modern mind. The insights concerning ancient religion should be kept in mind as we proceed to study other ancient documents.

Daniel is one of the two most important apocalypses in history. It supplies many of the elements that went into the making of Revelation, and it has remained an object of fascination for apocalyptic thinkers right up to the present. The *Animal Apocalypse* furnishes another full-blown apocalypse. It was written at the same time as Daniel, addresses the same historical situation, and yet has a different view of the significance of the Maccabean revolution and the actions of God in the world. The contrast reminds us that apocalypses and apocalypticism are varied, and we should expect such variety as we proceed.

Suggestions for Further Reading

Bickerman, Elias. *The God of the Maccabees: Studies on the Meaning and Origin of the Maccabean Revolt*. Leiden: Brill, 1979.

Collins, John Joseph. *Daniel: A Commentary on the Book of Daniel*. Hermeneia. Minneapolis: Fortress, 1993.

Davila, James R. "The Animal Apocalypse and Daniel." In *Enoch and Qumran Origins*, edited by Gabriele Boccaccini, J. Harold Ellens, and James A. Waddell, 35–38. Grand Rapids: Eerdmans, 2005.

Hengel, Martin. *Judaism and Hellenism: Studies in Their Encounter in Palestine during the Early Hellenistic Period*. 2 vols. London: SCM, 1974.

Portier-Young, Anathea. *Apocalypse against Empire: Theologies of Resistance in Early Judaism*. Grand Rapids: Eerdmans, 2011.

Tcherikover, Victor. *Hellenistic Civilization and the Jews*. Philadelphia: Jewish Publication Society of America, 1959.

Tiller, Patrick A. *A Commentary on the Animal Apocalypse of 1 Enoch*. Atlanta: Scholars Press, 1993.

4

The Book of Revelation

Our study is generally chronological, so studying Revelation now breaks the pattern. We do so for two reasons. In the two canonical apocalypses, Daniel and Revelation, we have the most influential apocalypses in history. They are the backbone of apocalypticism for all that follow them. Therefore it makes sense to read them together. Further, Revelation depends heavily on Daniel and Ezekiel in a literary sense, so we analyze it while those two canonical works are fresh in our minds.

Revelation is a coherent work by a single author, even though it does use some previous sources. For example, it preserves passages from Nero's time, though the book was composed during Domitian's reign, probably in 96 CE.

Revelation's author pretends to write about the Babylonians of the sixth century BCE, although the book really was written under and concerns the Romans at the end of the first century CE. Three other apocalypses from around the turn of the second century CE use the same device—*2 Baruch*, *4 Ezra*, and the *Apocalypse of Abraham*, as does 2 Peter in the New Testament (5:13). Throughout our analysis we speak of Rome, not Babylon, to forefront the true situation of the writer. It is unlikely that Revelation is pseudonymous. The author writes in his own name, John (Collins 1977b).

The Imperial Cult

The imperial cult is a key issue in Revelation (Price 1984). "Cult" means public, formal worship. It can take the form of animal sacrifice; offerings of grain, incense, or other items; or prayers and hymns. The imperial cult is the worship of Roma, Rome personified as a goddess, or of a specific emperor.

Revelation's author passionately opposed the imperial cult. Even when Christians did not participate in it, their complacence toward it was unacceptable. Religion and politics came together in the imperial cult; it expressed loyalty to Rome by its participants. For John, Roman religious claims were blasphemous because they infringed on God's sovereignty. Practically speaking, the imperial cult extended and reinforced Rome's imperial power and oppression. John was convinced that Rome was about to force the cult on everyone on penalty of death. That turned out not to be true.

Persecution

Modern Christians often imagine fierce opposition between Christianity and the Roman Empire right from the time of Jesus down to the adoption of Christianity as the official religion of the Roman Empire under the emperor Constantine in the early fourth century CE. They picture Christians being thrown to the lions accompanied by the cheers of hateful Roman crowds. This is misconceived (Potter 1992a; Frend 1965). There was no empire-wide persecution of Christianity until the middle of the third century BCE.

To gain a more accurate picture of Revelation's historical circumstances, we begin by remembering that there was no firm division between religion, politics, economics, kinship, and culture in the ancient world. Changes in religion had economic and political consequences, for example. The Roman world was tolerant of different religions. Polytheism was the rule. At the same time, if one refused to worship certain gods, that might have public import. Roman authorities repressed any sect they considered injurious to the state or social system.

The New Testament contains earliest Christianity's documents, so it is there that we look for evidence of Roman persecution in the first century CE. Jesus's execution was the elimination of an individual potentially dangerous to the Judean establishment and to Roman control of the region. No one but Jesus died. There was no attempt to wipe out Jesus's followers or their leaders. A bit later, Hellenistic Christians were expelled from Jerusalem, but the apostles and other Christians were allowed to stay. This was probably because the Hellenists (Greek-speaking Jews, probably from the Diaspora) were considered a threat to public order because of their views on Torah, while the apostles and other Aramaic-speaking Jewish Christians were not (Acts 6:8–8:1; 11:19–26). Jewish authorities did the expelling, and Paul was among them. Again, this was not a general persecution of Christians, even in Jerusalem.

Acts of the Apostles, the earliest church history, is more interested in obstacles raised by Jews against Christianity than in Roman repression. Acts is driven partly by its "Roman apologetic," an attempt to portray Christianity as harmless or even beneficial to the empire and to depict the Roman response to the new movement as benevolent. First Peter (2:13–17) and Paul (Rom. 13:1–7) seem conciliatory toward the empire (but see Horsley 1997).

The Gospels' apocalyptic discourses (speeches by Jesus) provide the best evidence for persecution (Matt. 24; Mark 13; Luke 21). They expect persecution from all sides, Jewish, Roman, and local, but their description is stylized and contains little detail. It is future and founded on the apocalyptic belief that there will be abundant suffering before the end comes (Dan. 12). Some parts of such predictions are probably written later, after some Christians had suffered for their faith. Their value as historical evidence is limited.

When Paul complains of being persecuted after he becomes a member of the new movement (2 Cor. 11:22–33), he mentions primarily Jewish examples. His activity in synagogues is disruptive, and synagogue leaders discipline him. At times, he seems also to have suffered Roman punishment, but that would also be for disrupting civic order.

In a couple of instances, Christian monotheism interfered with business interests. Paul drives a fortune-telling demon from a girl, ruining her owners' livelihood (Acts 16). He preaches against the lucrative idol-selling of Artemis of Ephesus, and provokes a hostile reaction (Acts 19:32–41). Two other New Testament documents, Hebrews and 1 Peter, attest to tension between Christians and their Greco-Roman environment. These are cases in which non-Christians resented Christians for reasons that are not clear. The two books are concerned that if Christians suffer, it should be purely on the basis of their faith and not for ordinary crimes. It sounds as if accusations against Christians often had nothing to do with Christianity per se. It was common for unusual sects or groups to attract such accusations—such as that they were sexually permissive or that they were inimical to the public welfare. The same is true today. In the case of the New Testament, where these occur, they seem to be local and on a small scale.

There are three Roman authors informative for our subject. Suetonius (lived from ca. 69 to after 130 CE) and Tacitus (ca. 56–117 CE), Roman historians, tell of Nero's persecution of Christians in 64 CE. Nero did not persecute them because they were Christian but on charges of arson. Rome had suffered a devastating fire, and Nero was being blamed. He deflected the blame onto the Christians. This shows that they were an identifiable group in Rome, that their existence was not forbidden, and that they were unpopular.

The third author, Pliny the Younger, governor of Bithynia—a Roman province in Asia Minor bordering the province of Asia, where the seven cities of Revelation were located—wrote to the emperor Trajan in around 112 CE. Locals were denouncing Christians, and he did not know what to do. He commented that Christianity was popular, that its adherents seemed to worship Christ as a god, and that as a result local temples and shrines were being abandoned and were suffering economically. Pliny's solution was to demand that the Christians offer incense and wine to the emperor's statue and curse Christ. This they refused to do, so he charged them with refusing to show loyalty to the emperor.

Trajan replied that there were no general rules for dealing with Christians. They were not to be sought out. If brought before the governor, they were to be punished if they refused to recant, because this showed intolerable stubbornness before Roman authority. Anonymous accusations were to be ignored. The impression is that there was no general law against Christians, and unless they caused trouble, they were left alone.

Roman writings say that Domitian, the emperor under whom Revelation was written, insisted on being worshiped. A strong case has been made that Domitian did no such thing (Thompson 1990). If Domitian did plan to enforce the imperial cult, then John had cause to worry, although nothing ever came of it. If not, it was his imagination rather than political reality that posed the problem.

There is little evidence of persecution in Revelation itself. Our author fears one to come. He can mention only one "martyr," Antipas, and it is not clear that Antipas died for being a Christian and certain that he did not die in a general persecution (2:13).

John feels that Christians misjudge Rome and are too complacent with Greco-Roman society. He wants them to perceive things differently. He is trying to shock them into his perspective: Rome is Satanic and opposed to God and those loyal to God. The author may have come from Palestine and have endured Roman brutality because of the Jewish revolt and the destruction of Jerusalem (Mussies 1980). The Greek of Revelation is heavily influenced by Aramaic and Hebrew, which supports this theory of John's origins.

The Combat Myth

Revelation adapts the combat myth that is central to many apocalyptic worldviews (Yarbro Collins 1976). Forsyth identifies Satan as the rebel god in the Christian version of the combat myth. We reproduce Forsyth's summary. He admits that it is not fully present in any one Christian source, but it is presupposed in one way or another by many Christian sources. This summary will help us not only with Revelation but also with our analysis of Jesus and with the rest of the New Testament.

> A rebel god challenges the power of Yahweh, takes over the whole earth as an extension of his empire, and rules it through the power of sin and death. He is the typical death-dealing villain who causes consternation among his subjects, and his depredations and cruelty make them long for a liberator. This dark tyrant, the "god of this world" as Paul called him, is eventually thwarted by the Son of God (or man) in the most mysterious episode of the Christian story,

Structure of Revelation

Descriptive Title (1:1–3)
Epistolary Frame (1:4–6)
Prophetic Sayings (1:7–8)
Inaugural Vision (1:9–3:22)
Eschatological Visions (4:1–22:5)
   Heavenly Throne Room Vision (4:1–5:14)
   First Great Cycle of Eschatological Visions (6:1–11:19)
      Seven Seals (6:1–8:5)
      Seven Trumpets (8:6–11:19)
   Second Great Cycle of Eschatological Visions (12:1–22:5)
      Seven Unnumbered Visions (12:1–15:4)
      Seven Bowls (15:1; 15:5–16:21)
      Babylon Appendix (17:1–19:10)
      Seven Unnumbered Visions (19:11–21:8)
      New Jerusalem Appendix (21:9–22:5)
Prophetic Sayings (22:6–20a)
Epistolary Frame (22:20b–21)

(Murphy 1998, xvii)

the crucifixion, which oddly combines both defeat and victory. As Luther could testify, the struggle with Satan continues, however, and we wait still for the end of his story in the end of history. The function of Christ, in almost the technical narrative sense of function, is to be the potential liberator of mankind from this tyranny, and the function of Satan is to be the adversary in this Christian variant of the ancient Near Eastern combat narrative. (Forsyth 1987, 6–7)

The Structure of Revelation

Revelation is a narrative within a letter, introduced as an apocalypse. It is not strictly chronological. When Christ unleashes the great eschatological events, they take place in two great cycles of visions that cover some of the same ground from different angles. This is called recapitulation. Having a grasp of Revelation's structure will help us to keep track of what is going on as we read the book.

Analysis of Revelation

Descriptive Title (1:1–3)

The opening words of Revelation define "apocalypse."

> The revelation of Jesus Christ, which God gave him to show his servants what must soon take place; he made it known by sending his angel to his servant John, who testified to the word of God and to the testimony of Jesus Christ, even to all that he saw. Blessed is the one who reads aloud the words of the prophecy, and blessed are those who hear and who keep what is written in it; for the time is near. (Rev. 1:1–3)

God reveals things to Jesus who reveals them to John by sending an angel to him. So a revelation is given to a human by a superhuman figure. The content of the revelation is what will soon take place and what John saw (including the heavenly world). Eschatological events are imminent.

For John, "testimony" (*martyria*) is a loaded word; he uses it nine times. Another five words derive from it. Another translation for *martyria* is "witness." Its original context is that of the law court. Since Revelation's author believes that the full power of the Roman Empire—legal, civil, and military—is soon to be brought to bear against Christians, he expects Christians to appear in Roman courts, as Jesus did. Christians' witness before Roman authorities may result in death. It is easy to see how the Greek word for witness, *martyria*, became the English word for sacrificing one's life for faith.

The introductory section ends with a blessing (one of seven) on the one who reads Revelation aloud and those who hear it. The author categorizes his apocalypse as prophecy.

Epistolary Introduction and Prophetic Pronouncements (1:4–8)

Revelation is in the form of a letter. For the analysis of Revelation's structure used here see Yarbro Collins (1992b) and Murphy (1998). Paul used the Hellenistic letter form (Doty 1973). Revelation 1:4–6 opens the letter, and 22:20b–21 closes it. Revelation adopts Paul's modifications of the letter form, so Paul's letters are his models. He operates in one of the same areas that Paul did. John's choice of the letter genre stresses his personal connection with his audience and emphasizes the historical circumstances he shares with them.

John sends the letter in his own name, and in that of God, the seven spirits with him, and Jesus. The addressees are seven churches in Asia Minor. Jesus is identified as "the faithful witness, the firstborn of the dead, and the ruler of the kings of the earth" (1:5). As witness, he has testified in a Roman court and died for it. As "firstborn of the dead," he is the first to be resurrected. Jesus's designation as ruler of the kings of the earth asserts his sovereignty. Jesus shares God's authority throughout the book. At its end, he and God occupy the same throne. Jesus is divine.

The epistolary section that closes the book prays that Jesus come (22:20b–21). This is a plea for the *parousia*. A "parousia" is an official visit of a ruler to a town or city, and it becomes a technical term for Jesus's second coming.

Jesus says that he will come back soon in 22:20a. While Jewish apocalypses look for the coming of God, Christian apocalyptic texts yearn for the second coming of Jesus.

Revelation follows the epistolary greeting with a doxology, a short expression of praise customary in Paul's letters (1:5b–6). Here it praises Jesus, who by his blood freed Christians from sin and made them a kingdom and priests. The doxology ends with praise to God and God's dominion. Again, these are issues of sovereignty. There is an allusion to Exod. 19:6, where at Sinai God makes Israel a priestly and royal nation. Both are important for John since he sees the Roman Empire as a rival kingdom with blasphemous religious claims.

A reference to the second coming occurs in a prophetic exclamation: "Look! He is coming with the clouds; every eye will see him, even those who pierced him; and on his account all the tribes of the earth will wail. So it is to be. Amen" (Rev. 1:7). Revelation is rife with allusions to the Hebrew Bible, yet it does not quote it directly. In this it follows the example of the Jewish apocalypses. Revelation draws its authority from the seer's visions, not from the sacred texts. That being said, Revelation has the richest allusions to the sacred writings of any New Testament book. It is a fitting ending to the Christian Bible not only because it deals with the end of history as we know it, but also because it brings together the entire Christian Bible. In the description of the second coming in Rev. 1:7 we have several biblical allusions. Jesus's coming on the clouds recalls the one like a son of man in Dan. 7. The reference to piercing and mourning over the pierced one alludes to Zech. 12:10. The figure in Zechariah is possibly messianic. While it is unclear whom Zechariah refers to, the referent is quite clear in Rev. 1:7; it is Jesus.

The second part of the prophetic exclamation reads: "'I am the Alpha and the Omega,' says the Lord God, who is and who was and who is to come, the Almighty" (Rev. 1:8). Alpha and omega are the first and last letters of the Greek alphabet. In an apocalyptic context, God's claim to be Alpha and Omega is especially meaningful. God is the beginning and end of all things. He is sovereign over all. History has a beginning and an end. God sees it as a whole. The language recalls Second Isaiah. There God declares his sovereignty on the basis of his knowing what is to come: "Declaring the end from the beginning and from ancient times things not yet done, saying, 'My purpose shall stand, and I will fulfill my intention'" (Isa. 46:10). There is an even closer parallel in Second Isaiah: "As God says, 'I am the first and the last; besides me there is no god'" (44:6; see 41:4; 48:12).

God is the one who was, who is, and who is to come. This is a play on the explanations of the divine name Yahweh in Exod. 3. The words "who is to come" are not in Exodus. They adapt the divine name to Revelation's new context, where the coming of God and Jesus is the center of future hopes.

Inaugural Vision Part One: Jesus as an Apocalyptic Figure (1:9–20)

John's initial vision has two main parts. In the first (1:9–20), John sees Christ, who tells him to deliver his book to the seven churches. In the second (chaps. 2–3), we hear messages tailored to each of the seven churches.

John delivers his visions directly to the seven churches through his apocalypse. He is one with them as he shares "the persecution and the kingdom and the patient endurance" (1:9). "Persecution" (*thlipsis*) is often translated "tribulation." Daniel 12 expects that there will be a period of trouble and suffering as has never been seen before. The idea of a final tribulation is the same idea. "Kingdom" reintroduces the idea of sovereignty. Those who join themselves to Christ become a new kingdom with the legitimate sovereign. Loyalty to God demands rejection of Rome. Since our author expects worldwide persecution, endurance is a main theme of the apocalypse. Endurance means to resist Rome's power even to the point of death.

John is on the island of Patmos as he writes. Apparently he cannot visit the churches, so he must write to them. He is on the island "because of [*dia*] the word of God and the testimony of Jesus" (1:9). Since Patmos was remote and thinly populated, it is more likely that John had been sent there as a punishment for causing disturbances than that he went there to preach. So he personally experiences Roman oppression. John writes to the churches that he was "in the spirit on the Lord's day" when he heard a voice coming from behind him that sounded like a trumpet. The trumpet is a theophanic touch. John's being in the spirit may indicate a trance. The Lord's day is Sunday. Since Jesus rose from the dead on Sunday, Christians shifted their observance of the Sabbath to Sunday from Saturday, the day commanded in the Ten Commandments. The voice instructs John to write his visions in a scroll. We have that scroll before us in the book of Revelation.

John turns and sees the one speaking to him. He sees seven golden lampstands, and Jesus is in their midst. John describes Jesus by combining elements drawn from the revelatory angel of Dan. 10, the one like a son of man in Dan. 7, and God in Dan. 7. The following table shows the biblical origins of each element.

John's Vision of Jesus

Revelation 1:13–16	Hebrew Bible
I saw one like the Son of Man,	I saw one like a son of man. (Dan. 7:13)
clothed with a long robe and with a golden sash across his chest.	I looked up and saw a man clothed in linen, with a belt of gold from Uphaz around his waist. (Dan. 10:5)
His head and his hair were white as white wool, white as snow;	His clothing was white as snow, and the hair of his head like pure wool. (Dan. 7:9)

his eyes were like a flame of fire,	. . . his eyes like flaming torches. (Dan. 10:6)
his feet were like burnished bronze, refined as in a furnace,	. . . his arms and legs like the gleam of burnished bronze. (Dan. 10:6)
and his voice was like the sound of many waters.	. . . and the sound of his words like the roar of a multitude. (Dan. 10:6) And there the glory of the God of Israel was coming from the east; the sound was like the sound of mighty waters. (Ezek. 43:2)
In his right hand he held seven stars, and from his mouth came a sharp, two-edged sword,	He shall strike the earth with the rod of his mouth. (Isa. 11:4; a messianic passage) He made my mouth like a sharp sword. (Isa. 49:2)
and his face was like the sun shining with full force.	. . . his face like lightning. (Dan. 10:6)

John combines Dan. 7, 10; Ezekiel; and Isaiah to present a fearsome and awesome Jesus. John fearfully falls to the ground. Jesus touches him and tells him not to fear. This fits the pattern of a theophany.

John describes his encounter with Jesus, saying, "When I saw him, I fell at his feet as though dead. But he placed his right hand on me, saying, 'Do not be afraid; I am the first and the last, and the living one. I was dead, and see, I am alive forever and ever; and I have the keys of Death and of Hades'" (Rev. 1:17–18). Jesus's words echo God's in Rev. 1:8 where he claims to be the Alpha and the Omega and of God in Isaiah where he says that he is the first and the last. Jesus is claiming divine power. He is the resurrected one, and he controls "Death and Hades." Jesus again commands John to write. He is to write what he sees, what the present situation is, and what is to happen (Rev. 1:19).

Jesus explains that the seven stars are the angels of the seven churches, and the seven lampstands are the seven churches. The correspondence between the stars, lampstands, angels, and churches links the visible and the unseen. Stars are heavenly beings.

The number seven pervades Revelation; it occurs fifty-four times (Aune 1997, xciii–xciv). Conventional wisdom has it symbolize completion. Yarbro Collins finds little in the ancient evidence to support that notion. Rather, seven may come from the idea that God created the world in six days and rested on the seventh. This is Sabbatarian eschatology. The most basic significance of the proliferation of sevens is that God controls all. There is a divine structure to eschatology. Its replication throughout the book makes that structure ubiquitous and overwhelmingly convincing.

Within John's environment, there is another source from outside Jewish tradition for seven stars. The ancient world thought that there were seven planets, including sun and moon. When Domitian's young son died, he commemorated him in a coin in which Domitian's wife, Domitia, was portrayed as the Queen of Heaven, while the son is shown surrounded by seven stars. The claim of divine power implicit in the coin's iconography is critiqued by Rev. 1. Jesus, not the imperial family, holds heavenly sovereignty. There may be a twist on astrology here as well. The ancient world, including the Jewish world, set much store by astrology. If Jesus controls the stars, he controls fate (Murphy 1998, 91).

The next two chapters of Revelation are a true gift to those interested in the relationship between apocalyptic visions and concrete historical circumstances. In Rev. 2–3, Jesus sends messages to seven angels, each the angelic patron of a church. This is a glimpse into what is going on in those churches, from the seer's perspective. The idea that each church has a patron angel is apocalyptic.

A key to understanding the seer's point of view is his relationship with the seven churches (Murphy 1998, 33–42). He claims for his book the status of prophecy, so he was a prophet. He was probably itinerant since he writes to seven churches, not just one. Itinerants were not unusual in early Christianity. To some degree he was an outsider. John was honored by some of the Christians he addresses but not by others. He clashed with some in the churches. There is a conspicuous absence of mention of church authorities, which suggests that John was not on the best of terms with them (Aune 1981, 26). That would not be unusual, for bishops are usually concerned about right order and control, and wandering prophets can be disruptive, as is shown in the contemporary Christian document known as the *Didache*. The seven churches form a rough circle. Our author may have been a circuit preacher.

Revelation's churches were in western Asia Minor, an important cultural, economic, and strategic area. Some were prominent cities, and some had installations for the imperial cult, a sign of their importance to both the region and to Rome (Hemer 1986).

Inaugural Vision Part Two: Messages to the Angels of the Seven Churches (2:1–3:22)

Ephesus. The message to the angel of the church at Ephesus reveals that some people have come to the church who claim to be apostles but are not such in the eyes of the seer (2:2). John is happy with the church in Ephesus because they agree with him that these are false apostles, but we learn nothing of their teachings.

Smyrna. To the church at Smyrna Jesus says that he knows that false Jews have slandered them. Such Jews are a "synagogue of Satan" who call themselves Jews but are not (2:9). The author does not consider Christianity to be a new religion. Jews who do not accept Christ are not true Jews. They are under Satan's control. They may be prominent citizens in Smyrna, where we know that there was an important Jewish community. Comfort with the satanic culture of Asia Minor is anathema for the seer. So John may have a couple of reasons for his wrath against Smyrna's Jews—their refusal to accept Christ and their accommodation to Hellenism.

Jesus warns that "the devil" is about to throw some of Smyrna's Christians into prison, and they may have to "be faithful until death." His expectation that the Smyrnean Christians are in imminent danger may be influenced by the fact that it was a center for the imperial cult. Its head official was the *neokoros*, the main overseer of the cult for the entire province (Potter 1992b).

Pergamum. Pergamum was also a site of the emperor cult. John calls the Roman altar there "Satan's throne" (2:13). The word "throne" occurs some forty-five times in Revelation. Sovereignty is a central issue in Revelation. Jesus reminds Pergamum's Christians that one of them, Antipas, was killed among them, "where Satan lives" (2:13). He calls Antipas a "faithful witness," showing that Antipas died because of his loyalty to Christ.

Jesus now becomes more specific. "I have a few things against you: you have some there who hold to the teaching of Balaam, who taught Balak to put a stumbling block before the people of Israel, so that they would eat food sacrificed to idols and practice fornication" (Rev. 2:14). The reference is to Num. 25. The foreign prophet Balaam counsels Balak, a Moabite king, to seduce the Israelites into idolatry and fornication so as to provoke God to punish them. The problem is how to relate this to the Pergamum church. Surely there is no one there who is encouraging idolatry or fornication.

The answer lies in Paul's letters. In 1 Cor. 8–10, Paul engages problems that the Corinthians have in dealing with pagan cults. Before they became Christians, they engaged in the religious life of their city. That included civic religious ceremonies, as well as more "private" activities, such as meals within a business or social network that involved eating meat sacrificed to idols and perhaps even cultic acts to honor gods who were patrons of families, groups, guilds, and voluntary associations. When they entered a new religious world that demanded exclusive worship of God, they had to determine what was acceptable and what was not. Paul lays out ground rules. It is always impermissible to take part in any cultic activities not honoring God, but eating meat that had been sacrificed to idols was not a problem. One could eat with a clear conscience unless it caused scandal to others.

Paul took a position diametrically opposite to that of the seer. The Jerusalem church was also more conservative than Paul. The council held in Jerusalem in 48 CE decided that gentile converts to Christianity could not eat meat sacrificed to idols (Acts 15:28–29).

That leaves the problem of "fornication." It is hard to believe that Christians in Pergamum were advocating fornication. But fornication is a frequent biblical metaphor for idolatry. Since the seer thinks of eating food sacrificed to idols as idolatry, "fornication" would be an appropriate accusation. Inclusion of the term tightens the parallel with the Balaam story.

Thyatira. Jesus is ambivalent toward the church at Thyatira. He begins with lavish praise. They are better now than in the beginning.

> But I have this against you: you tolerate that woman Jezebel, who calls herself a prophet and is teaching and beguiling my servants to practice fornication and to eat food sacrificed to idols. I gave her time to repent, but she refuses to repent of her fornication. Beware, I am throwing her on a bed, and those who commit adultery with her I am throwing into great distress, unless they repent of her doings; and I will strike her children dead. And all the churches will know that I am the one who searches minds and hearts, and I will give to each of you as your works deserve. But to the rest of you in Thyatira, who do not hold this teaching, who have not learned what some call "the deep things of Satan," to you I say, I do not lay on you any other burden. (Rev. 2:20–24)

This is a remarkable passage. The seer is very happy with the church, except that it accepts a woman prophet, Jezebel, who preaches eating food sacrificed to idols and fornication. This is a blatant contradiction. How could a church comprised of good Christians accept such a prophet? If the charges are literal, the Thyatiran church is an amazingly hedonistic group, and it would be bizarre for the seer to admire them. "Jezebel" was the name of the Israelite king Ahab's wife. She was a foreign princess who advocated the worship of Baal in Israel. She is one of the Bible's villains. It is unbelievable that any Christian prophet bore that name.

The content of the errant prophet's teaching is called by some the "deep things of Satan." Scholars do not agree on what this means. It may be a sarcastic parody of what the seer's opponents are actually saying. Perhaps they think they can eat sacrificial food because their understanding goes deeper than most. Paul claims in 1 Cor. 2:10 that to some Christians are revealed "the depths of God." Maybe John's opponents are claiming such revelation. Maybe they are Pauline Christians. Perhaps the opponents actually claim to know Satan's secrets and so to be immune to Satan. Perhaps they are gnostics who claim special knowledge and protection from Satan. We do not know.

Sardis. We know from other sources that Sardis was home to an important Jewish community, but Christ does not mention it. He says that the church there has a good reputation, but it does not deserve it. He threatens them with sudden and unexpected judgment (3:3).

Philadelphia. The message to Philadelphia again speaks of a synagogue of Satan who claim to be Jews but are not, whose members will in the end bow down before John's listeners (3:9). Jesus promises that he will shelter the Philadelphian Christians "from the hour of trial [*peirasmos*] that is coming on the whole world to test [*peirazō*] the inhabitants of the earth" (3:10). The seer envisages a worldwide persecution that will be eschatological testing.

Laodicea. The final message is to the church at Laodicea. It is judged to be lukewarm in its faith. This may indicate a lax attitude to Hellenistic culture.

Fig. 4. Restored synagogue at Sardis, one of the seven cities of Revelation. Although not used as a synagogue until the third century C.E., it attests to the ongoing and long-lasting status of the Jewish community there. (Todd Bolen/bibleplaces.com)

Throne Scene (4:1–5:14)

The throne scene grounds everything to follow in Revelation. Strictly speaking, the scene spans the book, for each vision originates there.

John is called up to heaven and sees God. The deity is described in the oblique ways we have seen in Ezekiel and elsewhere. Around the throne are twenty-four elders with crowns. They may symbolize the twelve tribes of Israel added to the twelve apostles. The usual theophanic elements of thunder and lightning are present. There are seven torches before God, interpreted as God's seven spirits, perhaps spies to keep track of happenings on the earth. Before God is a sea of glass, like crystal. The glass sea alludes to the firmament of Gen. 1, which is transparent so that the waters above can be seen by the earth's inhabitants below.

God has angelic attendants. Their description draws on the throne scenes of Ezek. 1 and Isa. 6. Around the throne, and on each side of the throne, are four living creatures, full of eyes in front and behind: the first living creature like a lion, the second living creature like an ox, the third living creature with a face like a human face, and the fourth living creature like a flying eagle. And the four living creatures, each of them with six wings, are full of eyes all around and inside. Day and night without ceasing they sing, "Holy, holy, holy, the Lord God the Almighty, who was and is and is to come" (Rev. 4:8).

This is a heavenly liturgy (Aune 1983a). As in Ezekiel, there are four "living creatures." While the creatures in Ezekiel each have the four faces—lion, ox, human, and eagle—here each creature has but one face. In Ezekiel each has four wings, but in Isaiah the seraphim have six. John sees six on the living creatures, so he combines Ezekiel and Isaiah. The eyes on the wings come from Ezek. 1. The song they sing is almost the same as the one sung by Isaiah's seraphim. In Isaiah, the seraphim sing, "Holy, holy, holy is the LORD of hosts; the whole earth is full of his glory." Revelation makes appropriate changes. God is called Almighty nine times in Revelation, a fitting appellation for a God more powerful than Rome. The earth being full of God's glory in Isaiah is a static image. Revelation changes this to the God who "was and is and is to come." The description plays on the explanation of the name Yahweh in Exod. 3, and it adds the elements of God's might and his "coming," both major apocalyptic concerns.

When the living creatures sing, the twenty-four elders throw their crowns down before God in submission of kings to the supreme emperor. The song acknowledges God's authority and power, which it connects with God's creative role (Rev. 4:11). Such a connection is common in the Hebrew Bible.

God has a scroll in his right hand. It is sealed with seven seals and has writing on the front and back, so it is packed with content, the eschatological events. No one can unseal the scroll, so the seer weeps, because the events it describes cannot take place unless it is opened. "Then one of the elders said to me, 'Do not weep. See, the Lion of the tribe of Judah, the Root of David, has conquered, so that he can open the scroll and its seven seals'" (Rev. 5:5). Jesus is described in messianic terms (Gen. 49:8–9). In Revelation, Jesus is the Davidic Messiah, but his conquest is bearing witness before Rome and suffering death for it (5:9). This turns the idea of conquest on its head.

Jesus has witnessed unto death. Because he was killed, he can open the scroll. His death has set the end-time events in motion. It was the central eschatological event.

John sees a Lamb that looks as though it has been slaughtered. It has seven eyes and seven horns. The eyes are the spirits before God in 1:4, which survey the earth. The Lamb takes the scroll from God, and there follows a series of short hymns of praise to God and the Lamb, first by the four living creatures and twenty-four elders, then by God's thousands of attendants, and finally by all creatures in heaven and earth. The hymns ascribe to God and the Lamb what kings would receive—power, glory, honor, might, and wisdom. This is a magnificent liturgy that gives God and the Lamb the honor due them. It is the mirror image of the imperial honors afforded the emperor, which are Satanic, and it negates them.

The First Great Cycle of Visions Part One: Seals (6:1–8:5)

First four seals. The Lamb opens the seals one by one. As he does, things transpire on earth. The first four seals release four horses on the earth, recalling

Zech. 1:7–11. The first two are warfare and death from battle, the third famine, and the fourth death by famine, pestilence, and animals. A fourth of the earth is killed as the fourth seal is opened.

Fifth seal. When the fifth seal is opened, the seer beholds souls under God's heavenly altar. They have been killed because of their "testimony," or "witness," and they pray for vengeance. They are told they must wait until the number to be killed is fulfilled. The idea is that a set number of people must die before the end. This becomes commonplace in apocalyptic expectation. Meanwhile, they receive a white robe, signifying that they have assumed a new, heavenly life.

Sixth seal. The sixth seal releases phenomena associated with theophanies and God's judgment. There is an earthquake, the sun goes dark, the moon turns red as blood, the stars fall to earth, the sky vanishes, mountains and islands disappear. People on earth tremble. All must be judged, "slave and free," but those most terrified are the rich, the powerful, the generals, the magnates, and the kings. They have most to fear (Rev. 6:17).

The seventh seal is temporarily delayed.

Liturgical interlude (7:1–17). Chapter 7 is a liturgical interlude before the seventh seal. When the Lamb finally opens the seventh seal, it leads into a series of seven trumpets. This telescopic structure shows that Revelation's visions do not proceed in a linear fashion. The same events are narrated more than once, presented in different forms.

The interlude is based on Ezek. 9. In Ezekiel, the prophet sees six angels ready to destroy Jerusalem's sinners, but they are prevented from doing so until a seventh angel puts a sign on the forehead of everyone who has not sinned. The scene implies that those sealed are not executed. In Rev. 7, John sees four angels at the four corners of the earth restraining four winds that will wreak havoc on the earth. The angels must wait until another angel seals the "servants of our God" on their foreheads. The number sealed is 144,000—12,000 from each of the twelve tribes of Israel.

Next the seer sees an innumerable multitude from every nation standing before the throne and the Lamb, singing praise to God and Jesus. They wear white robes and joyfully carry palm branches. They sing with the four living creatures, all the angels, and the elders. All worship God and the Lamb. An elder says that they have come through the great tribulation (*thlipsis*) and have washed their robes and made them white in the Lamb's blood.

There are two groups in the interlude, the 144,000 and the multitude. The tribulation is the time of great suffering preceding history's end. Since the second group has endured the tribulation, the first apparently has not. The seal on their foreheads has protected them. They represent a special group within the church. They have probably suffered death already, perhaps in Nero's persecution. This martyrdom has removed them from the earth before the tribulation.

The 144,000 are a special group within the church, so the question arises why they are said to be from the tribes of Israel. Revelation's author makes no clear distinction between Judaism and Christianity. Our use of the word "Christianity" is anachronistic for him, though convenient for us. The unity of what were to become two religions is expressed also by the twenty-four elders (4:4; twelve tribes and twelve apostles), and later, in the new Jerusalem, with twelve gates inscribed with the names of the twelve tribes and twelve foundations inscribed with the names of the twelve apostles (21:12–14).

John sees the great multitude before God's throne in the heavenly temple (7:15–17). They are now freed from the shortcomings of this flawed world—hunger, thirst, sun, heat, and tears. The Lamb is their shepherd (see Ezek. 34) and guides "them to springs of the water of life" (7:17). But things have not yet reached their completion. Apocalyptic transformation must involve the entire universe.

Seventh seal. At the beginning of Rev. 8, the Lamb opens the seventh seal. There is a period of silence for half an hour. This is primordial silence—silence that existed before the world began. It prepares the way for something new—the seven angels with the seven trumpets. The author says that these are the angels who stand before God (8:2). This is a special class of angel (Olyan 1993). Those closest to God are angelic leaders, or archangels.

The First Great Cycle of Visions Part Two: Trumpets (8:1–11:19)

The book of Revelation does not proceed in a simple, chronological manner. Parts of one cycle repeat or echo parts of the other. For example, both the trumpets in chapter 8 and the bowls in chapter 16 allude to the plagues on Egypt at the exodus. Both envisage cosmic events. In the sixth seal, the stars fall from the sky, but they are still there when the angels blow the trumpets. In the first trumpet, all the grass of the earth is destroyed, but in the fifth it is still there. Authors of ancient apocalypses were far less worried than we about consistency. They were more interested in an overall picture and effect. They were not literalists.

Liturgical interlude (8:1–5). Before the first angel blows his trumpet, there is another liturgical interlude. An angel offers incense on the golden altar before God's throne. The incense represents the prayers of the "saints." The word "saints" translates *hagioi*. It could as well be translated "holy ones." Here it does not mean angels, as in Daniel and most of the Hebrew Bible, but those loyal to God. It does not mean that each member is morally perfect; it means that they belong to God, the basic meaning of "holy." The angel takes coals from the altar and throws them onto the earth. They cause thunder, lightning, rumblings, and an earthquake. The scene recalls Ezek. 10:2 where God tells an angel to take fire from under his throne and scatter it over Jerusalem. The disasters that overtake the earth originate with God.

First trumpet. The first angel sounds his trumpet. Hail, fire, and blood are hurled upon the earth. These recall the third plague against Egypt (Exod. 9:22–26) and the fourth and seventh bowls of Rev. 16. A third of the earth and a third of the trees and all the grass burn up.

Second trumpet. When the second angel blows his trumpet, "something like" a great fiery mountain is thrown into the sea and a third of the sea becomes blood, a third of its creatures die, and a third of the ships are destroyed. The bloody sea is reminiscent of the first Egyptian plague, the Nile becoming blood, and the second bowl in Rev. 16.

Third trumpet. The third angel blows his trumpet and a blazing star falls on a third of the rivers and water springs. The star's name is "Wormwood" and a third of the waters become wormwood. Wormwood is a bitter plant. Bitter waters are undrinkable.

Fourth trumpet. The fourth angel sounds his trumpet, and a third of the sun, moon, and stars is darkened, as is a third of the day and night. The darkness of the sun, moon, and stars alludes to the ninth Egyptian plague and Revelation's fifth bowl.

Eagle's proclamation. At the conclusion of the first four trumpets, an eagle flies in mid-heaven and cries, "Woe, woe, woe to the inhabitants of the earth, at the blasts of the other trumpets that the three angels are about to blow!" (8:13). The next three trumpets are remarkably detailed. They are particularly important, as suggested by their angelic announcement as three woes.

Fifth trumpet. The fifth trumpet releases a catastrophe that recalls the locusts of Joel 2. An angel descends from heaven with a key to the bottomless pit. The angel opens the pit and smoke billows out, obscuring the sun and air. From the smoke emerge locusts who are told not to harm the earth's grass. They torture those without the seal for five months. Their torture is like a scorpion's sting. People will seek death but not find it.

The author describes the scorpions in detail. They are like warhorses, they have golden crowns, human faces, women's hair, lion's teeth, iron scales like military breastplates, and their many wings make noise like chariots rushing into battle. They have tails like scorpions with the power to torture. Their king is the angel of the abyss, the bottomless pit. His name is *'ăbadôn* in Hebrew ("destruction"), and in Greek *Apolluōn* ("destroyer"; 9:11).

Locust plagues were greatly feared in the ancient Near East, as they are today. Their effect on vegetation greatly affects humans. The author draws heavily on Joel 2 for his description. "Common to Joel and Revelation are the connection of the locust plague to the blast of a trumpet, the use of the term 'inhabitants of the land [earth],' the comparison of the locusts to an army, the darkening of the sun in Joel by the locust swarm and in Revelation by the smoke from which the locusts come, the comparison of the locust's teeth to lions' teeth and their sound to the rumbling of chariots" (Murphy 1998). Ironically they do not harm the vegetation. Their torture of humans may be just a warning of God's power and a chance to repent (see 9:20). This allows the scene to escalate in the next two trumpets.

The angel Abaddon is unique to Revelation. He rules the pit or abyss (*abyssos*). This calls to mind the ancient cosmology where there is a pit below the earth. In the Hebrew Bible it is called Sheol. The dead gather there, but there are no rewards or punishments. In apocalypses it becomes a place of postmortem punishments.

Since the locusts emerge from the abyss, one may consider them demonic. Although the angel Abaddon appears only here, the word appears in Job and Proverbs as a synonym for Sheol. The Greek translation furnished by the author, Apollyon, may be a subtle reference to the Greek god Apollo, a god with whom the Roman emperor Domitian identified (Fiorenza 1991, 72).

The fifth trumpet prompts a voice from the heavenly altar to order the release of the four angels bound at the river Euphrates. They invade the land, leading a cavalry of two hundred million, a gigantic number. In Ezek. 38–39 we met the anticipation that at the end of times an army consisting of all the nations would attack Israel in Jerusalem. Revelation transforms that into an army invading from the east that attacks the entire Roman Empire. The idea of an invading eastern army appears also in *1 Enoch* 56 (see *Testament of Moses* 3:2). The Parthian Empire lay to the east of the Roman Empire, and the two lived in tension. In some legends about Nero, he did not die but fled east and would return at the head of a Parthian army. There may be an echo of that notion here.

The cavalry horses draw the seer's attention. They do the damage, not their riders. The riders' armor is the color of fire, sapphire, and sulfur. The horses breathe fire, smoke, and sulfur. Their breath kills a third of humanity. This is an escalation over the warhorse-like locusts in trumpet four who merely torture humans. As if the horses were not terrifying enough, their tails are like serpents with heads that bite and harm. In this they resemble scorpions.

The next passage comments on the effect of these events. Even such great and fear-inspiring events did not cause humans to repent or give up idolatry, murder, sorcery, fornication, or theft (9:20–21).

Interlude, part one (10:1–11). We saw an interlude between the sixth and seventh seals (chap. 7), and there is another between the sixth and seventh trumpets (chap. 10). John sees a mighty angel descend from heaven, with a rainbow over his head, a face like the sun, and legs like fiery pillars (see the angels in Dan. 10 and 12). There is a little open scroll in his hand. With a foot in the sea and one on the land, signifying universal authority, he emits a sound like a lion's roar. As he does, seven thunders sound. John is about to write what they say but is told to conceal it. The angel swears that "the mystery of God" as announced "to his servants the prophets" will be revealed in the seventh trumpet (10:7). The verse relies on the principle enunciated in Amos 3:7: "Surely the LORD GOD does nothing, without revealing his secret to his servants the prophets."

A voice from heaven commands John to take and eat the little scroll. It is bitter to his stomach but sweet to his mouth. He is told he must prophesy again (10:11). The vision recommissions the seer. Eating the scroll recalls Ezek. 3, where the same metaphor symbolizes his receiving a prophetic message. In Ezekiel, the scroll is sweet, symbolizing his beautiful words. Revelation also has beautiful words, but the message is bitter. The secret of the little scroll is presumably contained in the rest of John's message in this cycle.

Interlude, part two (11:1–14). The last trumpet still does not sound. There is a second section of the interlude in 11:1–14, consisting of several parts. In the first, John is told to measure the temple. In the second, two witnesses prophesy in the great city for forty-two months. In the third, the beast that comes up from the bottomless pit conquers the witnesses and they lie dead in the city for three-and-a-half days. After that, God raises them up and brings them to heaven. In the fourth section, there is an earthquake in the city that kills a tenth of its inhabitants, and the rest glorify God.

John is told to measure the temple, altar, and worshipers but not to measure the court outside the temple, because the holy city is to be given over to the gentiles to trample for forty-two months. During that time, the two witnesses will witness for 1,260 days. The length of a month would be thirty days, so 1,260 days would be forty-two months, or three and a half years. The time of the witnesses prophesying and the gentiles trampling Jerusalem is the same. The witnesses are martyred at the end of that time. This has meaning in the world of politics and military realities. Something is protected (symbolized by the measuring), something is trampled, and during the trampling witnesses bear testimony. We are reminded of Rev. 7, where the 144,000 are protected from the tribulation, but they themselves are martyred, and where an innumerable multitude must come through the tribulation. We are also reminded of the fifth seal, where the martyred are under God's heavenly altar in his heavenly temple, now safe from persecution, but beg for vengeance.

The word "trample" recalls Dan. 8:13, where the cessation of the cult is Antiochus trampling the sanctuary. Daniel is told that the trampling will last for 2,300 mornings and evenings, equivalent to 1,150 days, not far from the 1,260 of Rev. 11. The time indications in Rev. 11 also recall the time, two times, and half a time from Dan. 7:25, again the length of time the Hellenistic emperor Antiochus IV stopped the cult. This is three and a half years, or forty-two months. Trampling by the gentiles also recalls Luke 21:24, where Jesus, in his apocalyptic discourse, warns that "Jerusalem will be trampled on by the Gentiles until the times of the Gentiles are fulfilled."

The seer expects a time when there are martyrs in heaven, but more are yet to join them. For the seer, Nero's persecution is past (64 CE), and he knows of a Christian martyr in Pergamum, Antipas the faithful witness (2:13). So he knows that part of the church is already martyred and now protected. These martyrs may correspond to the 144,000, sealed by the angel. The rest of the church must come through the tribulation. The two witnesses represent the testifying of the earthly church during this period, either of the whole church or just of church prophets. Eventually, they too will be martyred. During this time, the gentiles, that is, Rome, will rage against the church.

Another way to look at the measuring of the temple and the leaving out of its court is to see it as expressing two different aspects of the church. The temple with its altar and worshipers is the whole Christian church in union with God, ultimately invulnerable to Satan's onslaughts. The court, also called the holy city, is the church vulnerable to Roman power, the everyday experience of Christians in the empire (Fiorenza 1991, 77; Mounce 1977, 219–20). For an author who sees the church as a priestly people (1:6) as is Israel in Exod. 19, it is fitting that the church is a temple with sacred precincts. The abundance of temple imagery here and elsewhere in Revelation supports the notion that John is a Jewish Christian who had experienced the Roman destruction of the temple close-up and who had fled to Asia Minor after the war.

The second part of the vision examines the witnesses (11:4–6). Jewish law insists on two witnesses in capital cases, which may explain why there are two of them. They are the two olive trees and the two lampstands that stand before "the Lord of the earth" (11:4). This alludes to Zech. 4, where two olive trees are two anointed ones, messiahs, who represent the entire Judean community before God. The two witnesses do the same for the church. The lampstands make that clearer, for in Rev. 1 the seven lampstands are the seven churches.

The two witnesses prophesy. They project fire from their mouths to destroy their enemies, a reference to the power of their prophetic word. They shut up the sky and cause drought, and they turn water into blood and bring plagues on the earth. These are actions of Elijah and Moses, respectively. These two appear to Jesus when he is transfigured in the Gospels. They represent Israel's original leader (also a prophet) and one of Israel's main prophets. This brings across the seer's vision of the church as the true Israel. It is the true Israel in conflict with the nations. Moses struggled with Pharaoh, and Elijah fought Jezebel. Both fought against idolatry and defended God's exclusive sovereignty. A more restricted interpretation would see the two as representatives of church prophets.

In part three the witnesses have finished prophesying. The beast wars against them, prevails, kills them, and leaves them dead in the streets of "the great city that is prophetically [literally: "spiritually"] called Sodom and Egypt, where also their Lord was crucified" (11:8). For three and a half days, the inhabitants of the city gloat over them. Compared to their forty-two months of prophesying, the time is short. The contrast is underlined by the similarity—three and a half days contrasted with three and a half years. But it reminds us that evil is powerful. It temporarily overcomes the witness of the church and its prophets. However, what appears as defeat on earth is victory in the eyes of heaven. The city's inhabitants learn that lesson when the witnesses are raised and brought to heaven in the vision's fourth part. When they ascend, the city endures an earthquake that kills a tenth of its population. The rest repent by glorifying God, thus resolving the problem of sovereignty at the heart of John's concern. The entire earth now shifts from worshiping Rome to worshiping the true God and sovereign of the universe.

The time indications of Revelation, especially in chapter 11 and again in chapter 13, unite the different indications of the confrontation between the church and Rome and assure Christians that the period is foreordained by God, has a set ending, and will end in vindication.

In 12:17, Satan "makes war" on faithful Christians, and in 13:5–7, the beast "makes war" on the faithful and "conquers" them. The trampling of the holy city (11:2), the prophesying of the witnesses in a hostile environment when the beast makes war on them and kills them (11:3), the dragon's pursuit of the heavenly woman (12:6, 14), Satan's warring against the woman's children who are the church (12:17), and the beast's warring against and conquering the saints (13:5–7) are all the same events seen under different guises. They happen during a length of time based on the time, two times, and half a time of Daniel. That the beast "makes war" on the witnesses in 11:7 as he does on all Christians in 12:17 and 13:7 supports the theory that the witnesses represent not two individuals but the prophetic activity of the church, seen as an aspect of the whole church, especially embodied in Christian prophets and martyrs. (Murphy 1998, 265)

The identity of the great city in Rev. 11 is uncertain. Since it is where Jesus died, it seems to be Jerusalem. Its association with the temple also indicates Jerusalem. As the object of eschatological punishment, it may be Rome. The author says to interpret it "spiritually," that is, allegorically. That may permit us to consider it to be Rome as the center of the empire so that the reference to Jesus's death is stressed as a Roman act.

Seventh trumpet. The angel of chapter 10 promised that at the blowing of the last trumpet, the end spoken of by the prophets would come. This does happen. The seventh trumpet fulfills eschatological hope. Then there is a definitive break between chapter 11, the end of the first cycle, and chapter 12, where the second cycle begins.

The ending is swift. The angel blows the seventh trumpet, and a heavenly chorus sings an explanatory hymn. The kingdom of the world has become the kingdom of our Lord and of his Messiah, and he will reign forever and ever. (Rev. 11:15)

The world has been reclaimed by God and his Messiah. It will never revert to its former state. The twenty-four elders sing a confirming song (11:16–18). God has taken his power and begun to reign. The nations raged (see Ps. 2), but God's wrath defeated them. The destroyers of the earth are destroyed.

The definitive proclamation of God's sovereignty is dramatically portrayed in the opening of the heavenly temple now visible to all, symbolic of God's power breaking forth into the universe, accompanied by the usual cosmic signs—thunder and lightning, an earthquake, and hail (Rev. 11:19).

The Second Great Cycle of Visions (12:1–22:5)

The second cycle of visions consists of three groups of seven visions each. The first and the last are unnumbered, while the middle group consists of seven bowls of wrath poured upon the earth. This second cycle intensifies the author's antipathy to the empire and informs much of what he says from chapter 12 onward.

First unnumbered vision. The first vision occupies all of chapter 12. It begins with a great "portent" (*sēmeion*, "sign") in the sky. This reminds us of the importance of astrology in the ancient world (Malina 1995).

The first portent is a "woman clothed with the sun, with the moon under her feet, and on her head a crown of twelve stars. She was pregnant and was crying out with birth pangs, in the agony of giving birth" (12:1–2). This figure looks like the Queen of Heaven, a goddess of the ancient world. Jeremiah rails against Israel's homage to her (7:18; 44:17, 18, 19, 25). The Egyptian goddess Isis, popular in the Greco-Roman world, was depicted similarly. The woman in Revelation is in birth pangs, a common image for the coming of the end, but we are momentarily left in doubt about the identity of her child.

John immediately sees another sign in the heavens. It is of a "great red dragon, with seven heads and ten horns, and seven diadems on its heads. His tail swept down a third of the stars of heaven and threw them on the earth" (12:3–4). Children know this image. It is how they dress if they wish to dress as the devil at Halloween. Here we encounter the combat myth's sea monster again, the dragon. The Greek word in Rev. 12:3, *drakōn*, is the same as that used when Job places "sea" and "dragon" in apposition (7:12). Psalm 104:26 (Greek) translates Ps. 104:26 (Hebrew), changing "Leviathan" to "dragon." Though the sea is not mentioned in this initial sign in Rev. 12, water will feature later in the chapter. Satan is called a dragon fourteen times in Revelation (12:3, 4, 7 [twice], 9, 13, 16, 17, 18; 13:2, 4, 11; 16:13; 20:2). Dragons figure in the combat myth as inimical to the gods of order, both cosmic and political.

The Hebrew Bible does not identify the serpent in the Garden of Eden as Satan, but by the first century CE, the identification had been made. Revelation 12 melds the two figures.

The dragon has seven heads and ten horns. The four beasts from the sea in Dan. 7 have, collectively, seven heads and ten horns. The dragon has diadems on its horns, a royal band that was worn around headgear by Persian rulers.

The dragon sweeps a third of the stars to the ground. Daniel 8:10 tells us that Antiochus swept stars to the earth and trampled them when he prohibited the Jewish cult. Stars are heavenly beings and are God's army. When powerful emperors attack Judaism and Jews, they attack heaven. This is more than just figurative. Cosmic forces are at war when Seleucids or Romans attack Jews or Christians.

The dragon stands before the woman, ready to devour her child. The child comes forth as "a male child, who is to rule all the nations with a rod of iron" (12:5; a messianic image from Ps. 2:8–9) and is immediately snatched up to heaven (Aune 1997, 688–90). The vision does not match Jesus's ministry, since the boy is snatched up immediately, to return as conqueror. So John may have used a Jewish source (Charles 1920). The woman flees to the desert, where God nourishes her for 1,260 days. Christians would undoubtedly see Jesus in this child, and so it is natural to identify the woman as Mary. Scholars have suggested that the woman originally represents God's people, from whom the Messiah comes. The author may have both in mind. Multiple meanings are possible in apocalyptic texts (Collins 1998, 51–52).

The idea that the woman is also the church is supported by the fact that she flees to the wilderness and is nourished by God for 1,260 days, a number familiar from earlier in Revelation. It stands for the period during which the church endures Rome's blasphemous rule. The time of the woman's nourishment matches the time of the two witnesses in chapter 11. The woman is nourished by God in the wilderness, putting the church in another mythological context—that of Israel during the exodus.

What follows is an episode seminal to apocalyptic thinking.

> And war broke out in heaven; Michael and his angels fought against the dragon. The dragon and his angels fought back, but they were defeated, and there was no longer any place for them in heaven. The great dragon was thrown down, that ancient serpent, who is called the Devil and Satan, the deceiver of the whole world—he was thrown down to the earth, and his angels were thrown down with him.
>
> Then I heard a loud voice in heaven, proclaiming, "Now have come the salvation and the power and the kingdom of our God and the authority of his Messiah, for the accuser of our comrades has been thrown down, who accuses them day and night before our God. But they have conquered him by the blood of the Lamb and by the word of their testimony, for they did not cling to life even in the face of death. Rejoice then, you heavens and those who dwell in them! But woe to the earth and the sea, for the devil has come down to you with great wrath, because he knows that his time is short!" (Rev. 12:7–12)

There are two angelic armies at war, each with a superhuman leader. No such thing happens in the Hebrew Bible. Michael is Israel's protector and heavenly patron. He appears at the eschaton in Dan. 12. In Dan. 7, he is probably the one like a son of man. When he rules in heaven, Israel rules on earth. Now in Rev. 12 he secures his status in heaven. The power of evil can penetrate even heaven, and a real, cosmic war must be fought to eject it and keep it out. Michael, doing the hard work, leads the angels loyal to God against Satan and his angelic minions. The defeated dragon is the devil and Satan. He is the "ancient serpent" who deceived the whole human race.

A heavenly voice proclaims the meaning of these events. Michael's victory over Satan is possible because of Jesus's death and that of the martyrs. Victory over Rome is possible only when first Jesus and then Christians resist Rome and die as a result. The proclamation ends with a joyful cry over the heavenly victory but a warning to those who dwell on earth that the devil is now among them and is angry. Satan knows that his time is short; for now the church is in danger.

Now on earth, the dragon pursues the woman in the desert. Given the wings of an eagle, she escapes. This alludes to Exod. 19:4, where God tells Israel that he has borne them to him through the desert on eagles' wings. Having escaped from the serpent, the woman is nourished for a time, two times, and half a time, the same as 1,260 days. The dragon emits from its mouth a river to drown the woman, but the desert swallows it. This is another reference to the exodus, where water almost does Israel in, but God restrains the water. Finally, the dragon fumes off to attack the woman's children who obey God and preserve Jesus's testimony (12:17).

Second unnumbered vision. John sets the scene for the second vision by saying that the dragon stands on the seashore (12:18), an appropriate place for the villain of the combat myth. From the sea arises a beast with seven heads and ten horns, with diadems and blasphemous names on its heads. It resembles Satan. The beast from the sea is Rome, so the vision proves that Rome is like Satan. The names on its heads are blasphemous because the titles adopted by Roman emperors and the claims made by the empire are satanic. Imperial claims lie about God (the root meaning of blasphemy) and lie about the empire (Westbrook 1992, 549).

The connection with Dan. 7 is confirmed when we learn that the beast looks like a leopard, a bear, and a lion, the three animals of Dan. 7. "The dragon gave it his power and his throne and great authority" (13:2). Rome's power is a direct gift from the devil. That explains both its might and its hostility to those loyal to God. It also explains why loyalty to Rome is disloyalty to God.

One horn of the beast seems to have received a deathblow (13:3) but is cured. This reflects the Nero myth—the belief that Nero did not really die and would return, or that he did die and would come back to life (Klauck 2001).

The whole earth worships the dragon and the beast (13:4). Earth's desperate inhabitants believe fighting Rome is useless.

The beast utters proud and blasphemous words (compare to Antiochus IV in Dan. 7:8). It exercises authority for forty-two months (13:5; again, the same as a time, two times, and half a time, as well as 1,260 days, both in chapter 12 [12:6, 14], all Danielic references). It wars against the saints (church) and prevails. The whole earth worships it, with the exception of those with names written in "the book of life of the Lamb that was slaughtered" (13:8). Until

this point in Revelation, God has been the only object of the verb "worship."
Now the whole earth worships Satan and Rome.

Third unnumbered vision. This vision occupies the rest of chapter 13 (vv.
11–18). A beast arises from the land. It makes the earth worship the first beast,
so it leads the imperial cult. The land in question is Asia Minor, and so the
second beast represents those who tend the imperial cult in Asia Minor. It has
two horns like a lamb but speaks like a dragon. The imperial cult is superfi-
cially like the Christ cult, but its real message is different. Imperial religious
institutions may appear harmless, but they are not.

The land beast requires everyone to have the mark of the beast in order to
participate in the empire's economy. The mark is the name or the number of
the beast. This is a perversion of the seal given to the 144,000 in chapter 7.

The number of the beast is revealed as 666, the "number of a person" (13:18).
This refers to Nero. It is an instance of gematria, the practice of assigning
numerical values to words and names. Neither Latin nor Greek nor Hebrew
used numerals but let letters stand for numbers, so it was easy to reckon the
numerical value of any word. It was far more difficult, of course, to go from
a number to a word, since the possibilities would be practically unlimited.
Spelled one way in Hebrew, "Nero Caesar" would equal 666. Spelled another
way (without a concluding "n" at the end of Nero), it would equal 616. One
of the manuscript variants in Rev. 13:18 is indeed 616 (Metzger 1971, 676).
This confirms the identification of this figure as Nero.

Fourth unnumbered vision. In the fourth vision (14:1–5) we revisit the
144,000 who have the Father's name on their foreheads. The vision contrasts
with the Roman seal written on the foreheads or hands of Roman subjects.
The 144,000 are virgins, not having "defiled themselves" with women (Olson
1997). This is probably not to be taken literally, given the symbolic significance
of fornication elsewhere in the book. Rather, avoidance of defilement may
symbolize avoidance of idolatry. Perhaps their designation as first fruits of
redemption indicates their death as martyrs.

Fifth unnumbered vision. The fifth unnumbered vision (14:6–13) contains
three angels. The first warns that judgment is here and commands everyone
to worship God the creator. The second announces Rome's (Babylon's) fall.
The last asserts that anyone who worships the beast or its image, or receives
the beast's mark, will suffer eternal punishment consisting of fire and sulfur.
Their punishment will be witnessed by the angels and the Lamb.

Sixth unnumbered vision. The sixth vision (14:6–20) pictures one like the
son of man seated on a cloud holding a sickle. An angel tells him to reap the
earth in judgment. Another angel comes forth with his own sickle and also
reaps the earth and throws its fruit into God's wrathful winepress (14:19). It
is trodden, giving out an immense quantity of blood.

Seven bowls (15:1–16:21). The seventh unnumbered vision consists of seven
angels who hold seven bowls full of plagues to be poured out on the earth.

John says that these are the final ones, and with them, God's wrath is concluded (15:1).

We are accustomed to some element intervening between the sixth and seventh elements of a vision series. We also have an example of the interweaving of visions, since the seven trumpets were interwoven with the seven seals. There is a liturgical scene that is part of this picture of the seven angels. John sees the glassy sea again. It is surrounded by those who conquered the beast and its image and the number of its name (see chapter 13 for the same collocation). They are martyrs. They hold harps and sing the song of Moses (see Exod. 15) and the song of the Lamb. Their song praises God for his justice and declares that all will worship God because of the rightness of his judgments. This contrasts with everything that has been said about Rome. Rome is a counterfeit imitation of God. What Rome pretends to offer—a just society under the protection of a divine power—only God delivers. Rome produces nothing but injustice.

The seven angels receive seven bowls of wrath from the four living creatures. The heavenly temple fills with smoke from God's glory and none can enter until the plagues end (compare 1 Kings 8).

Chapter 16 contains the seven bowls. They overlap with the seven trumpets and contain references to the Egyptian plagues. The following chart (Murphy 1998, 337) lays out the parallels.

Parallels between the Trumpets, Bowls, and Egyptian Plagues

Trumpets Rev. 8:7–11:19	Bowls Rev. 16:1–21	Egyptian Plagues Exod. 7:14–12:32
1. On the earth: hail and fire mixed with blood; a third of vegetation burned	1. On the earth: painful sores on humans	First plague: water turns to blood Sixth plague: boils Seventh plague: thunder and hail
2. On the sea: a third of the sea turns to blood	2. On the sea: sea turns to blood	First plague: water turns to blood
3. On rivers and springs: a third of rivers and springs become bitter	3. On rivers and springs: rivers and springs turn to blood	First plague: water turns to blood
4. On the sun, moon, and stars: a third of their light darkened	4. On the sun: it scorches humans	Ninth plague: darkness
5. Abyss opened; smoke rises and darkens sun and air; locusts come from abyss and torture humans with stings	5. On the beast's throne: darkness and sores on humans	Sixth plague: boils Eighth plague: locusts Ninth plague: darkness

6. Angels held at Euphrates River released; demonic cavalry attacks humankind; fire, smoke, and sulfur come out of horses' mouths and kill a third of humankind	6. On the Euphrates River: river dries up so kings of east can come; frog demons come from mouths of dragon, beast, and prophet and assemble kings for battle against God	Second plague: frogs
7. Kingdom of God and Messiah come; punishment of wicked and reward of righteous; destruction of destroyers of earth; lightning, rumblings, thunder, earthquake, great hail	7. On the air: lightning, rumblings, thunder, earthquake, great hail; destruction of Babylon	Seventh plague: thunder and hail

Through the overlaps and parallels we can see both recapitulation and rootedness in biblical traditions. Of greatest interest to us are the last two bowls. The sixth contains the battle of Armageddon, and the seventh concerns the divine assault on Rome itself.

In 16:1, the angel's bowl is poured on the Euphrates River to allow the eastern armies to invade the Roman Empire. This was Rome's nightmare. There is also an allusion to the sixth trumpet, where a cavalry of two hundred million invades from the east. In the next verse, foul frog spirits come from the mouth of the dragon (Satan), the beast (Rome), and the false prophet (the provincial imperial cult). These are the three powers of chapter 13, arranged hierarchically. The three gather the world for battle "on the great day of God the Almighty" (16:14). They assemble at *harmagedōn*. The name derives from the Hebrew *Har Měgiddô*, "the mountain of Megiddo," referring to a fortress built on a rise in a strategic valley in Galilee where important ancient battles occurred (Ussishkin 1992). The idea of a great final battle derives from Ezek. 38–39 and Zech. 14.

The seventh bowl is God's attack on Rome, the "great city" (16:19). Cosmic elements are repeated and intensified—lightning, rumblings, thunder, and an unprecedented violent earthquake. The city splits in three, and cities around the empire collapse.

The Babylon appendix (17:1–19:10). The divine attack on Rome opens the way for two chapters dedicated to disclosing Rome's true nature.

Chapter 17 deals with international politics. Rome plays the prostitute with the nations of the earth. She sits on the beast of chapter 13, a scarlet beast with seven heads and ten horns, full of blasphemous names. She is decked out in vulgar and garish fashion.

> The woman was clothed in purple and scarlet, and adorned with gold and jewels and pearls, holding in her hand a golden cup full of abominations and the impurities of her fornication; and on her forehead was written a name, a

mystery: "Babylon the great, mother of whores and of earth's abominations."
And I saw that the woman was drunk with the blood of the saints and the blood
of the witnesses to Jesus. When I saw her, I was greatly amazed. (Rev. 17:4–6)

The picture is garish. Rome is all that is vile and repulsive to God. Now
displayed in her true colors, all pretense to being like God is a sham. Rome's
claim to divine honors is blasphemous and shocking. Stripped of her divine
pretensions, she is revealed to be nothing but the greatest prostitute. She is
the archenemy of anyone who dares worship the true God. She seeks their
suffering and death.

The angel offers to explain the mystery of the vision (17:7). The beast is
the one who "was, and is not, and is about to ascend from the bottomless pit
and go to destruction" (17:8). These words recall the Nero legend and are a
perversion of God's title, "the one who is, and who was, and who is to come"
(1:8). This is the same beast from the sea described in chapter 13.

The next passage interprets the seven heads. They are both seven mountains
and seven kings. Rome had seven hills. The angel says, "The woman you saw
is the great city that rules over the kings of the earth" (17:18). That the seven
hills are also kings has led to endless speculation about who they are. They
are Roman emperors, but there are numerous speculations about which ones
are meant. A chart of possibilities is offered in Attridge (Attridge and Meeks
2006, 2107). The ten horns represent kings allied with Rome. They surrender
sovereignty to the beast, Rome, and participate in the battle against the Lamb.
Eventually, the ten kings turn against the whore, Rome, and ravage her.

Chapter 17 deals with Rome's political alliances, while chapter 18 deals
with economics (Yarbro Collins 1980). The urban elite accounted for most
of the world's demand for luxury items. An angel announces that Babylon's
fall means the end of this system (18:3). Another heavenly voice commands
Christians to flee Rome lest they suffer from her punishments. There follow
laments over Rome's fall uttered by those who had the most to lose from it—
kings, merchants, and seafarers. Merchants will lose the profit from the traffic
in luxury goods. A list is given, culminating in the most objectionable—slaves
(18:12–13) (Koester 2008). The chapter culminates when an angel predicts
Rome's punishment for the deaths of prophets and saints (Christians), and
everyone slaughtered in the empire. Heaven rejoices that God has judged Rome
(19:1–5). Rome's punishment is eternal.

Christ's relationship with the church is depicted as a marriage feast between
the Lamb and his bride, the church, dressed in fine linen, explained as the "righteous deeds of the saints" (19:6–8). The seer tries to worship the interpreting
angel but is reproved. Only God deserves worship (19:10).

Vision one. In 19:11–16, the first vision of this set, Christ bursts out of
heaven on a white horse. His name is "Faithful and True," for he is truly
loyal to God. His eyes are like flame, he wears many diadems, and he has a

secret name, preserving his ultimate mystery. His robe is bloody, and his title is Word of God. Heaven's armies follow him on white horses. A sharp sword protrudes from his mouth; he will strike the nations with an iron rod. He treads the winepress of God's wrath. He is called King of kings and Lord of lords. Only this power can defeat Rome.

Vision two. An angel invites birds to eat a gruesome feast consisting of the dead flesh of God's enemies (19:17–18). The feast depends on the similar scene in Ezek. 39.

Vision three. The final battle takes only an instant (19:19–21). The beast and false prophet are thrown alive into the sulfuric lake. The rest of the evil army is killed.

Vision four. Satan's fate is next (20:1–3):

> Then I saw an angel coming down from heaven, holding in his hand the key to the bottomless pit and a great chain. He seized the dragon, that ancient serpent, who is the Devil and Satan, and bound him for a thousand years, and threw him into the pit, and locked and sealed it over him, so that he would deceive the nations no more, until the thousand years were ended. After that he must be let out for a little while.

This recalls Isa. 24:22, where sinful angels are shut up in a pit for a period before final punishment.

Vision five. After Satan is imprisoned, the martyrs, those beheaded, are raised from the dead (20:4–10). This is not the general resurrection; it is the first of two resurrections (20:5). The martyrs reign with Christ for the thousand years of Satan's confinement. This thousand-year period when Satan is bound and the martyrs reign with Christ is known as the millennium, from the Latin *mille*, meaning thousand, and *annos*, meaning year. Exactly what it means and when it will happen has occupied apocalyptic thinkers ever since Revelation was written.

Vision six. At the end of the millennium, Satan will be released and will deceive the nations and rally them (20:7–10). Gog and Magog make their appearance. The battle is decided in an instant, as fire descends from heaven and destroys Satan's army. Satan is cast into the lake of fire to join the sea beast and the land beast in eternal torture.

Vision seven. The seventh vision contains general resurrection (the second resurrection) and final judgment (20:11–15). God sits on a great white throne on earth; all are raised and judged by him for their deeds; the book of life is opened; death and Hades are thrown into the lake of fire, the "second death"; all who are not in the book of life are thrown into the fiery lake.

The place of ultimate consummation is not heaven but earth. Building on the Jewish ideal of God's people gathered around God's earthly temple, Revelation pictures the final consummation as God on earth in the new Jerusalem,

Revelation: Apocalypse and Apocalypticism

- Revelation fits the definition of apocalypse perfectly.
- Revelation is not pseudonymous, unlike most apocalypses. John stresses his relationship with those to whom the apocalypse is addressed.
- John sees an apocalyptic Jesus with features based on Dan. 7; 10; Ezek. 43; and Isa. 11, 49.
- The tribulation is under way.
- The eschatological events have their origins at God's throne.
- Clashing sovereignties (God and Rome) are central.
- The author envisages a worldwide persecution of Christians.
- The dragon (Satan) gives to Rome its power. The unseen world determines the seen world.
- The great battle of Armageddon is described (Satan, Rome, and the imperial cult are defeated).
- There are two resurrections.
- The millennium occurs.
- There is a last judgment.
- New heavens and a new earth appear.
- The New Jerusalem is described.

bestowing on humanity all the benefits God intended at creation. John sees a new heaven and a new earth. The first heaven and earth have passed away, "and the sea was no more" (21:1). The disappearance of the sea is fraught with meaning (see *Testament of Moses* 10). No longer is God's order at risk. The enemy is forever vanquished.

God comments on what has been accomplished. The relationship between God and his universe has radically changed. Whereas before this we have heard primarily from the seer, angels, elders, heavenly choruses, and so on, now we hear from God himself: "'See, I am making all things new.' Also he said, 'Write this, for these words are trustworthy and true.' Then he said to me, 'It is done! I am the Alpha and the Omega, the beginning and the end'" (Rev. 21:5–6). God promises water to the thirsty, a covenantal relationship with those who conquer, that is, resist Rome, and punishment in the fiery lake for sinners, a punishment termed the second death (21:7–8).

New Jerusalem appendix (21:9–22:5). The new Jerusalem is impossibly idealistic. It measures fifteen hundred miles on a side, and has walls that exceed two hundred feet in height. It has twelve gates inscribed with the names of the twelve Israelite tribes and twelve foundations inscribed with the names of the twelve apostles, representing the union of Israel and Christianity. It is constructed of precious metals and jewels. The new Jerusalem has no temple, because God and Christ take its place (21:22). He and the Lamb live among their people. Sinners and Satan are no longer present.

The divine throne brings fertility to the new earth. The water of life flows down the city's street. The tree of life from the Garden of Eden grows in Jerusalem, bringing health to the nations. There is no more night; there is no need for sun in God's presence. God's people reign with him and the Lamb forever.

Epilogue (22:6–21)

Prophetic sayings (22:6–20a). John identifies himself as the receiver of the visions. He tries again to worship the angel and is rebuffed. Worship belongs to God alone. John is told not to seal the book, because the time of the fulfillment is near (22:10).

In 22:12–13, Christ applies to himself the divine title Alpha and Omega and declares that he is coming soon (see also 22:16–17). A blessing is pronounced on those in the new Jerusalem. They pray for Christ's parousia.

Epistolary greeting (22:20b–21). The concluding epistolary greeting matches its epistolary beginning (1:4–6).

Suggestions for Further Reading

Aune, David E. *Revelation*. 3 vols. Nashville: Thomas Nelson, 1997.

Barr, David L., ed. *Reading the Book of Revelation: A Resource for Students*. Atlanta: Society of Biblical Literature, 2003.

Friesen, Steven J. *Imperial Cults and the Apocalypse of John: Reading Revelation in the Ruins*. Oxford and New York: Oxford University Press, 2006.

Kraybill, J. Nelson. *Apocalypse and Allegiance: Worship, Politics, and Devotion in the Book of Revelation*. Grand Rapids: Brazos, 2010.

Murphy, Frederick J. *Fallen Is Babylon: The Revelation to John*. Harrisburg: Trinity Press, 1998.

Price, S. R. F. *Rituals and Power: The Roman Imperial Cult in Asia Minor*. Cambridge: Cambridge University Press, 1984.

Schüssler Fiorenza, Elizabeth. *Revelation: Vision of a Just World*. Minneapolis: Fortress, 1991.

Yarbro Collins, Adela. *The Combat Myth in the Book of Revelation*. Missoula, MT: Scholars Press, 1976.

———. *Crisis and Catharsis: The Power of the Apocalypse*. Philadelphia: Westminster, 1984.

5

Ancient Jewish Apocalypses

Judaism of the late Second Temple period and immediately afterward offers a wealth of apocalypses and other texts containing apocalyptic sections and elements. They illustrate the importance of apocalypticism in Jewish thought and life from the third century BCE to the second century CE. The most important is the book of Daniel. We now consider others, beginning with *1 Enoch*.

First Enoch is a collection of documents, each of which originally circulated independently. We separate out the book's components and examine each in its own right. Each component incorporates smaller units, a couple of which are themselves apocalypses. A case in point is the *Animal Apocalypse*, which we have already studied.

The following is the conventional division of *1 Enoch* into five originally independent main parts:

Book of the Watchers (*1 Enoch* 1–36)—third century BCE
Similitudes of Enoch (*1 Enoch* 37–71)—first century CE
Astronomical Book (*1 Enoch* 72–82)—third century BCE
Book of Dreams (*1 Enoch* 83–90)—second century BCE
Epistle of Enoch (*1 Enoch* 91–108)—second century BCE

The *Book of Dreams* contains the *Animal Apocalypse* (*1 Enoch* 85–90), and the *Epistle of Enoch* contains the *Apocalypse of Weeks* (*1 Enoch* 93:3–14;

91:12–17; its order is disturbed in the Ethiopic, but it is in proper order in the Aramaic fragments from Qumran).

The Enoch Community

Enoch is the perfect pseudonym for an apocalyptic seer (VanderKam 1995). Genesis says, "Enoch walked with God; then he was no more, because God took him" (Gen. 5:24). Every other ancient figure in Gen. 5 dies. Enoch's escaping death demands explanation. The Enoch tradition sees it as the reason Enoch can receive and impart heavenly secrets. "Walking" is a Jewish metaphor for behavior. One Hebrew word for law, *hălākâ*, literally means "walking."

VanderKam traces connections between Enoch in Genesis and ancient Mesopotamian heroes (VanderKam 1984; Collins 1998, 44–47). Enoch is the seventh in the line of Adam in Gen. 5, and he is said to have lived for 365 years, an allusion to the length of a solar year. The *Sumerian King List* has as its seventh king Enmeduranki (or Enmeduranna). His city was ruled by the sun god Shamash (the Hebrew for "sun" is *šemeš*). The connection between Enoch and Enmeduranki is the association of each with the sun and being number seven in the list. During the late Second Temple period, there was a calendrical dispute between Jewish groups over whether the year ought to be determined by the sun or the moon or a combination, and *1 Enoch* advocates a solar year.

The seventh sage in Mesopotamian mythology, Utuabzu, contemporary with Enmeduranki, ascended to heaven, as did Enoch. Another Mesopotamian hero, Atrahasis (also called Utnapishtim), the hero of the Mesopotamian flood story, was shown the secret of the gods, the impending flood. This is similar to *1 Enoch* 83, where Enoch foresees the flood in a dream.

Ancient cultures competed with each other by claiming that important aspects shared by various cultures—astronomy, for example—were invented by their culture and borrowed by others (Collins 1998, 46). The process can work in the opposite direction—one culture can copy another to enhance its own history and status. Attaching Enoch to an ancient Mesopotamian king and sage supports Enoch's pedigree and his claim to sacred, esoteric knowledge.

There is certainly an Enoch tradition, for *1 Enoch* is a composite work, made up of documents written at different times and circumstances, all attributed to Enoch. In the second century CE, we have yet another Jewish apocalyptic work, called *2 Enoch*, and in the fourth or fifth century we have a Jewish mystical text called *3 Enoch*. If there was not an actual Enochic community or school, there was a succession of writers who interacted with each other's work.

Numerous scholars have noticed that the Enoch literature does not put much if any stress on Torah. It may represent a Judaism not fully consonant with what we think as mainstream, centered on Torah and priesthood. The discussion is ongoing and has not resulted in consensus. A school of thought sees "Enochic Judaism" as different from and opposed to more mainstream Judaism as represented by Torah and the Jerusalem priesthood (Boccaccini, Ellens, and Waddell 2005; Boccaccini and Collins 2007; Boccaccini et al. 2009; Nickelsburg 1998; 2001; 2007; Collins 2003b; 2007; 2008; Bachmann 2011; Reed 2005).

The Enochic literature is clearly apocalyptic, since it sees the world as radically disordered, it employs apocalyptic insight into the unseen world, and it expects an eschatological end. The lack of mention of the larger story centered on Sinai stands in stark contrast with other Jewish apocalypses as well as the literature of the apocalyptic community of Qumran. The religion of the Enoch literature is Jewish, but it is not Mosaic. It is covenantal, but the laws on which it is built are not those of Torah but are broader, rooted in the universe as a whole. One can compare it to the wisdom tradition in its relative lack of interest in the Sinai covenant and the particular history of Israel. It attests to variety within Second Temple Judaism, a variety that has been overshadowed by the dominance of Mosaic Judaism (Collins 2008).

The *Book of the Watchers* (*1 Enoch* 1–36)

Explanation for Evil

The *Book of the Watchers* is comprised of the first thirty-six chapters of *1 Enoch*. A "watcher" is a kind of angel. "Watcher" may indicate function, such as the guarding of heaven or surveillance of the earth. The Enochic book recounts the story of the heavenly watchers who violate God's order by coming down from heaven and disrupting creation. This is an account of the origin of evil different from that in the Adam and Eve story. Sin and evil are the fault of the angels, not humans.

The angelic explanation of evil has roots in Genesis. Genesis 6:1–4 preserves a mythological fragment in which "sons of God" are attracted to women and take them as wives. The text juxtaposes this to the presence of Nephilim on the earth—legendary warriors and heroes, which may imply that the Nephilim are the watchers' offspring. The situation provokes divine action, and God limits life to 120 years, lest this semidivine form of life be combined with great length of life (Gen. 1:3). *First Enoch* builds this fragment into a full narrative.

Structure

The *Book of the Watchers* falls into three divisions. Chapters 1–5 introduce the book and also lay the groundwork for the entire collection. They introduce the seer, Enoch, describe the imminent appearance of God in judgment, and exhort readers to obey God as does the universe. Chapters 6–16 speak of the descent of the watchers and its results (6–11), recount the watchers' request to Enoch that he plead for them before God (12–16), and tell of his efforts to comply. In the remainder of the book (17–36), Enoch tours the cosmos and observes places fraught with eschatological significance.

Analysis of the Book of the Watchers

Opening (chaps. 1–5). The opening words of the *Book of the Watchers* are these:

> The words of the blessing of Enoch, wherewith he blessed the elect and righteous, who will be living in the day of tribulation, when all the wicked and godless are to be removed. And he took up his parable and said—Enoch a righteous man, whose eyes were opened by God, saw the vision of the Holy One in the heavens, which the angels showed me, and from them I heard everything, and from them I understood as I saw, but not for this generation, but for a remote one which is for to come. (*1 Enoch* 1:1–2)

Angelic intermediaries show Enoch the heavenly realms and tell him "everything." They explain the revelation and disclose that it concerns the end time, including rewards and punishments. We thus have esoteric knowledge whose ultimate origin is heaven, given to a human being through heavenly intermediaries, knowledge that is both spatial and temporal. The real writer believes himself to live in the end time. Obviously *1 Enoch* is pseudonymous.

"Elect" and "righteous" recur frequently in *1 Enoch.* "Elect" means chosen by God, and "righteous" means in alignment with God's will.

"Blessing" recalls Moses's blessing of the twelve tribes (Deut. 33:1), and the opening of eyes echoes the Balaam story (Num. 22:31). The author enhances Enoch by making him resemble these prophetic figures.

The rest of chapter 1 describes a theophany, an appearance of God. God comes from his heavenly abode. The watchers are afraid, mountains melt, and there are earthquakes and destruction. God's coming means punishment for the wicked and protection for the righteous. He is accompanied by his heavenly hosts, "tens of thousands of his holy ones."

Chapters 2–5 are addressed to sinners. They describe the orderliness of creation, obedient to God's commands. In contrast, the wicked have not obeyed God. They have fallen prey to pride and have spoken "hard words" against God's majesty. They will be punished eternally and mercilessly. In contrast, the righteous will obtain mercy. "They shall inherit the earth" is an allusion to Ps. 37:11, used also by the people of Qumran (and Jesus [Matt. 5:5]).

The story of the watchers (chaps. 6–11). Chapters 6–11 recount the story of the sinful watchers. It combines two originally separate accounts, one where the angelic leader is Shemyaza, and another where it is Azazel. In *1 Enoch* 6 as in Gen. 6, the angels see beautiful women, descend, and take them as wives. They also teach the women heavenly secrets—charms, enchantments, and the use of roots and plants. The offspring of the angels and the women are giants who consume all that belongs to humans and then humans themselves. They sin against animals and finally turn on one another. At last, the earth itself raises a cry against them.

In chapter 8, Azazel makes his own mischief. He teaches humans metal-working, by which they make weapons, jewelry, and cosmetics. This leads to fornication and warfare. Other angels teach humans astrology and the signs of the earth and of the clouds. None of the knowledge conveyed to humans by the angels was meant to be open to them. This is an instance of a broader mythological theme, found in various cultures, that humans have acquired knowledge that the gods did not intend them to have. It is not surprising that sex and violence feature so prominently in this story. These are two things that have troubled humanity from time immemorial. Humanity cries out in the midst of this iniquity, and their cry ascends to heaven.

Apocalypses are purposely vague about real-world references. Generally, *1 Enoch* 6–7 explains why the world is not as God intended. There may be more specific historical situations behind these stories, but, if so, they are veiled. Nickelsburg suggests that the giants represent Hellenistic kings who ruled after Alexander the Great and who wreaked havoc through their wars, especially during the third century BCE when the *Book of the Watchers* was written (Nickelsburg 2001, 170; Collins 1982). There were five wars in the third century between the Ptolemies and the Seleucids. Such wars must have taken their toll on Palestine's inhabitants. The Hellenistic emperors must have seemed superhuman to those who witnessed their power and endured their oppression.

Later (15:2–3), God chides the angels for leaving heaven and asking Enoch, a human, to intercede for them. This reverses the proper order of things—they should be interceding for humans. Some detect criticism of the Jewish priesthood, who did not maintain their proper holiness, perhaps because of improper marriages (Suter 1979).

Four archangels—Michael, Uriel, Raphael, and Gabriel—observe the earth's distress (chap. 9). Humanity begs for their intercession. The angels describe the misdeeds of the fallen angels and the damage they have done, appealing to God as creator and the one who has foreseen everything, urging him to give them instructions.

God springs into action in chapter 10. He is like an emperor giving brisk orders to his ministers and generals. Uriel is dispatched to Noah with instructions on how to escape the coming flood. Raphael is to bind Azazel hand and foot, cast him into darkness, and make a place in the desert where he will be covered over with weighty boulders to await the final judgment (see Isa. 24:21–22). Raphael is to heal the earth. Azazel bears primary responsibility for the ruin of the earth: "And the whole earth has been corrupted through the works that were taught by Azazel: to him ascribe all sin" (*1 Enoch* 10:8–9).

God sends Gabriel to destroy the fruit of the union between angels and humans. Michael confines Shemyaza until the last judgment when he will endure a fiery punishment like that of Azazel. Michael destroys the offspring and spirits of the angels and women. He cleanses the earth from evil and instead plants righteousness.

Utopia ensues (chaps. 10–11). The righteous bear thousands of children. They live normal lengths of youth and old age. All are righteous. The earth is fertile beyond natural possibilities. All worship God, and the earth is cleansed from defilement. There is no more sin and punishment, and God promises never to punish the earth this way again. God opens the heavenly storehouses of blessing, which descends upon the earth, along with lasting truth and peace.

Enoch and the watchers (chaps. 12–16). Enoch appears in chapter 12, where righteous watchers order him to bring to the wicked watchers news of their condemnation. The watchers beg Enoch to plead their case before the Lord (chap. 13). Enoch retires to an isolated place to write out their petition and falls asleep. He has a vision of a journey to heaven and the rest of the universe, which occupies the rest of the book. His intercession for the watchers fails.

Chapter 14 is a throne vision. Enoch tells the watchers that their cause is hopeless and then is swept up to heaven by clouds, wind, stars, and lightning and arrives at God's heavenly abode. Enoch's approach to God's dwelling and his depiction of the dwelling itself stretches human language. It is both understandable and beyond understanding. Enoch's approach expresses the awe and trepidation expected when one approaches a great emperor or enters the temple of a great god. His reactions are appropriate—quaking and fear.

God's dwelling is like no place on earth—walls of crystal, surrounded by fire, a clear ceiling with stars and lightning with fiery cherubim between them. It is hot as fire and cold as ice. Enoch sees a still greater house: "And in every respect it so excelled in splendor and magnificence and extent that I cannot describe to you its splendor and its extent" (14:16–17). The floor of the house is fire, as is the ceiling. The ceiling contains lightning and fire. Finally, Enoch beholds God's throne. The heavenly architecture recalls the Jerusalem temple. Earth and heaven correspond.

Enoch's throne scene draws on other such scenes, particularly those of Ezek. 1, Isa. 6, and Dan. 7. God's throne is crystal, reflecting the idea that the firmament is transparent, and it has wheels, as in Ezekiel, since it is God's chariot. Fire flows from it, as in Dan. 7. Also like Dan. 7, the throne is surrounded by cherubim and tens of thousands of angels. God's clothing is white and bright as the sun. Not even angels can behold God's majesty. Most frightening, God summons Enoch to hear his word. Enoch collapses in terror but is aided by a "holy one."

In chapter 15, God commands Enoch to carry his condemnation to the watchers again. He chides them for having left their assigned place in heaven, lain with women, defiled themselves, begotten violent and destructive giants, and renounced their spiritual, eternal existence. The situation is described again how evil spirits proceeded from the dead bodies of their offspring and afflicted the earth, causing misfortunes, violence, and oppression. This was because the giants resulted from an illegitimate mixing of heaven and earth. The passage conveys God's displeasure with the state of the world, dominated by Hellenistic empires.

God continues his speech in chapter 16, elaborating on the destructive activities of the evil spirits, which continue with impunity until the eschaton. God explains that secrets revealed by the angels to the women, although destructive, are ultimately "worthless," and that the key heavenly secrets are safe.

Enoch's tour of the universe (chaps. 17–36). Chapters 17–36 contain Enoch's tour of the universe, much of which has eschatological significance. Spatial and temporal elements of apocalyptic revelation are fused. Chapters 17–18 show Enoch touring places of natural elements like stars, winds, thunder and lightning, river sources, and the origin of the sea. In chapter 18, Enoch encounters his first eschatologically significant areas. There are seven mountains, one of which is like God's throne. Then Enoch sees a "horrible place" with neither floor nor ceiling. It is a fiery abyss. Within it he sees stars and the "host of heaven" that did not follow their proper times and paths. They will be imprisoned for ten thousand years.

The fiery abyss is the watchers' destination. They had intercourse with women, and their spirits mislead humankind, including persuading them to worship demons as if they were gods, an explanation of idolatry (see Deut. 32:17; 1 Cor. 10:20). They will stay in the abyss until the end, when they will be destroyed. Meanwhile, their women will be sirens, figures from Greek mythology who seduce mariners into shipwreck. Enoch claims that he alone has seen this vision.

Chapter 20 lists seven archangels and their tasks. Michael is placed over the "best" part of humanity, Israel. Gabriel has charge of paradise, the serpents, and the cherubim. Gabriel is especially close to God.

Chapter 21 shows Enoch observing two more places of punishment. One is for seven angels who transgressed God's will. The second is the prison for the angels. Both are "horrible," fire-filled places with no set borders.

Chapter 22 shows where dead humans await the final judgment. They occupy four hollow places. The places show that a measure of judgment has already taken place. The angel Raphael's explanation of the different groups actually contains only three, indicating a corruption in the text. The righteous abide in a place of bright water. Of the other two places, one contains the wicked who have not yet suffered for their wickedness, and the other a place for sinners who have suffered and so will not suffer full punishment.

In chapter 23, Enoch observes the source of punishing fire. In chapters 24–25, Enoch again sees seven mountains; Michael tells him that one will be

Fig. 5. The Kidron Valley, between Jerusalem and the Mount of Olives, was traditionally identified as a site for the last judgment. These Jewish tombs belong to those who want a front-row seat at that event. (Chris Miller)

God's throne at the end. The mountain is surrounded by fragrant trees, one of which stands out for fragrance and appearance. Humans are forbidden to taste of it. Only the righteous will partake of it, and they will do so at the end. It is the tree of life from the Garden of Eden. It will be transplanted to God's temple. God is the eternal king and will bring the righteous with him to his place, where they will live a long life, as their ancestors did, but free of suffering and care. The apocalyptic end looks like creation's beginning.

Chapters 24–25 bring Enoch to the eschatological Jerusalem. It is recognizable through geographical features—the Kidron valley to the east of the city, and the Mount of Olives farther east. This is the site of the final judgment. The wicked will be judged in the presence of the righteous. Even today one can see innumerable graves on the Mount of Olives, facing Jerusalem. Confident people, sure of their own righteousness, have secured a place there so that they have a front-row seat at the final judgment.

The remaining chapters feature Enoch's visits to the rest of the universe. Especially interesting is chapter 32, where he visits the Garden of Eden and sees the tree of knowledge of good and evil. These chapters complete Enoch's tour. His knowledge is complete and reliable.

The *Astronomical Book* (*1 Enoch* 72–82)

This book dates from the third century BCE, as does the *Book of the Watchers*. Together, they are our oldest Jewish apocalyptic works. Except for the fact that it attests to an interest in cosmological knowledge, most of which was already out of date when it was written, the *Astronomical Book* does not contain much we need to investigate. The author claims that his knowledge comes through the angel Uriel, and that it describes the order of the universe that will hold true until the new creation, which will be eternal (72:2). It is concerned with whether there should be a 360- or a 364-day year.

In chapter 80, Uriel informs Enoch about the deterioration of the universe that happens at the end of time. Sinners' lives will be shortened and the earthly order will change. The growth of seed will slow, rain will be withheld, trees will be barren, the moon will alter its order, the sun will shine inordinately brightly, and the stars will not follow their proper order. Sinners will err in reading the stars, and they will mistake the stars to be gods. They will be punished and destroyed (80:8). Behind these sins it is easy to discern calendrical disputes and idolatry.

The angel invites Enoch to read the heavenly tables containing the deeds of humankind throughout history. Enoch utters a beatitude over the righteous who will not be judged.

In the work's final chapter, Enoch instructs his son. He describes the solar year, divided into four parts of three months (thirty days), each introduced by a separate day. This results in 364 days, a solar year. Sinners do not reckon in this way and so they err. Enoch reveals that each part of the year is the responsibility of particular angels, whose names he discloses.

The *Dream Visions* (*1 Enoch* 83–90)

Dream Visions is in two parts. The first is a fragment about the flood (*1 Enoch* 83–84), and the second is the *Animal Apocalypse* (*1 Enoch* 85–90), which we discussed in chapter 3.

The *Apocalypse of Weeks*

Embedded within the *Epistle of Enoch* (*1 Enoch* 90–104) is the *Apocalypse of Weeks*. The Ethiopic version of *1 Enoch* has disturbed the order of this apocalypse. Its proper order would be 93:1–10 followed by 91:11–17. This is confirmed by the Aramaic fragments from Qumran.

The *Apocalypse of Weeks* divides history into ten periods, which it terms "weeks." Of these, the seventh is a turning point, and it reflects the time of the real author. The date of the writing is disputed, but since it is mentioned in the book of *Jubilees*, written sometime in the second century BCE, it cannot be after that time. The time of the real author is probably related to the Hellenistic Reform in Jerusalem and consequent events.

The *Apocalypse of Weeks* refers to biblical history, and it sees a pattern of alternating good and bad periods, which do not correspond strictly to the alternation of weeks. Enoch received his information from a heavenly vision, through the words of the angels, and from the heavenly tablets. When Enoch recounts the vision, he says that he is reading it "from the books." The content of the ten weeks is as follows:

First Week: (A good week.) Enoch comes in the seventh generation from Adam; a time of righteousness.

Second Week: (A bad week.) A time of wickedness. The "first end," the flood, comes. A man is saved from within it (Noah). Wickedness increases and a law is made for the sinners.

Third Week: (A good week.) God chooses Abraham as the "plant of righteous judgment" and his posterity, Israel, as the eternal "plant of righteousness."

Fourth Week: (A good week.) Visions of the holy and righteous are seen, the eternal law (Torah) is given, and an "enclosure" is made for it, the desert tent that prefigures the temple.

Fifth Week: (A good week.) The temple is built.

Sixth Week: (A bad week.) Hearts are blinded and forsake wisdom. A man "ascends" (Elijah). At the week's end, the temple is destroyed and the people are dispersed (the Babylonian exile).

Seventh Week: (A good week, in the end.) The time of the real author. At the beginning, an "apostate generation" arises. At the week's end are chosen "the elect righteous of the eternal plant of righteousness, to receive sevenfold instruction concerning all his creation."

Eighth Week: (A good week.) The righteous execute judgment on the wicked with a sword. The righteous become prosperous. A temple is built for "the great king in glory forevermore," and all humans look to the "path of righteousness."

Ninth Week: (A good week.) Righteous judgment encompasses the world. Evil deeds disappear. The world is slated for destruction.

Tenth Week: (A good week.) There is a "great eternal judgment" in which the angels are judged. The first heaven passes away and a new one appears. The "powers of the heavens shall give sevenfold light." There follow weeks without number in which there is only righteousness and sin is not mentioned.

The *Apocalypse of Weeks* may be incomplete, and there may have originally been a reference to resurrection at its end, corresponding to the reference in 92:3 (Collins 1998, 65).

The *Epistle of Enoch*

The *Epistle of Enoch* is not an apocalypse, but it has an apocalyptic outlook, including moral and social dualism, postmortem rewards and punishments, God's preordination of events (92:3), judgment (100:4), and vengeance on the wicked at the hand of the righteous (98:12). We do not see Enoch touring heaven, but he has seen the heavenly tablets (103:1–2) and writings of the angels. He presumes special revelation (Collins 1998, 66–67).

The *Epistle* alternates between Enoch's words to the righteous and to the sinners, demonstrating moral and social dualism. Enoch acknowledges that the righteous suffer at the hands of the sinners, and he assures them that God will soon intervene to reward the righteous and punish the wicked. Chapter 92 tells the righteous, "Let not your spirit be troubled on account of the times; for the Holy and Great One has appointed days for all things" (92:2). The resurrection of the righteous will be to peace and light and goodness and grace (92:3–5, 10).

A period of violence will intervene between the present and the end. There will be increased unrighteousness, apostasy, blasphemy, uncleanness, and transgression (91:5–7). Then "a great chastisement" will descend from heaven onto earth and bring all to a halt.

Enoch singles out idolatry as especially heinous (91:9), perhaps reflecting the events of the Hellenistic Reform, and perhaps Antiochus's persecution. References to violence may allude to the civil war in Judea between Hellenizers and their opponents.

The *Epistle of Enoch* offers a specific description of the sinners. First, he notes economic sins.

> Woe to those who build their houses with sin; for from all their foundations shall they be overthrown, and by the sword shall they fall. And those who acquire gold and silver in judgment suddenly shall perish. Woe to you, you rich, for you have trusted in your riches. And from your riches shall you depart, because you have not remembered the Most High in the days of your riches. (94:7–8)
>
> Woe to you who acquire silver and gold in unrighteousness and say: "We have become rich with riches and have possessions, and have acquired everything we have desired. And now let us do what we purposed: for we have gathered silver, and many are the husbandmen in our houses. And our granaries are brim full as with water." Like water your lies shall flow away; for your riches shall not abide but speedily ascend from you; for you have acquired it all in unrighteousness, and you shall be given over to a great curse. (97:8–10)

Sinners' wealth is attained through unrighteousness and economic injustice. The wicked will perish by the sword and incur fiery punishment and will "perish in wrath and in grievous judgment forever," while the deceased righteous will rise to a world full of wisdom and free of sinners (91:9–10). Enoch encourages the righteous.

> Fear not the sinners, you righteous; for again will the Lord deliver them into your hands, that you may execute judgment upon them according to your desires. Woe to you who fulminate anathemas which cannot be reversed: healing shall therefore be far from you because of your sins. Woe to you who requite your neighbor with evil; for you shall be requited according to your works. Woe to you, lying witnesses, and to those who weigh out injustice, for suddenly shall you perish. Woe to you, sinners, for you persecute the righteous; for you shall be delivered up and persecuted because of injustice, and heavy shall its yoke be upon you. (*1 Enoch* 95:3–7)

Lying witness and weighing out injustice refer to the legal realm, where the wealthy have an unfair advantage. Enoch encourages the righteous with the prospect that in the future they will witness the sinners' demise and their own "lordship over them." He then attacks the wicked.

> Woe unto you, you sinners, for your riches make you appear like the righteous, but your hearts convict you of being sinners, and this fact shall be a testimony against you for a memorial of your evil deeds. Woe to you who devour the finest of the wheat, and drink wine in large bowls, and tread underfoot the lowly with your might. Woe to you who drink water from every fountain, for suddenly you shall be consumed and wither away, because you have forsaken the fountain of life. Woe to you who work unrighteousness and deceit and blasphemy: it shall be a memorial against you for evil. Woe to you, you mighty, who with might oppress the righteous, for the day of your destruction is coming. In those days many and good days shall come to the righteous—in the day of your judgment. (*1 Enoch* 96:4–8)

The rich and mighty appear righteous. They are the pillars of society. They enjoy respect. God appears to have favored them. This is all a chimera. The foundation of their success is not righteousness but sin. The day of judgment will witness eschatological reversal. Things will be as God wills, with the righteous exercising lordship and the sinners exposed.

Disagreements about ideology may also be at issue. Given *1 Enoch*'s relative lack of interest in Mosaic Torah, these may not be legal disputes per se. They do show some sort of intellectual conflict.

> Woe to you who rejoice in the tribulation of the righteous; for no grave shall be dug for you. Woe to you who set at nothing the words of the righteous, for you shall have no hope of life. Woe to you who write down lying and godless words; for they write down their lies that men may hear them and act godlessly towards their neighbor. Therefore they shall have no peace but die a sudden death. (*1 Enoch* 98:13–16)

Legal disagreement does appear in 99:2, and the law may be the Torah: "Woe to them who pervert the words of uprightness and transgress the eternal law" (*1 Enoch* 99:2; see also 104:10).

The *Book of the Watchers* attributes evil to the watchers (angels). The *Epistle* insists that humans are responsible for human sin (98:4). There is, then, a contradiction on this important point within *1 Enoch*.

The *Similitudes of Enoch*

The *Similitudes of Enoch* occupies chapters 37–71 of *1 Enoch*. It is not present at Qumran. It probably dates to the first century CE. The book consists of three "similitudes" or "parables" (chaps. 38–44, 45–57, and 58–69), which means simply figurative language, or, as Collins notes, a complex set of analogies, between heavenly and human figures, for example. The *Similitudes* are framed by an introductory chapter (37) and two concluding chapters that are two separate and not entirely compatible endings to the book (70–71).

Apocalyptic Wisdom

The *Similitudes* is an apocalypse. Enoch receives revelation, a "vision of wisdom." Enoch's visions are explained by an angel. Their content includes eschatology and the unseen world. Enoch boasts, "Till the present day such wisdom has never been given by the Lord of Spirits as I have received according to my insight" (37:4–5). The authority of the *Similitudes* surpasses that of any previous revelation.

Chapter 42 enshrines the concept of apocalyptic wisdom. It is in the form of a hymn.

> Wisdom found no place where she might dwell;
>   Then a dwelling-place was assigned her in the heavens.
> Wisdom went forth to make her dwelling among the children of men,
>   And found no dwelling-place:
> Wisdom returned to her place,
>   And took her seat among the angels.
> And unrighteousness went forth from her chambers:
>   Whom she sought not she found,
> And dwelt with them,
>   As rain in a desert
>   And dew on a thirsty land.

Wisdom belongs in heaven and has no home on earth. One must have access to heaven to get wisdom. Wisdom belongs to the heavenly Son of Man. It is shared with the righteous even during this life but especially in the world to come. Those who have died already have access to the heavenly spring of wisdom.

Sirach, a wisdom (sapiential) work, has the opposite view. It is also expressed in hymnic form. Wisdom tours the universe.

> Among all these I sought a resting place; in whose territory should I abide? "Then the Creator of all things gave me a command, and my Creator chose the place for my tent. He said, 'Make your dwelling in Jacob, and in Israel receive your inheritance.' Before the ages, in the beginning, he created me, and for all the ages I shall not cease to be. In the holy tent I ministered before him, and so I was established in Zion. Thus in the beloved city he gave me a resting place, and in Jerusalem was my domain." (Sir. 24:7–11)

Later, Sirach says, "All this is the book of the covenant of the Most High God, the law that Moses commanded us as an inheritance for the congregation of Jacob" (24:23). For Sirach, wisdom is present in the Torah. It comes from God, and it has its home in Jerusalem. Israel has access to it. This is not apocalyptic wisdom. It is traditional wisdom with a theological bent. These two kinds of wisdom—apocalyptic and sapiential—express different concepts of the universe, God, and knowledge.

The *Similitudes* has as a general theme the impending judgment. The righteous will enjoy fellowship with the angels and a renewed life on earth (41:2; 45:5; 51:4), and the wicked will descend to Sheol for eternal punishment. The wicked are the kings, the powerful, and the wealthy. Eschatological reversal is in the offing. Presently the righteous do not enjoy recognition. At the judgment, they will be revealed as the righteous. This corresponds to the revelation of their heavenly patron, a figure who goes by the titles Son of Man, Righteous One, Chosen One, and Messiah. He is presently hidden in heaven, but at the end of time he will be revealed (Collins 1980).

This heavenly figure has drawn much attention in scholarship, especially because of his similarity to the Son of Man in the Gospels. The figure in the *Similitudes* and the one in the Gospels are independent developments of Dan. 7. In Dan. 7, one like a son of man, that is, one who looks like a human—a common descriptor for an angel—receives sovereignty from God on his throne in heaven, while the people of the holy ones (Israel) receive sovereignty on earth. In Dan. 7, the one like a son of man is probably Michael. There is a similar close relationship between Enoch's Son of Man, called elect and righteous, and the righteous on earth who share the same description (Collins 1980).

There are three major judgment scenes in the *Similitudes*, one in each of the parables. Each is modeled on Dan. 7; they are three versions of the same event. God sits on his throne, while the Son of Man sits on his own throne and judges.

The kings, the powerful, and the wealthy do not acknowledge the Lord of Spirits and his Son of Man, and they oppose the righteous (see Dan. 1–6).

At the judgment, the powerful finally understand the consequences of their sinfulness and beg for another chance, but it is too late.

First Parable (Chaps. 38–44)

The first parable (38–44) opens by saying that judgment is coming. The righteous "will appear," the Son of Man "will appear" to the righteous, and light "will appear" to the chosen. "The secrets of the righteous shall be revealed." In the near future, it will be clear who is righteous. The powerful cannot even look upon the righteous in their new state. This is eschatological reversal. Power relations are upended.

Chapter 39 says that when the watchers descended, Enoch "received books of zeal and wrath, and books of disquiet and expulsion." Creation was alienated from God.

Enoch is carried up to heaven and sees the dwelling places of the deceased righteous. They abide with the angels. They intercede for their counterparts on earth—the hidden, righteous community. Enoch sees the Son of Man and "his dwelling-place under the wings of the Lord of Spirits." Soon, "righteousness shall prevail in his days." The "days of the Son of Man" (an expression found also in the Gospels) will be the opposite of the present.

Enoch joins the heavenly liturgy. The deceased righteous are in the company of God's angels, and with the angels they praise God for creation and for his foreknowledge, and they proclaim, "Holy, holy, holy, is the Lord of Spirits: He fills the earth with spirits." The song depends on the one Isaiah heard the angels singing in Isa. 6. Enoch heard the same hymn in *1 Enoch* 14, altered for context. In Isa. 6, the angels sing, "Holy, holy, holy is the Lord of hosts; the whole earth is full of his glory" (Isa. 6:3). The author of the *Similitudes* changes Isaiah's words to emphasize that God is the source of the spirits that fill the earth. The *Similitudes* regularly refer to God as the Lord of Spirits.

Angelology is a focus of chapter 40. Like Ezekiel, Enoch sees four presences before God. Enoch learns their secret names and functions. The first is Michael, and he continually praises God. He is merciful and long-suffering. He restrains God's wrath to grant humanity a chance to repent. The second is Raphael, who praises the Righteous One and the righteous ones. He has control over all diseases and wounds. The third is Gabriel. He intercedes for those dwelling on earth. He is over the "powers"—cosmic powers and superhuman beings. The fourth presence is Phanuel. He fends off the satans and forbids them to come before God to accuse humans. He "is set over the repentance unto hope of those that inherit eternal life."

In the next chapters, Enoch learns more about the universe. He sees the mansions in which the righteous dwell (see John 14:2–3), and he witnesses the wicked being dragged off to punishment. He learns the secrets of thunder and lightning, of wind and rain, of clouds and dew. He learns the routes of the sun and moon. The workings of the heavenly luminaries are tied to God's retributive scheme. The sun "changes often for a blessing or a curse." The division between day and night corresponds to the division between the righteous and the wicked.

Second Parable (Chaps. 45–57)

The second parable (45–57) also deals with judgment, particularly of the kings and powerful. Chapter 45 supplies a summary. Those who deny the Lord of Spirits will have no place, either in heaven or on earth, except the places of punishment. On the day of judgment, the Elect One, identical with the Son of Man, takes his throne to judge. Then he descends and dwells with the righteous; heaven and earth are transformed; sinners are destroyed.

Enoch now sees God and the Son of Man in a scene dependent on Dan. 7: "And there I saw One who had a head of days, and His head was white like wool, and with Him was another being whose countenance had the appearance of a man, and his face was full of graciousness, like one of the holy angels" (46:1). Enoch asks his angelic guide about the Son of Man. The Son of Man is surpassingly righteous, he reveals mysteries, the Lord of Spirits chose him, and he will defeat the powerful and the kings and the sinners. The sinners are earthly rulers. They presume to raise their hands against the stars and against the Most High. They trust in their own power and wealth, deny God, and make their own gods. They persecute those true to the Lord of Spirits.

Chapter 47 shows the positive side of judgment. The prayer and blood of the righteous ascend to God. The holy ones (angels) add their intercessory prayer. The Lord of Spirits takes his throne, the books of judgment are opened, and his heavenly retinue stands before him (see Dan. 7). The righteous rejoice because "the number of the righteous had been offered" (47:4), meaning that there was a preset number of righteous who had to be killed, and the number had finally been achieved.

Enoch sees heavenly fountains of wisdom and righteousness. The "thirsty" drink. Heaven is the scene of all wisdom and righteousness. Then we learn that the Son of Man either existed or was present in God's mind before all creation (48:2–3). God reveals him to the righteous. The wicked are given over to the righteous and are punished because they have denied the Lord of Spirits and his Messiah (the Son of Man). To the Son of Man is ascribed endless glory and might, and his function as judge is reaffirmed.

In chapter 51, Sheol yields up its inhabitants. This refers to resurrection. The rest of the second parable consists of Enoch's journey around the cosmos. Cosmological knowledge contains eschatological knowledge.

In the west, Enoch sees metal mountains—gold, silver, iron, copper, soft metal, and lead (chap. 52). They will melt when God comes at the eschaton. At that time, the strength of these metals will mean nothing.

Next Enoch beholds a deep valley in which people deposit gifts for God. The wicked are banished from the earth. Enoch sees angels preparing "instruments of Satan," instruments to punish the wicked. The Elect One causes the righteous "to appear," and they are no longer oppressed by the wicked. In the next chapter (54), Enoch observes a deep valley full of fire into which the kings and the mighty are hurled. He spots huge chains reserved for Azazel and his hosts, who will be covered with boulders till the final judgment. On the final day, the four archangels will cast the wicked angels into the fire. This is "vengeance on them for becoming subject to Satan, and leading astray those who dwell on earth" (54:6).

God releases the waters above the firmament and the waters below the earth; the wicked recognize their sinfulness and perish. The scene parallels the Genesis flood. As in Genesis, God relents and swears never to destroy humankind this way again. He places a sign in the heavens as a symbol of his promise. In Genesis, this is a rainbow. God decrees that next time all will be judged by his Elect One, who will sit on a throne.

Enoch sees angels with scourges (56). The interpreting angel tells him these are to punish the offspring of the evil angels. The angels return and attack the Persians and the Medes in the east. They stir up the kings to attack the holy land, but Jerusalem hinders them. The kings turn on one another and slaughter each other (56:7). The scene recalls the great final battle in Ezek. 38–39.

Countless wagons loaded with people converge on Israel (57). The angels in heaven take notice and the pillars of the earth tremble. It is the return of Israel's exiles, a common feature of eschatological scenarios.

Third Parable (Chaps. 58–69)

The opening paragraph of the third parable (58–69) extols the future state of the righteous. They are in the light of the sun and of eternal life. Their days are unending. The righteous seek out "the secrets of righteousness."

Chapter 60 introduces a fragment of the Book of Noah, since the seer in this section speaks of his grandfather as the seventh in line from Adam, a figure whom we know as Enoch. In chapter 60, the heavens shake and this distresses the angels. The seer is filled with fear. The angel speaks of the two primordial monsters—Leviathan in the sea and Behemoth on the land—who rise up at the eschaton and feast. The seer asks for information about the beasts and is told that this is hidden knowledge. But then he learns a good deal, not only about the monsters, but about the cosmos in general—thunder, lightning, wind, rain, the moon, and stars. The seer also learns that natural elements have guardian angels. For example, there is a spirit of the snow and one of the dew.

In chapter 61 the angels use measuring cords to search out and gather the righteous. This is equivalent to seeking out the "secrets of the depths of the earth" (61:5). They are brought together with the angels, the various types of whom are specified, to praise God. This is followed in chapter 62 with another version of the judgment scene. The wicked—the kings, the mighty, and the exalted—appear before God, who commands them to behold the Righteous One, seated on a glorious throne. The wicked recognize his power and sovereignty and are afraid. He was until now hidden. They beg for mercy. The elect take pleasure in seeing God's wrath destroy the wicked with the sword. The wicked are gone forever, and the righteous live with the Son of Man. They don glorious clothes that never fade.

In chapter 63, focus is on the wicked—the kings, the mighty, the powerful, and those who possess the earth. They finally recognize God's sovereignty. They praise God and beg for mercy. They praise him for his deep and innumerable secrets. They understand that they were wrong to depend on their own strength and royalty. It is too late. They are driven from God's presence to eternal punishment. Enoch also sees "in that place," the place of punishment, the angels who descended from heaven and illegitimately taught secrets to humans (chap. 64).

Chapter 65 reintroduces Noah. He goes to his grandfather, Enoch, because he is terrified at the impending destruction. Enoch tells him that the destruction is necessary because people on earth have

> learned all the secrets of the angels, and all the violence of the Satans, and all their powers—the most secret ones—and all the power of those who practice sorcery, and the power of witchcraft, and the power of those who make molten images for the whole earth: And how silver is produced from the dust of the earth, and how soft metal originates in the earth. For lead and tin are not produced from the earth like the first: it is a fountain that produces them, and an angel stands therein, and that angel is pre-eminent. (65:6–8)

Noah will survive the destruction because he is innocent "concerning the secrets." Noah's seed will include kings and righteous ones.

God orders the angels of punishment, also called the angels of the waters, to hold back the waters so that the ark can be built. In a change from Genesis, where Noah builds the ark, here the angels build it. The evil angels are thrown into the valley of fire that Enoch saw to the west, near the metallic mountains. Hot streams are produced that smell of sulfur, and they are the source of hot springs used by the wealthy of the earth. This is a possible reference to hot springs at Callirrhoe, where the rich sought cures. Herod himself used the springs. Those springs will, through the agency of angels, turn scalding and torture those who sought bodily comfort in them. The source of their luxury will become an instrument of punishment.

Chapter 69 contains dense angelology where twenty-one angelic leaders are named. Problems on earth are attributed to the angels. Among the problems are angelic rebellion; illicit sharing of heavenly secrets with humans; Eve's sin;

knowledge of weaponry; war; writing; and the afflictions of demons, serpents, and the fruit of the womb so that it dies.

An angel named Kasbeel is the angel of "the oath." The oath is the power of God by which the entire universe came to be and is maintained. The oath is powerless unless one is in possession of the secret name. To have control of oath and name is to possess God's omnipotence. Michael guards the name. With the oath and name secure, the universe remains safe, and the angels who have charge of the universe rejoice. The idea that the oath might fall into the wrong hands raises the apocalyptic idea that the universe is under abiding threat.

Two Endings (Chaps. 70–71)

There are two different endings to the *Similitudes*, the first in chapter 70 and the second in chapter 71. Chapter 70 is short. Enoch is brought to heaven into fellowship with the angels and the righteous who have died.

Chapter 71 gives a fuller picture of heaven. Enoch sees angels, streams of fire, and God himself, before whom he prostrates himself. Michael takes him by the hand, lifts him up, and shows him the secrets of righteousness and the secrets of the cosmos. Then Enoch sees a structure made of crystals, surrounded by fire, and guarded by the cherubim, seraphim, and ophanim. He sees the four archangels coming in and out of the crystal house. Finally, they come out with God himself, and Enoch prostrates himself, is transformed, and blesses God. There is a startling moment where the angel tells Enoch that he, Enoch, is the Son of Man. This puzzled the original translator so much that he emended the text to read, "This is the Son of Man," as if the angel were indicating a third person (Charles 1913). However, we wonder why Enoch would now be identified with the Son of Man when there was no hint of this anywhere in the *Similitudes*. The easiest solution is to see Chapter 71 as an addition to the original book.

Fourth Ezra

Fourth Ezra is one of the most tightly constructed and coherent apocalypses extant. It was written around the turn of the second century CE in response to the Roman destruction of Jerusalem and its temple. Like other works then, it speaks of Rome but does so in terms of Babylon (Stone 1981). The Babylonian experience was so traumatic for Israel that it became a paradigm for the Roman catastrophe, which was equally traumatic.

Fourth Ezra is chapters 3–14 of *2 Esdras*, found in the Apocrypha of the Christian Old Testament. It is Jewish, while the two chapters at the beginning of *2 Esdras* and the two that end it are Christian additions.

Ezra's Change of Heart

Fourth Ezra is in seven sections. In the first three, Ezra argues with the angel Uriel about the destruction of Jerusalem and Israel's sufferings. The fifth and sixth sections are more conventional apocalyptic visions. In the seventh section, Ezra receives ninety-four books of revelation. *Fourth Ezra*'s central section consists of Ezra's vision of the new Jerusalem.

A central problem is why Ezra changes from one who challenges God in the manner of Job to a more conventional seer, who accepts divine revelation without resistance. The key lies in the central section. That section begins with Ezra's challenge to God, but then he encounters a woman mourning over the death of her son. Ezra gives the woman advice, and then she is transformed into the new Zion.

Ezra's change of heart should not cause us to underestimate the genuineness of Ezra's challenges to God. Taken together with the book as a whole, they constitute a powerful theodicy, a defense of God's justice. The author's choice of using the name of Ezra makes the theodicy even more powerful. Ezra is a Jewish hero. He was a righteous scribe and priest who brought the written Torah to Judah from Babylon in the mid-fifth century BCE. *Fourth Ezra* also gives Ezra a key role in the restoration of Torah after Jerusalem's destruction (seventh section; chapter 14). Ezra's struggles with God's justice are likely genuine expressions of the author's own deeply felt struggles. A challenge to God's ways is more convincing in one whose loyalty to God is unquestionable than from a lesser figure.

Section One (3:1–5:19)

This section introduces the seer. He allegedly writes thirty years after the destruction of Jerusalem by the Babylonians, which would place its fictive setting around the middle of the sixth century BCE. The number thirty depends on Ezekiel, and need not be taken literally. It is likely that the work was really composed in the last decade of the first century or the beginning of the second century CE.

As he lies in his bed, Ezra becomes agitated because he sees that Israel suffers while Babylon (Rome) lives in luxury. This is unfair. Israel is sinful; Rome is more so. This injustice leads him to review history for answers. His historical review takes the form of a prayer; Ezra seeks direct confrontation with God, as did Job.

Ezra begins history with Adam, who disobeys God. God "immediately" . . . "appointed death for him and for his descendants" (3:7). God is quick to punish and favors extreme retribution. All humanity follows Adam, and God does nothing to stop them. Later, God destroys sinful humanity with the flood, sparing only the righteous Noah and his family.

Humanity soon returns to sinfulness. God chooses Abraham from humanity. God loves Abraham, makes a covenant with him, and reveals to him "the end of times." In apocalypses, major righteous figures of the past like Moses and Abraham often receive secret, eschatological knowledge, even when the Bible makes no mention of it.

God gives Israel the Torah, accompanied by cosmic disturbances that highlight the event's immense importance. The giving of the Torah is good, but ineffective: "Yet you did not take away their evil heart from them, so that your law might produce fruit in them" (3:20). The result is ceaseless sin. The evil heart is like the evil inclination (*yeṣer*) in humans that surfaces in the Dead Sea Scrolls and later in Rabbinic literature.

God chooses David to build him a city, Jerusalem, and sacrifices are offered in it. Its citizens continue to sin, because they still have an evil heart. God surrenders the city to the Babylonians. This brings the author up to his fictive present. Ironically, the nation that has done most to please God is the lowliest. So where is God's justice?

The angel Uriel asks Ezra whether he considers himself capable of understanding God's ways. Ezra naively answers, "Yes." The angel challenges him to solve one of three problems. He asks Ezra to weigh fire, measure wind, or to call back a day that has passed. Ezra is stymied. The angel pushes further, challenging him to tell him about the depths of the sea, the water above the firmament, the entrances to Hades, or the ways into paradise. Again, Ezra is at a loss. Uriel asks Ezra how he can possibly understand God's ways if he cannot understand even the things with which he has grown up—rain, wind, and days. Ezra protests that it would be better not to exist at all than to suffer and not comprehend why. This is the quandary of humanity apart from apocalyptic knowledge—humanity has enough knowledge to cause it anguish, but not enough to answer its crucial questions.

Unmoved, the angel continues to put Ezra in his place. He asks Ezra whether the forest should make war on the sea, or the sea to fight the forest. Ezra answers that the place of one is not the place of the other. Uriel turns the metaphor against Ezra, saying that one who belongs on earth cannot presume to understand what is in the heavens. Ezra objects that he is not asking about heaven, but about what humans experience on earth.

This fascinating dialogue between Uriel and Ezra is a sophisticated discussion of epistemology—what can humans know and how can they know it? Ezra thinks that his questions are straightforward. They concern not divine secrets or cosmic knowledge, but everyday experience. He does not grasp that understanding everyday experience is impossible without esoteric knowledge available only through direct revelation. He is in fact asking about what is above the heavens, but he does not get the connection. He is asking about God and God's plans. Unaided human reason is incapable of that knowledge unless it is granted from on high. Ezra does not think of himself as an apocalyptic seer, but he learns that he must become one to find answers to his earthly questions.

Finally the angel imparts traditional apocalyptic knowledge. He reveals that the present world is so inundated with evil that it cannot be where the righteous will live in God's grace. A grain of evil has been planted in Adam's heart, and the harvest must come before the present age is ended. Then the new age can come. This lays out the doctrine of the two ages.

Ezra wants to know when the end of the old world and the arrival of the new will happen. The angel counsels patience, for God's times are unalterable. The new world will come "when the number of those like yourselves is completed" (4:36). The angel confirms that there is much less time left than has passed already.

Uriel describes the end. The earth is terrified, knowledge and wisdom disappear, the earth becomes desolate, the sun shines at night and the moon during the day, wood drips blood, the stones speak, and the stars fall. The cosmos unravels and chaos advances. The angel says, "These are the signs I am permitted to tell you" (5:13).

Section Two (5:20–6:34)

Ezra begins with a prayer challenging God (5:23–30). God chose Israel out of all humanity. Ezra asks why, then, it has been handed over to the nations. He even suggests that God hates Israel.

Uriel objects to Ezra's presumption that he loves Israel more than God does. Ezra says he wishes only to understand God's ways. At first Uriel answers as in the first dialogue. He says that Ezra cannot comprehend. Ezra persists. The angel tells him that the earth is growing old. Ezra requests that God directly supplement the eschatological knowledge supplied in the previous dialogue. God tells him not to be disturbed if the ground begins to shake. The end will terrify the earth.

God says that first comes the completion of Zion's humiliation. A seal will be placed on the passing age, bringing it to an end. Books of judgment will be opened. Year-old children will speak as adults, and women will give birth to fully formed babies after three or four months. Cultivated land will be desolate, and full storehouses will be empty. A trumpet will sound, striking terror into everyone's heart. Friends will make war on friends, the earth will be terrified, and fountains will cease to flow. The righteous will rediscover truth, overcome corruptibility, and live apart from deceit and without the presence of the wicked.

Section Three (6:35–9:25)

Ezra's opening prayer goes through the six days of creation, noting God's power and purpose. Noteworthy is the mention of the mythical sea monster Leviathan and the land monster Behemoth. In the sixth day, humanity was created. God's creation culminated in Israel's existence and was for Israel's sake. The seer remembers that God had said the other nations were as spittle to him (Isa. 40:15). Now the gentiles rule Israel. He asks how long the present situation will last.

Uriel says that one must navigate the "narrow" passages of the present age so as to arrive at the blissful future. Ezra should not concentrate on the sufferings of the present but look to the future.

Ezra objects that most humans will not enjoy the future age. The angel is unmoved: "Let many perish who are now living, rather than that the law of God that is set before them be disregarded!" (7:20). The righteous will see God's wonders and experience Jerusalem's renewal. The Messiah will appear, rule for four hundred years, and die along with the rest of humanity. This is followed by seven days of primordial silence, preface to the new creation.

Next comes the last judgment. Everyone is raised from the dead and is judged by God on his throne. One of two destinations awaits each individual—the pit of torment or paradise. Those raised from the dead see a world different from the one to which they were accustomed. Natural elements have passed away— sun, moon, stars, clouds, thunder, lightning, water, air, darkness or morning, seasons, heat, cold, hail, rain, and dew. The judgment will take seven years. God assures Ezra that he has revealed these secrets to no one except Ezra (7:44).

Fourth Ezra provides no comfort for the weak and sinful. Perhaps few apocalypses do, but this work is particularly contemptuous of the sinful. Ezra finds no comfort in divine wisdom. His response borders on despair. Humans are tormented because they are headed for punishment and they know it.

Ezra learns that those who die before the end will immediately begin to experience reward or punishment. *Fourth Ezra* is detailed about this in-between state. Asked by Ezra whether intercession in the afterlife is possible on behalf of others, the angel says that death is final. One's fate is determined at that point. Despairingly, Ezra addresses Adam, asking him why he has done such damage to humankind (7:118).

Ezra appeals to God's mercy. He hopefully regales God with descriptions of his nature—merciful, gracious, patient, bountiful, compassionate, a giver of goodness—all to no avail. Ezra argues that human sinfulness gives God a chance to show mercy. This mercy is necessary, for all have sinned. "For in this, O Lord, your righteousness and goodness will be declared, when you are merciful to those who have no store of good works" (8:36; see Rom. 5:6–8).

Ezra again asks when the end will come. God lists the usual signs— "earthquakes, tumult of peoples, intrigues of nations, wavering of leaders, confusion of princes" (9:3). Political issues dominate. Then the righteous experience salvation in the land of Israel.

Section Four (9:26–10:59)

The fourth section again begins with Ezra's prayer expressing unhappiness with God's ways. Then he meets a woman in mourning over the loss of her son. She explains that she lived with her husband for thirty years childless, and that then she received a son. On his wedding day he died. Ezra tells her that her grief is nothing compared with that of Zion. His advice to her is the following: "If you acknowledge the decree of God to be just, you will receive your son back in due time, and will be praised among women" (10:16). Ironically, he becomes the spokesperson for theodicy. He defends God's justice.

As Ezra speaks, the woman's face shines and flashes like lightning. Suddenly she is transformed into a city being built. Uriel explains that the woman is Zion, her thirty years of barrenness are when no sacrifice had yet been offered in her, the life of her son is the time of the temple, and his dying symbolizes Jerusalem's destruction. Uriel instructs Ezra to tour the city and to stay until the following night, when God will reveal more to him about the "last days."

Section Five (11:1–12:51)

This vision contains no confrontation between Ezra and God. Ezra sees an eagle arising from the sea with twelve wings and three heads. As in Dan. 7, the sea is the origin of forces opposed to God. The eagle is Rome. It is noteworthy that at the same time in history, there is a Jewish (4 Ezra) and a Christian (Revelation) apocalypse each of which portrays Rome as some sort of beast emerging from the sea, depending on Dan. 7. What happens with the eagle mirrors Roman history, from Julius Caesar to the Flavians, whose dynasty ended in 96 CE. Then Ezra sees a lion indicting the eagle. It accuses the eagle of atrocities, including conquering the entire earth, subjecting it to terror, oppressing everyone, using deceit, harming the meek, and destroying the righteous. God has taken notice. The eagle is burned up and the entire earth is terrified (12:3).

God explains that the eagle is the fourth beast that Daniel saw arise from the sea. The lion is the Messiah, David's descendant (Gen. 49:9). He will judge and destroy the wicked, the Roman Empire in particular. He will free the righteous and bring them salvation in the land of Israel. He then instructs Ezra, "Therefore write all these things that you have seen in a book, put it in a hidden place; and you shall teach them to the wise among your people, whose hearts you know are able to comprehend and keep these secrets" (12:37–38).

Section Six (13:1–58)

Ezra sees one like a human being, an allusion to the one like a son of man in Dan. 7. He also emerges from the sea. He flies around the world on clouds; wherever he looks, everything trembles, and when he speaks, those who hear him melt. An innumerable multitude gathers from all over the earth to war against him. He carves out a great mountain for himself and flies onto it. When the peoples attack, fire from his mouth annihilates them. The man descends the mountain, and a peaceable multitude gathers to him comprised of the happy, the sorrowful, the bound, and some who bring other people as offerings.

Ezra receives an interpretation of the vision. The sea usually symbolizes forces opposed to God, but here it represents the mysterious and powerful universe of which only God has full knowledge and control. The man's origin in the sea indicates that he is the one "whom the Most High has been keeping for many ages" (13:26). This man will liberate God's creation.

In the end, God will deliver the righteous. In those days, humans will make war on each other, and "then my Son will be revealed, whom you saw as a man coming up from the sea" (13:32). Three times God calls the one like a man his Son (13:32, 37, 52), a messianic term (Yarbro Collins and Collins 2008). When the Son appears, the nations unite against him.

> But he shall stand on the top of Mount Zion. And Zion shall come and be made manifest to all people, prepared and built, as you saw the mountain carved out without hands. Then he, my Son, will reprove the assembled nations for their ungodliness (this was symbolized by the storm), and will reproach them to their face with their evil thoughts and the torments with which they are to be tortured (which were symbolized by the flames), and will destroy them without effort by means of the law (which was symbolized by the fire). (13:35–38)

The final battle transpires at Jerusalem. The Son judges the sinful nations and decrees their torture. God's law destroys them.

The eschatological victory won, a peaceable multitude gathers to the Son. They are the lost tribes of Israel. The northern tribes disappeared when the Assyrian Empire conquered and deported them in 721 BCE. Since then, tradition has speculated about their fate. Eschatological scenarios frequently envisage their ultimate return.

Section Seven (14:1–48)

God's voice comes out of a bush. God draws the specific parallel between Ezra and Moses. God says about Moses, "I told him many wondrous things, and showed him the secrets of the times and declared to him the end of the times. Then I commanded him, saying, 'These words you shall publish openly, and these you shall keep secret'" (14:5–6). Moses published the Torah but also received secret revelation. God tells Ezra that he will soon be taken up to be with his Son and the other righteous. He should instruct the wise among the people and prepare to depart. The end is imminent, and as it gets closer, conditions on earth will get worse.

Ezra asks God to allow him to reconstruct revelation, which was burned in the destruction of Jerusalem, to make it available to humans yet to be born. God agrees. He tells Ezra to be in the wilderness for forty days, the same length of time Moses passed on Mount Sinai receiving the Torah. He is to take with

Fourth Ezra: Apocalypse and Apocalypticism

- It has the form of an apocalypse.
- Two worlds are described: the present is sinful and corruptible; the future is perfect and radically different from this one in its cosmic nature, social makeup (no evil), and lack of ills.
- There is strict social and ethical dualism.
- Adam's sin affects all of humanity.
- Humanity's evil inclination leads to rampant sinfulness.
- Apocalyptic knowledge is necessary to understand history and the present.
- A messiah is described in some detail in two different scenarios, and in passing in another.
- Esoteric knowledge surpasses Torah.
- The end is near.
- There is a set number of people who must live before the end.
- It is difficult to get into the next world.
- Solomon's temple is destroyed, clearing the way for the next steps in history; ultimately, there is an eternal, eschatological temple.
- There are complex visions that must be interpreted.
- God's enemies are destroyed by superhuman means.
- The sea plays a role, both positive and negative.
- There appear the two primordial monsters, Leviathan and Behemoth.
- Angels, especially Uriel, are very active, revealing and debating with Ezra.
- There is a last judgment, with eternal rewards and punishments.
- Resurrection occurs.
- There is a temporary messianic kingdom.
- The state of the dead between death and the last judgment is described.
- Apocalyptic knowledge is given to Abraham.
- The end is characterized by typical cosmic and social signs.
- Israel is reunited, including all twelve tribes.

him five highly trained scribes. God explains, "I will light in your heart the lamp of understanding, which shall not be put out until what you are about to write is finished. And when you have finished, some things you shall make public, and some you shall deliver in secret to the wise" (14:25–26).

In the wilderness, Ezra drinks a cup, is filled with wisdom, and begins to dictate. The scribes take turns writing, but Ezra works without a break. At the end of forty days, the Most High tells him, "Make public the twenty-four books that you wrote first, and let the worthy and the unworthy read them; but keep the seventy that were written last, in order to give them to the wise among your people. For in them is the spring of understanding, the fountain of wisdom, and the river of knowledge" (14:45–47). The secret revelation is

Fig. 6. The Romans built the fortress Antonia to control the temple. This photograph of a model illustrates both the Hellenistic features of Herod's temple and how visible Roman power was to the Jews, even as they worshiped at their most sacred space. (Chris Miller)

superior to the public revelation. While the written Torah is given to everyone, the secret revelation is given only to the wise. God says it is these last books that truly contain understanding, wisdom, and knowledge. Apocalyptic knowledge surpasses Torah.

Second Baruch (The Syriac Apocalypse of Baruch)

Second Baruch and Fourth Ezra

Second Baruch was written around the same time as *4 Ezra* and in response to the same set of circumstances—the destruction of Jerusalem in 70 CE. Like *4 Ezra*, its fictional setting is the original destruction by the Babylonians. Baruch was Jeremiah's scribe; he experienced the Babylonian destruction firsthand. Also like *4 Ezra*, *2 Baruch* is in seven sections. The two books address a number of similar issues and do not always agree. For example, *4 Ezra*'s seer blames Adam for human sinfulness, while *2 Baruch* insists that each person is the Adam of his or her own soul. The original language of both works was Hebrew, and both were written in Jewish Palestine. As is the case with Daniel and the *Animal Apocalypse*, we have two apocalypses written at about the same time and addressing the same circumstances. In each case, the result is two quite different works.

Fourth Ezra and *2 Baruch* are clearly related in some way, but just how is debated. It is possible that *2 Baruch* was written as an alternative to *4 Ezra.* Unlike Ezra, Baruch accepts God's will throughout the apocalypse. His questions aim at understanding God's ways, but he does not resist as does Ezra. Similarly, there is not the degree of tension between human reason and apocalyptic revelation that we find in *4 Ezra.*

Section One (1:1–9:2)

Baruch experiences Jerusalem's destruction firsthand and shows that it is not a victory for God's enemies but is God's act. The book begins with God's word coming to Baruch (a prophetic formula) and announcing that the sins of those in Judah exceed those of the northern tribes of Israel. Baruch is ordered to depart from Jerusalem along with Jeremiah and the rest of the righteous, because their works and prayers preserve the city.

Baruch reacts to the news of Jerusalem's destruction with grief. He asks questions that reveal how he sees Jerusalem's religious and cosmic significance. He thinks that if Jerusalem is gone, the name of Israel will be forgotten, there will be no one to sing God's praises, no one will learn the Torah, and the world itself might revert to primordial silence.

God answers that punishment will be temporary, and the world is not about to pass from existence. The earthly Jerusalem is not the one about which he made promises. That one is in heaven. It was revealed to Adam, Abraham, and Moses. When Adam sinned, he lost the vision of the heavenly Jerusalem as he did paradise. God relativizes the value of the earthly Jerusalem by denying that his promises concerning Zion really apply to it (Murphy 1985). The destruction is an eschatological event, but Baruch allows it too much significance.

The earthly Zion is not equivalent to the heavenly, but it still is God's earthly dwelling. God and the righteous must depart before it can be destroyed. Then angels destroy the city. Baruch is now swept up by the Spirit to view Jerusalem's destruction. The angels hide the temple's sacred vessels "until the last times," when they will be restored. The temple will be rebuilt in eschatological times.

Section Two (10:1–20:6)

Jeremiah is to travel to Babylonia with the exiles, a detail at variance with the biblical account, while Baruch awaits God's revelation amidst Jerusalem's ruins. The revelation concerns "what will befall at the end of days" (10:2). Baruch laments before the temple, inviting nature and humanity to join him. He blames the temple priests for being poor stewards of God's sanctuary and tells them to fling the temple keys into heaven, relinquishing priestly authority (10:18). The lament tells God's enemies that temple accoutrements will be burned rather than surrendered, and it bemoans their prosperity in the face of Zion's suffering. Baruch expresses confidence that the pleasant situation of the enemies will come to an end. It is only through God's long-suffering that they have not already been destroyed.

Baruch is to be present at the consummation of history to tell the nations the reason for their punishment. He can do this because he has witnessed the Babylonians' violation of the temple. If they ask how long they must suffer, Baruch is to tell them that for as long as they have enjoyed the fine wine (prosperity and happiness) they must now taste the dregs (punishment), for God is "no respecter of persons." If his own people cannot escape justice, then surely his enemies cannot do so.

Sounding a bit like Ezra, Baruch raises objections. He says that there are many sinners and sinful nations in the present, but they will not be at the consummation to get what they deserve. He also asks what good righteousness has done for the just, for they are among the exiles. He declares that God's ways are inscrutable. Even if the future vindicates the righteous, most are not in that category. He includes himself in the latter group, as did Ezra. Finally, Baruch notes that the world was made for humanity and not the converse, but that now humanity departs while the world remains.

God answers as in *4 Ezra*. Humans had the Torah as a guide but deliberately sinned. The present is tough for the righteous, but the future holds bliss. Baruch objects that life is too short to achieve righteousness. God insists that length of life is irrelevant. Adam lived for the better part of a millennium and sinned. Moses lived a mere 120 years and was just. Baruch counters that there are many more people who follow Adam's example than there are like Moses. God reminds Baruch that he, not Baruch, judges, and that Baruch should turn his attention to the end of things.

Chapter 20 proclaims that the destruction of Jerusalem serves God's purposes in that it hastens the eschaton. It is God who has "taken away Zion" (20:2).

Section Three (21:1–34:1)

Baruch's opening prayer praises God as the creator of all, omniscient and omnipotent. He seems more optimistic than before about how many righteous there are, claiming that there are "not a few" (21:9).

Baruch's dissatisfactions go beyond the immediate crisis of Jerusalem. He is unhappy with the nature of the world itself. He says, "If there were this life only, which belongs to all men, nothing could be more bitter than this" (21:13). Human life is changeable, and no matter how good things might be at any given moment, they are bound to deteriorate. Strength turns to sickness, satiety to famine, and beauty to ugliness. "The nature of man is always changeable" (21:15). Without a "consummation," all would be in vain. This complaint fits Baruch's frequent denotation of the world and humanity as "corruptible." It is an almost philosophical distinction between change and permanence, and it would hold even if sin were not the issue (Murphy 1986).

God's long-suffering will soon run out. The Messiah will appear. The two primordial monsters—Leviathan in the sea and Behemoth on the land—will be food for the humans who are left. The earth will enjoy miraculous fertility. Health will reign, and manna will descend from heaven. This is "the consummation of time" (29:8). After this, the Messiah will return to heaven. A temporary messianic kingdom appears also in 4 Ezra 7.

There will be a general resurrection. "All those who have fallen asleep in hope of him shall rise again" (30:2). The souls of the wicked will despair, knowing that their torment has arrived.

The section ends with Baruch's speech. He exhorts the people to mourn for Zion and says, "Lo! the days come, when everything that is shall be the prey of corruption and be as though it had not been" (31:5). He says that the people will be protected if they have the Torah in their hearts. In a little while the building of Zion (Solomon's temple) will be shaken in order to be rebuilt (the second temple). That second building will also be destroyed and will be "desolate until the time" (32:3). Finally, it will be "renewed in glory" forever (the eschatological temple).

Section Four (35:1–47:1)

Baruch receives a complex vision of a forest in a plain surrounded by mountains (chap. 36). A vine and a fountain arise and cast down the forest. One fallen cedar is brought to the vine, which chastises it because the cedar represents a conquering and oppressive empire. In the author's real situation, this is Rome. The cedar is told to lie in ashes with the rest of the forest and be tormented, and that the future holds still more torment. The vision ends with the vine prospering in the plain, now full of flowers.

The interpretation does not fit the vision. It employs the four-kingdom schema seen in Dan. 2 and 7. This has no counterpart in the vision. The fourth kingdom is the ultimate oppressor of the world and of Israel. The vine and fountain are the Messiah. The cedar is the last leader of the fourth kingdom. He is brought before the Messiah on Mount Zion, judged, and executed. There follows a messianic era, where the Messiah reigns in the holy land with the people. "And his principate will stand for ever, until the world of corruption is at an end, and until the times aforesaid are fulfilled" (40:3). Again there is a temporary messianic kingdom that is not history's ultimate goal. Even though the evil empire is gone, it will still be a "world of corruption." Again we find that sin is not the only problem in this world. The world itself is imperfect, corruptible, and temporary.

Baruch asks who will participate in the messianic kingdom. He knows that there are some who were once subject to the law but abandoned it (apostates), and others who once did not know the law but adopted it (proselytes to Judaism). God answers in ethnic terms. Those who left the people and mingled with the seed of people who themselves mix with other peoples are lost. Those who separate from the peoples and join the unmingled people of Israel will be saved. "Corruption" takes the former. Ethnicity is flexible, and one can leave or join the chosen people (Johnson Hodge 2007).

Baruch's exhortation concludes the section. The exhortation takes the form of a testament, since God has told Baruch that he will die. He commands the people to obey the law. If they do so, they will leave this world and enter the next. The present world is beset by sin and by imperfection both. But they must remember that God is "no respecter of persons" (44:4).

> Because whatever is now is nothing, but that which shall be is very great. For everything that is corruptible shall pass away, and everything that dies shall depart, and all the present time shall be forgotten, nor shall there be any remembrance of the present time, which is defiled with evils. For that which runs now runs unto vanity, and that which prospers shall quickly fall and be humiliated. For that which is to be shall be the object of desire, and for that which comes afterwards shall we hope; for it is a time that passes not away, and the hour comes which abides forever. And the new world comes which does not turn to corruption those who depart to its blessedness, and has no mercy on those who depart to torment, and leads not to perdition those who live in it. (44:8–12)

Section Five (47:2–52:7)

Baruch's opening prayer extols God's omniscience and omnipotence. He implores God's mercy. Israel trusts Torah, and it does not mingle with the nations. God insists on strict retribution. He describes the chaos of the end time. Wisdom disappears, and humans attack each other and practice oppression. God highlights the social upheaval that accompanies the end, not the physical manifestations that apocalypses often stress.

In 48:42–43, Baruch blames Adam and Eve for humanity's situation. He reminds God that humanity is his creature, and that from the time of Adam's creation, God has known humanity. But this is not his more fundamental view. Elsewhere he unequivocally blames individuals for their own fate. Of course, tension between force of historical circumstance and individual responsibility is a hallmark not only of apocalypticism but of human philosophical and theological thought in general.

Where Ezra had to be forced by the angel and God to concentrate on the righteous instead of on sinners, Baruch turns to the righteous of his own initiative (48:48). For them, the present world is transitory and full of labor, but the next world will be unending and full of light.

Baruch asks what form people will take in the new world. Will they have the same bodies, these that are caught up in evils and imprison people? God answers that when the dead are raised, they will appear initially as they did in life. Everyone will be recognizable, so all will know who is good and bad. This serves the cause of retribution. Then sinners will become even worse in appearance than now. Those who obeyed the law will become glorious, and they will enter "the world which does not die" (50:3). While the wicked waste away, the righteous attain the splendor of the angels and the stars. They will see the world now hidden; time will not age them. They will see paradise, the living creatures beneath God's throne, and the angelic armies. Their glory will surpass even that of the angels.

Section Six (53:1–77:17)

Baruch sees a cloud arise from the sea. At its summit is lightning. The cloud produces twelve downpours. Some are black and some are bright, but the black outnumber the bright. After the twelve waters, more black waters, now mixed with fire, devastate the earth. The lightning casts the cloud to earth and assumes universal dominion. Twelve rivers arise from the sea, surround the lightning, and submit to it.

Baruch's prayer for interpretation praises God's omniscience and omnipotence. God reveals his ways to the righteous. Baruch praises God's justice in punishing the sinners, something that Ezra never does. This leads him to comment once more on Adam. Although Adam was the first to sin and brought "untimely" death on everyone, still each individual is responsible for his or her eternal fate (54:15). "Adam is therefore not the cause, save of his own soul, but each of us has been the Adam of his own soul" (54:19).

Ramiel interprets the vision. The cloud is human history. Each downpour is a different period. As Ramiel says later, "The Most High made division from the beginning, because he alone knows what will befall" (69:2).

The first waters, which are black, represent Adam's period and his sin. This brought the world untimely death, grief, anguish, pain, disease, "the begetting of children," and "the passion of parents" (56:6). This exceeds what the Bible attributes to the sin of Adam and Eve. Genesis says that the woman will have pain in childbearing, but 2 Baruch blames procreation and sexual passion on Adam's sin. He is also blamed for the angels' rebellion when they descended from heaven and had sexual intercourse with women. This radically rereads the story of the watchers.

The second waters are bright. They are Abraham's time. In accord with other Jewish tradition, Abraham obeyed Torah, an anachronism. Abraham receives apocalyptic knowledge—the last judgment, a renewed world, and life everlasting (57:1–2).

The third waters are black and symbolize the sinfulness of all nations, particularly Egypt.

The fourth waters are bright. They represent Moses's time. Cosmic disturbances accompany the giving of the Torah, indicating its importance. Moses also receives apocalyptic knowledge, but this time it is remarkably full. The extent of what is revealed to him about the universe, unseen powers, and future events makes him one of the most important apocalyptic seers in history.

The fifth waters, which are black, denote the time of the judges. The Amorites sinned during that time, and Israel was entangled in their sins. Amorite sin is primarily religious—incantations, mysteries, and pollution.

The sixth waters are bright and correspond to the time of David and Solomon. Their era is romanticized, as is common in Jewish and Christian tradition. The temple was built. Enemy blood was shed, which is justified because the enemies were sinful. Israel ruled over nations. It was a time of peace, prosperity, and wisdom. The holy land was favored by God above all lands.

The seventh waters are dark and represent the reign of Jeroboam I, king of the northern kingdom of Israel after the split between north and south (Judah). Jeroboam sinned especially in founding two cultic sites in the north, one at Bethel and one at Dan. The sinful northern tribes were exiled. The author throws in a general judgment of gentiles: "Regarding the Gentiles it was tedious to tell how they always wrought impiety and wickedness, and never wrought righteousness" (62:6).

The eighth waters are bright and stand for the reign of Hezekiah, one of the few kings the Bible considers righteous.

The ninth waters are black, representing Manasseh's kingship. Manasseh succeeded Hezekiah. He violated the cult of Israel's God and indulged in foreign religious practices. The Bible blames him for the Babylonian exile (2 Kings 24:2–3).

King Josiah, represented by the tenth waters, which are bright, is another biblical hero. He followed the example of Hezekiah and reversed the evils of Manasseh. Ramiel says that he will enjoy eternal reward, and that it is on account of people like him that the future world will come.

The black eleventh waters are Baruch's present. Zion is delivered up; the gentiles boast over it; Israel will dwell among the gentiles in exile and shame; because of Zion's defeat, the gentiles' idolatries are the more prevalent; and the Babylonian king boasts before God. But he shall fall in the end. Even in Zion, there is "the smoke of impiety" everywhere (67:6).

The twelfth waters signify the future for Baruch, and they are bright. They begin with tribulation for the righteous, but then they will be saved and witness their enemies' fall. They will rejoice and Zion will be rebuilt, but "not fully as in the beginning" (68:6). This expresses dissatisfaction with the second temple. Afterwards, there will be "the fall of many nations" (68:7).

Finally, there is a downpour of waters that follows the twelve previous downpours and is blacker than any of them. It is equivalent to the tribulation. This must take place at the end of the Second Temple period. Society breaks down. The poor have more than the rich, the lowly rule over the honorable, there is incessant fighting, the wise are silent, there is an earthquake, famine,

Second Baruch: Apocalypse and Apocalypticism

- *Second Baruch* is an apocalypse. Baruch is the seer. God or Ramiel is the revealer. Baruch learns about the future and about the unseen world.
- Jerusalem and its temple are destroyed by God's angels.
- There is the periodization of history.
- A set number of people must live in the world before the eschaton.
- There is a messianic age. It is temporary; during that time the Messiah rules and presides over a transition to the permanent renewal.
- The messianic age is near.
- The present world is full of evil and is deteriorating.
- There are two worlds. The present is full of suffering, especially for the righteous. The future holds eternal reward for the good and eternal punishment for the wicked.
- There is a general resurrection. The book speculates on what shape the risen will assume.
- Apocalyptic secrets were revealed to Adam, Abraham, and Moses.
- Frequent reference is made to the last times and the consummation.
- The dominion of the gentiles will soon end.
- Length of life is unimportant.
- There is social dualism: righteous and sinners.
- The delay of the eschaton is due to God's long-suffering.
- General judgment occurs.
- Leviathan and Behemoth will be food for the elect in the future.
- The heavenly manna will come down to earth once more.
- Those in the land of Israel will be saved.
- There are two main visions complete with interpretation.
- Baruch's testament includes a typical apocalyptic exhortation.
- The wicked will be punished with fire.
- God is on a throne, beneath which are four living creatures, surrounded by a myriad of angels.
- Wisdom comes from heaven. In the final evil time, it disappears from the earth.
- Knowledge of history's meaning comes only through revelation.
- There will be an ingathering of all Israel—those of the north and those of the south—so that the twelve tribes will be reconstituted.
- God's justice overrides his mercy.
- Adam affected all of subsequent history, but personal responsibility is defended forcefully.
- One should rejoice in present suffering; it cannot compare to the bliss to come.
- Humans cannot know the full extent of the mysteries of the universe.
- God's revelation is a gift.
- The end will be marked by social disruption and natural disasters.
- This world is marked by innumerable evils, such as disease, pain, and so on. The new world will lack these things.

and fire. The writer's distress over this inversion of society betrays his upper-class prejudices. Those who escape these evils must ultimately face the Messiah as judge. The holy land will protect its own.

The Messiah judges the nations. Those who have oppressed Israel, he slays. Those who have not, he spares. "And it shall come to pass, when he has brought low everything in the world, and has sat down in peace for the age on the throne of his kingdom, that joy shall then be revealed, and rest appear" (73:1). The messianic age is perfect. There is healing, and no more untimely death, disease, anxiety, hatred, or envy. Beasts minister to people. Women no longer have pain in childbearing. Farmers do not get weary. (These last two undo curses of Genesis.) Buildings are built speedily and almost effortlessly. Finally, "that time is the consummation of that which is corruptible, and the beginning of that which is not corruptible" (73:2). The messianic period is not the ultimate consummation. The messianic era does not fully belong to the age of corruptibility, nor is it yet the age of incorruptibility. It is in between.

Section Seven (77:18–87:1)

The final section is the letter sent to the exile. It adds little to our investigation of apocalyptic themes.

The *Apocalypse of Abraham*

The *Apocalypse of Abraham* survives only through a Slavonic translation, but it was probably originally written in Hebrew and comes from Jewish Palestine. Like *4 Ezra* and *2 Baruch*, it is an apocalyptic response to Jerusalem's destruction by the Romans (Stone 1981). Like them, it sees the destruction through the prism of the Babylonian disaster. Unlike them, it spends far less time on the destruction and the resulting need for theodicy. It is unique among the Jewish apocalypses in that it describes a cosmic journey of the seer with the attendant interest in cosmology but also displays an interest in history. Normally, apocalypses are one or the other—cosmological or historical.

The *Apocalypse of Abraham* resembles Daniel in that it consists of two main parts, the first of which is not properly speaking an apocalypse. Rather, it is the story of Abraham's confrontation of his father Terah's idolatry (chaps. 1–8). Chapters 1–8 define Abraham and his descendants as those who reject idolatry.

Chapter 9 begins the apocalypse. God will reveal to Abraham "the ages which have been created and established" and the future, focusing on what will happen to the good and the bad. Abraham is to offer animal sacrifices on a high mountain. The sacrifices echo Gen. 15, while the high mountain is an allusion to the sacrifice of Isaac in Gen. 22. Abraham fasts to prepare for revelation.

Abraham, hearing God's voice but seeing nothing, fears greatly and falls to the ground. God sends Jaoel to him. Although Jaoel is an angel, he seems a step above any other angel. He is like Metatron, a godlike figure in rabbinic literature, who raised disagreement among rabbis, some going so far as to call him the "little Yahweh," while others saw him as a threat to monotheism (Segal 1977). Jaoel's name means "Yahweh is God," and it is possible that there is an allusion to Exod. 23:21, where God tells Israel to follow and obey the angel in whom his name dwells. Jaoel's self-introduction shows him to be a master of the heavenly world. He exists with God in the seventh heaven, and he says that his name is "a power in virtue of the ineffable Name that is dwelling in me" (chap. 10). He has a variety of jobs. He must restrain the cherubim, who tend to attack one another. The cherubim and seraphim are God's bodyguards and are fearful. They are like semi-wild dogs who serve their master's purpose but who are unpredictable.

Jaoel teaches the angels their song of praise. He restrains Leviathan, the sea monster, and he has charge of every reptile. He has authority over Hades. It is he who burned Abraham's father's house, and he has now been sent to guide and protect Abraham and his posterity. He works with Michael but seems superior even to him.

Chapter 11 describes Jaoel in terms that recall God and the angels in Daniel and Ezekiel. His hair is white like snow. His body is like precious stones. His turban is like a rainbow. He wears the royal color purple and bears a kingly scepter. He counsels Abraham not to be afraid. He will remain visible until the sacrifice, and after that he will be invisible, but Jews should believe that Jaoel is with them, even though they cannot see him.

Jaoel and Abraham travel across the desert to God's mountain, Horeb (Sinai). The journey takes forty days, a figure that conjures up much in Israel's history—including the giving of the Torah through Moses, the wandering in the wilderness, and Elijah's journey across the desert under similar circumstances. Abraham fasts to prepare for what is to come. Jaoel's appearance is his food and Jaoel's teaching is his drink. At the mountain, Abraham objects that he has no animal sacrifice. The angel tells him to look around him, and Abraham sees a heifer, a she-goat, a ram, a dove, and a pigeon. The scene recalls Gen. 15 and 22. Abraham is not to sacrifice the birds, for they will transport Jaoel and him into the heavens and throughout the universe. Jaoel promises Abraham that he will see heaven, earth, the sea, the abyss, the underworld, the Garden of Eden, Eden's rivers, and the entire world that the rivers encircle (chap. 12).

In Gen. 15:11, Abraham chases away birds of prey that threaten to eat the sacrificial meat. The apocalypse turns these birds into a single bird, which warns Abraham that he has no business in this holy place. It tells Abraham to flee, for if he continues to ascend to the heights, he will perish. Jaoel reveals that the bird is Azazel, one of the two main leaders of the fallen angels in the *Book of the Watchers*. Jaoel rebukes Azazel, reminding him that he has relinquished his own right to be in the heavenly places. Earth is now his place. He leads humanity astray, but God has not given the righteous into his hand. Azazel's heavenly garments, which have been confiscated, are preserved in heaven for Abraham. Ironically, Azazel, an angel from heaven, is now stuck on earth, while Abraham, an earthly mortal, will have access to heaven. Jaoel says to Azazel, "The mortality which was his has been transferred to you" (chap. 13).

In chapter 14 Jaoel reminds Abraham that Azazel rebelled against God and spread heavenly secrets not meant to be shared with humans. He is to be eternally punished. Abraham is to have nothing to do with him, nor should he fear him. He should ignore him.

The angels of sacrifice carry the sacrifices aloft, and Jaoel and Abraham ride the birds into the heavens (chaps. 15–16). Abraham observes a crowded and busy world, full of angelic figures who look like men, praising God, speaking an unknown language, and passing into and out of existence. It is an intensely bright and fiery scene. Abraham grows fearful and asks Jaoel why he has brought him to such a place. Jaoel tells him that he will stay with him, so he ought not fear. God himself is about to approach them, but Abraham will not see him. He will only hear him.

In chapter 17, God approaches. Fire surrounds them, and God's voice is heard, sounding like many waters and like the sea. The place pitches violently. The angel worshipfully bows his head. Abraham cannot even cast himself on the ground, for there is no ground. Jaoel instructs him to sing and worship. The apocalypse reveals the song's words. It praises God for his divine nature and lists his exalted powers and traits. It concludes with a prayer that God reveal what he has promised.

Chapter 18 is a throne scene. The fire of the floor rises into the heights. Abraham hears the divine voice and observes a fiery throne beneath the fire. The throne is surrounded by "all-seeing ones," angels who may be related to the watchers or perhaps to the eye-filled wheels of Ezek. 1. Then Abraham sees the four living creatures, each with four faces—human, lion, eagle, and ox. These derive from Ezek. 1; each has four heads, so that there are a total of sixteen faces. They have six wings, which corresponds with the seraphim of Isa. 6; the creatures of Ezekiel have only four. The wings serve the same functions as in Isaiah. After completing their song, they threaten one another. Jaoel turns their faces away from one another and teaches them a song of peace whose author is God.

Now Abraham sees behind the creatures a fiery throne whose wheels have eyes all around, as in Ezek. 1. The wheels themselves are superhuman figures, and later Jewish tradition sees them as an order of angels called the 'ôphanîm, "wheels." Over the wheels is a fiery throne, surrounded by fire, surrounded by angels. The divine voice, like a human voice, comes from within the throne.

In chapter 19 God tells Abraham to look down from where he is, in the seventh heaven, telling him, "See how on no single expanse is there any other than he whom you have sought, or who has loved you." This reaffirms Abraham's monotheism. He obviously was right to be against his father's idolatry. In the seventh heaven, Abraham sees fire, light, dew, many angels, and "a power of invisible glory over the living creatures which I saw; but no other being did I see there." This is God's abode, and no other may share it with him. The seventh heaven is the highest. (There is an eighth heaven mentioned in the next verse, but this is an error.)

Abraham looks down to the sixth heaven, which is full of angels who do the bidding of the fiery angels above them. On the fifth, he observes the stars, whom the earth obeys. This may be an endorsement of astrology. God tells Abraham to count the stars, for the number of his posterity will exceed their number (see Gen. 15).

Abraham tells God that he had been accosted by Azazel before his ascent into heaven. He notices that Azazel is not present in heaven. He asks God what God's relationship to Azazel is now. God does not answer immediately, but the heart of the vision is about to transpire, and Azazel's role is clearer there.

Abraham continues to look down, and the text summarizes all that he sees, without specifying the heavens. The description is dense.

> The earth and its fruits, and what moved upon it and its animate beings; and the power of its men, and the ungodliness of their souls, and their righteous deeds and the beginnings of their works, and the lower regions and the perdition therein, the Abyss and its torments. I saw there the sea and its islands, and its monster and its fishes, and Leviathan and his dominion, and his camping-ground, and his caves, and the world which lay upon him, and his movements, and the destructions of the world on his account. I saw there streams and the rising of their waters and their windings. And I saw there the garden of Eden and its fruits, the source of the stream issuing from it, and its trees and their bloom, and those who behaved righteously. And I saw therein their foods and blessedness. And I saw a great multitude—men and women and children half of them on the right side of the picture and half of them on the left side of the picture. (21:3–7)

God explains that Abraham has seen the world as God intended it. The people on the right side of the picture are Israel, and those on the left are everyone else. It is puzzling that Israel is said to be "with Azazel." This may indicate that Israel is sinful. The complex scene has been rewritten by Christians, and it is probably they who have arrayed Israel with Azazel.

God tells Abraham to observe who seduced Eve, and he will then understand Israel's situation at the end of the age. Abraham sees Adam and Eve, figures of gigantic proportions, embracing each other and eating the fruit. Behind them stands a serpent with humanlike hands and feet, and with six wings. God informs Abraham that the serpent is Azazel. Thus Azazel could be considered the source of all evil, as in the *Book of the Watchers*. Abraham asks God why he has given such power over humans to Azazel, and God responds that Azazel has power only over those who are willing. Abraham asks why God created humanity with evil in its heart, for humans act according to their created nature. So again we have a tension between evil being caused by Azazel, the evil human inclination, and personal choice.

The seer observes humanity's sinfulness. His vision begins with Adam and Eve and moves on to Abel's murder at the hand of his brother Cain, a murder inspired by "the Adversary," a reference to Azazel ("satan" means "adversary"). He sees multiple evils caused by "the lawless one," another reference to Azazel. He sees impurity and those who pursue it, pollution and jealousy, and the place of fire in the lower parts of the earth. He sees theft. He sees men having sexual relations with men. (We cannot fairly equate this with modern ideas of homosexuality, for ancient ideas of sexuality were very different from our own, and we should not oversimplify [D. Martin 2006].) He sees desire. He sees "the likeness of the image of jealousy," a reference to the idol in the Jerusalem temple (Ezek. 11). It is an idol like his father used to make, and he sees a boy sacrificed before it. God reveals that this is the Jerusalem temple, founded by God for his glory and service, but turned into a site of rebellion against God. God says that he foresaw this pollution and the human sacrifice and that he therefore decreed judgment at the beginning of creation. Abraham asks God why he has permitted such evil, if he knew it in advance. God explains that it is a product of human free will.

Abraham sees the people from the right side of the picture invade the left side and destroy its temple. Abraham immediately recognizes this as the destruction of Jerusalem and its temple by the nations. God points to the sins of those in the temple itself. The statue and the illicit sacrifices have angered God.

Abraham asks about the righteous. God says that Israel did have some good leaders (David, Hezekiah, Josiah), but that most quickly turned to their own interests. Abraham asks how long this dismal state of affairs will persist. God says that there are four ages of a hundred years each. This is a reference to the four kingdoms of Dan. 2 and 7. The time scheme this section indicates is hard to decipher; the text may be corrupt. In addition to the four eras, God mentions an hour at the end that is equivalent to a hundred years, and then he says that the end time itself will be divided into twelve parts.

There follows a Christian interpolation in chapter 29. It speaks of a man who arises from Israel and whom many from the left and from the right (Jews and gentiles) worship, and whom some from both left and right physically abuse.

God speaks of the beginning of the age of righteousness to come. The lawless gentiles will suffer at the hands of Israel's righteous. God will bring ten plagues (as in the exodus) on the earth. Then a set number of Jews, a number kept secret by God, will go to the holy land and will offer proper sacrifices and prayers. The temple cult is reestablished in righteousness. The righteous will rejoice in God continually, and they will punish the wicked who have oppressed them. They will spit in the face of their enemies. God will be with Abraham forever.

Abraham suddenly finds himself back on earth, but the revelation continues. God specifies the ten plagues as distress; conflagration of cities; destruction and disease of animals; worldwide hunger; destruction through rulers; an earthquake and the sword; hail and snow; lethal attacks of wild beasts; alternating hunger and pestilence; punishment by the sword and through flight; thunder and another earthquake (chap. 30).

The final phase of the end time contains the sound of the trumpet "out of the air," and God sends his "Elect One," who will gather the oppressed people of God from throughout the earth. God will burn those who have oppressed and wronged the righteous. Azazel plays an active role in their punishment.

The apocalypse ends with God telling Abraham that his seventh generation (perhaps that of Moses in Egypt) will be enslaved in a foreign land, but that God will wreak vengeance on Israel's enemies.

The Book of *Jubilees*

Jubilees rewrites Genesis and part of Exodus. It is a revelation dictated by the angel of the presence to Moses on Mount Sinai, written down by Moses. *Jubilees* focuses on law. Apocalypses do not generally rewrite Scripture or concentrate on legal specifics, so this is unusual. Collins considers *Jubilees* a borderline case in terms of its genre, but he concludes that it does fit the definition of an apocalypse (1998, 83). Moses receives special revelation from God through an angel. The revelation is of the future, including two eschatological scenarios, and of the unseen world. History is divided and foreordained according to set periods. Final judgment is in view throughout the book.

Jubilees's interpretations go well beyond Torah's text. Its laws are said to be written on heavenly tablets (3:10, 31; 4:5, 32; etc.) (Collins 1998, 81). It was popular in the community of the Dead Sea Scrolls. It is fascinating in its simultaneous dependence on Scripture and its freedom in rewriting that Scripture.

Jubilees is well acquainted with *1 Enoch*. VanderKam shows that it knows the *Book of the Watchers* and the *Astronomical Book* as well, and it is possible that it knows the *Book of Dreams*, the *Apocalypse of Weeks*, and the *Epistle of Enoch* (VanderKam 1978; Collins 1998, 80). Its version of the origin of evil is similar to that in the *Book of the Watchers*, but with a twist. *Jubilees* makes the descent of the angels a good thing, commanded by God. Ironically, their task was to impart knowledge to humanity, the very thing for which they are blamed elsewhere. Once on earth, they went astray with women. As in *1 Enoch*, when the offspring of the angels and women died, spirits emerged from their bodies. These are the evil spirits that afflict humankind. In *1 Enoch*, no limit is placed on them. In *Jubilees* 10, Mastema, leader of the spirits, must plead with

The *Apocalypse of Abraham*: Apocalypse and Apocalypticism

- The *Apocalypse of Abraham* fits the definition of an apocalypse.
- Abraham makes a heavenly journey.
- He sees the universe from the vantage of the seventh heaven.
- There are seven heavens. The seventh is for God and his closest, fiery angels.
- The heavenly world is unlike this one; it heaves up and down; it has no solid earth on which Abraham can throw himself in fear; it is fiery and inhabited by fiery creatures.
- The vision of God's throne combines elements of Isa. 6 and Ezek. 1.
- Jaoel is a powerful angel, perhaps the most powerful. He reveals things to Abraham. His appearance is like that of God and the angels in Daniel.
- God does most of the revealing to Abraham.
- The work envisages the ultimate and eternal punishment of the wicked and the reward of the righteous.
- Azazel's role is detailed; he rebels against God and imparts heavenly secrets to those who should not get them; he leads the unrighteous astray; he was the serpent in Eden who seduced Adam and Eve; he tries to stop Abraham from receiving revelation; he plays a role in the punishment of sinners.
- Azazel's heavenly garments, left behind when he left heaven, are reserved for Abraham.
- Abraham, accompanied by Jaoel, fasts to prepare for his visions.
- The angelic figures surrounding God, both the cherubim and the four living creatures, must be controlled; they tend to attack one another.
- Leviathan has destructive power, but he is kept in check by Jaoel.
- Jaoel burns Terah's house.
- Jaoel and Michael protect Israel.
- Heavenly beings are described in strange and mystical ways.
- There are heavenly songs that must be sung. Abraham himself sings one.
- The stars control the earth.
- Eternal punishment is located in the abyss or in the lower regions of the earth.
- God plans all, including the judgment, from the beginning; Abraham sees the picture of creation that God had in his own mind and by which he fashioned everything.
- The end time is characterized by the usual sorts of social and cosmic upheavals.
- There is the usual dualism. The opposition between Israel and the gentiles is highlighted.
- Sin is caused by humans; they have free will.
- Abraham asks "how long," and God answers cryptically; his answer involves the number four (as in the four kingdoms) and twelve (perhaps traceable to Persian traditions).
- The righteous will come back to the land of Israel; they will have a hand in the punishment of the righteous.
- The final scene of the eschaton includes the blowing of a trumpet from the air, the coming of the Elect One with God's power, and the gathering of God's people from throughout the earth.

God to allow some of the spirits to remain on earth. God allows 10 percent to do so. So *Jubilees* places greater emphasis on human responsibility than does the *Book of the Watchers*, which fits its emphasis on law.

Especially important is the Sabbath. The Sabbath is a key topic of debate in late Second Temple Judaism. *Jubilees* portrays the patriarchs as having obeyed the Torah, despite the anachronism. In his testamentary speech (chaps. 20–23), "Abraham warns his sons to practice circumcision, renounce fornication and uncleanness, refrain from marriage with Canaanite women, avoid idolatry, eat no blood, and perform washings before and after sacrifice" (Collins 1998, 80).

Nudity is an issue in *Jubilees* (3:31), something that would be of concern during the Hellenistic Reform. In 50:12, making war is forbidden on the Sabbath. This also was an issue during the Maccabean revolt (1 Macc. 2:39–41). *Jubilees* dates to the Hasmonean period.

Jubilees advocates a solar calendar with a 364-day year. The following passage shows why this is so important both here and elsewhere.

> Command the children of Israel that they observe the years according to this reckoning—three hundred and sixty-four days, and these will constitute a complete year, and they will not disturb its time from its days and from its feasts; for everything will fall out in them according to their testimony, and they will not leave out any day nor disturb any feasts. But if they do neglect and do not observe them according to His commandment, then they will disturb all their seasons, and the years will be dislodged from this order, and they will disturb the seasons and the years will be dislodged and they will neglect their ordinances. And all the children of Israel will forget, and will not find the path of the years, and will forget the new moons, and seasons, and sabbaths, and they will go wrong as to all the order of the years. For I know and from henceforth will I declare it to you, and it is not of my own devising; for the book lies written before me, and on the heavenly tablets the division of days is ordained, lest they forget the feasts of the covenant and walk according to the feasts of the Gentiles after their error and after their ignorance. For there will be those who will assuredly make observations of the moon—how it disturbs the seasons and comes in from year to year ten days too soon. For this reason the years will come upon them when they will disturb the order, and make an abominable day the day of testimony, and an unclean day a feast day, and they will confound all the days, the holy with the unclean, and the unclean day with the holy; for they will go wrong as to the months and sabbaths and feasts and jubilees. For this reason I command and testify to you that you may testify to them; for after your death your children will disturb them, so that they will not make the year three hundred and sixty-four days only, and for this reason they will go wrong as to the new moons and seasons and sabbaths and festivals, and they will eat all kinds of blood with all kinds of flesh. (6:32–38)

Without the correct calendar, one cannot serve God. Feast days can even become abominations. Failure in this regard leads to other transgressions, such as the all-important rule not to consume blood. The author thinks that use of the lunar calendar is due to gentile influence. This would fit the early Hasmonean period.

God foreordains history. The structure of the book, broken into jubilees, forty-nine-year periods, shows the fixed structure of history. The work supplies two eschatological scenarios. The first is in chapter 1. God tells Moses that Israel will forsake him. But there is hope.

> "After this they will turn to me [God] in all uprightness and with all their heart and with all their soul, and I will circumcise the foreskin of their heart and the foreskin of the heart of their seed, and I will create in them a holy spirit, and I will cleanse them so that they shall not turn away from me from that day unto eternity. And their souls will cleave to me and to all my commandments, and they will fulfill my commandments, and I will be their Father and they will be my children. And they all will be called children of the living God, and every angel and every spirit will know that these are my children, and that I am their Father in uprightness and righteousness, and that I love them. And write down for yourself all these words which I declare to you on this mountain, the first and the last, which shall come to pass in all the divisions of the days in the law and in the testimony and in the weeks and the jubilees unto eternity, until I descend and dwell with them throughout eternity." And He said to the angel of the presence: "Write for Moses from the beginning of creation till my sanctuary has been built among them for all eternity. And the Lord will appear to the eyes of all, and all shall know that I am the God of Israel and the Father of all the children of Jacob, and King on Mount Zion for all eternity. And Zion and Jerusalem will be holy." And the angel of the presence who went before the camp of Israel took the tables of the divisions of the years—from the time of the creation—of the law and of the testimony of the weeks of the jubilees, according to the individual years, according to all the number of the jubilees according to the individual years, from the day of the new creation when the heavens and the earth shall be renewed and all their creation according to the powers of the heaven, and according to all the creation of the earth, until the sanctuary of the Lord will be made in Jerusalem on Mount Zion, and all the luminaries be renewed for healing and for peace and for blessing for all the elect of Israel, and that thus it may be from that day and unto all the days of the earth. (1:15–29)

Here is history in a nutshell. The passage describes the perfect future in covenantal terms, highlighting the relationship between God and Israel. The righteous are children of God. The renewal of Israel is accompanied by the renewal of creation, earthly and heavenly. Jerusalem is God's eternal dwelling place.

The other eschatological scenario occurs in chapter 23. The chapter paints a dismal picture of the state of the world after Abraham. It highlights the decreasing length of human life. It speaks of innumerable calamities, illnesses, wickedness, famine, warfare, the breakdown of society, and transgression of the law. Three-week-old children will appear as elderly. Finally, God will

Jubilees: Apocalypse and Apocalypticism

- *Jubilees* has the form of an apocalypse.
- There is cosmic and social dualism.
- Angels and demons are active and affect human life.
- The content comes from revelation given by God through the angel to Moses.
- There is judgment to come.
- There will be a new creation.
- Israel will be renewed.
- Zion will be renewed and holy for all eternity.

punish the wicked by means of the gentiles, a possible allusion to the conflict between Jews and Seleucids. Then things begin to change.

> In those days the children shall begin to study the laws and to seek the commandments, and to return to the path of righteousness. And the days shall begin to grow many and increase amongst those children of men till their days draw nigh to one thousand years, and to a greater number of years than before was the number of the days. And there shall be no old man nor one who is not satisfied with his days, for all shall be as children and youths. And all their days they shall complete and live in peace and in joy, and there will be no Satan nor any evil destroyer, for all their days shall be days of blessing and healing. And at that time the Lord will heal His servants, and they shall rise up and see great peace and drive out their adversaries. And the righteous shall see and be thankful and rejoice with joy forever and ever, and shall see all their judgments and all their curses on their enemies. And their bones shall rest in the earth, and their spirits shall have much joy, and they shall know that it is the Lord who executes judgment and shows mercy to hundreds and thousands and to all that love him. (23:26–31)

The renewal of Israel and the new creation is precipitated by the emergence of those who study the laws. Collins points out that this might correspond to a period in the history of the Dead Sea Scrolls community before the rise of their prophetic leader, the Teacher of Righteousness. For twenty years, they looked for the proper way, knowing that Israel was displeasing God. The Teacher then arose and interpreted Torah for them and revealed that they were the true Israel. *Jubilees* is not a sectarian book, but it was a favorite book at Qumran. It may be a product of the same movement, but at an early stage.

In *Jubilees* 23, the emergence of this Torah-abiding group leads to the renewal of humanity. They now live to an advanced age. At death, their bodies are buried but their spirits live on in joy. This is not resurrection, but may be termed a spiritual resurrection. Note that there are few indications of bodily resurrection at Qumran as well. In *Jubilees*, Satan is gone, Israel no longer has enemies, and it enjoys peace and healing. Expectation of judgment underlies all of *Jubilees* (5:19). Only the righteous will enjoy the future, perfect creation.

Jubilees presents a world in which angels and demons are active (Collins 1998, 82–83). Good angels control the universe, serve in God's presence, reveal important truths to humankind, and protect the righteous from demons. Evil spirits are God's and humankind's enemies, and they are led by Mastema or Beliar (1:20). Thus there is cosmic dualism, corresponding to social dualism.

Suggestions for Further Reading

Boccaccini, Gabriele, and John Joseph Collins, eds. *The Early Enoch Literature*. Boston: Brill, 2007.

Collins, John Joseph. *The Apocalyptic Imagination: An Introduction to Jewish Apocalyptic Literature*. 2nd ed. Grand Rapids: Eerdmans, 1998.

Kulik, Alexander. *Retroverting Slavonic Pseudepigrapha: Toward the Original of the Apocalypse of Abraham*. SBLTCS 3. Atlanta: Society of Biblical Literature, 2004.

Murphy, Frederick J. *The Structure and Meaning of Second Baruch*. Atlanta: Scholars Press, 1985.

Nickelsburg, George W. E. *1 Enoch: A Commentary on the Book of 1 Enoch*. Hermeneia. Minneapolis: Fortress, 2001.

———. *Jewish Literature between the Bible and the Mishnah: An Historical and Literary Introduction*. 2nd ed. Minneapolis: Fortress, 2005.

Stone, Michael. *Fourth Ezra: A Commentary on the Book of Fourth Ezra*. Hermeneia. Minneapolis: Fortress, 1990.

6

Ancient Jewish Literature Related to Apocalypticism

N ot every Second Temple Jewish work is an apocalypse. Nonetheless, even those that are not apocalypses often contain apocalyptic features. This chapter will look at a few such documents.

The *Testament of Moses* (Also Known as the *Assumption of Moses*)

Ancient sources speak of a *Testament of Moses* and an *Assumption of Moses*. Scholars assume that the *Testament of Moses* before us is one or both of those works. The end of the text has been lost, so we do not know whether it ever included an assumption of Moses into heaven. In its present state, the work does not narrate Moses's death, although that would be logical. The work is a testament—a last declaration of an important figure before his death. These are Moses's last words to his successor, Joshua. It is based upon Deut. 32–34. Testaments were a common literary form in ancient Judaism and Christianity (Collins 1984b). They usually contain predictions of the future, replete with eschatological elements.

Although not an apocalypse, the *Testament* uses pseudonymity. It also uses *vaticinia ex eventu* (prophecy after the event), assuming that all history is laid out beforehand and conforms to God's plan. The work expects radical apocalyptic change. Deuteronomy is mentioned in the first chapter as the repository of Moses's "prophecies."

In chapter 1, Moses instructs Joshua:

> And receive this writing that you may know how to preserve the books which I shall deliver unto you; and you shall set these in order and anoint them with oil of cedar and put them away in earthen vessels in the place which he made from the beginning of the creation of the world, that his name should be called upon until the day of repentance in the visitation when the Lord will visit them in the consummation of the end of the days. (1:16–18)

Moses designates himself mediator of the covenant. Jerusalem will be the place of the preservation of God's true revelation all the way to the eschaton, the "consummation of the end of days." God planned this at creation.

The *Testament of Moses* was originally written during the Maccabean revolt and was later adapted to Herod's time. The description in chapter 8 of a persecution of Judaism matches the situation of the persecution of the Seleucid Antiochus IV. The story of Taxo in chapter 9 combines elements of the story of the elderly martyr in 2 Macc. 6 and of the seven brothers in 2 Macc. 7 who were martyred. However, chapter 6 refers to the time of Herod in the late first century BCE. This led Charles to posit that the chapters were out of order, but most think that the testament originally applied to Antiochus's persecution and was later reapplied to Herod's time (Charles 1913). Chapters 8 and 9, which originally described Antiochus's persecution, were now seen as a period of persecution to follow Herod's rule and that of his sons (chap. 6) as well as a period when the ruling class, particularly the priests, oppressed the people (chap. 7). The culmination of history would happen after that (chap. 10).

We focus on chapter 10, but before treating it in more detail, there are several things worth noting. Moses covers the period of the judges quickly and then speaks of the split of the north from the south. The "ten tribes" of the north set up their own laws and cultic system and eventually fall into idolatry, for which they are exiled. In chapter 3, the southern tribes blame their own exile to Babylonia on the sins of the north, and the northern tribes agree. The initial response of the tribes as a whole is to blame God for not fulfilling his promises about Israel's possession of the holy land, but they then remember Moses's prophecies of what would happen to them if they broke the covenant. They are experiencing the covenantal curses. It is not surprising that a work written in Moses's name emphasizes the law and covenant. The theology of the book is Deuteronomistic—obedience brings blessing, disobedience brings punishment.

Chapter 4 speaks of one who intercedes for Israel, probably Daniel (see Dan. 9), and of a foreign king who has compassion on Israel and allows them to return to Judah and rebuild. The king is Cyrus the Great. Moses says that some of the exiles will return and rebuild the walls, but that they will lament because they are unable to offer sacrifices. This manifests disapproval of the

Second Temple cultic establishment. Meanwhile, the ten northern tribes continue to live among the gentiles. The belief that the ten tribes survive somewhere makes it possible that they will return to the land in the end and all twelve tribes will be reunited.

Chapter 5 and 6:1 refer to the Hasmoneans. Our author does not approve of them. They defile the sanctuary. Jews are "divided as to the truth," which may be a reference to the Hellenistic Reform and of the Hasmonean period in general. The Hasmoneans are not legitimate priests. In addition to polluting the altar, they are venal and open to bribery. They claim both kingship and priesthood (6:1).

Chapter 6 concerns Herod and his sons. The chapter says he is not of the "race of priests," and it speaks of his oppression, destruction of the nobility, and secret prisons. His reign lasts thirty-four years (37–4 BCE). His sons are said to rule for shorter periods. The description of Herod's reign is so vivid it makes us think that the author writes close to this time. Herod's sons ruling for shorter periods is inaccurate, for Herod Antipas ruled Galilee and Perea from 4 BCE to 39 CE, forty-three years. This part of the testament was written just after Herod's death. The text "predicts" that a "king of the west" will come and conquer the Palestinian Jews and crucify many. This fits the war of Varus, the Roman governor of Syria who ruthlessly crushed rebellions in Jewish Palestine after Herod's demise.

After Herod, Moses predicts a ruling class that is self-indulgent, rapacious, and inimical to the poor. The ruling class, much of which was priestly, demands that others keep their distance from them lest they be polluted. This may reflect disagreements over purity that we see in the Gospels, in the Dead Sea Scrolls, and in other materials concerning the Pharisees and Sadducees.

Chapter 8 describes a persecution to come, modeled on the one by Antiochus IV, and chapter 9 tells the story of Taxo and his seven sons. Taxo willingly endures martyrdom and encourages his sons to do the same, "for if we do this and die, our blood shall be avenged before the Lord" (9:7).

Chapter 10 portrays the eschaton. The suffering under Herod and his sons issues in the establishment of God's kingdom. God's kingdom spreads through all creation. The world is not under God's control, as it should be. God must take it back. When he does, the entire universe will be the kingdom of God.

"Satan shall be no more" (10:1). This is the other side of the coin from God's universal reign. Although Moses has not spoken of Satan earlier, this line reveals that the world is under Satan's control, and that Satan must be vanquished for God's kingdom to come (see our treatment of Mark's Gospel). Sorrow will depart with Satan.

The reader learns that the hands of the chief angel will be "filled." The angel is a heavenly priest, and his full hands mean that he is offering sacrifice to God. Then this priestly angel will avenge Israel on its enemies.

Apocalyptic Elements in the *Testament of Moses*

- After the reign of Herod and his sons, there will be a persecution of Judaism.
- Martyrdom of the faithful will spur God to action to avenge them.
- Satan is gone.
- Sorrow is gone.
- The sea is gone.
- The chief angel offers God sacrifices.
- The same angel will avenge Israel on its enemies.
- God comes forth from his throne and his habitation.
- There are the usual cosmic signs: the earth shakes, mountains are laid low, the sun stops giving its light, the moon turns to blood, the stars are disturbed, the sea sinks into the abyss, fountains and rivers dry up.
- God punishes the gentiles and destroys their idols.
- Israel will be with the stars and look down on their enemies being punished in Gehenna.

There is a fearful theophany. God, the "heavenly one," rises from his place and wrathfully comes to earth. We get the usual apocalyptic signs: the earth shakes, mountains are laid low, hills shake and fall, the sun goes dark and the moon becomes red, the stars are disturbed, and the sea "shall retire into the abyss." This last detail is particularly significant in view of the combat myth. The sea represents chaos and everything opposed to God. The sea also disappears in the renewal of creation in Rev. 21:1.

God comes to defeat the gentiles and annihilate their idols. Israel is happy and is brought up to the stars on the wings of the eagle (see Exod. 19). Israel looks down on their enemies suffering in Gehenna, a place of postmortem punishment.

Joshua is near despair as he contemplates Moses's death. He does not feel equal to the task of shepherding the people. Moses encourages Joshua, for leadership comes not from one's own character but from God's choice. Similarly, God's dedication to Israel is not because Israel is worthy but because of God's free election. All of history has played out as God planned from the beginning, "and nothing has been neglected by him even to the least thing, but all things he has foreseen and caused all to come forth" (12:4–5). Moses's last words to Joshua in the extant text lay out Deuteronomistic theology: obedience to God will bring blessings, and disobedience will bring punishment.

The *Psalms of Solomon*

The *Psalms of Solomon* are a collection of noncanonical psalms. Although they speak cryptically about the situation they address, many referents are transparent. They are written after the Roman Empire, through the person of Pompey the Great, expanded to swallow Palestine—Jerusalem and Judea in particular. The psalms convey the trauma of Pompey's actions. Originally he was in the eastern Mediterranean to fight piracy. While he was there, two warring Hasmonean brothers, Hyrcanus II and Aristobulus II, appealed to him to resolve their power struggle. Pompey did so in a way unsatisfactory to Aristobulus, and the upshot was a siege of Jerusalem in which one of the rival Jewish factions opened the gates of the city to admit the Romans. Pompey polluted the sanctuary by entering it. This is spoken of as the gentiles trampling the sanctuary. Rome had now gobbled up Jewish Palestine. It was 63 BCE.

The psalmist was a member of the upper class. He says in *Psalms of Solomon* 1 that he was prosperous and thought himself righteous. The conquest of Jerusalem by Pompey was a shock. It was even more shocking to him that citizens of the city cooperated in its fall. He decides that Jerusalem has received due punishment for its sins, and he is especially harsh in his treatment of its priestly ruling class, the Hasmoneans. In the *Psalms of Solomon*, Jerusalem is characterized by an upper class that is oppressive, deceitful, hypocritical, and pretends to obey Torah but in fact sins sexually and economically. They seek their own good, not God's service. They amass wealth, take the homes of others, and then play the role of society's pillars and respectable ones. The priests are no better than the upper class in general, and they add to their sins pollution of the sanctuary. They pollute the altar with menstrual blood (indicating disagreement over purity rules) and by their own immorality.

The psalms are permeated with the notion that God will ultimately protect the righteous and punish the wicked. He has already punished Pompey by having him killed on Egyptian shores (2:26). Pompey is the typical foreign ruler who considers himself "great," when he should acknowledge that all power comes from God.

None of what we have said makes the *Psalms of Solomon* apocalyptic. It is traditional Deuteronomistic theology. God influences history directly, but that is universally assumed in Israel's literature. We see no angels or demons, cosmic disruption, or visions interpreted by angels. What is of great interest for the study of apocalypticism, however, is the messianism expressed in the final two psalms, 17 and 18. Eschatological scenarios do not necessarily involve a messiah, but when they do, it is often a figure with a Davidic profile. Examination of the final two psalms in this collection supplies a rich view of what a Davidic messiah looks like.

Psalm 17 begins, "O Lord, you are our king forever and ever" (17:1). The psalmist sees God's sovereignty challenged by Rome and so affirms God's rule. Then he immediately speaks of God's establishment of the Davidic monarchy that he swore would last forever. Davidic rule does not challenge God's kingdom as do other monarchies; it embodies it. When our author writes, Israel has lacked a Davidic king for centuries.

Fig. 7. The Roman takeover of Palestine by Pompey in 63 BCE brought improvements like aqueducts, but such structures were also reminders of Roman domination. (Chris Miller)

Sinners rose up in Jerusalem and cast out legitimate priests, whom the author calls "us." They grabbed what God had not promised them, the kingship. This alludes to the Hasmoneans, who were legitimate priests but who had no traditional claim to kingship. The psalm says that they "set a [worldly] monarchy in place of that which was their excellence" (17:7).

The Hasmoneans "laid waste the throne of David in tumultuous arrogance" (17:8). God raised against them "a man who was alien to our race" (17:9), Pompey, who laid waste the land, slaughtered young and old alike, exiled many, and humiliated the nobility. He filled the land with gentile customs, and many Jews complied. The righteous had to flee, some to the desert and others elsewhere. Fleeing to the desert occurs frequently in Jewish history, beginning with the exodus.

The author's view of the Jews who do not flee is dim. They cooperate with the gentiles to the detriment of the Torah; none of them is righteous, from the rulers to the judges to the people. The very heavens refuse to give them rain, and the fountains dry up.

A new Davidic king will solve Israel's problems in one fell swoop. The psalmist prays that God raise up such a king, when God deems it suitable. He must be filled with power from God so that he can expel the gentiles who trample Jerusalem. He will also "thrust out sinners from the inheritance"— unfaithful Jews will taste his wrath and be separated from the people (17:26). Using biblical messianic allusions, the psalmist says that the king will break

Apocalyptic Elements in the *Psalms of Solomon*

- There is an idealistic restoration of the Davidic monarchy.
- In the end, all Jews are righteous; there is social dualism.
- The kingdom of God comes to earth.
- All nations come to Jerusalem to worship.
- There is a lack of social justice.
- Jerusalem is entirely holy (see Zech. 14 and Ezek. 40–48).
- The tribes are restored to their original territories, as distributed by Joshua.
- All nations are conquered and ruled over by the Messiah.
- The king speaks the words of the angels.
- God is a warrior.

his enemies with a rod of iron (Ps. 2:9) and destroy the godless nations with his word. The nations will flee and the sinners will be reproved.

The king's task is not entirely negative. He must reconstitute a pure and faithful people. He must tolerate no unrighteousness. Then all Israel will be children of God. Like Joshua, the king is to settle the tribes on their land. The reform recaptures the idealized past. Things will be as God originally intended. They will be ethnically pure. No non-Jew will live with them.

Davidic jurisdiction surpasses the social and geographical borders of Israel. The king judges and rules the nations "in the wisdom of his righteousness" (17:31).

The king makes Jerusalem "holy as of old," and the nations stream to worship Israel's God. They flock to behold the king's glory and God's. They bring back Israel's exiled as offerings. The king is famous for righteousness and is taught by God himself. In his days, there will be no unrighteous in Israel, and he will be God's Messiah. His strength rests not in conventional means—horses and soldiers and wealth. Rather, he relies on God. He will be sinless. Nations and sinners will fear him. He will defeat rulers by his word. He will possess God's Holy Spirit. No one will be able to prevail against him. He will be Israel's perfect shepherd. There will be no oppressors and no oppressed in Israel. The king's "words will be like the words of the holy ones [angels] in the midst of sanctified peoples" (17:49).

This powerful messianic psalm ends as it began: "The Lord himself is our king forever and ever" (17:51).

The *Psalms of Solomon* ends with the eighteenth psalm. It also is messianic, and it adds little to what the seventeenth has already said about the Messiah. It concentrates more on God's relationship with Israel and lauds God for his love and mercy toward the chosen people and for his favor to the poor. It finds in God's just judgments chastisement that turns Israel from folly and ignorance, thus treating Israel like a firstborn son. It prays that God purify Israel in preparation for the advent of the Messiah. The Messiah will "establish them all before the Lord" (18:9).

The *Sibylline Oracles*

A sibyl was a female prophet. There were many sibyls in the ancient world, some quite famous, such as the sibyl of Cumae in Italy, the sibyl of Delphi near the shrine of Apollo, and the sibyl of Erythraea in Asia Minor. The sibyls, while in ecstasy, uttered oracles directly from the gods. The oracles were often long, poetic constructions. Their prophecies had a political, religious, and frequently an eschatological outlook. As with so many such compositions, they show evidence of the rewriting and combining of sources. They were used, sometimes cynically, for the advancement of politicians and political causes. Many ancients placed much weight on sibylline oracles, and written collections of such oracles appeared in various places. Rome was the site of an important collection. It was destroyed when the temple of Jupiter burned down in 83 CE, but a new collection was subsequently assembled. Augustus, fearing the political implications of such oracles, had many of them destroyed, but he did save a selection. Those that he kept, he edited for his own benefit.

Both Jews and Christians used the form of sibylline oracles to promote their religious and political ideas. Eschatology played an important role in these works. Here we examine several Jewish sibylline oracles as examples of how this form both lets the authors' audiences make sense of their world and preserves their hopes and expectations.

The Jewish sibylline oracles originated primarily in the Diaspora. Their presentation often pays close attention to Hellenistic monarchs and to the relation of gentiles to Jews and to Israel's God, sometimes giving them a prominent role in God's plans. The very fact that these oracles are placed in the mouth of the gentile sibyl rather than the usual Jewish hero indicates that they aimed to bring Jewish religious, political, and mythological views before a wider Hellenistic audience, or at least that they were meant to influence how Jews thought about their place and its God on the broad stage of world history. Jewish criticism of their gentile neighbors traditionally focused on idolatry and immorality, especially sexual immorality. The Jewish sibylline oracles must be seen in context as part of a Hellenistic world that had frequent recourse to revelation to comment on political and social realities. We have Egyptian and Persian examples of this. Aspects such as periodization of history and eschatological climaxes as well as concern with royal and imperial politics appear in all categories of such revelations (Collins 1998, 118; Eddy 1961).

The main collection of Jewish and Christian sibylline oracles contains twelve books, although because of peculiarities of the manuscript tradition they are numbered 1–8 and 11–14 (Collins 1998, 118). Our concern is with the Jewish sibyllines. Books 3–5 are Jewish and date from the period we are considering—the Second Temple period and slightly beyond, extending to the second revolt against Rome in 132–135 CE. Books 1–2 are basically Jewish with Christian editing (Collins 1974a; 1982; 1998, 116–26).

Sibylline Oracles *1 and 2*

These two texts really comprise one work. They contain a tenfold division of history into "generations" that spans the two works. In this division of history, and in the eschatological scenario contained in *Sibylline Oracles* 2, the works are similar to apocalypses. As prophecies of the sibyl, they claim to be revelation from God. These two works are mostly Jewish but contain Christian interpolations and rewritings. The Jewish work was probably written before 70 CE. The only mention of a specific geographic location is Phrygia in northern Asia Minor.

The division of history is not detailed. Rather, it presents a generalized criticism or praise of humanity in each of ten generations. Its most specific references are to events in Genesis, particularly the story of Adam and Eve, and that of Noah and the flood. The work was not inspired by a historical crisis. It is a moralistic composition that rails against humans' evil deeds and exhorts them to proper behavior. Noah delivers a sermon in which he concentrates on human participation in bloodshed and warfare, but there is another section that consists of a lengthy quotation of an ancient Jewish wisdom work called the *Sentences of Pseudo-Phocylides*. That work provides general instruction on how to live a proper life, taking up diverse topics such as honesty, mercy, moderation, justice, and money.

There is a major Christian interpolation in the seventh of the ten generations. To that generation belong the Greek Titans, who in Greek mythology are gods, children of the sky, and among whom is numbered Chronos. In this oracle the Titans are simply unusually strong humans. They assault heaven, but God "shuts them out." Their behavior provokes God, and he is tempted to respond with another flood but keeps his promise of no more devastating floods.

Then comes a Christian section. Jesus is said to be God incarnate. He fulfills and does not destroy the Torah. Reference is made to John the Baptist and his execution by Herod Antipas. The "Hebrews" will not believe in Jesus, but gentiles will. He brings eternal life to those whom he chooses, and he punishes the lawless. He teaches, heals, drives out demons, and walks on water. The document describes Christ's sufferings and lays them at the feet of the Jews. The Romans are not mentioned. Christ dies, goes to preach the resurrection to those in the underworld, rises, and ascends. Christianity arises. The Jewish temple is destroyed and the Jews are driven from their land. This all happens at the end of *Sibylline Oracles* 1. At the beginning of *Sibylline Oracles* 2, we read of the tenth generation, so the eighth and ninth are lost.

The eschatological portions of *Sibylline Oracles* 2 also remind us of the extent to which Jewish eschatological traditions served Christian interests. For the most part, these portions are Jewish, but they have been touched up by Christians. They require little alteration to be useful to Christians. Verses 154–73 reveal the signs that will precede the eschaton. Children will be born already old. There will be famines, pestilence, and warfare. It will be a time of great sorrow. Children will turn against parents and even eat them. The destruction of mothers will spell the end of humankind, although evildoers of that time will not realize it. Instead of prophets, there will be deceivers. Beliar will come and work misleading signs. Righteous people and the Hebrews will be plundered. The ten lost Israelite tribes will come from the east, seeking their kinsmen. The nations will perish.

Next, the Hebrews assume rule over the earth. God will cause sleep to overcome most humans, but some will stay awake to witness his coming. Those who are awake are "blessed servants." "He" (God or Christ) will come when stars, moon, and sun all shine at midday. Uriel opens the doors of Hades and leads all the dead out. God sits on the throne of judgment.

Christ is imperishable and thus comparable to God. He comes on a cloud, recalling the one like a son of man in Dan. 7. He takes his place at God's right hand and judges good and bad. The holy men from ancient Israel also come to God—Moses, Abraham, Isaac, Jacob, Joshua, Daniel, Elijah, Habakkuk, Jonah, "and those whom the Hebrews killed." This may refer to the tradition that all the ancient prophets suffered violence at the hands of their fellow Israelites, a tradition that contradicts history and the biblical texts, but which enjoyed currency in late Second Temple Judaism. Then the text makes the remarkable statement, "He will destroy all the Hebrews after Jeremiah." This is a disturbing condemnation of the Jewish people.

Righteous and unrighteous alike pass through a flaming river. The righteous will be saved, while sinners perish. The sins of the unrighteous are catalogued in a long list, demonstrating the author's concern with morality. The list of sins is broad, indicating that the author is not driven by a specific historical crisis, but is rather distressed at the immorality surrounding him. Issues of social justice are present—as when the rich exploit the poor. The author shows analytical sophistication as he accuses some almsgivers of getting the wherewithal for their generosity from their dishonest dealings (271–72). Disregard for parents concerns him, as do sexual sins. Violence, hypocrisy, abortion, sorcery, and idolatry are all condemned. Persecution of the righteous marks the sinners.

The depiction of the sufferings of the wicked at God's hand is luridly detailed, as is the reward of the righteous. The collection ends with a plea for mercy for the author. He was rich, sinned, and now needs forgiveness.

Sibylline Oracles 3

Collins shows that this text is comprised of material written over a two-century period (1998, 118–19; 1983, 21–33). The oldest parts date to the middle of the second century BCE, and the later parts come from around the first century CE. What he calls the "main corpus" is verses 97–349 and 489–829. The oracles are generally "loosely structured" (Collins 1998, 119). Verses 350–488 are oracles against the nations and some of them date from the first century BCE. Verses 1–97 "are diverse in origin" and perhaps originally formed a conclusion of a different text (Collins 1998, 119; Kurfess 1965, 707). The following outline summarizes Collins's (1988, 118–19) findings on the nature of each oracle, bringing some order into this complicated document.

Introductory oracle: 1–96. Perhaps displaced here from the conclusion of another book.

Main corpus: 97–349; 489–829. Loosely structured collection. Mid-second century BCE.

Oracles with a common pattern: 162–95; 196–294; 545–656; 657–808. Sin; punishment; coming of king or kingdom.

Oracles against nations: 350–488. Some from mid-first century BCE.

The four oracles that follow a pattern each end with the advent of a king or kingdom (162–95; 196–294; 545–656; 657–808) (Collins 1998, 119). The final kingdom is the kingdom of God. Since there are four kingdoms, this may reflect the four-kingdom scheme we have seen in Dan. 2; 7; and elsewhere, except that in the other cases the kingdom of God follows the four and is not one of them. In any case, the fourfold sequence makes essentially the same point—the kingdoms of this world will end and God will be sovereign over all.

Sibylline Oracles 3:1–96: Initial oracle. We examine *Sibylline Oracle* 3 in the order in which it is now preserved. It begins with a section (1–96) that presents a complete, self-contained scenario in its own right. Since the issue in this section is God's sovereignty, it is a suitable introduction to the book as a whole. The section begins with the sibyl's claim that she is forced to prophesy by God enthroned on the cherubim.

Next the sibyl turns to humanity. Humans are created in God's image, and yet they do not walk in God's ways. We have not encountered this rationale for exhortation to proper behavior before. The sibyl then proclaims God's authority: "There is one sovereign God, ineffable, whose dwelling is in heaven" (11). God is self-creating, unseen but seeing all, eternal, incapable of being seen by humans or even having them pronounce his name. He is "the mighty, heavenly God, the World-Ruler" (19). He created all, including the heavenly luminaries and human beings. Unlike idols, he is not made of stone or metal.

Humans commit the ultimate folly when they worship animals and idols made of stone and metal.

Humanity errs in other ways as well. People are liars, idolaters, adulterers; they are selfish and will not share with the needy; women take on lovers for money; and they engage in all manner of immorality. The political sign that God's coming is near is that Rome will take control of Egypt, which the sibyl says has not yet happened. (Augustus defeated Antony and Cleopatra in the battle of Actium in 31 BCE, and at that time Rome definitively subjugated Egypt.) Once that happens, God's kingdom will come and he will rule all through a "prince." Then there is a typical eschatological scenario. "Latin" people in particular are punished. There is cosmic turmoil. Fire floods the earth from heaven. Cities will be destroyed, and the sibyl enumerates particular ones that are doomed. Beliar appears and deceives many with his power over the mountains, sea, sun, and moon. He even raises the dead. Beliar appears as an antichrist. Even some Jews fall prey to his wiles. God consumes Beliar with fire, and a "widow" then rules the earth; she casts various types of metal, a symbol of earthly power, into the sea.

At that point, God will "roll up the heaven" like a scroll (82). The firmament will fall to earth, and all will be burned up. The heavenly luminaries will be gone, as will the seasons that they ruled. A sun will rise that will never cease, and God's judgment will take place.

The sibyl sees the world as a mess because of its failure to follow God's ways. Humans violate God's sovereignty by idolatry and they offend him through immorality. The Romans are the worst. God's judgment is inevitable and imminent.

Sibylline Oracles *3:97–161: Part of the main collection.* The first oracle of the main collection is 97–161. It is remarkable in that it treats Greek mythology as a historical account. This is an instance of euhemerism, the belief that the stories of the gods were really embellishments of historical figures, kings, and heroes. The theory goes back to Euhemerus of Messene around 300 BCE (Collins 1998, 119). The sibyl traces "history" beginning with the building of the Tower of Babel (Gen. 11), when humans angered God by attempting to build a tower to reach into heaven (probably a critique of the Mesopotamian ziggurats). Then the sibyl gets into Greek mythology.

After God divides humanity into nations, thus creating the potential for conflict, Chronos, Titan, and Iapetus are kings. Despite their divine nature in Greek stories, here they belong to the tenth generation of humanity. The three are the children of Gaia and Ouranos. These names mean "earth" and "heaven." The stories are about humans, but people have projected this onto a cosmic scale, making them cosmic powers. When their father dies, Chronos and Titan fight each other. A lengthy section follows, recounting the successive battles of the Greek figures. After this, there is a listing of eight kingdoms that follow, ending with Rome. Collins suggests that, since the sibyllines often speak of ten kingdoms, that the kingdom of God would follow Rome, and the kingdom of Chronos should be counted here.

Sibylline Oracles *3:162–95: First oracle with the common pattern*. The second oracle of the main collection is 162–95. It is one of the four that Collins says follow the pattern of sin-disaster-kingdom. It goes through the succession of kingdoms, beginning with that of Solomon, ultimately going through the kingdoms of the Greeks and Macedonians and ending with Rome. The Roman period is characterized negatively. It is full of oppression and immorality. This situation prevails until "there shall reign over Egypt a king, who shall be of Greek origin, and then the nation of the Mighty God shall be again powerful, that nation which shall be to all mortals the guide of life" (192–95). This Hellenistic Egyptian king introduces the restoration of Israel. In this sense, he is a salvific figure. Israel is that part of humanity whose God is the true God, and which therefore is a model for the entire human race.

Sibylline Oracles *3:196–294: Second oracle with the common pattern*. The next oracle is 196–294. It also is part of the original collection and follows the pattern of sin-disaster-kingdom. It contains far more information about Israel's fate than the oracles we have examined thus far. It speaks first of God's punishment inflicted on the kingdoms preceding Israel, naming that of the Titans, the Greeks, the Phrygians, and so on. The sibyl predicts misfortune for those "who dwell around the great temple of Solomon" (214), a reference to Israel. These people are godly people, descended from godly people. Their righteousness is defined as refraining from such practices as astrology, augury, sorcery, the deep mysteries of earth and sea, magic, and enchantments. All of these attempts to find and control secret knowledge and cosmic powers challenge God's authority. The righteous lead strictly moral lives, not engaging in common sins. Noteworthy is the element of social justice, where the righteous rich give a portion of their wealth to the poor. This is seen as "fulfilling the command of the Mighty God, the ever abiding strain" (246).

The sibyl predicts that Moses will lead the people out of Egypt, that God will give them his law, and that they will suffer evil because they disobey that law. They will commit idolatry; as punishment they will be driven away from God's sanctuary, and their land and the sanctuary will be destroyed. The people will go into exile, where the natives will be angered by their peculiar customs. This last point offers a small window into how at least some Jews were treated in the Diaspora. Their exile will last seventy years, a number derived from the prediction of Jeremiah.

When Israel obeys the Torah once again, God will send them a king and will judge everyone. Then there will be a royal line that will not fail. Israel will return to Judah and rebuild the temple. The Persians will help rebuild the temple, and it will be as it was before. God will encourage the rebuilding in a revelatory dream.

Sibylline Oracles *3:295–488: Oracles against nations.* Verse 295 introduces a lengthy oracle that condemns each of the nations by name. Collins notes that the oracles in the section are collected from a number of sources. The section begins with the sibyl revealing that God had told her to prophesy concerning each land so that their kings might know what is in store for them. She begins with Babylon and Assyria, the two nations responsible for the exile of the southern kingdom of Judah and the northern kingdom of Israel, respectively (301–13). Babylon receives the most attention, as usual, since the northern kingdom had disappeared into the mists of history, while the south returned to Judah from exile in Babylonia to carry on Israel's history and traditions. Horrible punishments await Babylon, commensurate with its grievous sin in destroying God's temple. Egypt is the object of the next oracle, and it also will suffer punishment (314–18).

Next to receive news of doom are Gog and Magog, located in Ethiopia. Their presence here is remarkable, for while Babylonia, Assyria, and Egypt are historical entities who played key roles in Israel's history, Gog of Magog is a mythological leader who appears in the eschatological battles of *Ezek.* 38–39; Magog is a land to the north of Israel and Gog is its prince. In *Sibylline Oracles* 3, Gog and Magog are both leaders from Africa. This leads the sibyl to attack another African nation, Libya.

The sibyl then turns to an enemy from the west who destroyed the temple, an apparent reference to Rome. The sibyl predicts the fall of many cities of the Roman Empire in both Europe and Asia. Rome itself will return threefold what it has stolen from Asia, and each Asian forced into Roman slavery will have twenty Italians to serve him and to suffer poverty and bondage like they inflicted on their Asian victims. Rome's punishment will bring joy to Europe and Asia. We have seen in our discussion of Revelation that many in Asia profited from Roman rule and expressed their loyalty and gratitude through the imperial cult (allowing also for the possibility that they did so for purely practical reasons). The *Sibyllines* give a different view. Here the Romans are invaders, destroyers, oppressors, and violators of other nations. The sibyl foresees a time of social concord when all live under God's law and there is no more war, division, or oppression.

There follows a long and complex section detailing in prophetic form political and military events in the Hellenistic world. Easily recognizable are the exploits of Alexander the Great and his successors which bring war and suffering to the world. Along the way, the sibyl takes a swipe at Homer, who distorted history through his poetic art and brought gods into the picture of warfare between peoples (419–32). Without him, the stories of the heroes and the gods would have perished, which the sibyl thinks would have been a good thing. So Homer also will get what he deserves in the end, and, although that is not specified by the sibyl, it is not positive.

Sibylline Oracles *3:489–544: Part of the main collection.* Verses 489–91 signal the beginning of another oracle (489–544). The sibyl cries that God has compelled her to prophesy concerning many lands. The sibyl is interested primarily in the Hellenistic world. Gog and Magog reappear. Much of the oracle is dedicated to the barbarian assault on the Greeks. It is God's punishment. In the end, "all Hellas [Greece] shall lie under the yoke of slavery" (537). Following this, God inflicts pestilence and drought and fire on all of humanity, and a third dies.

Sibylline Oracles 3:545–656: *Third oracle with the common pattern.* The next oracle is 545–656. It is the third of the four that have the pattern of sin-disaster-kingdom and is addressed to the Greeks. They may have suffered at the hands of the Romans, but that does not excuse them of their own tyranny. They commit idolatry and have done so since the time of their ancient kings a millennium and a half ago. Now they are to be punished, even if they belatedly turn to the true God. God's just sentence must be executed. Then a new race will arise who will have God's law and who worship him alone. They serve God in his temple. They live happily in their own land, and their prophets benefit all of humanity. They do not create human artifacts but direct their prayers to heaven (a reference to Judaism's lack of an engraved image for God). They "respect the purity of marriage" and do not engage in sex with boys, critiques of the Hellenistic culture around them.

Then an Egyptian king will arise, the seventh of his line. At that time, a powerful king comes from the east and overwhelms the earth. He defeats all kingdoms, Egypt in particular. Then he rides on the sea and comes "to God, the great King, the Eternal" and worships him. Humanity's accomplishments are as nothing and are burned up. God then gives them abundant food and drink.

The sibyl counsels people to offer sacrifices to God, to be righteous, and to refrain from oppression. But the sibyl predicts that humans will engage in terrible actions that will bring God's punishment. Kings will engage in destructive warfare, barbarians will ravage Greece, and humans will fight over gold and silver. Their bodies will be devoured by vultures and beasts, and the earth will swallow their remains. The earth will revert to an uncultivated state. Finally, people will burn their own weapons, and God will send a king from the east who will put an end to war. Some will die at his hands but others will be among the faithful. All these things he will do in obedience to God.

This oracle draws the line between Jews and non-Jews vividly. It does so in the traditional terms of idolatry and morality, especially sexual immorality. It is distinctive, however, that the king who brings salvation is not even Jewish, much less Davidic.

Sibylline Oracles 3:657–808: *Fourth oracle with the common pattern.* The final oracle of the four oracles that have the pattern of sin-disaster-kingdom is verses 657–808. It begins with Israel living in its own land in peace and prosperity. Then the kings of the earth, tired of fighting one another, turn against Israel and encamp around Jerusalem. This is the familiar eschatological idea that the nations will gather against Israel at the end of time. God attacks the nations and fills the earth with dead bodies. They are guilty not only because they attack Israel, but because "they knew not the Law" (686). The beasts consume the bodies, an element found also in Ezek. 39; Rev. 19; and other eschatological scenarios.

After the destruction of its enemies, Israel once again lives in peace around the holy sanctuary in Jerusalem. God protects them as an encircling fire, recalling Zech. 1. The rest of the world takes notice: "See how the Eternal loves these men" (711). The gentiles stream to Jerusalem to worship the one they now recognize as the one true God. They study God's Torah and worship him. They repent of their past idolatry and burn their weapons. They castigate Greece for its arrogance and for its attack on Jerusalem.

Then comes God's judgment. He burns up the "stubborn men" who refuse to acknowledge his sovereignty, but for the rest there is untold fertility of the land, lack of war, friendship between kings, abundance of livestock, and a common law for all living on the earth. Then the sibyl delivers an exhortation. This section contains some implicit common Jewish criticisms of gentile society. They are no longer to engage in unlawful service but are to serve only God. They are to shun adultery and sexual activity between males. They are not to slay their own infants, a reference to the practice of exposure of unwanted babies.

The nations now come to Jerusalem to worship the true God. There is an idyllic time when there is an abundance of earthly goods, animals of prey coexist peacefully with their former victims, and the dangers of the earth vanish. Signs precede this ideal age. Visions of swords will be seen in the sky at dawn and dusk, dust will fall from heaven onto earth, the light of the sun and moon behaves strangely, the rocks drip with blood, and visions of a battle appear in the clouds. This is the "consummation of war" accomplished by God (807). The oracle ends with the assertion, "All must sacrifice to the Mighty King" (808). This shows that a major issue for the author is the evil of sacrificing to any being other than God.

This oracle draws a clear distinction between Jews and gentiles. The view of gentiles is a typical one: they are idolatrous, immoral, and engage in endless violence against one another. Sacrifice to beings other than God is heinous. The oracle brings together several elements that are familiar from apocalypses. The nations gather against Israel in Jerusalem to annihilate it. God attacks and destroys them. Then Israel lives again in peace and prosperity. The nations convert to the true God by seeing what God has done for Israel. There then comes idyllic peace and prosperity when all worship God and all are under his law.

Several times in *Sibylline Oracles* 3 there appears an Egyptian king who is a virtual messiah (Collins 1998, 119–22). He is called the seventh of the Greek kings, and he is also called a king from the sun, an appellation that is found elsewhere in Egyptian literature. Due to the reign of the seventh king, Egypt throws away its idols (606–8). In 652–66, by order of the true God, he cleanses the earth of war. Designating a gentile as such a salvific figure recalls Isaiah's assessment of Cyrus the Great, who is explicitly hailed as a messiah in Isa. 45:1, and who is praised in this very oracle (286–94).

Sibylline Oracles 4

This book shows signs of having been edited over time. Its periodization of history includes ten periods and four kingdoms. The last period coincides with the last kingdom and assumes Greek domination. Then the work goes on to consider the Roman Empire, which is neither one of the four kingdoms, nor the final, eschatological kingdom. Some of the work was written before Roman domination of Jewish Palestine and some after. There is little specifically Jewish in the original document, so Collins considers it to be an example of "Near Eastern resistance to Hellenism" (1998, 240; 1974b).

The book begins with the sibyl contrasting her presentation of the reliable word of the one true God with the false prophet of the pagan god Phoebus. The traditional contrast of idols fashioned by humans and the almighty creator of the universe is invoked. The sibyl has been given the task of foretelling all that is to happen throughout the ten "generations" of the earth. Remarkably for a Jewish work, the sibyl proclaims as happy those who do not put stock in any earthly temples or literal, bloody sacrifices. This is unusual. It is part of how the author deals with the destruction of the temple by the Romans (for a similar view of 2 Baruch, see Murphy 1984). She shifts attention to morality, designating as evil such things as murder, dishonesty in business, males having sexual relations with males, and hypocrisy. In God's judgment, the wicked will be consigned to the fire, while the righteous will "remain upon the fruitful field" (45). This is to happen in the tenth generation.

Now the sibyl reviews all ten generations. The Assyrians rule for six, beginning with the great flood. Then the Medes take over, ruling for two generations. During their rule, cosmic signs happen—night in the middle of the day, the falling to earth of the stars and moon, a mighty earthquake, the ruin of many cities, the appearance of islands, the Euphrates being full of blood, all ending in war between the Medes and the Persians. Ordinarily, such signs would signal the onset of the final days, but here they do not.

The Persians defeat the Medes, who flee across the Tigris. The time of Persian rule is dismal, full of wars, schisms, and the ruin of cities. It lasts one generation.

Then come the Greeks. They bring doom to Asia, Egypt, and as far east as Bactria, near India. Greek conquest is soon followed by the rise of Rome, which now brings us outside the scheme of the ten generations, indicating that the original document was a protest against Greek rule and was then edited to take account of Roman rule. "Italy" enslaves the Greek world. Romans overcome Jerusalem and destroy its temple, which places this section of the work after 70 CE.

Then there is a reference to Nero. In our discussion of Revelation, we have mentioned the Nero legends that arose after his suicide in 68 CE. Rumors circulated that he did not really die. This passage from *Sibylline Oracles* 4 speaks of Nero fleeing over the Euphrates to Parthia like a fugitive slave, accurately accuses him of matricide, and notes that this led to much bloodshed in Rome. After this, a Roman leader attacks Jerusalem and destroys its temple and "godly men," Israel. Vespasian first received charge of the Jewish war from Nero; he attacked Jerusalem, and then he became emperor in 69 CE and turned the war over to his son Titus, who took the city and destroyed the temple.

The author expects this to be followed by Nero's return, "the exile from Rome" (138), who attacks the west with a huge army. Rome falls, and the wealth Rome pilfered from Asia is returned, an element we observed in *Sibylline Oracles* 3 as well. This is divine retribution. Soon the world becomes entirely ungodly, practicing all sorts of evils; God will destroy them all.

This leads to a plea by the sibyl that her hearers become righteous. If they do, God will relent. In apocalypticism, and generally in the *Sibyllines* as well, history and the coming judgment are foreordained. Humans cannot change this. This is a major difference between apocalypses and the classical prophets. The prophets preached repentance, through which God's punishment could be averted. *Sibylline Oracles* 4 is closer to the prophetic than the apocalyptic tradition in this aspect.

If humankind persists in its evil ways, God will burn up all humans. Then he will quench the fire and raise up humans again. The ungodly he will send to hell. The righteous he will bring onto a renewed and pleasant earth.

The third *Sibylline Oracle* shows how a single document can be edited to respond to a situation later than its original writing. It was used first to make sense of Greek domination and then of Roman oppression. It is a political as well as a religious work. In its final form, it sees a resolution of the destruction of Jerusalem and its temple through the punishment of Rome through Nero and the forces of the east, and ultimately through God's direct intervention. After God's judgment and the removal of the ungodly from earth, the righteous will live in God's favor in a renewed world.

Sibylline Oracles 5

Sibylline Oracles 5 consists of six oracles (Collins 1998, 234–38). The four central oracles follow a common pattern in which there is a condemnation of nations (Egypt in one and three; Asian nations in two and four), "the return of Nero as an eschatological adversary" (Collins 1998, 234), the coming of a "savior figure," and destruction, usually by fire. The tone of the work is anti-Roman and pessimistic, especially since it ends with a scene of destruction. The four central oracles were written after the destruction of Jerusalem and its temple in 70 CE but show no knowledge of the Jewish revolution that took place afterward in the Diaspora under Trajan (115–17 CE). The final oracle (435–531) does refer to that event, and so was written after it. The initial oracle of the book (1–51) is the latest, since it refers to Hadrian and perhaps even to Marcus Aurelius (Collins 1998, 234).

This collection of oracles is similar to apocalypses in that it depends on direct revelation to a seer (sibyl) of crises to come, refers to a final eschatological crisis in which nature plays a role, speaks of cosmic destruction, contains themes that occur in apocalypses such as the Nero legend, and contains social dualism. It does not, however, mention life after death.

The first oracle (1–51) introduces the whole collection. Its first verse displays anti-Romanism, for it characterizes what follows as the "woeful chronicle of the sons of Latium" (1), the Romans. The rest of the first oracle is primarily a listing of Roman emperors, using the numerical equivalent of their initials to designate them. Of note is the treatment of Nero. He is described as "athlete, charioteer, murderer, and doer of a thousand extravagant acts" (31). His failed attempt to cut a canal across the isthmus of Corinth is cited. Referring to the beliefs about him after his death, the sibyl says, "Even when he disappears, he shall be malignant" (33). He will return claiming divinity, but God will oppose him.

Vespasian comes in for special mention as "a destroyer of godly men" (36) because of his war against the Jews in Palestine. He was called away from the war to be emperor. His son, Titus, took over the military leadership and ultimately inherited the throne from his father. Remarkably, the destruction of the temple is not mentioned explicitly, giving support to Collins's suggestion that this was originally a pro-Roman oracle that was later adapted to its present context. *Sibylline Oracles* 11–14 and 1–2 are also pro-Roman, showing that not all Jews everywhere were anti-Roman, nor were they always anti-Egyptian. The Jewish war and the destruction of Jerusalem turned many Jews against Rome.

The second oracle (52–110) is against Egypt. Egypt is castigated for mistreating the Jews. It has fallen from the stars and will not ascend to heaven. It is taken to task for idolatry, as usual. "The Persian" will come upon it, a possible allusion to Nero, who will come from Persia leading hordes from the east. When he has completely devastated Egypt, he will attack Jerusalem, "the city of the blessed" (107). At that point, God will intervene by sending a king to defeat him and to carry out judgment on kings and unrighteous men.

The third oracle (111–78) follows the pattern of the second—oracle against the nations, return of Nero, appearance of a redemptive figure, and destruction. This oracle takes aim at various cities and regions of Asia especially. The section on Nero details the suffering the world endured through him. He is called "godlike" because he took his own divinity more seriously than did other Roman emperors except for Caligula. He attempted to pierce the Isthmus of Corinth. The sibyl calls his supposed divine ancestry false. His mother met a bad end, and he was fearless, shameless, and loathed by all. He is blamed for the destruction of the Jewish temple (he was emperor at the beginning of the Jewish war) and burned many Jews, destroying the holy temple and the righteous people.

The savior figure is represented by a bright star that descends to earth from heaven. Stars were often considered to be angels. The oracle of Balaam speaks of a savior as a star in a passage that held messianic significance at Qumran and elsewhere (Collins 1998, 236). The name Bar Kokhba, a messianic figure in the revolt against Rome in 132–135 CE, means son of a star. In this oracle, the star burns up the sea, whose god is Poseidon whom the Romans honor, and burns Italy and Babylon (Rome). The burning of the sea carries overtones of the sea as God's enemy in the ancient Near Eastern combat myth. The Romans are guilty because on their account "many faithful saints of the Hebrews have perished, and the true people" (161).

Rome is guilty of numerous sins. They engage in magic, adultery, intercourse with boys, and injustice. Rome is "effeminate" (167). This would be a great insult to an ancient male. The worst thing in patriarchal societies is to be like a woman. Rome has overestimated itself, claiming unique status. God will destroy Rome and prove it wrong. Its destination is Hades.

The fourth oracle turns again to Egypt. Once master of the world, it will suffer at the hands of its traditional enemy, Ethiopia, and others. In the end, they too will perish. When Nero returns (214), God will give him power and he will overcome Egypt. All this happens because the world is in chaos due to Jerusalem's fall: "For all men blood and horrors are in store because of the great city and the righteous people, brought safe through all, whom Providence exalted" (225–27). The destruction of humanity is a suitable penalty for the attack on the holy city and its people. The sibyl takes the Fates to task for bringing evil on the world and for their false counsel, but eventually they will be the instrument of good news.

Next come words of salvation. They have been edited by Christians, since they speak of a man coming from the sky who is nailed to a tree by his hands. It is possible, however, that this passage originally did speak of a non-Christian savior figure, since that is common in these oracles.

The savior figure arrives when Persia is at peace and "the godlike heavenly race of the blessed Jews, who dwell around the city of God at the center of the earth," are also at peace. The Greeks will no longer trample the holy land. The Jews will offer hymns and sacrifices to God. Evil will go into hiding. Fire rains from heaven, crops are destroyed, the land lies desolate, and there is no animal worship, for which the Egyptians were notorious. The righteous will be blessed, for they worship the one God.

The fifth oracle is directed primarily against Asian cities (286–433). Their idolatry arouses the sibyl's wrath. God hurls a "fiery meteor" from heaven, and all nature is disturbed. Dead bodies pile up from God's assault. Cyme, the site of a famous sibyl, is called "foolish," since our sibyl considers all other sibyls false. As she continues her jeremiad against Asian cities, the sibyl pauses for a moment to mention God's grace on Judea, a land divinely blessed from the beginning and which was given special responsibility to know and do God's will.

When God's reign begins, all is darkness. People will finally look to God in heaven who is the King and who "watches" from heaven. He will have no compassion on his enemies, who sacrifice to Hermes and stone deities. There is only one sensible response: "Let justice, wisdom, and glory hold sway over the just, lest the immortal God in anger destroy the whole bloodstained race of men and their shameless kin. We must love the Father, the Wise, the Everlasting" (358–60). If God finds no one who worships him alone, he will destroy the entire human race.

Next comes Nero. He invades the west from the east, a matricide who will take over the empire, surpass all people in cunning, assume absolute power, and ruin the earth. He will burn all people.

The earth is filled with war, which ends when nature itself reacts. The righteous alone are left, and they enjoy peace at long last. Punishment overtakes the sinners. Their sexual sin is highlighted—abuse of boys, incest, prostitution, and even bestiality.

The sibyl laments the destruction of Jerusalem's temple "for the second time," this time by the Romans (the first was by the Babylonians). The temple was surrounded by people who refused false worship and adored only the one God. An "unholy king" defiled and destroyed it, and then met his own death.

A king is sent by God who conquers all and destroys the evildoers. He rebuilds the city and the temple in splendor and makes it "more radiant than the sun and moon" (421). It has a giant tower that reaches to heaven, probably the temple itself, that commands recognition of this city as God's. All people, from east to west, sing hymns to God. This happens through "God the sender of thunder, the Creator of the great Temple" (433).

The sixth and final oracle of this collection is in 434–531. The sibyl preaches doom for Babylon and then foresees that all the earth will be enveloped in warfare. The Egyptian gods Isis and Serapis, very popular gods in the Greco-Roman world, will be abandoned. The sibyl exhorts listeners to build God's true temple. They are to renounce idolatry and engage in true service to the one God. This God is Father, King, and supreme. He sustains all souls and is eternal. A temple to the true God will be raised in Egypt, and all will be well. But then the dreaded Ethiopians, traditional foes of the Egyptians, attack and destroy the temple. This provokes God's anger and war arises in heaven. The constellations are heavenly beings who war with one another and fall fighting onto the earth, leaving the sky starless and the earth devastated.

This is the gloomy ending of *Sibylline Oracle 5*. Although there are oracles of salvation within these oracles, they are overshadowed by visions of war, suffering, catastrophe, cosmic dissolution, and divine punishment. They rail against idolatry and sexual immorality, typical complaints of Jews against gentiles. A true temple is built in Egypt. God favors Judea, Jerusalem and its temple, and the people of Israel, but until some future time God's favor does not save them from political oppression and suffering.

Testaments of the Twelve Patriarchs

Study of the *Testaments of the Twelve Patriarchs* is beset with problems. In its present form, it is Christian. Some hold that the work is originally Christian (de Jonge 1953), while others maintain that it is originally Jewish and has been edited by Christians (Slingerland 1977). We take the latter view, for while it is impossible to separate neatly the Jewish work from the Christian adaptations, still, most of the work has nothing distinctively Christian about it.

A second problem is that the *Testaments* has undergone a complex textual history (de Jonge 1953). It has affinities to other Jewish texts and traditions and may have existed in various forms. The final work incorporates pre-existent works, partially attested at Qumran and in the Cairo Geniza (a storeroom in a Cairo synagogue) (Collins 1998, 134–36).

A third difficulty concerns dating. The final form of the work must be during Christian times, but it is more difficult to guess when the Jewish work was more or less complete. The long disquisitions on ethical matters—virtues and vices—sound Hellenistic and are uncharacteristic of Jewish apocalypticism. The closest we come to such teaching is in the wisdom literature, but even there we do not find such long and well-argued pieces of ethical import. This suggests that the work is the product of the Diaspora, rather than the Palestinian homeland (Collins 1998, 136).

Perhaps we can turn difficulties into insight. The very mix of elements in this multifaceted work teaches us something about apocalypticism in Judaism in the late Second Temple period and in early Christianity. It shows that an apocalyptic worldview, even when not the centerpiece of a given document, can still be an integral part of that work's worldview and can be taken almost for granted. For example, there are frequent references in the *Testaments* to *1 Enoch*. The author(s) knew it well and respected it greatly. Also, references to Beliar are common in the work, and he is opposed to the good angel. This takes place both in the ethical sections and in the eschatological sections. Resurrection is taken for granted. The predictions of the future usually issue in eschatological scenarios. A dual messiahship is expected, one priestly and the other royal, with the priestly ascendant, as at Qumran.

Another insight is that ancient documents were often not static, fixed entities. They were written, edited, rewritten, and adapted to new situations and new ways of thinking.

Certain themes span this collection of testaments. The first is extensive ethical instruction, concentrating on individual sin and virtue and bolstered by examples and counterexamples in the patriarchs' lives. Predictions of the future warn against sin, encourage virtue, and set out sanctions for human behavior. This recalls wisdom literature (Collins 1998, 136–37; 1993b). Another theme is the legitimation of the Levitical priestly leadership. There is also frequent reference to Judah's leadership, although Judah is considered inferior to Levi.

Testaments usually speak of the future, and these are no exception. The eschatological sections generally follow the pattern of sin, followed by exile, followed by restoration. This is a pattern familiar to the book of Deuteronomy.

Worthy of close analysis are chapters 2–5 of the *Testament of Levi*, for they constitute a complete apocalypse. The apocalypse shows some internal inconsistency, as Collins indicates, since the number and order of the heavens are somewhat confused. In this apocalypse, Levi ascends into heaven and has an experience that solidifies his priestly status.

In chapter 2, Levi recalls the circumstances of his vision. He has just participated in the sack of Shechem, condemned by Jacob in the Bible because it violated a treaty Jacob had concluded with the Shechemites. In subsequent Jewish tradition, however, the sack of Shechem was approved of, probably because it was the dwelling place of the Samaritans, traditional enemies of the Jews. In the *Testament of Levi*, this is the occasion of Levi being invited into heaven by an angel, so Levi's role in the sack is praiseworthy and becomes part of the reason he is selected eternal priest. Levi falls asleep and is possessed by God's spirit. In this state, he perceives the pervasive wickedness of humankind. Levi sees three heavens, but it is said that there are four more, seven in all. Levi travels through the first heaven, in which there is a sea hanging. This draws on the ancient idea that there are waters above the firmament. In this case, they separate the lowest heaven from the other two. Levi marvels at the light in the second heaven, and then he enters the highest heaven, where the light is still brighter. There he stands in God's presence. The angel informs him that he will learn God's mysteries, which he must then impart to humans so that they may be saved.

In the following chapter, the heavenly levels number seven. They appear in the following order in the text:

1. The lowest is gloomy because it houses the iniquities of humans. It is full of fire, snow, and ice in preparation for the day of judgment, and there dwell the spirits of retribution, also ready for the last day. This heaven intervenes between humans on earth and the upper heavens, blocking human view into what lies beyond.
2. In the second heaven are the angelic armies ready to wage war on Beliar and his allies.

3. Above them are "holy ones" (presumably in the third heaven). These are angels.
4. In the highest heaven (unnumbered, but apparently the seventh) is God, "far above all holiness."
5. Below the highest heaven is one (the sixth) in which the archangels expiate the sins of ignorance of the righteous through bloodless sacrifice.
6. In the next heaven (the fifth) are messenger angels who bring information to the archangels.
7. In the next heaven (the fourth) are thrones and dominations, types of angels, who continually praise God.

The angel explains to Levi that God looks down through the heavens and could cause all to fear. Since humans do not have a clear view into heaven, they do not know enough to fear God, and so they sin. This is an ingenious explanation of why humans dare to affront the deity. Only a clear view into the heavens of the sort that has been granted to Levi will set humans straight. Since he has made this apocalyptic journey and learned God's mysteries, Levi alone is qualified to guide humankind.

Chapter 4 describes judgment in traditional apocalyptic terms—cosmic chaos, Hades swallowing up the dead, and persistent human iniquity. Only those who heed Levi's wisdom will be saved.

In chapter 5, the angel opens the gates of the highest heaven and allows Levi to behold God on his throne. God bestows on him the priesthood "until I come and sojourn in the midst of Israel." This will be the culmination and goal of history. The angel gives Levi a sword and instructions to destroy Shechem. Levi asks the angel's name so that he can call on him in time of tribulation. The angel gives him no name but describes himself as the one who intercedes for Israel, probably Michael. Levi awakes and blesses God and the angel.

Despite the numerous difficulties in interpreting the *Testaments of the Twelve Patriarchs*, it testifies to the extent to which apocalyptic thinking can mix with other forms to create a rich document. Concerns with ethical behavior, the inculcation of moral virtue, political and religious power and hierarchy, the place of Israel among the nations, the judgment of human iniquity—all come together and are illuminated by the conception of the world as ultimately controlled by God but opaque to sinful humans, enlightenment available only through the Jewish priesthood bolstered here by Levi's apocalyptic vision, and the hope that in the future God will dwell with Israel and that the ideal priest and king will rule.

Christians found this work congenial to their interests. All they needed to do was to add details that transformed the eschaton into the coming of Christ.

Collins lays out the ways in which the *Testaments* is like and unlike apocalypses (Collins 1998, 137). Apocalypses see the future as unalterable, although individuals can determine their own fate by being on the right side of the eschatological struggle. The *Testaments* follows a more traditional Deuter-onomistic, covenantal scheme whereby what happens in the future is at least to some extent determined by human action. Virtue brings reward, and sin brings punishment. Like apocalypses, the *Testaments* is pseudonymous. The source of revelation in apocalypses is the conveyance of secrets to a seer by a superhuman figure. In the *Testaments*, the patriarch's insights are the content of information, typical of testaments, although there are frequent references to *Enoch* as well, usually concerning predictions of the future, predictions that look apocalyptic. In some cases, the patriarchs receive privileged information, the best example being Levi in the *Testament of Levi* 2–5.

Also apocalyptic is the frequent reference to Beliar (once to Satan), and to his heavenly rival, the angel of peace. These tempt or support individuals in their ethical struggles, and they also play an eschatological role—after death each takes to himself his own kind of humans (Collins 1998, 139–40).

Testament of Levi 18 brings together elements useful to Jewish apocalyptic thought, but the chapter is either a Christian product or has been extensively reworked by Christians. Following the disloyalty of the Jewish priests, an es-chatological figure arises who is both priest and king. God reveals the divine word to him. He judges the whole earth. His star rises in heaven "as of a king," perhaps an allusion to Balaam's star and scepter prophecy. Heaven and earth rejoice. Divine knowledge is poured out on the earth, and the "angels of the glory of the presence of the Lord" (18:5) rejoice in him. The heavens open, and sanctification pours out upon him, and he receives consecration and understand-ing "in the water" (a reference to Jesus's baptism in the Jordan River and the descent of the Spirit on him at that time). He mediates God's glory to humans, and he saves the gentiles. He opens the gates of paradise, sin is abolished, and the righteous have rest. Those who are holy eat of the tree of life and possess the Holy Spirit. He binds Beliar, his children receive power to tread on poison-ous serpents (see Mark 16:18). God, Abraham, Isaac, Jacob, and Levi exult.

Many other passages of this lengthy work are worth investigation, but we have said enough to indicate how apocalyptic thought can inform other sorts of writing, especially testaments, and serve a variety of purposes.

Conclusion

There are still other documents from ancient Judaism worthy of study, but space prevents us from examining them here. We have looked at some of the more significant ones to give an idea of the widespread nature of apocalyptic thought at this time, even beyond apocalypses. We have added to our store of knowledge the kinds of things to expect from apocalyptic belief—scenarios, images, themes, and so on. We are now well equipped to investigate how the early Christian movement made use of these materials.

Suggestions for Further Reading

Atkinson, Kenneth. *I Cried to the Lord: A Study of the Psalms of Solomon's Historical Background and Social Setting*. Boston: Brill, 2004.

Collins, John Joseph. *The Apocalyptic Imagination: An Introduction to Jewish Apocalyptic Literature*. 2nd ed. Grand Rapids: Eerdmans, 1998.

———. "The Sibylline Oracles." In *The Old Testament Pseudepigrapha*, edited by J. H. Charlesworth, 317–472. New York: Doubleday, 1983.

———. *The Sibylline Oracles of Egyptian Judaism*. Missoula, MT: Society of Biblical Literature, 1974.

De Jonge, Marinus. *Jewish Eschatology, Early Christian Christology, and the Testaments of the Twelve Patriarchs: Collected Essays of Marinus de Jonge*. New York: Brill, 1991.

Hollander, Harm W., and Marinus de Jonge. *The Testaments of the Twelve Patriarchs: A Commentary*. Leiden: Brill, 1985.

Nickelsburg, George W. E. *Jewish Literature between the Bible and the Mishnah: An Historical and Literary Introduction*. 2nd ed. Minneapolis: Fortress, 2005.

Slingerland, H. Dixon. *The Testaments of the Twelve Patriarchs: A Critical History of Research*. Missoula, MT: Scholars Press, 1977.

7

The Dead Sea Scrolls

Finding the Scrolls

In 1947, a Bedouin boy discovered ancient manuscripts in a cave in the Judean hills to the northwest of the Dead Sea. His discovery sparked a series of searches that occupied the better part of a decade and resulted in the discovery of a total of eleven caves containing the remains of about eight hundred texts dating from the first century CE and the first couple of centuries BCE. Some texts were almost complete, preserved carefully in jars, while others had to be pieced together from tiny fragments, many buried deep in the sand of the caves' floors. Some documents were in multiple copies, while others survived only as a few scraps. The number of manuscripts and fragments is enormous, and the library contains around eight to nine hundred works in all. The work of bringing order to this chaos has been laborious, time consuming, and has involved innumerable scholarly decisions and interpretations. It involves solving what is probably the most complex jigsaw puzzle in history. The work continues to this day (Collins 1992b).

The manuscript find has been hailed as the greatest archaeological discovery of the twentieth century. It is easy to imagine the excitement of the scholars who first gained access to an ancient library untouched for almost two thousand years. The excitement was even greater in that the scrolls promised to shed light on two of the world's great religions—Judaism and Christianity—and to illumine the relationship between them. Occasionally, extravagant claims have been made that the scrolls would undermine the foundations of Christianity or would yield secrets about Jesus that would completely change how we think

Fig. 8. Cave 4 near Qumran yielded the richest store of manuscripts of the Dead Sea Scrolls. (Chris Miller)

of him. Such claims have always proven false. Nonetheless, the scrolls have made invaluable contributions to our understanding of late Second Temple Judaism and of early Christianity by providing firsthand, detailed evidence for an ancient Jewish apocalyptic community.

The long and fascinating story of the discovery of the scrolls, their retrieval, the problems of possession of them, and of their interpretation has often been told (Vermès 2004, 1–8; VanderKam and Flint 2002, 1–19). Part of the story is that for years many scrolls were entrusted to few scholars to edit and publish. This kept them from the public and from the larger academic community, causing frustration and bitterness. Everything changed in the early nineties; photographs of the scrolls suddenly became available to all, opening the floodgates to research and publication, and the flood continues to this day.

Overview

Scholarly opinion generally agrees that the scrolls are the library of a Jewish apocalyptic sect living in community (called the *yaḥad*, from the Hebrew for "one") near the caves in a settlement whose ruins are still visible today. The settlement is now called Qumran, derived from the Arab name for the ruins (Vaux 1973; Magness 2002; 2004; Patrich 2000; Pfann 2000). It was occupied, except for a brief break, for about two centuries—from around the middle of the second century BCE to its destruction by the Romans in 68 CE—during the war between the Jews and Romans.

The scrolls are fascinating for many reasons. They manifest a variety of perspectives on many subjects, but their worldview and social organization are relatively consistent and can be recovered, at least in their main lines. Other Jewish apocalyptic literature exists in something of a vacuum. Although we can comment generally on how apocalyptic texts may have fit into their environment, we are reduced to a good deal of educated guessing. In the case of the scrolls, we have the rare situation where we know something of the community that preserved them.

Josephus says that there were three Jewish "philosophical schools" (*haireseis*) in his day—the Pharisees, the Sadducees, and the Essenes. We know of the Essenes from reports by Philo, a Jewish philosopher of Alexandria who flourished in the early first century CE, and Pliny the Elder, a Roman writer of the first century CE, as well as from Josephus (Vermès and Goodman 1989). The Dead Sea Scrolls witness to a community like that of the Essenes and correspond to their geographical location, so most think that the people of the scrolls are Essenes.

The beginning of the sect's settlement at Qumran has generally been dated to around the mid-second century BCE (Vaux 1973; Magness 2002, 63–66). Archaeology suggests that the settlement was destroyed by the Romans in 68 CE. There was a brief gap in settlement under Herod the Great. So, in all, the *yaḥad* occupied Qumran for around two centuries, embracing the time of Jesus and early Christian beginnings.

The scrolls contain a variety of kinds of texts. First, there are biblical manuscripts. Before the discovery of the scrolls, the oldest extant biblical manuscripts dated from the Middle Ages. Experts have now demonstrated fluidity in the texts during the late Second Temple period (Bernstein 2000; VanderKam and Flint 2002, 103–53).

Of the nonbiblical texts, there are documents that are sectarian, ones that are not by the sect, and a third category of texts whose origin is debated. The sectarian texts demonstrate an origin in the sect's particular situation, both social and historical. Two obvious examples of this are the two main rulebooks (*serek*), the *Community Rule* and the *Damascus Rule*. They yield information about the sect's history, rules for living, social structure, ideology, and ways of praying. Other such texts are the *Thanksgiving Psalms*, some of which may reflect the experience of the sect's founder (the Teacher of Righteousness) or another of its early leaders. Unique to the sect are biblical commentaries that interpret biblical texts line by line, applying them to the sect's present. They are called *pĕšārîm*, plural of *pešer*, which is Hebrew for "interpretation." The *War Scroll* is also sectarian.

The scrolls also contain nonbiblical texts known from other contexts that contain nothing making them sectarian. Such works include *Jubilees* and most of *1 Enoch* (the *Similitudes* [*1 Enoch* 37–71] are missing at Qumran; instead we find the *Book of the Giants*). Finally, there are texts of disputed origin.

An example is the *Temple Scroll*, a long text that lays out how the temple is to be ordered until it is replaced by the eschatological temple.

When we consider that the Qumran library consists of so many texts, written in different circumstances over a considerable period of time, it is not surprising to find variety within the collection, even among works composed by the sect itself. We should not think of the sect as homogeneous over time and space. It is more accurate to think of it in looser terms, as a movement. It had adherents both at Qumran and outside the settlement. The scrolls show signs of serious disagreement even within the community itself. Collins recently published *Beyond the Qumran Community* (Collins 2010). The title indicates the necessity of moving beyond conceptions of the community as monolithic, homogeneous over time, and unified. Nonetheless, despite this caveat against overgeneralization, many agree on some mainline interpretations.

Who collected the library found in the caves? The likeliest candidates are those who wrote the sectarian scrolls. These writers and their fellows had a great interest in collecting biblical scrolls as well as much other material that they thought illuminating. Hints in the scrolls supply enough information to hazard informed guesses about this community.

Why Did the Sect Form?

Around the middle of the second century BCE, a group of Jewish men separated themselves from the rest of Palestinian Jewish society in order to live the Torah more faithfully, according to their interpretation. They vigorously disagreed with how the Jerusalem establishment interpreted and lived Torah. They settled at Qumran, west of the Dead Sea. They lived a life of celibacy and common property. They thought in apocalyptic terms and awaited God's direct intervention in history when he would fight with and for his chosen ones at Qumran. They would overcome the foreign overlords (first the Hellenistic rulers and then the Romans) and their Jewish allies, and God would establish them in Jerusalem as the rightful priests and the true Israel.

The scrolls also attest to another form of Essene life, one in which members did not completely withdraw from society, but lived a distinctive lifestyle in the region's villages. There is reason to believe that the groups that did not withdraw were actually an earlier form of the broader movement. Recently, another form of organization has been suggested that puts a special group of ten men as the epitome of the sect that travels between Essene settlements and unites them in practice and theology (Collins 2010; Stout 2011).

The group was a sect. A sect is a minority within society that shares society's outlook in some ways but not in others. A sect's differences with the larger society demand its separation from it in some way—geographically, as at Qumran, or in terms of lifestyle, as with Essenes living in villages, or both.

Both branches may have held a joint yearly meeting at Qumran to reinforce their unity and rededicate themselves to the new covenant God made with them. They were the community of the new covenant. The phrase comes from Jer. 31, where the prophet says that God will make a new covenant with Israel since Israel has broken the old. Jeremiah had in mind a renewal of the covenant so that it is within the hearts of the people; he did not mean a new religion, which is how Christians later interpreted the phrase.

It is not known for sure why the people of Qumran separated themselves from the rest of Jewish society. One theory is the Maccabean hypothesis. It posits that when the Seleucid emperor Antiochus IV tried to stamp out Judaism beginning in 167 BCE, the Maccabees forged a coalition with several different groups in Judaism. That coalition was not to survive the war against Antiochus; it broke up into the three groups mentioned by Josephus. We first hear of these groups—Pharisees, Sadducees, and Essenes—in the immediate postwar period. Each had a different interpretation of Torah and espoused a different way of being Jewish. Some Essenes found their differences with the Hasmonean establishment after the war to be intolerable and so eventually withdrew to the Judean desert. Some scholars identify this faction with the *ḥăsîdîm*, the "righteous" or "pious ones," who are called scribes, dedicated to the Torah, and mighty warriors, who allied with the Maccabees in the first stages of the Jewish revolt against the Seleucids in 167 BCE (1 Macc. 2:42; 7:12–16; 2 Macc. 14:6) (Cross 1995). Others are more specific, attributing Daniel and the Enochic writings to this group (Hengel 1974, 1:175–80). The *ḥăsîdîm* theory is speculative, since we know so little about them (Kampen 1988). The attribution of Daniel and the Enochic materials to the same group is unlikely, given their incompatible attitudes to the Hasmoneans.

The differences that caused the people of Qumran to withdraw from Jerusalem are debated. One suggestion is that they objected to the Hasmoneans assuming the high priesthood, though they were not from one of the traditional high priestly families. Some refine this thesis, noting that in some of the scrolls, the priests of Qumran claim Zadokite lineage. That is, they believed that they were descended from Solomon's high priest, Zadok. Ezekiel insisted in Ezek. 44 that only the Zadokites were full priests. Priesthood in the Second Temple period did not accord with Ezekiel's restrictive definition, but the Zadokites were the most prominent group of priests throughout the period (Hunt 2006). But none of the scrolls say explicitly that this is why the sect separated itself. Further, references to Zadokites in the scrolls may not date to the sect's origins (Davies 2000).

A key scroll in this regard is MMT (*Miqṣat Ma'ăśê Ha-Tôrâ*; "Some Observances of the Law"). It is fragmentary, so even its form is subject to debate. Its editors think that it was a letter written by the founder of the sect, probably the Teacher of Righteousness, to a high Jerusalem official, probably one of the Hasmonean king-priests (Qimron and Strugnell 1985; Qimron 1994). In its present form it consists of a calendar (incomplete) based on solar reckoning. It was not the calendar followed in Jerusalem. We have seen in our discussion of *1 Enoch* how important such a discrepancy was (Talmon 2000; VanderKam 1998; 1979). Contained within the Qumran library were nonsectarian works that also assumed a solar calendar—*Jubilees* and *1 Enoch*. It is possible that the sect isolated itself because it could not live in a community so at odds with God's will. Each feast celebrated in Jerusalem, and even many of the sacrifices in the temple, offended God. The *Damascus Rule* warns its readers not to enter the temple, for its sacrificial fires were lit "in vain" (6:13–14).

MMT contains a list of disagreements between the writer and his addressee on matters of law. Some might seem trivial to modern readers, but we must remember that every culture, ancient and modern, has symbolic issues not readily understandable to outsiders, but that represent key values to the society concerned. The writer seeks to persuade his addressee to agree with his interpretations. If the addressee had agreed, perhaps the community never would have left society, or, if they were already at the site, perhaps they would have returned. But the Jerusalem authorities did not bend. As the writer addresses the Jerusalem leader, he refers to a third group whose interpretation of Torah diverges from that of the sect. Many think that this group is the Pharisees (Baumgarten 2000; VanderKam and Flint 2002, 276–80; Harrington 2000).

The sectarians were a small minority in Israel. There was little to no chance that they could wrest Jerusalem from Hasmonean control through force of arms, although they were not pacifists. This is where apocalypticism served them well. First, they interpreted the present evil time as the age of wrath spoken of by Daniel in his apocalypse. They also called it the age of wickedness. They considered the present age as dominated by an evil cosmic force, personified in Belial, the prince of evil angels opposed to God. They saw Israel's foreign overlord (first the Hellenistic empires and then Rome) as in league with Belial. The idea of a superhuman power at the head of evil, angelic, demonic, and human forces finds no place in the Hebrew Bible. It first occurs in the context of apocalypticism. Dualism was part of the sect's worldview from its earliest days (Collins 1997, 45–47).

The sect anticipated a fierce battle at the end of this age in which God, his angels, and the faithful Jews of the sect would fight Belial, his angels, and all other humans, including an alliance of Israel's foreign enemies and unfaithful Jews (Collins 1997, 130–49; 2000c). The *War Scroll* foretells the specifics of the war and instructs Israel how to participate in it.

The *Damascus Rule* begins with a brief outline of the sect's history. At first, the sect consisted of people unhappy with Israel's situation, but unsure of what action to take (Hengel 2000). For about twenty years, they were "like men groping for the way" (1:9–10). Then there arose one to whom God revealed the things in which Israel had gone astray and what to do about it (1:11–12). This foundational figure is the Teacher of Righteousness (*môreh ha-ṣedek*).

He gave direction to the sect, supplied them with the proper interpretation of Torah, disclosed how the ancient prophets had foretold the present—in particular the emergence of the sect as the community of the new covenant—and formed a tightly structured, apocalyptic community.

Apocalypticism in the Scrolls

There is not a single apocalypse among the scrolls that we can ascribe to the sectarians themselves. There are a couple of texts that may have been apocalypses, though it is hard to tell because of their fragmentary state. The afterlife, so important to apocalypticism, is left vague in the scrolls. Resurrection is barely mentioned, if at all. Nonetheless, the sect did have at least eight copies of Daniel in its library, and four of the five sections of *1 Enoch* are found there. Recent work has been done on the connection between the Enoch literature and the community of the Dead Sea Scrolls (Boccaccini, Ellens, and Waddell 2005).

There are other indications of the apocalyptic nature of the sect. There are among the scrolls bits of other texts, generally referred to as pseudo-Danielic material, that seem to relate to Daniel in some way but are not directly from that apocalypse. Notable is the inclusion of the story of the watchers in the brief synopsis of history that begins the *Damascus Rule*. They are listed among history's sinners (2:18).

Apocalypticism is not limited to apocalypses. The scrolls exhibit key apocalyptic ideas and images integral to its worldview. The case has been made by Collins and others (Collins 1990; 1997; Nickelsburg 2000; VanderKam 2000). To demonstrate the apocalyptic nature of the Qumran community, we begin by considering the main elements of apocalypticism. Then we look more closely at specific important texts from Qumran to see how they incorporate these elements.

The Qumran community was priestly in nature. Priests lead the community and priestly concerns are paramount for them. In the eschatological future, there will be two messiahs, one priestly and one kingly, of the line of David. The priestly messiah will take precedence over the kingly one (VanderKam and Flint 2002, 265–73; Collins 1997, 71–90). In many places in the scrolls, issues of sacrifice, atonement, and purity arise (Kugler 2000).

Apocalypses draw their authority from direct revelation. In this way, the community of Qumran is authentically apocalyptic. The *Damascus Rule* says that God gave the Teacher of Righteousness direct revelation that served as a foundation for the sect.

Apocalyptic revelation has a spatial and a temporal aspect. The spatial aspect means that the seer receives special knowledge about the unseen world—the world of angels and demons, of God and Satan. Claim to such knowledge permeates the scrolls. The sect, probably through the Teacher of Righteousness and other leaders, knows about the angelic and the demonic world. The *Thanksgiving Hymns* speak of the psalmist standing among the angels and learning of things that can be accessed only in this way. Passages we will observe consider that the community lives among the angels, members of the unseen world. One text (*Songs of the Sabbath Sacrifice*) describes the liturgy that takes place in heaven. The community knows about the unseen world not only through the inspiration of its own leaders and its own communal experience, but also through Daniel, Enoch, and Ezekiel, whose books they cherished and interpreted.

Belial is the prince of the bad angels, and the sectarians know of his activities, who his allies are, and what his future holds. In *Community Rule* 3–4, Belial is the Angel of Darkness opposed to the Prince of Light. All humanity is divided between them, showing a correspondence between social and cosmic dualism.

The temporal aspect of apocalyptic revelation has to do with what will happen in the future. The scrolls contain numerous passages that speak about eschatological events.

There are things to consider that go beyond the definition of the genre of apocalypse. They are always or commonly found in apocalypses and among apocalyptic thinkers. They include things like dualism, the origin of evil, periodization of history, concepts of the afterlife, resurrection, messianism, and angelology and demonology.

In apocalypticism, dualism permeates and defines all aspects of the universe. People are either righteous or wicked. For Qumran, only members of the *yaḥad* can be righteous, because only they know God's will. In the angelic world, there are good angels and bad angels. The good angels are led by Michael, the bad by Belial. In the realm of behavior, there are only two choices—righteousness and disobedience to God. In Persian religion, there is a similar dualism, but the Persian version can be more radical than what we find in any Jewish sources. In Persian religion, Zoroastrianism, dualism can extend to the highest levels, so that there are two gods, evenly matched, one good and one bad. There is a less extreme form of Zoroastrian dualism in which the split between good and evil does not extend to the highest level. Rather, at top is a sole, good god.

Jewish thought could not fully accommodate the idea that there is any power in the universe equal to that of its God. Therefore the scrolls tell of a universe whose dualism is transcended by God and is therefore not absolute. In a passage that comes the closest to a systematic expression of Qumran's worldview, the *Instruction on the Two Spirits* (1QS 3–4) (Collins 1997, 10–11), God creates the Angel of Darkness (Belial) and the Prince of Light (Michael) and allows both to exist until the eschaton, at which time God triumphs and purges evil. Angelic dualism corresponds to social and ethical dualism. All humanity falls into the camp of the good angel or the bad one. Human behavior follows suit. In a surprising twist, good and bad also struggle within each human until the end. We examine this *Instruction* below in treating the *Community Rule*. Here we note simply that it is "thoroughly apocalyptic" (Collins 1997, 38).

The *Instruction*'s concept of the origin of evil does not fit neatly into other schemes we know. It is not due to the fall of the angels, as in *1 Enoch*. Like the wisdom tradition, the scrolls in general stress human responsibility, but there are shades of determinism in this passage. Nonetheless, the ultimate solution seems to place the blame for sin on the individual, who can choose. Like Sirach, a wisdom work, humans have an evil inclination (*yeşer*), which they can resist. The *Damascus Rule* 2–3 leads us through history, blaming those, including the watchers, who did not resist this evil *yeşer*, thus supporting human responsibility. Unlike *4 Ezra*, which blames God for leaving the evil inclination in the human heart, but more like Sirach, who also defends human responsibility and the ability to resist the evil *yeşer*, the *Instruction on the Two Spirits* holds in tension free will and determinism. Wisdom influence on Qumran has long been noted, as is evident in 4Q *Sapiential Work A*. But Collins rightly rejects the idea that the introduction of a psychological, inner conflict between good and evil overrides the mythological and cosmic dimensions of the *Instruction* (Collins 1997, 40–41).

That Qumran preserved *Jubilees* shows its interest in history's divisions. We find a similar concern in various texts written by the sectarians. The *Damascus Document* provides a rough chronology. There are frequent assertions in the scrolls that God foreknows everything to happen. The eschatological war's progress is laid out in detail in the *War Scroll*. The present is the age of wrath.

Apocalyptic scenarios may or may not have a messiah. Daniel and the *Book of the Watchers* do not. Because of Christian interest in the messiah, the topic has drawn more attention than it otherwise would have done. Messiahship is not a major preoccupation of the scrolls (Evans 2000b). Nonetheless, several texts from the scrolls demonstrate messianism, although they are not entirely consistent. The relative value of messianism at Qumran is evident in that not only does it not dominate the scrolls, but the places where it does appear do not all agree (Collins 1995; Evans 2000b). There was no univocal "doctrine" of the messiah in the sect.

A probable reconstruction of the most common expectation in the scrolls is that the sectarians expected two messiahs, a king of David's line and a priest. This reminds us that in the Hebrew Bible the two main people who would be anointed were the king and the high priest. We also find reference in the Bible to the anointing of a prophet (Isa. 61) and of the patriarchs. There is evidence that Qumran expected a third figure, a prophet. Although the eschatological prophet is not called a messiah, there is one passage in which Israel's prophets are called messiahs (*Damascus Rule* 6:1). In a document describing a meal that will take place when the messiahs are present, the priestly one takes precedence over the kingly one (1QSa). This fits the priestly nature of the community. The messiahs are humans who fulfill the necessary leadership roles for the future Israel.

After the Babylonian exile, some hoped for a restoration of the dyadic leadership that had preceded it—king and priest. When that hope was disappointed, hopes for a royal leader seem to have gone into abeyance for a while. Even Daniel and the books of the Maccabees do not expect a messianic figure. We see a resurgence of messianic hope around the middle of the first century BCE that lasts until at least the first half of the second century CE. The scrolls provide us evidence of messianic hope in the first century or two BCE and into the first century CE. Collins provides a comprehensive examination of the evidence of the scrolls on this topic (Collins 1995).

Hope for an afterlife is unclear in the scrolls. The reason may be that the sectarians thought that they already lived in the presence of the angels. This is realized eschatology. Jewish apocalypses sometimes picture the end as the righteous joining the angelic host. The sectarians of Qumran had already done this (Collins 1997, 129).

Now that we have an overview of the community's apocalypticism and its history, we turn to specific texts. Our analysis cannot be exhaustive. We focus on passages that illumine the apocalyptic nature of the sect.

The *Community Rule*

This is one of two long rule books in the scrolls, the other being the *Damascus Rule*. It is present in multiple manuscripts (eleven in cave 4), and parts of it were incorporated into some versions of the *Damascus Rule*, resulting in hybrid texts. It is of great importance to the sect and underwent many changes, some big, some small, over time. The *Rule* breaks into three main parts: entry into the community, rules, and a psalm of the Master (the sect's leader).

Part 1, the entry into the covenant, may be a sermon for an annual covenantal renewal ceremony at Qumran. It gives a splendid overview of the nature of the sect. In particular, it contains what is a distinctive passage in the scrolls, the *Instruction on the Two Spirits* (Collins 1997, 38–41).

The section begins with a sketch of the Master's obligations. His primary responsibility is to teach the community to live by the correct interpretation of Torah, that is, teaching them to live "in accordance with all that has been revealed concerning their appointed times, and that they may love all the sons of light, each according to his lot in God's design, and hate all the sons of darkness, each according to his guilt in God's vengeance" (1). This line shows the importance of the liturgical rules for the community and for the proper keeping of feasts and of daily religious observances ("appointed times"). It shows that the sect believes that its proper interpretation of these things is revealed. Finally, it betrays a social and angelic dualism—there are sons of light and sons of darkness; some humans belong to the lot of Belial, and others to the lot of God (*Community Rule* 2). The community must carry out this ritual throughout the dominion of Belial. During this time, Belial carries on a campaign against Israel, according to *Damascus Rule* 4:13. Dimant notes that the idea of a period dominated by Belial is "the very heart of sectarian thought" (1984, 493).

The next section proclaims that everyone who enters the covenant must live according to God's laws as interpreted by the sect, and that they must do so "during the dominion of Belial." This is the same as the age of wrath, a phrase taken from Daniel. Belial exercises power on earth, but it will end soon.

In the next section, the priests bless the righteous, that is, the members of the sect who act in accord with God's will, and the Levites curse those who belong to the "lot of Belial." Blessings and curses are part of covenant making. The present is called the time of the "dominion of Belial." The righteous are to receive freedom from evil. They also receive wisdom. The Levites say to the wicked, "Be damned in the shadowy place of everlasting fire."

After the priests warn against backsliding, the text instructs the sect to celebrate this entrance into the covenant yearly. Members "enter" in strict hierarchical order—priests, Levites, and laypersons.

Then comes another warning against backsliding. Those who enter the covenant and then fail to live accordingly will not be cleansed by ablutions. Using priestly language declares that members become truly pure only by obedience to God's laws; external washing (for which there is archaeological evidence at Qumran) is but a symbol of internal cleansing. Through obedience one is cleansed of one's sins and makes atonement for failings. This priestly sect, deprived of cultic means of making atonement for sins, has substituted obedience for atoning sacrifice.

The rest of columns 3 and 4 is taken up with the *Instruction on the Two Spirits*. The Master is to teach members "the nature of all the children of men according to the kind of spirit which they possess, the signs identifying their works during their lifetime, their visitation for chastisement, and the time of their reward." The text then claims that all is within God's control. He has established the design for everyone. This and other parts of the instruction sound like predestination, but it is not so simple.

All of humanity is ruled either by the Prince of Light (also called the Angel of Light or the Angel of Truth) or by the Angel of Darkness. Each angel rules his own in terms of their nature and their deeds. Those belonging to the Angel of Light do good deeds, and those of the lot of the Angel of Darkness do bad deeds. The ultimate reward of the righteous will be peace, long life, and "eternal joy in life without end." The wicked will receive "a multitude of plagues by the hand of all the destroying angels, everlasting damnation by the avenging wrath of the fury of God, eternal torment and endless disgrace together with shameful extinction in the fire of the dark regions." There could be no clearer statement of the social and cosmic dualism typical of apocalypses, of the idea of future rewards and punishments, and of knowledge of the nature of the unseen world. Social dualism is caused by the rule of the Angel of Light (the same as Michael and Melchizedek [king of righteousness]) and the Angel of Darkness (called elsewhere Belial and Melchiresha [king of evil]). The entire system has been created and decreed by God. Both good and bad angels have been created by God, so this is not absolute dualism. Although God created both types of angels, God loves those in the light and hates the ways of the Angel of Darkness.

There is an unusual twist to this dualism. It extends to each individual in the sense that each has a share in both the light and the darkness. One belongs to either of the two angels to the extent that one has a greater portion in one or the other. There is a struggle within each person throughout life. As the text says, "Until now the spirits of truth and injustice struggle in the hearts of men and they walk in both wisdom and folly" (*Community Rule* 4). At the end, those with a greater portion in the darkness will suffer eternal punishment, while those with a greater portion in the light will be purified by God, "and all the glory of Adam shall be theirs." In other words, they will recover the state of Adam before the fall. The apostle Paul has a similar view (Murphy-O'Connor 2009).

Rules lay out how a person can enter the sect; they demonstrate the community's hierarchical structure. Separation is key. One must separate from outsiders. In the final stage of admission, the person must cede all possessions to the group. Radical separation fits the priestly view of separation of the holy from the profane, and it also fits the idea that Qumran is a sect, emphasizing the boundaries between itself and the wider world, particularly the world of unfaithful Israel. It also suits apocalyptic dualism. Zadokite priests are arbiters of Torah. This gives the priests, and the Master in particular, total authority over the behavior of the members as well as over the structure of the community, its relationship with outsiders, and group ideology. The claim to absolute authority is not unusual in such settings. A radically dualistic view of the world cannot be upheld unless discipline is strict, and that is best accomplished by absolute leadership. There follows a penal code. It helps to enforce strict decorum, maintenance of hierarchy, sectarian unity, and loyalty.

The next section speaks of atonement and how it may be achieved by a priestly community without access to Jerusalem, the only site where sacrifice can be legitimately offered to God. The Torah unequivocally demands sacrifice to purify Israel and its sanctuary from the guilt that would otherwise jeopardize God's presence in the temple and among the people. For generation after generation, the people of the Dead Sea Scrolls occupied Qumran, with no possibility of fulfilling God's will in that regard. To make atonement possible, this text proclaims that suffering for God's will, perfect obedience to the Torah, and prayer now replace sacrifices. The community makes possible the presence of the angels among them and the maintenance of the covenant with God. The presence of the angels in the community proves that God favors them and not the Jerusalem establishment.

At points throughout the document, the writer uses Scripture to make his point. There is a noteworthy citation of Scripture (italicized) in this section.

> And when these become members of the Community in Israel according to all these rules, they shall separate from the habitation of unjust men and shall go into the wilderness to prepare the way of Him; as it is written, *Prepare in the wilderness the way of . . . , make straight in the desert a path for our God* (Isa. xl, 3). This (path) is the study of the Law which he commanded by the hand of Moses, that they may do all that has been revealed from age to age, and as the prophets have revealed by his Holy Spirit.

A Christian reader will notice immediately that the same quotation is applied to John the Baptist in the Synoptic Gospels. It is taken to mean that John prepares the way for Jesus by preaching in the desert. The people of Qumran saw this verse as referring to themselves. They had gone into the desert to keep the Torah perfectly. When God comes to fix the world, he will find a community obedient to his will.

The document now turns to the Master's duties. He is to teach proper interpretation of the Torah and to enforce its observance. A telling sentence is the following: "He shall conceal the teaching of the Law from men of injustice, but shall impart true knowledge and righteous judgment to those who have chosen the Way." The insiders have special knowledge and hide it from outsiders.

The *Community Rule* ends with a psalm of the Master. He promises to pray at the proper times and to be constantly mindful of God's law. He will bless God's name continually. He will return good for evil in his dealings even with unjust men, but that is only for the present, for, as he says, "I will not grapple with the men of perdition until the Day of Revenge, but my wrath shall not turn from the men of falsehood, and I will not rejoice until judgment is made." Also speaking of the Master, the text declares: "Everlasting hatred in a spirit of secrecy for the men of perdition!" For now, he keeps his hatred secret, but there will be a "Day of Revenge."

The Master promises not to keep Belial in his heart. Even the Master must beware of Belial. But God has wiped out the Master's transgression through divine righteousness. This is the closest parallel we have to the apostle Paul's idea of God's righteousness. True righteousness comes through God's grace, not human action.

Contained within this psalm is a key passage for our topic:

> My eyes have gazed
> on that which is eternal,

Apocalypticism in the *Community Rule*

- Secret wisdom is revealed to the Master and by him to the community.
- The Master and members must not share this wisdom with outsiders.
- There is social and cosmic dualism.
- The ruler of the bad angels is Belial, and the good angel is probably Michael.
- The present is the time of Belial's dominion, also called the age of wrath.
- A day of judgment will come for the men of perdition.
- The people of Qumran will help to fight the men of perdition when the time comes.
- The sectarians have access to the heavenly world even now, since they have inherited the lot of the angels and the angels are present with them.

> on wisdom concealed from men,
> on knowledge and wise design
> (hidden) from the sons of men;
> on a fountain of righteousness
> and on a storehouse of power,
> on a spring of glory
> (hidden) from the assembly of flesh.
> God has given them to His chosen ones
> as an everlasting possession,
> and has caused them to inherit
> the lot of the Holy Ones.
> He has joined their assembly
> to the Sons of Heaven
> to be a Counsel of the Community,
> a foundation of the Building of Holiness,
> and eternal Plantation throughout all ages to come. (*Community Rule* 11:5–9)

The Master has had access to the eternal wisdom hidden from humanity. The people of the scrolls are in community with the angels. The angels are present with them even in this age of wrath. This is realized eschatology.

The *Damascus Rule*

The other main rule among the scrolls is the *Damascus Rule*, so called because it speaks of the sectarians as if they were in exile in Damascus. Most take this symbolically as referring to the settlement of the sect in the Judean desert at Qumran. The two manuscripts of the *Damascus Rule* had already been known from medieval manuscripts discovered in the storeroom (*genizah*) of a synagogue in Cairo and published in 1910.

Fig. 9. The caves where the Dead Sea Scrolls were found are near these ruins. Most think that this is where the celibate branch of the sect lived. (Jim Yancey)

There are many similarities between the *Damascus Rule* and the *Community Rule*. We are dealing with the same sect, broadly speaking. At the same time, there are significant differences. One main difference is that the rules in the *Damascus Rule* assume that the sectarians are living in villages, marrying and having children, and interacting with Jews who do not belong to the sect and with gentiles as well. The *Community Rule* assumes that its members are all celibate, male, and separate from society. There were two main branches of the sect. The celibate branch lived at Qumran, while those who married lived in the villages of Jewish Palestine, and even in Jerusalem itself. There was an Essene gate in Jerusalem's walls, and there may have been an Essene quarter in Jerusalem.

The *Damascus Rule* falls into two main divisions. The first is an exhortation and the second a list of rules. The exhortation begins with a brief history of the sect. It starts with God's abandonment of Israel and the temple in the time of Nebuchadnezzar, the sixth century BCE. God gave them up to the sword, but he saved for himself a remnant because of his covenant with the patriarchs. Then, 390 years later, in the age of wrath, he raised up the beginnings of the Qumran community. For twenty years they did not know what they were supposed to do, but they knew that Israel was unfaithful to God, and that even they were guilty. Then God raised up for them the Teacher of Righteousness, and "he made known to the latter generations that which God had done to the latter generation, the congregation of traitors, those who departed from the way." The

Teacher is the recipient of special revelation. He lives in the "latter generation," and he sees that Israel has betrayed God. This revelation tells the Teacher what is going on—that Israel is unfaithful, that he lives in an age of wrath, that he is being inspired to interpret the Torah faithfully in ways concealed from everyone else, and that he can understand God's intentions for the present and future. All of this fits the sect's apocalyptic mindset. (Riesner 1992)

Conflict with Hasmonean rulers is evident throughout the scrolls, and conflict with the Pharisees receives attention, too. The *Damascus Rule* speaks of a "Scoffer" who is a rival of the Teacher of Righteousness. The language derives from the Bible (Isa. 28:22; Pss. 10:5; 73:8; 74:10, 22). The Scoffer lies and leads Israel astray, thus incurring the curses of the covenant. Others, called the "seekers of smooth things" (Isa. 33:10) are probably the Pharisees who, according to the sect, seek the easy way in Torah interpretation. The sect's enemies pursue the righteous with the sword and incur God's wrath. These bearers of the sword must be Hasmoneans and their allies. Using priestly terminology, the writer declares that they are defiled before God.

The exhortation provides a brief view of a broader history, prefacing it with the claim that God knows everything in advance, and that he rewards the obedient and hates and punishes the disobedient. Punishment comes in the form of "power, might, and great flaming wrath by the hand of all the Angels of Destruction." The review of history shows that all who follow their own evil inclination are punished, while those who do not enjoy God's favor. Within this history, the watchers who came down from heaven and their giant children are among the wicked ones. The narrative culminates in the emergence of the sect, to which God revealed "the hidden things in which all Israel had gone astray." Only the members of the sect, who possess this special revelation, can please God, because the rest of Israel does not even know what they are doing wrong. God forgave the sectarians, built them "a sure house in Israel," referring to their community. They are "destined to live for ever and all the glory of Adam shall be theirs." All these things are God's "wonderful mysteries." In the present, "until the age is completed," all sectarians "shall do according to that interpretation of the Law in which the first [men] were instructed."

Isaiah 34:14 speaks of terror, the pit, and the snare coming upon Israel. The *Damascus Rule* interprets this as pertaining to the present and representing sexual immorality, wealth, and defilement of the temple. These are the sins of those in Jerusalem, and they are signs that the power of Belial has been unleashed against Israel.

The text specifies some of the sins of Jerusalem's inhabitants. An intriguing parallel with Jesus is that it is considered fornication to take a second wife when the first is still alive. Interpretation of this passage is uncertain. Since polygamy does not seem to have been an issue at this time, this may be a reference to divorce. If it does demonstrate a negative attitude to divorce, it, along with a passage in the prophet Malachi and the teaching of Jesus, are the only three places in ancient Jewish texts where divorce incurs disapproval. Both Jesus and this text refer to Genesis and the idea that the couple leave their families and become a new entity. In studying Jesus, we will suggest that Jesus's position is due to an apocalyptic viewpoint—that civilization has declined and that the original state of the world must be recaptured. In the scrolls, several references to the glory of Adam suggest that such thinking is familiar to the sect.

Members are to avoid outsiders and show love and justice to insiders. Concern for the poor is evident, and, drawing on Lev. 19, the text declares "they shall love each man his brother as himself." In the case of Qumran, this admonition has a sectarian twist. One's brother is another member of the sect.

Numbers 24:17 reads as follows: "I see him, but not now; I behold him, but not near—a star shall come out of Jacob, and a scepter shall rise out of Israel; it shall crush the borderlands of Moab, and the territory of all the Shethites." This is widely given a messianic interpretation in Jewish tradition. At Qumran, the star is the interpreter of the law and the scepter is the prince of the congregation; they are to come at the eschaton (*Community Rule* 7). This reflects Qumran's dual messiahship. The interpreter of the law is the priestly messiah, and the prince is the Davidic messiah. When God and the messiahs come, the disobedient will be "visited for destruction by the hand of Belial." A few lines down, the messiahs are mentioned again. No one who has entered the community and then betrayed it will be a member of the sect "from the day of the gathering in of the Teacher of the Community until the coming of the Messiah out of Aaron and Israel." The messiah out of Aaron is a priest, and the messiah out of Israel is a prince.

The "gathering in" of the Teacher of Righteousness is his death. The *Damascus Rule* says that there will be about forty years between his death and the end of those who deserted to "the Liar," the Teacher's rival in Jerusalem. During those forty years, God's wrath is kindled against Israel. This is an instance of trying to predict the end time. If the Teacher led the community for about forty years, this means that from the time of the original community's groping for the way (twenty years) to the end (eighty years, including the career of the Teacher and the forty years following) would be a hundred years. By that reckoning, the end will come 490 years after Nebuchadnezzar's sack of Jerusalem. That would make it 96 BCE. Of course, this ancient calculation is more symbolic than literal, both because the ancient authors were unable to be so precise in their dating, and because the number 490 comes from Dan. 9, where Jeremiah's prediction that the exile will last for seventy years becomes seventy weeks of years, or seventy times seven, or 490. For the sectarians, this will be the real end of the exile. The Second Temple establishment was not the real fulfillment of Jeremiah's promise of an end to the exile (Knibb 1976; N. T. Wright 1996). That would come when God's remnant replaced the sons of darkness in Jerusalem.

Apocalypticism in the *Damascus Rule*

- The present is the time of the dominion of Belial, also called the age of wrath and the age of wickedness.
- The coming of the messiahs of Aaron and Israel is described.
- The sect's history is reckoned using the 490 years of Dan. 9 as a guide.
- God raised up the Teacher of Righteousness for them, gave special revelation to the Teacher, and had him share it with the group.
- The Teacher of Righteousness learns through revelation the demonic nature of the present and the proper interpretation of the Torah, as well as God's choosing of the remnant, the sect. All these are God's mysteries.
- The sectarian nature of the group is demonstrated through the strict rules that bind them together, through the love that they show to one another, and through strict regulation of relations with outsiders.

The rules following the exhortation show special interest in the Sabbath. They also show that the community for which this rule was written consisted of married members who had interactions with other Jews and with gentiles. The present is the time of the dominion of Belial. The righteous follow the rules during the "age of wickedness until the coming of the Messiah of Aaron and Israel." There are probably two more references to the two messiahs at the end of this scroll, but damage to the scroll makes certainty impossible.

The *Messianic Rule*

Vermès (2004, 159) calls this a "messianic rule" because "(1) it was intended for all the congregation in the *last days*; (2) it is a Rule for a Community adapted to the requirements of the messianic war against the nations; (3) it refers to the presence of the priest and the Messiah of Israel at the Council, and at the meal described in column 2." The text clarifies regulations regarding the time when the messiahs come and the war against the nations is near or underway.

The document begins by saying that it is for "all the congregation of Israel in the last days." The congregation of Israel means the sect, for the text goes on to say that it concerns those who "walk according to the law of the sons of Zadok the Priests and of the men of their covenant who have turned aside [from the] way of the people." These are the ones who atone for the land.

The text lists rules pertaining to ages at which a person assumes specific responsibilities in the sect. No "simpleton" is to "hold any office in the war destined to vanquish the nations."

Further on it says that no one suffering from a physical imperfection or having any uncleanness is to enter the assembly, for "the Angels of Holiness are [with] their [congregation]."

The rule describes a meal at which the priest and the Messiah of Israel are present. The "(priest-) Messiah" will come at the head of all Israel, and at the head of the priests, who then sit in a hierarchical order. Then comes the Messiah of Israel, and all of the laymen sit before him. The preeminence of the priest is clear, and he is to be the first to pronounce blessing over the bread and wine. Only then may the Messiah of Israel do so. After those two leaders, the rest of the members recite a blessing in the order of their "dignity," that is, their status within the community.

The eschatological elements in this text are evident. The messiahs are present and the war against the nations is near or in progress. The coming of the messiahs makes no real difference to the nature of the community. The priest still presides over all. The rules for admission into the community and growth within it are still in force. The community continues to be the location of God's angels on earth and the only place where true atonement is possible. The eschatological community will mirror what the community is in the present.

The *War Rule*

Like many texts preserved in the scrolls, this one has a complicated editorial history. Broadly speaking, the most probable solution is the one adopted by Vermès, that columns 1 and 15–19 are the original work and depend on Dan. 11:40–12:3. They speak of a final battle against the Kittim. The word "Kittim" was identified with Cyprus originally, but it came to mean any of the powers from the direction of the Mediterranean Sea. The scrolls applied it to both the Seleucids and the Romans, depending on the historical circumstances. Vermès argues that military details in the *War Rule* indicate that the writer knew Roman practices of warfare, so he dates this scroll during the Roman period, perhaps around the turn of the first century CE. This original document was supplemented by the heavily detailed description of a forty-year eschatological war in columns 2–14.

A great final battle between God's forces and those of his enemies is common in apocalypticism, as we have seen. Despite the widespread belief in a final battle, no text, Jewish or Christian, rivals the *War Rule* in the detail with which it portrays that struggle. We look first at the columns that Vermès believes made up the original document and then go on to examine the rest of the text.

The text begins by saying it is for the Master at the time when the sons of light will be "unleashed" against the sons of darkness and their leader, Belial. Also arrayed against Israel are some of its traditional biblical enemies, such as Moab and Edom, and, finally, the Kittim, and the ungodly of the covenant.

The ungodly of the covenant are Jews who do not belong to the sect. At the beginning of the battle, the "exiled sons of light" return from the desert (Qumran) and establish a military camp before Jerusalem. After the battle, they "go up." Vermès takes this to mean that they go up to Jerusalem. That is probable, both because the verb "to go up" is often applied to the trip to Jerusalem, since it is thought of as built on a mountain (Mount Zion), and because further on in the document the sect controls Jerusalem. They sacrifice there and render service at the sanctuary.

The maneuvers of the king of the Kittim are based on Dan. 11. He goes first to Egypt and then proceeds against the kings of the north, and he tries to cut down Israel as he goes. This mimics the movements of Antiochus IV as described in Daniel and in the books of the Maccabees. This time it means victory for Israel. Israel's triumph is certain.

> This shall be a time of salvation for the people of God, an age of dominion for all the members of His company, and of everlasting destruction for all the company of Belial. The confusion of the sons of Japheth shall be [great] and Assyria shall fall unsuccoured. The dominion of the Kittim shall come to an end and iniquity shall be vanquished, leaving no remnant; [for the sons] of darkness there shall be no escape. [The sons of righteous]ness shall shine over all the ends of the earth. They shall go on shining until all the seasons of darkness are consumed, and, at the season appointed by God, His exalted greatness shall shine eternally to the peace, blessing, glory, joy, and long life of all the sons of light. (*War Rule* 1:5–9)

Now that the author has left no doubt about the battle's outcome, he describes the battle in more detail. He paints a vivid picture of carnage and violence. Men and "gods" contend on the same battlefield. This is not just nation against nation, or human army against human army. The angels participate on both sides, so that there is a "clamour of gods and men." This is a time of tribulation for the righteous, but it will end in "eternal redemption." The war will take place in seven parts. During three of them, the sons of light dominate, and during three the sons of darkness prevail. In the seventh part, God defeats Belial's army, both its angels and its humans.

All this transpires in column 1. If we now skip to column 15, we are following the original document. Columns 15–19 reinforce the themes of a battle that involves both humans and angels. One side is led by Belial and represents the forces of darkness, and the other is on the side of God. Column 17 makes this dualism more symmetrical by introducing the angel Michael, Israel's angel, into the battle.

> This is the day appointed by Him for the defeat and overthrow of the Prince of the kingdom of wickedness, and He will send eternal succour to the company of His redeemed by the might of the princely Angel of the kingdom of

Michael. With everlasting light he will enlighten with joy [the children] of Israel; peace and blessing shall be with the company of God. He will raise up the kingdom of Michael in the midst of the gods, and the realm of Israel in the midst of all flesh.

The parallel kingdoms—Michael's in the heavenly places and Israel's on earth—recall Dan. 7, where the one like a son of man receives dominion in heaven, while the people of the angels (Israel) receive dominion on earth. The most likely candidate for the identity of the one like a son of man in Dan. 7 is Michael, who appears as Israel's angel in Dan. 10 and 12.

We turn now to columns 2–14. They are filled mostly with details that we need not investigate. They share the basic premises of the original document—there will be a war between the forces of light and darkness, the war will involve humans and angels, and God will claim ultimate victory. In column 7, there is a prohibition against women, men with physical deformities and ailments, or anyone who is unclean entering Israel's military camp because the angels are present with them and rules of ritual cleanness apply.

In column 10 there is a psalm. Particularly noteworthy is the depiction of the community.

> Who is like Thy people Israel
> which Thou hast chosen for Thyself
> from all the peoples of the lands;
> the people of the saints of the covenant,
> instructed in the laws,
> and learned in wisdom . . .
> Who have heard the voice of Majesty
> and have seen the Angels of Holiness,
> whose ear has been unstopped,
> and who have heard profound things? (*War Rule* 10:9–11)

It is not military might that makes Israel victorious; it is obedience to God's laws. They have received mysteries granted to no other people. They have seen the holy angels and heard deep things, references to special revelation from God and to their community with the angels.

In column 11 there is a passing reference to Gog, Israel's enemy in Ezek. 38–39. Here Gog and his assembly is another way of referring to Belial and the Kittim. The coming war with the Romans fulfills Ezekiel.

Column 12 celebrates the angelic might God has at his disposal. He commands thousands of powerful angels. The author knows this because he has heard the kinds of descriptions of heaven that are present in Dan. 7, for example. Because God will send them to help his people, they can "despise kings" and "scorn the mighty."

Column 18 recognizes that God has created everything, even Belial.

Apocalypticism in the *War Rule*

- The author knows about the future war through special revelation.
- The author consulted Daniel to help him discern what was to come. He saw the war as a fulfillment of Ezek. 38–39.
- A final battle occurs between the forces of light and darkness.
- Belial leads the forces of darkness and Michael the forces of light.
- Victory comes through God's direct intervention.
- Dominion is exercised in heaven by Michael and on earth by Israel.
- The war brings about destruction of the forces of evil.
- There is social and cosmic dualism.
- The war is foreordained, down to its details.
- God creates all, even Belial. God's sovereignty is absolute.
- There is an emphasis on angels.

Belial, the Angel of Malevolence, Thou hast created for the Pit; his [rule] is in Darkness and his purpose is to bring about wickedness and iniquity. All the spirits of his company, the Angels of Destruction, walk according to the precepts of Darkness.

There is no doubt that the *War Rule* qualifies as apocalyptic, even though it is not an apocalypse. It is likely that the author saw his predictions about the final war as special revelation. The psalm in column 10 speaks of insight into the angelic world and of deep knowledge transmitted to the sectarians.

The *Pesharim* (Biblical Commentaries)

The Qumran sect invented a new genre—a line-by-line commentary on Scripture. This form was to become popular in both Judaism and Christianity. The interpretation of the biblical books assumes that the biblical writers wrote about the future, not their own time. Specifically, they wrote about the sect. The early Christians had precisely the same outlook. Many interpretations at Qumran are not so much exegesis as a seemingly arbitrary assignment of meaning to parts of the text that seem to have little justification in the text itself. The text is read as if it were a riddle to be solved through inspiration.

The Qumran *pesharim* are testimony that true understanding of Scripture came through direct revelation. This is stated most clearly in the commentary on the prophet Habakkuk. Column 5 begins with an interpretation of Hab. 1:5, which speaks only of God doing something hard to believe. The interpreter sees this as a reference to the fact that the leaders in Jerusalem did "not [listen to the word received by] the Teacher of Righteousness from the mouth of God." It also refers to members of the new covenant who did not believe in the covenant of God. It refers to the "unfaithful at the end of days."

> They, the men of violence and the breakers of the Covenant, will not believe when they hear all that [is to happen to] the final generation from the Priest [in whose heart] God set [understanding] that he might interpret all the words of His servants the Prophets, through whom he foretold all that would happen to his people and [his land].

This is an explicit statement that God gave the Teacher of Righteousness special revelation so that he might understand how the prophets foretold the Teacher's present and the future of the sect and the world. Even the fact that most did not believe him was foretold in Scripture.

Later in the commentary the author develops this theme.

> God told Habakkuk to write down all that would happen to the final generation, but He did not make known to him when time would come to an end. And as for that which He said, *that he who reads may read it speedily*: interpreted [*pišrô*, from *pešer*, meaning "interpretation"] this concerns the Teacher of Righteousness, to whom God made known all the mysteries of His servants the Prophets.

Even the prophets were unaware of the precise meaning of their own words. They wrote for the future, and their words were wrapped in mystery until God enabled the Teacher of Righteousness to unveil their true meaning.

The prophets and psalms were seen by the Teacher and the sect to foretell events in the sect's history. In a sense, all of those predictions concern eschatological events, since the sect saw itself as living in the age of wrath and caught up in the near-final clash between the sons of light and the sons of darkness. The prophets and psalms foretell the work of the Teacher and his conflict with the Jerusalem authorities, specifically the one known as the Wicked Priest and Liar (probably the Hasmonean ruler Jonathan), as well as the continuing hostility between Qumran and Jerusalem. They speak disparagingly of the reigns of various Hasmonean kings, as well as of the Greeks and the Romans.

We need not analyze all historical references in the *pesharim*. Instead, we point out where something specifically eschatological and/or apocalyptic is foretold. Since we have already quoted the commentary on Habakkuk, we begin there.

Habakkuk

The Habakkuk *pesher* asserts that God inspired the prophets to write of future events, events concerning the Qumran sect. God then inspired the

Teacher of Righteousness to discern the hidden, mysterious meaning within those prophetic texts. The events concerning the Teacher and the sect were to take place in the "final generation."

Habakkuk 1:12–13a concerns the fact that God will not destroy Israel at gentile hands. Rather, the nations will be judged at the hands of the elect within Israel. This alludes to the fact that the people of Qumran will participate in the final battle. They are not pacifistic. Those in Israel who are repentant will be forgiven and purified. All this happens in the "age of wickedness."

Speaking of the "appointed time," Habakkuk says, "It shall tell of the end and shall not lie" (2:3). From this vague indication, the interpreter says, "Interpreted, this means that the final age shall be prolonged, and shall exceed all that the Prophets have said; for the mysteries of God are astounding." Apparently, the end did not come when some in the sect expected. The age of wickedness was being stretched out, beyond expectations. Even this delay is interpreted as foretold by Habakkuk and is another of God's amazing mysteries. Disconfirming evidence is interpreted as confirming evidence.

Habakkuk 2:3 says, "If it tarries, wait for it, for it shall surely come and not be late." Interpreted, this concerns the men of truth who keep the law, whose hands shall not slacken in the service of truth when the final age is prolonged. For all the ages of God reach their appointed end as he determines for them in the mysteries of his wisdom.

The sect comprises the "men of truth." As with all sectarians, they believe they have "the truth" while no one else does. The present age, which should lead to the final showdown between God and Belial, is longer than expected. Nonetheless, the sect believes that things always happen as God has foreordained. Nothing can interfere with God's plan. One cannot fully understand the divine plan, since God's ways are mysterious.

Nahum

The commentary on the prophet Nahum contains numerous historical references. It speaks of Greek kings (Seleucids) and of Hasmoneans (Alexander Jannaeus in particular). The author expects that the Hasmoneans will be defeated and punished by the Kittim, who in this case are the Greeks. He sees Nah. 3:6–7a, which speaks of a group which earns the contempt of humanity when God "casts filth" on it, as referring to the seekers of smooth things, probably the Pharisees.

> Interpreted, this concerns those who seek smooth things, whose evil deeds shall be uncovered to all Israel at the end of time. Many shall understand their iniquity and treat them with contempt because of their guilty presumption. When the glory of Judah shall arise, the simple of Ephraim shall flee from their assembly; they shall abandon those who lead them astray and shall join Israel.

The Pharisees are rivals of the sect. Their interpretation of Torah is dominant in mainstream Palestinian Judaism. The sect sees this not as a simple difference in interpretation. Rather, the sect has the truth and is the only group that deserves the name Judah and Israel. The interpreter uses the name Ephraim, the name of one of the twelve tribes and a general designation of the apostate northern kingdom of Israel in the Bible, to denote the Jewish community that does not follow the sect's teachings. This passage expects a resolution of the differences in Torah interpretation at the end. The sect will be proven right.

Isaiah

A fragmentary commentary on Isaiah speaks of the coming of the Davidic Messiah at the end of days. It interprets part of Isa. 11, a messianic passage.

> [Interpreted, this concerns the Branch] of David who shall arise at the end [of days]. . . . God will uphold him with [the spirit of might and will give him] a throne of glory and a crown of [holiness] and many-coloured garments. . . . [He will put a sceptre] in his hand and he shall rule over the [nations]. And Magog . . . and his sword shall judge [all] the peoples.

Despite the gaps in the fragment, the general direction is clear. It concerns the end. The Davidic Messiah will rule through God's support; he will rule the nations. This is in some way a fulfillment of the famous eschatological battle involving Gog of Magog in Ezek. 38–39.

Psalm 37

The commentary on Ps. 37 speaks of hostility endured at the hands of the Jerusalem establishment, perhaps by the Teacher of Righteousness. It quotes the psalm, "But the humble shall possess the land and delight in abundant peace" (4Q171 2:11). This means that the repentant poor will escape Belial and rejoice in the land. The "poor" are those who depend on God and contrast with the powerful.

The *pesher* develops this idea of the poor at the end of time.

> Interpreted, this concerns the congregation of the Poor, who [shall possess] the whole world as an inheritance. They shall possess the High Mountain of Israel [for ever], and shall enjoy [everlasting] delights in His Sanctuary. [But those who] shall be *cut off*, they are the violent [of the nations and] the wicked of Israel; they shall be cut off and blotted out for ever. (4Q171 3:10–12)

This passage supplies a striking depiction of the perfect situation following the consummation of history. The ideal fulfillment is the sect's possession of

Jerusalem, Mount Zion, and the temple. All who oppose the sect, Jew and gentile alike, will be annihilated. Jerusalem will be the center of everything. Those who take delight in their sanctuary service rule the world.

Two Messianic Texts

Two important texts use Scripture to shed light on the Qumran's messianism. The first is called a florilegium, or a midrash—a creative interpretative work in which numerous biblical texts are brought together to shed light on each other. It begins with 2 Sam. 7:10, which speaks of God planting Israel in the land and protecting it from its enemies. This occurs in a section of the Deuteronomistic History that is an expression of support for the Davidic dynasty. This is royal ideology, which we discussed in chapter 2, in which David wishes to build God a house (temple), and God responds that he will build David a house (dynasty), while David's son Solomon will build the temple. The sect refers this promise to itself. They reinterpret the house to mean their own community, thought of as a temple (Gärtner 1965). The uncircumcised and the unclean cannot enter this human temple, "for there shall My Holy Ones be."

The enemies mentioned in 2 Sam. 7 become in this text

> the children of Belial who cause them to stumble so that they may be destroyed [by their errors,] just as they came with a [devilish] plan to cause the [sons] of light to stumble and to devise against them a wicked plot, so [that they may be subject] to Belial in their [wicked] straying.

When 2 Sam. 7 speaks of David's son, the florilegium's interpretation is, "He is the Branch of David who shall arise with the Interpreter of the Law [to rule] in Zion [at the end] of time." This accords with the expectation of two messiahs, one priestly and one Davidic. After a section in which the disobedience of the priests, sons of Zadok and of Levi, is seen to be foretold in Scripture, the text ends by interpreting Ps. 2:1. Psalm 2 is a messianic psalm, which speaks of the opposition of the nations to the Lord and his Messiah. It is seen as a prediction of the attack of the nations against the "elect of Israel in the last days." It is a time of trial for the elect, during which Belial exercises power. The author sees this as fulfilling Dan. 12:10, a passage which also refers to the time after the end-time tribulation when the righteous become pure.

The second of the messianic texts is called a testimonium. It is an anthology of biblical texts. It begins with excerpts from Deut. 5 and 18. The quotation of Deut. 18 has Moses speaking of a prophet like himself who will arise in the future and whom Israel must listen to. Those who do not will be cut off from the people. The next quotation is from Num. 24:15–17. It is Balaam's famous oracle, which tells of a star and a scepter that will arise in Israel. We have seen that the star is the priestly Messiah while the scepter is Davidic. Balaam speaks of the military victories of the one to come. Combined with the reference to Deut. 18, this testimonium expects three eschatological figures—a priest, a king, and a prophet.

The next quote is taken from the blessing of Levi in Deut. 33:8–10. The priestly tribe is faithful to the Torah and offers incense and sacrifices to God.

Finally, Josh. 6:26 invokes a curse on anyone daring to rebuild Jericho. John Hyrcanus did indeed rebuild Jericho, but the sins of the Hasmoneans go far beyond this. The author says, "Behold, an accursed man, a man of Belial, has risen to become a fowler's net to his people, and a cause of destruction to all his neighbors." Then his brother arises and rules. This refers to the Hasmoneans Jonathan and Simon. They "have committed an abomination in the land, and a great blasphemy among the children [of Jacob. They have shed blood] like water upon the ramparts of the daughter of Zion and within the precincts of Jerusalem."

A Messianic Fragment

Publication of 4Q521 caused a stir because it seems to express expectation of a messiah in the mold of Jesus. It speaks of a messiah who declares God's word and brings the world under the commandments of the holy ones. The rest of this fragment combines elements from Isa. 61 and Ps. 146. The latter declares that "he" will liberate captives, give sight to the blind, and bring wholeness to the physically disabled. The former says that "he" will heal the wounded, raise the dead, and bring good news to the poor. The collocation of such elements recalls the Gospel presentations of Jesus, but the Qumran fragment leaves unclear whether it is the Messiah or God who accomplishes these things. The fragment fascinates those interested in rooting Christian conceptions in Jewish soil. The scenario depicted is not mirrored elsewhere in the scrolls, so it is hardly representative.

The Heavenly Prince Melchizedek (11Q13)

This is a truly remarkable document, for a number of reasons. Its hero is Melchizedek, a shadowy figure who is spoken of only in Gen. 14, where he is king and priest of Jerusalem, at the time a Jebusite city, not part of Israel, and Ps. 110, where someone is declared a priest "according to the order of Melchizedek." Hebrews 7 uses this story to create a priesthood for Jesus, since he was of the tribe of Judah, not Levi, and so could not be a Levitical priest. In this text, Melchizedek is equivalent to Michael, since he is the head of the sons of heaven. The form of the document is a midrash, a weaving together of biblical texts. The midrash is remarkable in the detail with which it describes Melchizedek's end-time activities.

Melchizedek is portrayed as the end-time judge, doing his work on the Day of Atonement at the end of the tenth Jubilee cycle. Based on a couple of biblical passages, he is called ʾēl and ʾĕlōhîm, each of which could mean "god" but could also mean "judge." Melchizedek's activity is extensive in the end time. He is the judge who condemns Belial, restores property as promised for the Jubilee year (Lev. 25), proclaims release to the captives (Isa. 61), and takes the righteous into his own lot, giving them liberty and forgiveness. He is God's avenger. He saves people from Belial. He is the "anointed of the spirit" who reigns at the end of time.

The Thanksgiving Hymns

This is a lengthy collection of psalms whose overarching theme is gratitude to God. Because they are prayers, it is difficult to derive specific historical knowledge from them. But that is not our purpose. We are interested in whether they assume an apocalyptic worldview. They do.

It has been surmised that many of these psalms reflect the experience of the Teacher of Righteousness. The psalms praise God for much of what we have already discovered in the other scrolls. The Teacher, or the sect in general, has been gifted with special revelation through which he has secured a unique relationship with God. That transformation has resulted in communion with the angels, separation from other humans, opposition from outside the community, and at times division within the community. Belial figures in the psalms, and there are explicit apocalyptic visions related in Psalms 9 and 10. They speak of a man being born accompanied by miraculous occurrences. All pregnant wombs give birth at the same time. This may refer to a messiah. The foundations of the earth shake, the heavens roar and frighten the dead, the abysses are in turmoil, hell and Abaddon open, the pit receives the wicked, the wrath of Belial is unleashed on the whole world, a fire consumes all vegetation, fire devours the foundations of the earth and all dry land, rocks and mountains melt, the torrents of Belial invade Abaddon and the abyss, and the land cries out and its inhabitants perish. The horrifying scene ends as follows:

> For God shall sound His mighty voice,
> and His holy abode shall thunder
> with the truth of His glory.
> The heavenly hosts shall cry out
> and the world's foundations
> shall stagger and sway.
> The war of the heavenly warriors shall scourge the earth;
> and it shall not end before the appointed destruction
> which shall be for ever and without compare. (1QH 11:34–36)

Conclusion

We turn to Collins's guidance in summarizing our findings (Collins 1997, 150–51). He lists the most important apocalyptic features of the scrolls' world-view as the following. The sect lives in a world in which there rages a war between good and evil. The sect is caught up in this and plays a key role on the side of good. The dichotomy is social—the sect against everyone else—and cosmic, with Belial (the Angel of Darkness; Melchiresha) arrayed against Michael (the Prince of Light; Melchizedek). History is predetermined. The sect lives at a time when Belial is in the ascendant, so it is an age of wrath and an age of wickedness; but God will soon intervene. The "end of days" preceding God's intervention is divided between a time of testing which is present, and the messianic period to come. The messianic period leads into an all-out war between good and evil in which the sect participates alongside Michael and God's angels; God's forces ultimately win the war. Specifics are hard to come by after this, although a renewed Jerusalem is logical. The sect may have expected a final, complete conflagration. References to resurrection are few and ambiguous. Blissful eternal life shared with the angels awaited the righteous, while eternal punishment was the fate of the wicked. The sect subscribed to realized eschatology because they already possessed communion with the holy ones.

Collins brings further clarity into the picture by comparing Qumran beliefs with other apocalyptic points of view, noting continuities and new elements. Like Daniel and most of *1 Enoch*, the scrolls believe in superhuman forces that interact with humans. Michael and Belial are key to how the sect views the universe. In particular, earthly evil was caused by the intervention of evil cosmic figures. Nothing in the earlier texts, however, approaches the systematic development of dualism found in the *Instruction on the Two Spirits* in *Community Rule* 3–4. This is due at least partly to Zoroastrian influence. Daniel and *1 Enoch* are bereft of the messianic hope found in the scrolls. Like the historical apocalypses in general, Qumran sees history in terms of preset periods. The scrolls display a characteristically apocalyptic interest in angelology, but show no interest in cosmic geography. Their experience of the heavenly world is immediate, communal, and cultic. Even in their earthly life, they participate in it mystically.

A final and revealing difference between Qumran and what we find in earlier apocalypses brings us back to where we began, with the observation that in Qumran we find a trove of diverse texts allowing us to reconstruct, though provisionally, the actual social life of a community (or rather, a number of related communities). Collins remarks directly on that—the interaction between text and social life, between revelation and behavior. While Daniel, *1 Enoch*, and other apocalypses speak of a single seer getting a once-for-all revelation, reduced to writing and passed on to others, the sect of Qumran was gifted with a more immediate source of direct contact with God and God's revelation. The sect had an ongoing source of revelation contained both in a continually evolving series of texts and the living presence of leaders who knew God's will. They imagined themselves living already in communion with the angels, with the sort of direct access to the heavenly enjoyed or claimed by no one else. In a Weberian sense, one might think of this as original charisma being routinized, but that would not do it justice (Weber, Henderson, and Parsons 1947). The commerce with the heavenly world never became routine for these elect.

Suggestions for Further Reading

Boccaccini, Gabriele, J. Harold Ellens, and James A. Waddell, eds. *Enoch and Qumran Origins: New Light on a Forgotten Connection.* Grand Rapids: Eerdmans, 2005.

Collins, John Joseph. *Apocalypticism in the Dead Sea Scrolls.* New York: Routledge, 1997.

———. *Beyond the Qumran Community: The Sectarian Movement of the Dead Sea Scrolls.* Grand Rapids: Eerdmans, 2010.

———, and Robert A. Kugler, eds. *Religion in the Dead Sea Scrolls.* Grand Rapids: Eerdmans, 2000.

Cross, Frank Moore. *The Ancient Library of Qumran.* 3rd ed. Sheffield: Sheffield Academic Press, 1995.

Magness, Jodi. *The Archaeology of Qumran and the Dead Sea Scrolls.* Grand Rapids: Eerdmans, 2002.

VanderKam, James C., and Peter W. Flint. *The Meaning of the Dead Sea Scrolls: Their Significance for Understanding the Bible, Judaism, Jesus, and Christianity.* San Francisco: HarperSanFrancisco, 2002.

Vermès, Géza. *The Complete Dead Sea Scrolls in English.* Rev. ed. London: Penguin, 2004.

8

The Gospels, Q, and Acts of the Apostles

L ike the Hebrew Bible, the New Testament contains only one apocalypse, the book of Revelation. This does not indicate lack of apocalyptic influence. On the contrary, apocalypticism permeates the New Testament. In this chapter, we look closely at the four Gospels, as well as Q (one of the sources of Matthew and Luke), and Acts of the Apostles.

Approaching the New Testament

The New Testament begins with four Gospels. Matthew is the first, followed by Mark, Luke, and John. Intensive research in the nineteenth century convinced most scholars that Mark was the first Gospel written, not Matthew. The same research demonstrated that Matthew and Luke used Mark as one of their sources. So close are the first three Gospels that they can be placed side by side and compared in books called Gospel parallels (Throckmorton 1992). For this reason, they are called the Synoptic Gospels, "synoptic" coming from the Greek, meaning to "see together."

The "Synoptic Problem" is the puzzle of how the first three Gospels relate to each other (Ehrman 2008, 92–100; Murphy 2005, 19–22). The most widely accepted solution is the "Two-Source Solution." It holds that Matthew and Luke used Mark as their main source and supplemented it with another source, now lost to us. Scholars call the lost source "Q," from the German word *Quelle*, meaning "source." Reconstructions of Q are possible based on detailed comparison of Matthew, Mark, and Luke. Material common to Matthew and Luke that they did not take from Mark is probably from Q. Q consists mostly of sayings of Jesus, along with a limited amount of other material, such as the curing of the centurion's servant and material on John the Baptist. The way that Matthew and Luke "redact" or adapt their sources, Mark and Q, tells us much about their points of view. This study is called redaction criticism (Perrin 1969). It makes sense for us to look at Mark first, since then we can determine how Matthew and Luke rewrote Mark with respect to apocalyptic elements.

Acts of the Apostles was written by the same author who wrote the Gospel of Luke. Therefore we treat it right after analyzing Luke.

The Gospel of John differs in many ways from the Synoptics. We consider it at the end of this chapter.

The Gospel of Mark

Mark as Eschatological History

Mark is not an apocalypse but a gospel. The ancient literary genre closest to gospel is biography (Ehrman 2008, 69–74; Vorster 1992). Yarbro Collins (1992a) notes the similarities between Mark's Gospel and ancient biography, but while biography's purpose is to elucidate an individual's character, Mark focuses on eschatological events. Jesus is central to those events, but Yarbro Collins finds "eschatological history" a more satisfactory description of Mark's genre than straight biography. Each part of her case deserves attention, because each is relevant to our judgment of Mark as apocalyptic. We treat them briefly here and in more detail below (Yarbro Collins 2007, 42–44).

First, Mark considers the beginning of his story to be the beginning of the "good news." The Greek is *euangelion* and the Old English is *godspel*, which becomes "gospel" in modern English. The good news is that God's plan for history is entering its final and decisive stage. John the Baptist is Jesus's forerunner, in fulfillment of ancient prophecies. God's plans expressed in ancient prophecy encompass more than just John's appearance. They include the entire Gospel.

Second, Jesus's activity is modeled on that of Israel's heroes such as Moses, Elijah, Elisha, and David. In that sense, the Gospel is like Israel's historical narratives.

Third, Mark 13, the "apocalyptic discourse," lays out God's plan for the end of the world as we know it: the beginning of the birth pangs (13:8); the preaching of the gospel worldwide (13:10); the tribulation (13:19); arrival of the Son of Man (13:24–27); the end (13:7). The divine plan is mentioned in 8:31; 13:7, 20; 14:36, 49.

Fourth, within a Hellenistic context, Mark would have been recognizable as a history closely paralleled with the biography of a famous politician.

Finally, the Gospel has similarities to lives of philosophers, since Jesus is a teacher and interpreter of the law.

Overall, Mark can be seen as an eschatological historical monograph. This genre does justice to all of Mark's features—its historical aspects, its biographical features—while making interest in an individual subservient to his role in history, and a strong eschatological orientation.

The Gospel

Mark begins, "The beginning of the good news [gospel] of Jesus Christ, the Son of God" (1:1). The Greek word "gospel," *euangelion*, had political connotations, particularly when used in propaganda of leaders who touted their reigns as legitimate and as good news for the world. Depending on the extent of the claims made in such propaganda, the good news could take on eschatological overtones. For example, the political/religious use of such language with reference to the emperor Augustus appears in the following inscription.

> It seemed good to the Greeks of Asia, in the opinion of the high priest Apollonius of Menophilus Azanitus: "Since Providence, which has ordered all things and is deeply interested in our life, has set in most perfect order by giving us Augustus, whom she filled with virtue that he might benefit humankind, sending him as a savior [*sōtēr*], both for us and for our descendants, that he might end war and arrange all things, and since he, Caesar, by his appearance [*epiphanein*] (excelled even our anticipations), surpassing all previous benefactors, and not even leaving to posterity any hope of surpassing what he has done, and since the birthday of the god Augustus was the beginning of the good tidings for the world that came by reason of him [*ērxen de tō kosmō tōn di'auton euangeliōn hē genethlios hēmera tou theou*]," which Asia resolved in Smyrna. (The Priene inscription, quoted from Evans 2000a)

Augustus is credited with bringing peace to the world and being the greatest benefactor of all. He is called a god and his birthday is the beginning of the "good news." The calendar should begin with his birthday. (The Christian world today counts Jesus's birth year as the beginning of the present era.) Augustus is called "savior." He has "appeared," the Greek for which, *epiphanein*, is of the same root as the throne name of Antiochus IV Epiphanes, implying divinity. Since Augustus's adoptive father, Julius Caesar, had been divinized by the Roman Senate after his death, Augustus also received the title "Son of the Divine Julius," or simply, "Son of God." Vergil, the famous Roman poet who wrote during the time of Augustus and in praise of him, wrote in his *Fourth Eclogue* about the birth of Augustus as the renewal of the world and of history.

For Mark's Gospel, the good news concerns Jesus's messiahship: "The beginning of the good news of Jesus Christ, the Son of God" (1:1). "Christ [*christos*]" is Greek for "messiah." In Israel's traditions, this is a royal title. "Son of God," Mark's key designation for Jesus, appears together with messiahship several times in the Gospel. We find this conjunction elsewhere in Jewish literature as well (Ps. 2; 2 Sam. 7 implicitly; *Similitudes of Enoch* [*1 Enoch* 37–71]; *4 Ezra* 11–13). The king of Israel is the son of God, as we learned in chapter 2. It is fitting, therefore, that the kingdom of God, central to Jesus's preaching throughout the Synoptics, comes through the agency of the Son of God, the Messiah.

The very first verse of Mark would carry political and eschatological overtones to the ancient reader or hearer. It would delegitimate the Roman order and replace it with God's sovereignty, the kingdom of God. This is a seditious document. It is sometimes thought that Pilate put Jesus to death because he misunderstood that the kingdom Jesus preached was not of this world and therefore not a threat to Rome. On the contrary, Pilate understood perfectly the implications of Jesus's claims and actions.

John the Baptist

Mark turns to prophecy to show that what is taking place was foreseen long before by the prophets and so was planned by God.

> As it is written in the prophet Isaiah,
>> "See, I am sending my messenger ahead of you,
>> who will prepare your way [the verse is actually from Malachi];
>> the voice of one crying out in the wilderness:
>> 'Prepare the way of the Lord,
>> make his paths straight,'"
>
> John the baptizer appeared in the wilderness, proclaiming a baptism of repentance for the forgiveness of sins. And people from the whole Judean countryside and all the people of Jerusalem were going out to him, and were baptized by him in the river Jordan, confessing their sins. (1:2–5)

We have no direct evidence from first-century Jewish Palestine for a similar baptism. That this sort of baptism is unique to John is implied by the fact that he carries the title "the Baptist," showing that he is the only one who does this sort of thing. John's baptism is not simply a ritual washing for participation in temple worship. Nor is it the sectarian version of such a washing, which would allow members of the Qumran sect to take part in communal meals (Meier 1994, 2:19–99). John's baptism is a once-for-all ritual that prepares for the Lord's definitive coming (Klawans 2000, 138–43).

John is a prophet, and he predicts something that will come to pass within a few more verses of the Gospel—the coming of one stronger than he, who will baptize with the Holy Spirit (1:7–8). John's anticipation of the bestowal of the Spirit reflects an expectation that the activity of God's Spirit in the world will be part of history's consummation (see, for example, Isa. 11:1–2; Joel 2:28–32; Acts 2:17–22; the Dead Sea Scrolls).

John the Baptist looks like Elijah. He is in the wilderness, dressed in camel's hair and with a leather girdle around his waist. This recalls Elijah in 2 Kings 1:8. In the Christian arrangement of the books of the Hebrew Bible, the last book is Malachi. The final words of that book tell of the return of Elijah. Elijah's earthly career ended with his being swept up into heaven in a fiery chariot (2 Kings 2:11–12). This led to speculation about why he was taken up in this way (Allison 1984; Faierstein 1981; Malchow 1984; Fitzmyer 1985). Malachi answers by assigning him a special task:

> Lo, I will send you the prophet Elijah before the great and terrible day of the LORD comes. He will turn the hearts of parents to their children and the hearts of children to their parents, so that I will not come and strike the land with a curse. (Mal. 4:5–6)

The disorder of the world is social disorder, which must be rectified lest God inflict punishment on the land. The Christian Old Testament ends with Malachi's prediction of Elijah's coming before the judgment, and the New Testament begins with the Gospels, each of which starts with the appearance of John the Baptist, who Mark implies is Elijah and whom Matthew explicitly identifies with Elijah twice (11:14; 17:13). Thus the entire Old Testament leads to the appearance of John the Baptist. But his appearance is not an end in itself. John's purpose is to prepare for Jesus's arrival. While Malachi expected that Elijah would prepare for God's (the Lord's) coming as judge, the Synoptic Gospels change this to John the Baptist, Elijah returned, preparing the way for Jesus.

In 1:14, John is arrested. The Greek word for "arrest" is *paradidōmi*. It can also mean "to betray" or "to hand over." It occurs frequently in the Gospel, most often with Jesus as the object. Jesus is betrayed or "handed over" to the authorities and is ultimately executed. The same happens to John. In 1:14, he is arrested (handed over) and dies at the hands of Herod Antipas (Mark 6), a Jewish client-ruler of the Romans. John's fate foreshadows that of Jesus and of Jesus's followers, who will also be handed over (13:9–13). God has planned it all. John, Jesus, and Jesus's followers all die because they oppose Satan and his human collaborators (Duling and Perrin 1994, 301). This fulfills the idea that before the end, there will be a period of unprecedented suffering. Jesus's death and resurrection introduce not the golden age but a period of suffering as good and evil collide.

The parallel between John's death and that of Jesus occurs in the transfiguration as well (9:2–13). Jesus ascends a mountain with his three closest disciples, Peter, James, and John, where he is gloriously transformed before them. Jesus is described in terms reminiscent of the Ancient of Days (God) in Dan. 7 and the angel of Dan. 10. The scene is apocalyptic in that a private revelation is given to three select disciples and discloses the unseen world. Moses and Elijah appear with Jesus and converse with him. As Jesus and the disciples descend from the mountain, Jesus tells them to keep this quiet until the Son of Man rises from the dead.

Jesus's disciples ask him, "Why do the scribes say that Elijah must come first?" He answers, "Elijah is indeed coming first to restore all things." Jesus then says that the Son of Man (meaning himself) must suffer and rise from the dead. The passage ends with Jesus saying, "But I tell you that Elijah has come, and they did to him whatever they pleased, as it is written about him." He refers to John the Baptist's death. The prediction of Elijah's coming and of the Son of Man's resurrection puts everything into an eschatological context.

Jesus's Arrival and Baptism

The climax of the introductory section is Jesus's arrival. In a vision visible only to himself ("he saw"), the heavens open and the Spirit comes down and rests on him in the form of a dove. Jesus, but no one else (the voice addresses him, not the crowd), hears God call him God's Son, confirming the first line of the Gospel. Jesus's true identity, best expressed through the title Son of God, is a secret that will become known only when Jesus dies. Even those to whom the secret is revealed, the apostles, do not really get it. Throughout the Gospel they display consistent lack of understanding, particularly with respect to Jesus's suffering and death. This is Mark's "Messianic Secret." Mark puts Jesus's suffering and death at the center of his work. Until it happens, no one can really understand who Jesus is. Human misunderstanding is actually part of God's plan. Jesus dies as a result of his battle to bring in God's kingdom and his conflict with Satan, Satan's demons, and humans (religious authorities and Romans) who resist the kingdom.

Jesus's baptism is a commissioning scene, appointing him to a particular position (Son of God) giving him a task. The rest of the Gospel shows what Jesus's task is. It is to defeat Satan and bring in God's kingdom. As in Yarbro Collins's distinction between biography and eschatological history, Jesus's identity is significant because of what it implies for the eschatological event of the coming of God's kingdom.

Jesus's Conflict with Satan

Immediately after his baptism, the Spirit "drives" Jesus into the wilderness. The language is noteworthy. God has an urgent plan for the end time. Jesus has been commissioned, and God pushes him to get on with it.

In the wilderness, Jesus encounters Satan and is "tempted" or "tested" by him. The Greek participle for "tempted," *peirazomenos*, corresponds to the noun used in the Lord's Prayer, *peirasmos*, where Jesus instructs his disciples to pray to be delivered from temptation (Matt. 6:13; Luke 11:4). The word occurs frequently in eschatological contexts. As the end draws near, the faithful are tested in multiple ways, including opposition by hostile powers, often demonic. Jesus begins his own career by confronting Satan on Satan's own turf, the wilderness, and by undergoing this initial eschatological testing, but his fight with Satan will continue. Matthew's form of the Lord's Prayer makes deliverance from temptation more specific by requesting deliverance from "the evil one," Satan (6:13).

God supports Jesus in his struggle against Satan. Even in the wilderness God sends angels to serve him. This recalls how God treated Elijah in the desert (1 Kings 19:4–8).

Jesus plunges into the fray immediately upon his return from the wilderness. After John's arrest, Jesus goes to Galilee, "proclaiming the good news of God, and saying, 'The time [*kairos*] is fulfilled, and the kingdom of God has come near; repent, and believe in the good news'" (1:14–15). *Kairos* bears the sense of meaningful time, time with special content and consequence. Time's fulfillment implies that history has a specific structure, and it is time for something important to happen. This is apocalyptic periodization of history.

Jesus reveals the content of the good news: the kingdom of God has drawn near. God is about to reassert divine sovereignty over the cosmos and human history. The precise meaning of "kingdom of God" has been debated for centuries, but in an apocalyptic gospel such as Mark, it must be eschatological (Willis 1987; Meier 1994, 2:289–506). The verb translated "has come near" is ambiguous. It can mean something has come near but not yet arrived, or that it has become present. In this verse, it means something in between. In the ministry of Jesus, the kingdom has begun to break into history, but it will not fully arrive until Satan's power is broken and the righteous are rescued. Meanwhile, Jesus confronts Satan, as must the church. To accept Jesus's message, one must "repent" (verb: *metanoeō*; noun: *metanoia*), which literally means "change one's way of thinking" or "change one's way of looking at the world." If successful, Mark's Gospel will move its readers to see things in light of the imminent kingdom.

After calling the first four disciples, Jesus enters a synagogue and teaches. A man possessed by an unclean spirit enters and cries, "What have you to do with us, Jesus of Nazareth? Have you come to destroy us? I know who you are, the Holy One of God" (1:24). Jesus exorcizes the man. The congregation exclaims, "What is this? A new teaching—with authority! He commands even the unclean spirits, and they obey him" (1:27). Jesus's interaction with the demon is typical of Mark's Gospel. Demons recognize him because they belong to the unseen realm. The demon knows that the Holy One, Jesus, has come to destroy him. Humans do not have insight into the unseen world as

Jesus and the demons do. They recognize Jesus's authority over the demons, but they do not know its significance.

After Jesus cures Peter's mother-in-law, there is a summary statement in which Jesus performs many cures and casts out many demons. It ends, "He [Jesus] would not permit the demons to speak, because they knew him" (1:34; cf. 3:11–12).

After choosing the twelve apostles, his inner circle, Jesus goes home.

> Then he went home; and the crowd came together again, so that they could not even eat. When his family heard it, they went out to restrain him, for people were saying, "He has gone out of his mind." And the scribes who came down from Jerusalem said, "He has Beelzebul, and by the ruler of the demons he casts out demons." And he called them to him, and spoke to them in parables, "How can Satan cast out Satan? If a kingdom is divided against itself, that kingdom cannot stand. And if a house is divided against itself, that house will not be able to stand. And if Satan has risen up against himself and is divided, he cannot stand, but his end has come. But no one can enter a strong man's house and plunder his property without first tying up the strong man; then indeed the house can be plundered. (3:19–27)

Why do some think that he is out of his mind? Surely his cures and exorcisms are not irrational. Perhaps Jesus's contact with and apparent power over the demonic world is viewed skeptically by some who therefore think him mentally unbalanced. His family either agrees or are embarrassed, for they seek to restrain him.

The Jerusalem scribes think that Jesus is in league with Satan and so can control Satan's allies. This assumes the apocalyptic idea of an army of demons at Satan's command. Jesus rebuts their charge by pointing to its illogicality. Why would Satan oppose his own forces?

Jesus's exorcisms bind Satan, the "strong man." The world is Satan's house. Plundering it is rescuing those under Satan's rule. This recalls Melchizedek rescuing people from Belial in the Dead Sea Scrolls (11Q13). Jesus has begun shifting sovereignty of the world from Satan to God.

In Mark 5 we read of another exorcism. As usual, the unclean spirit recognizes Jesus and shouts, "What have you to do with me, Jesus, Son of the Most High God? I adjure you by God, do not torment me" (5:7). The demon thinks that Jesus will execute the punishment expected for evil angels and spirits in apocalypses, and he begs Jesus not to do so. Jesus demands to know the spirit's name and learns, "My name is Legion, for we are many" (5:9). This associates Rome with the evil power of Satan. "Legion" refers to the largest division of the Roman army, usually consisting of around six thousand men. Jesus casts the demons into a herd of pigs, an animal unclean for Jews, which then rush into a lake and perish. The incident reinforces the idea that Jesus is here to fight Satan and his human allies.

In Mark 6, Jesus sends out the twelve. He gives them "authority over the unclean spirits" (6:7). They are to preach repentance, cure diseases, and cast out unclean spirits. They carry on all aspects of Jesus's ministry except for preaching the kingdom. Although they have been given the kingdom's "secret" (see below on 4:11), they still don't comprehend and so are not competent to preach it yet. Nonetheless, the apostles' preaching of repentance prepares people for the kingdom, and their attack on demons spreads God's sovereignty.

Parables and the Secret Kingdom

Understanding that Mark has an apocalyptic viewpoint helps to explain his parable section, chapter 4. After telling the parable of the sower (4:3–8), Jesus says, "Let anyone with ears to hear listen!" (4:9). This implies that only certain people are privy to the parable's meaning.

> When he was alone, those who were around him along with the twelve asked him about the parables. And he said to them, "To you has been given the secret of the kingdom of God, but for those outside, everything comes in parables;
> in order that
>   'they may indeed look, but not perceive,
>   and may indeed listen, but not understand;
>   so that they may not turn again and be forgiven.'" (4:10–12)

Most readers of the Gospels assume that Jesus told parables as a way of getting his message across. Not so here. Rather, he uses parables to hide his message, lest his hearers understand, repent, and be forgiven. This is strange, to say the least. Jesus quotes Isa. 6:9–10. It predicts that Israel will not accept Isaiah's message. Jesus expects a similar rejection. This fits Mark's Messianic Secret.

This needs fuller explanation. Apocalypses are dualistic; they divide humanity into the righteous and the wicked, those who understand and those who do not. Mark 4 falls into this pattern. Ironically, even those who should understand, the disciples, do not. This supports Mark's idea that the message will become fully clear only upon Jesus's death. The rest of the Gospel shows that Mark sees the church as inhabiting a hostile world that does not accept Jesus's proclamation. This must be due to God's plan. Later in the chapter, Jesus offers explanations of the parables to his disciples only (4:33–34). Mark explains his own knowledge that Israel as a whole did not accept Jesus into part of God's plan. They did not accept the message because it was hidden from them, at least at first.

Other parables reinforce the idea that Jesus tells parables not to clarify things but as mysteries, signaling the end. However, in 4:22 he says that everything now secret will come to light. Ultimately, all will understand.

The parable of the growing seed (4:26–29) also means that the coming of the kingdom is not fully understood, even by those who help to bring it about.

The farmer sows seed, which then grows, although the farmer "does not know how" (4:27). Then comes the harvest (a common eschatological image). The parable of the mustard seed, while not necessarily apocalyptic, becomes so in its present context. It points to a situation in which the smallest becomes the largest, to a time in which the small beginnings of the kingdom, the church, lead to a time when all take refuge in it.

Jesus, Elijah, and Elisha

Mark implies that John the Baptist is Elijah. Jesus himself also has some of the characteristics of Elijah and his prophetic successor Elisha. Jesus preaches repentance, as Elijah was expected to do (Mal. 4:6). He also multiplies food and raises the dead, both of which Elijah and Elisha did (1 Kings 17:8–24; 2 Kings 4:18–37, 42–44). Echoes of Elijah and Elisha in Jesus's ministry enhance the eschatological tone of the Gospel, as when John the Baptist is portrayed in ways reminiscent of Elijah (Meier 1994).

When Herod Antipas asks about Jesus's activity (6:14), he learns that some say that John the Baptist has been raised from the dead and has empowered Jesus. Others say that Jesus himself is Elijah, and still others that he is a prophet. John the Baptist was an eschatological prophet as Elijah would be when he came again. What Jesus says and does makes him look like a prophet to his contemporaries, and the content of his message makes him an eschatological prophet.

It is striking that Jesus never identifies himself directly as the Son of God or as the Messiah in Mark. At best he accepts the appellation when others use it (Messiah in 8:29; Messiah and Son of God in 14:62). He does accept the role of prophet in 6:4, where he says, "Prophets are not without honor, except in their hometown, and among their own kin, and in their own house."

Jesus and the Sea

Jesus stills a storm at sea in 4:35–41, thereby displaying divine power. The sea was a powerful image in apocalypses (Dan. 7; 4 Ezra 13; Rev. 13) and similar texts (Testament of Moses 10:5). Jesus speaks to the sea and rebukes it, and it calms down (Ps. 89:9). He treats it as if it were a person, albeit a cosmic one. Ultimately, the imagery springs from the combat myth. When Jesus dominates the sea in Mark, he acts for God and opposes God's ancient mythological enemy. This is parallel to his defeat of Satan. We have seen in Rev. 12 and 13 that Satan and Rome are portrayed as God's enemies in the combat myth. Jesus is God's agent. His exercise of authority is analogous to his performing exorcisms.

The same point is made by the next sea story (6:45–52). There the apostles make a night voyage on the sea without Jesus and encounter strong winds. Jesus walks on the sea while it is riled up. This echoes Ps. 77:19: "Your way was through the sea, your path, through the mighty waters; yet your footprints were unseen," originally a reference to the Red Sea miracle. The apostles mistake him for a ghost. Jesus calms their fears, embarks with them, and the wind immediately ceases. They do not understand because they have not understood the meaning of the multiplication of loaves, narrated in the previous passage (6:30–44). The multiplication of loaves points to Jesus's identity as God's eschatological agent and carries overtones of the work of Moses (manna in the desert) as well as of Elijah and Elisha. Like the God of order in the combat myth, Jesus controls the sea.

Son of Man

The phrase "Son of Man" is frequent in Mark's Gospel, occurring fourteen times. Scholars commonly categorize the Son of Man sayings into three groups—eschatological, suffering, and earthly (Bultmann 1972). The earthly material applies the title to Jesus twice during his ministry, once when he claims the power to forgive sins (2:10), and once when he exercises authority over the Sabbath (2:28). The suffering Son of Man refers to Jesus's suffering, death, and resurrection (8:31; 9:9, 12, 31; 10:33, 45; 14:21 [twice]; 14:41). The eschatological Son of Man comes at the end of time to judge (8:38; 13:26; 14:62).

The eschatological Son of Man. After portraying his own suffering messiahship, put in terms of the Son of Man, and presenting his followers with a dire view of their own future suffering, Jesus says, "Those who are ashamed of me and of my words in this adulterous and sinful generation, of them the Son of Man will also be ashamed when he comes in the glory of his Father with the holy angels" (8:38). This alludes to the one like a son of man in Dan. 7:13–14. Here Jesus has assumed the identity of the Son of Man, who judges people at the end of time according to whether they are scandalized by his suffering and death as the Son of Man and are afraid to undergo suffering and death as the price for following him.

When Jesus is on trial, the high priest asks him, "Are you the Messiah, the Son of the Blessed One?" (14:61). Jesus answers, "I am; and 'you will see the Son of Man seated at the right hand of the Power,' and 'coming with the clouds of heaven'" (14:62). The single quotation marks here indicate the translator's decision that the verse quotes Dan. 7 and Ps. 110. As in Dan. 7, the Son of Man comes with the clouds of heaven. As in Ps. 110:1, the Son of Man sits at God's right hand. Jesus is both the Son of Man who is being condemned to death and the Son of Man who will come at the eschaton to vindicate his own ministry. The two go together and explain one another.

The apocalyptic Son of Man appears toward the end of Jesus's apocalyptic discourse in chapter 13. After the traditional apocalyptic disturbance of the sun, moon, and stars, Jesus says, "Then they will see 'the Son of Man coming in clouds' with great power and glory. Then he will send out the angels, and gather his elect from the four winds, from the ends of the earth to the ends of heaven" (13:26–27). Here is another reference to Dan. 7, with references to the Son of Man, power, glory, clouds, and angels. He comes to gather "his elect," "his chosen," a word used frequently in apocalyptic contexts. This eschatological scenario represents Jesus's second coming and the final separation of those who accept him and his ministry from those who do not.

Mark expects the eschatological Son of Man to come soon. He has Jesus say in 13:30, "Truly I tell you, this generation will not pass away until all these things have taken place." Jesus knows that the eschaton will come soon, although he does not know exactly when: "But about that day or hour no one knows, neither the angels in heaven, nor the Son, but only the Father" (13:32).

The suffering Son of Man. There are numerous references in Mark to the suffering Son of Man. Three such sayings (8:31; 9:12; 10:33) structure the second major section of the Gospel (8:22–10:52). The first follows what is traditionally called "Peter's Confession," which occurs at the beginning of the second section. Jesus asks the disciples who the people say he is. "And they answered him, 'John the Baptist; and others, Elijah; and still others, one of the prophets'" (8:28). Their answer corresponds to what Herod heard about Jesus (6:14–15). This answer is inadequate. Jesus asks his disciples, "But who do you say that I am?" Peter answers, "You are the Messiah" (8:29). We might expect Jesus's immediate approval of Peter's insight, but that does not happen. (Matthew adds it.) Instead, Jesus orders Peter to silence, in accordance with Mark's Messianic Secret. There follows the first prediction of the suffering Son of Man.

> Then he began to teach them that the Son of Man must undergo great suffering, and be rejected by the elders, the chief priests, and the scribes, and be killed, and after three days rise again. He said all this quite openly. And Peter took him aside and began to rebuke him. But turning and looking at his disciples, he rebuked Peter and said, "Get behind me, Satan! For you are setting your mind not on divine things but on human things." (8:31–33)

Jesus speaks "openly." Given Mark's Messianic Secret and the fact that he has not spoken of his suffering and death even to the disciples, Jesus's openness is something new and to be noted. The accent in this passage is on suffering, not resurrection, but the resurrection is nonetheless crucial.

Peter "rebukes" Jesus, a strong word indicating severe disagreement. He refuses to accept suffering as part of messiahship. Jesus in turn "rebukes" Peter. Peter does not accept God's plan. Apocalypticism is dualistic and allows only one of two possibilities—acceptance or rejection. Jesus concludes that Peter must be on Satan's side, not God's.

The other two predictions of the suffering Son of Man that structure this section make the same points (9:30–31; 10:33–34).

An important Son of Man saying occurs toward the end of this section. At the end of a passage in which Jesus tells his disciples that their role is to be servants, not rulers, Jesus says, "For the Son of Man came not to be served but to serve, and to give his life a ransom for many" (10:45). Mark's Christology stresses not Jesus's glory and power, but his suffering, as he battles with Satan and human forces opposed to God's kingdom. This is not atonement imagery—Jesus suffering the penalty for human sin—but is connected with Jesus's battle. Jesus guarantees that the struggle will be won and thereby people will be ransomed from Satan, a slavery image (Stevens 1987; Yarbro Collins 2009). Jesus's followers must carry on the same battle and pay the same price.

Jesus, the Jewish Authorities, and the Destruction of the Temple

Finally, Jesus goes to Jerusalem and confronts its authorities (11:1–16:8). He enters triumphantly, and his arrival is taken by the crowds to signal the advent of the Davidic kingdom (11:10). The next day, Jesus enters the temple and attacks the money changers and merchants. Echoing Jeremiah's words in Jer. 7:11 and 26, he accuses those in charge of the temple of turning it into a den of thieves (11:17; see Zech. 14:21). The scene is framed by Jesus's cursing of the fig tree (11:13–14, 20–21), symbolizing his condemnation of the temple authorities and the destruction of the temple resulting from their actions. Confronted by the priests, scribes, and elders who demand to know by what authority he acts, Jesus associates himself with John the Baptist once again, his eschatological forerunner. The leaders are reluctant to criticize John, since the crowd considers John a true prophet (11:27–33).

There follow a number of clashes between Jesus and the leaders. The Jerusalem authorities ought to be God's representatives, but they have been unfaithful, and Jesus predicts their ouster, using a parable about wicked tenants of a vineyard (12:1–12; alluding to the portrayal of Israel as God's vineyard in Isa. 5). When Pharisees and Herodians try to trap him about paying taxes to Caesar, he exposes their hypocrisy, for they carry Roman coinage bearing the emperor's likeness. Jesus says, "Give to the emperor the things that are the emperor's, and to God the things that are God's" (12:17). Giving to God what belongs to God is precisely what the leaders fail to do, as Jesus's vineyard parable makes clear. Ironically, they carry Caesar's coin and image, so they accept Roman sovereignty. Here again we have a clash of sovereignties, and Jesus's opponents fall on the wrong side. Next, Jesus argues that the Sadducees' refusal to believe in resurrection is wrong (12:18–27). He thereby defends the apocalyptic belief of resurrection against religious authorities in Jerusalem. There follow passages about the most important commandments in the Torah (12:28–34) and about whether the Messiah is David's son (12:35–37).

All of this lays the groundwork for Jesus's prediction of the temple's destruction. He begins by attacking the Jerusalem scribes who use their status for prideful purposes (12:38–40). Among his accusations is that they "devour widows' houses." In the next passage, a widow deposits into the temple treasury a tiny amount of money, which represents all of her possessions (her *bios*, "life"; 12:41–44). Jesus contrasts her to the rich, who contribute "out of their abundance." This leads directly to Jesus's prediction of the temple's destruction (13:1–2). Seen in this context, the widow's story makes a point quite different from what we normally hear. Most frequently it is used to demonstrate her self-sacrifice and generosity, something that should be imitated. But Mark's point is that the temple establishment eagerly gobbles up contributions, even from those who can least afford it. They "devour" the little that widows have. The rich exploit the poor. This condemnation leads directly into Jesus's discourse on the temple's destruction.

Criticism of the temple leadership was common in the Second Temple period. It is especially common in eschatological and apocalyptic contexts, such as the Dead Sea Scrolls, the *Animal Apocalypse*, Tob. 14, the *Psalms of Solomon*, and the *Testament of Moses*. Mark's Jesus also situates his criticism of temple leadership and prediction of the temple's destruction in an apocalyptic context. Immediately after the prediction that the temple will soon be destroyed, Jesus and his disciples cross the Kidron Valley to the Mount of Olives, where Jesus delivers his apocalyptic discourse (13:3–37) (Beasley-Murray 1993). Mark claims that the eschaton is near, but time is left before it comes. Mark's audience should use this time to preach the gospel, despite persecution by Jewish and gentile authorities (13:9–13). Those who do so and endure "to the end" will be saved when the Son of Man comes.

Jesus lists the typical apocalyptic signs of the end, with the caution that "the end is still to come." He lists false prophets and messiahs, wars and rumors of wars, earthquakes, and famines. Using an image familiar in apocalypticism (see Rev. 12; Qumran), he says, "This is but the beginning of the birth pangs" (13:8). He lists persecution and social discord that will result from the preaching of the gospel. Then he predicts the "desolating sacrilege set up where it ought not to be (let the reader understand)" (13:14). The aside implies that only the elect will understand Jesus's meaning. The desolating sacrilege alludes to Dan. 9:27; 11:31; 12:11, where it refers to the statue of Zeus set up in the temple by Antiochus IV in the second century BCE. It may also refer to Caligula's failed attempt to set up his own statue in the temple in the first century CE. For Jesus, it is a future event, signaling the onset of eschatological sufferings. The listeners must flee at that time, "for in those days there will be suffering such as has not been from the beginning of the creation that God created until now, no, and never will be" (13:19).

After the suffering come cosmic events:

> the sun will be darkened,
> and the moon will not give its light,

and the stars will be falling from heaven,
and the powers in the heavens will be shaken. (13:24–25)

After these traditional eschatological events, the Son of Man comes to gather his elect. The apocalyptic discourse ends with Jesus telling his disciples that the end is near, but even he does not know when it will be (13:30–32). He exhorts them to be ready. The final words of the discourse are, "Keep awake" (13:37).

Jesus's Death and Resurrection as Apocalyptic Events

Jesus celebrates Passover with his disciples, and during the course of the meal he says, "Truly I tell you, I will never again drink of the fruit of the vine until that day when I drink it new in the kingdom of God" (14:25). Jesus expects not a "spiritualized" kingdom, but one in which he will feast and drink wine with his disciples, after his death and resurrection. Dragged before the high priest, Jesus finally admits his messiahship publicly, and he immediately refers to the coming of the Son of Man at the eschaton (14:62). This brings to mind the entire Son of Man complex, covering Jesus's ministry, suffering, death, resurrection, and return to save the elect and condemn those who have not accepted him. It brings the entire gospel into view and frames it eschatologically. The high priest does not know it, but by his own sarcastic words he has doomed himself.

As Jesus hangs on the cross, darkness covers the land. When he dies, the temple curtain is torn in two. The meaning of this is not transparent, but given Jesus's opposition to the temple leadership and his prediction of the temple's destruction, it may symbolize that destruction and connect it directly to the leaders' rejection of Jesus and God's kingdom. It may also symbolize the idea that access to God is no longer through the cultic establishment but through Jesus—his death in particular. Finally, Jesus's resurrection, announced by the angel in 16:6, is both a vindication of Jesus and a foretaste of the eschaton.

What "Must" Happen

Mark frequently uses the verb "must [*dei*]." It conveys the idea that what transpires in the Gospel has been decreed by God. The frequency of its usage colors the entire book, so we reproduce all of its uses here. Several of them have to do with key events, and so they can be called end-time events foreordained by God.

> 7:10: For Moses said, "Honor your father and your mother"; and, "Whoever speaks evil of father or mother *must* surely die."
> 8:31: He began to teach them that the Son of Man *must* undergo great suffering, and be rejected by the elders, the chief priests, and the scribes, and be killed, and after three days rise again.

9:11: They asked him, "Why do the scribes say that Elijah *must* come first?"

9:19: He answered them, "You faithless generation, how much longer *must* I be among you? How much longer *must* I put up with you?"

9:35: He sat down, called the twelve, and said to them, "Whoever wants to be first *must* be last of all and servant of all."

10:17: As he was setting out on a journey, a man ran up and knelt before him, and asked him, "Good Teacher, what *must* I do to inherit eternal life?"

10:43: It is not so among you; but whoever wishes to become great among you *must* be your servant.

10:44: Whoever wishes to be first among you *must* be slave of all.

13:7: When you hear of wars and rumors of wars, do not be alarmed; this *must* take place, but the end is still to come.

13:10: The good news *must* first be proclaimed to all nations.

13:14: When you see the desolating sacrilege set up where it ought not to be (let the reader understand), then those in Judea *must* flee to the mountains.

13:15: The one on the housetop *must not* go down or enter the house to take anything away.

13:16: The one in the field *must not* turn back to get a coat.

14:31: He said vehemently, "Even though I *must* die with you, I will not deny you." And all of them said the same.

Of these verses, the ones that could easily be called apocalyptic are: 8:31: Jesus must suffer, die, and rise from the dead; 9:11: Elijah must come first; 9:19: Jesus must be with this generation; 13:10: the gospel must be preached to all nations (in the apocalyptic discourse); 13:14, 15, 16: no one should delay when fleeing Jerusalem as the end approaches; 14:31: Peter thinks he also may have to die.

The remaining verses have to do with proper behavior for Jesus's followers. These are not in themselves apocalyptic, but they help to form a community that fits Jesus's status and function. Jesus demands denunciation of wealth and becoming a slave to all.

Mark as an Apocalyptic Gospel

Jesus's mission involves not just enemies in the visible world but also of the unseen world. He confronts and battles Satan and demons. He is the only human with insight into this unseen world; only inhabitants of the unseen world—angels, demons, and God—really understand who Jesus is and what these final battles mean.

When Jesus tries to convey to his disciples what is happening, he commands them to secrecy. He uses parables to hide his message from outsiders. But just as the secret doctrines of apocalypses will eventually be known to all, Jesus declares that what is hidden will eventually be revealed.

Jesus expects the usual apocalyptic eschatological events—wars, earthquakes, famine, unprecedented suffering, persecution, disturbance of heavenly

Mark as an Apocalyptic Gospel

- John the Baptist comes in fulfillment of Isaiah, indicating all is to happen according to God's preordained plan.
- John the Baptist looks like the prophet Elijah, who Malachi says is to come before God's great day of judgment.
- Jesus announces the imminence of the kingdom of God and helps to bring it in (God's sovereignty is at issue).
- The kingdom will come in power in the near future.
- The rich will find it nearly impossible to enter the kingdom, but God can make it possible (10:17–25).
- The "gospel" is a political statement.
- Jesus battles Satan and the demons to bring in the kingdom.
- Apocalyptic drama occurs in three parts (John the Baptist is handed over and dies; Jesus is handed over and dies; Christians are handed over and die).
- The Son of Man comes at the end to judge.
- An apocalyptic discourse is presented in chapter 13.
- Apocalyptic signs are described: the temple destroyed; wars and rumors of wars; earthquakes; famines; false prophets; false messiahs; sun, moon, and stars disturbed; Son of Man comes to judge.
- Jesus battles earthly forces opposing the kingdom—the temple establishment and the Romans.
- Jesus is resurrected.
- Jesus defends the idea of a general resurrection against the Sadducees.
- The transfiguration gives the disciples insight into Jesus's heavenly identity, which can be made public only after Jesus's death and resurrection.
- Secrecy: parables keep the secret of the kingdom.
- There is dualism: insiders and outsiders; the way humans think (like Satan) and the way God thinks.
- Jesus's messiahship is intimately linked to suffering.
- Jesus connects suffering to the eschaton.
- History is determined by God's plan, visible in the apocalyptic discourse, and implied in references to the prophets.
- Jesus controls the sea.

bodies, and a final separation of the elect from the wicked. He also anticipates his own resurrection and defends general resurrection. Jesus has introduced the last days. The eschatological events have been set in motion. All will culminate in the coming of the Son of Man on the clouds of heaven, a scenario dependent on Dan. 7.

Fig. 10. Herod's temple plays a central role in each of the four canonical Gospels. (Chris Miller)

Q

Matthew and Luke used two main sources for their Gospels—the Gospel of Mark and Q (Tuckett 1992). Much controversy surrounds Q. To begin with, it no longer exists, as far as we know. Nonetheless, the vast majority of interpreters take the two-source solution to the Synoptic Problem as a working hypothesis. A smaller number dedicate their studies to a study of Q itself. To study Q, one must reconstruct it. The reconstruction is itself an academic endeavor, so reconstructions differ. The basic method of reconstructing Q is common to all such efforts. A comparison of Matthew, Mark, and Luke yields material Matthew and Luke have in common that they did not obtain from Mark. This material is at least a rough approximation of Q.

A basic problem is deciding which, if either, of Matthew or Luke is closer to Q in wording, order, and so on. Most have decided that Luke is closer than Matthew in the order in which he incorporates Q material into his Gospel. For that reason, the convention has developed to number Q verses according to chapter and verse numbers in Luke's Gospel.

Any reconstruction of Q demands numerous decisions about individual verses and, at times, larger sections. Here we depend on the work of others. There are several good reconstructions of Q available, some freely accessible on the internet. There are also websites dedicated to the study of Q. All reconstructions end up being primarily collections of sayings of Jesus, although there is some narrative. One narrative is the story of the cure of the centurion's servant. Another is narrative material concerning John the Baptist.

There is no passion narrative in Q, at least as most reconstruct it. Of course, we cannot be sure.

New Testament scholarship has tended to posit a different community behind every document. This would mean that there was a community whose view of Jesus is embodied in Q and whose discipleship conformed with the view of Jesus implied by Q. Our first task in studying a document is to comprehend its structure, theology, Christology, and outlook. Then we might speculate on what a community that produced such a document might look like.

Scholars have subjected Q to meticulous analysis and developed theories about its editorial history. This has led to speculation about stages in its development, and that speculation has involved the issue of just how apocalyptic the work is, how apocalyptic its various stages are, and, correspondingly, how apocalyptic the Q community was at various stages in its history. In this book we treat Q as a whole, not trying to distinguish layers (Kloppenborg 1987; Horsley 1991; 1998; Goff 2005; Collins 1993b). As it stands, it is clearly apocalyptic.

Q as Apocalyptic

Horsley insists that Q not be treated simply as a collection of sayings (Horsley 1998, 305). Q is organized according to a series of discourses and must be read accordingly. Horsley sees Q as primarily an exhortation concerning social, economic, and political behavior that is sanctioned by "prophetic threats of reward and punishment (e.g., Q 6:20–49; 12:2–12, 22–31)" (Horsley and Draper 1999, 86). Horsley organizes the text into the following discourses (Horsley and Draper 1999, 87–88). Chapter and verse numbers accord with the Gospel of Luke, as explained above.

> 3:7–9, 16–17: Promising/threatening opening
> 6:20–49: Jesus's opening speech; the kingdom is for the poor; instructions for interaction within the kingdom community
> 7:18–35: Fulfillment of Israel's long-held hopes
> 14:26–27, 34–35; 15:4–7; 16:13, 17, 18: Community discipline
> 17:1–6, 23–37: Preparedness for sudden judgment
> 9:57–10:16: Mission
> 11:2–4, 9–11: Petitioning God for the kingdom
> 11:14–26: Reassurance about kingdom's presence; condemnation of this generation (scribes and Pharisees)
> 12:2–12: Exhortation to confidence in confession
> 12:22–31: No need for anxiety caused by poverty if in pursuit of kingdom
> 12:39–40, 42–46: Sanctions
> 12:49–59: Crisis caused by Jesus's mission
> 13:18–21: Kingdom as encouraging through parables of growth
> 13:28–29, 34–35; 14:16–24: Kingdom as condemnation of rulers in Jerusalem
> 17:23–37: Exhortation to maintain group discipline
> 22:28–30: Positive, anticipatory ending; kingdom is renewal of Israel

Tying all of the Q document together is the kingdom of God. For Q, the kingdom is the renewal of Israel. The form of sayings and themes corresponds to their function within the text, which relates to their functions in the community. Those aimed internally, at church behavior and discipline, utilize "traditional covenantal exhortation and popular wisdom." Condemnations for Jesus's opponents use prophetic forms and motifs. Material on the killing of the prophets occurs in the sections against the Jerusalem establishment, as does the material about "this generation." Material on the coming of the Son of Man and the suddenness of judgment with both positive and negative effects is followed by the promise of societal renewal, which sanctions the entire document. Q is concerned with "a renewed social order," which "entails social conflict" (Horsley and Draper 1999, 90). Horsley suggests "sayings of the prophets" as a good description of the work.

Jesus and the Baptist: Part One

Two blocks of material in Q concern John the Baptist. The first is about John's preaching and baptizing. The second concerns John's questioning of Jesus from prison.

The first Baptist block begins the entire work. The apocalyptic features of John's preaching are more vivid than in Mark. He fiercely condemns his hearers as vipers and demands to know who warned them to flee from the wrath to come. John warns that membership in Israel counts for nothing in the face of God's wrath. Those who do not bear the fruit of repentance are doomed. "Even now the axe is laid to the root of the trees; every tree therefore that does not bear good fruit is cut down and thrown into the fire" (Q 3:9).

John's depiction of the stronger one to follow him continues in this vein. The one to come is a judge. He baptizes with fire, probably both a negative (punishment) and positive (refinement) image, depending on one's state of repentance. Wheat goes to the granary; chaff will be burned.

Jesus against Satan

In Q's next section, Jesus confronts Satan in the desert. He is subjected to three temptations. "Tempt" means eschatological testing. In the first and third temptations (Luke's order), Satan challenges Jesus to prove his sonship to God through acts of power—changing stone into bread and casting himself from the highest point of the temple, trusting the angels to rescue him. For the latter, Satan dares to quote Scripture to undergird his argument. Jesus refuses the temptation in both cases, redefining divine sonship as loyalty to God and quoting Scripture to that effect. In the middle temptation, Satan offers Jesus the kingdoms of the world in return for his worship. There could not be a clearer choice between sovereignties. Jesus's choice is uncompromising, and he supports it with reference to Scripture. One may worship God alone. Only

One is truly sovereign. Yet Satan is in a position to offer sovereignty at this point, since he is ruler of this world. The world's empires are satanic. They are his to bestow.

By experiencing Jesus's confrontation with Satan, the reader has gained insight into the usually unseen world of angels and demons. He or she can now understand how visible events, such as Jesus's career, are part of something larger that involves God, angels, demons, cosmic struggle, and the course and goal of history. Insight into the unseen world imparts true understanding of what is happening before one's senses.

The Renewed Community

The next section lays out the nature of the renewed community Jesus expects. It becomes the basis of Matthew's Sermon on the Mount (Matt. 5–7) and Luke's Sermon on the Plain (Luke 6). It is primarily wisdom material, but it contains advice appropriate to an apocalyptic community. It encourages the formation of a community that, although in tension with society, is nonresistant and witnesses to a different set of values than those of its environment.

Seen as a whole, one must read Q in light of its introduction.

> Then he looked up at his disciples and said:
>   "Blessed are you who are poor,
>   for yours is the kingdom of God.
>   "Blessed are you who are hungry now,
>   for you will be filled.
>   "Blessed are you who weep now,
>   for you will laugh.
>   "Blessed are you when people hate you, and when they exclude you, revile you, and defame you on account of the Son of Man. Rejoice in that day and leap for joy, for surely your reward is great in heaven; for that is what their ancestors did to the prophets." (Q 6:20–23)

These are the Beatitudes. They are so familiar to modern Christians that they have lost their ability to shock, but they are radical. They embody eschatological reversal. Too easily they are heard as a benevolent egalitarianism. Rather, at the eschaton, present conditions will be reversed. God is so angry at human society that the only solution is to turn it on its head. It will require more than small adjustments.

Jesus's hearers ought to rejoice in opposition and suffering. It authenticates their message. They are in solidarity with the prophets, who also suffered. They do not fit in and they ought not to. This wholesale disapproval of the current state of affairs is typical of apocalypses. The mention of heaven also suits an apocalyptic outlook. Postmortem rewards and punishments are the hallmark of apocalyptic eschatology.

Jesus and the Baptist: Part Two

The second block of John material occurs in Q 7. In the light of the first block of John material, it also should be read apocalyptically. John's inquiry to Jesus recalls the first block, for he asks whether Jesus is the "one to come" or whether they ought to look for another. The one to come is eschatological. Jesus answers with an enumeration of his miracles—healings, exorcisms, raisings of the dead, and the preaching of the good news to the poor. Jesus's miracles are like those in Isaiah, and so can be seen as fulfillment of prophecy (Harvey 1982, 113; Sanders 1985, 160–63). Exorcism is not associated with messiahship in Jewish sources, but it is compatible with the idea that the Messiah institutes God's rule and that the coming of God's kingdom means the defeat of Satan (see *Testament of Moses* 10; Dead Sea Scrolls). Jesus's preaching fulfills Isa. 61, which says that the prophet's task is to bring good news to the poor. Jesus blesses anyone not taking offense at him. This warns John not to disapprove of his ministry.

Jesus's answer can easily be read within an apocalyptic framework. The world is as it is because it is not as God wished it. Sickness, demon possession, death, and political oppression demonstrate that God seems to have lost sovereignty over the universe. Reversal of these evils signals the presence of the kingdom of God.

The next verses demonstrate that the Jesus movement has been alienated from the Baptist's movement. There were many things that John and Jesus shared, but they also differed in key ways. When Jesus lists his activities in response to John's question, he enumerates things he did but John did not. Jesus goes so far as to claim that John is not in the kingdom: "The least in the kingdom of God is greater than he" (Q 7:28).

Mission

Q's missionary discourse has apocalyptic elements (Q 9:57–10:16). The message is that the kingdom of God has come near, and the mission is driven by the need to reveal knowledge of how to be saved. The mission is urgent. The missionaries must move fast. There is little time. They should shake the dust from their feet and move on if they do not meet quick success. "Harvest" indicates that the climax has come. Judgment is next, and it seems imminent. Punishment and reward are hell and heaven.

Jesus praises God for hiding the truth from the wise and revealing it to babes, his followers. No one can know the Father except the Son and those to whom he decides to reveal him. Prophets and kings have not been granted to see and know what Jesus's followers do. This is apocalyptic secrecy.

Q's readers petition for the kingdom through reciting the Lord's Prayer. This is an eschatological prayer, pleading for the coming of God's kingdom and for deliverance from temptation, the end-time testing (Brown 1965). It seeks political and economic changes, pleading for the discharge of debts and pledging to do the same for those indebted to the petitioners.

Q devotes considerable space to the Beelzebul controversy (Q 11). Beelzebul is the "prince of demons." The idea that there is an organized body of demons and that they have a leader is apocalyptic. Demons possess people, and Jesus has the power to expel them. Jesus interprets this as the approach of God's kingdom. Beelzebul has a kingdom, and Jesus's exorcisms attack that kingdom. Jesus easily refutes the idea that he casts out demons by Beelzebul's power. If it is not by Beelzebul's power that he does so, it must be by God's might. In an apocalyptic world, there are only two sides.

Condemnation of Opponents

The rest of Q 11 condemns Jesus's human opponents, mainly the scribes and the Pharisees. The section begins and ends with an announcement of judgment. What comes between are specific accusations, the most important one of which ends the section. It is that the leaders do not enter the kingdom themselves, and they prevent others from doing so (Q 11:52). They are, in fact, Satan's accomplices.

Jesus characterizes the entire contemporary generation as evil. Such a sweeping generalization sounds apocalyptic. Jesus recalls Jonah's preaching to the Ninevites. The Son of Man, Jesus, is the present-day Jonah, but he is greater than Jonah. Jesus claims that the Ninevites, Jonah's audience who repented at his preaching, will arise at the judgment and condemn Jesus's unrepentant hearers. Both John and Jesus exceed past prophets. The queen of the south will also rise from the dead and condemn the present generation. She also will realize that Jesus is greater than Solomon.

The penultimate charge is that the present generation builds the prophets' tombs and thereby join themselves to their ancestors who killed the prophets. At the same time, they reject and persecute the prophets sent to them, members of the Q community. They are responsible for the persecution of all the prophets, past and present.

Instruction for Insiders

Q's insiders face hostility, and this section instructs them on how to handle it and reassures them of God's support. Their proclamation means that what had been secret is now made known (Q 12:2). Jesus tells them not to fear the one who can harm their body in this life, but to fear God, who can cast into hell. They are warned that they must make faithful confession of the Son of Man and of the Holy Spirit. If they remain faithful to the Son of Man, the Son of Man will confess them before the angels. When they are brought to trial, the Holy Spirit will inspire them with what to say.

After a section that tells them that their poverty should not hold them back, because God cares for them, they are again warned of coming judgment. Two sections contain a warning that the judgment is to come unexpectedly (Q 12:39–40, 42–46). The first says that it will come unannounced like a thief, and the second that the master (Jesus) will also come without warning.

Jesus's Mission as Crisis

Q heightens the tone of crisis connected to Jesus's ministry. He comes to cast fire on the earth. He comes not to bring peace but a sword. His ministry causes familial conflict. Followers must act like a debtor being dragged before a judge—they must use the little time left to settle with the plaintiff.

Entrance into the kingdom will be hard. The door is narrow, not wide. Many will not make it. The Lord will be the householder who refuses to rise and let them into the house, claiming he never knew them.

The kingdom's advent will be negative for those who refuse to listen to Jesus. They will see Abraham, Isaac, Jacob, and all the prophets feasting together with the sons of the kingdom while they are left outside. This assumes resurrection, postmortem rewards, and awareness of being in the prophetic tradition. Jesus warns, "Some are last who will be first, and some are first who will be last" (Q 13:30). Jerusalem is condemned. It has had its last chance. Jesus brought it news of the kingdom; the next time it will see him will be at his triumphal entry. For now, Jerusalem's house is desolate.

The banquet parable follows, with its message that the invited refuse to come, and unlikely ones fill the banquet hall. This expresses how the Q community sees the religious establishment. The community is on the outside now, but in the end they will be the insiders.

Jesus emphasizes again how difficult it is to follow him—one must reject one's own family and carry one's cross. In the midst of these exhortations comes a verse that has perplexed scholars: "The law and the prophets were until John; since then the good news of the kingdom is preached and everyone enters it violently" (Q 16:16). The transparent elements are that John's ministry is a watershed between an earlier period and the time when the gospel is preached. Also, there is an element of violence in the present. Since John is less than the least in the kingdom, he does not belong to the second period. The violence suffered is probably the persecution of the Q community, seen as part of the end-time sufferings.

Q 17:23–37 describes the end. The hearers are warned not to listen to false warnings about it, for the Son of Man "in his day" will be like lightning that flashes across the sky from east to west. As in the day of Noah, when the earth's population carried on their lives as if nothing were going to happen, so in the days of the Son of Man the end will come unexpectedly. The days of Lot teach the same lesson. Fire and brimstone rained down on them without

Q and Apocalypticism

- There is belief in heaven and hell.
- An imminent judgment is expected.
- Secrets are revealed to the world.
- Exorcisms demonstrate the coming of the kingdom.
- Jesus and Satan are in conflict.
- An entire generation is condemned.
- The Holy Spirit is present in an eschatological role.

warning. That is what the day of the Son of Man will be like. Trying to save one's life will result in losing it.

Q includes the parable of the pounds before the final closing. To prepare for the end, one must bear fruit.

The last line of the document reads, "You are those who have stood by me in my trials; and I confer on you, just as my Father has conferred on me, a kingdom, so that you may eat and drink at my table in my kingdom, and you will sit on thrones judging the twelve tribes of Israel" (Q 22:28–30). This pictures a this-worldly kingdom. "Judging" is not judicial but is used in the sense contained in the book of Judges. It means ruling the tribes. For the first time since the Assyrian exile in 721 BCE, there will be twelve tribes, a restored Israel. The Q community, who had been last, will now be first.

In its present form, Q is permeated with apocalypticism. Since Q was used by Matthew and Luke as a source, it is early, probably at least as old as Mark, which was written around 70 CE, and perhaps older. Q is a product of an early apocalyptic community. It saw Jesus as a prophet and more than a prophet who commanded a certain way of life representing the renewal of Israel, who fought with the religious establishment, battled with Satan, and warned of imminent judgment followed by heaven or hell. He and the Baptist were God's messengers. Jesus's death and resurrection are not mentioned. Jesus's importance lies in his urgent message.

Since Q contains so much community instruction, it affords a glimpse into what this apocalyptic community was like. The community lived strictly—trying to follow ethical demands that called for nonresistance to hostility and oppression, leaving judgment up to the Son of Man, being aware of a cosmic struggle with Satan, expecting imminent judgment with heaven and hell on the other side of it, accepting poverty and being completely dependent on God, being conscious of the presence of the Holy Spirit in their midst whose role was to support them in their eschatological trials, loving their enemies, practicing mercy, doing intense missionary work, proclaiming the secrets imparted to them by Jesus, acknowledging the Son of Man, and so on.

The Gospel of Matthew

Matthew's Gospel uses Mark and Q as its two main sources. Much of what is said about Mark and Q concerning apocalypticism applies to Matthew as well, and we need not repeat it. We concentrate on how Matthew edits his sources with respect to their apocalyptic aspects.

Matthew, like Mark, makes the kingdom of God central to his Gospel. It is the content of Jesus's preaching, teaching, and actions. Divine sovereignty remains a major concern. Matthew's Jesus announces the kingdom's nearness and helps to inaugurate it through preaching, teaching, miracle working, and exorcising. Jesus's battle against Satan and his demons is preserved by Matthew. Jesus's struggle against earthly forces that oppose God's plan—the Jewish establishment, both the priestly establishment in Jerusalem and the Pharisaic establishment, as well as the Roman imperial system—is as important in Matthew as in Mark (Carter 2001).

Jesus's death and resurrection remain eschatological events in Matthew, as in Mark. Matthew emphasizes them still more as eschatological happenings.

The Kingdom of God

Matthew mostly follows Mark in what the kingdom means. However, there are subtle but important shifts that we note as we proceed.

God's Plan, Foretold by the Prophets

Two ways that Matthew changes Mark most obviously are at the beginning and end of his Gospel. Matthew starts with a two-chapter infancy narrative, lacking in Mark. The Gospel ends with the "Great Commission," where Jesus sends his apostles on a mission to the whole world (28:16–20). We start with the former.

In Mark, God has a plan for the final days, now in progress. The existence of a divine plan is evident from Mark's quotation of prophets, and from chapter 13, where the progressive steps of the last days are enumerated. Matthew enhances this aspect of Mark. He does so, among other ways, through "formula quotations." These are quotations from biblical prophets introduced by formulas that declare that what happens fulfills prophecies. There are five formula quotations in the first two chapters alone. In those chapters, the following events happen in order to fulfill Scripture: the virgin birth, Jesus's birth in Bethlehem, the flight to Egypt, Herod's killing of the male babies, and settling in Nazareth. These five quotations, and the many others which pepper the Gospel itself, keep the reader cognizant that every step of Jesus's career is divinely determined.

Matthew begins his Gospel with a genealogy proving Jesus's membership in the people of Abraham as well as his Davidic lineage. Jesus is a true member of Israel with messianic credentials. The very first words of the Gospel, translated by the NRSV as "an account of the genealogy," are *biblos geneseōs*. This alludes to the first book of Torah, Genesis. It implies that God's plan for the world goes back to its beginning, and that Jesus's coming indicates that the culmination of that plan is near. Another indication that God controls history is that there are exactly fourteen generations between Abraham and David, David and the Babylonian exile, and the exile and Jesus. The number fourteen may be due to the fact that it is the numerical value of the name "David." Matthew highlights Jesus being the Son of David.

Matthew's view takes in all history from Abraham on (who first appears in Gen. 11), and, if the allusion to Genesis in Matthew's opening is given weight, his view takes in creation itself. Throughout the Gospel, Matthew refers to the end of the age, so his view of history takes in all of history, from beginning to end. It is apocalyptic in scope.

Jesus's Teaching Goes Out to All Nations

The Gospel ends with the Great Commission (28:16–20). Jesus orders the disciples to baptize all nations, teaching them to observe all he has commanded them, and assuring them that he will be with them "to the end of the age" (28:20). Teaching to observe commands is Torah language. It recalls Deuteronomy, where Moses tells the Israelites to teach their children Torah (Deut. 5:31). The eschatological notice here in Matthew both enhances and adapts Mark's brief command in Mark 13:10 that the disciples preach the gospel to all nations. It gives it further content, the teaching of Jesus's interpretation of Torah.

The commission envisages a community based on Jesus's renewal of Israel and encompassing the entire world. It gives the impression that the end is further off than Mark thought. The worldwide mission must take time. Mark's expectation that the end will come before all the hearers of Jesus's message die seems unrealistic. Nonetheless, Matthew thinks of the present as an "age" that will "end." This retains an apocalyptic viewpoint.

John the Baptist

Like Mark, Matthew connects John the Baptist with biblical prophecy. John remains the one in the wilderness preparing the way of the Lord predicted by Isaiah. As in Mark, John resembles Elijah. Whereas Mark's Gospel only hints at the identification of John and Elijah, Matthew states it explicitly twice (11:14; 17:11–13).

Matthew finds more information about the Baptist in Q, and some of it enhances John's apocalyptic profile.

When he saw many Pharisees and Sadducees coming for baptism, he said to them, "You brood of vipers! Who warned you to flee from the wrath to come?

Bear fruit worthy of repentance. Do not presume to say to yourselves, 'We have Abraham as our ancestor'; for I tell you, God is able from these stones to raise up children to Abraham. Even now the ax is lying at the root of the trees; every tree therefore that does not bear good fruit is cut down and thrown into the fire. (3:7–10)

The Baptist uses "wrath [*orgē*]" to designate the coming judgment. His description of the judgment is vivid—trees being cut down and thrown into the fire. Ethics are present in that trees that bear good fruit survive the fiery judgment. Membership in Israel is not enough to save his hearers from judgment. The lines between good and bad in apocalyptic contexts are not usually drawn between those who are in Israel and those who are not, or between those who are Christian and those who are not. The lines cut through those entities (Levine 1999). Matthew's complaints against the scribes and Pharisees are catalogued in chapter 23.

Matthew finds material in Q to enhance John's eschatological preaching. When Mark's John speaks of the stronger one to follow him, he says simply that he will baptize people with the Holy Spirit. This has eschatological significance and draws on biblical roots (Isa. 11:1–2; Joel 2:28–32). With the aid of Q, Matthew's John goes further. The stronger one "will baptize you with the Holy Spirit and fire. His winnowing fork is in his hand, and he will clear his threshing floor and will gather his wheat into the granary; but the chaff he will burn with unquenchable fire" (Matt. 3:11–12). Mark's Jesus left unclear what baptism by the Holy Spirit means. Matthew's John connects it to fiery judgment.

Jesus against Satan and the Demons

In Mark, Jesus's first act after his baptism is to withdraw to the desert to be tempted by Satan. He does the same in Matthew. The Greek word for temptation, *peirasmos*, connotes that this is an eschatological test. Mark gives no details of the confrontation. Matthew does. He finds them in Q, so we have already examined them.

Matthew preserves many of Mark's confrontations between Jesus and demons, with some changes. He has no interest in the Messianic Secret. In Mark 3, Jesus is accused of being in league with Satan, and Jesus refutes the charge. Matthew, using material from Q, makes the connection between Jesus's exorcisms and the coming of the kingdom. He argues that if he is not in league with Satan, then he is fighting Satan, which means the kingdom of God has come near (12:22–32). He also admits that there are other Jewish exorcists. Jesus is not unique in that respect. The eschaton approaches with outbreaks of divine power that happen even outside the Jesus movement.

Matthew, like Mark, dedicates a chapter to parables (Matt. 13; Mark 4). He adds a parable accompanied by an interpretation (13:24–30, 36–43). Jesus seldom interprets his parables in the Synoptics, so an interpretation stands out (McIver 1995; Luomanen 1998; Doty 1971). The parable tells of the wheat and the weeds (13:24–30). A householder plants wheat. An enemy comes at night and plants weeds among the wheat. The householder's slaves inform him of the situation and ask whether they should pull up the weeds. The householder says not to do so, lest they also pull up the wheat. They should wait until the harvest, and then burn the weeds and gather the wheat into the master's barn.

There follows an allegorical interpretation (13:36–40). Each element of the parable finds a referent outside the parable, and all point to its apocalyptic intent. The householder is the Son of Man; the field is the world; the good seed is the "children of the kingdom"; the enemy who sows the weeds is the devil; the harvest is the end of the age; the reapers are the angels. At the end of the age, the Son of Man sends the angels who gather the evildoers to be thrown "into the furnace of fire, where there will be weeping and gnashing of teeth. Then the righteous will shine like the sun in the kingdom of their Father" (13:42–43).

Humans live in an age in which the Son of Man and Satan compete for souls. All of history is set within an arena of struggle between God, through the Son of Man, and Satan. At the end of the age lies the last judgment, with its postmortem rewards and punishments, eternal burning or astral immortality. Angels aid the Son of Man in the last judgment. Matthew draws the image of gnashing of teeth from Q. Luke mentions it once (13:28); Matthew uses it six times, demonstrating intense interest in the last judgment and punishment of the wicked.

In subsequent exorcisms, Matthew redacts Mark with an eye to downplaying exorcism in favor of healing. In the first synagogue scene in Mark (1:21–28), Jesus casts out a demon. Matthew omits the exorcism. In the summary section of Mark 1:32–34, healings are mentioned, but the emphasis falls on exorcisms. In Matthew's version, the exorcisms are present, but they blend with the healings and serve the purpose of a formula quotation:

> That evening they brought to him many who were possessed with demons; and he cast out the spirits with a word, and cured all who were sick. This was to fulfill what had been spoken through the prophet Isaiah, "He took our infirmities and bore our diseases." (8:16–17)

Sickness could be caused by spirit possession, and Matthew seems to have that in mind. The formula quotation highlights illness only. Jesus's healing activity is one of Matthew's main themes. He often associates it with Jesus's identity as Son of David. Matthew shifts the emphasis from exorcism to healing, without losing the idea that Jesus was an exorcist and that his exorcisms are associated with his work on behalf of God's kingdom. Healings are eschatological events for Matthew and he wishes to enhance their presence in Jesus's ministry and connect them with Davidic messianism. Harvey argues that the sorts of miracles that Jesus chose to perform are eschatological: "Such cures were not only unprecedented; they were characteristic of the new age which, as we have seen, was expected in one way or another by the majority of the contemporaries of Jesus. To use the jargon of New Testament scholarship, they were eschatological miracles" (Harvey 1982, 113; Sanders 1985, 160–63).

The Sermon on the Mount

The famous Sermon on the Mount, present only in Matthew, is not a fiery, apocalyptic sermon, but it does presume an apocalyptic context. The sermon has often been called the charter of the kingdom. Matthew gathers material from various sources (Mark, Q, M, oral tradition) in order to present Jesus's ethical demands. They are stringent. At their base is the idea that one must bear fruit to enter the kingdom. Words are not sufficient. Membership in the community is not enough. Even doing miracles, healing, prophesying, and exorcising do not suffice. Matthew's most succinct statement of what is required can be found in the last judgment scene, where the Son of Man explains that how one treats the neediest determines one's eternal fate (25:31–46).

The sermon begins with the Beatitudes. They promise that the present order will be reversed in the kingdom, an example of eschatological reversal. The poor in spirit will receive the kingdom, those who mourn will be comforted, those who hunger and thirst for righteousness will be satisfied, and so on. The first will be last and the last will be first (19:30; 20:16). This is not only apocalyptic; it is militant.

Getting into the kingdom is hard: "Enter by the narrow gate; for the gate is wide, and the way is broad that leads to destruction, and many are those who enter by it. For the gate is small, and the way is narrow that leads to life, and few are those who find it" (7:13–14). Jesus says later, "Many are called, but few are chosen" (22:14). These are not reassuring words. They are a challenge and a warning. They find a close echo in *4 Ezra* 7:12–14. Matthew's strict attitude suits an apocalyptic outlook.

After insisting that hearers bear good fruit, Jesus says that many who seek to enter the kingdom of heaven on the basis of things like miracle working will be turned away (7:21–23).

Matthew and Mission

In chapter 10, Jesus sends out his disciples on a mission to Israel. Matthew's version of Jesus's instructions for the mission are more elaborate than those in Mark 6:6–13. Matthew constructs his discourse mostly from material in Mark and Q. He introduces the missionary discourse as follows:

Then Jesus went about all the cities and villages, teaching in their synagogues, and proclaiming the good news of the kingdom, and curing every disease and every sickness. When he saw the crowds, he had compassion for them, because they were harassed and helpless, like sheep without a shepherd. Then he said to his disciples, "The harvest is plentiful, but the laborers are few; therefore ask the Lord of the harvest to send out laborers into his harvest." (9:35–38)

Jesus preaches the kingdom, which was eschatological and aimed at the renewal of Israel. The notion that Israel is a flock whose shepherds are negligent is common in the texts we have already examined. Matthew employs the metaphor of the harvest, a common eschatological metaphor and one particularly beloved of Matthew. He uses it in the parable of the wheat and the weeds and its interpretation (13:30, 39) and in the parable of the vineyard tenants (21:34). Matthew, following Q, asserts that the harvest is ready; the eschaton is near.

When Mark's Jesus first chooses the twelve apostles, he does so that they might "proclaim the message, and . . . have authority to cast out demons" (3:14–15). Later, Jesus sends them out and "gave them authority over the unclean spirits" (6:7). "They cast out many demons, and anointed with oil many who were sick and cured them" (6:13). Matthew's Jesus gives his disciples the same three tasks—preach, cure, and cast out demons. Later in the discourse he clarifies that the message is that the kingdom has come near (10:7) and says, "Cure the sick, raise the dead, cleanse the lepers, cast out demons" (10:8). Such specific instructions make the parallel between Jesus's mission and that of his disciples clear. They carry on his eschatological activities. Matthew stresses curing the sick.

From Q's mission section, Matthew introduces the issue of the last judgment in his mission discourse, something not present in Mark. Speaking of towns that do not accept the message, Jesus says, "Truly I tell you, it will be more tolerable for the land of Sodom and Gomorrah on the day of judgment than for that town" (10:15). In 10:17–25, Matthew brings in material from Mark's apocalyptic discourse concerning persecution of Christians. People will treat Jesus's followers no better than they have Jesus himself. If they have gone so far as to associate Jesus with Beelzebul, they will certainly malign those of Jesus's household (10:25).

Jesus expects the end to come before their mission is completed. He tells them, "When they persecute you in one town, flee to the next; for truly I tell you, you will not have gone through all the towns of Israel before the Son of Man comes" (10:23). Scholars have a difficult time with this verse. How could Matthew have a saying of Jesus expecting the end to come before his disciples finish their mission to Israel, given his instructions to them at the end of the gospel to make disciples of all nations? The most common solution is to view 10:23 as a vestige of an earlier period. The solution leaves the puzzle of why Matthew would have preserved a saying if he saw Jesus as mistaken (Levine 1988). We cannot solve this problem here. Suffice it to say that it testifies to a stage of the Matthean tradition where there is an imminent second coming of Jesus. Matthew chose to retain this urgent notice.

In another section from Q, Matthew's Jesus urges his apostles to be fearless as they preach in the face of deadly hostility. They are to preach publicly what Jesus tells them secretly. Matthew wants the whole message to be made known so that no one has an excuse for rejecting it.

Knowing his disciples will face the same opposition he has, Jesus exhorts them not to fear: "Do not fear those who kill the body but cannot kill the soul; rather fear him who can destroy both soul and body in hell" (10:28). The rest of the passage (10:26–33) exhorts Matthew's audience to fearlessness in holding on to their faith in the face of antipathy and persecution.

The missionary discourse assumes a militant tone as it winds down. Jesus asserts that he has come not to bring peace but a sword (10:34). His mission will set members of families against one another. His followers must be willing to give up family to follow him. Taking up one's cross is necessary to being a disciple. "Those who find their life will lose it, and those who lose their life for my sake will find it" (10:39). The missionaries are like Jesus. Those who oppose Jesus oppose them, and those who support them support Jesus. The tone is one of alienation from the world. A battle is being waged; those who side with Jesus suffer for it.

Condemnation of Jerusalem's Religious Leaders

Criticism of religious leaders permeates Matthew. It grows strident as Jesus enters Jerusalem and confronts them on their home turf. He first enters Jerusalem not triumphantly, but humbly as the Son of David (21:1–17). He curses the fig tree, symbolic of Israel and its leaders who refuse to receive him (21:18–22). The chief priests and the elders challenge his authority, and he wins the verbal combat by associating himself with John the Baptist, the eschatological prophet accepted by the people (21:23–27). Jesus then tells the parable of the two sons in which the one who initially pledges obedience but then does not end up doing the father's will represents Israel. The other son, who says no at first but then obeys, represents Jesus's followers who are not typical religious people. Next comes the parable of the wicked tenants, which portrays the refusal of Israel's leaders to give to God the fruit of their labors. They must be replaced: "Therefore I tell you, the kingdom of God will be taken away from you and given to a people that produces the fruits of the kingdom" (21:43).

All this leads to the banquet parable. It appears in very different forms in Matthew and Luke. It is not present in Mark.

The Kingdom of God Is Like a Banquet

Matt. 22:2–14	Luke 14:16–24
The kingdom of heaven may be compared to a king who gave a wedding banquet for his son. He sent his slaves to call those who had been invited to the wedding banquet, but they would not come. Again he sent other slaves, saying, "Tell those who have been invited: Look, I have prepared my dinner, my oxen and my fat calves have been slaughtered, and everything is ready; come to the wedding banquet." But they made light of it and went away, one to his farm, another to his business, while the rest seized his slaves, mistreated them, and killed them. The king was enraged. He sent his troops, destroyed those murderers, and burned their city. Then he said to his slaves, "The wedding is ready, but those invited were not worthy. Go therefore into the main streets, and invite everyone you find to the wedding banquet." Those slaves went out into the streets and gathered all whom they found, both good and bad; so the wedding hall was filled with guests. But when the king came in to see the guests, he noticed a man there who was not wearing a wedding robe, and he said to him, "Friend, how did you get in here without a wedding robe?" And he was speechless. Then the king said to the attendants, "Bind him hand and foot, and throw him into the outer darkness, where there will be weeping and gnashing of teeth. For many are called, but few are chosen."	Someone gave a great dinner and invited many. At the time for the dinner he sent his slave to say to those who had been invited, "Come; for everything is ready now." But they all alike began to make excuses. The first said to him, "I have bought a piece of land, and I must go out and see it; please accept my regrets." Another said, "I have bought five yoke of oxen, and I am going to try them out; please accept my regrets." Another said, "I have just been married, and therefore I cannot come." *So the slave returned and reported this to his master. Then the owner of the house became angry and said to his slave, "Go out at once into the streets and lanes of the town and bring in the poor, the crippled, the blind, and the lame."* And the slave said, "Sir, what you ordered has been done, and there is still room." Then the master said to the slave, "Go out into the roads and lanes, and compel people to come in, so that my house may be filled. For I tell you, none of those who were invited will taste my dinner."

Luke is closer to the original form of the parable, for Matthew's allegorizing of it results in a story that has a confused narrative line. Matthew has turned a rather simple narrative into one that represents in a one-to-one fashion events outside the parable—God's relationship with Israel and his subsequent relationship with the church.

In Luke, the master's slaves receive "regrets" from those invited to their master's banquet. The master fills the banquet with those who were not originally invited. The lesson is that the kingdom is like a feast in which those who come are not the expected ones and those who were expected to be there are not. This fits Jesus's general disapproval of self-righteous people and his care for the "sinful." The verse italicized in the table above was probably added by Luke himself, for it echoes 14:13 and reflects Luke's concern for the poor and sick. There is nothing in Luke's version of the parable that sets Jew against gentile. The parable is not about that.

Matthew's version introduces elements that are out of place in the story, but that suit his allegorical meaning better. The master becomes a "king," making him a more fitting figure to represent God. The invited guests kill the slaves sent to invite them to the feast. This reflects the theme that Israel persecutes the prophets, here represented by the master's slaves. The king sends his troops and destroys their city. This refers to the destruction of Jerusalem, a result of its rejection of the prophets, including Christian missionaries. The king then has his slaves bring into the feast everyone they could find, "both good and bad." This reflects Matthew's view of the church as a mixture of good and bad, as in the parable of the weeds in chapter 13.

In accord with his interest in the last judgment, Matthew adds a section to the parable that also creates an awkward narrative. The king enters the feast and surveys the guests. One does not have on wedding garments, so he orders his servants, "Bind him hand and foot, and throw him into the outer darkness, where there will be weeping and gnashing of teeth. For many are called, but few are chosen" (22:13–14). One might wonder why the guests would be expected to have the proper clothing, since they have been dragged in from the street. But for Matthew, the allegory is what is important. The wedding garments signify worthiness to be at the feast. Matthew's parable levies a terrible penalty for failure. It amounts to damnation, and Matthew takes the opportunity to remind his audience how hard it will be to attain salvation.

Condemnation of the Scribes and Pharisees

Matthew constructs a context in which Jesus's apocalyptic discourse must be understood. He begins by composing chapter 23, consisting entirely of condemnation of the scribes and Pharisees. Most of the material comes from Q, but scribes and Pharisees are groups Matthew attacks throughout his Gospel. Matthew's Jesus attacks these groups for hypocrisy with respect to Torah. He recognizes their God-given authority but claims that they do not practice what they preach. They follow the minutiae of the Torah, which Jesus praises, but they neglect justice, mercy, and faith, which are central (23:23). Jesus acknowledges the authority of Israel's teachers, but they abuse it. First, they do not acknowledge Jesus's authority or even that of God. They ought to profess but one father, their heavenly Father, but they ignore him by their mistreatment of the Torah. They ought to have but one teacher, the Messiah, Jesus (23:10). This amounts to saying that anyone who does not follow Jesus cannot be following the Torah. This is made plain in a verse that immediately follows Jesus's insistence that one must listen to the Messiah: "But woe to you, scribes and Pharisees, hypocrites! For you lock people out of the kingdom of heaven. For you do not go in yourselves, and when others are going in, you stop them" (Matt. 23:13). The scribes and Pharisees use religious status to prevent others from entering the kingdom. They are God's eschatological enemies. They are the human equivalent of Satan.

Matthew ends the discourse by saying that the scribes and Pharisees are responsible for killing the prophets. They claim that had they lived at the time of their ancestors, they would not have joined them in resisting God's word. They "prove" this by their honoring the prophets through monuments. Jesus turns their argument on its head by concentrating on their descent from those who had indeed killed the prophets and making the implicit argument that they are like their ancestors (Matt. 23:29–36) (Johnson Hodge 2007, 19).

Jesus now looks to the future. He is in fact referring to the time of Matthew's church. He predicts that the Jewish leaders will persecute those sent to them by Matthew's community. Prophets were common in early Christianity (Aune 1983b); Matthew's church was Jewish and used Jewish titles like "scribe" and "sage" and "prophet" for some of their members. When Jesus says that he will send such emissaries to them, he is speaking of the church's relatively unsuccessful missionary efforts among Jews. They may indeed have encountered the sorts of synagogue discipline Matthew describes, such as flogging. Paul tells us firsthand that he endured such punishments (2 Cor. 11:24). That would have been a natural response on the part of synagogue leaders to those who would disrupt their communities.

Matthew positions this chapter of condemnation immediately before his apocalyptic discourse (chap. 24), which begins with Jesus's prediction of the temple's destruction. The condemnation of Israel's leaders brings on the temple's destruction. The temple symbolized God's presence with Israel, and it was maintained by the priestly establishment. The Gospel demonstrates that Israel has not been true to its side of the covenant with God, and so the temple now symbolizes something untrue. It must go out of existence. Matthew makes this tragically clear in the way he has Jesus end this chapter.

> Jerusalem, Jerusalem, the city that kills the prophets and stones those who are sent to it! How often have I desired to gather your children together as a hen gathers her brood under her wings, and you were not willing! See, your house is left to you, desolate. For I tell you, you will not see me again until you say, "Blessed is the one who comes in the name of the Lord." (23:37–39)

Apocalyptic Discourse

Matthew begins his rewriting of Mark 13 with subtle but significant changes. In Mark, Jesus predicts the destruction of the temple, and his disciples ask when it will take place and what will be the signs announcing it. Matthew changes this to, "Tell us, when will this be, and what will be the sign of your coming [*parousia*] and of the end of the age?" (Matt. 24:3). Matthew's disciples look explicitly for Jesus's second coming, the central event in the Christian eschaton, and for the "end of the age," one of Matthew's favorite phrases highlighting his apocalyptic worldview. The disciples connect Jesus's second coming and the end of the present age. They assume that it is all planned.

The rest of the apocalyptic discourse follows Mark in the main. Matthew has already transferred some of what Mark has in his apocalyptic discourse to his missionary discourse (Matt. 10), so those elements are not present here. Matthew has already employed them to stress the eschatological significance of Christian mission.

Matthew agrees with Mark that the approaching end will include the usual apocalyptic signs—false messiahs and prophets, wars and rumors of wars, famines and earthquakes. All are birth pangs, a common apocalyptic metaphor. Jesus says, "Then they will hand you over to be tortured [*eis thlipsin*]" (24:9). The more frequent translation for *thlipsis* is "tribulation," which highlights its apocalyptic connotations. Mark has already included communal dissent as part of the church's end-time suffering, predicting that members of one's own family will betray one. Matthew makes some internal dissent clearer, including "lawlessness" and the cooling of love. He agrees with Mark that "the one who endures to the end will be saved" (24:13; cf. Mark 13:13). While Mark has the statement that the gospel must be preached to all nations in the middle of his prediction of the church's sufferings, Matthew puts it in a more effective spot, at the end of this section, and makes it even more of a programmatic statement: "This good news of the kingdom will be proclaimed throughout the world, as a testimony to all the nations; and then the end [*telos*] will come" (Matt. 24:14). *Telos* can mean simply "end," but it often means a goal, a fulfillment, or a conclusion. The "end" is God's goal. It is that to which all history, Israel's history in particular, advances. It is of ultimate significance to the whole world.

Matthew follows Mark closely in the next section of the discourse. When the end comes, the readers must flee Jerusalem. There will be false messiahs and prophets with signs and omens, leading astray even "the elect." Like Mark, Matthew says that the second coming will be with undeniable signs, comparable to a lightning flash that lights up the sky from east to west. Matthew's Jesus moves on to the usual celestial signs—failure of the sun and moon and falling of the stars. Then the Son of Man comes on the clouds with his angels, who gather the elect. Matthew adds a trumpet call to announce the rescue of the elect from the earth.

Matthew follows Mark in warning the community that when these signs happen, "he is near, at the very gates. Truly I tell you, this generation will not pass away until all these things have taken place" (Matt. 24:33–34; cf. Mark 13:29–30). Jesus does not know exactly when the kingdom will arrive: "About that day and hour no one knows, neither the angels of heaven, nor the Son, but only the Father" (24:36).

Matthew concludes the apocalyptic discourse with three passages from Q. Luke has them distributed throughout his Gospel, and since Luke follows the order of Q more closely than Matthew, Matthew probably brought them to this spot to conclude the discourse. The first compares the eschaton to the biblical flood (24:37–41). As the earth's population did not expect the flood, so the eschaton will catch the earth's population unaware. The second passage from Q compares the coming of the Son of Man to a thief in the night (24:42–44); it is unexpected and unpredictable.

The final passage from Q also speaks of readiness for Christ's second coming. It compares the Christian awaiting the second coming to a slave awaiting his master's return from a journey. The slave does not know when the master will return. He must perform his duties properly so that whenever the master comes, he will be found faithful at any and all times. Q goes on to say that the unprepared slave will be punished, even cut to pieces. Matthew adds that the master will "put him with the hypocrites, where there will be weeping and gnashing of teeth" (24:51). The reference to hypocrites fits neatly with Matthew's condemnation of the scribes and Pharisees in chapter 23. Weeping and gnashing of teeth recalls the five other instances of this phrase with which Matthew punctuates his Gospel.

Eschatological Parables and the Last Judgment

Matthew follows the apocalyptic discourse with two parables flanking a picture of the last judgment (chap. 25). Actually, this forms part of the apocalyptic discourse since there is no formal break between chapters 24 and 25.

The first parable is unique to Matthew and precedes the story of the last judgment. It is the story of the ten bridesmaids who await the groom in the night with lamps to light his way (25:1–13). Five bring extra oil for their lamps in case he is delayed, and five do not. Sure enough, the groom is late. The five with oil joyfully accompany the groom into the wedding banquet, while the five unprepared bridesmaids are excluded. Those who expect the eschaton to be soon and are willing to expend effort for a short time to be ready for it may or may not have their dream fulfilled. They cannot be sure. The solution is to live one's life always ready for the end, no matter how long it takes. Matthew prepares his church for the long haul.

The second parable is from Q and follows the picture of the last judgment (25:14–30). It is the parable of the talents (Matthew: a gigantic amount of money) or pounds (Luke: a much smaller amount of money). Matthew may have increased the amount of money to demonstrate the huge stakes of the last judgment. In the parable, a rich man goes on a journey, leaving three slaves with varying amounts of money. Two invest the money and are rewarded by the master. One buries it, afraid to lose it. The master disapproves of this and, in Matthew's version, orders that the "worthless slave" be thrown "into the outer darkness, where there will be weeping and gnashing of teeth" (25:30). Yet again we encounter this expression that Matthew finds so useful. One must produce good fruit or expect the worst. Luke (and probably Q) takes a gentler view when he expects that the one who did not invest the money will simply have it taken away from him and given to the slave who had originally received the most (19:24). Matthew stresses the necessity of action.

These two parables flank the only picture the New Testament offers of the last judgment (25:31–46). It is unique to Matthew, testifying again to his abiding interest in the last judgment. It begins, "When the Son of Man comes in his glory, and all the angels with him, then he will sit on the throne of his glory. All the nations will be gathered before him, and he will separate people one from another as a shepherd separates the sheep from the goats, and he will put the sheep at his right hand and the goats at the left" (Matt. 25:31–33). We have a close parallel to this scene in the *Similitudes of Enoch* where there are three scenes with a son of man sitting on a throne and judging the nations. Enoch's son of man is also styled the Messiah and God's son. Matthew owes much to Jewish apocalypticism for this scene. The judgment is on all the nations here. It is universal. The use of sheep and goats in this scene recalls Ezek. 34, a judgment scene involving sheep and goats.

The basis for judgment in Matthew is ethical. How one treats the needy determines whether one will enter God's kingdom. Both the good and the bad, the sheep and the goats, are surprised at this. Matthew intends to correct a false impression on the part of his audience. Whatever else they thought might bring salvation—be it inclusion in a chosen people, proclamations of faith, or even exercise of spiritual powers—none of these things determines their salvation. Rather, the Son of Man will judge on the basis of care for the hungry and the thirsty, the naked, the sick, and those in prison. This offers a glimpse into what Matthew expected of his church. Apocalyptic expectation was not just a matter of being part of a community that awaited Jesus's parousia. It was behavior that ensured that when Christ did return, he would find his followers engaging in activity suited to the kingdom. The kingdom for Matthew has to do with a particular sort of society. People fit for the kingdom are not necessarily those whom one might expect. They may not be the well educated, the religious leaders, the miracle workers, or prophets. Ethical, merciful, and socially just behavior of a radical nature constitutes being ready for the end.

The Death of Jesus

Matthew rewrites Mark's account of Jesus's death and resurrection to enrich its apocalyptic tone. When a crowd comes to the Garden of Gethsemane to arrest Jesus, he refuses to resist. When one of his followers strikes a member of the crowd with a sword, Jesus rebukes him. Jesus says, "Do you think that I cannot appeal to my Father, and he will at once send me more than twelve legions of angels? But how then would the scriptures be fulfilled, which say it must happen in this way?" (26:53–54). God commands an angelic army.

Using the Roman word for an army division, Jesus specifies just how many angelic divisions he could muster to fight his enemies. But Scripture, and so God, have determined otherwise.

True to his interest in portraying everything as going according to God's plan, Matthew adds that it was to fulfill prophecy that Judas received thirty pieces of silver for betraying Jesus and that the money was used to buy a field to bury foreigners (Zech. 11:12–13; Jer. 18:2–3; 32:6–15).

Matthew rewrites Jesus's death to emphasize its eschatological features and to characterize it as the turning of the ages.

Jesus Dies on the Cross: Matthew and Mark

Matt. 27:50–54	Mark 15:37–39
Then Jesus cried again with a loud voice and breathed his last. At that moment the curtain of the temple was torn in two, from top to bottom. The earth shook, and the rocks were split. The tombs also were opened, and many bodies of the saints who had fallen asleep were raised. After his resurrection they came out of the tombs and entered the holy city and appeared to many.	Then Jesus gave a loud cry and breathed his last. And the curtain of the temple was torn in two, from top to bottom.
Now when the centurion and those with him, who were keeping watch over Jesus, saw the earthquake and what took place, they were terrified and said, "Truly this man was God's Son!"	Now when the centurion, who stood facing him, saw that in this way he breathed his last, he said, "Truly this man was God's Son!"

Jesus's death in Mark is stark. The bare narrative line is that Jesus asks God why he has abandoned him, and then he screams and dies. When the centurion sees that he dies "in this way [*houtōs*]," he recognizes that he is the Son of God.

Matthew completely changes this. Immediately upon Jesus's death there is the apocalyptic earthquake. Then there is a resurrection of saints. This is extraordinary. Jesus is not the first to be raised from the dead. The risen ones appear to many in Jerusalem, but, somewhat awkwardly, Matthew says that this did not happen until Jesus himself had been raised. So this transports us to three days after Jesus's death. Then, suddenly, the narrative returns to Jesus's death. The centurion in charge of the execution and those with him, reacting to "the earthquake and what took place," pronounce Jesus to be the Son of God.

Matthew's rewriting of Mark results in a disjointed narrative. He surrounds Jesus with apocalyptic happenings—the earthquake, splitting of rocks, resurrections, and apparitions. While Mark presents the centurion's confession of Jesus's identity as due to Jesus's suffering and shocking death, Matthew makes his confession depend on witnessing of the apocalyptic events attesting to the eschatological significance of Jesus's death. The events following Jesus's death indicate that his death is the turning of the ages (Meier 1979).

Only in Matthew do priestly authorities set a guard over the tomb; they know about Jesus's prediction that he will rise from the dead. The appearances of angels in the empty tomb stories of the other Gospels are fairly tame. Angels are simply beings who look human and convey information to humans. Matthew adds a new section, not present in the other Gospels, in which the angels are part of a vivid apocalyptic scene: "Suddenly there was a great earthquake; for an angel of the Lord, descending from heaven, came and rolled back the stone and sat on it. His appearance was like lightning, and his clothing white as snow. For fear of him the guards shook and became like dead men" (28:2–4).

Other Apocalyptic Elements

The two ages. Matthew believes that there are two ages, the present age and the age to come. In 12:32, Jesus decrees that those who sin against the Holy Spirit will not be forgiven, "either in this age or in the age to come." In the parable of the weeds and wheat, the judgment will not take place until the harvest, which occurs "at the end of the age" (13:39, 40, 49). At the beginning of the apocalyptic discourse, Jesus's disciples ask him when the end of the age will come (24:3). In the Great Commission, Jesus assures his apostles that he will be with them till the end of the age (28:20).

Peter's confession. In Mark, when Jesus asks his apostles who they think he is, Peter confesses that he is the Messiah. Peter does not accept that Jesus's messiahship includes suffering, so Jesus condemns him for being on Satan's side. Matthew retains all this, but right after Peter's confession of Jesus as Messiah, Jesus praises him and says that this insight could not have come from any human being but must have been given directly to Peter by God. Peter will be the rock on which Jesus builds his church. The foundation of the church is the special revelation that Jesus is the Messiah and Son of God.

Jesus as Son of Man. Each Gospel uses the figure of the Son of Man somewhat differently. The Synoptic Gospels all have three categories of Son of Man sayings—eschatological, suffering, and earthly. Matthew takes over all of these categories from Mark, but his particular emphasis is the eschatological Son of Man, the one who comes at the end of time to judge. This is clearest in chapter 25, where Jesus is pictured as the Son of Man, seated on a throne and judging.

Healing and the Son of David. We have already noticed Matthew's emphasis on healing as an important part of Jesus's Davidic messiahship. This reaches a climax when Jesus is in the temple. The blind and the lame came to him in the temple, and he cured them. But when the chief priests and the scribes saw the amazing things that he did, and heard the children crying out in the temple, "Hosanna to the Son of David," they became angry and said to him,

Matthew and Apocalypticism

- Jesus is resurrected.
- There is a general resurrection at Jesus's death.
- Jesus's death is an apocalyptic event.
- Emphasis is on the end of the age.
- There are two ages.
- There is a last judgment.
- The entirety of history, from creation to the last judgment, is in view.
- The history of the church is depicted as a struggle between the Son of Man and Satan.
- Jesus battles Satan through exorcisms.
- Healings are an activity of the Son of David and described as end-time manifestations.
- Jesus is the Messiah.
- Jesus takes possession of the temple as Son of David and healer.
- Worldwide mission is part of the eschatological events.
- There is an apocalyptic discourse.
- Jesus's relationship with John the Baptist.

"Do you hear what these are saying?" Jesus answered, "Yes; have you never read, 'Out of the mouths of infants and nursing babies you have prepared praise for yourself'?" (Matt. 21:14–16) Matthew's scriptural references show the importance he attaches to this episode and prove that even the details of these events were planned by God and are integral to the eschatological events.

Jesus's triumphal entry into Jerusalem is messianic. His entry fulfills what Zechariah prophesied. Jesus is the humble king. The crowds recognize Jesus as the Son of David and quote Ps. 118 to praise him. The scene represents the Davidic Messiah who comes to his royal city to take possession of it. It fulfills Israel's messianic hopes.

Luke

Like Matthew, Luke uses Mark and Q as his two main sources. Our task is to see what Luke makes of the apocalyptic materials he uses. Are they relegated to a minor status, or does Luke maintain an apocalyptic outlook even as he adapts it? In our analysis, we use the Acts of the Apostles, since the same person wrote both Luke and Acts.

The effect on Christian belief of a delayed parousia has long been a topic of discussion among New Testament scholars. Many hold that Luke addresses the delay of the parousia by downplaying its imminence without rejecting the expectations of his sources. He shifts from the belief that Jesus is to return soon to an understanding that Jesus will eventually return, but perhaps not until sometime in the distant future. Although there are details in Luke's Gospel that indicate a delay in the parousia, the narrative arc of the entire story in Luke and Acts is one of eschatological fulfillment. All that God promised to Israel is now to be. All can be encapsulated in the single word "salvation."

Tannehill presents Luke-Acts as a tragic story (1985). It starts on an optimistic, high note, and it finishes in disappointment. Chapters 1–2 present Jesus's coming as the fulfillment of all divine promises to Israel, but throughout the Gospel, Israel refuses to accept Jesus, and in the end, the temple authorities reject him. But Acts affords Israel a second chance. Beginning with the apostles' preaching in Jerusalem, the message is once more offered to Israel. In Acts, although many thousands of Jews believe, as a whole they do not. Therefore, the missionaries, particularly Paul, turn from the Jews to the gentiles (Acts 13:46–47). Paul's last words to his Jewish hearers, gathered together in Rome—center of the gentile world—are, "This salvation of God has been sent to the Gentiles; they will listen" (Acts 28:28).

In traditional Jewish eschatological scenarios, Israel accepts God's salvation, and then the nations take notice and worship Israel's God. Here the pattern is disrupted by Israel's refusal to believe.

God's promises to Israel include the coming of the Messiah in the person of Jesus. He is Son of God and son of David (1:32–33). His reign will be eternal. His coming is heralded even when he is in the womb, for John the Baptist, while also in the womb, is said by the angel Gabriel to come in the spirit and power of Elijah to precede him (1:17). Mary proclaims that his coming means the lifting up of the lowly and the downfall of the powerful, the filling of the hungry and the rejection of the rich (1:46–55). She sees this as fulfillment of God's promises to her ancestors. John's father, Zechariah, declares that now Israel's enemies will be defeated and Israel will be free to worship its God freely (1:68–79). Jesus describes his own work in terms of the prophet in Isa. 61, who brings good news to the poor, proclaims liberty to the captives, ends oppression, and declares God's Jubilee year of forgiveness (4:18–19). The infancy narrative comes to a close with the prophet Simeon's recognition that in Jesus he has seen God's salvation revealed to the whole world, to the glory of Israel (2:29–32). Simeon's words to Mary foreshadow something less joyful—conflict within Israel over Jesus and sorrow for Mary herself (2:34–35).

In a programmatic scene in the synagogue at Nazareth, Jesus presents his ministry in terms of the anointed prophet of Isa. 61, as mentioned above (4:16–21). Later in the scene, Jesus foretells that Israel will reject him as it did Elijah and Elisha, who then served the gentiles. His hearers then turn against him (4:23–29). The Gospel goes on to portray Jesus as God's prophet, filled with God's Spirit, who brings healing and forgiveness, all of which is seen as salvation, to Israel.

Much of Luke's Gospel is set as a long journey to Jerusalem, where he must bring his message of salvation. A clear beginning is indicated in 9:51, where he sets "his face to go to Jerusalem." Along the way, Jesus has an interaction with the Pharisees that demonstrates Herod's hostility toward him. The Pharisees warn him that Herod is after him.

> He said to them, "Go and tell that fox for me, 'Listen, I am casting out demons and performing cures today and tomorrow, and on the third day I finish my work. Yet today, tomorrow, and the next day I must be on my way, because it is impossible for a prophet to be killed outside of Jerusalem.' Jerusalem, Jerusalem, the city that kills the prophets and stones those who are sent to it! How often have I desired to gather your children together as a hen gathers her brood under her wings, and you were not willing! See, your house is left to you. And I tell you, you will not see me until the time comes when you say, 'Blessed is the one who comes in the name of the Lord.'" (13:32–35)

As he arrives at Jerusalem, Jesus knows that it will reject him.

> As he came near and saw the city, he wept over it, saying, "If you, even you, had only recognized on this day the things that make for peace! But now they are hidden from your eyes. Indeed, the days will come upon you, when your enemies will set up ramparts around you and surround you, and hem you in on every side. They will crush you to the ground, you and your children within you, and they will not leave within you one stone upon another; because you did not recognize the time of your visitation from God." (19:41–44)

Finally, when Jerusalem rejects Jesus, he is killed and raised again, fulfilling God's promise of victory over death itself.

The risen Lord appears to two disciples on their way to Emmaus, bitterly disappointed that Jesus has not restored the kingdom to Israel but has ended his career in defeat on the cross. Jesus explains that they have not understood the Scriptures, and that his suffering, death, and resurrection were part of God's plan (24:36–49).

In Acts of the Apostles, the apostles and disciples and all the church receive the same divine Spirit as Jesus possessed. This happens at *Pentēcostē*, and it is a fulfillment of the end-time hopes of Joel (2:1–21). The church carries on Jesus's mission. It brings salvation by healing, exorcising, preaching forgiveness, proclaiming forgiveness, and witnessing that God has in Jesus fulfilled the greatest eschatological promise, resurrection from the dead. This is repeatedly presented as the center of the prophetic message of the church.

Peter informs his fellow Israelites that Jesus is the prophet foretold by Moses in Deut. 18:15, and that to reject him is to be cut off from Israel (3:17–26). Jesus is also the one in whom the ultimate salvation of resurrection is fulfilled, as it was foretold by David. The rest of Acts shows that although many Jews do believe, most do not, and so the great eschatological moment of Israel's visitation by God to fulfill all promises is missed.

Luke thinks that the time of the church is now different from that of the ministry of Jesus. The church extends Jesus's ministry. It continues its efforts toward Israel, but it is fast becoming a gentile church. The end time is still part of its belief and preaching, but it is very busy spreading throughout the Greco-Roman world. The parousia is still to come, but the church has much work to do, empowered by God's eschatological Spirit, and that work will take some time.

Luke comes to terms with the delay of the parousia through a series of small changes to his sources. He wants only to dampen imminent expectation. Everything we deem apocalyptic—resurrection, postmortem rewards and punishments, and so on—remains an integral part of his worldview.

Conzelmann provides a framework within which to place all of the elements of Luke's theology (1960). Luke divides salvation history into three parts. The first is the period of Israel; the second, Jesus's ministry; and the third, the church. Between the first and second periods is an interim consisting of John the Baptist's ministry and the descent of the Spirit on Jesus. Between the second and third periods is an interim stretching from Jesus's ascension (unique to Luke) to the descent of the Spirit at Pentecost. Who possesses the Spirit and when is important. In the first period it is the prophets, in the second it is Jesus, and in the third it is the church. Whoever has the Spirit speaks and acts for God. The period of Israel has the Hebrew Bible as its book, the period of Jesus has Luke's Gospel, and the period of the church has Acts of the Apostles, a history of the earliest church written by Luke.

Perrin (Duling and Perrin 1994, 377) states the case for Luke's treatment of the parousia:

> To be sure, certain Lukan passages stress the near expectation of the parousia (compare Luke 3:9, 17; 10:9; 21:32), and the author even seems to add to them (Luke 10:11; 18:7–8). Yet, these passages should be interpreted in relation to what is clearly Luke's more dominant view: the parousia will take place in some *indefinite* future.

We begin with the passages that support the idea that Luke tries to downplay the parousia's imminence. Horsley gives a noteworthy example of one such passage. We show all three Synoptic Gospels in parallel to make the point.

Jesus's Inaugural Preaching in the Synoptic Gospels

Matt. 4:17	Mark 1:14–15	Luke 4:15
From that time Jesus began to proclaim, "Repent, for the kingdom of heaven has come near."	Jesus came to Galilee, proclaiming the good news of God, and saying, "The time is fulfilled, and the kingdom of God has come near; repent, and believe in the good news."	He began to teach in their synagogues and was praised by everyone.

For each of the evangelists, Jesus's initial preaching sets the stage for all that follows. Luke's redaction tames Jesus's inaugural preaching. He displaces the themes of the approach of the kingdom, fulfillment of time, repentance, and good news. Luke abandons none of these themes, but he does not include them at this decisive point.

Perrin's analysis of Luke's apocalyptic discourse shows that it lengthens the time between the destruction of Jerusalem and the eschaton (Duling and Perrin 1994). Mark expects the eschaton to come soon after the temple's fall (Mark 13:14–27). Luke makes the military details of Jerusalem's destruction more specific but omits the mention of false prophets and adds a reference to an interim period, which he calls the "times of the Gentiles" (21:24).

Luke makes a noteworthy change to Q's parable of the pounds. Q places this parable toward the end of his work to warn that preparedness for the end involves investment now. In introducing this parable, Luke says, "As they were listening to this, he went on to tell a parable, because he was near Jerusalem, and because they supposed that the kingdom of God was to appear immediately" (Luke 19:11).

Horsley observes that Luke turns from apocalyptic and prophetic expressions to concentrate on concrete history. Luke is perhaps the most political of the evangelists, paying close attention to the realities of the Greco-Roman world and the power arrangements of the Roman Empire. His shift from describing Rome's destruction in Danielic terms as a "desolating sacrilege" to "when you see Jerusalem surrounded by armies, then know that its desolation has come near" (21:20) illustrates this (Horsley 1998, 339–40). For Luke, the destruction of Jerusalem ought to be seen less in apocalyptic terms than in its meaning for a historical shift in the Christian mission from Jews to gentiles. That plays itself out in detail in Luke's next volume, Acts of the Apostles. Apocalypticism is still present; it is a question of emphasis.

In a much-discussed passage, Luke displays a degree of ambivalence toward apocalyptic speculation:

> Once Jesus was asked by the Pharisees when the kingdom of God was coming, and he answered, "The kingdom of God is not coming with things that can be observed; nor will they say, 'Look, here it is!' or 'There it is!' For, in fact, the kingdom of God is among you." (17:20–21)

Verses 20–21 claim that there are no signs that will reveal when the kingdom is to arrive. Its statement that the kingdom is "among you" is unclear. The Greek word for "among," *entos*, means most frequently "among" or "in the midst of." It was once common to translate as "within you," making the kingdom a psychological reality—a matter for personal, individual transformation. That interpretation has fallen out of favor. It is more likely that this verse pictures the kingdom as something that will come suddenly, so that it is unexpectedly there. In any case, it is noteworthy that Luke follows this up with a section from Q that vividly portrays the eschaton in great detail with all the traditional apocalyptic elements we have come to expect (17:22–37). Luke tries simultaneously to discourage speculation on the time of the end and to create in the minds of the readers a vivid and even frightening image of the end.

Horsley concludes his treatment of Luke as follows: "For all his deletion and downplaying of apocalyptic language and excitement, however, Luke is not devoid of prophetic motifs that evoke a sense of fulfillment and crisis, motifs also found in Jewish apocalyptic literature of the time" (Horsley 1998, 340).

Luke inherits an apocalyptic worldview but lives in a world that does not entirely match that worldview. His main problem is that the parousia is delayed. More than any other work we have studied, his outlook is urbane and cosmopolitan, displaying an impressive grasp of imperial politics and the worldwide implications of Jewish rejection of this new religious movement. Apocalyptic elements in Luke's thought are not dispensable. But he rethinks them in terms of a broader, historically driven theology.

Acts of the Apostles

The Role of the Apostles

The first chapter of Acts contains a programmatic statement by Jesus that pertains directly to our interests.

> When they had come together, they asked him, "Lord, is this the time when you will restore the kingdom to Israel?" He replied, "It is not for you to know the times or periods that the Father has set by his own authority. But you will receive power when the Holy Spirit has come upon you; and you will be my witnesses in Jerusalem, in all Judea and Samaria, and to the ends of the earth." When he had said this, as they were watching, he was lifted up, and a cloud took him out of their sight. While he was going and they were gazing up toward heaven, suddenly two men in white robes stood by them. They said, "Men of Galilee, why do you stand looking up toward heaven? This Jesus, who has been taken up from you into heaven, will come in the same way as you saw him go into heaven." (Acts 1:6–11)

At first glance, the apostles' question seems misguided. Is restoration of Israel's kingdom really the point of Jesus's ministry? Did Jesus not come to preach something more "spiritual"? Significantly, Jesus does not correct them. Rather he says that they should not be concerned about "the times or periods that the Father has set by his own authority" (1:7). God still plans to restore Israel to its rightful place in the world, but they are wrong to worry about when that will be. God has planned out history, and it will take place as he wills.

Jesus tells the apostles to get on with their task of witnessing to Jesus's resurrection in Jerusalem, Samaria, and to the ends of the earth. Acts of the Apostles tells the tale of the ever-widening Christian movement. The book begins in Jerusalem and ends in Rome. By arriving at the center of the known world in the person of Paul, the message of Christianity will have arrived at the ends of the earth and have come from the heart of Judaism.

Witnessing to the resurrection is, of course, witnessing to an apocalyptic event. Another such event is Jesus's ascension into heaven, from which he will eventually return to earth. But as the apostles stand on the Mount of Olives gazing into the heavens into which Jesus has disappeared, "two men in white," angels, chide them for staring (1:10–11). The angels do not want the apostles to sit around waiting for the parousia. It will come in its time, but they cannot know when that will be.

Acts 2 tells the story of Pentecost. The Jewish Feast of Weeks—in Greek, *Pentēcostē*, meaning "fiftieth" because it is celebrated on the fiftieth day after Passover—is the occasion of the descent of the Spirit onto the nascent church, gathered together anxiously in Jerusalem. Once they receive the Spirit, they abandon their fear and begin to preach. Their audience hears them each in their own native tongue and was amazed by the miracle. Peter steps to the fore and proclaims this to be the fulfillment of Joel's prophecy.

Luke makes several crucial changes to the text of Joel to clarify the eschatological significance of Pentecost. While Joel speaks of the spirit being poured out on Israel "afterward," Luke changes that to "in the last days" (2:17). Luke also adds the phrase "and they shall prophesy" (Acts 2:18). For Luke, the Spirit is always a prophetic spirit. Following Joel more closely, Luke includes the usual apocalyptic signs of portents in the heavens and signs on the earth. There will be blood, fire, and smoke. The sun turns to darkness, and the moon to blood. What happens is apocalyptic, and Jesus's resurrection, ascension, and pouring out of the Spirit have set things in motion.

Peter quotes Ps. 16:8–11, taking it as a composition of David. David praises God for not abandoning his soul to Hades. Taking this as a prediction of resurrection, and knowing that David was not raised, Peter applies it to Jesus. Thus Luke finds in Scripture a prediction of Jesus's resurrection. Having risen from the dead, Jesus has ascended to God's right hand in heaven, from where he now sends the Spirit down upon the church. God has now made Jesus Lord and Messiah.

God's Plan

It is not only Jesus's resurrection that God foreordained. He also planned Jesus's death. Peter says, "This man, handed over according to the definite plan [Greek: *boulē*] and foreknowledge of God, you crucified and killed by the hands of those outside the law" (2:23). *Boulē* is important in Acts, denoting God's plan for salvation history. God planned Jesus's prophetic and messianic career—his suffering, death, and resurrection, as well as his ascension and sending of the Spirit on the church.

When the Christians pray, they also refer to God's plan. They first praise God as creator; then they quote Ps. 2 about the gentiles raging against God and his Messiah to describe what the Jerusalem authorities, Herod, and the Romans had done to Jesus; and then they acknowledge again that this was what "your plan [*boulē*] had predestined to take place" (4:28). They pray for boldness and for signs and miracles to be performed in Jesus's name to advance the mission.

When Paul delivers one of his major missionary speeches, to inhabitants of Pisidia of Antioch, he sketches out what God has done in salvation history, leading up to Jesus. Along the way, in speaking of David's death, Paul says, "David, after he had served the purpose [*boulē*] of God in his own generation, died" (13:36). Through Jesus, God fulfills all the promises to the ancestors and to the prophets. Foremost is salvation, including forgiveness of sin and resurrection from the dead. In that same sermon, Paul says that Jesus's resurrection was promised by God to Israel's ancestors (13:32–39). This reappears when Paul speaks before the Sanhedrin. The Pharisees believed in resurrection, but the Sadducees did not. In the midst of the council, Paul exclaims, "I am a Pharisee, a son of Pharisees. I am on trial concerning the hope of the resurrection of the dead" (23:6). Paul puts this at center stage even when making his case to the Roman governor Felix, where he says it twice (24:14–15; 24:20–21). Paul also speaks before King Agrippa, who is Jewish: "I stand here on trial on account of my hope in the promise made by God to our ancestors, a promise that our twelve tribes hope to attain, as they earnestly worship day and night. It is for this hope, your Excellency, that I am accused by Jews! Why is it thought incredible by any of you that God raises the dead?" (26:6–8). Later in the speech, Paul says that everything connected with Jesus was predicted by Moses and the prophets (26:22–23).

At the end of Acts, Paul preaches to the Jewish community in Rome. He tells them that "it is for the sake of the hope of Israel that I am bound with this chain" (28:20). A few days later, "he explained the matter to them, testifying to the kingdom of God and trying to convince them about Jesus both from the law of Moses and from the prophets" (28:23). Some believed and some did not. Finally, Paul quotes Isa. 6 to the effect that they will listen but never understand. Paul tells them that the Spirit was right when it said this about them. Paul therefore turns to the gentiles (28:28).

When speaking to the elders at Ephesus, Paul reminds them that he had given them the entire Christian message: "For I did not shrink from declaring to you the whole purpose [*boulē*] of God" (20:27).

Enemies of the movement use *boulē* themselves, an instance of dramatic irony. When the Jerusalem Sanhedrin deliberates on what to do about the new movement, the Pharisee Gamaliel counsels, "Keep away from these men and let them alone; because if this plan [*boulē*] or this undertaking is of human origin, it will fail; but if it is of God, you will not be able to overthrow them—in that case you may even be found fighting against God" (5:38–39).

Boulē occurs once in Luke's Gospel with this meaning. In 7:30, Luke adds the comment, "By refusing to be baptized by him [John the Baptist], the Pharisees and lawyers rejected God's purpose [*boulē*] for themselves."

The Role of the Church

Luke transforms traditional apocalyptic thinking into a scheme designed to legitimize the church. He at times downplays apocalyptic fervor. In Acts, he alters apocalyptic thought to support an extended mission. Apocalyptic elements provide a foundation for the church while not allowing the fervor of imminent expectation to interfere with the church's work.

Jesus's death and resurrection introduce not the eschaton but a distinctive phase of salvation history. The direct connection established in Acts 2 between the risen Christ, now at God's right hand, and the church, upon which Jesus pours the Spirit, makes the church God's agent in the world. It witnesses to Christ's resurrection. Christ's resurrection fulfills all that the prophets have foretold, a theme that Luke carries throughout Acts. Luke has turned the church into an ongoing eschatological reality, joined to the reality of Jesus's resurrection through the Spirit, and looking forward to the ultimate consummation of history. It is all God's plan, and this plan ties together the entire sweep of history, from Israel's prophets, to Jesus, and to the church (Murphy 2005, 211–12).

Peter calls on his Jewish audience to repent. If they do, "times of refreshing" will come from God, and God will send the Messiah to them again (3:20). Jesus "must remain in heaven until the time of universal restoration that God announced long ago through his holy prophets" (3:21). The term "universal restoration" (*apokatastasis*) is found only here in the entire Bible. It may be related to the Stoic cosmic cycle in which periodically the entire universe is consumed in a fiery cataclysm and then is reconstituted. For Luke, it means that the world is returned to its proper state, in accord with God's will. It may, then, be another of Luke's adaptations of an apocalyptic scheme to his idea of salvation history.

The Gospel of John

The Gospel of John is not apocalyptic. However, it ultimately springs from an apocalyptic setting—the Jesus movement and early Christianity—and it displays vestiges of its origins. Like Luke, John purposely rewrites apocalyptic elements that he has inherited, particularly references to the Son of Man.

John's Christology depends on a cosmology in which this world is under Satan's control. It is dark and alienated from God. Jesus is a man from heaven. He is a stranger to this world (Meeks 1972). More than that, he is actually God (1:1; 5:18; 20:28), a claim not made explicitly by the Synoptic Gospels. He comes from the glorious place of light and truth. John builds his theology up from dualistic oppositions: light/dark, truth/falsehood, heaven/earth, belonging to God/belonging to this world, up/down. Because this scheme fits the Gnostic worldview, Gnostics of the second century and later adopted John as their favorite Gospel. Some scholars have argued that the Gospel itself was Gnostic (Käsemann 1968). That view has been discredited, even though John gave the Gnostics grounds for their more advanced cosmological systems.

Jesus is the Savior from the other world. Those who unite themselves to him here and now become members of the world above, as soon as they accept him. They are born a second time, into the world of light and life. Jesus's death and resurrection become his passage back into that world. After his resurrection and before passing into the world above definitively, Jesus breathes the Holy Spirit upon his followers so that they can continue his mission and presence here on earth. That means coming out of the world alienated from God and being one with Jesus and the Father—coming from darkness into light. Sociologically, it means belonging to John's church, which distinguished itself from other Christian churches by its Christology.

In reconceiving the Son of Man, John makes two main contributions. First, the Son of Man is the same person as the one who comes down from heaven (3:13). Only through him can one have access to the Father. Second, references to the suffering Son of Man in the Synoptic Gospels are transformed into the Son of Man who is "lifted up." John plays on the double meaning of lifted up—lifted up on the cross and lifted up in the sense of being exalted. Jesus's crucifixion is his glorification because it means his leaving this world and going back to his origin (1:14; 8:28; 12:34).

The Gospel's prologue says, "From his [Jesus's] fullness we have all received, grace upon grace. The law indeed was given through Moses, grace and truth came through Jesus Christ. No one has ever seen God. It is God the only Son, who is close to the Father's heart, who has made him known" (1:16–18). These verses contrast Judaism and Christianity, with the advantage to Christianity. "Grace and truth" allude to God's covenantal qualities in the Hebrew Bible, loving-kindness (ḥesed) and faithfulness (ʾĕmet). This is supposed to come through Moses. But the prologue claims that not even Moses saw God (despite what the Hebrew Bible says; Deut. 34:10). Since only the Son, Jesus, the Word of God, has seen the Father, only he can grant access to the Father.

As Jesus himself says in his Last Supper discourses, "I am the way, and the truth, and the life. No one comes to the Father except through me. If you know me, you will know my Father also. From now on you do know him and have seen him" (14:6–7).

John joins these two ideas—that Jesus is the stranger from heaven and that the lifting up of the Son of Man is his return to the world above—in his conversation with Nicodemus, a member of the Jerusalem Sanhedrin.

> No one has ascended into heaven except the one who descended from heaven, the Son of Man. And just as Moses lifted up the serpent in the wilderness, so must the Son of Man be lifted up, that whoever believes in him may have eternal life. For God so loved the world that he gave his only Son, so that everyone who believes in him may not perish but may have eternal life. (3:13–16)

Jewish tradition is full of individuals who went to heaven, including Moses. Jewish apocalyptic tradition is especially important in this regard (Himmelfarb 1993, 1983). Even Paul claims to have ascended to the third heaven (2 Cor. 12:1–4). John rejects all such claims. Jesus, the Son of Man, is the only link between heaven and earth. Only he has been in heaven.

Jesus originates in heaven. He is not simply a person from earth who has made the trip. He travels in the opposite direction from apocalyptic seers. He first comes down and then goes up, whereas they need to ascend to heaven before they come back down. Although Jesus is fully human, he is a native of the world above. Anyone who believes this can share that world and have eternal life. This happens right now. This is "realized eschatology":

> Indeed, God did not send the Son into the world to condemn the world, but in order that the world might be saved through him. Those who believe in him are not condemned; but those who do not believe are condemned already, because they have not believed in the name of the only Son of God. And this is the judgment, that the light has come into the world, and people loved darkness rather than light because their deeds were evil. (3:17–19)

Condemnation, judgment, has already happened to those who do not believe what the Gospel has to say about Jesus.

Although John espouses realized eschatology, apocalyptic elements survive in his Gospel. Later in chapter 3 the evangelist says, "Whoever believes in the Son has eternal life; whoever disobeys the Son will not see life, but must endure God's wrath" (3:36). The ideas of a last judgment and God's future wrath have not disappeared. This is the only occurrence of the word "wrath" in John, so it is hardly prominent, but it is present.

In chapter 5, John takes up the idea that the Son of Man is the end-time judge.

Just as the Father raises the dead and gives them life, so also the Son gives life to whomever he wishes. The Father judges no one but has given all judgment to the Son, so that all may honor the Son just as they honor the Father. . . .

Very truly, I tell you, the hour is coming, and is now here, when the dead will hear the voice of the Son of God, and those who hear will live. For just as the Father has life in himself, so he has granted the Son also to have life in himself; and he has given him authority to execute judgment, because he is the Son of Man. Do not be astonished at this; for the hour is coming when all who are in their graves will hear his voice and will come out—those who have done good, to the resurrection of life, and those who have done evil, to the resurrection of condemnation. I can do nothing on my own. As I hear, I judge; and my judgment is just, because I seek to do not my own will but the will of him who sent me. (5:21–30)

Apocalyptic eschatology is so tied to early Christian expectation that John must include it somewhere. As he explains that the Father has delegated responsibility for judgment to the Son, apocalyptic elements creep into the Gospel. This passage envisages literal resurrection. Graves will open; the dead will rise; there will be postmortem rewards and punishments.

In a later passage, we again encounter literal resurrection:

Martha said to Jesus, "Lord, if you had been here, my brother [Lazarus] would not have died. But even now I know that God will give you whatever you ask of him." Jesus said to her, "Your brother will rise again." Martha said to him, "I know that he will rise again in the resurrection on the last day." Jesus said to her, "I am the resurrection and the life. Those who believe in me, even though they die, will live, and everyone who lives and believes in me will never die. Do you believe this?" She said to him, "Yes, Lord, I believe that you are the Messiah, the Son of God, the one coming into the world." (11:21–27)

Resuscitation is at issue here, not resurrection from the dead in the eschatological sense. Resuscitation is what Martha wants in verse 22. She wants her brother back. Ironically, Jesus points to the general resurrection at the end of time. Martha understands the allusion (11:24), but it does not give her what she wants. Jesus resorts to his usual, theologically loaded revelation about his own role and significance. In what sounds like a riddle, he uses death and life in two different senses—physical and spiritual. One who believes him will die physically but not spiritually. He or she will lose physical life but will gain eternal life. John still believes in traditional resurrection, but since Christians already have eternal life, it is a bit anticlimactic.

John transforms the apocalyptic elements of early Christianity into something new. And yet even he retains elements of the apocalyptic milieu in which every form of Christianity had roots. When Jesus realizes that his death is near, he says, "Now is the judgment of this world; now the ruler of this world will be driven out" (John 12:31).

Conclusion

Our analysis shows the prevalence of an apocalyptic worldview in Mark, Q, Matthew, and Luke. Matthew and Luke adopt the apocalyptic aspects of Mark and Q but adapt them to their own purposes. Acts of the Apostles also incorporates that worldview, though it reads more like a history than an apocalyptic proclamation. Still, it is a history planned by God and guided at every step by the Spirit. John subscribes to realized eschatology, but apocalyptic elements do emerge in several places.

Suggestions for Further Reading

Allison, Dale C. *The End of the Ages Has Come: An Early Interpretation of the Passion and Resurrection of Jesus*. Philadelphia: Fortress, 1985.

Aune, David E. *Apocalypticism, Prophecy, and Magic in Early Christianity: Collected Essays*. Tübingen: Mohr Siebeck, 2006.

Ehrman, Bart D. *The New Testament: A Historical Introduction to the Early Christian Writings*. 4th ed. New York: Oxford University Press, 2008.

Horsley, Richard A. "The Kingdom of God and the Renewal of Israel: Synoptic Gospels, Jesus Movements, and Apocalypticism." In *The Encyclopedia of Apocalypticism*, edited by John Joseph Collins, Bernard McGinn, and Stephen J. Stein, 1:303–44. New York: Continuum, 1998.

———. "Wisdom and Apocalypticism in Mark." In *In Search of Wisdom: Essays in Memory of John G. Gammie*, edited by Leo G. Perdue et al., 223–44. Louisville: Westminster John Knox, 1993.

Murphy, Frederick J. *An Introduction to Jesus and the Gospels*. Nashville: Abingdon, 2005.

Perkins, Pheme. *Resurrection: New Testament Witness and Contemporary Reflection*. Garden City, NY: Doubleday, 1984.

9

Jesus the Apocalyptic Prophet

This chapter has a somewhat different nature than the others in this book. In the others, our objects of study have been literary documents. Here it is a historical person, Jesus of Nazareth. Our literary sources serve primarily as evidence for that person. In chapter 8, we treated the Gospels, our main sources for Jesus, but our purpose was to determine the apocalyptic nature of each document. We did not assess them as potential evidence for Jesus himself. We now use those same documents for this rather different historical purpose. We seek not a complete presentation of the historical Jesus, but one that highlights his apocalyptic characteristics and goals. There are innumerable studies that provide fuller accounts of Jesus (Horsley 2010a; Meier 1991; Sanders 1995). That being said, apocalypticism is central to how we view Jesus. When considering him from this angle, we go a long way in painting a satisfactory historical portrait of him.

Sources

The Gospels were written by people of great faith in Jesus, and most scholars think that they were written for believers, for the specific uses of the church. Historians must read them critically and, to the degree that it is possible, objectively, according to the methods and assumptions of historical inquiry. This can go against the grain of some believers, but for others it has proven a way to deepen their faith. They integrate critical analysis with their own faith-filled reading of the text to arrive at insights that leave them enriched in their faith and better informed historically.

Some may wonder why we treat Jesus separately from the Gospels. What more can we know about him apart from them? True, the Gospels are almost our only source for Jesus. Nonetheless, even a quick glance at the canonical Gospels confronts us with basic decisions if we are to use these texts for the purposes of history. For example, it is difficult to imagine that the historical Jesus was both as he is in the Synoptic Gospels (Matthew, Mark, and Luke) and as he is in the Gospel of John. In the Synoptic Gospels, Jesus says little about himself. In John, he speaks of little else. In the Synoptics, Jesus preaches and teaches mostly about the kingdom of God. In John, that phrase occurs only in 3:3, 5. Jesus's characteristic way of teaching in the Synoptics is in parables, while in John, there are no parables in the form of short stories. John's Gospel contains little that is apocalyptic, while the Synoptics present Jesus in an apocalyptic light. In the Synoptics, exorcisms are the most common form of miracle performed by Jesus, while they are entirely absent from John.

Faced with radical differences in the pictures of Jesus in John and the Synoptics, historians find the Synoptic presentation more plausible. John's Jesus is highly exalted, almost a god on earth. The Synoptics have a "lower" (less exalted) Christology, supplying the historian with more material from which to reconstruct a believable human Jesus.

Mark wrote his Gospel first, and Luke and Matthew used him as the main source for their Gospels. So for the purpose of historical inquiry they do not constitute three independent sources. Matthew and Luke used another source, no longer extant, which we call Q (from the German *Quelle*, "source"), which does give us an early source independent of Mark. Most of it consists of sayings of Jesus.

Material unique to Luke or Matthew is designated L or M, respectively. These are not literary sources properly speaking. When they are reconstructed, they do not look like coherent sources as does Q. They just mean that the material they contain was peculiar to the evangelist. He obtained them from oral tradition, as far as we know. In some instances, he may have composed them himself.

The *Gospel of Thomas*, also a collection of Jesus's sayings, dates in its present form from the second century. Some claim that in an earlier form it dates as early as Q and that where *Thomas* has material similar to what we find in the Synoptics, it occasionally preserves that material in an older form (Patterson 1993). Others think that the *Gospel of Thomas* depends on the Synoptic Gospels and so is not independent. Even those who think of the document as early in parts and are willing to use it for reconstruction of the historical Jesus find only a small amount of material to add to what others already accept as authentic.

Paul supplies us with an independent source, but he preserves little about the historical Jesus. He does give us independent attestation for the fact that Jesus was against divorce, had an inner circle of twelve, was born subject to the Torah, celebrated a Last Supper with his disciples, and so on.

Beyond what we find in the New Testament, Q, maybe the *Gospel of Thomas*, and perhaps a couple of brief mentions in the Jewish historian Josephus, there are no extant sources dating to the first century CE that contribute to our knowledge about the historical Jesus. There are gospels from the second century and later, but they present pictures of Jesus that no one takes as reliable historical sources. Many of them make no such claims; they present the risen Christ, not the pre-resurrection Jesus. Others are legendary accounts of Jesus's childhood.

Non-Christian ancient sources are of little to no help in the historical quest for Jesus. Second Temple Jewish sources do not mention him, except perhaps for Josephus, as mentioned. The Christian interpolations we have observed in such Jewish works as the *Testaments of the Twelve Patriarchs* and the *Apocalypse of Abraham* are of no historical value for this subject. Rabbinic sources are too late. The earliest of them that speak of Jesus are from centuries after his time and are legendary. Roman sources contain no information they could not have obtained by observing the fledgling religion in their midst.

Criteria of Authenticity

During the course of Jesus research over the years, scholars have developed several criteria to help decide what is historically authentic and what is not in the Jesus material that has come down to us (Meier 1991, 1:167–95; Murphy 2002, 334–36).

Criterion of dissimilarity. This criterion states that if there is something in the Jesus tradition dissimilar to what we would expect from Second Temple Judaism or from the early church, it has a claim to authenticity. For example, although the idea of divine kingship is common in Israel, as we have already seen, the phrase "kingdom of God" is not, nor is the idea of "entering" the kingdom. This manner of speaking seems characteristic of Jesus.

N. T. Wright suggests a refinement of the criterion of dissimilarity that works well in the case of the observations above about the kingdom of God. If there is something in the Jesus tradition that makes sense within Second Temple Judaism but that is still distinctive of Jesus and also connects with something that we find in the early church, it has a claim to authenticity (Wright 1996). Jesus's use of the kingdom of God fits this criterion. Given the emphasis on God's kingship in Israelite and Jewish tradition, it is fitting that Jesus thinks in these terms. At the same time, his use of the concept has certain distinctive elements, as shown above. This criterion is limited by our imperfect knowledge of ancient Judaism and Christianity.

Criterion of embarrassment. The example of John the Baptist shows that there are things in the Gospels that are embarrassing to the church. These include the crucifixion, the betrayal by Judas, the baptism by John, the accusation that Jesus is possessed by Beelzebul, and the accusation that he acts like a glutton and a drunkard. The church would not have fabricated such things. This is perhaps the most useful criterion.

Multiple attestation. The more independent sources in which an item appears, the greater the chance that it is authentic. Since the Synoptic Gospels are not independent of one another, an item occurring in all three does not count as independent attestation. Independent sources would be Mark, Q, John, Paul, L, M, and maybe Thomas.

Meier expands this criterion to include multiplicity of genres. If something in the tradition is attested in a variety of forms of tradition, such as narratives, sayings, editorial comments, and so on, it has a greater claim to authenticity. Healing miracles and exorcisms, for example, are not only recounted in the Gospels, they are also spoken about.

Criterion of coherence. Once a body of material is established as authentic using the stricter criteria, one can apply a standard of coherence to judge additional material. Material that is coherent with the established core has a claim to being authentic.

Criterion of linguistic and environmental context. Some material may be excluded because it is anachronistic or does not fit the historical and cultural context of first-century Jewish Palestine. For example, the wordplay involving the Greek word *anōthen* in John 3, where Nicodemus takes it to mean to be born "again" while Jesus means to be born "from above," works in Greek, but not in Aramaic, Jesus's native language.

Criterion of rejection and execution. No picture of Jesus can be adequate that does not account for his being opposed and ultimately executed by those exercising power in ancient Judea.

Criterion of result. When Jesus died, a movement survived. It eventually became independent of Judaism. Although most scholars do not believe that Jesus intended that his movement become a new religion, its survival of his death and its trajectory toward a communal entity independent of Judaism had roots in his own activity and teaching. He may not have intended for his community to become separate from Judaism, but he did intend to found a community within Judaism.

The limitations of the criteria of authenticity. Scholars differ on the usefulness of the criteria of authenticity. Meier builds his entire presentation on the criteria (Meier 1994). Others, including Sanders, prefer another route (Sanders 1985). Sanders believes that it is best to begin with a plausible theory of Jesus's life and mission, and then to see whether it does justice to the evidence. His starting assumption is that Jesus was an eschatological prophet announcing the restoration of Israel. He also assembles a list of things that are in themselves very likely—such as that Jesus was baptized by John, had disciples, and died by crucifixion in Jerusalem—and asks whether they fit his picture of Jesus.

Another approach is that of James D. G. Dunn (2003). He notes that the Gospels do not offer direct evidence for the historical Jesus. Rather, they show the effect that Jesus had on his followers. Yet this is what is really important about Jesus. It is what has been the foundation of what believers down through the ages have thought about Jesus. And ultimately these pictures rest on the interpretations of Jesus by those who actually lived and worked with him, so they are more reliable than skeptics often suggest.

Our method is eclectic. Historical interpretation is never simple, nor is it a science in the way that we find in the natural sciences. Our historical reconstructions borrow something from each of the approaches sketched above. They do not contradict each other; rather, they complement one another.

Apocalyptic or Non-Apocalyptic Jesus

The main question that divides students of the historical Jesus today is whether or not he was an apocalyptic prophet. Around the turn of the twentieth century, Johannes Weiss insisted that Jesus must be seen within the context of ancient Jewish eschatological expectation (1971). Weiss argued that Jesus expected an imminent eschaton. When it did not come, he thought that his own death would bring it about. Albert Schweitzer held essentially the same position (2000). For the time being, the idea of Jesus as an apocalyptic figure had won the day. With some exceptions, the majority of scholars accepted this view. The most prominent New Testament scholar of the twentieth century, Rudolf Bultmann, conceived of Jesus in this manner (1958; 1972).

In the second half of the twentieth century, opposition arose against seeing Jesus as an eschatological prophet. Its strongest voices were Robert Funk and John Dominic Crossan (Crossan 1991; Funk 1969; 1996). The founding of the Jesus Seminar in 1985 offered scholars of similar convictions the opportunity to work collaboratively to rethink the historical Jesus. They developed a picture of a non-apocalyptic Jesus and claimed that majority opinion had swung in their direction (Funk 1998; Funk and Hoover 1993).

Others disagreed. E. P. Sanders published a seminal work in 1985, *Jesus and Judaism*, depicting Jesus as a prophet of Jewish eschatological restoration (1985). In 1991, John Meier began publishing a massive, four-volume study of the historical Jesus entitled *A Marginal Jew* (Meier 1991–2009). Meier's portrait is of an eschatological prophet modeled somewhat on the prophet Elijah. Other major scholars have followed suit, including Allison and Ehrman (Allison 1998b; Ehrman 1999).

In 2001, *The Apocalyptic Jesus: A Debate* was published (Miller 2001). It brought together Allison with three scholars who do not think that Jesus was an apocalyptic prophet—Marcus Borg, John Dominic Crossan, and Stephen Patterson (Allison 1998b; Crossan 1991; Patterson 1998). Allison's writings are a reliable guide to the view of Jesus as an eschatological prophet, and our treatment here is indebted to his presentations.

Jesus and John the Baptist. No one doubts that Jesus began his career in association with John the Baptist. That is the picture presented by each of the Synoptics, as well as by Q and the Gospel of John. So it is independently attested by three sources (the Synoptics being considered one source). Few doubt John was an apocalyptic preacher. Material preserved in Mark, Q, and John confirms that. The Baptist preaches repentance, predicts the coming of a powerful one after him, and speaks of imminent, fiery judgment (Q 3:7–9, 16–17; Mark 1:4, 7–8).

Mark says little about the relationship between John and Jesus. Jesus shows up to be baptized along with great crowds, and John gives him no special attention. Jesus has a vision in which God declares him to be his Son, but there is no indication that anyone except Jesus saw or heard anything. Jesus then begins a ministry permeated with apocalypticism.

Later sources show embarrassment concerning Jesus's relationship with John and a concern to prove that Jesus outranks John. Matthew's own material has John say that he should not baptize Jesus but that Jesus should baptize him, assuming that the superior baptizes the inferior (3:14). Luke uses subtler means, avoiding a statement that John actually baptized Jesus, although he implies it. The Gospel of John goes still further—John does not baptize Jesus at all. In John's Gospel, the Baptist explicitly and repeatedly declares his subordination to Jesus (3:24–30; 1:19–36). In John's prologue (1:1–18), two sections argue strongly that John is inferior to Jesus (1:6–8, 15). Immediately after the prologue, John's Gospel has emissaries from Jerusalem interrogate the Baptist about his identity (1:19–27). He vigorously denies that he is the messiah and insists that he is merely the forerunner and announcer of the greater one to come, Jesus. In John 3 and 4, Jesus pursues a ministry independent of and in competition to that of John (John 3:22–30). When John's disciples tell him this, John forcefully declares Jesus's superiority (John 3:27–30). The Gospel says both that Jesus baptized and that he did not. This suggests that he did indeed baptize, but that his baptizing dropped out of the tradition when it seemed to put him too much on the Baptist's level (cf. John 3:22 and 4:1–2).

Each of the four Gospels, therefore, betrays discomfort with the idea that Jesus began his career by being baptized by John, and perhaps even by initially engaging in an independent ministry based on John's. The criterion of embarrassment is one of the strongest indicators of authenticity, and Jesus's baptism qualifies as a cause of embarrassment to the early church.

Jesus began his public life by accepting John's baptism for repentance in the face of God's imminent intervention in history. This indicates that Jesus subscribed to John's eschatological message.

Jesus's baptism can be problematic for believing Christians even today for another reason, since it seems to imply that Jesus thought of himself as sinful and needing repentance. As historians, we have no basis on which to judge whether someone is sinful or not, either in the present or the past. But it is legitimate for historians to inquire whether Jesus *thought* he was sinful. Does his acceptance of John's baptism indicate this? Not necessarily. The ancients thought more in terms of the group than the individual. Jesus was a member of Israel. If the judgment was near, and if Israel was preparing for it through a baptism meant to protect the community from God's wrath, it would have been natural for Jesus to join in, even if he did not feel personally sinful.

There are indications in the New Testament that John had regular followers (for example, Mark 2:18; 6:29; John 3:25), but we do not know if he was engaged in community-building activities. It seems more likely that he was preparing individuals to go back to their homes and await the end (Crossan 1994). Jesus's vision was different. Jesus worked to form a community that would constitute the nucleus of a new Israel when the end came. His work of preaching, teaching, healing, and exorcising all served the end of building that community and preparing it for a new state of affairs, which he called the kingdom of God. For him, it was near. At some point Jesus split from John and began his own ministry. He still had tremendous respect for John, but perhaps he felt that his own ministry fell further along in the eschatological timetable.

John seems to have disapproved of Jesus's career. Our evidence comes from Q, and here we look at it in Matt. 11. In Matt. 11, having heard what Jesus was doing, he sends for Jesus asking whether he is really the one for whom Israel waits or whether they should turn elsewhere. Jesus responds by listing his healing activities and blessing the one who did not take offense at him. This may be a message to John not to be among those who take offense. Meier judges Jesus's answer to be authentic to the historical Jesus (Meier 1994, 402). Jesus perceives the power of God breaking through in his ministry. The eschatological clock is ticking and has left John behind, something that confuses and perhaps even angers John. He does not see what Jesus is doing as what he had predicted.

Jesus says that John was a prophet and more than a prophet, but that the least in the kingdom of God is greater than he (Matt. 11:11). This picture demonstrates that even two people who agree on some essentials—an imminent eschaton, a coming judgment, the need for repentance, the need to warn others of what is happening, and the conviction that they have special knowledge—can disagree on other matters, go their separate ways, pursue different tactics, and give important things different value. That mentor, John, disapproves of Jesus, but that the mentee, Jesus, continues to honor his mentor is probably a familiar story in human history.

Jesus speaks of the different natures of his and John's careers in terms that seem authentic: "For John came neither eating nor drinking, and they say, 'He has a demon'; the Son of Man came eating and drinking, and they say, 'Look, a glutton and a drunkard, a friend of tax collectors and sinners!'" (Matt. 11:18–19). The saying matches what we know of the careers of the two men. John was an ascetic living in the desert, while Jesus is frequently depicted at meals and seems to do a fair amount of eating and drinking. It is hardly likely that the church would have made up a saying in which Jesus is called a glutton and a drunkard. No one thinks that Jesus was really dissolute, but even slanders often have some basis in reality. Jesus's enemies may have used his eating and drinking against him. He did not act the way prophets are supposed to act.

Matthew 11 contains the following enigmatic statement: "From the days of John the Baptist until now the kingdom of heaven has suffered violence, and the violent take it by force. For all the prophets and the law prophesied until John came; and if you are willing to accept it, he is Elijah who is to come" (11:12–14). Luke's version is as follows: "The law and the prophets were in effect until John came; since then the good news of the kingdom of God is proclaimed, and everyone tries to enter it by force" (16:16). The very fact that this statement appears in different forms in Matthew and Luke indicates that Jesus's early followers had trouble with it. Its meaning is not transparent. It divides history into major sections, typical of apocalypticism. The first part is associated with the law and the prophets, while the second associates the kingdom of God and violence in some way. Matthew seems to indicate that those who belong to the kingdom suffer violence. Luke has a different take, stressing enthusiastic reaction to the kingdom.

The saying implies that Jesus thinks apocalyptically in that he divides history into sections, associates the second with the kingdom of God, and connects the kingdom with suffering violence, which may correspond to the end-time suffering. He locates the turn between the two ages with John the Baptist's ministry, which would be natural, since that seems to be what got him into the eschatology business. Matthew adds the identification of the Baptist with Elijah, whose eschatological return was predicted in Mal. 4. He also adds the asides "if you are willing to accept it" and "let anyone with ears listen!" (Matt. 11:14–15), both indicating that Matthew reads the statement in an apocalyptic context, in which understanding mystery is important.

Jesus the prophet. Allison notes that Jesus was compared to several eschatological figures. One, of course, is John the Baptist (Miller 2001, 23). Reports coming to Herod and to Peter said that people thought of him in connection with John (Mark 6:16; 8:28). Acts of the Apostles reports that when the Sanhedrin was discussing the Jesus movement after Jesus's death, the Pharisee

Gamaliel compared it to that of Theudas, an eschatological prophet who thought of himself as a new Moses who would split the Jordan River. He led an uprising that was crushed by the Roman governor Fadus, who administered the area in 44–46 CE. Gamaliel also mentions Judah the Galilean who resisted the Roman census of 6 CE as slavery and who insisted that only service to God was proper. He urged his followers not to shrink from bloodshed and to expect God's help (Murphy 2002, chap. 8).

Allison offers five arguments that, taken together, make it reasonable to picture Jesus as an apocalyptic prophet: (1) Jesus's early followers thought the end was near; (2) Jesus's followers quickly claimed that they had encountered the risen Jesus; (3) in Jesus's suffering and resurrection Jesus's followers recognized the familiar apocalyptic pattern of suffering followed by vindication, so they expected the kingdom to come soon; (4) the Roman world of the time was suffused with prophetic eschatology, and Jews were no exception; and (5) Jesus was associated in various texts with eschatological figures—John the Baptist, Theudas, and Judas the Galilean.

Sanders adds more. Jesus chose twelve apostles. It is noteworthy that we know almost nothing about most of them. Most Christians cannot even name them all. The New Testament lists are not even entirely consistent. What is important is not the men but the number. It is symbolic. Its symbolism is transparent when Jesus tells his apostles, "Truly I tell you, at the renewal of all things, when the Son of Man is seated on the throne of his glory, you who have followed me will also sit on twelve thrones, judging the twelve tribes of Israel" (Matt. 19:28; cf. Luke 22:30). Horsley (1993) maintains that "judging" means not a judicial function but "ruling," as in the book of Judges. The scene in Q has Jesus speaking to all twelve apostles, including Judas. Such a saying would not have been fabricated by the early church with Judas as part of the audience, so it has a powerful claim to authenticity.

By Jesus's time, most of the tribes were long gone. The northern kingdom, consisting of nine or ten tribes, depending on how they are counted, had been exiled by the Assyrians in 721 BCE and were never heard from again. Numerous eschatological scenarios look forward to the reunion of all Israel, north and south, all twelve tribes. By assembling twelve leaders for a reconstituted Israel, Jesus aligns himself with those who entertain such hopes.

Sanders interprets eschatologically Jesus's actions in the temple at the end of his career. He rejects the notion that Jesus was simply protesting the presence of commercial activity in the sacred precincts. Tipping over the tables of the money changers and forbidding the selling of animals would bring to a halt the entire proceedings of the temple. Jesus's tipping over the tables was a prophetic symbolic action representing the temple's destruction. Sanders shows the widespread dissatisfaction with the temple and its establishment in Second Temple times, and he notes passages where an eschatological destruction and rebuilding of the temple are expected.

Were Sanders's theory built only on the detail that Jesus tipped over tables in the temple, the idea of its destruction would not be compelling. However, there are numerous references to Jesus's speaking of the temple's destruction. He does so in each of the Synoptic Gospels' apocalyptic discourses, as well as in John 2:19–21. In the accounts of Jesus's trial before the Sanhedrin, witnesses attest to several different forms of the statement Jesus allegedly made about the temple's destruction. The different forms as well as the insistence that these were false accusations show the extent to which the early church had trouble coming to terms with what he did say. He seems to have said something about the temple's destruction and its being rebuilt, not by human hands. If he said anything like that, it would obviously be an eschatological statement.

Jesus began as a disciple of John the Baptist, and after his death the church was permeated with apocalypticism. It would be strange indeed, then, if he himself were not apocalyptic in outlook.

Jesus's resurrection. The followers of Jesus believed that they had encountered Jesus risen from the dead three days after his crucifixion. Allison sees this as strong evidence not only that they themselves thought apocalyptically, but that Jesus himself had prepared them to do so. After all, even if they had visions of Jesus after his death, why would they necessarily have thought of this in terms of resurrection? Could they not have been seeing a ghost, or a simple vision, or some sort of phantasm? Why resurrection?

Jesus's references to his own death and resurrection frequently encounter skepticism on the part of scholars, since the references conveniently fit Christian belief. But it is more than likely that Jesus anticipated his own death as he approached a hostile Jerusalem with a mission he knew threatened its rulers. If Jesus thought in apocalyptic terms, he probably expected an imminent eschaton in which resurrection would play a part. If he spoke of this to his disciples, and it is hardly to be imagined that he did not, they may have had a quick interpretation ready when he died and an explanation handy when they encountered him again.

Jesus may have expected a general resurrection, since we have no evidence in Judaism for anything else, but certainly not the resurrection of a single person. When Jesus, Elijah, and Elisha "raise" the dead, this is resuscitation, not resurrection in the eschatological sense. But in Jesus, the earliest church encountered a single resurrection. Matthew seems confused about this, since his rewriting of Mark's version of Jesus's death entails the resurrection of others. Paul associates Jesus's resurrection with a general resurrection in 1 Cor. 15. He goes so far as to say that if there is no general resurrection, then Jesus was not raised.

Jesus's exorcisms. Jesus's public career began with his being baptized by John. He may even have been one of John's disciples (Meier 1994, 116–30). He quickly went his own way. Mark indicates that he immediately went out to the wilderness to be tempted by Satan. We cannot know whether this is accurate. It fits Mark's interest in Jesus's battle with the demons, so it may be suspect for that reason. Our question is whether it accurately reflects Jesus's way of think-ing. The fact that Jesus is credited with so many exorcisms suggests that it is.

Jesus's most frequent action in the Synoptic Gospels is exorcism. Not only are there a multitude of exorcisms in the Synoptics, but there are also summaries of Jesus's activities in which exorcisms are featured. Mark emphasizes exor-cisms, while Matthew plays them down a bit in favor of healings (themselves put within an eschatological context by Matthew), but still features them. The same is true of Luke. Exorcisms are mentioned in Jesus's sayings as well as in the words of other characters in the Gospels. This is multiple attestation in terms of form. Meier says that if we reject Jesus's exorcisms, we may as well give up on knowing anything about Jesus.

We do not know how common exorcism was in Jewish Palestine in Jesus's time (Twelftree 1993). Jesus admits in Mark and Q that other Jews exorcise (Mark 9:38–40; Matt. 12:27; Luke 11:19; Q 11:19). Jesus sees the unnamed exorcist in Mark 9 as fighting the same battle that he is waging. If, as the story says, the exorcist exorcises in Jesus's name, he may himself see it as part of Jesus's battle. There are no prophetic or messianic figures that we know of who do exorcisms. However, there are a couple of apocalyptic passages that connect the coming of the ideal world with the defeat of Satan (*Testament of Moses* 10; *Jubilees* 23; *Testament of Levi* 18; the last was probably reworked by Christians). It is probable that Jesus himself brought together these two things—exorcism and the defeat of Satan at the end of times. This would fit the criterion of double dissimilarity. His joining of these two things is unknown in the Judaism of his day, but it would make good sense in that context.

Jesus tells his disciples of a vision he had: "I watched Satan fall from heaven like a flash of lightning" (Luke 10:18). The book of Revelation describes such a scene, when the archangel Michael drives Satan from heaven. Rebellious angels under the leadership of angels such as Azazel and Shemyaza appear in the *Book of the Watchers*. Luke's saying is bereft of christological content and fits Jesus's exorcisms, since it attests to Satan's presence on earth as well as his defeat, something Jesus speaks of in Q as well (Matt. 12:27; Luke 11:19). It has a strong claim to authenticity.

In both Mark and Q Jesus is accused of exorcising by the power of Beel-zebul. In both places, Jesus sees his exorcisms as a binding of Satan, as part of Satan's rule coming to an end as God's kingdom approaches. One saying in this complex has a strong claim to authenticity: "If it is by the finger of God that I cast out the demons, then the kingdom of God has come to you" (Luke 11:20). "Finger of God" occurs only here in the New Testament. It is not characteristic of Luke or any other part of the New Testament. It alludes to Exod. 8:19, where Pharaoh's magicians admit that they cannot replicate the plague of the gnats. There are only two other occurrences of the phrase "finger of God" in the Bible, both referring to God's writing the Torah on stone tablets. This argues for authenticity.

Fig. 11. This is a mountain near the north shore of the Sea of Galilee. Jesus seems to have spent most of his ministry in the small villages of Galilee before he went to Jerusalem. He would have been very familiar with this kind of spare countryside. (Jim Yancey)

The kingdom of God. One of the most widely accepted aspects of Jesus's ministry is that he preached the kingdom of God. In Mark's Gospel, Jesus emerges from the desert and immediately preaches: "The time is fulfilled, and the kingdom of God has come near; repent, and believe in the good news" (1:15). The "good news," another translation for the "gospel" (*euangelion*), is that God's kingdom is near. This is an apocalyptic pronouncement. Time fulfilled implies a foreordained history that has reached its critical point. The kingdom of God as something that can "come near" implies that the kingdom is equivalent to the new world of apocalypticism. It is not here, but it is close. Repentance is the appropriate reaction to such news. Mark places these words here as a programmatic statement for his Gospel, so their authenticity is questionable. Nonetheless, they accord with Jesus's apocalyptic outlook.

Everyone agrees that the kingdom of God was at the center of Jesus's teaching, but there is disagreement about just what he meant by the phrase. As we saw in chapter 2, the kingship of God is a common idea in ancient Judaism. But Jesus had a distinctive way of speaking about it. The very phrase "kingdom of God" is not all that frequent in ancient Jewish texts. More common is the proclamation "Yahweh reigns," in the Psalms, for example. The use of "kingdom" as the object of "enter" is also unusual, yet Jesus speaks this way repeatedly. Since the kingdom could hardly be a specific place on earth to which one might travel in the present and then enter, it must be future. This again is most like the new world idea in apocalypticism.

Those who advocate a non-apocalyptic Jesus think that he thought of the kingdom in non-apocalyptic terms. They appeal to such sayings as the following: "Once Jesus was asked by the Pharisees when the kingdom of God was coming, and he answered, 'The kingdom of God is not coming with things that can be observed; nor will they say, "Look, here it is!" or "There it is!" For, in fact, the kingdom of God is among you'" (Luke 17:20–21). These verses could read as an assertion that the kingdom of God is not apocalyptic, but they need not. They could in fact be making a point similar to that of Jesus when he says that the end will come like a thief in the night, without warning. The idea that "the kingdom of God is among you" may refer to the suddenness with which it appears. Indeed, Luke 17 follows these verses with warnings about the suddenness and unexpectedness of the kingdom's advent and the necessity to maintain an attitude of readiness.

A perennial debate concerning Jesus's conception of the kingdom of God is whether he thinks of it as present or future. The fact that the debate has lasted for so long shows that there is evidence on both sides. The most likely solution to the problem is that Jesus saw the kingdom as in some sense both present and future. He saw his own work as helping to bring in the kingdom. He preached its nearness, warned people to prepare for and be ready for it, fought Satan through exorcisms, brought God's healing power into the world, exhorted people to repent, opposed earthly powers that resisted the kingdom, and so on. But the kingdom was yet to come in its fullness. He needed his disciples to help him, and he might have foreseen a time when they would have to carry on that work without him. He expected an imminent climax to the struggle he was carrying on. The coming kingdom, identical with the new world of other apocalyptic schemes, would be ideal and would be this-worldly. It would be a utopia, conceived of in terms of ancient Judaism, which had an abundance of resources to draw on to imagine what was to come. Sanders's hypothesis about what Jesus expected, a renewed and restored Israel, is probably accurate.

The majority of scholars consider some form of the Beatitudes authentic. If so, they shed light on how Jesus conceived of the kingdom of God.

The Beatitudes

Matthew 5:3–12	Luke 6:20–26
Blessed are the poor in spirit, for theirs is the kingdom of heaven.	Blessed are you who are poor, for yours is the kingdom of God.
Blessed are those who mourn, for they will be comforted.	Blessed are you who are hungry now, for you will be filled.
Blessed are the meek, for they will inherit the earth.	Blessed are you who weep now, for you will laugh.
Blessed are those who hunger and thirst for righteousness, for they will be filled.	Blessed are you when people hate you, and when they exclude you, revile you, and defame you on account of the Son of Man.
Blessed are the merciful, for they will receive mercy.	
Blessed are the pure in heart, for they will see God.	Rejoice in that day and leap for joy, for surely your reward is great in heaven; for that is what their ancestors did to the prophets.
Blessed are the peacemakers, for they will be called children of God. Blessed are those who are persecuted for righteousness' sake, for theirs is the kingdom of heaven.	But woe to you who are rich, for you have received your consolation.
Blessed are you when people revile you and persecute you and utter all kinds of evil against you falsely on my account. Rejoice and be glad, for your reward is great in heaven, for in the same way they persecuted the prophets who were before you.	Woe to you who are full now, for you will be hungry. Woe to you who are laughing now, for you will mourn and weep.
	Woe to you when all speak well of you, for that is what their ancestors did to the false prophets.

Matthew has nine beatitudes, Luke only four. Luke balances the four beatitudes with four woes, while Matthew has no woes. Meier argues persuasively for the authenticity of the first three beatitudes.

Comparison of Matthew's and Luke's forms of the parables shows them to be rather different. Luke speaks of those who are literally poor, hungry, and unhappy, while Matthew softens this. However one interprets "poor in spirit," it is a step away from literal poverty. Hunger and thirst for righteousness is not the same as literal hunger and thirst. "Righteousness" is a favorite word of Matthew's, since it belongs in a context concerned for obedience to Torah (see, for example, Matt. 5:17–20). One can construct an argument for either Matthew or Luke or both changing Q's version of the beatitudes. Assuming for a moment that either Matthew or Luke is more faithful in his reproduction of Q, one could argue that Matthew changed it to make it less radical and more appropriate as a teaching vehicle in his church. His use of poor in a figurative way is commonplace in ancient Jewish piety. Alternatively, one could imagine that Luke took beatitudes like Matthew's and made them more challenging and more attuned to his interest in the division between rich and poor, a tendency found elsewhere in his Gospel.

It is likely that the original form of the beatitudes in Q was closer to Luke's form than to Matthew's, and that Q's form is close to what the historical Jesus said. Luke's form fits the radical nature of Jesus's ministry and message better than Matthew's. Broadly speaking, Jesus aligned himself with the poor and powerless, confronting the rich and powerful. He seems to have kept their company more often, and it was the upper class that opposed and ultimately killed him. The disciples themselves are shocked by Jesus's statements, "How hard it will be for those who have wealth to enter the kingdom of God!" and "It is easier for a camel to go through the eye of a needle than for someone who is rich to enter the kingdom of God" (Mark 10:23, 25).

Both Matthew and Luke consider the Beatitudes important to Jesus's message. Matthew places them at the beginning of his Sermon on the Mount (Matt. 5–7), while Luke positions them similarly, at the beginning of his Sermon on the Plain (Luke 6). The Beatitudes are instances of eschatological reversal. They point out the unfortunate situation of Jesus's hearers in the present and predict that their situation will be reversed when the kingdom comes. This is an apocalyptic way of looking at things. The kingdom is not here. It has yet to come. But its coming is certain, and it will mean radical change in the world. Note that we are speaking of a this-worldly kingdom. Apparently, people will still eat and drink. This recalls Jesus's words at the Last Supper: "Truly I tell you, I will never again drink of the fruit of the vine until that day when I drink it new in the kingdom of God" (Mark 14:25). Jesus utters these words when he is about to be arrested and killed. Even if scholars are unwilling to argue that Jesus knew the details of what was in his immediate future, most think that at this point he knew that something terrible was about to happen, and he may have seen it in terms of the impending eschaton when the righteous would suffer. Nonetheless, he looked forward to a time to come when he would be drinking wine in God's kingdom. This also is eschatological reversal.

Reversal is common throughout the Gospels. Assertions like "But many who are first will be last, and the last will be first" (Matt. 19:30; cf. Matt. 20:16; Mark 10:31; Luke 13:30); "Whoever wants to be first must be last of all and servant of all" (Mark 9:35); "For all who exalt themselves will be humbled, and those who humble themselves will be exalted" (Luke 14:11); and "For those who want to save their life will lose it, and those who lose their life for my sake, and for the sake of the gospel, will save it" (Mark 8:35) punctuate the Gospels. We recall also parables such as the rich man and Lazarus, where a desperately poor man goes to heaven and is with Abraham, while the rich man by whose gate he used to lie goes to hell (Luke 16:19–31). Another example is the parable of the Prodigal Son, where the younger son, the one who wasted his inheritance, is honored, while the older son who had been dutiful all his life remained outside the feast (Luke 15:11–32). The parable of the Pharisee and the tax collector makes a similar point. It is the sinner, not the pious person, who is justified in God's eyes (Luke 18:10–14). Such material reveals that Jesus was profoundly dissatisfied with the human condition as he found it and was particularly critical of those people who considered themselves religious.

According to Boomershine, Jesus uses the apocalyptic tradition in a dialectical, not a rhetorical, way (Boomershine 1998). Boomershine draws on this theoretical distinction as formulated by Stanley Fish (1994). Rhetoric appeals to shared ground between writer and reader. It confirms the assumptions held by the reader. Dialectic challenges the assumptions of the reader and makes his or her world uncomfortable and unsure. Jesus's beatitudes attack the comfort of the rich and the self-satisfied. His parables challenge the self-righteous, the wealthy, and the powerful.

The Lord's Prayer is usually thought to be authentic. It is found in Q.

The Lord's Prayer

Matthew 6:9–13	Luke 11:2–4
Our Father in heaven,	Father,
hallowed be your name.	hallowed be your name.
Your kingdom come.	Your kingdom come.
Your will be done, on earth as it is in heaven.	
Give us this day our daily bread.	Give us each day our daily bread.
And forgive us our debts,	And forgive us our sins,
as we also have forgiven our debtors.	for we ourselves forgive everyone indebted
And do not bring us to the time of trial,	to us.
but rescue us from the evil one.	And do not bring us to the time of trial.

This is the only prayer that Jesus teaches his disciples. The shorter form is closer to what was in Q and likely to what Jesus himself said.

The prayer easily fits an eschatological context (Brown 1965). Jesus expects an eschatological kingdom of God. Here he expresses that in a prayer. The petition form means that the kingdom is not here and that it must come to be through divine agency.

The hallowing of God's name means to make it holy, to honor it appropriately. It means to recognize God as God, for God is the source and very definition of holiness in ancient Judaism and Christianity (Gammie 1989). The behavior of those who profess faithfulness to God affects his holiness, for if his worshipers do not act in ways appropriate to God's holiness, then they pollute it. The clearest expression of this is in Ezek. 36. The historical setting of Ezekiel is the Babylonian exile, and the hallowing of God's name that he anticipates corresponds to the restoration of Israel. Israel had defiled God through their actions. The prophet expects that Israel will begin to obey God, and that God will bring Israel back to Judah and build the ideal Jerusalem and temple. These are all elements that belong to eschatological scenarios of the Second Temple era. Matthew is close to Ezekiel when he explains hallowing God's name as doing God's will on earth as it is in heaven.

The combination of the coming of the kingdom and the hallowing of God's name is found in the ancient Jewish prayer, the Qaddish. Scholars are unsure about when the Qaddish began to be used. We know only that it was part of a prescribed rabbinic order of prayers in the Talmudic period. Nonetheless, its similarity to the Lord's Prayer is striking and shows a pattern of thought shared by Jesus and other Jews:

> Magnified and hallowed be his great name in the world [or age] that he has created according to his good pleasure; may he cause his kingdom to reign [i.e., may he establish his kingdom] . . . in your lives [i.e., in your lifetime] and in your days and in the lives of the whole house of Israel, very soon and in a near time [i.e., in the near future]. (Meier 1994, 297)

Meier urges reading the three petitions of the Lord's Prayer in this "strong eschatological perspective" (Meier 1994, 301). The prayer for bread may refer to the eschatological banquet. If the whole prayer should be read in terms of the coming kingdom, then the reference to bread shows that the kingdom is not disembodied. It has to do with bread. In Mark 14:25, we learned that wine will not be lacking, either. Jesus's second petition makes the forgiveness of people at the last judgment dependent on their own forgiveness of those who owe them. Jesus states this in economic terms. In Matthew, we ask God to forgive us our "debts" as we forgive those who owe us "debts." Luke asks for forgiveness from "sins" if we forgive "debts."

Q's plea to be spared "trial" (*peirasmos*) is also eschatological. It refers not to individual temptation concerning specific sins. Rather, it refers to the time of testing that accompanies the final showdown between good and evil and marks the end of time. Matthew is on the mark when he adds a petition to be kept from "the evil one," probably a reference to Satan.

Q contains another kingdom saying that adds detail to what Jesus expected. There is not a great deal of difference between Matthew and Luke in this episode, so we simply quote Matthew: "I tell you, many will come from east and west and will eat with Abraham and Isaac and Jacob in the kingdom of heaven, while the heirs of the kingdom will be thrown into the outer darkness, where there will be weeping and gnashing of teeth" (Matt. 8:11–12). The setting is a banquet. The patriarchs are there, so resurrection is in view. This is the great eschatological banquet present in some Jewish eschatological scenarios. The biggest point of contention in interpretation is whether those who come from east and west are Jews or gentiles. Sanders is correct in thinking that Jesus subscribed to the traditional Jewish eschatological scenario by thinking that once Israel was saved, the gentiles would acknowledge Israel's God. Actually, there are many passages where the two go together. Exiled Jews come back to the land of Israel along with the gentiles. There is no reason that Jesus may not have that in mind. In any case, we have here the hope of an eschatological banquet attended by the risen patriarchs, with some others included and some not.

Having examined many of Jesus's kingdom sayings, Meier offers the following summary of what Jesus's thoughts were regarding the kingdom of God.

> Taken together they clearly indicate (1) that Jesus expected a future, definitive coming of God to rule as king; (2) that this hope was so central to his message that be bade his disciples make it a central petition of their own prayer; (3) that the coming kingdom would bring about the reversal of present unjust conditions of poverty, sorrow, and hunger; (4) that this final kingdom would bring an even more astounding reversal: it would include at least some Gentiles, not as conquered slaves but as honored guests, would share the eschatological banquet with the Israelite patriarchs (risen from the dead?); and (5) that, despite the possibility of his impending death, Jesus himself would experience a saving reversal: he would share in the final banquet, symbolized by the prophetic event of the Last Supper. The last two points make it clear that the final kingdom is in some sense transcendent or discontinuous with this present world. (Meier 1994, 337)

Meier asks whether Jesus sets a deadline for the kingdom (Meier 1994, 336–48). He finds three passages relevant to the question. He begins his search for an answer with Matt. 10:23: "When they persecute you in one town, flee to the next; for truly I tell you, you will not have gone through all the towns of Israel before the Son of Man comes." Meier argues that this saying must come from the early church, not from Jesus. The context is a missionary discourse composed by Matthew in which the church's missionary activity is seen as part of the end-time events. A mission broader than that undertaken by Jesus is envisaged. The coming of the Son of Man is really a reference to Jesus's parousia (Meier 1994, 339–41).

Meier reads Matt. 10:23 as did Matthew himself, and he accurately represents the meaning of the verse in its present context. Still, the content of the mission originally envisaged in the saying is not entirely clear. Jesus did not undertake a mission to anyone but Palestinian Jews, nor did he intend to go beyond that circle. In much the same way that Paul thought that by missionizing key towns and cities in his orbit of influence he was missionizing the whole area, Jesus may have thought that his own mission and that of the apostles during his lifetime was covering all the towns of Israel. We take the view that Jesus expected an eschatological Son of Man to come as judge, a Son of Man who was not Jesus himself. If we read Matt. 10:23 this way, then Jesus expected the end quite soon.

In Mark 9:1 Jesus says, "Truly I say to you, there are some of those who are standing here who shall not taste death until they see the kingdom of God after it has come with power." The saying fits with an imminent expectation, even if it allows for delay.

The final saying Meier considers that may have Jesus setting a time for the end is Mark 13:30. Again he judges it inauthentic. He finds it too dependent for its meaning on its present position in Mark's apocalyptic discourse. But the criterion of embarrassment leads some to see the saying as authentic, since Jesus admits to not knowing the precise time of the end. Jesus's attitude fits with his general reluctance to pin down the time of the end.

The Son of Man. This is a title prominent in the Synoptic Gospels, Q, and John. It fulfills the criterion of multiple attestation. At the same time, it has been at the center of scholarly debate that has lasted decades. The main issue is whether any of the Son of Man material goes back to Jesus, or whether it is entirely a creation of the early church. The scholarly literature on this is immense, and the arguments for and against authenticity are complex. We cannot do them justice here. We simply sketch out our position.

This is an important topic because among Jesus's sayings about the Son of Man are ones that speak of an eschatological figure to come who will judge humankind on the basis of whether they accepted Jesus. It was once a widespread position that these eschatological sayings were uttered by Jesus.

Several unusual features of the Son of Man sayings set the title apart from others applied to Jesus. The Son of Man sayings all appear on Jesus's lips. No one else ever utters them. When Jesus does speak of the Son of Man, other characters never react to the title. It apparently means nothing to them. The title never appears outside the Gospels except in Revelation and Acts of the Apostles. It is not used by the later church. The sayings always seem to be speaking of someone other than Jesus, although the Gospels intend their readers to conclude that Jesus is the Son of Man.

Rudolf Bultmann, a dominant figure in New Testament studies in the twentieth century, was a pioneer in form criticism, a method in which individual traditional forms are isolated from the Gospels where they occur, categorized according to form and use, and examined for signs of modifications in transmission (Bultmann 1972). He divided material about the Son of Man into three categories—earthly, suffering, and eschatological. In the first, Jesus speaks of the Son of Man's authority to forgive sins and his authority over the Sabbath. In the second category, Jesus speaks of the necessity that the Son of Man suffer, die, and rise from the dead. In the last category, the Son of Man is a heavenly figure who comes to judge people on the basis of whether they accepted Jesus or not.

Bultmann considered two Son of Man sayings of Jesus authentic.

> Those who are ashamed of me and of my words in this adulterous and sinful generation, of them the Son of Man will also be ashamed when he comes in the glory of his Father with the holy angels. (Mark 8:38)

> And I tell you, everyone who acknowledges me before others, the Son of Man also will acknowledge before the angels of God; but whoever denies me before others will be denied before the angels of God. (Luke 12:8–9)

In each case, Jesus speaks as if the Son of Man were someone other than himself. Matthew 10:32–33 furnishes us with a variant of these sayings in which the Son of Man now becomes Jesus.

> Everyone therefore who acknowledges me before others, I also will acknowledge before my Father in heaven; but whoever denies me before others, I also will deny before my Father in heaven. (10:32–33)

Bultmann decided that Jesus did expect a heavenly judge to come at the end of time, a judge modeled on the one like a son of man in Dan. 7. Although most scholars do not think that there was a fixed title "Son of Man" in first-century Judaism, two documents from that time—*Similitudes of Enoch* and *4 Ezra*—also draw on the one like a son of man in Dan. 7 to depict an eschatological figure, spoken of as the messiah and the son of God. When Jesus was perceived as risen from the dead, the church expected that he would return to earth, an event called his parousia, from *parousia* indicating an official visit of an important political figure to a city. This expectation arose early. It is already present in the earliest document to be included in the New Testament, 1 Thessalonians, written around 51 CE. In that letter, Paul expects to be alive when Jesus returns. The figures of Jesus returning and the Son of Man coming to judge merged in early Christian belief. Over time, the title Son of Man expanded to take in Jesus's earthly ministry as well as his suffering, death, and resurrection. Both of these developments took place by the time the Gospel of Mark was written, around 70 CE.

We can go further. In 1 Thess. 4, Paul attributes his eschatological scenario to Jesus. This is unusual for Paul, who seldom relies on Jesus's teaching. By the time that Paul wrote, it may be that Jesus's idea of the Son of Man, a figure separate from himself, had already merged with the idea that Jesus himself would return as judge. That would explain why in this passage Paul expects Jesus, not the Son of Man, to come to rescue believers from God's wrath.

Jesus and the Gentiles

Modern Christians and Jews take for granted that Judaism and Christianity are separate religions, and few ethnic Jews identify as Christians. In the beginning it was not so. Jesus was a Jew, as were all of his followers. Even after he died, his followers did not immediately begin to missionize gentiles. Acts of the Apostles assumes that there were no gentile believers in Jesus until the conversion of the centurion Cornelius in chapter 10, more than a third of the way through this first history of earliest Christianity. When Peter does admit gentiles into the church, he is severely criticized by other believers, who are all Jewish. He defends himself in Acts 11, and in Acts 15 a meeting in Jerusalem presided over by Jesus's brother James (Jacob) decides to let gentiles into the church without demanding that they obey Torah. At the meeting, Pharisaic believers insist that gentiles must take on the Torah, but they lose the debate. Later in Acts 11 we see the first real mission to the gentiles, and then Paul begins a systematic missionary effort to convert them in Acts 13.

If Jesus had worked with the gentiles or even planned a mission to them for some later period, it is impossible to imagine that Luke, Acts's author, would have written in this way. Jesus did not settle these questions. It is unlikely that he even discussed them with his disciples. When church members meet in Jerusalem in Acts 15, and when Paul wrestles with this question himself, they never quote Jesus. They had nothing to quote. Jesus's mission was to Israel, not the gentiles. His task was to renew Israel, as was the task of other Israelite and Jewish prophets—not to preach to the nations.

The Gospels supply little to no evidence that Jesus ever directed his attention to gentiles. There are but two stories in which he interacts with them, the healing of the centurion's servant in Q and the healing of the Syrophoenician woman's child in Mark (used by Matthew but not by Luke, perhaps because Luke found it too negative toward gentiles). In each case, Jesus does not come into contact with the one cured. He cures them from a distance. In the centurion story, Jesus expresses surprise that the faith of a gentile is stronger than what he has found in Israel. The story about the woman's daughter in Mark and Matthew is harsher toward gentiles.

Jesus Heals a Gentile Girl

Mark 7:24–30	Matthew 15:21–28
From there he set out and went away to the region of Tyre. He entered a house and did not want anyone to know he was there. Yet he could not escape notice, but a woman whose little daughter had an unclean spirit immediately heard about him, and she came and bowed down at his feet. Now the woman was a Gentile, of Syrophoenician origin. She begged him to cast the demon out of her daughter. He said to her, "Let the children be fed first, for it is not fair to take the children's food and throw it to the dogs." But she answered him, "Sir, even the dogs under the table eat the children's crumbs." Then he said to her, "For saying that, you may go—the demon has left your daughter." So she went home, found the child lying on the bed, and the demon gone.	Jesus left that place and went away to the district of Tyre and Sidon. Just then a Canaanite woman from that region came out and started shouting, "Have mercy on me, Lord, Son of David; my daughter is tormented by a demon." But he did not answer her at all. And his disciples came and urged him, saying, "Send her away, for she keeps shouting after us." He answered, "I was sent only to the lost sheep of the house of Israel." But she came and knelt before him, saying, "Lord, help me." He answered, "It is not fair to take the children's food and throw it to the dogs." She said, "Yes, Lord, yet even the dogs eat the crumbs that fall from their masters' table." Then Jesus answered her, "Woman, great is your faith! Let it be done for you as you wish." And her daughter was healed instantly.

In both versions, Jesus is harsh toward the gentile woman. He does not want to cure her child. He speaks of gentiles as "dogs" and of Jews as "children." When he cures her daughter in Mark, it seems he does so only because she accepts the inferior position he assigns to non-Jews.

Matthew's rewriting makes Jesus's attitude even harsher. At first, he will not even answer the woman. He does so at the insistence of his disciples who are annoyed by her. He tells her that he has not come for gentiles but for Israel. Jesus repeats this saying in 10:5, where he tells his disciples whom he is sending on a mission not to go to the gentiles or Samaritans. Matthew retains Mark's reference to gentiles as dogs.

Whatever one's judgment on the authenticity of the stories of the centurion's servant and the gentile woman's daughter, they give little support to the position that Jesus worked with gentiles. Did gentiles have a place in his thinking? Sanders offers a solution (Sanders 1985, 212–21). Jewish eschatological scenarios often included the gentiles worshiping Israel's God at the end of time. That often followed the renewal of Israel and its relationship with God. Acts of the Apostles took the position that since most Jews did not accept Jesus, the eschatological schedule had to be adjusted. The message would be brought to the gentiles ahead of schedule (Acts 13:46–47; 28:25–28). Paul also reverses the order of how humanity is reconciled to God. It should have been Jew first and then gentile, but since Israel did not believe, Paul went to the gentiles (Rom. 11). He expected that once the gentiles were converted, Israel would change its heart and accept God's favor.

It may well be that Jesus left the gentile question up to God. Jesus's task concerned Israel alone. He may have believed that after Israel's renewal, the gentiles would believe. The problem would take care of itself.

Jesus's Miracles

We have already treated Jesus's exorcisms. The remaining miracles are often divided into healings and nature miracles. The latter category includes miracles like walking on water, calming the sea, multiplying bread, and raising the dead. The sea miracles can be explained by the church's desire to exalt Jesus. They echo hymns to God found in Psalms. For example, Jesus's walking on water recalls Ps. 77:19: "Your way was through the sea, your path, through the mighty waters; yet your footprints were unseen." His calming the sea echoes Ps. 89:9–10: "You rule the raging of the sea; when its waves rise, you still them. You crushed Rahab like a carcass; you scattered your enemies with your mighty arm." This portrayal of God and so of Jesus draws on the ancient combat myth. It is reflected in the Gospel stories when Jesus speaks directly to the sea and rebukes it in the calming episode.

The other nature miracles can be explained similarly. Elijah and Elisha both raised the dead and multiplied food. In 1 Kings 17, Elijah raises a widow's son, and Jesus does the same in Luke 7. In 2 Kings 4, Elisha multiplies food. We can see just how closely the story concerning Jesus was shaped by the one about Elisha by comparing Mark and 2 Kings.

Multiplying Food: Elisha and Jesus

Mark 6:35–44	2 Kings 4:42–44
When it grew late, his disciples came to him and said, "This is a deserted place, and the hour is now very late; send them away so that they may go into the surrounding country and villages and buy something for themselves to eat." But he answered them, "You give them something to eat." They said to him, "Are we to go and buy two hundred denarii worth of bread, and give it to them to eat?" And he said to them, "How many loaves have you? Go and see." When they had found out, they said, "Five, and two fish." Then he ordered them to get all the people to sit down in groups on the green grass. So they sat down in groups of hundreds and of fifties. Taking the five loaves and the two fish, he looked up to heaven, and blessed and broke the loaves, and gave them to his disciples to set before the people; and he divided the two fish among them all. And all ate and were filled; and they took up twelve baskets full of broken pieces and of the fish. Those who had eaten the loaves numbered five thousand men.	A man came from Baal-shalishah, bringing food from the first fruits to the man of God: twenty loaves of barley and fresh ears of grain in his sack. Elisha said, "Give it to the people and let them eat." But his servant said, "How can I set this before a hundred people?" So he repeated, "Give it to the people and let them eat, for thus says the Lord, 'They shall eat and have some left.'" He set it before them, they ate, and had some left, according to the word of the Lord.

The stories share the following elements: a prophet is faced with a short-age of food to feed people; he commands his attendants to feed a crowd; the crowd is miraculously fed and satisfied; there is food left over.

When biblical stories so obviously shape a narrative about Jesus, it throws suspicion on the Jesus stories as having been composed for theological pur-poses. So some may not consider them strong grounds on which to base con-clusions about the historical Jesus. Such stories do, however, attest to the early church's desire to interpret Jesus's ministry in biblical terms, which often have eschatological overtones. The process also raises the question of whether this begins with Jesus himself. That is, we can ask whether Jesus saw his own min-istry in biblical and eschatological terms. Our analysis supports the conviction that he did. Meier's research shows that not only did Jesus consider himself to be an eschatological prophet, he also saw himself in terms of Elijah and Elisha. We know that Malachi expected Elijah to return to earth before God's great judgment in order to renew Israel. Such expectations left their mark not just on Christianity but on Judaism as well.

Jesus was a healer. Historians cannot answer the question of whether Jesus actually performed miracles. That falls outside of any historian's purview. Believers have their own answers to such questions and do not need historians to instruct them one way or the other. What historians can do is ask what Jesus and his contemporaries thought was happening. It is plain that Jesus and others believed that he was indeed doing miraculous healings.

As historians we can also ask what Jesus and his contemporaries thought his miracles signified. They attested to power seldom encountered in human beings, although Jesus was not unique as an ancient miracle worker. Our special interest is in whether Jesus would have seen his miracles as having eschatologi-cal significance. Harvey has made a persuasive case that he would have done so (1982; cf. Sanders 1985, 160–64). The miracles that Jesus chose to perform were not common—curing the blind and the lame, for example—and they were ones mentioned by Isaiah. Jesus may have made a deliberate choice to do these miracles in fulfillment of prophecies by Isaiah.

Jesus's Movement as Millenarian

Many religious phenomena occur not just in one culture or period, but in many. Cross-cultural comparison is a powerful tool for understanding religious phenom-ena, as long as differences of circumstances, culture, and history are respected. Generalizations must be grounded in specifics. Recently Allison has compellingly defended the picture of Jesus as a millenarian prophet. We reproduce below the elements of Jesus's program that Allison finds to be typically millenarian (1998b, 61–64). Practically every element listed is represented in Jesus's teach-ing and activity and in the movement that he began. A millenarian movement

- addressed the disaffected or less fortunate in a period of social change that threatened traditional ways and symbolic universes; it indeed emerged in a time of aspiration for national independence
- saw the present and near future as times of suffering and/or catastrophe
- was holistic, that is, envisaged a comprehensive righting of wrongs and promised redemption through a reversal of current circumstances
- depicted that reversal as imminent
- was both revivalistic and evangelistic
- may have promoted egalitarianism
- divided the world into two camps, the saved and the unsaved
- broke hallowed taboos associated with religious custom
- was at the same time nativistic and focused upon the salvation of the community
- replaced traditional familial and social bonds with fictive kin
- mediated the sacred through new channels
- demanded intense commitment and unconditional loyalty
- focused upon a charismatic leader
- understood its beliefs to be the product of a special revelation
- took a passive political stance in expectation of a divinely wrought deliverance
- expected a restored paradise that would return the ancestors
- insisted on the possibility of experiencing that utopia as a present reality
- grew out of a precursor movement

Conclusion

This chapter makes the case that Jesus was an eschatological, apocalyptic prophet. A process of playing down eschatological elements in Jesus's teaching is observable already in Luke and John. Through the ages and into the modern period, many Christians have not known what to do with apocalypticism. Though some have made it a central feature of their belief and social structure, many others have relegated it to secondary status. For the latter, apocalypticism is a side issue. For the former, it is central to the Christian message.

Suggestions for Further Reading

Allison, Dale C. "The Eschatology of Jesus." In *The Encyclopedia of Apocalypticism*, edited by John Joseph Collins, Bernard McGinn, and Stephen J. Stein, 2:267–302. New York: Continuum, 1998.

———. *Jesus of Nazareth: Millenarian Prophet*. Minneapolis: Fortress, 1998.

———, and Robert J. Miller. *The Apocalyptic Jesus: A Debate*. Santa Rosa: Polebridge, 2001.

Ehrman, Bart D. *Jesus: Apocalyptic Prophet of the New Millennium*. New York: Oxford University Press, 1999.

Horsley, Richard A. *Jesus and the Powers: Conflict, Covenant, and the Hope of the Poor*. Minneapolis: Fortress, 2010.

Meier, John P. *A Marginal Jew: Rethinking the Historical Jesus*. 4 vols. New York: Doubleday, 1991–2009.

Sanders, E. P. *The Historical Figure of Jesus*. New York: Penguin, 1995.

———. *Jesus and Judaism*. Philadelphia: Fortress, 1985.

10

The Apostle Paul

The New Testament contains thirteen letters attributed to Paul. Seven are accepted by everyone as authentic. The authorship of the others is debated. We use just the seven undisputed letters in this chapter as sources for Paul's own thought. The others will be treated in the next chapter. Each of the seven letters except Romans is written to a church that Paul founded. The seven are as follows:

Romans
1 Corinthians
2 Corinthians
Galatians
Philippians
1 Thessalonians
Philemon

Paul: Before and after His Call

Paul fascinates those interested in early Christianity and Christian theology more broadly. He is the second most important figure in early Christianity, after Jesus himself. His influence on history and theology was assured by the importance of his letters for Augustine (354–430 CE) and Martin Luther (1483–1546), two giants of Christian history and theology.

Paul and his theology are known through his authentic letters. Acts of the Apostles can be of some value for determining the chronology of Paul's career, but it is of little to no help in reconstructing his theology (Murphy-O'Connor 1996). Paul's letters are occasional: they address specific occasions in the churches. None presents his theology systematically. To gain an overview of Paul's thought, one must piece together a picture that transcends what he offers in any one of his letters. Of course, any such reconstruction is subject to critique and involves a good deal of interpretation. We begin by offering an overview and then go on to analyze individual letters. We focus on apocalyptic elements in Paul's thought, so ours is not a complete presentation of his theology. Since we use 1 Thessalonians extensively in our general discussion, we do not treat it separately.

Paul was a Jew of the Diaspora, born in the Hellenistic city of Tarsus in Cilicia, a region of southeast Asia Minor. His native language was Greek, and he had a good basic Greco-Roman education. He was a Pharisee and was fiercely dedicated to Torah and the traditions of his ancestors. He was very well versed in Scripture.

Paul began as an enemy of the Jesus movement, which at that point was an inner-Jewish movement. He saw it as inimical to Judaism and tried to crush it. He says in Gal. 1 that he had a vision of the risen Christ that radically changed him and caused him to join the movement and leave "Judaism" (a rare use of the term in the New Testament; the only other is in Acts 13:43). Paul's vision occurred shortly after Christ's death. Paul's earlier antagonism toward Jewish Christ-believers may have been caused by their attitude toward Torah. Some thought that gentiles could be members of Israel without obeying Torah, a position Paul himself adopts after his call, and one that the Jerusalem church confirmed, according to Acts 15. This would explain why his vision of the risen Christ, which he says caused his change of attitude (Gal. 1:13–24), so quickly became a reassessment of Torah (Phil. 3:2–11).

Some avoid the term "conversion" for Paul; he did not see himself as converting to another religion. In his description of his change of attitude and conviction toward Christ, his language recalls a prophet's commission (Gal. 1:15–16; Jer. 1:5; Isa. 49:1–6) (Stendahl 1976, 7–23; Nock 1933; Gaventa 1986). Because of his vision, Paul now had to admit Jesus was raised from the dead. That meant that believers' claims about Jesus must be true. Jesus was the Messiah. Paul had to make sense of this. Central to his thought was that Christ's coming meant that the gentiles were now to be accepted as part of God's chosen people. Through his revelation, he received a divine commission to bring this message to the gentiles. This placed him in the center of the dispute about whether gentile converts to the new movement needed to obey Torah. He was convinced that they did not. His position set him at odds not only with nonbelieving Jews but also with believers who considered Torah necessary for all believers, including gentiles. Acts 15 shows that the Jerusalem church at the time consisted entirely of Jewish believers, some of whom were Pharisees who insisted on gentile converts obeying the entire Torah.

Paul was an apocalyptic thinker, which raises the question of whether he thought in such terms before his vision. Since we have no written sources from the Pharisees, we do not know for sure whether any of them thought in apocalyptic terms. Acts of the Apostles says that when Paul appeared before the Jerusalem Sanhedrin, he instigated an argument within it by raising the issue of resurrection. Acts's author explains, "The Sadducees say that there is no resurrection, or angel, or spirit; but the Pharisees acknowledge all three" (Acts 23:8). (The Sadducees were an aristocratic party in Jerusalem associated with the high priest.) Belief in resurrection, angels, and spirits fits an apocalyptic worldview, so there may have been Pharisees who saw the world apocalyptically. Paul may have been one of them.

In this book we avoid applying the word "Christian" to Paul because he never uses the term, nor does he see believers in Christ as constituting a new religion, different from that of Israel. Instead, he speaks of those who are "in Christ," or those who believe, or those who have faith. They are brought into the fellowship of God's chosen people, the children of Abraham. In this chapter we use the term "believers" to designate those in Christ. This implies no judgment about what we would call non-Christians, especially Jews who did not believe in Christ. Paul uses the word "church" for local communities in Christ. The Greek *ekklēsia* for "church" may derive from one of the Hebrew words for Israel's assembly in the Bible: *qāhāl*.

The New Perspective on Paul

Scholars have long debated what holds together Paul's complex and often confusing theology. The doctrine of "justification by faith" has been a favorite candidate over the ages, due to Martin Luther's influence. "Justification" or "righteousness" means being right with God. It can have legal overtones— being declared innocent before the divine tribunal. According to Luther, Paul's main problem was the individual's inability to fulfill God's law and so be declared righteous or justified. God solved this by making salvation available through pure grace, apart from the law. One need only have faith, thus the Latin motto, *sola fidei*, "by faith alone." Righteousness is "imputed" to a person. The late Krister Stendahl, a Swedish-Lutheran bishop and highly esteemed biblical scholar, questioned Luther's interpretation at its roots, clearing the way for new interpretations of Paul (1963). Stendahl showed that Paul's problem was not the individual's guilty conscience but the salvation-historical issue of how to include the gentiles in God's favor. Stendahl's work marked a new beginning in Pauline studies dubbed the "new perspective" on Paul.

Some scholars have gone further with Stendahl's insights. Stendahl notes that Paul's letters are addressed to gentiles. These scholars argue that what Paul says about Torah applies only to gentiles and not to Jews. Gentiles relate to God through faith in Christ, while Jews continue to relate to God through Torah (Johnson Hodge 2007; Stowers 1994; Gager 1983). This is a logical leap that the present author does not share. Paul can say things about Torah that are generally true no matter who the audience. His statements about Torah are often so sweeping and absolute that it is difficult to see them as limited to his gentile hearers, so that he would say very different things if addressing Jews. For one thoughtful appraisal of the radical new perspective by one who appreciates its insights but has reservations, see Setzer (2005).

Paul, an Apocalyptic Thinker

A landmark in interpretation of Paul is the work of Albert Schweitzer. This is the same Schweitzer who portrayed Jesus as immersed in apocalypticism. Schweitzer's two books on Paul, *Paul and His Interpreters* (German: 1911) and *The Mysticism of Paul the Apostle* (German: 1930), insist that the proper context in which to read Paul is Jewish apocalypticism (Schweitzer 1912; 1931).

De Boer distinguishes between two types of Jewish apocalypticism found in Paul. The first is cosmological and the second forensic (1989; 1998). The first depicts the world as under the control of cosmic powers inimical to God. Examples are *1 Enoch* 1–16 (the *Book of the Watchers*) and the *Testament of Moses* 10. God will soon intervene to defeat these powers and reassert divine sovereignty. Forensic Jewish eschatology emphasizes a final judgment, conceived of in legal terms. Representatives are *4 Ezra* and *2 Baruch*. The Dead Sea Scrolls combine both views. De Boer concludes that cosmological apocalypticism is more fundamental to how Paul structures his thought but that both are present in his letters.

When Paul's vision forced him to reassess his position and decipher what Christ's resurrection meant, his explanatory framework was apocalypticism. Within this context, Christ's resurrection signaled that the end-time events had begun. Paul refers to his vision of the risen Christ as a "revelation" (*apocalypsis*; Gal. 1:12). He later receives another "revelation" ordering him to consult the Jerusalem church (Gal. 2:2). In 2 Corinthians he says that he has had numerous "visions and revelations" (*optasias kai apokalypseis*; 12:1). Paul was an apocalyptic seer, even though he never wrote an apocalypse.

The Parousia, the Eschaton

Paul has an intense interest in Jesus's second coming (*parousia*) (Plevnik 1997; 2009). He addresses it in his earliest extant letter, 1 Thessalonians, written around 51 CE to a gentile church he recently founded. Paul summarizes their new beliefs: "You turned to God from idols, to serve a living and true God, and to wait for his Son from heaven, whom he raised from the dead—Jesus, who rescues us from the wrath that is coming" (1:9–10). There are two parts to this statement. The first claim is that Paul's audience, consisting of non-Jews, were polytheists before they converted (an appropriate term since they really did switch religions). In Paul's eyes, gentiles worship stones and wood statues that are not even alive, much less divine, while Jews worship a living God. Paul's language—to turn from idols and serve "a living and true God"—echoes traditional Jewish polemic. Paul uses a traditional Jewish argument against polytheism.

The second part of Paul's statement portrays the church as awaiting Jesus's second coming and so introduces a specifically Christian note. When Jesus returns to earth from heaven he will protect the church from God's wrath, an eschatological event. Expectation of Christ's imminent second coming pervades 1 Thessalonians.

Later in the letter, Paul addresses a problem that arose in the Thessalonian church after his departure. Some church members died, but they had thought that Jesus would return from heaven while they were all still living. Paul must have left them with the impression that the parousia was very close, and that he himself did not expect such deaths. Acts and 1 Thessalonians show that Paul's stay in Thessalonika was fairly brief, and he did not have much time to answer all possible questions there. This also casts light on Paul's theological thinking—he did it while in the heat of battle, so to speak. He developed his ideas while engaging his churches' problems.

Paul explains that the dead will not miss out when Jesus comes back. On the contrary, the dead in Christ will be gathered to Christ in advance of those still living. Paul implies that he and most of his audience will be among the living when Jesus returns.

> For since we believe that Jesus died and rose again, even so, through Jesus, God will bring with him those who have died. For this we declare to you by the word of the Lord, that we who are alive, who are left until the coming [*parousia*] of the Lord, will by no means precede those who have died. For the Lord himself, with a cry of command, with the archangel's call and with the sound of God's trumpet, will descend from heaven, and the dead in Christ will rise first. Then we who are alive, who are left, will be caught up in the clouds together with them to meet the Lord in the air; and so we will be with the Lord forever. (4:14–17)

Note the eschatological trappings—a cry of command, a trumpet sound, the archangel's call. Paul attributes what he says to "the Lord," which for him always means Jesus, except when he is quoting Scripture. Paul seldom claims that his teaching originates with Jesus, but here he has concrete details from Jesus about the eschaton. This reconfirms that Jesus thought in apocalyptic terms.

In 1 Thess. 2:19, Paul tells the church that he has wanted to visit them, but Satan made it impossible. At the parousia, Paul will point to the Thessalonian church as his accomplishment (2:19). Satan is trying to ruin Paul's work.

In 1 Thess. 3:13, Paul prays that the Thessalonians may be blameless at the parousia. He says that Christ will return with all his saints, "holy ones" (3:13). In the Hebrew Bible, "saints," or "holy ones," usually means angels. Modern parlance uses it of extraordinarily holy people who have died. Paul's usage is different from both; for him it usually means everyone in Christ. Believers who have died will come back with Christ at his second coming.

Paul offers another description of the eschaton in 1 Cor. 15.

> As all die in Adam, so all will be made alive in Christ. But each in his own order: Christ the first fruits, then at his coming [*parousia*] those who belong to Christ. Then comes the end, when he hands over the kingdom to God the Father, after he has destroyed every ruler and every authority and power. For he must reign until he has put all his enemies under his feet. The last enemy to be destroyed is death. . . . When all things are subjected to him, then the Son himself will also be subjected to the one who put all things in subjection under him, so that God may be all in all. (15:22–28)

Paul lays out the order of eschatological events. First, Christ is raised. This has already happened. Then, at Christ's parousia, believers who have died will be raised. Between Christ's resurrection and the general resurrection, Christ will overcome God's cosmic enemies, the last of whom is death personified. Finally, Christ will deliver universal sovereignty to God.

The Resurrection

Paul's argument in 1 Cor. 15 concerning resurrection leads into his description of the end.

> If Christ is proclaimed as raised from the dead, how can some of you say there is no resurrection of the dead? If there is no resurrection of the dead, then Christ has not been raised; and if Christ has not been raised, then our proclamation has been in vain and your faith has been in vain. We are even found to be misrepresenting God, because we testified of God that he raised Christ—whom he did not raise if it is true that the dead are not raised. For if the dead are not raised, then Christ has not been raised. If Christ has not been raised, your faith is futile and you are still in your sins. Then those also who have died in Christ have perished. If for this life only we have hoped in Christ, we are of all people most to be pitied. But in fact Christ has been raised from the dead, the first fruits of those who have died. (1 Cor. 15:12–20)

Paul, disturbed that the Corinthians do not believe in general resurrection, writes awkwardly and repetitively. He does so to leave no room for misinterpretation because the issue is so important. His basic point is that Christ's resurrection makes no sense apart from the apocalyptic concept of general resurrection.

The Corinthians have difficulty with the idea of bodily resurrection. Plato considered the body a prison for the soul. Release from the body brought freedom. Stoicism held that at death a person's *logos* (reason, intellectual individuality, soul) rejoined the universal *Logos* and individuality was lost. Corinthian believers did not accept any resurrection beyond that of Jesus, which was unique.

Paul explains that the risen body, though continuous with the bodies humans have now, is also different. Resurrection bodies will be spiritual. This seems a contradiction until we realize that "spiritual" has a different meaning for the ancients than for moderns. Spiritual does not mean nonmaterial. It can be a different, much finer kind of material. Paul uses the analogy of a "dead" seed becoming a living plant to express at once the continuity and discontinuity of the old body with the new (Engberg-Pedersen 2010).

Two Worlds

Belief in two worlds—the present world and the world to come—is central to apocalypticism (De Boer 1989; Hanson 1976b; Vielhauer 1965; Russell 1964). The present world is alienated from God. It is dominated by cosmic forces hostile to God—Satan and his minions, for example—or by human sin, as in *4 Ezra* or *2 Baruch*. Because it is alienated from God, the present world has many faults—including sickness, death, social strife, sin, and disobedience to God. The future world undoes the present world. Everything wrong with the present world is repaired in the new. The world to come is under God's sovereignty.

As Paul sees things after his revelation (Gal. 1:16), all humanity apart from Christ is alienated from God. Therefore, all humanity needs redemption. No one can escape this world on his or her own. If Paul had an apocalyptic viewpoint before his revelation, then his mistake was to think that through the Torah Israel could be right with God, despite the world's fallen nature. He would be vindicated at God's coming. Paul's vision compelled him to modify his view. If God raised Jesus from the dead, then his old way of thinking was inadequate, because it had no role for Jesus.

Despite the fact that for Paul the end time had begun, the world remained mostly the same. This anomaly became a major wrinkle in Christian adaptations of Jewish apocalyptic thinking. Paul confronted a world that looked like the old world; yet, despite appearances, definitive changes had taken place. One concise theological way of summarizing the problem is the dichotomy "already/not yet." Some eschatological things were already present, and some were not yet here. Another is "eschatological reservation," the idea that although certain eschatological events had already transpired, crucial events were yet to come.

Figures one and two illustrate our overview of Paul's thought. Figure one schematizes salvation history, while figure two shows Jesus as the way between the old and new worlds.

Fig. 12. Pauline theology.

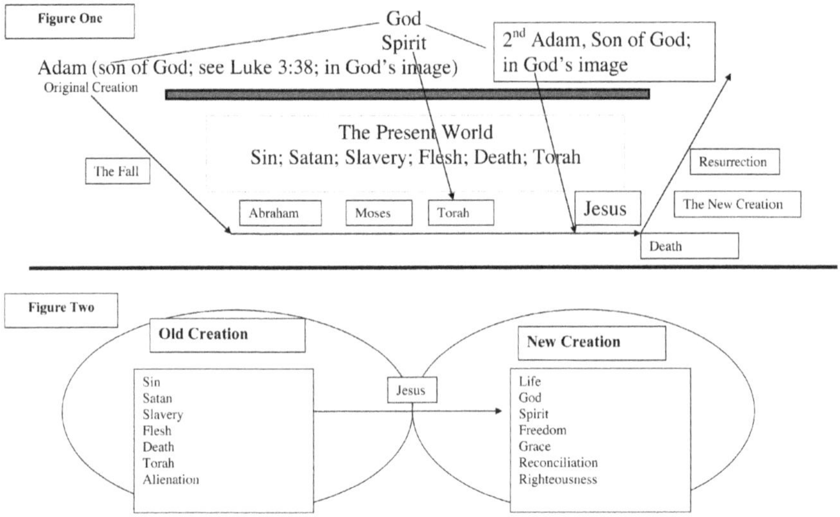

Adam Christology

Adam Christology figures largely in Paul's thought, and it is tightly interwoven with his apocalyptic convictions. We explain Adam Christology here; a fuller understanding of it will emerge as we go through his letters (Barrett 1962; Hooker 1990; Murphy-O'Connor 2009).

True to his concentration on Scripture, Paul looks to Genesis to understand what is wrong with the world and what role Adam played in bringing about a situation not intended by God. Paul's reading of Genesis is as follows. In the beginning, God created Adam and the rest of creation as he wanted them to be. Adam was in a right relationship with God. He was in the image of God (Gen. 1:27). Although Paul does not use the phrase here, Adam was a "son of God." (Paul does use the term "sons of God" for those in a proper relationship with God in Rom 8. Luke 3:38 calls Adam a son of God.)

Adam received a single command from God—not to eat of the tree of the knowledge of good and evil—and he disobeyed. As a result, he was banished from the Garden of Eden. This meant entering the world humans now inhabit. Circumstances in this world are not as God originally planned. It is deeply flawed. Genesis 3 enumerates changes that Adam and Eve, the serpent, and even the earth endure. The section reads like a description of the world all humans know, full of pain and toil and ending in death. Because of Adam's disobedience, the very earth is cursed. Humans must struggle to make it produce. Most importantly, death enters the world. Paul implies that Adam is no longer in God's image. The Dead Sea Scrolls speak of those who become right with God regaining the "glory of Adam," meaning Adam as he was before the fall. Paul's thought is similar.

Since Paul combines forensic and cosmological apocalyptic thinking, he easily slips from the forensic model to a cosmological one. Death becomes a cosmic, personal force. The same happens with sin, which becomes a cosmic force functionally equivalent to Satan. Note that Paul speaks of "sin" more often than "sins." Rather, he speaks of sin, a personal power that holds humanity in its grasp.

The world humans inhabit is a deeply distorted version of the one God created. But through the Christ-event, God made it possible for humans to regain what Adam lost. ("Christ-event" is a convenient theological shorthand for what Christians believe has happened in Christ.) God, through Christ, creates a new world.

Paul's list of adjectives, nouns, and phrases characterizing the present world is long and rich (Patte 1983). Figures one and two list some of those terms. In this world, humans are enslaved to Satan, sin, death, and the flesh. They are alienated from God. In this context, "flesh" does not mean body as opposed to soul. The origin of this use of "flesh" is biblical. The Bible sometimes speaks of "flesh and blood" to emphasize the distance between God and humans. Paul goes beyond biblical usage by interpreting "flesh" apocalyptically, to indicate humanity radically alienated from God. "Flesh" is the first of the two apocalyptic worlds.

In Christ, God has accomplished a new creation. Christ is the new Adam, and those in Christ are a new humanity. The new world is already present to believers, but the old world has not yet passed away. Proof that the new world is present is the presence of the Spirit. "Spirit" means God's active presence, another common biblical image.

Things are soon to change definitively. The present world will end. The world to come will reverse all that is bad about the present world. This is the meaning of Paul's flesh/spirit dichotomy.

The New Adam

God could not tolerate forever the state of affairs caused by Adam's sin. The solution was to start anew. God would create a new Adam to inaugurate a new humanity. The new Adam would be without sin, as the old Adam had begun. Since the new Adam was not in the image of the old, and since the new Adam was sinless, he did not deserve to live in the world that resulted from Adam's sin. God commanded him to enter that fallen world anyway.

Jesus obeyed. By obeying, he subjected himself to slavery to sin and death. By carrying through his obedience to the last, he became the head of a new humanity, one characterized by obedience.

The new Adam undid what the old Adam had done, so Paul conceived of the new Adam's activity as analogous to but antithetical to the first Adam's act. As disobedience resulted in alienation from God, so obedience would result in being set right with God. This is the same as justification, which is also righteousness, being reconciled to God, and being in the new creation. As death entered the world through a human being, so the possibility of life entered through a human being (1 Cor. 15). There are now two creations and two humanities, at the head of each of which is a human being (Barrett 1962). Each humanity is descended from one of the two Adams.

Each person now decides which humanity to belong to (Murphy-O'Connor 2009). One can remain in the old Adam or join the new humanity of the new Adam. To be "in Christ," Paul's characteristic way of designating believers, means to be in the new Adam. Of course, this involves ancient conceptions of what it means to be human that do not sit easily with modern ways of thinking. While we often think in individualistic terms, the ancients tend to think in terms of groups (Malina 1981, 51–70). Paul thinks broadly about different sorts of humanities.

By entering this world, Jesus became a slave to sin and death, even though he was innocent. When Jesus died, he left this world behind. God vindicated him by raising him from the dead. By his death he left the old creation, and by his resurrection he entered the new. He reentered a perfect relationship with God. He was made right with God again. He regained his divine sonship. He reattained the image of God. He regained what Adam had lost, including lordship—Adam was meant to rule over the earth, while Jesus became Lord of all.

Through Jesus's death and resurrection, God brought the new creation into existence. Others get there by dying and rising with Christ. Christ's death and resurrection is the road by which he left this world and entered the next, and he opened up this route for others. In baptism, believers die with Christ (Rom. 6). They leave this world. They are dead to it. However, they have not yet been raised. They have not definitively entered the future world. Believers are in-between. What they do not yet possess has been dubbed the "eschatological reservation."

Paul expects a general resurrection and a last judgment, when God's wrath (*orgē*) at sin will be unleashed. Wrath is a technical, apocalyptic term (1 Thess. 1:10). When Christ returns, he will save believers from eschatological wrath. Salvation is future, and Paul usually (with few exceptions) puts the verb "to save" in the future tense.

Paul adapts the idea of the two worlds by making them coexist in the lives of Christians. Believers struggle to stay in the new creation and to battle the effects of the old creation in themselves and in their communities. In this sense, Paul's thought parallels that of Qumran (*Community Rule* 3–4).

The New Adam and General Resurrection

In 1 Cor. 15, Paul argues with Corinthians who do not believe in general resurrection. There is no indication that they do not believe in Jesus's resurrection. Paul's argument, examined in more detail below, is that the two are inextricably related. As he says, "As all die in Adam, so all will be made alive in Christ" (1 Cor. 15:22). He thinks of resurrection as part of Adam Christology.

Some Corinthians cannot conceive of bodily resurrection because they cannot imagine what a resurrected body would be like (1 Cor. 15:35). Paul explains that it is continuous with this body but is very different. He eloquently expresses the relationship by the metaphor of a seed, apparently dead, which turns into a living plant. The two are very different, but one comes from the other. Humans do receive new bodies, but they are of a radically different nature than their former, mortal bodies. He shows himself a citizen of the Greco-Roman world by claiming that there are different sorts of bodies that can be observed even now. Human bodies are different from heavenly bodies like the sun, moon, and stars. The heavenly luminaries are also sentient, bodily, personal beings—angels—but they have little in common with human bodies.

Within this argument, Paul again resorts to Adam Christology. As mortal bodies are transformed into spiritual bodies (remembering that "spiritual" does not mean immaterial), humans are similarly transformed when passing from the old Adam to the new.

> Thus it is written, "The first man, Adam, became a living being"; the last Adam became a life-giving spirit. But it is not the spiritual that is first, but the physical, and then the spiritual. The first man was from the earth, a man of dust; the second man is from heaven. As was the man of dust, so are those who are of the dust; and as is the man of heaven, so are those who are of heaven. Just as we have borne the image of the man of dust, we will also bear the image of the man of heaven. (1 Cor. 15:45–49)

Again Paul depends on Genesis. When God breathed into Adam, the creature of dust became a living being (Gen. 2:7). Jesus, on the other hand, did not come to be in this way. Paul leaves us a bit in the dark here, but he must have some notion of Jesus being created apart from the alienated world and then sent into it, becoming flesh and even becoming sin (2 Cor. 5:21). So he originated in heaven with God. When he was born, died, and rose, he became the way to God for all. In that sense, he was a life-giving being. By being in Christ, humans live forever. Adam came first, the new Adam came later. This contradicts an ancient metaphysical view, that of Platonism, for example, that the physical is modeled on the spiritual and therefore derives from it. Spiritual comes first and then physical. In the case of the two Adams, the order is reversed. The old Adam came first, and the new Adam has come much later. Being in the old Adam or the new Adam relates to whether one is physical or spiritual. But we know that for humans to be spiritual they must have the Spirit of Christ, and if they do, they are in Christ and in the new world. In language not entirely typical of Paul, he turns this dichotomy into one contrasting earth (dust) and heaven (home of God's Spirit), but this is because he is influenced by Adam being made of the dust of the earth.

Finally, Paul bumps up against his already/not yet tension. In other contexts, he says believers are already dead to the old world and living in the new; they are no longer in the flesh but are in the Spirit. Nonetheless, he never says that we are already raised. That is part of the eschatological reservation. Similarly, here he refuses to say that we are in the image of the new Adam. That is still future. Some of it is clarified by our discussion of God's image below.

God's Image

Adam Christology in Paul is associated with the word "image [*eikōn*]." The following list collects the instances of Paul's usage of the word, omitting only Rom. 1:23, which does not pertain to our topic.

> For those whom he foreknew he also predestined to be conformed to the image of his Son, in order that he might be the firstborn within a large family. (Rom. 8:29)
> For a man ought not to have his head veiled, since he is the image and reflection of God; but woman is the reflection of man. (1 Cor. 11:7)
> Just as we have borne the image of the man of dust, we will also bear the image of the man of heaven. (1 Cor. 15:49)
> And all of us, with unveiled faces, seeing the glory of the Lord as though reflected in a mirror, are being transformed into the same image from one degree of glory to another; for this comes from the Lord, the Spirit. (2 Cor. 3:18)
> In their case the god of this world has blinded the minds of the unbelievers, to keep them from seeing the light of the gospel of the glory of Christ, who is the image of God. (2 Cor. 4:4)

Paul explicitly uses "image" in the context of Adam Christology in 1 Cor. 15:49. Adam was created in God's image, according to Gen. 1:26–27. When Adam disobeyed, he lost God's image. God made a fresh start, creating a new Adam, Christ, who was in God's image. When God commanded him to forego the advantages of being in such a state and to enter the fallen world brought into being by Adam's disobedience, Christ did so to such an extent that Paul can speak of him as having *become* sin (2 Cor. 5:21). In this state, he could not be in God's image. Paul could not be stronger about Jesus completely and genuinely entering this world enslaved to sin. Christ then died to this world and rose into the new, regaining the image of God.

The already/not yet of Paul's apocalyptic thought is a factor in Paul's concept of believers' relation to God's image. He says that they "have borne" (past) the image of the old Adam, and they "will bear" (future) the image of the new (1 Cor. 15:49). In baptism, believers are no longer in Adam's image. Paul is reticent to say explicitly that they are already in Christ's image, since he always has in mind the eschatological reservation—what has not yet happened. Paul leaves believers' present situation ambiguous, at least as concerns their being in God's image.

God wishes to bring humanity into the image of the new Adam and so into God's own image: "For those whom he foreknew he also predestined to be conformed to the image of his Son, in order that he might be the firstborn within a large family" (Rom. 8:29). Christ is the Son of God, so to be in Christ's image is to be a child of God. This makes all Christ-believers one large family, with Christ as "firstborn," the first to rise from the dead into the new world. It is Christ's resurrection that makes him a Son of God. This agrees with Rom. 1:4: Christ "was declared to be Son of God with power according to the spirit of holiness by resurrection from the dead."

Second Corinthians 3:18 presents the process of conforming to Christ's image as gradual and perhaps even mystical. As believers contemplate Christ's image, they are transformed into it. Life in Christ is in one sense a once-for-all affair. Dying with Christ in baptism moves one from the old world to the new. Nonetheless, experience teaches that before one literally dies and is raised from the dead, one lives in both worlds and is in danger of sliding back into the old world.

The word "image" occurs also in 1 Cor. 11 where Paul discusses proper attire for women in liturgical gatherings. Paul insists that women should cover their heads and that men should not. Paul combines arguments of various sorts in this passage, and we need not unravel the entire complex. We trace only what relates to our examination of "image." In 11:3, Paul says, "But I want you to understand that Christ is the head of every man, and the husband is the head of his wife, and God is the head of Christ" (11:3). Paul then says that it is disgraceful for a man to pray or prophesy with a head covering, and it is equally disgraceful for a woman to do the same with an uncovered head. He says, "For a man ought not to have his head veiled, since he is the image and reflection (eikōn kai doxa) of God; but woman is the reflection (doxa) of man" (11:7). Doxa, translated "reflection" here, actually means "glory," a word frequently applied to God and God's world and common in apocalyptic contexts.

This passage places in parallel being in the image of someone and being someone's head. Tying the two together, Paul could have said that Christ is in the image of God, men are in the image of Christ, and women are in the image of men. The last statement might be suggested to Paul by Genesis. He could have assumed that Gen. 1 means that humanity, though a unity, consists of male and female, and given the order of the words in the text, men come first. Or he could be influenced by the second creation story, where Eve is made from Adam's rib. The latter is supported by 1 Cor. 11:8, where he says that woman was created from man. We examine that passage below.

The last passage concerning image (2 Cor. 4:4) occurs in the same context as does the one about being gradually transformed into Christ's image. It is polemical; Paul argues that his opponents do not understand his gospel because they are incapable of perceiving the glory of God in the risen Christ, who is in God's image. Their failure results from their being blinded by "the god of this world." Again, in the end, Paul appeals to apocalyptic perception.

Paul's Letters

This section examines Paul's letters to determine the role of apocalypticism in his thought. The structure of Paul's letters is as follows (Doty 1973):

Salutation
Writer(s)
Addressee(s)
Greetings
Thanksgiving
Prayer
Body
Final Greetings

The three parts of the salutation, usually very brief in a Hellenistic letter, are often expanded by Paul to foreshadow or even begin the argument of the letter. Paul's salutation often contains significant characterizations of the sender and receiver. Paul's greetings, which usually combine Hellenistic and Jewish elements, also serve to begin Paul's argument. The usual Hellenistic greeting *chairein*, meaning something like "be well" or "be healthy," is changed by Paul to the similar-sounding *charis*, meaning "grace" or "gift." "Grace" epitomizes Paul's gospel, since it means God's free gift of favor through Christ. To this Paul adds "peace," a typically Jewish greeting. Likewise, Paul can modify the usually short thanksgiving, prayer, body, and final greetings to help convey his message.

Galatians

Galatians is addressed to a gentile church founded by Paul. Other missionaries arrived there after him and advocated the view that the Galatians must obey the Torah, or at least parts of it. Scholars sometimes call these missionaries "Judaizers," echoing Paul's language, which refers to them as those who would impose on the Galatians Jewish customs and laws (2:14; *ioudaizein*). Their position contradicts Paul's certitude that being righteous, that is, being in the right relationship with God, comes from faith in what God has done through Christ. Paul claims that if people could have overcome their alienation from God through obedience to Torah, then the death of Christ would have been unnecessary (2:21). Paul sets up a stark contrast between Torah and faith in Christ throughout the letter (Tobin 2004, 64–70). Justification, theoretically, comes from one or the other, but not both. For Paul, it can come only through Christ.

Paul's attitude toward Torah is one of the thorniest issues in his theology (Dunn 1990; Sanders 1977; Räisänen 1983; Tomson 1990). His basic theological dilemma is that he believes that the Torah is God-given, good, and spiritual. It is for him a vital source of information about what God thinks. Nonetheless, since his vision of the risen Christ, he no longer believes that Torah is able to overcome the alienation between God and humans created by Adam's sin. That can be done only in Christ. So, then, what function does the Torah serve? Whatever else Torah does, it does not liberate from the slavery of the present world. Torah-obedient Jews not in Christ still inhabit a world alienated from God; they are behind the barrier that separates the fallen world from God (Betz 1992, 874–75; Gombis 2007).

Paul's apocalyptic outlook underlies his argument in Galatians. In presenting the "apocalyptic gospel" of Galatians, Martyn points to three apocalyptic elements that are important to the letter—the two-world idea, God's intervention into the world to bring redemption, and the concept of a crucified cosmos and a new creation (Martyn 2000; 1985). We examine Galatians to see how these and other apocalyptic elements contribute to Paul's argument.

In Galatians Paul alters the usual Hellenistic greetings:

> Paul an apostle—sent neither by human commission nor from human authorities, but through Jesus Christ and God the Father, who raised him from the dead—and all the members of God's family who are with me, To the churches of Galatia: Grace to you and peace from God our Father and the Lord Jesus Christ, who gave himself for our sins to set us free from the present evil age, according to the will of our God and Father, to whom be the glory forever and ever. Amen. (1:1–5)

A faction in the Jerusalem church believed that all believers should obey Torah (see Acts 15), a position Paul vigorously rejects. Part of Paul's argument against this is to deny any subordination to the Jerusalem church. He denies categorically that he owes his apostolic commission to any human, not even to the Jerusalem church or its leaders; it is directly from Jesus and God, who raised Jesus from the dead. His commission and his gospel came from a direct "revelation" (*apokalypsis*) of Jesus Christ (1:11–12), disclosing the apocalyptic mechanism by which he has his information. Paul concludes his lengthy self-characterization by saying that the letter comes not just from him but from "all the members of God's family" with him, a reminder to the Galatians that they are not just individual believers, nor is Paul an isolated voice, but all are members of a single family who must share the same views.

Paul outlines the gospel revealed to him. The grace and peace he offers come from "the Lord Jesus Christ, who gave himself for our sins to set us free from the present evil age, according to the will of our God and Father" (1:3–4). If Jesus liberated the Galatians "from the present evil age," then Torah had nothing to do with it.

In 1:11–2:10, Paul proves his independence of the Jerusalem church. He narrates his own commissioning by the risen Christ, which took place through a "revelation [*apokalypsis*] of Jesus Christ" (1:12), totally apart from any contact with Jerusalem. Paul says that he had been an exemplary follower of Torah and of his fathers' traditions (perhaps Pharisaic), but that God "called me through his grace [*charis*], and was pleased to reveal [*apokalypsai*] his Son to me, so that I might proclaim him among the Gentiles" (1:15–16). Apart from a brief two-week visit to Jerusalem, Paul carried on his gentile mission for many years without contact with the Jerusalem leaders. Then he received a "revelation [*apokalypsis*]" to go to Jerusalem to consult with them (2:2). They accepted his Torah-free gospel to the gentiles, although there were some Jerusalem believers who disagreed (2:7–10). True to his apocalyptic views, Paul insists that he acts according to special revelations.

Paul insists on his independence from Jerusalem, but he does ultimately go there to make sure that his message and that of the Jerusalem church coincide, so his stance toward them is ambivalent (2:1–2). He wants his gospel to be acknowledged by the whole church, lest schism cast doubt on his gospel and harm the churches. It is noteworthy that both in his original commission and in his subsequent dealings with the Jerusalem church he explicitly relies on revelations from God. He went to Jerusalem because God told him to do so. Paul's apocalyptic outlook applies not just to his doctrine but also to his actions. God's direct revelations to him not only make him think differently, they also direct and sustain his missionary efforts.

Betz discerns the structure of a legal argument in Galatians. After narrating the facts of the case (chaps.1–2), Paul states his proposition (2:15–21) and then brings forth proofs for it (3:1–4:31) (Betz 1992; Tobin 2004, 64–70). In the proposition, Paul sets up an either/or contrast between Torah and faith as the way to be "justified," that is, to be in God's favor. In the narration leading to the proposition, he tells of his interactions with the Jerusalem church and then recalls a confrontation between himself and Peter at Antioch. There he castigated Peter for separating himself from gentile believers for a meal so as not to offend Jewish Christians who had come from James, head of the Jerusalem church. He calls these people the "circumcision faction." He tells Peter in what amounts to the proposition of his legal argument,

> We ourselves are Jews by birth and not Gentile sinners; yet we know that a person is justified not by the works of the law but through faith in Jesus Christ. And we have come to believe in Christ Jesus, so that we might be justified by faith in Christ, and not by doing the works of the law, because no one will be justified by the works of the law. (2:15–16)

At the end of the proposition, he says forcefully, "I do not nullify the grace of God; for if justification comes through the law, then Christ died for nothing" (2:21).

Paul proves his proposition by six arguments (Tobin 2004, 64–70). The first appeals to the Galatians' own experience (3:1–5). When they originally heard Paul's message, they received the Spirit, observable through the occurrence of miracles in their midst. The Spirit signals the presence of the new age. Their possession of the Spirit had nothing to do with Torah.

Paul's next argument is based on Scripture (3:6–14). In Gen. 15:6, he finds that Abraham "believed God, and it was reckoned to him as righteousness" (Gal. 3:6). How can Abraham be righteous if he lives in the old world? Paul answers, "The scripture, foreseeing that God would justify [make righteous] the gentiles by faith, declared the gospel beforehand to Abraham, saying, 'All the Gentiles shall be blessed in you'" (3:8). In this amazing statement, Paul makes Abraham an exception to all those trapped in this alienated world. He has an anticipatory (proleptic) possession of righteousness because the gospel has been preached to him and he has believed. This makes him like later believers—or rather, it makes them like him. In the ancient world, one was thought to be like one's ancestor (Johnson Hodge 2007). Abraham's righteousness is not due to his obedience to Torah, which itself did not come until centuries later, but is based on his belief in the gospel. The same is true for Galatian believers. Those in Christ have become like Abraham through faith in the gospel, and so they are designated his offspring (3:7). They have become part of the chosen people, who have Abraham as their father.

The second part of this argument contrasts the blessings available through faith with the curse to which are subject all who live under Torah (3:10–14). This is one of the most difficult passages in Paul's letters (Gombis 2007). Paul reads Deut. 27:26, which threatens a curse on those who do not obey all of Torah, as characterizing the Torah in general. Through the word "curse," Paul connects this passage to Deut. 21:23, which says that a person hung on a tree (a form of crucifixion) is cursed. Since Jesus was crucified, he has taken on himself the law's curse. The curse no longer hangs over the heads of those with faith because it has already been taken on and therefore disarmed by

Jesus. To take on Torah would be to return to the curse. It would be to move from the new world of blessing to the old world of alienation.

Paul's next argument relies on rules of inheritance (3:15–18). The Torah was given to Israel 430 years after Abraham, so it could not change the condition upon which the promise given to Abraham was based—faith. The promise is an inheritance of Abraham's descendants. Not even circumcision, enjoined on Abraham in Gen. 17, could qualify the promise, for it came after Abraham's faith and declaration of righteousness. Paul further argues that the biblical promises are to Abraham's "seed," a singular noun, so the recipient is one, not many, and so it must be Christ.

Paul's next arguments are more explicitly apocalyptic. Torah is from God, so Paul must account for its purpose. Galatians 3:19–4:11 can be read as one long argument that struggles to reconcile the divine origin of Torah with its being unable to deliver humanity from the slavery of the old world.

Paul sometimes employs the rhetorical device of diatribe to lay out the full implications of his arguments. In diatribe, a fictive dialogue partner asks questions and raises objections to the author's arguments. In 3:19, this partner asks, "Why then the law?" It is an obvious question, since the law is powerless to deliver humanity from slavery in the old world. Paul answers that Torah was "added because of transgressions, until the offspring would come to whom the promise had been made" (3:19). The answer could mean that the law kept humans within reasonable bounds of behavior. Or it could mean that Torah would show the need for liberation. In any case, Torah cannot interfere with the promise given to Abraham on the basis of faith. The law was never capable of "making alive," of bringing righteousness. It could never spring the apocalyptic trap in which humanity found itself.

Paul's interlocutor is not satisfied. He objects, "Is the law then opposed to the promises of God?" (3:21). This provokes Paul's strong reaction: "Certainly not!" Still, by raising the question, Paul admits that such a conclusion might seem logical. Put apocalyptically, is it possible that the Torah might actually prevent one from entering the new world? On one level, the answer is "Yes." The entire letter makes this point. However, this would happen only if one were to make the mistake that has been refuted in the proposition (2:15–16). The law was never the way to fulfillment of God's promises. To think that it was would be to cancel out faith in Christ. It is an either/or proposition. Before his call, Paul thought pleasing God meant obeying Torah. Now he knows that the only way to gain God's favor and so be justified is through faith in Christ. "If a law had been given that could make alive, then righteousness would indeed come through the law" (3:21). In the alienated world, Torah cannot do what it seems it ought to do. The law was never able to "make alive," to "make righteous."

So then, what was Torah's real purpose? Paul says that Scripture revealed the true state of things, that everything was "imprisoned . . . under the power of sin, so that what was promised through faith in Jesus Christ might be given to those who believe" (3:22). In this sense, the Torah itself is an apocalyptic revelation, if read correctly. To get the full import of this statement, one must realize that "faith" (*pistis*) and "to believe" (*pisteuein*) come from the same root. "To believe" means "to have faith." Paul uses these words in relation to faith in what God has done in Christ, not in some less specific sense, such as belief in the existence of God. Obviously, Jews believe in God, so "faith" cannot mean simply this. If Torah had not left humanity imprisoned under sin, there would have been no occasion for faith in Christ, for the content of that faith is that God has freed us through Christ.

Paul continues in the same vein: "Now before faith came, we were imprisoned and guarded under the law until faith would be revealed [*apokalyphthēnai*]" (3:23). Since faith is faith in Christ, it was not possible until Christ came. Jewish life before "faith," meaning before acceptance of what God did in Jesus, amounted to being guarded like children under the care of a *paidagōgos*, a slave whose job it was to protect and discipline children until they became adults. That job is now unnecessary. Faith has "been revealed." All of this can be known only through direct revelation.

Before Jesus, those under the law were "enslaved to the elemental spirits of the world" (4:3). "Elemental spirits" (*stoicheia*) refers to superhuman powers. Such powers include the gods and goddesses previously worshiped by Paul's hearers (Tobin 2004, 66). Believers are now free of those powers because God sent Jesus "to redeem those under the law, so that we might receive adoption as children. God has sent the Spirit of his Son into our hearts, crying, 'Abba! Father!' So you are no longer a slave but a child, and if a child then also an heir, through God" (4:5–7).

Jesus was born "under the Torah" so that he could "redeem [*exagorazō*] those under the Torah." What does Paul mean by "redemption"? And why would someone under the Torah need it? The verb contains the root *agora*, which denotes the main marketplace of a Hellenistic city. Jesus has "purchased" those enslaved to the elemental spirits of the universe. His use of this verb is prompted by the image of slavery. The elemental spirits are cosmic powers. Humans are enslaved to them. Christ has purchased them.

It is shocking that Paul equates deliverance from the elemental spirits of the universe with liberation from Torah. How could Paul draw such an outrageous equivalence? It makes sense only if read in the context of the radical change Paul experienced under the influence of special revelations. Only these could possibly have had the power to alter his view of Torah so profoundly. They did not change his conviction that Torah is God-given. But they did lead to his thorough reappraisal of Torah's function, and he sketches that function with the aid of his apocalyptic worldview.

The result of humans being purchased from slavery is that they become "sons of God." We retain a literal translation of the Greek *huioi tou theou* rather than the more inclusive (and accurate) "children of God" to highlight the connections between Paul's usage in different contexts. For example, believers are sons of God as Jesus is Son of God. The word "sons" ultimately must be read as inclusive of women and men both. God is redeemed humanity's Father.

The next section of Paul's argument charges the Galatian community with desiring something that will push them back into the old world. They were once enslaved to "beings that by nature are not gods" (4:8). Through Christ, they have escaped. Now they wish to go back. Certainly they do not think of it this way. They do not understand how Paul can equate their desire to obey Torah with their former life of polytheism. He argues that when they want to celebrate the days, months, seasons, and years of the Jewish liturgy, they are looking to improve their relationship to God. That very wish demonstrates that they do not really understand how they got into the proper relationship with God in the first place, and their lack of understanding endangers their status.

In 4:21–31, Paul offers a sixth proof—an allegorical interpretation of a biblical passage. He begins, "Tell me, you who desire to be subject to the law, will you not listen to the law?" (4:21). He then allegorically interprets the story of Abraham's two sons, Isaac, born to his free wife Sarah, and Ishmael, born to Sarah's slave Hagar. It is really the story of two covenants. "Covenant" (Greek: *diathēkē*; Hebrew: *běrît*) means "agreement" or "pact" between two parties. It is one of the main ways the Bible conceptualizes the relationship between humanity and God. Paul says that the covenant associated with Hagar denotes the earthly Jerusalem of his day—non-Christ-believing Judaism. She and her children are in slavery. Sarah represents the heavenly Jerusalem; Paul and his hearers are her children and are free. They have a new covenant with God.

Paul concludes, "So then, friends, we are children, not of the slave but of the free woman. For freedom Christ has set us free. Stand firm, therefore, and do not submit again to a yoke of slavery. Listen! I, Paul, am telling you that if you let yourselves be circumcised, Christ will be of no benefit to you" (4:31–5:2). Receiving circumcision, the sign of the old covenant, is to relinquish freedom and accept slavery again, because the old covenant belongs to the old world. The word "again" is important. Accepting circumcision is a return to slavery. They will have slipped back into the old world. Ironically, their end position would be equivalent to their starting position. Slavery to superhuman powers is the same as obedience to Torah.

Paul now gets quite heated about circumcision, and he utters several statements that clarify things further.

> For in Christ Jesus neither circumcision nor uncircumcision counts for anything; the only thing that counts is faith working through love. (5:6)

"In Christ" is equivalent to being in the new world. There, circumcision counts for nothing. The new world is characterized by "freedom." Paul warns that this means freedom both from Torah and from the cosmic powers. It does not mean that one can do whatever one wants. Believers ought to be "slaves to one another" by loving one another. They ought to walk according to the Spirit and not according to the flesh.

Paul lays out the "obvious" behaviors that characterize the flesh and those that are typical of the Spirit. He sums them up by saying, "If we live by the Spirit, let us also be guided by the Spirit" (5:25). If we are truly members of the new creation, we must act that way.

The Flesh: Behaviors	The Spirit: Behaviors
Fornication, impurity, licentiousness, idolatry, sorcery, enmity, strife, jealousy, anger, quarrels, dissensions, factions, envy, drunkenness, carousing, and things like these (5:19–21)	Love, joy, peace, patience, kindness, generosity, faithfulness, gentleness, and self-control (5:22–23)

> It is those who want to make a good showing in the flesh that try to compel you to be circumcised—only that they may not be persecuted for the cross of Christ. Even the circumcised do not themselves obey the law, but they want you to be circumcised so that they may boast about your flesh. May I never boast of anything except the cross of our Lord Jesus Christ, by which the world has been crucified to me, and I to the world. For neither circumcision nor uncircumcision is anything; but a new creation is everything! As for those who will follow this rule—peace be upon them, and mercy, and upon the Israel of God. (6:12–16)

If circumcision would allow Paul's hearers to avoid persecution, perhaps it is a case of them wanting to appear as Jews to Roman or local authorities. Judaism was accepted in the Roman Empire. Christianity occupied an ambiguous status, and that occasionally caused them problems.

Paul insists that he has left the old world and entered the new. He does this by the vivid image of being crucified with Christ (6:14; cf. 2:19). In 2:19 he says that he is crucified to the law, and in 6:14 that he is crucified to the world and the world to him. There can be no clearer statement of transfer from the old world to the new, which, ironically, for Paul is equivalent to saying that he is dead to the law and the law to him. Paul's list of behaviors characterizing the two worlds recalls the similar lists at Qumran that characterize the lot of God and the lot of Belial (*Community Rule* 4).

Binary Opposites in Galatians Describing the Two Worlds

The Old (Fallen) World	The New World
Flesh	Spirit
World	In Christ
Slavery	Freedom
Slavery	Redeemed (bought back)

The Old (Fallen) World	The New World
Torah (circumcision; feasts)	Freedom from Torah
Works of the Torah	Faith
Works of the Torah	Grace
Death	Life
Satan	God
Being ungodly	Being justified (made righteous)
World	New creation

Romans

Six of the seven authentic Pauline letters are to churches Paul founded. Romans is the sole exception. Paul wrote to Rome because he wanted to extend his mission to the western part of the empire, and he wanted to make sure that he had the support of the church at Rome. For that reason, he explained his gospel to them. This letter comes closest of all of Paul's epistles to a complete explanation of that gospel (Stendahl 1993; Tobin 2004; Fitzmyer 1993; Stowers 1994).

The argument in Romans can be divided into several main parts. In chapters 1–4, Paul proves that all humanity, Jew and gentile, has failed to be right with God. God rectified this in Christ, through whom justification is available to everyone. In chapters 5–8, he discusses believers' present situation (justification) and what the future holds (salvation). In chapters 9–11, Paul takes up the question of unbelieving Israel. In the rest of the letter Paul engages in parenesis, that is, moral teaching and exhortation. The role of chapter 16 has been disputed, since it occupies different spots in the letter in different manuscripts, but we take it as the epistolary conclusion.

Paul's apocalyptic gospel (chaps. 1–4). Paul begins his letter with a statement of the gospel that sounds different from how he usually puts it, so he is probably drawing on tradition. A few verses further along he restates the gospel in his own terms. Paul begins with a more traditional formulation because he wants to assure his hearers that he subscribes to accepted Christian belief. But he also adapts that profession of faith to his own theology, which is heavily informed by his apocalyptic idea of two worlds.

> Paul, a servant of Jesus Christ, called to be an apostle, set apart for the gospel of God, which he promised beforehand through his prophets in the holy scriptures, the gospel concerning his Son, who was descended from David according to the flesh and was declared to be Son of God with power according to the spirit of holiness by resurrection from the dead, Jesus Christ our Lord. (1:1–4)

God's gospel, his plan to save humanity, was promised in advance by the biblical prophets. Paul makes little of Jesus's Davidic lineage in his letters, so we may consider this a traditional element, that is, it is something he has inherited from the tradition, not peculiar to his own thought. Davidic lineage is "according to the flesh" while Jesus's sonship is "according to the spirit of holiness." This makes Davidic lineage relatively unimportant, since it is "according to the flesh." It is a distinction belonging to the old world, not the new. In the world of the Spirit, Jesus is God's Son. That is the kinship that counts. Paul claims that Jesus's sonship was "by resurrection from the dead." When Jesus agreed to enter the old world, he relinquished divine sonship. Through his birth, suffering, death, and resurrection, he exited the enslaved world and reentered God's realm. It was not until his resurrection that he could again be considered Son of God. Those in Christ travel the same journey and so also belong to the new world, with the eschatological reservation. They are not yet raised from the dead, so their journey is incomplete.

In 1:17–18, Paul restates the gospel, now untrammeled by the need to couch it in traditional terms.

> For I am not ashamed of the gospel; it is the power of God for salvation to everyone who has faith, to the Jew first and also to the Greek. For in it the righteousness of God is revealed through faith for faith; as it is written, "The one who is righteous will live by faith." (1:16–17)

Later Paul says, "All, both Jews and Greeks, are under the power of sin" (3:9). In the old world, all are under the power of sin. In the new world, the power of God prevails. In the old, humanity is condemned. In the new, it receives salvation. It is power against power (Tobin 1987). It is a cosmic struggle. It is not just an individual effort to be good. The gospel is God's power against sin's power.

Chapters 2–3 seem to say that people in the old world are able to be on the right side of God even without Christ. A closer look reveals that this is not true. Paul's intent is to show that even in the old world there is no real difference between Jew and gentile, and that all were incapable of being right with God. Righteousness was impossible for both. He begins by showing that theoretically Jew and gentile were equally capable of pleasing God, but they failed.

Paul's dichotomy of Jew and Greek is equivalent to Jew and gentile. Throughout Romans, this dualism—Jew/Greek—is operative, but on two levels. On one level, the distinction is relatively unimportant. This is the more significant level. It has to do with whether one is righteous. On another level the distinction is important, although not of ultimate significance. This has to do with God's special relationship with Israel. A refrain in Romans is "Jew first and then Greek." This primacy is historical, not salvific.

In Rom. 1:18–2:16, Paul says that the wrath of God is being unleashed on the gentiles. Although they could have known from creation the truth about God—that there is one God, creator of the universe—they failed to recognize that. As a result, they became idolaters. From traditional Jewish anti-polytheistic views Paul knows that idolatry leads to immorality, and he catalogues sins that grow from idolatry (D. Martin 2006). Although gentiles could have been on God's right side through what is called natural theology— theological insight grounded in observation of nature—they failed (Collins 1977a). In 2:17, Paul turns his sights on the Jews. They had not only nature but God's revelation to point them in the right direction, but they also failed, so they were no better than the gentiles.

Chapter 3 brings the argument to its point. In 3:1–2, Paul says, "Then what advantage has the Jew? Or what is the value of circumcision? Much, in every way. For in the first place the Jews were entrusted with the oracles of God." A few verses further on, he says, "What then? Are we [Jews] any better off? No, not at all; for we have already charged that all, both Jews and Greeks, are under the power of sin" (3:9). Here are the two levels. To be a Jew is a wonderful thing. One has the Torah, the divine oracles, for one thing. But this does not bring liberation from enslavement to sin. Ultimately all, Jew and Greek, "are under the power of sin." That is the essence of the old world.

Note the absolute terms in which Paul expresses himself. He does not say everyone commits a lot of sins. He says that all humans are under the "power of sin." How does Paul know this? Because "it is written" (3:10). Paul produces a concatenation of biblical texts to prove his point, beginning, "There is no one who is righteous, not even one" (3:10; Eccles. 7:20). No one is on the right side of God. No one can change this. Not even the Jew who knows the Torah can escape because, ironically, the Torah reveals that all are under the power of sin. "'No human being will be justified in his sight' by deeds prescribed by the law, for through the law comes the knowledge of sin" (3:20).

Faced with this situation, God has done something new. Paul introduces his explanation, which will stretch through the end of chapter 8, with the words, "But now, apart from the law, the righteousness of God has been disclosed, and is attested by the law and the prophets" (3:21). Righteousness, unattainable in the old world by either Jew or Greek, is now available to both. It is "the righteousness of God through faith in Jesus Christ for all who believe. For there is no distinction, since all have sinned and fall short of the glory of God; they are now justified by his grace as a gift, through the redemption that is in Christ Jesus" (3:22–24).

Chapter 4 argues that since Abraham was righteous before being circumcised, circumcision is irrelevant to righteousness. The same holds for those in Christ. "It [righteousness] will be reckoned to us who believe in him who raised Jesus from the dead, who was handed over to death for our trespasses and was raised for our justification" (4:24–25).

Present and future (chaps. 5–8). Chapter 5 lays out the already/not yet of Paul's theology. He begins, "Therefore, since we are justified by faith, we have peace with God through our Lord Jesus Christ, through whom we have obtained access to this grace in which we stand; and we boast in our hope of sharing the glory of God" (5:1–2). Those in Christ now possess justification. That means peace with God. That means grace. We are now no longer in the fallen world but in Christ.

Because of what we now have, "we boast in our hope of sharing the glory of God" (5:2). What we now have makes us confident of what we will have, but we do not yet have it. This turns Paul's attention to the future and shows why we have such a strong basis for our hope.

> If while we were enemies, we were reconciled to God through the death of his Son, much more surely, having been reconciled, will we be saved by his life. But more than that, we even boast in God through our Lord Jesus Christ, through whom we have now received reconciliation. (5:10–11)

For believers, the future brings salvation. "Salvation" is the noun for what is accomplished by the verb "to save." The root meaning of the word (*sōtēria*) is rescue from something bad. In this case, the bad thing is God's eschatological wrath.

The rest of Rom. 5 concerns Adam Christology. Paul's first step in this section is to expound on what happened through Adam.

> Therefore, just as sin came into the world through one man, and death came through sin, and so death spread to all because all have sinned—sin was indeed in the world before the law, but sin is not reckoned when there is no law. Yet death exercised dominion from Adam to Moses, even over those whose sins were not like the transgression of Adam, who is a type of the one who was to come. (5:12–14)

Verse 12 introduces a problem that is still debated. How does sin get transmitted to all humans? We know from Rom. 2–3 that all humanity before Christ was under the power of sin. Those chapters seem to say that this is because all humans sinned. Does Rom. 5:12 mean that sin and death spread to everyone because everyone had in fact freely sinned? Or does it mean that through Adam everyone was enslaved by sin and so was unable not to sin? Does it mean, as later interpreted by Augustine and the Catholic Church, that a state of original sin was established into which all humans are born?

Most would identify the last of these solutions as later doctrine, not Paul's meaning. The real choice is between the first two. To choose the first—that everyone in fact freely sinned and that this is why the world is alienated from God—would be to deprive Adam of the role he plays in Paul's theology. It seems more in line with Paul's apocalyptic thought to choose the second: he sinned, and the entire world and his progeny were enslaved. They had no choice. Paul emphasizes not individual sin but the common state of humanity. Certainly all humans sinned, but no human could avoid sin. This is the reason that Paul far more frequently speaks of sin in the singular, not the plural. He is interested more in sin as a cosmic force than in individual sins, although there is a connection between the two. He thinks apocalyptically, and so talks about the universal effects of sin and tends to generalize about individual sin.

Paul asks whether there was sin before Torah. His answer is that sin was present, since Adam had disobeyed God, but that sin could not be "reckoned," "counted up," before the Torah. The law provided a way to identify sin. It brought greater knowledge of sin. But it did not account for the presence of sin in the world. That predated Moses. And since sin predated Torah, so did death. This was true for everyone, even though their sins were not like Adam's transgression. Adam's sin is unique because it introduced sin into the world. In 5:20, Paul says that Torah caused sin to multiply, a sin that was already present. By broadening knowledge of sin, it created more opportunities for sin.

Romans 6 takes up practical implications of simultaneously existing in two contradictory realms. Paul again uses diatribe. The questioner asks whether one ought to sin more so that grace can abound more. Sin creates opportunities for grace. Paul responds with his usual "By no means!" In baptism, believers have died with Christ. They have died to this world. They have died to sin. Christ has proceeded to the next stage. God has raised him from the dead. That has not yet happened to believers. The "not yet" of the already/not yet pattern prevents Paul from completing the parallelism between Jesus and Christians. We die with Christ, but we have not yet risen with Christ. Paul turns the second part of the parallel toward behavior: "We have been buried with him by baptism into death, so that, just as Christ was raised from the dead by the glory of the Father, so we too might walk in newness of life" (6:4). We have died to the world and sin. We must strive to live as if completely in the new.

Paul draws clear connections between believers' new status and their behavior. They are not to sin. Rather,

> Present yourselves to God as those who have been brought from death to life, and present your members to God as instruments of righteousness. For sin will have no dominion over you, since you are not under law but under grace. (6:13–14)

There are two powers in the universe, and people must be enslaved to one or the other (6:15–23) (D. Martin 1990). They can be slaves of sin, and get death as a reward, or slaves of God, and receive righteousness as wages.

Paul uses the analogy of marriage to show that death to this world means freedom from the law (7:1–4). As a woman is freed upon her husband's death from the law binding her to her husband, so a death (Christ's and our own in baptism) brings about freedom from the law. Paul applies this to believers by describing their situation before and after their faith.

> While we were living in the flesh, our sinful passions, aroused by the law, were at work in our members to bear fruit for death. But now we are discharged from the law, dead to that which held us captive, so that we are slaves not under the old written code but in the new life of the Spirit. (7:5–6)

Being captive to the law is equivalent to being in the old world. The law actually arouses sinful passions that result in death.

Romans 7:7–25 has been a source of much confusion. It is misleading if "law" always means Torah and if the chapter is about Paul's own life. Paul is speaking not of himself but of all humanity. Generally speaking, by "law" Paul means divine commands. It is the same whether he means God's command to Adam or God's commands through Moses.

To explain, Paul again resorts to diatribe and has his fictive listener ask a nonsensical question. "What then should we say? That the law is sin?" (7:7). Paul exclaims, "By no means!" How could his thought have veered so close to absurdity?

Paul says that the law is not sin, but that humanity would not have known sin except for the law. He uses as an example one of the Ten Commandments. If the law had not forbidden coveting, humans never would have known what coveting was. Divine law provides education in sin. It points it out. By pointing it out, it provides more ways to sin. He goes further: "But sin, seizing an opportunity in the commandment, produced in me all kinds of covetousness. Apart from the law sin lies dead" (7:8). Ironically, divine commands are tools of sin. Sin is disobedience, and without divine rules, there is no opportunity for disobedience.

Paul now gets into "history," but it is not his own personal history. It is the history of humanity.

> I was once alive apart from the law, but when the commandment came, sin revived and I died, and the very commandment that promised life proved to be death to me. For sin, seizing an opportunity in the commandment, deceived me and through it killed me. So the law is holy, and the commandment is holy and just and good. (7:9–12)

Paul was never "alive apart from the Torah." He was always under Torah until he accepted Christ. But if "I" is taken as humanity and if "law" means any command of God, then we can make sense out of this statement. We need only read Genesis. In the beginning, God created Adam and Eve. At first there was no commandment from God. Then God commanded them not to eat of the tree of the knowledge of good and evil. Now they had an opportunity to sin. A law gave sin the chance to come to life and spring into action. The consequence was death. God had meant for the commandment to bring life. The commandment promised life but brought death. "For sin, seizing an opportunity in the commandment, deceived me and through it killed me" (7:11).

Ironically, this affirms divine law. "So the law is holy, and the commandment is holy and just and good" (7:12). Commands from God are always holy and just and good. That sin, or Satan, can use them for its own purposes only proves that they are good. If they were not, it would make no difference if one disobeyed them.

Paul's fictional interlocutor asks, "Did what is good, then, bring death to me?" (7:13). Again Paul exclaims, "By no means!" He goes on, "It was sin, working death in me through what is good, in order that sin might be shown to be sin, and through the commandment might become sinful beyond measure" (7:13). Sin, not law, is responsible for death.

The next section vividly illustrates what Paul means, and it has misled many a commentator who see it as an account of Paul's own personal struggles with his own sin and scruples.

> For we know that the law is spiritual; but I am of the flesh, sold into slavery under sin. I do not understand my own actions. For I do not do what I want, but I do the very thing I hate. Now if I do what I do not want, I agree that the law is good. But in fact it is no longer I that do it, but sin that dwells within me. For I know that nothing good dwells within me, that is, in my flesh. I can will what is right, but I cannot do it. For I do not do the good I want, but the evil I do not want is what I do. Now if I do what I do not want, it is no longer I that do it, but sin that dwells within me.
>
> So I find it to be a law that when I want to do what is good, evil lies close at hand. For I delight in the law of God in my inmost self, but I see in my members another law at war with the law of my mind, making me captive to the law of sin that dwells in my members. Wretched man that I am! Who will rescue me from this body of death? Thanks be to God through Jesus Christ our Lord!
>
> So then, with my mind I am a slave to the law of God, but with my flesh I am a slave to the law of sin. (7:14–25)

Paul's first statement explains it all. The law is spiritual, but humanity is "of the flesh, sold into slavery under sin." When God sent the Torah into the fleshly world, it was recognized as being from God, so it was by definition good and "spiritual." Torah was in the fallen world but not of it. Torah could not put humanity right with God because it entered a world enslaved to sin, and law simply gave humanity further chances to disobey (see 8:3).

If we take Rom. 7:14 as our interpretive principle for the rest of the passage, all falls into place. Humanity sees the law as good, but it cannot fulfill the law because humanity is alienated from God, kept in captivity by sin as a cosmic force. Humanity cannot understand its own condition because it can recognize the good but cannot live it. If that is true, then humanity concludes, "It is no longer I who do it, but sin that dwells within me."

The transition between verses 24 and 25 is critical. Given the hopeless condition of humanity, it cries out, "Who will rescue me from this body of death?" (7:24). By "body" Paul means "self." By "body of death" Paul means the self entrapped in the old world. Verse 25 supplies the answer: "Thanks be to God through Jesus Christ our Lord!" (7:25). Greek often leaves out the verb "to be," and it should be supplied in the translation of this verse. A better expression of Paul's intent might be, "Thanks be to God, *it is* through Jesus Christ our Lord." Deliverance comes through Jesus.

Paul concludes, "So then, with my mind I am a slave to the law of God, but with my flesh I am a slave to the law of sin" (7:25). Were it simply an intellectual choice, humanity would easily choose the right service, the right slavery. But one's flesh is a slave to sin. Flesh is the entire human being seen as part of the fallen world.

Chapter 8 concludes the long argument of Rom. 5–8 in particular and 1–8 in general. Throughout the chapter there is a clear distinction between the two worlds—flesh and spirit. Those in Christ have in some sense "made it." They have escaped the world of the flesh and are now in proper relationship with God.

> For God has done what the law, weakened by the flesh, could not do: by sending his own Son in the likeness of sinful flesh, and to deal with sin, he condemned sin in the flesh, so that the just requirement of the law might be fulfilled in us, who walk not according to the flesh but according to the Spirit. (8:3–4)

Torah was unable to free humans from the old world because Torah was "weakened by the flesh." Torah was powerless to help humans to obey it. Setting the Torah before a humanity unable to perform it only creates the impossible situation described in Rom. 7.

God devises a means of rescuing humanity. He sends his Son "in the likeness of sinful flesh" and "to deal with sin," and he "condemned sin in the flesh." Paul hints at a sacrificial model for interpreting Christ's death. "To deal with sin" translates *peri hamartias*, which is a term for the sin offering in the sacrificial cult.

Paul is bolder in 2 Corinthians: "For our sake he made him to be sin who knew no sin, so that in him we might become the righteousness of God" (5:21). This is an astounding statement. Jesus "knew no sin" when he was created as the second Adam, the perfect human. He did not deserve to die, but he made himself subject to death by entering this world. In 2 Cor. 5:21, Paul states this as harshly as can be imagined. Jesus goes from not knowing sin to actually *being* sin; he became the epitome of fallen humanity.

If Paul is unafraid to say that Jesus became sin, then it is not surprising that he could think of Jesus as a sacrifice for sin and Jesus's death as dealing with sin in the same sense as do sacrifices. In that case, Paul means in Rom. 8:3–4 that Jesus is condemned to death for human sin. He takes on responsibility for sin and pays the penalty, death, for it. Paul thinks of this as a legal requirement of the law ("the just requirement of the law"; *dikaiōma*) that must be satisfied. Once that is done, humans are no longer burdened with responsibility and guilt (8:4). This is not unlike what we saw in Gal. 3, where Jesus takes on the curse of the law.

Paul encourages believers to set their minds on things of the Spirit, things of the new world. There should be a correspondence between where one is (which world), how one behaves, and how one thinks. If one belongs to the world of the flesh, one has no freedom. As Paul says,

> For this reason the mind that is set on the flesh is hostile to God; it does not submit to God's law—indeed it cannot, and those who are in the flesh cannot please God. But you are not in the flesh; you are in the Spirit, since the Spirit of God dwells in you. Anyone who does not have the Spirit of Christ does not belong to him. (8:7–9)

Paul's claim that his readers are not in the flesh but in the Spirit makes no sense unless read in the context of the two worlds. It makes no sense to read "flesh" as material as opposed to immaterial, for example. Obviously the addressees have physical bodies. Paul means that believers are not in the old world but in the new world. The Spirit's presence within Christians is proof of this.

Paul contrasts being in debt to the flesh to being in debt to the Spirit. He is introducing yet another metaphor to delineate the readers' relationship to the two worlds. This one is from economics.

The two worlds can also be characterized in terms of life and death. "For if you live according to the flesh, you will die; but if by the Spirit you put to death the deeds of the body, you will live" (8:13). They have died to sin, to the "deeds of the body," to the fallen world, to the old self; as a result, they will live.

Now the focus shifts:

> For all who are led by the Spirit of God are children of God. For you did not receive a spirit of slavery to fall back into fear, but you have received a spirit of adoption [*huiothesia*, incorporating the word *huios*, "son"]. When we cry, "Abba! Father!" it is that very Spirit bearing witness with our spirit that we are children of God, and if children, then heirs, heirs of God and joint heirs with Christ—if, in fact, we suffer with him so that we may also be glorified with him. (8:14–17)

Paul contrasts slavery with sonship, as in Galatians. Translating literally (as shown in the interpolation above) brings out the parallel with Christ. By escaping slavery, believers have become sons of God. The Spirit within them bears witness to that by causing them to cry out the Aramaic word *Abba*, "Father," perhaps a throwback to Jesus's own way of praying (see Mark 14:36). Sons are heirs. Jesus inherits the new world, and so do his siblings. Believers suffer with Christ now. Full glorification is in the future.

Paul imparts a vision of future consummation that is powerful, vivid, and ties up some loose ends of his apocalyptic vision.

> I consider that the sufferings of this present time are not worth comparing with the glory about to be revealed to us. For the creation waits with eager longing for the revealing of the children of God [*huioi tou theou*: "sons of God"]; for the creation was subjected to futility, not of its own will but by the will of the one who subjected it, in hope that the creation itself will be set free from its bondage to decay and will obtain the freedom of the glory of the children of God. We know that the whole creation has been groaning in labor pains until now; and not only the creation, but we ourselves, who have the first fruits of the Spirit, groan inwardly while we wait for adoption, the redemption of our bodies. For in hope we were saved. Now hope that is seen is not hope. For who hopes for what is seen? But if we hope for what we do not see, we wait for it with patience. (8:18–25)

Paul expects great things. The sufferings of the present are not worthy to be compared to them. What is coming can be summed up in a single word, "glory," and Paul uses the loaded word "reveal" (*apokalyptō*). Paul is speaking of the eschaton, using apocalyptic language.

The "sons of God" are to be revealed at the eschaton. Ultimately, the new world is made up of persons, collectively called "sons of God," as Christ is Son of God. As is typical of apocalypticism, humanity and the universe are closely intertwined. Genesis says that the earth was cursed because of Adam's sin. The created universe awaits liberation, too.

Paul lists the stages of movement from the old to the new world:

> For those whom he foreknew he also predestined to be conformed to the image of his Son, in order that he might be the firstborn within a large family. And those whom he predestined he also called; and those whom he called he also justified; and those whom he justified he also glorified. (8:29–30)

God knows in advance those who are to be members of the new world. He "predestined" them to be conformed to Christ's image. All who belong to the new world are children of God. The Father, Christ his Son, and those in Christ's image are now one "large family."

Shifting to other images, Paul uses the verb "called"; that is, he uses an image that does justice both to Christian mission and to God's special relationship to those he predestines to be saved. Next comes justification (the law-court image) and finally glorification, which is the consummation of all. In his enthusiasm, Paul seems to have advanced the eschatological clock, since he puts "glorified" in the past tense.

Now that believers have justification, what can hinder them? Nothing. The first list Paul gives of things that cannot stop them is of descriptions of everyday things—"hardship, or distress, or persecution, or famine, or nakedness, or peril, or sword" (8:35). His other list sounds more apocalyptic—"neither death, nor life, nor angels, nor rulers, nor things present, nor things to come, nor powers, nor height, nor depth, nor anything else in all creation" (8:38–39). "Powers" are supernatural, unseen powers, while things like rulers, height, and depth may also be cosmic powers.

Israel (chaps. 9–11). In Rom. 9–11, Paul reviews Israel's status, using Scripture. He addresses not Jews but gentiles. His audience thinks that they have replaced Israel. Nothing could be further from the truth. God intends to save both Jew and Greek.

Paul begins by listing what God has given to Israel and, through Israel, to the world.

> I am speaking the truth in Christ—I am not lying; my conscience confirms it by the Holy Spirit—I have great sorrow and unceasing anguish in my heart. For I could wish that I myself were accursed and cut off from Christ for the sake of my own people, my kindred according to the flesh. They are Israelites, and to them belong the adoption, the glory, the covenants, the giving of the law, the worship, and the promises; to them belong the patriarchs, and from them, according to the flesh, comes the Messiah, who is over all, God blessed forever. Amen. (9:1–5)

Paul's first statement is moving. He would rather be excluded from the new world, separated from Christ, and lose everything that he has worked to bring to others, than have Israel not be saved. To be cut off from Christ would be to be accursed. But Israel is his "kindred according to the flesh." Paul's love for his people is overwhelming, even though it is a distinction that applies essentially to the old world.

Paul lists the gifts Israel has from God that prepare the way for Christ.

The adoption (*huiothesia*): God's election of Israel as God's son.

The "glory": a priestly term for God's presence, especially in the temple.

The covenants: between God and Abraham, Isaac, Jacob, Jacob's twelve sons, Israel (through Moses), David, and the Davidic dynasty.

The giving of the law: Torah given through Moses on Mount Sinai.

The worship: Jerusalem, its temple and priesthood, and its sacrificial liturgy.

The promises: all that God promised to Israel.

The patriarchs: Abraham, Isaac, Jacob, and Jacob's twelve sons from whom Israel is descended.

The Messiah "according to the flesh": Christ was a Jew and he was the Messiah; Paul qualifies this, because usual ideas of messiahship do not play the role in his theology that they do elsewhere in Jewish and Christian thought.

Can all of this be insignificant? Does it not describe God's work throughout history, and does it not have profound implications for gentiles as well as Jews? Then how could it possibly be that Israel is now excluded from God's intent for humanity? It cannot be. It is a question Paul must address.

Paul begins by discussing the nature of ethnicity. Who can really be said to descend from Abraham? To a modern mind that thinks in terms of biology, that might seem a simple question, even if built on complicated science. But the issue is not really so clear, even today. Ethnicity is not a matter of biology alone. Biology is usually involved, although to what extent is debatable. Other factors determining ethnicity include common language, history (real or invented), homeland and diaspora communities, lineages (some more accurate than others; many invented and transmitted through generations), dress and food, religion, customs, and so on. It is possible to be of a given ethnicity without any true biological foundation for it, as counterintuitive as that might be. Descendants are thought to share the nature and traits of their ancestor (Johnson Hodge 2007).

Paul argues that not all who are "biologically" descended from Abraham are really his descendants (9:6–16). Abraham had two sons (actually more), Isaac and Ishmael. God's "purpose of election" was passed down only through Isaac, the younger son, not the elder Ishmael as one would expect. Paul explains, "This means that it is not the children of the flesh who are the children of God, but the children of the promise are counted as descendants" (9:8).

Paul then brings up the "similar" case of Rebecca, Isaac's wife, and her sons (9:10–16). God decreed that when she bore twins, the elder (Jacob) should serve the younger (Esau). This was not because of any merit or demerit on either of their parts. God pronounced it while they were still in the womb.

Resorting again to diatribe, Paul has his conversation partner question whether God is therefore unfair (9:19). Paul parries that God can do whatever he wants with his creation (9:20–24). Indeed, God has reserved glorification for "us whom he has called, not from the Jews only but also from the Gentiles" (9:24). Being right with God rests not in being Jewish, but in being called by God.

Next Paul quotes Isaiah to the effect that God will determine that some who were his people are no longer his people, and that some who were not his people will be his people. This means that not all Israel will be saved, but only a "remnant" (9:27).

Paul next puzzles over the fact that Israel has not obtained righteousness, while gentiles have. It is a passage much misinterpreted, because it has often been seen in the light of Luther's analysis, which runs as follows: Israel pursued righteousness based on works, and the gentiles pursued it through faith. Israel thought it could earn righteousness by its own efforts, while the gentiles realized that righteousness was a gift and could not be earned. These are two different sorts of religion, one legalistic and the other grace-filled.

This misinterprets Paul. When Paul says that the gentiles pursue righteousness through faith, he means faith in what God has done in Christ. When he speaks of Israel pursuing righteousness "as if it were based on works," he means obedience to Torah, not works in general. These are not two types of religion, one built on personal effort and the other on grace. Rather, it is a question of whether one wins favor with God through non-Christ-believing Judaism or through Christ. If we view these as separate religions for a moment (Paul did not), then, as has been said by other scholars, the ultimate problem with Judaism is that it is not Christianity (Sanders 1977).

Paul denies that Israel is lost. Its refusal to believe is the first step in an eschatological process still in motion. Israel has missed the justification available in Christ, but it is only for the moment. Its lack of belief has resulted in the gentile mission, Paul's in particular. Paul works hard among the gentiles, hoping that Israel will ultimately recognize the truth, become "jealous," and will therefore come to faith.

Paul seeks to make his gentile readers humble about their newfound status before God. He first uses the image of the olive tree (11:17–24). Israel was originally God's olive tree, root, and branch. When Christ came and the gentiles believed while the Jews did not, Israel was cut off of God's olive tree and the gentiles grafted in. Paul warns the gentiles not to let their pride displease God so that they themselves are cut off. After all, it would be easier to cut off the nonnative branches and regraft the original branches than it was to cut off the original branches and graft in wild branches in the first place.

In 11:25–26, Paul reveals to his readers "a mystery." This is a technical term in apocalypticism for secret knowledge available only through revelation.

> So that you may not claim to be wiser than you are, brothers and sisters, I want you to understand this mystery [*mystērion*]: a hardening has come upon part of Israel, until the full number of the Gentiles has come in. And so all Israel will be saved; as it is written, "Out of Zion will come the Deliverer; he will banish ungodliness from Jacob." "And this is my covenant with them, when I take away their sins."
>
> As regards the gospel they are enemies of God for your sake; but as regards election they are beloved, for the sake of their ancestors; for the gifts and the calling of God are irrevocable. Just as you were once disobedient to God but have now received mercy because of their disobedience, so they have now been disobedient in order that, by the mercy shown to you, they too may now receive mercy. For God has imprisoned all in disobedience so that he may be merciful to all. (11:25–32)

In biblical eschatological scenarios, it is common that God rescues Israel and then the gentiles come to believe in Israel's God. Paul reverses this order, as does Acts of the Apostles. Now, because of Israel's unbelief, the gentiles are the first to come into God's favor. Then Israel will believe. This will happen when a set number of gentiles come to be in Christ. The set number fits the general idea that God planned things in advance. The specific idea of a pre-ordained number of people to be saved matches similar ideas in *4 Ezra* 4:36 and Rev. 6:11.

Paul knows that all Israel will be saved because "it is written." He calls Israel God's enemies "for your sake." That is, God has consigned Israel to the old world for the sake of the gospel being preached to the gentiles. Despite that, even as enemies, they remain beloved because of their ancestors, "for the gifts and the calling of God are irrevocable" (11:29). Israel's election is eternal. Paul ends with the same message that pervades the letter: "For God has imprisoned all in disobedience so that he may be merciful to all" (11:32).

The rest of Romans is taken up with *parenesis*, a technical term for teaching and moral exhortation. Paul uses apocalyptic ideas here as sanctions for proper behavior. He begins with a general directive: "Do not be conformed to this world [*aiōn*], but be transformed by the renewing of your minds, so that you may discern what is the will of God—what is good and acceptable and perfect" (12:2). The word for "world," *aiōn*, is the root of the English word "eon." It means "age" and appears in apocalyptic contexts for God's division of history into eras. Paul uses it twenty-one times in his letters. In this exhortation, Paul acknowledges that those in Christ are still beset with temptations. They must struggle against the tendency to live in accord with the world around them. In Rom. 7, Paul insisted right living was a cognitive exercise, among other things. Here again he stresses the importance of using one's mind to understand one's new obligations.

In Rom. 12:19, Paul instructs his audience not to seek vengeance, but to leave it to God's eschatological wrath, already at work in the world. Government is legitimate and is God's instrument for keeping order in human society. It is even a tool of God's wrath: "It is the servant of God to execute wrath on the wrongdoer. Therefore one must be subject, not only because of wrath but also because of conscience" (13:4–5).

Paul's exhortations are the more urgent because he expects the end to come soon: "Besides this, you know what time it is, how it is now the moment for you to wake from sleep. For salvation is nearer to us now than when we became believers. . . . Put on the Lord Jesus Christ, and make no provision for the flesh, to gratify its desires" (13:11, 14). As salvation draws near (but still future), it is not time to act as though one still belonged to the world of the flesh.

Paul ends the letter with apocalyptic flourishes.

> The God of peace will shortly crush Satan under your feet. The grace of our Lord Jesus Christ be with you. . . . Now to God who is able to strengthen you according to my gospel and the proclamation of Jesus Christ, according to the revelation of the mystery [*apokalypsin mystēriou*] that was kept secret for long ages but is now disclosed, and through the prophetic writings is made known to

all the Gentiles, according to the command of the eternal God, to bring about
the obedience of faith—to the only wise God, through Jesus Christ, to whom
be the glory forever! Amen. (16:20, 25–27)

Philippians

Philippians does not contain many apocalyptic elements, but it does have
a famous passage that sheds light on Paul's apocalyptic thought. Ironically,
it is a passage of which Paul may not be the author, although some think he
did compose it (Yarbro Collins 2003, 364n20; R. Martin 1967). It is a hymn,
and it is susceptible to more than one interpretation. The one espoused here
is not the majority opinion, but it is plausible, and given how well it fits with
Paul's thought elsewhere, we propose it as closest to Paul's intention.

Philippians 2:6–11 speaks of Jesus,

> who, though he was in the form of God,
>   did not regard equality with God
>   as something to be exploited,
> but emptied himself,
>   taking the form of a slave,
>   being born in human likeness.
> And being found in human form,
>   he humbled himself
>   and became obedient to the point of death—
>   even death on a cross.
> Therefore God also highly exalted him
>   and gave him the name
>   that is above every name,
> so that at the name of Jesus
>   every knee should bend,
>   in heaven and on earth and under the earth,
> and every tongue should confess
>   that Jesus Christ is Lord,
>   to the glory of God the Father.

Majority opinion sees the hymn as about Christ's preexistence, that is,
his existence in heaven as God before becoming incarnated as a human. It
is kenotic Christology, *kenōsis* being the Greek word for "emptying." Christ
emptied himself of his divinity, or at least of his divine powers, in order to
assume human limitations. Then God restored his proper status, Lord of the
universe.

There is another possibility, one to which we subscribe. The hymn can be
read as an expression of Adam Christology if read against the background
of Gen. 1–3. Terminology differs between Genesis and the hymn, but that is
hardly surprising in such a creative piece. In Genesis, Adam was created in the

"image" (*eikōn*) of God (Gen. 1:27). In the hymn, this corresponds to saying that Jesus, the new Adam, was in the "form" (*morphē*) of God. In Genesis, Adam sinned because being in God's image was not enough for him. He wished to be equal to God. It is important that we translate the Greek word *harpagmos* as something not possessed but to be grasped at, rather than something possessed to be exploited. Either translation is valid, but the first fits our interpretation. Adam desired an equality that he did not have. Jesus was the opposite. Like Adam, he was in God's image, but not equal to God. Unlike Adam, he did not grasp at equality with God. He did not commit the sin that Adam committed.

Becoming a fallen human means that Jesus takes on the form of a slave, because the old world is enslaved to sin. Paul's terms "human form" and "human likeness" do not imply that he denies Christ's full humanity. Just the opposite—Jesus becomes completely human in the image of the old Adam, with its attendant slavery to sin. Christ carries this humbling of himself to the ultimate. Not only does he die; he endures ultimate humiliating death, on a cross. It was a punishment Romans often used on slaves.

Because of Jesus's obedience, even to death, God exalted him, giving him a name above every other being in the universe, so that all must worship him. The name is "Lord." It is a title applied to God in the Bible, but for Paul this does not amount to Jesus being equal to God. Throughout his letters, Paul consistently separates the divinity of the Father from the lordship of Christ. In 1 Cor. 15, we saw that God put all things under Jesus's feet—that is, he subjected the entire universe to Jesus's authority as Lord—but that God was always superior to Jesus, and in the end Jesus will deliver the kingdom to God. Significantly, the eschatological scenario Paul sketches in 1 Cor. 15 involves explicit Adam Christology. Jesus's ultimate dominion over the cosmos corresponds with Adam's dominion over every living thing in Genesis. Since being in the image of God in Gen. 1:26 is juxtaposed with dominion over living creatures, it is likely that Jesus becoming Lord is related to his regaining of God's image for himself and for those who are "in" him.

Adam Christology in Philippians 2:6–11

Genesis 1–3	Philippians 2:6–11
Adam is in the image of God	Jesus is in the form of God
Adam grasps at being equal to God	Jesus does not grasp at being equal to God
Adam's disobedience introduces humanity to slavery and death	Jesus's obedience subjects him to slavery and death
Adam lost his lordship over the earth	Jesus gains lordship over the universe and regains the image of God

Other details in Philippians confirm that Paul thinks apocalyptically. The fact that they occur in passing shows how Paul always has such thoughts in the back of his mind, even when they are not the focus of discussion. At the beginning of the letter, Paul urges his audience to be ready for "the day of Jesus Christ," referring to Christ's parousia and coming judgment (1:6, 10).

In chapter 3, Paul addresses the issue of obedience to Torah, again in the context of circumcision. Paul calls his past allegiance to Torah "garbage" that he has thrown out so that he might be in Christ. Now that Paul has left Torah behind, he is in a new state and looks forward to a future that will consummate in resurrection. He wants to

> be found in him, not having a righteousness of my own that comes from the law, but one that comes through faith in Christ, the righteousness from God based on faith. I want to know Christ and the power of his resurrection and the sharing of his sufferings by becoming like him in his death, if somehow I may attain the resurrection from the dead. (3:9–11)

Further on, Paul again employs apocalyptic language against other Christians whom he thinks do not live properly in Christ. He calls them "enemies of the cross of Christ" (3:18). This is because they set their minds on "earthly" things. Judaizers pursue earthly things because Torah belongs to the old world. To counter this, Paul presents the proper attitude for one in Christ.

> But our citizenship is in heaven, and it is from there that we are expecting a Savior, the Lord Jesus Christ. He will transform the body of our humiliation that it may be conformed to the body of his glory, by the power that also enables him to make all things subject to himself. (3:20–21)

1 Corinthians

A major problem in the Corinthian church is that of spiritual gifts, that is, powers given through the Spirit for the good of the church. They include such things as the ability to prophesy, do miracles, heal, teach, speak in tongues, and so on. These demonstrate the Spirit's presence. The Corinthians value these gifts for their own sake rather than for what they can do for the church. They even compete, considering one person as of greater status than another in the church because of such gifts, thus tearing the church apart. The great irony is that gifts that belong to the new world end up being used in ways that typify the old world.

There are other problems that Paul must address. He deals with them all by showing that they should be seen from the point of view of the new creation. Anything that does not build up the church cannot be compatible with being in Christ.

The thanksgiving section of 1 Corinthians thanks God for the Corinthians' spiritual gifts, but does so in the context of the eschaton. Paul's strategy is to get them thinking about how they will be judged by Christ with respect to their attitudes toward spiritual gifts, so that you are not lacking in any spiritual gift as you wait for the revealing [*apokalypsis*] of our Lord Jesus Christ. He will also strengthen you to the end, so that you may be blameless on the day of our Lord Jesus Christ. God is faithful; by him you were called into the fellowship of his Son, Jesus Christ our Lord. (1:7–9)

The reference to Jesus's "apocalypse," revealed at the end of time, is the same as his parousia. That, in turn, is the same as "the day of our Lord Jesus Christ." Christ comes as judge, an implicit threat. The Corinthians' attitude undermines "fellowship," the solidarity and oneness that should characterize those in Christ, and it is God who called them into that fellowship.

Paul is upset that some in the Corinthian community are proud of their "wisdom" and lord it over others. For Paul, this is behavior suitable for this "age" (*aiōn*), not for those in Christ.

Fig. 13. Ruins at Corinth. Paul spent around eighteen months in Corinth, and he wrote at least seven letters to this church. (Jim Yancey)

The offenders reason as the world reasons, but worldly wisdom cannot know God. The existence of factions proves that the readers still live in the old world.

The irreconcilable opposition between this world and being in Christ is powerfully articulated in terms of Christ's cross. Paul sees the cross as the ultimate negation of the values of the present *aiōn* or *kosmos*.

> When I came to you, brothers and sisters, I did not come proclaiming the mystery of God to you in lofty words or wisdom. For I decided to know nothing among you except Jesus Christ, and him crucified. And I came to you in weakness and in fear and in much trembling. My speech and my proclamation were not with plausible words of wisdom, but with a demonstration of the Spirit and of power, so that your faith might rest not on human wisdom but on the power of God. (2:1–5)

True wisdom is an apocalyptic *mystērion* of God. In one realm there is worldly wisdom, "plausible" to those in the image of the old Adam, but incompatible with Christ's cross. In the other realm is God's mystery that reveals the power of the Spirit. The mystery of God is the gospel. Jew and gentile alike have ways of judging Paul's gospel, one on the basis of wisdom (gentiles) and the other on the basis of signs (Jews), but both standards belong to this world.

Paul counters worldly wisdom with another wisdom, not of this world, that he does impart to those sufficiently mature to receive it.

> Yet among the mature we do speak wisdom, though it is not a wisdom of this age [*aiōn*] or of the rulers of this age, who are doomed to perish. But we speak God's wisdom, secret [*en mystēriō*] and hidden [*apokalyptō*], which God decreed before the ages [*aiōn*] for our glory. None of the rulers of this age [*aiōn*] understood this; for if they had, they would not have crucified the Lord of glory. But, as it is written,
>
> > "What no eye has seen, nor ear heard,
> >   nor the human heart conceived,
> > what God has prepared for those who love him"—
>
> these things God has revealed to us through the Spirit; for the Spirit searches everything, even the depths of God. For what human being knows what is truly human except the human spirit that is within? So also no one comprehends what is truly God's except the Spirit of God. Now we have received not the spirit of the world, but the Spirit that is from God, so that we may understand the gifts bestowed on us by God. And we speak of these things in words not taught by human wisdom but taught by the Spirit, interpreting spiritual things to those who are spiritual. (2:6–13)

The wisdom Paul imparts is opposed to this world's wisdom. It is the wisdom of God's realm, not of this world's "rulers" (*archōn*), a word probably meaning not humans but superhuman powers. God's wisdom is secret, mysterious, hidden, and foreordained before creation. He quotes Scripture to underscore that God's plans for humankind surpass human imagination. He brings this around to spiritual gifts. One can truly understand God's ways only through God's Spirit. There is a spirit of the world that is useless in helping humans to understand God. The spiritual gifts can actually be dangerous for them if they do not have the right "mind" about them. Paul closes, "but we have the mind of Christ" (2:16).

In chapter 3, Paul condemns factionalism, seeing it as proof that his readers still belong to the world of the flesh, not the Spirit. The difficulty of holding together the already and the not yet of Christian existence makes Paul's language imprecise here. He uncharacteristically uses flesh as a stage of immaturity on the way to a more mature existence, although ultimately he maintains his strictly binary opposition between the two modes of existence—flesh and Spirit. Corinthian factionalism is built on loyalty to particular missionaries. Paul rejects this. Judgment of each leader takes place in the final judgment. All is seen against the backdrop of the impending eschaton.

Paul sees an absolute opposition between God's wisdom and that of the world: "Do not deceive yourselves. If you think that you are wise in this age [*aiōn*], you should become fools so that you may become wise. For the wisdom of this world [*kosmos*] is foolishness with God" (3:18–19).

In chapter 4, Paul warns his readers not to judge anyone. The time for judgment is when "the Lord comes."

In dealing with a case of immoral behavior, Paul instructs them to turn the offender over "to Satan for the destruction of the flesh, so that his spirit may be saved in the day of the Lord" (5:5). Paul intends to eject the sinner from the church so that he is back in Satan's realm. The church is the scene of the new creation, while everything outside it is Satan's realm. That experience may awaken the person to the danger in which he has placed himself, and he may repent.

First Corinthians 7 discusses sexual relationships. Some in Corinth doubt whether sexuality, even within marriage, is compatible with their new status. Paul himself foregoes sex for the sake of his apostolate (chap. 9). He addresses the Corinthians' questions by making three basic points. The first is that the world is rapidly coming to an end, and the best way for believers to spend their time is to get ready for the end. The second is that not all have the dedication and strength to live celibate lives. Those who do not must give vent to their passions in the only legitimate way, through marriage. The third is that all in Christ occupy a realm that can no longer be identical with living in the world of the flesh, so "natural" relationships no longer have the significance that they once did (Wimbush 1987).

Paul's practical advice is that ideally believers should refrain from marriage, since it distracts from their new existence. Marriage, circumcision, and slavery are of no significance in Christ. No effort should be wasted on changing one's worldly status. Twice Paul expresses the nearness of the end: "The appointed time has grown short" (7:29); "the present form of this world is passing away" (7:31). Nonetheless, Paul is realistic. Sexual urges are powerful. If one cannot forego sex, then one should marry. Otherwise, Satan will tempt one through lack of self-control (7:5).

Chapters 8–10 offer another glimpse of how Paul views the unseen world. Here he discusses the Corinthians' relation to the world outside Christ to which they once belonged (Theissen 1982). They must now learn how to pursue their public and business lives, which, in the Greco-Roman world, meant navigating many occasions in which religion played a role. They are gentile, and this was not a problem when they were polytheists. Meat sold in the marketplace might have been sacrificed in pagan rituals. Dinner parties might involve such meat being served. Social engagements might include pagan sacrifices or other rituals. One's social life might involve worship of idols. What could newly minted believers do and what was now improper? Paul advises that they may eat food sacrificed to idols, since idols have no power over those in Christ. Nonetheless, if this scandalizes church members, one should relinquish one's freedom. Paul's principle is always whether something builds up the church or tears it down. But it is always improper to worship any being that is not God.

Paul acknowledges the existence of superhuman beings that are the object of pagan worship. There are many so-called gods and lords (8:5). They do exist. Paul claims these gods and lords are demons, a view present in Deut. 10:20 and 32:17.

We discussed other aspects of 1 Corinthians in our general treatment of Paul's apocalyptic theology above. Specifically, we examined his views of resurrection and of the eschaton in 1 Cor. 15, and the Adam Christology implicit at the beginning of chapter 11 and within chapter 15.

2 Corinthians

This letter is a composite of several letters written over time. There are competing theories about what constitutes each letter incorporated into the final version. We adopt the theory advocated by Perrin in his introduction to the New Testament (Duling and Perrin 1994, 231). The order of the fragments in the collection is not chronological.

Letters Incorporated into 2 Corinthians

Letter 1 (2:14–6:13; 7:2–4)	A church member attacks Paul; Paul's relations with the church problematic
Letter 2 (chaps. 10–13)	The "tearful letter" referred to in 2:3–4 and 7:8; Paul's attempt to fight the "super-apostles"
Letter 3 (1:1–2:13; 7:5–16)	A letter of reconciliation
Letter 4 (chap. 8)	A letter of introduction for Titus for a collection for the Jerusalem church
Letter 5 (chap. 9)	Another letter about the collection

Paul had already written 1 Corinthians to the church in Corinth, and in that letter he mentioned a previous one (1 Cor. 5:9), now lost. So Paul wrote at least seven letters to Corinth.

Although Paul founded the Corinthian church and had a longstanding relationship with them, their dealings were never without problems. When he wrote 1 Corinthians, he was on good terms with them and was able to offer them advice and instruction. But there were already problems of authority, for he begins the letter by castigating them for breaking into factions, one loyal to him, one to Peter, one to Apollos, one to Christ. By the time he wrote the letters collected in 2 Corinthians, things were worse. Since we have only one side of the argument—Paul's—we must reconstruct the other side (Georgi 1986).

Letter 1: Paul's defense (2:14–6:13; 7:2–4). Paul begins his engagement with the Corinthian problems by writing a letter, Letter 1. Paul enlists several apocalyptic elements in passing in Letter 1. His appeal rests on his relationship with his audience, as well as on his theology. They are apparently falling into the same errors as in 1 Corinthians. They value the things the world does—wisdom, spiritual gifts, good appearance, eloquence, and so on. They may disparage Paul because in their opinion he falls short on these things. He is not quite up to the Corinthians' standards.

Throughout the letter Paul speaks to them of the sufferings he undergoes for his ministry. Suffering is a truer sign of apostleship than what his opponents in Corinth stress. The things of which the Corinthians boast belong to the world of the flesh, not the new world. Letter 1 of 2 Corinthians continues the gospel of the cross as Paul expounded it and used it in 1 Corinthians.

Basic to Paul's argument is that his ministry fits God's world, and so it clashes with this world's standards. By claiming this, he turns the opponents' arguments on their head. They claim that Paul's unattractive, deathlike appearance, his weakness, his sickness, his sufferings, and the resistance he encounters all show him to be an unworthy representative of God's message. He is likely to be guilty of underhandedness, fraud, and obfuscation. His gospel is complicated and misleading. He serves himself, not God. Paul makes the opposite case. By what they value, his opponents prove that they are still trapped in the fleshly world (4:10–12; chapters 10–11).

Paul may seem to his audience like one punished by God, but he is actually a person "sent from God and standing in his presence" (2:17). This is a claim to almost angelic status and authority. In Jewish apocalypses certain angels stand in God's presence, and at times they are sent from God to humans. The very word "angel" (Greek: *angelos*; Hebrew: *māl'ak*) means "messenger." In Luke 1, Gabriel says that he stands in God's presence and that he has been sent by God (Luke 1:19).

Paul was taking up a collection on behalf of the poor of the Jerusalem church (see Gal. 2:10), and some in the church suspect him of fraud (Georgi 1991; Duff 1991, 80–81). Paul's defense implies that someone is accusing him of dishonesty (6:3; 7:2; see 1 Thess. 2:3–12). The Corinthians' suspicions are fueled by the fact that Paul has never brought to them letters of recommendation.

In response to the complaint that he has produced no letters of recommendation, Paul answers that the Corinthian church itself is his letter, written "not with ink but with the Spirit of the living God, not on tablets of stone but on tablets of human hearts" (3:3). Paul founded the church, the church has the Spirit, and this validates Paul's ministry. What more could they desire in terms of credentials? Paul contrasts the physical letter to the Spirit in their hearts (3:2–3).

This leads to a contrast between the written Mosaic covenant and the new, spiritual covenant. The Torah is spiritual and from God, so it has a degree of glory, even though it cannot accomplish reconciliation with God. Paul concludes, "If what was set aside came through glory, much more has the permanent come in glory!" (3:11). Since "the present form of this world is passing away" (1 Cor. 7:31), so is the old covenant expressed in Torah.

According to Paul, nonbelieving Jews remain unaware of what is central to Scripture: "Indeed, to this very day whenever Moses is read, a veil lies over their minds; but when one turns to the Lord, the veil is removed. Now the Lord is the Spirit, and where the Spirit of the Lord is, there is freedom" (3:15–17). "Lord" means Jesus. One can understand Scripture only if Christ is the hermeneutical key. When one turns to Christ, the veil over one's mind is removed and one sees Scripture's meaning. The presence of the Spirit is the same as the presence of Christ. The Spirit is always Christ's Spirit. And when "the Spirit of the Lord," that is, the Spirit of Christ, is present, "there is freedom." By freedom Paul means escape from the enslavement that is the essence of the world.

Paul speaks of believers having unveiled faces as they gaze at the glory of "the Lord," that is, Christ (3:16–18). As they gaze, they are transformed into "the same image" from one degree of glory to another.

Paul relates all of this to his ministry. His opponents complain that his theology is obfuscating. He retorts, "And even if our gospel is veiled, it is veiled to those who are perishing. In their case the god of this world has blinded the minds of the unbelievers, to keep them from seeing the light of the gospel of the glory of Christ, who is the image of God" (4:3–4). Insiders know and understand Paul's gospel. Typical of apocalypticism, Paul's message is veiled to outsiders, and this is accomplished by "the god of this world."

Paul's message, ultimately one of glory, is in his own ministry in this world carried in "clay jars" so that there is no confusion about what the message is (4:7–12). Paul lists his weaknesses and sufferings as examples of his efforts to keep the focus on God's work and not on his own.

Paul offers help with his dense argumentation. He tells his readers that he is saying all this so that they will be able to answer those who concentrate on "outward appearance" (*tous en prosōpō*) rather than on what is in the heart. Paul's argument is brought together in apocalyptic terms.

> From now on, therefore, we regard no one from a human point of view ["according to the flesh"]; even though we once knew Christ from a human point of view, we know him no longer in that way. So if anyone is in Christ, there is a new creation: everything old has passed away; see, everything has become new! (5:16–17)

Those in Christ are a new creation. Our analysis is supported by an important article written by Martyn in 1967. Here is a key paragraph from his exposition of 2 Cor. 2:14–6:10.

> He [Paul] is saying that there are two ways of knowing and that what separates the two is the turn of the ages, the eschatological event of Christ's death/resurrection. There is a way of knowing that is characteristic of the old age [*gnoskein* or *eidenai kata sarka*], and by clear implication there is a way of knowing which is proper either to the new age or to that point at which the ages meet. (Martyn 1967, 274)

Martyn notes that Paul has no problem describing what knowing *kata sarka* (according to the flesh) means. It embodies the values endemic to the old world. Knowing *kata pneuma* (according to the Spirit) is more difficult, because believers have not fully and definitively entered that world. There is the ever-present already/not yet of Paul's apocalyptic thought. So Paul resorts to knowing *kata stauron* (according to the cross). This is a way of knowing appropriate to the juncture of the ages. Paul uses language employed by Paul's two types of opponents in Corinth, who may be of a Gnostic bent in 1 Corinthians and consider themselves divine men in 2 Corinthians (Georgi 1986). Neither group thinks eschatologically. By using the language of his opponents—according to the flesh and according to the Spirit—Paul draws them into his argument. By interpreting these ways of knowing eschatologically, Paul moves the argument onto an apocalyptic plane. Paul's opponents' achievements and credentials then seem empty, and Paul's weakness becomes strength.

Letter 2: The tearful letter (chaps. 10–13). Letter 1 was unsuccessful. Paul tried a visit to Corinth, but it was a disaster. He departed in humiliation. So he writes another letter, which we possess partially in chapters 10–13. Later he refers to it as his letter full of tears (2:4). Paul is still upset about the same things as in Letter 1. This letter fragment begins with a statement confirming our comments in the previous paragraph.

> I myself, Paul, appeal to you by the meekness and gentleness of Christ—I who am humble when face to face with you, but bold toward you when I am away!—I ask that when I am present I need not show boldness by daring to oppose those who think we are acting according to human standards [according to the flesh]. Indeed, we live as human beings [in the flesh], but we do not wage war according to human standards [according to the flesh]; for the weapons of our warfare are not merely human [fleshly], but they have divine power to destroy strongholds. We destroy arguments and every proud obstacle raised up against the knowledge of God, and we take every thought captive to obey Christ. (10:1–5)

Even those in Christ are forced to live "in the flesh," but Paul refuses to conform to this world. Instead, he reflects Christ's humility. Still, if he needs to show strength in order to get the Corinthians back into line, he can and will do it. But his strength comes from rational argumentation, which reflects God's power. He will not engage his opponents in a contest of who has the most spiritual power or persuasive eloquence.

Paul discloses what his opponents are saying: "For they say, 'His letters are weighty and strong, but his bodily presence is weak, and his speech contemptible'" (10:10). He condemns such an attitude. It serves the ego of the opponents, not the mission of Christ's apostles.

It seems strange that Paul's readers would resent his not charging them for his apostolic services (11:7). His detractors may be saying that Paul himself does not deem them worth the price. Paul will not change his ways.

And what I do I will also continue to do, in order to deny an opportunity to those who want an opportunity to be recognized as our equals in what they boast about. For such boasters are false apostles, deceitful workers, disguising themselves as apostles of Christ. And no wonder! Even Satan disguises himself as an angel of light. So it is not strange if his ministers also disguise themselves as ministers of righteousness. Their end will match their deeds. (11:12–15)

Paul's attack is ferocious. These so-called apostles are not only wrong; they are satanic. And Satan is forever trying to hinder Paul.

Paul makes a clever rhetorical move in the next section. Having renounced engaging his opponents on their own ground, fleshly wisdom, he reverses himself and now says he will do what they are doing. He will boast "according to the flesh" (11:18). Then, instead of boasting in the things of which they boast, he boasts of the opposite. The true signs of an apostle are not eloquence, power, or appearance, but misfortunes, persecutions, hardships, betrayal, and so on. As he says, "If I must boast, I will boast of the things that show my weakness" (11:30). This reveals God's power, not Paul's, and it conforms to Christ's death (12:9).

Paul moves on to another level of credentials—mystical experiences. He traveled to heaven and received mysterious revelations. He is so reticent about it that he speaks of it in the third person, but it is clear that he refers to himself. He does know that he was in the third heaven (12:2). Different apocalypses can have different numbers of heavens. Seven is not uncommon, from which we get the modern expression about being in "seventh heaven." Paul says also that he was in "Paradise" (12:4), and some apocalypses locate paradise in one of the heavens.

While in heaven, Paul "heard things that are not to be told, that no mortal is permitted to repeat" (12:4). This adds secrecy to Paul's mystical knowledge. Nonetheless, Paul does not want to use this to convince his readers in Corinth. He ought to be able to proceed with them on the basis of the truth of his message and his arguments, not on the basis of such credentials.

> But if I wish to boast, I will not be a fool, for I will be speaking the truth. But I refrain from it, so that no one may think better of me than what is seen in me or heard from me, even considering the exceptional character of the revelations [*apokalypseis*]. Therefore, to keep me from being too elated, a thorn was given me in the flesh, a messenger of Satan to torment me, to keep me from being too elated. (12:6–7)

Despite his reluctance to use his mystical experiences as an argument, Paul lets the readers know that they have been many and were "exceptional." Paul's ambivalent attitude to these sorts of credentials is evident in how he concludes his argument: "I have been a fool! You forced me to it" (12:11).

Paul's thorn is a puzzle. It is probably an illness. It may have something to do with his less-than-healthy appearance. His letters often refer to his ill health. Paul takes it as God's way of keeping him humble, despite the gifts God has bestowed on him. God uses Satan to make the point.

Letter 3: Letter of reconciliation (1:1–2:13; 7:5–16). Eventually things turned out well in Corinth, as Letter 3 demonstrates. Paul says that his suffering was for their salvation, so they might share Paul's consolation. Salvation means the ultimate consummation of the apocalyptic scheme. Paul's suffering represents and brings about distance from this world of the flesh. They should look to Paul to see how that works: "Indeed, we felt that we had received the sentence of death so that we would rely not on ourselves but on God who raises the dead" (1:9). When Paul and the Corinthians arrive at "the day of the Lord Jesus Christ," they will be able to boast in one another because they will have lived life according to Paul's gospel.

Paul turns to the proper treatment of his main opponent in Corinth. The church has already punished him. Paul wants to get past the episode. Anything else would prolong the conflict and give Satan an opportunity to stir up more trouble within the community: "And we do this so that we may not be outwitted by Satan; for we are not ignorant of his designs" (2:11).

Letters 4 and 5 (chaps. 8 and 9). These letters do not add appreciably to our understanding of Paul's apocalyptic worldview.

Jesus and Paul: Contrasting Apocalyptic Thinkers

Jesus and Paul were both first-century Jews. The movement Jesus founded grew into the church that Paul served so fervently and fruitfully. Both thought in terms of Jewish apocalypticism. But they were also quite different from each other.

Ancient Judaism was diverse. Jesus and Paul fell into opposite sides of a basic distinction between ancient Jews: one was a lifelong inhabitant of a rural area in the homeland, Galilee; the other, a citizen of the wider world of the Jewish Diaspora. Both groups of Jews were Hellenistic, but to different degrees and in different ways. Paul's Hellenization was more obvious. Hellenism was primarily an urban phenomenon, and Paul was urbane. He hailed from southeastern Asia Minor, from the area of Cilicia, the city of Tarsus. Tarsus was a Hellenized city and a university town. Paul's native language was Greek. His letters show evidence of a Greek education. He knew and used the letter form well, knew some Greek philosophy at least secondhand, and employed Greek rhetorical forms.

Jesus was born and spent most of his life in Galilee. He came from Nazareth, a town of several hundred people never mentioned in the Hebrew Bible or by Josephus. Sepphoris, one of the most important Hellenistic cities in Palestine, was within four miles of Nazareth, yet Jesus apparently never visited it. Jesus seems to have restricted his activity to Galilee's towns and villages except for his final visit to Jerusalem. His native language was probably Aramaic; he likely spoke no Greek, or at best a smattering of it.

Both Jesus and Paul thought in apocalyptic terms, but the result was markedly different. Jesus focused on the coming kingdom of God. Sanders conceives of this as a this-worldly state of affairs in which God properly rules the world he created (Sanders 1985; Horsley 1993). Under God's rule, things will be as they ought to be, as God intended. One aspect of that is the restoration of Israel, with twelve tribes reconstituted and "judged" or "ruled over" by the twelve apostles. In God's kingdom, people will eat and drink wine. They will sit at table with Abraham, Isaac, and Jacob.

Paul also thought in apocalyptic terms, but he did not expect an earthly restoration of Israel. For Paul, the old and new worlds were profoundly different. Resurrection would mean that one would be on an entirely different plane of existence. One would be completely transformed and live forever with the Lord "in the air." One would no longer have this physical body but a spiritual one.

We have repeatedly stressed the complex and varied nature of apocalypses and apocalypticism. To encounter such complexity in Jesus and Paul should not be surprising.

Suggestions for Further Reading

Dunn, James D. G. *The Theology of Paul the Apostle*. Grand Rapids: Eerdmans, 1998.

Engberg-Pedersen, Troels. *Paul and the Stoics*. Louisville: Westminster John Knox, 2000.

Gager, John G. *Reinventing Paul*. New York: Oxford University Press, 2000.

Murphy-O'Connor, Jerome. *Becoming Human Together: The Pastoral Anthropology of St. Paul*. 3rd ed. Atlanta: Society of Biblical Literature, 2009.

———. *Paul: A Critical Life*. New York: Clarendon, 1996.

Plevnik, Joseph. *What Are They Saying about Paul and the End Time?* New York: Paulist Press, 2009.

Sanders, E. P. *Paul and Palestinian Judaism*. Philadelphia: Fortress, 1977.

Stendahl, Krister. "The Apostle Paul and the Introspective Conscience of the West." *Harvard Theological Review* 56, no. 3 (1963): 199–215.

———. *Paul among Jews and Gentiles, and Other Essays*. Philadelphia: Fortress, 1976.

Tobin, Thomas H. *Paul's Rhetoric in Its Contexts: The Argument of Romans*. Peabody, MA: Hendrickson, 2004.

11

The Rest of the New Testament

Contested Pauline Letters

Of the thirteen letters attributed to Paul in the New Testament, seven are undisputed with respect to their authenticity. We used only those seven as we analyzed Paul's thought. We now turn to the other six. They are witnesses to later Christian thinkers who considered themselves in the tradition and spirit of Paul, even though we may judge otherwise. Our interest is in their apocalyptic elements.

2 Thessalonians

The problem in 1 Thessalonians is that some church members have died, but Christ has not yet come back. They apparently expected that Christ would come back soon, before any of them died. Paul implies that he expects that he and his readers will be alive at the parousia (4:13–18). Second Thessalonians has the opposite problem. Some in the church think that the parousia is not only close but that it has already arrived. The author refers to a "spurious" letter from him (supposedly Paul) saying just that (2:2). The author of 2 Thessalonians thinks that the end is not close; a lot has to happen first. It is hard to believe that Paul could have written twice to the church, within a short period of time (since the letters are so similar), and yet that the church's problem is the opposite in each case.

The first two chapters of 2 Thessalonians are intensely apocalyptic. They speak of the present suffering of the church as its "affliction" (*thlipsis*), the word found frequently for the terrible suffering of the end time. The author awaits vindication, and he paints it in lurid hues:

> When the Lord Jesus is revealed from heaven with his mighty angels in flaming fire, inflicting vengeance on those who do not know God and on those who do not obey the gospel of our Lord Jesus. These will suffer the punishment of eternal destruction, separated from the presence of the Lord and from the glory of his might, when he comes to be glorified by his saints and to be marveled at on that day among all who have believed, because our testimony to you was believed. (1:7–10)

Paul is an apocalyptic thinker, but he does not engage in this kind of almost gleeful pleasure in contemplating the horrible fate of those who are not Christian.

Chapter 2 addresses the more specific problem of the church, that some think the parousia has already come. His solution is to remind his audience of what must come before the parousia.

> Let no one deceive you in any way; for that day will not come unless the rebellion comes first and the lawless one is revealed [*apokalyphthē*], the one destined for destruction. He opposes and exalts himself above every so-called god or object of worship, so that he takes his seat in the temple of God, declaring himself to be God. Do you not remember that I told you these things when I was still with you? And you know what is now restraining him, so that he may be revealed [*apokalyphthēnai*] when his time comes. For the mystery [*mystērion*] of lawlessness is already at work, but only until the one who now restrains it is removed. And then the lawless one will be revealed [*apokalyphthēsetai*], whom the Lord Jesus will destroy with the breath of his mouth, annihilating him by the manifestation of his coming [*parousia*]. The coming of the lawless one is apparent in the working of Satan, who uses all power, signs, lying wonders, and every kind of wicked deception for those who are perishing, because they refused to love the truth and so be saved. For this reason God sends them a powerful delusion, leading them to believe what is false, so that all who have not believed the truth but took pleasure in unrighteousness will be condemned. (2:3–12)

The author expects a "lawless one" to come at the end of time. Someone is now restraining him; the author does not say who. Then comes a rebellion and the revelation of the lawless one. The passage is pervaded with the language of secrecy and revelation.

We have not yet addressed the issue of the antichrist. We do so below in greater detail. For now, it is sufficient to note that many Christian apocalyptic scenarios envisage a figure, usually human, who will appear at the end of time and who will be opposed to Christ. The behavior of the "lawless one" in 2 Thessalonians contains much that the antichrist represents throughout history, even though the term is not used here—he is in some sense human;

he claims to be God; he usurps God's temple; he takes on God's authority and power, both political and religious; he deceives; he has the power of Satan behind him; and when he appears, the second coming of Christ is near. When the antichrist rules, Satan is active. His power and deception fill the world and doom people because they are swept up, deluded by his falsehood. When that happens, Christ's parousia will happen as well, and Christ will destroy the lawless one.

The author's readers need not worry, however. They are the "first fruits for salvation" (2:13) through God's choice (an apocalyptic idea), and the Lord will protect them from Satan (3:3).

Colossians

Of all the disputed Pauline letters, Colossians has the most support as being authentic. Nonetheless, we judge it to be pseudonymous. Its Greek is quite different from what we are used to from Paul, because it is composed of long, involved sentences contrasting with Paul's more rapid style. Its vocabulary contains many words not used elsewhere by Paul. More important than style is substance. When compared with Paul's seven undisputed letters, Colossians displays a shift on key points of theology. Fortunately, those shifts affect the apocalyptic viewpoint, so they give us another opportunity to observe how an apocalyptic worldview is transformed and adapted to suit an author's purposes.

This letter addresses a church not founded by Paul. Christians have entered the church preaching a gospel with which the author disagrees. As usual, we have only one side of the argument, so we cannot know just what the author's opponents believed and preached. The issue has been debated for a long time without general consensus. The author calls it "philosophy and empty deceit, according to human tradition, according to the elemental spirits of the universe, and not according to Christ" (2:8). He exhorts them not to yield to his opponents' insistence that they follow certain observances concerning food, drink, festivals, new moons, and Sabbaths (2:16). They are but a "shadow" of what is to come, while "the substance belongs to Christ" (2:17). The opponents also insist on self-abasement and worship of angels, and they rely on "visions" and have a "human way of thinking" (Greek: "by the mind of his flesh") (2:18). Against all this, the author holds up the image of Christ, in whom the fullness of God dwells, through whom everything was created, even the powers of the universe.

Broadly sketched, the author's opponents advocate a religion with Jewish elements—dietary rules, feasts and Sabbaths, and other observances. Worship of angels implies some sort of mystical experience, perhaps supported by asceticism (self-abasement). The mysticism seems to go beyond what Paul encountered in Galatia, and it is what prompts the author's reflections on the nature of Christ, who has become a cosmic figure, the one through whom the entire universe was created.

If the author of this letter is not Paul, it is someone well acquainted with Paul's theology. He adopts much of it but changes it subtly. The major change is that while Paul insists that the resurrection is future for believers, this author shifts it to the past. Believers have not only died with Christ; they have already risen with him. Their lives are hidden in heaven with Christ. We saw Paul struggle with this tension in his own theology. In Rom. 6 Paul says we have died with Christ, but he carefully refrains from saying we have risen with him. That is for the future. Given the extreme care with which Paul usually frames such issues, it is striking when this author can say explicitly and with no apparent second thoughts that we have already been raised with Christ.

The author's willingness to take the step that Paul would not is due to the nature of the theology he fights, particularly its mystical side. The author faced opponents who advocated not only Jewish ways but mystical experiences. This author needed not only renunciation of ways thought to belong to this fleshly world, but something more positive that he could hold up to his readers as more valuable than connection to angels or other powers. Presence with Christ in heaven was about as good as it could get—the ultimate trump card. So this author moved the eschatological calendar forward, beyond what Paul had dared to do.

We turn to some of the letter's details to observe how he simultaneously adopts the basics of Paul's apocalyptic reasoning while changing it to meet his own new situation. The author has read Paul's argument in Galatians. Before attacking his opponents' position, the author lays out the basics of his own theology.

The Colossians are gentiles. At one time they had no share in the blessings that were to come through Israel's God. Now they do, through Christ. For this author, this is a "mystery" (1:26, 27; 2:2; 4:3). His fullest statement of it is in 1:26–27: "The mystery [*mystērion*] that has been hidden throughout the ages and generations but has now been revealed to his saints. To them God chose to make known how great among the Gentiles are the riches of the glory of this mystery [*mystērion*], which is Christ in you, the hope of glory." The mystery Paul reveals in Rom. 11 is similar to the one here insofar as it concerns the relationship between Jews and gentiles before and after Christ. But it is also different. In Romans, the mystery is that hardening has come upon Israel so that the gentiles will be brought into God's favor, while for Colossians it is that the gentiles are now reconciled to God.

The mystery in Colossians reveals the new relationship the readers have with each other in Christ, and it also preserves hope, an eschatological reservation that is not unlike Paul's own. This is not fully realized eschatology; it is something between Jesus's or Mark's thoroughgoing eschatology and John's realized eschatology. A scale of eschatologies measured by the degree to which one presently enjoys the benefits of what would traditionally be in the future would be the following:

Thoroughgoing eschatology (Jesus; Mark; Revelation)
Already/not yet (Paul)
Already/not yet, but resurrection in the past (Colossians)
Already: realized eschatology (Gospel of John)

Like Paul, this author thinks that believers have already escaped the old world dominated by powers opposed to God: "He has rescued us from the power of darkness and transferred us into the kingdom of his beloved Son, in whom we have redemption, the forgiveness of sins" (1:13–14). Like Paul, he thinks that adopting the practices urged by his opponents will result in living "according to the elemental spirits of the universe" (2:8), in other words, slipping back into the old world. Both Paul and this author see the believers as being in a state where they are no longer bound by the old world but are in jeopardy of slipping back into it. But this is for different reasons. For Paul, it is because adoption of the Torah betrays the confidence that reconciliation comes only through what God has done in Christ. For the author of Colossians, it is because they are in danger of giving up their status of being with Christ in heaven right now, sharing in the ultimate spiritual blessings, in return for the paltry benefits they think they can get through their hoped-for relationships with other superhuman powers. The problem is different. So is the solution. But because both have to do with Jewish practices and both involve apocalyptic views of old and new worlds, they sound alike.

Along the way, the author shifts another Pauline idea away from apocalypticism. Paul almost always speaks of sin in the singular as a cosmic power. One could generally substitute "Satan" where Paul has "sin" and have the same meaning. Our author speaks of "sins," individual acts against God (*paraptōma*), and says that through Christ believers have "forgiveness" (2:13). Paul never uses the Greek verb *charisetai* in this sense ("to forgive") in his authentic letters as he does here. The shift lessens Paul's picture of a humanity freed by God's act in Christ from enslavement to cosmic sin.

The picture of Christ shifts a bit, as well. Paul does have some idea of the preexistence of Christ, according to our interpretation, if taken within his Adam Christology. There must have been a time before Jesus entered the fallen world, since he agreed to do so. This was his act of obedience. Colossians moves in the direction of Johannine Christology and that of the later church when it says that all creation, including superhuman powers like "thrones or dominations or rulers or powers" were created through Christ (1:16). This makes the same claim as does the prologue to John's Gospel, and it depends on Jewish speculation on wisdom as both an attribute of God and as a semiautonomous

cosmic power alongside but in harmony with God. Because of this, the fullness of God dwells in Christ, so when believers are united with Christ they are
united with God. This also makes it possible for Christ to reconcile all things
to God—all came into being through him and in him God's fullness dwells.
Christ holds it all together. The author applies that directly to the inclusion
of the gentiles in God's favor (1:22). Paul does not use "reconciliation" in this
specific sense—the inclusion of the gentiles. It is another instance of a subtle
semantic shift that betrays a non-Pauline hand.

Paul and the author of Colossians both speak of Christ as being the "firstborn." Paul applies this only to Jesus's resurrection. The Colossians author
uses it that way, too, but he also applies it to the fact that all things were created in Christ, so Christ is before all things and so is in this additional sense
"firstborn."

In its exhortation, Colossians uses some familiar Pauline language. The
author warns of God's wrath if the Colossians do not make the right decisions, speaks of their old and new selves, and talks of the image of God, and
of Jesus being in God's image (1:15; 3:10).

Ephesians

Whoever wrote Ephesians had a wide knowledge of Paul's letters and was
particularly engaged with Colossians. One intimately familiar with Paul's
letters will find references to one or another of them in every verse of Ephesians, yet in most cases those references will alter Paul's meaning. The letter
reads somewhat as a pastiche of the Pauline corpus, but it also has a central
agenda and does hold together on its own. The best manuscripts lack the name
"Ephesus," leading to the hypothesis that the letter was not originally addressed
to that church but was perhaps a cover letter for a collection of Paul's epistles.

Since Ephesians follows Colossians closely, it makes some of the same
changes in Paul's theology as does that letter. The resurrection is again in the
past and has become more spatial than temporal. Believers are now with Christ
in heaven. We again meet the cosmic Christ. The author, like the author of
Colossians, speaks of a mystery kept secret for the long ages and only now
revealed. The mystery is similar to that of Colossians. It is that the gentiles
have now been included within Israel and that the dividing line between Jew
and gentile is forever broken down. The letter adapts apocalyptic images to
reinforce the new identity of these converted gentiles.

The author informs his readers that what has happened to them is the
"mystery of his [God's] will, according to his good pleasure that he set forth in
Christ, as a plan for the fullness of time" (1:9–10). As an assurance of this, his
audience received the Holy Spirit as a seal, a Pauline idea expressed in Rom. 5
and elsewhere and also used by Colossians. The author wishes for his readers
"a spirit of wisdom and revelation [*apokalypsis*]" (1:17), indicating that he

wishes them to think the way he does. The author uses the word "mystery" seven times in this short letter, only one of which (5:32) does not apply to the breaking down of the division between Jew and gentile.

We see the cosmic Christ in Ephesians: "God put this power to work in Christ when he raised him from the dead and seated him at his right hand in the heavenly places, far above all rule and authority and power and dominion, and above every name that is named, not only in this age but also in the age to come" (1:20–21). This echoes Colossians as well as the hymn in Phil. 2 and the eschatological scenario of 1 Cor. 15. Added to the cosmic lordship expressed in the Philippians hymn are the specification that Jesus is above "all rule and authority and power and dominion," superhuman powers in the universe, and the mention of the two ages. Both have apocalyptic meaning, and both apply to the letter's interests. Through Christ the gentiles are brought into communion with Israel. This new era of undivided humanity is the new age. This is all symbolized and realized in the heavenly, cosmic Christ, who rules over all, thus uniting the universe.

To reinforce the significance of his gentile audience's inclusion in the new world, in union with Israel, the author characterizes the old and new worlds in ways that utilize apocalyptic motifs.

> You were dead through the trespasses and sins in which you once lived, fol-
> lowing the course of this world, following the ruler of the power of the air,
> the spirit that is now at work among those who are disobedient. All of us
> once lived among them in the passions of our flesh, following the desires of
> flesh and senses, and we were by nature children of wrath, like everyone else.
> But God, who is rich in mercy, out of the great love with which he loved us
> even when we were dead through our trespasses, made us alive together with
> Christ—by grace you have been saved—and raised us up with him and seated
> us with him in the heavenly places in Christ Jesus, so that in the ages to come
> he might show the immeasurable riches of his grace in kindness toward us in
> Christ Jesus. (2:1–7)

Echoes of Paul's other letters are audible. The old world is the world of death, it is subject to cosmic powers alienated from God, it enslaves one to the passions of one's flesh, it subjects one to God's wrath, it is inhabited by those who are disobedient, and it is all according to "the course of this world." Following the sorts of changes in Paul's apocalyptic worldview that Colossians had already made, this author asserts that believers are already raised with Christ and sit with him in heaven to emphasize what his hearers already possess and to stress how permanent that is. It seems less liable to reversal than is Paul's state of reconciliation, since Paul is so careful about his eschatological reservation. Although the author has shifted emphasis from the temporal to the spatial, he maintains the temporal aspect, for he speaks of "the ages to come."

The mystery must now be lived out by the audience of the book. It is known to them and has never been known before; it must be proclaimed and advanced by the church. This is central to the church's mission.

> Surely you have already heard of the commission of God's grace that was given me for you, and how the mystery was made known to me by revelation [*apokalypsis*], as I wrote above in a few words, a reading of which will enable you to perceive my understanding of the mystery of Christ. In former generations this mystery was not made known to humankind, as it has now been revealed to his holy apostles and prophets by the Spirit: that is, the Gentiles have become fellow heirs, members of the same body, and sharers in the promise in Christ Jesus through the gospel.
> Of this gospel I have become a servant according to the gift of God's grace that was given me by the working of his power. Although I am the very least of all the saints, this grace was given to me to bring to the Gentiles the news of the boundless riches of Christ, and to make everyone see what is the plan of the mystery hidden for ages in God who created all things; so that through the church the wisdom of God in its rich variety might now be made known to the rulers and authorities in the heavenly places. This was in accordance with the eternal purpose that he has carried out in Christ Jesus our Lord, in whom we have access to God in boldness and confidence through faith in him. (3:2–12)

The apocalyptic framework is evident. God has a plan that is a mystery hidden for ages that is now revealed. The cosmic powers, the "rulers and authorities in the heavenly places," are opposed to the unity brought about between Jew and gentile through Christ. The church must announce this unity to them, and it must also live in such a way that the new state of the gentiles is embodied in their behavior. They are no longer like gentiles alienated from Israel and God. In their preaching the mystery and living in accord with it, they are engaged in battle with these forces.

> Now this I affirm and insist on in the Lord: you must no longer live as the Gentiles live, in the futility of their minds. They are darkened in their understanding, alienated from the life of God because of their ignorance and hardness of heart. They have lost all sensitivity and have abandoned themselves to licentiousness, greedy to practice every kind of impurity. That is not the way you learned Christ! For surely you have heard about him and were taught in him, as truth is in Jesus. You were taught to put away your former way of life, your old self, corrupt and deluded by its lusts, and to be renewed in the spirit of your minds, and to clothe yourselves with the new self, created according to the likeness of God in true righteousness and holiness. (4:17–24)

Paul's apocalyptic idea of a new self and a new creation in God's image supports a new life. The old world has been left behind. The readers are at war with its demonic princes.

Finally, be strong in the Lord and in the strength of his power. Put on the whole armor of God, so that you may be able to stand against the wiles of the devil. For our struggle is not against enemies of blood and flesh, but against the rulers, against the authorities, against the cosmic powers of this present darkness, against the spiritual forces of evil in the heavenly places. Therefore take up the whole armor of God, so that you may be able to withstand on that evil day, and having done everything, to stand firm. Stand therefore, and fasten the belt of truth around your waist, and put on the breastplate of righteousness. As shoes for your feet put on whatever will make you ready to proclaim the gospel of peace. With all of these, take the shield of faith, with which you will be able to quench all the flaming arrows of the evil one. Take the helmet of salvation, and the sword of the Spirit, which is the word of God. (6:10–17)

The Pastoral Epistles

The "Pastoral Epistles" are 1 and 2 Timothy and Titus. They claim Paul's authorship, but few accept the attribution. They are called "pastoral" because their addressees are not churches, as in Paul's undisputed letters, but individual pastors. They differ from Paul's authentic letters in many ways—form, language, content, historical situation, and so on. They cannot contribute to our understanding of Paul's apocalyptic thought. Rather, they supply evidence for how Paul's thought was adapted by later writers. Since these three letters are so similar to each other, it is justifiable to see them as a whole, written by one person, addressing a single situation.

The Pastoral Epistles evince little real apocalyptic thought. Certain ideas and mythological assumptions from apocalypticism appear in passing, but they do not capture the author's attention. For example, the author assumes that there is a Satan who is active outside the church. Those who act in ways contrary to the proper behavior demanded of respectable and pious people are following the ways of Satan (1 Tim. 3:6–7; 5:15). Engagement in theological disputes and taking a position the author sees as erroneous is also to be under the devil's influence (2 Tim. 2:26). The author says that he has turned someone over to Satan (1 Tim. 1:20), perhaps a reference to excommunication as in 1 Cor. 5:5. Despite these references, the author does not dwell on Satan's activity, nor does he give the impression that he or his readers have a lively sense of being besieged by the devil or engaged in cosmic battle.

The "day" or "that day" are mentioned in passing as well. The day of judgment is present and is the horizon against which all human action must be considered. But again, it is not imminent. If anything, it seems distant (2 Tim. 1:12, 18; 4:8).

The author opposes certain teachings current among his readers. As usual, we have but one side of the argument, so we cannot know in detail just what his opponents espouse. Jewish law, theology, and practices are part of it. Relevant to our purposes are two church members, Hymenaeus and Philetus, who "have swerved from the truth by claiming that the resurrection has already taken place" (2 Tim. 2:18).

The Remainder of the New Testament

We have now examined the book of Revelation, the four Gospels, Acts of the Apostles, Q, the historical Jesus, the seven undisputed Pauline letters, and the six letters attributed to Paul but disputed by scholars regarding their authenticity. This leaves eight more texts that are part of the New Testament.

First Peter

This letter is attributed to Peter, but most question the attribution. The author writes to gentile converts to Christianity. Their new status causes problems for them in their environment, since they can no longer participate in society as they once did. The author portrays that participation as conforming to the sinful ways of their own past. They are meeting hostility from their non-Christian neighbors, who accuse them of various crimes. It is not unusual for those who are considered outsiders to society to be unjustly accused of crimes, either in the ancient world or the modern one.

The author's advice is to fit into society as well as possible without engaging in acts that contravene their new life in Christ. If they suffer accusation and punishment, it must not be on account of normal crimes; it should be for the name of Christ (4:12–19). They should obey the civil authorities and society's laws (2:13–17), but they should never engage in sinful behavior, even if it is normal in their environment (4:1–6).

The author lays the groundwork for his instruction by teaching his readers about their present status. It is a provisional situation. It is lived out between their conversion to Christianity and the eschaton. This is an interim time and is not permanent.

> Blessed be the God and Father of our Lord Jesus Christ! By his great mercy he has given us a new birth into a living hope through the resurrection of Jesus Christ from the dead, and into an inheritance that is imperishable, undefiled, and unfading, kept in heaven for you, who are being protected by the power of God through faith for a salvation ready to be revealed [*apocalyptō*] in the last time [*en kairō eschatō*]. In this you rejoice, even if now for a little while you have had to suffer various trials [*peirasmos*], so that the genuineness of your faith— being more precious than gold that, though perishable, is tested by fire—may be found to result in praise and glory and honor when Jesus Christ is revealed [*apocalyptō*]. Although you have not seen him, you love him; and even though you do not see him now, you believe in him and rejoice with an indescribable and glorious joy, for you are receiving the outcome of your faith, the salvation of your souls. (1:3–9)

The author depicts their sufferings as "various trials," or "temptations" (*peiras-mos*). *Peirasmos* is frequently used in apocalyptic contexts for the end-time trials and sufferings. The language of revelation uses the familiar verb *apocalyptō*. Salvation for the readers will come at the last time, expressed in two words frequent in apocalyptic contexts: "last time." The entire section sets an end time for the sufferings of the readers. Their present sufferings are tests to see if they are worthy of this eschatological salvation. It provides them with a context within which to interpret their unfortunate present experiences.

The letter's next section underscores how fortunate the readers are to be living when they do. They are near the end of time, a period foreseen by the prophets.

> Concerning this salvation, the prophets who prophesied of the grace that was to be yours made careful search and inquiry, inquiring about the person or time that the Spirit of Christ within them indicated when it testified in advance to the sufferings destined for Christ and the subsequent glory. It was revealed to them that they were serving not themselves but you, in regard to the things that have now been announced to you through those who brought you good news by the Holy Spirit sent from heaven—things into which angels long to look! (1:10–12)

The prophets foretold Christ's sufferings and glory. Like Qumran, this letter portrays the ancient prophets as foretelling the recent past. Since the readers live after the Christ event and benefit directly from it by being reborn into a new hope resulting from Christ's resurrection, the prophets have served them. Even angels are jealous of the readers who experience a new status and the hope of an imminent eschaton that spells salvation for them.

What has happened in Christ is for the sake of the readers, and it is painted in apocalyptic colors: "He was destined before the foundation of the world, but was revealed at the end [*eschaton*] of the ages for your sake. Through him you have come to trust in God, who raised him from the dead and gave him glory, so that your faith and hope are set on God" (1:20–21).

As they await the eschaton, the letter's listeners should get along with their surrounding culture as far as possible. Their attitude toward civil authorities should be one of obedience and respect (2:13–17). They are to accept human institutions and act toward the emperor and his governors as legitimate au-thorities. The section ends with the brief exhortations: "Honor everyone. Love the family of believers. Fear God. Honor the emperor" (2:17).

Most of the rest of the letter is exhortation to Christian behavior. It includes the form scholars call a *Haustafel*, a set of rules for the household, containing specific instructions for each category of person—slaves, wives, and husbands. Baptism is "an appeal to God for a good conscience," made through Christ's resurrection, "who has gone into heaven and is seated at the right hand of

God, with angels, authorities, and powers made subject to him" (3:21–22). Jesus is a cosmic figure with other superhuman figures subject to him.

Chapter 4 says that the gospel has been preached to the dead to give them a chance to live in the Spirit. Salvation is to be available even to them, since they did not have a chance to receive the benefits of Christ's resurrection before their death (4:6). This is the origin of the doctrine of the "harrowing of hell," something that caught the Christian imagination in later times.

Plunging back into moral exhortation, the author leads with the proclamation, "The end [*telos*] of all things is near" (4:7). *Telos* connotes a goal as well as a simple ending, and it is not unusual in apocalyptic contexts. In the midst of exhortation, the author inserts apocalyptic motivations. His hearers are to act properly so that "when the chief shepherd appears, you will win the crown of glory that never fades away" (5:4). This refers to Christ's parousia. They are to remain alert and on guard, for "like a roaring lion your adversary the devil prowls around, looking for someone to devour" (5:8). Their task is to "resist him, steadfast in your faith, for you know that your brothers and sisters in all the world are undergoing the same kinds of suffering" (5:9). They can rejoice, knowing that there is an end in sight when they will receive their hope, eternal life in Christ (5:10). The readers are to make sense of their situation by recognizing that it is part of a worldwide drama in which those who belong to Christ can endure the present temporary sufferings because they know that in the end, at the eschaton, they will receive their reward.

Second Peter

A second New Testament letter is attributed to Peter, and again scholars doubt the attribution. The author writes because the community of his readers is beset by what he considers to be deceptive and immoral teachers. Whether or not they were actually immoral (the author mentions lust, greed,

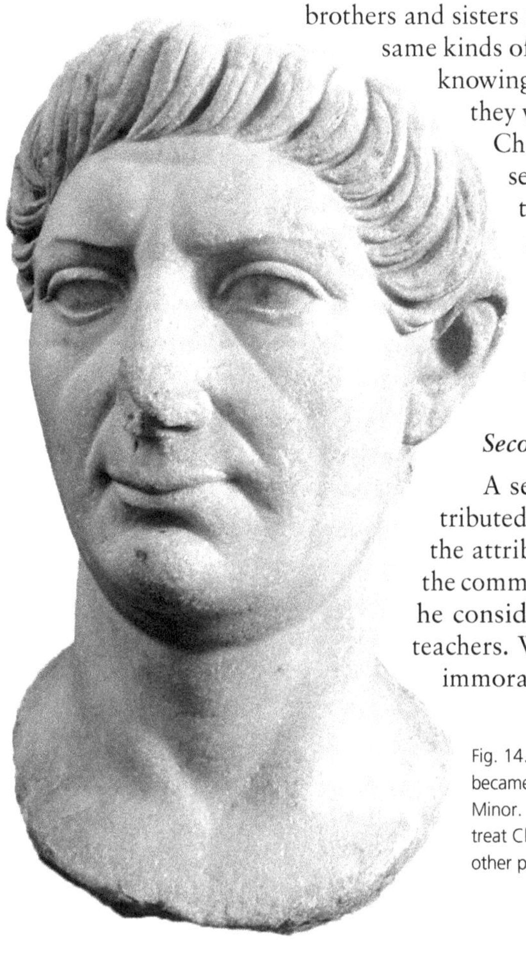

Fig. 14. Under the reign of Trajan, Pliny the Younger became governor of Pontus-Bithynia in northern Asia Minor. He wrote to Trajan to determine how he should treat Christians there. First Peter is written to, among other places, Pontus and Bithynia. (Todd Bolen/bibleplaces.com)

and licentiousness) is impossible to judge, since such accusations were routine in the ancient world against those of a different philosophy or religion (L. Johnson 1989; Knust 2006). That they had different teachings is hardly to be doubted.

The author threatens punishment against the false teachers and any who pay them heed. He adduces examples drawn from the Bible and outside of it to prove that God punishes the wicked. The first speaks of the sinful angels who were consigned to dark places to await ultimate judgment, a scene that could be taken either from the Isaiah Apocalypse (Isa. 24–27) or the *Book of the Watchers*.

Before his final exhortation, the author addresses a matter bearing directly on our concerns. There are those who are mocking the very idea that there will be a parousia. Ironically, the author takes such doubt as proof that the last days are here.

> You should remember the words spoken in the past by the holy prophets, and the commandment of the Lord and Savior spoken through your apostles.
>
> First of all you must understand this, that in the last days scoffers will come, scoffing and indulging their own lusts and saying, "Where is the promise of his coming? For ever since our ancestors died, all things continue as they were from the beginning of creation!" They deliberately ignore this fact, that by the word of God heavens existed long ago and an earth was formed out of water and by means of water, through which the world of that time was deluged with water and perished. But by the same word the present heavens and earth have been reserved for fire, being kept until the day of judgment and destruction of the godless.
>
> But do not ignore this one fact, beloved, that with the Lord one day is like a thousand years, and a thousand years are like one day.
>
> The Lord is not slow about his promise, as some think of slowness, but is patient with you, not wanting any to perish, but all to come to repentance. But the day of the Lord will come like a thief, and then the heavens will pass away with a loud noise, and the elements will be dissolved with fire, and the earth and everything that is done on it will be disclosed. (3:2–10)

Apocalyptic elements are obvious—radical change in the world, future destruction of the world by fire, judgment, destruction of the wicked, sudden coming of the day of the Lord, and the passing away of heaven and earth. Our author declares their truth on the basis of what has been promised by the prophets, Jesus, and the apostles.

Most consider this letter to be one of the latest texts to be included in the New Testament. It is certainly late enough for the parousia to be questioned because Jesus was long gone and yet had not returned. Meanwhile, the world had not changed. How long must they wait? The author arrives at a clever solution. Appealing to Ps. 90:4, he shows that God's conception of time does not match that of humans. Even if a thousand years should pass, that is but a day to the Lord.

Hebrews

This work is often referred to as the letter of Paul to the Hebrews. However, even some ancients recognized that the document is not by Paul, nor does it claim to be. Although it has some formal claim to be a letter, it lacks an epistolary beginning. And though it claims to be to the Hebrews, there is no strong indication in the work that it is written to Jews, despite its use of the Jewish sacrificial cult to explain what has happened in Jesus. Generically, it is clearly a homily, perhaps written to the Roman church; since its author is so familiar with Alexandrian thought, it was perhaps composed there.

In our interpretation of this complex and closely argued homily, we depend on the seminal article of George MacRae (1978). He observes that interpreters have long seen that there were two kinds of temple interpretation involved in the work, but that the tension has usually been resolved by insisting on one or the other as paramount. MacRae's central insight is that if the homiletic genre of Hebrews is taken as the key to its meaning, then one type of temple symbolism is used by the homilist to support the wavering hope of his audience, who concentrate on the other type.

The two types of temple symbolism are that of the cosmic temple and that of the apocalyptic heavenly temple. The first is held by the Alexandrian writer, while the second is how the addressees think. The cosmic temple interpretation sees the universe as constructed in the form of a temple. As Josephus, the first-century-CE priest-historian expresses it, the earthly temple is tripartite—a porch, a holy place, and the holy of holies. God is present in the holy of holies, so that symbolizes heaven (*Ant.* 3.123, 180–81). The holy place is the earth, and the porch is the sea. Philo, a famous Jewish philosopher from Alexandria, contemporary with Jesus, has a similar interpretation (*QE* 2.90–96). However, influenced by his Neoplatonic philosophy, he speaks of the outer rooms as the sensible world, while the inner sanctuary is the realm of the Platonic Forms, accessible only through the mind. This can be more clearly understood through the parable of the cave in Plato's *Republic*, where humans see only the shadows of the true realities, called the Forms. When one sees a horse, one is seeing but the shadow of what is really real—"Horse," as a noetic (that is, accessible only through the philosophically trained mind) Form. Transposed to the cosmos, heaven corresponds to the world of the Forms, while humans on earth see only the shadows of what is really real.

We have seen the importance of throne scenes in the Hebrew Bible and in apocalypses. The idea of a full temple present in heaven is evident in several apocalypses, two examples being *1 Enoch* 14 and Rev. 4–5 and throughout that work.

Rather than choose one or the other of these views as that of Hebrews, MacRae demonstrates that both are used and blended. The author uses his own Alexandrian ideas to bolster the fading apocalyptic hopes of his audience. In so doing he blends the apocalyptic temple idea, which they believe, with his own. We follow MacRae in his main lines, but there are some differences in deciding which temple symbolism is operative in which passages.

One of the central goals of religion is to gain and maintain a positive access to God. One must be in touch with God to please him so that he bestows his favor on one's worshiping group. All religions have rituals, practices, and rules to keep this access open. Central to the ancient Jewish way was its cult. Torah commands sacrifices to be performed in the temple. Priests sacrifice animals and use their blood to purify the sanctuary so that God will remain there, and to make up for sin. The Day of Atonement (Lev. 16) prescribes a complex yearly ritual to atone for the inadvertent sins of the high priest and of the community. It involves his entering the sanctuary twice with purifying blood and sprinkling the ark of the covenant with it. He enters once for his own sins and once for the sins of the people.

Hebrews claims that the Jewish cult does not work. But it provides a copy of something that does work. For him, Jesus Christ is the true high priest, the shedding of his blood the effective sacrifice that purifies the people and allows them access to God, and the sanctuary he enters the true one, heaven. Unlike the Jewish sacrifices, his is once-and-for-all. It need never be repeated, and Jesus remains in heaven as the believers' high priest. The real purpose of the cult described in the Bible, which is indeed God's Word for this author, is simply to provide a schema through which believers can understand the work of Christ—how it works and why it was necessary.

Although the author speaks of the desert tent, he is really referring to the Jerusalem temple. He speaks of the tent because that is what is before him in the biblical text, and he is an exegete, a biblical interpreter.

In 9:1–10, we get a detailed description of the items of the Jewish cult. In speaking of the Day of Atonement, the author claims that the symbolism of access to the holy of holies being restricted to the high priest, and to him only once a year, is that "the way to the sanctuary is not yet disclosed" (9:8). The same verse explains that the way will not be revealed "as long as the first tent is still standing." He explains the meaning of the first tent.

This is a symbol of the present time, during which gifts and sacrifices are offered that cannot perfect the conscience of the worshiper. . . . But when Christ came as a high priest of the good things that have come, then through the greater and perfect tent (not made with hands, that is, not of this creation), he entered once for all into the Holy Place, not with the blood of goats and calves, but with his own blood, thus obtaining eternal redemption. (9:9–11)

In 9:9, there is the cosmic temple, with the outer rooms representing the present age, which will ultimately pass away—an apocalyptic idea. The two symbolisms are blended here. In 9:10–11, we see a tent not built with hands and not of this creation, through which Jesus passes in order to enter the true sanctuary, heaven. He does so with his own blood. He is both priest and sacrificial victim. This is more the apocalyptic idea, since it envisages a complete temple in heaven.

Jesus will return to earth, but not because there is any more work to do to open the way to heaven.

> He has appeared once for all at the end of the age to remove sin by the sacrifice of himself. And just as it is appointed for mortals to die once, and after that the judgment, so Christ, having been offered once to bear the sins of many, will appear a second time, not to deal with sin, but to save those who are eagerly waiting for him. (9:26–28)

The homilist refers to the parousia, and he admits that his listeners are eager for it.

Meanwhile, he offers his audience a vivid picture of Christ having entered heaven, having achieved purification for them, and sitting at the right hand of God as their permanent high priest. As he says earlier, "Now the main point in what we are saying is this: we have such a high priest, one who is seated at the right hand of the throne of the Majesty in the heavens, a minister in the sanctuary and the true tent that the Lord, and not any mortal, has set up" (8:1–2). This is the vision the homilist offers his hearers, who have grown weary in their eschatological hope. If they can see the present reality of having Jesus in heaven as their high priest, then they know their apocalyptic hope is valid and firm and to be trusted.

In the same chapter, the author once again blends the cosmic and apocalyptic temples.

> They offer worship in a sanctuary that is a sketch and shadow of the heavenly one; for Moses, when he was about to erect the tent, was warned, "See that you make everything according to the pattern that was shown you on the mountain."
> But Jesus has now obtained a more excellent ministry, and to that degree he is the mediator of a better covenant, which has been enacted through better promises. For if that first covenant had been faultless, there would have been no need to look for a second one. (8:5–7)

The author builds on the scene in Exodus where God shows Moses the "blueprints" for the temple (Exod. 25:40). There is a pattern according to which the temple must be built. Later tradition turns this into a heavenly temple that is the model for the earthly one. The idea that heaven contains a full temple is apocalyptic. The idea that the Jewish temple is a "sketch and shadow" of the real one is Platonic, where the really real is in the world of the Forms and what is on earth is merely shadows of the Forms. Of course, such shadows cannot be effective. They can only hint at what is real.

We cannot pass over the rest of chapter 8 without acknowledging some content that is highly objectionable in its treatment of Judaism. The author considers Jeremiah's idea of a new covenant (Jer. 31) and takes it to mean that since Jews have failed to live up to the covenant, God is making a new one, meaning a new religion. This goes beyond Jeremiah's meaning. Jeremiah meant the new covenant as a renewal of God's relationship with Israel, as did the people of the Dead Sea Scrolls later. Our author sees it as a death sentence for Judaism. He says, "In speaking of 'a new covenant,' he has made the first one obsolete, and what is obsolete and growing old will soon disappear" (8:13). This is supersessionism, the idea that Christianity has surpassed and replaced Judaism, which no longer has any purpose and should no longer exist. Today it is explicitly rejected by mainline churches. A good example is the Catholic text *Nostra Aetate*, one of the documents of Vatican II.

MacRae goes on to examine the concepts of hope and faith in Hebrews. The homilist describes faith as insight into the unseen world. He wants that insight to support their hope for the future. He says,

> Now faith is the assurance of things hoped for, the conviction of things not seen. Indeed, by faith our ancestors received approval. By faith we understand that the worlds were prepared by the word of God, so that what is seen was made from things that are not visible. (11:1–3)

Faith—belief in what we cannot see, virtual insight into the unseen world—supports apocalyptic hope.

In 11:13–16, the author says that the Israelite and Jewish heroes he lists in this chapter all hoped for what they could not see. They knew that they were strangers on earth, and that their true home was heaven. That hope is now more firmly grounded because Jesus has actually entered heaven and become the believers' "pioneer," the one who has gone before to open the way. He says it well in chapter 6: "We have this hope, a sure and steadfast anchor of the soul, a hope that enters the inner shrine behind the curtain, where Jesus, a forerunner on our behalf, has entered, having become a high priest forever according to the order of Melchizedek" (6:19–20). Christians cannot see this, but they have faith in it.

Hebrews espouses a high Christology, like that of John and Colossians. Like them, it claims that creation happened through Jesus. Jesus is superior to the angels and to Moses. But he is genuinely human as well. Being both human and divine, he is the prefect mediator between God and humans, the essence of the priestly role. This is why only he can accomplish access to God.

Hebrews blends apocalyptic and cosmic temple ideas and thereby strengthens the addressees' apocalyptic hope through his cosmic temple notion. He subtly interweaves two sorts of symbolism, one more native to him and the other more native to his audience. We now look for what else in the book confirms that the author uses apocalyptic elements in his sermon.

In chapter 6, the homilist lists the things he considers basic to Christian belief. Among them are "resurrection of the dead, and eternal judgment" (6:2). Also, Christians have "tasted the goodness of the word of God and the powers of the age to come" (6:5). Speaking of their eschatological hopes, he says, "We want each one of you to show the same diligence so as to realize the full assurance of hope to the very end" (6:11).

In calling his audience to stand firm, he quotes Isa. 26:20 and Hab. 2:3–4: "In a very little while the one who is coming will come and will not delay" (10:37). Toward the end of his treatment, he urges his audience to believe in God's eschatological promise.

At that time his voice shook the earth; but now he has promised, "Yet once more I will shake not only the earth but also the heaven." This phrase, "Yet once more," indicates the removal of what is shaken—that is, created things— so that what cannot be shaken may remain. Therefore, since we are receiving a kingdom that cannot be shaken, let us give thanks, by which we offer to God an acceptable worship with reverence and awe; for indeed our God is a consuming fire. (12:26–29)

James

James's concern is with ethical exhortation, and its teaching contains echoes of Jesus's teaching. James has often been taken to be Jesus's brother (Gal. 1:19). The author is not a sophisticated theologian, and the work contains no discussion of theological issues as such. There are passing references to aspects of an early Christian worldview that draw on apocalypticism. They are used primarily as sanctions for righteous behavior.

James is negatively disposed to the rich. In 1:9–11 there is an echo of Jesus's beatitudes, where James proclaims that the rich will wither away while the poor will be raised up. A direct warning to the rich in 5:1–6 sounds apocalyptic: "Your gold and silver have rusted, and their rust will be evidence against you, and it will eat your flesh like fire. You have laid up treasure for the last days" (5:3). It says that the harvesters' cries have reached God. Harvest is a frequent apocalyptic image for the last judgment. It continues, "You have lived on the earth in luxury and in pleasure; you have fattened your hearts in a day of slaughter" (5:5).

Antipathy toward the rich is matched by a positive attitude toward the poor: "Listen, my beloved brothers and sisters. Has not God chosen the poor in the world to be rich in faith and to be heirs of the kingdom that he has promised to those who love him?" (2:5). As in Jesus's beatitudes, God's kingdom is for the poor.

James's basic standpoint for the poor and against the rich echoes the teaching of Jesus as well as the teaching of many Jewish and Christian apocalypses.

James displays belief in demons (2:19), hell (3:6), judgment (2:13), the devil (4:7), and Christ's parousia (5:7). The basic apocalyptic worldview is taken for granted. The author of James warns that the parousia is near, so he believes in the imminent eschaton (5:9), and that serves as a sanction for his exhortations.

Jude

This letter has been attributed to Jude, Jesus's brother. It counters false teachers whom Jude accuses of sexual immorality. Again, since such accusations are common in attacks on opponents in the ancient world, it is uncertain how much credence to place in such rhetoric (L. Johnson 1989; Knust 2006). The author warns that false teaching and immoral behavior will bring punishment. To prove that, he refers to examples in literature inside and outside the Bible. Of special interest is that he cites the example of the watchers from *1 Enoch* 1–36 (6). He also quotes the same section of Enoch to warn of God's coming as judge (14–15). He looks forward to eternal life, and he pleads with his audience to save those in spiritual danger, which is equivalent to "snatching them out of the fire" (22). James believes in angels (8–9), the devil (9), punishment by eternal fire (7), reward of eternal life (21), and a final judgment he calls "the great Day" (6).

Jude's polemic against these teachers is heated. His use of apocalyptic references brings the full weight of Christian teaching about judgment, reward and punishment, and eternal hellfire to bear against them.

1, 2, and 3 John

These three short documents were written by someone who belonged to the church or one of the churches that had the Gospel of John as its foundational text (Brown 1982). They are very similar to that Gospel in language, cadence, and theology. At the same time, they display substantive differences from the Gospel. One area of difference is in their relationship to apocalyptic thought.

The three texts are so similar to each other that they probably have the same author, were written at about the same time, and concern the same issues. The first text does not have the generic form of a letter (greetings, prayer, thanksgiving, body, final greetings), while the other two do. The second and third texts are short and contain nothing apocalyptic. First John does contain key passages and ideas that pertain to apocalypticism. It is written to a Johannine community with a concrete problem that the author wishes to address, but it forgoes the letter form, perhaps because it is more of a sermon to be read aloud in the congregation.

First John reverses the de-apocalypticizing that the Gospel of John accomplishes. This means reemphasis on Christ's parousia, the last judgment, a negative attitude toward this world, the passing away of this world, and revelation of truth in the present and of eschatological events to come.

The author does not make apocalyptic concerns the object of his discussion or argument. Rather, they are a rationale for a particular stance toward the world and a sanction for belief and behavior that the author urges. The author rails against persons who have left the Johannine community and have adopted a doctrine incompatible with the truth. It is plausible that the opponents deny that Jesus was human. They perhaps think that he is a heavenly being that only appeared to be human. That doctrine would fall under the category of Docetism, from the Greek word *dokeō* meaning "to seem." Jesus only seemed to be human but really was not. This matches some Gnostic documents, but we would need more information to know whether the opponents are truly Gnostic. The author of 1 John takes vigorous exception to such a view.

Despite its high Christology, the Gospel of John does not eliminate Jesus's humanity. He eats, drinks, suffers, and dies. The Gospel's prologue states clearly that the Word became flesh (1:14). The author of 1 John is right, then, in seeing the denial of Jesus's human nature as contrary to the theology of his community, at least as articulated by John's Gospel. In this, he continues the Gospel's teaching. In other ways, however, he has changed it.

The first way that the author changes the Gospel's teaching regards the atonement. Atonement means being put at one with God. This can be done in different ways, depending on the religious system. Even within a single religion, ideas of atonement vary. In Christianity, atonement usually happens through the crucifixion. The fullest expression of this in the New Testament is in Hebrews, but it appears elsewhere as well. Paul uses it in passing, as we have seen. First John states it succinctly: "The blood of Jesus his Son cleanses us from all sin" (1:7). Again, "He [Jesus] is the atoning sacrifice for our sins, and not for ours only but also for the sins of the whole world" (2:2; see 4:10). Given the sectarian stance of John's Gospel, it would be strange if it held that the work of Jesus would have anything to do with cleansing the sins of those who are not "us."

More to our purposes, the author of 1 John is more willing to resort to apocalyptic thought than is the Gospel's author. The idea that the readers do not belong to the world and the contrast of the world and the community in terms of light and dark conform to the Gospel's usage. This is not necessarily apocalyptic, though it could be. It could just as easily be Gnostic. What is apocalyptic is the statement in 2:8 that "the darkness is passing away and the true light is already shining." This is part of an exhortation to reject the world, which is a place of darkness, alienation from God, and immorality. The author states this forcefully.

Do not love the world or the things in the world. The love of the Father is not in those who love the world; for all that is in the world—the desire of the flesh, the desire of the eyes, the pride in riches—comes not from the Father but from the world. And the world and its desires are passing away, but those who do the will of God live forever. (2:15–17)

"The world" has been entered by the writer's opponents, and what the author says about the world forms part of his argument against them. The idea that the world is passing away can be apocalyptic.

A third time in a short space the author reminds his readers about the world's passing away: "Children, it is the last hour! As you have heard that antichrist is coming, so now many antichrists have come. From this we know that it is the last hour" (2:18). For the author, the antichrists are his opponents. Their beliefs and activities are signs of the end. This is the first time we have come upon the term "antichrist," although we have met the idea already, in Revelation and 2 Thessalonians, for instance. The term usually designates someone that comes at the end of time, pretends to be good but is really bad, assumes overwhelming power over the earth, and is ultimately defeated by God and Christ (McGinn 1994).

The author also mentions Christ's parousia, his second coming. They ought to heed what he says so that they are ready to face Christ when he returns: "And now, little children, abide in him, so that when he is revealed we may have confidence and not be put to shame before him at his coming [*parousia*]" (2:28). The language of revelation appears in this verse and is common throughout the document, occurring seven times in this short text. The Greek verb used, *phaneroō*, is less common in apocalyptic contexts than *apokalyptō*, but the author uses it in an apocalyptic sense when he speaks of the original revelation of Christ in the world (1:2; 3:5, 8; 4:9), of his parousia (2:28; 3:2), and of the revelation of what his readers themselves will be at the eschaton (3:2).

The author mentions the last judgment in 4:17. For his readers, it should be an event that they anticipate with boldness and confidence, because they imitate Christ in love. This is tied to the author's attack on his opponents, since they allegedly do not have love for the community and so will not be ready for the last judgment.

Also apocalyptic is the mention of the devil throughout the text. Those to whom the author writes have already conquered "the evil one," the devil (2:12–15). The author sees humanity dualistically, and he expresses this in terms of individuals' relationships to the devil.

Everyone who commits sin is a child of the devil; for the devil has been sinning from the beginning. The Son of God was revealed for this purpose, to destroy the works of the devil. Those who have been born of God do not sin, because God's seed abides in them; they cannot sin, because they have been born of God. The children of God and the children of the devil are revealed in this way: all who do not do what is right are not from God, nor are those who do not love their brothers and sisters. (3:8–10)

This passage recalls the teaching on the two spirits in the *Community Rule* of Qumran because it sees humanity as divided in two parts. One is under the devil's control and one has escaped that control through being born again as described by John's Gospel (John 3). The cosmic dualism involved is not just between God and the devil, but between Jesus and the devil. Jesus is "revealed" to combat the devil. This echoes the dualism in the *Community Rule*, where the angel of light leads the righteous and the angel of darkness leads those opposed to God.

Similar ideas are expressed at the end of the document.

We know that those who are born of God do not sin, but the one who was born of God protects them, and the evil one does not touch them. We know that we are God's children, and that the whole world lies under the power of the evil one. And we know that the Son of God has come and has given us understanding so that we may know him who is true; and we are in him who is true, in his Son Jesus Christ. He is the true God and eternal life. Little children, keep yourselves from idols. (5:18–21)

The "evil one" is the devil. That the entire world lies under the devil's power is apocalyptic. The idea that believers constitute a world apart—that is, a world free of the devil's power—matches Paul's thought on this subject, although how that plays itself out in the two authors is quite different.

The Antichrist

We first encounter the term "antichrist" in the letters of John. For the letters' author, the antichrist was anyone who denied that Jesus came in the flesh. Any sort of Docetist or Gnostic would qualify for this condemnation. Polycarp, bishop of Smyrna in Asia Minor in the second century, follows 1 John in seeing the antichrist as those who deny Jesus has come in the flesh, but he adds that such people belong to the devil (*To the Philippians* 7:1).

The antichrist as an eschatological figure who opposes Christ is present in some sense in the New Testament, although he is not labeled such. As in the case of the Messiah, one cannot restrict one's evidence for the antichrist to passages that use the term explicitly (McGinn 1994). Most believe, for example, that 2 Thess. 2:3–12; Rev. 13; and other texts refer to the antichrist even though they do not employ the term.

We have seen above that 2 Thessalonians contains a fairly complete picture of an antichrist figure. He is a lawless one who is human, deceives people, takes a throne in the Jerusalem temple, claims God's authority, depends on

Satan's power, and is a sign that the parousia of Christ is near. In Rev. 12–13, we have a sort of "unholy trinity" in the dragon who is cast out of heaven, the beast that arises from the sea, and the beast from the land. We also have a numerical equivalent for the name of the beast—666. Within Revelation itself, the dragon is Satan, the beast from the sea is a Roman emperor or the Roman Empire, and the beast from the land is the imperial cult in Asia Minor. Later tradition is not entirely consistent on which of these is the antichrist, but it is most frequently seen as the beast from the sea. He is worshiped, exercises dominion over the whole earth, has the power of Satan behind him, is human, and is defeated by Christ and thrown into the fiery lake. It is he who, in collaboration with Satan, makes war on Christians.

Conclusion

We have now studied the entire New Testament. We have found abundant apocalyptic elements throughout that collection. We have seen that Jesus was an apocalyptic prophet, that Paul thought in apocalyptic terms, and that Q, one of the major sources for Matthew and Luke, was apocalyptic in outlook. With a) their foundational documents so thoroughly steeped in apocalypticism, b) their object of worship a preacher of eschatological hopes, and c) their life lived in what they often perceived as a hostile world, it is not surprising that early Christians even beyond the apostolic period continued to be engaged with apocalypticism, or that apocalypticism has continued to be a part of Christianity right up to the present.

Suggestions for Further Reading

Allison, Dale C. *The End of the Ages Has Come: An Early Interpretation of the Passion and Resurrection of Jesus*. Philadelphia: Fortress, 1985.

Aune, David E. *Apocalypticism, Prophecy, and Magic in Early Christianity: Collected Essays*. Tübingen: Mohr Siebeck, 2006.

MacRae, George W. "Heavenly Temple and Eschatology in the Letter to the Hebrews." *Semeia*, no. 12 (1978): 179–99.

Marcus, Joel, and Marion L. Soards, eds. *Apocalyptic and the New Testament*. Sheffield: JSOT Press, 1989.

Plevnik, Joseph. *Paul and the Parousia: An Exegetical and Theological Investigation*. Peabody, MA: Hendrickson, 1997.

VanderKam, James C., and William Adler. *The Jewish Apocalyptic Heritage in Early Christianity*. Minneapolis: Fortress, 1996.

Yarbro Collins, Adela. *Early Christian Apocalypticism: Genre and Social Setting*. Semeia. Vol. 36. Decatur, GA: Scholars Press, 1986.

12

The Ongoing Legacy
of Apocalypticism

Apocalypticism is alive and well. It thrives in many forms and for a variety of reasons. In many cases, modern people, such as fundamentalists or conservative evangelicals, explicitly think in apocalyptic terms, relying heavily on the canonical books of Daniel and Revelation. Apocalypticism gives meaning to their lives, particularly in a society they perceive as hostile to their beliefs and values. In other cases, the influence of apocalypticism is more subtle, influencing core beliefs of "mainstream" forms of Christianity—resurrection, heaven, hell, rewards and punishments after death, and the last judgment. Believers are often not even aware that such beliefs come from apocalypticism.

John Joseph Collins lays out positive and negative elements of the apocalyptic phenomenon (2005b). This chapter presents his reflections and carries his observations further in light of our studies.

Collins enumerates four objections to apocalyptic literature: Its symbolism is strange, its interpretation is difficult, the failure of specific prophecies can lead to disillusionment, and its moral dualism is too simplistic and can be dangerous.

First, its symbolism is strange. It stands out from biblical literature and most of what modern believers and scholars are accustomed to. Many revelations are in the form of dreams, in which strict logic does not apply, and in which one thing might stand for another. Even though the apocalypses are literary productions, visionary experience may stand behind many of them. Further, apocalyptic texts draw heavily on ancient mythology, unfamiliar to moderns.

Familiarity with such mythology helps to understand what is being said, how it is being said, and why it takes this form. An ancient person would have such patterns and stories at his or her disposal, as part of general cultural knowledge. They would also be more familiar with and comfortable with dreams and visions and communications from the other world.

To interpret apocalypticism's rich and complex symbols literalistically is to distort the nature of apocalyptic language. Apocalyptic language not only evokes the deepest fears and hopes of people in a particular historical circumstance, it does so over time and in many different circumstances. It is multivalent. The images lack specificity that would restrict them to one situation. The lasting relevance of Daniel and Revelation witnesses to this.

Since moderns generally do not make use of such images, they easily misunderstand them. They might see them as irrelevant to their own situation and the products of a feverish mind, or they might take them too literally and fail to take into account that this is not simple, descriptive language with an uncomplicated referential relationship to entities outside of itself. Neither approach does justice to the nature of apocalyptic language. One must read these documents within their contexts of origin to make good sense of them.

This book aims to aid modern readers to understand the context of ancient apocalypticism and so to make sense of it for ourselves. That does not mean that we become apocalyptic thinkers necessarily, but it does mean that we understand the ancient texts better—a worthwhile effort given their ongoing importance in modern religion, liturgy, theology, literature, and art. We will also understand better those who do think apocalyptically, particularly conservative evangelicals and fundamentalists on the American scene. We will also understand ourselves better. Even the so-called "mainstream" churches, such as Roman Catholicism, Episcopalianism, Lutheranism, the nonfundamentalist segments of the Presbyterians and Baptists, and so on, draw extensively in their language and symbols from apocalypticism. Thus it can foster mutual understanding between groups that seem foreign to one another. It can also shed light on texts from the Hebrew Bible, which are foundational for both Judaism and Christianity.

Modern believers are not free of mythology, nor should they be. We noted in chapter 1 that mythology furnishes a way of speaking of unseen realities that can be spoken of adequately in no other way. To reduce such language to a simplistic referential model, even in theology, where human reason is brought to bear on religious belief, is to impoverish both belief and reason, and it is to lack appreciation of the complexity of human thought and language.

In our first chapter, we noted that human language and knowledge rely heavily on analogy and metaphor. We think and learn in terms of comparing things (including experiences and intellectual concepts) to one another. This is true even of scientific thinking, which, although it appears at first glance to be a matter of numbers and formulas and empirical observations, also employs metaphors to make sense of it all.

When it comes to matters such as God, creation, humanity as a whole, good, evil, sin, and the spiritual in everyday life, we must use analogies and metaphors; we never leave them behind entirely. Anthropomorphism, speaking of God in human terms, is intrinsic to religion. This book has contributed to the reader's realization that Jewish and Christian symbols and theologies are deeply rooted in the ancient period. We seek such understanding not to discard them as useless baggage from a distant past. That was the goal of some prominent biblical scholars of the last century, including that towering figure, Rudolf Bultmann (1962; 1954). We have begun, specifically in biblical studies, to recognize the continuing power of mythology in our lives, individual and communal. This brings a richness and a self-awareness to our religious thought absent before. It allows us to be aware of how such thought developed so that we can both benefit from it and be critical of it. Religion embodies human attempts to respond to the divine. As such, it is inevitable that it will contain much that is praiseworthy, but it will also contain elements that need critical thought and modification. The study of religion, along with other activities such as theologizing, exploring history, and conducting descriptive and comparative studies, will supply believers with tools to identify, discuss, and mitigate those aspects that might not be so praiseworthy and that have results that many might see as contrary to the broader purposes of religion.

Collins's second potential criticism of apocalypticism is that when interpreted in a literalistic way, apocalyptic literature can seem a rather inferior sort of writing—a form of awkward allegory. It is true that parts of apocalypses refer to people, places, and events in the world outside the literature. Apocalypses speak of specific cities, like Jerusalem and Rome, specific kings, such as Antiochus IV and Nero, and specific events, such as the destruction of Jerusalem's temple or Jesus's crucifixion. The four terrible beasts that arise from the sea in Dan. 7 do refer to the empires of the Babylonians, the Medes, the Persians, and the Greeks. But to conclude that most or all apocalyptic images can be decoded in this way is to make a leap that exceeds the evidence. It is also to ignore what is gained by speaking of empires in terms of mythological, cosmic beasts.

When Daniel speaks of Antiochus IV, he does indeed speak of a human being who is a king, but Antiochus is much more than that. He is a cosmic power that challenges God himself. The visible world is indissolubly joined to the unseen world. Kings, empires, and peoples all live in a world that is far richer and deeper than that perceived by the five senses (Horsley 2010a). Some humans gain access to that world. They become apocalyptic seers or sibylline prophets. Their very access to that world shows how thinking simply in terms of the empirical world does not do justice to the way the cosmos works. To some degree or another, all modern believers share this view. Life is not just what we see and feel and taste. It is also "spiritual," a favorite modern word that is overused and often distorts ancient thought. We must take into account "supernatural" realities, another word that distorts ancient perceptions. When any believer explains the ultimate meaning of things, it involves an unseen world that affects and is affected by this world.

A third possible criticism of apocalypticism is its interest in predicting the future, particularly when such prediction assumes the form of identification of concrete dates and times. This leads to disillusionment when prophecies fail to materialize. It can contribute to skepticism about religion by both insiders and outsiders. Collins shows that there is surprisingly little attempt at such specific prediction in the ancient sources. The timing of future events, particularly eschatological happenings, is usually left rather vague. An exception is Daniel, which at the end has several successive times when the end is supposed to come. Despite the inaccuracies of its predictions, Daniel has been one of the most popular apocalypses of all time, being included in the Hebrew Bible and used by both Jews and Christians (Collins and Yarbro Collins 2005c). The modern obsession with dating the end carries apocalyptic thinking further than the ancient sources support. On the other hand, the innumerable failures of apocalyptic prophecies to materialize have never led to the disappearance of apocalyptic thought. If anything, they have caused thinkers to redouble their efforts to advocate an apocalyptic viewpoint.

There are other indications of date-searching in ancient apocalypticism as well. The *Damascus Rule* among the Dead Sea Scrolls gives a rough date for the end, but it is rather vague. The sectarians used interpretation of Scripture, the *pesher* on Habakkuk, to show that a delay of the consummation had been foreseen by prophecy. The book of Revelation gives no absolute date for the end, but it repeatedly says that it will be "soon." When it did not happen, it did not in the least dampen the enthusiasm of many Christians for this book. Jesus and Paul expected an imminent end, but later Christians incorporated it into a broader conception of the divine plan. Again, none of these examples approaches the enthusiasm for and the supposed precision of specific dates that has been so evident throughout Christian history and that so often catches public attention today.

In the first chapter, we noted that the sociologist Leon Festinger developed a theory of cognitive dissonance relating to failed prophecy (Festinger, Riecken, and Schlachter 1964). If one belongs to a prophetic group that demands commitment expressed in concrete action and deep identification of the person with the group, and if the prophecies of that group do not come true, then a common response is that the adherents believe in the prophecies even more strongly and often engage in missionary work to convince others as well, so that they may have more support in their beliefs. Mathew Schmalz has shown that Festinger oversimplifies (1994). He examines several failures of the prophecies of the Jehovah's Witnesses and demonstrates that they have utilized a variety of strategies to deal with failed prophecy that have not always corresponded to those in Festinger's theory, including such things as changing the substance of the prophecy and undergoing institutional change. Nonetheless, the broader point stands that failure of prophecy does not necessarily spell failure for the group that believed in it. In fact, Christianity itself is a group that persisted despite failed prophecies about Jesus coming back soon, as a fair reading of the New Testament makes clear.

The reason that groups perdure even when their prophecies do not come to fruition is perhaps because of their understanding that specific prophecies are a product of a broader and more basic belief in unseen forces that control their fate and that of the entire universe. The most common expression of such conviction is a personal God who has plans for the universe that will right wrongs, reward the righteous, and punish the wicked. This makes sense of life. Even the stripped-down version of religious belief subscribed to by many during the Enlightenment, including some of the foremost founding fathers of the United States—Benjamin Franklin and Thomas Jefferson, for example—held these basic convictions. Although humans can err in terms of interpreting the sacred texts, the main lines of religious belief need not be annihilated by such mistakes. And the debt that all such theologies owe to apocalypticism must be acknowledged.

Collins supplies another piece of the puzzle as well. Most apocalypses show signs of having been composed during some sort of a crisis—military, religious, economic, or social (Poirier 2003; Horsley 2010b). Apocalyptic writers find the crisis so pressing that they anticipate God's intervention to change things radically. In most cases, they cannot imagine that God will stand for the status quo for much longer, for it is much too offensive to him.

Collins's last potential criticism of apocalypticism is the nature of moral dualism. Apocalypses almost always divide humanity into the good and the bad, the righteous and the wicked. The problem with this sort of thinking must be clear to anyone who is not already caught up in it. Surely the vast majority of humans, perhaps all, are a mixture of good and bad. Of course some are better than others and some are remarkably bad. To prove the point, people usually resort to extreme examples such as the evil Hitler and the holy Mother Teresa. But most people do not reach these extremes. Saints would be the first to reject the idea that they are fully good, and, nearly impossible as it is to comprehend and still less to accept, even the most evil of people may think that they are good. It is often said in religion that one must hate the sin but love the sinner. No one is beyond redemption.

Moral and social dualism is harmful to mutual understanding and encourages dehumanizing and even demonizing those who disagree with us, who belong to a different ethnicity or nationality, who profess a different religion, or who have different politics. It militates against a healthy self-criticism. It is far better, as Abraham Lincoln said, to seek to be on God's side than to claim that God is on our side. Apocalyptic thought lends itself too easily to radical and often unjust condemnation of the other. Contemporary political and social life in America provides abundant examples of that. It makes it much easier to go to war, for it demonizes the enemy.

Collins also considers the positive legacy of apocalypticism. Apocalypticism has provided a rich store of images to religious language. Almost everyone in the Western world is familiar with some aspect of apocalyptic language, even if he or she is unaware of its origins.

Beyond this contribution, Collins discusses other ways in which apocalypticism contributes to religious thought. He first recaptures the meaning of the apocalyptic worldview, and it is worth quoting him as a reminder of the main aspects of apocalypticism.

> The essential elements of this worldview are a lively belief in the role of supernatural forces in shaping human behavior and an equally lively belief in the certainty of a definitive final judgment that will not only set matters right on earth (if the earth is thought to endure) but also provide everlasting reward or punishment for individual behavior. (2005a, 161–62)

Collins sees three categories in which apocalypticism still has something to say to us. First, there is the idea that some aspects of life are beyond human control. Second, there is the conviction of transience—this life is transitory and there is something beyond it that is lasting. Third, there is the notion of transcendence. This life has a significance beyond itself, and resolution of issues of justice will be resolved in the future life.

As noted above, the New Testament scholar Rudolf Bultmann, who was as much a philosopher and a theologian as a biblical exegete, argued that the Christian message enshrined in the New Testament could speak to modern, science-minded humans only if shorn of its mythological exterior (Bultmann 1970). He subscribed to the idea put forward by David Strauss in the nineteenth century that myths are simply vehicles for ideas which themselves can be stated more forthrightly (Strauss 1972). Bultmann, when he exercised such demythologizing, ended up with a worldview corresponding to, indeed isomorphic with, an existentialist view of the world (Arnett 1963). Biblical scholars now reject his conclusions. But they go further. Mythology is not just a mask for dialectical thought. It is a language of its own that cannot be simply reduced to ethical precepts or metaphysical claims. The narrative is not dispensable. It never will be. Any churchgoer or reader of the Bible can attest to that. All attempts to reduce religion to a philosophical system or a code of ethics have failed because they have neglected the essential narrative element of religion.

Do People Really Believe These Things?

Readers of this book who are fundamentalist or conservative evangelicals or even apocalyptically oriented Catholics may be offended by this question. Of course they believe these things, and the Bible shows them to be true. Any other approach is untrue to the biblical word. But such readers will not be surprised by the question, at least if their lives carry them beyond the confines of their religious communities, which it usually does. They know that, although there are tens of millions of prophecy believers in the United States and still more who believe the absolute inerrancy of the Bible, society as a whole does not share their views. They see numerous instances of rejection of their positions in ethics and in both personal and public customs and behavior, politics, and intellectual discourse. It is natural that such challenges do not simply crush their convictions but have led them to grapple with the challenges and seek ways to convince others that their views accord with God's will for humanity and the universe.

For those outside such churches, attempts to decipher biblical prophecy in detail as predicting current events and to take literally biblical eschatological thought seem strange, although from time to time the public at large becomes fascinated by one or another form of such expectation. To those who write off contemporary expressions of apocalypticism, they perhaps need to be reminded of several important things.

No Christians or Jews will deny that their beliefs are rooted in the Bible. Yet many, perhaps the majority, now read the Bible critically. They consider the Bible as the product of limited human beings constrained by their historical circumstances and with limited understandings. They take ancient literary genres seriously and understand that they are not simply equivalent to modern ones in all respects, and that those who wrote the Bible may think and feel differently than we on many issues. Their very logic and cultural assumptions are different from those of moderns. The Roman Catholic Church has made this its official position on biblical study, as is clear in the document of Vatican II on revelation, as well as in the important publication *The Interpretation of the Bible in the Church* (Fitzmyer 1995). But such critical, sometimes called liberal, interpretation of the Bible undermines the Bible, according to some. Hence the heat raised by the issue of the scientific study of evolution, which for some seems to contradict the Bible (although most—including the Catholic Church—argue that it does not, and so have accepted the scientific evidence).

Clearly, there will be no easy conversation between the two broadly designated groups. Nonetheless, it is crucial that those who reject apocalypticism consider certain important points, and it has been the goal of this book to make such consideration possible based on facts rather than impressions.

First, most religions look strange to outsiders but self-evident to insiders. Much that is believed even by non-apocalyptic Christians is odd to outsiders—that Jesus is both God and human, that he died for our sins (the doctrine of the atonement, that his suffering and death were necessary for God to forgive us), that he rose from the dead, that Jesus is truly present in the consecrated bread and wine, that there is an afterlife including a heaven and a hell, that

Christianity is founded on the worship of someone executed as a political offender in the most shameful manner, and so on. To the average Christian, these are not shocking ideas. They are easily accepted and are self-evident. The insider/outsider dynamic in examining religions is crucial (McCutcheon 1999). Depending on how one handles it, it will be an insurmountable obstacle to understanding the other, or it will be something that enables one to take the other's beliefs seriously as another way of making sense of the world. Hopefully, this book serves the latter aim.

Finally, all Christians and Jews should take seriously the degree to which apocalyptic thought in Judaism and Christianity in the late Second Temple period has influenced later embodiments of the religion, to the present day. Because all Jewish and Christian believers owe so much to apocalypticism, it stands to reason that the more they know about this often troubling worldview, the better they will understand their own beliefs. Knowing the roots of one's belief enriches it. If this book has contributed to that process for any of its readers, then it has been a success.

Suggestions for Further Reading

Collins, John Joseph. "The Legacy of Apocalypticism." In *Encounters with Biblical Theology*, 155–66. Minneapolis: Fortress, 2005.

Daley, Brian. "Apocalypticism in Early Christian Theology." In *The Encyclopedia of Apocalypticism*, edited by Bernard McGinn, 3–47. New York: Continuum, 1998.

Works Cited

Allison, Dale C., Jr. 1984. "Elijah Must Come First." *Journal of Biblical Literature* 103 (2): 256–58.

———. 1998a. "The Eschatology of Jesus." In *The Encyclopedia of Apocalypticism*, edited by John Joseph Collins, Bernard McGinn, and Stephen J. Stein, 2:267–302. New York: Continuum.

———. 1998b. *Jesus of Nazareth: Millenarian Prophet*. Minneapolis: Fortress.

Arnett, William M. 1963. "Rudolf Bultmann's Existentialist Interpretation of the New Testament." *Asbury Seminarian* 17: 28–38.

Attridge, Harold W., and Wayne A. Meeks. 2006. *The HarperCollins Study Bible: New Revised Standard Version, Including the Apocryphal/Deuterocanonical Books with Concordance*. 1st ed., fully rev. and updated. San Francisco: HarperSanFrancisco.

Aune, David E. 1981. "The Social Matrix of the Apocalypse of John." *Biblical Research* 26: 16–32.

———. 1983a. "The Influence of Roman Imperial Court Ceremonial on the Revelation of John." *Biblical Research* 28: 5–26.

———. 1983b. *Prophecy in Early Christianity and the Ancient Mediterranean World*. Grand Rapids: Eerdmans.

———. 1997. *Revelation*. 3 vols. Nashville: Thomas Nelson.

Bachmann, Veronika. 2011. "The Book of the Watchers (1 Enoch 1–36): An Anti-Mosaic, Non-Mosaic, or Even Pro-Mosaic Writing?" *Journal of Hebrew Scriptures* 11 (1): 1–23. www.jhsonline.org.

Bader, Chris. 1999. "When Prophecy Passes Unnoticed: New Perspectives on Failed Prophecy." *Journal for the Scientific Study of Religion* 38 (1): 119–31.

Barclay, John M. 1996. *Jews in the Mediterranean Diaspora: From Alexander to Trajan (323 BCE–117 CE)*. Edinburgh: T&T Clark.

Barrett, C. K. 1962. *From First Adam to Last*. New York: Scribner.

Baumgarten, Albert I. 2000. "Pharisees." In *Encyclopedia of the Dead Sea Scrolls*, edited by Lawrence H. Schiffman and James C. VanderKam, 2:657–63. New York: Oxford University Press.

Beasley-Murray, George Raymond. 1993. *Jesus and the Last Days: The Interpretation of the Olivet Discourse.* Peabody, MA: Hendrickson.

Bernstein, Moshe J. 2000. "Scriptures." In *Encyclopedia of the Dead Sea Scrolls,* edited by Lawrence H. Schiffman and James C. VanderKam, 2:832–42. New York: Oxford University Press.

Betz, Hans Dieter. 1992. "Galatians, Epistle to the." In *The Anchor Bible Dictionary,* edited by David Noel Freedman, 2:872–75. New York: Doubleday.

Bickerman, Elias. 1979. *The God of the Maccabees: Studies on the Meaning and Origin of the Maccabean Revolt.* Leiden: Brill.

Boccaccini, Gabriele, Giovanni Ibba, Jason von Ehrenkrook, James Alan Waddell, and Jason Zurawski, eds. 2009. *Enoch and the Mosaic Torah: The Evidence of Jubilees.* Grand Rapids: Eerdmans.

Boccaccini, Gabriele, J. Harold Ellens, and James A. Waddell, eds. 2005. *Enoch and Qumran Origins: New Light on a Forgotten Connection.* Grand Rapids: Eerdmans.

Boccaccini, Gabriele, and John Joseph Collins, eds. 2007. *The Early Enoch Literature.* Boston: Brill.

Boyer, Paul. 1992. *When Time Shall Be No More: Prophecy Belief in Modern American Culture.* Cambridge: Harvard University Press.

Brown, Raymond E. 1958a. "The Pre-Christian Semitic Concept of 'Mystery.'" *Catholic Biblical Quarterly* 20: 417–43.

———. 1958b. "The Semitic Background of the New Testament *mysterion.*" *Biblica* 39: 426–48.

———. 1961. "The Pater Noster as an Eschatological Prayer." *Theological Studies* 22 (2): 175–208.

———. 1982. *The Epistles of John.* Garden City, NY: Doubleday.

Bultmann, Rudolf. 1954. "The Christian Hope and the Problem of Demythologizing." *Expository Times* 65 (9): 276–78.

———. 1958. *Jesus and the Word.* New York: Scribner.

———. 1962. "On the Problem of Demythologizing." *Journal of Religion* 42 (2): 96–102.

———. 1970. "On the Problem of Demythologizing." In *New Testament Issues,* 35–44. New York: Harper & Row.

———. 1972. *History of the Synoptic Tradition.* Oxford: Blackwell.

Carter, Warren. 2001. *Matthew and Empire: Initial Explorations.* Harrisburg, PA: Trinity Press.

Charles, R. H. 1920. *A Critical and Exegetical Commentary on the Revelation of St. John.* 2 vols. Edinburgh: T&T Clark.

———, et al., eds. 1913. *The Apocrypha and Pseudepigrapha of the Old Testament in English, with Introductions and Critical and Explanatory Notes to the Several Books.* 2 vols. Oxford: Clarendon.

Clifford, Richard. 1972. *The Cosmic Mountain in Canaan and the Old Testament.* Cambridge: Harvard University Press.

———. 1975. "History and Myth in Daniel 10–11." *Bulletin of the American Schools of Oriental Research* 220: 23–26.

———. 1984. *Fair Spoken and Persuading: An Interpretation of Second Isaiah.* New York: Paulist Press.

———. 1998. "The Roots of Apocalypticism in Near Eastern Myth." In *The Encyclopedia of Apocalypticism,* edited by John Joseph Collins, 1:3–38. New York: Continuum.

Cohn, Norman. 1970. *The Pursuit of the Millennium: Revolutionary Millenarians and Mystical Anarchists of the Middle Ages.* New York: Oxford University Press.

Collins, John Joseph. 1974a. *The Sibylline Oracles of Egyptian Judaism.* Missoula, MT: Society of Biblical Literature.

———. 1974b. "Place of the Fourth Sibyl in the Development of the Jewish Sibyllina." *Journal of Jewish Studies* 25 (3): 365–80.

———. 1977a. "The Biblical Precedent for Natural Theology." *Journal of the American Academy of Religion* 45: 36–67.

———. 1977b. "Pseudonymity, Historical Reviews and the Genre of the Revelation of John." *Catholic Biblical Quarterly* 39: 309–28.

———. 1977c. *The Apocalyptic Vision of the Book of Daniel.* Harvard Semitic Monographs. Missoula, MT: Scholars Press.

———. 1977d. "Cosmos and Salvation: Jewish Wisdom and Apocalyptic in the Hellenistic Age." *History of Religions* 17 (2): 121–42.

———. 1980. "The Heavenly Representative: The 'Son of Man' in the Similitudes of Enoch." In *Ideal Figures in Ancient Judaism,* edited by John Joseph Collins and George W. E. Nickelsburg, 111–33. Chico, CA: Scholars Press.

———. 1982. "The Apocalyptic Technique: Setting and Function of the Book of the Watchers." *Catholic Biblical Quarterly* 44: 91–111.

———. 1983. "The Sibylline Oracles." In *The Old Testament Pseudepigrapha,* edited by J. H. Charlesworth. New York: Doubleday.

———, ed. 1984a. *Apocalypse: The Morphology of a Genre.* Semeia 14. Missoula, MT: Scholars Press.

———. 1984b. "Testaments." In *Jewish Writings of the Second Temple Period: Apocrypha, Pseudepigrapha, Qumran Sectarian Writings, Philo, Josephus,* edited by Michael E. Stone, 325–55. Philadelphia: Fortress.

———. 1987. "The Kingdom of God in the Apocrypha and Pseudepigrapha." In *Kingdom of God in 20th-Century Interpretation,* 81–95. Peabody, MA: Hendrickson.

———. 1990. "Was the Dead Sea Sect an Apocalyptic Community?" In *Archeology and History in the Dead Sea Scrolls,* edited by John Joseph Collins and Lawrence H. Schiffman, 25–51. Sheffield: JSOT Press.

———. 1991. "Genre, Ideology, and Social Movements in Jewish Apocalypticism." In *Mysteries and Revelations,* edited by John Joseph Collins and J. H. Charlesworth, 11–32. Sheffield: JSOT Press.

———. 1992a. "Daniel, Book of." In *The Anchor Bible Dictionary,* edited by David Noel Freedman, 2:29–37. New York: Doubleday.

———. 1992b. "Dead Sea Scrolls." In *The Anchor Bible Dictionary,* edited by David Noel Freedman. 2:85–101. New York: Doubleday.

———. 1993a. *Daniel: A Commentary on the Book of Daniel.* Hermeneia. Minneapolis: Fortress.

———. 1993b. "Wisdom, Apocalypticism, and Generic Incompatibility." In *In Search of Wisdom,* edited by Leo G. Perdue, Bernard Brandon Scott, and William Johnston Wiseman, 165–85. Louisville: Westminster John Knox.

———. 1995. *The Scepter and the Star: The Messiahs of the Dead Sea Scrolls and Other Ancient Literature*. New York: Doubleday.

———. 1998. *The Apocalyptic Imagination: An Introduction to Jewish Apocalyptic Literature*. 2nd ed. Grand Rapids: Eerdmans.

———. 2000a. *Between Athens and Jerusalem: Jewish Identity in the Hellenistic Diaspora*. Grand Rapids: Eerdmans.

———. 2000b. "Apocrypha and Pseudepigrapha." In *Encyclopedia of the Dead Sea Scrolls*, edited by Lawrence H. Schiffman and James C. VanderKam, 1:35–39. New York: Oxford University Press.

———. 2000c. "Powers in Heaven: God, Gods, and Angels in the Dead Sea Scrolls." In *Religion in the Dead Sea Scrolls*, edited by John Joseph Collins and Robert A. Kugler, 9–28. Grand Rapids: Eerdmans.

———. 2000d. *Between Athens and Jerusalem: Jewish Identity in the Hellenistic Diaspora*. 2nd ed. Grand Rapids: Eerdmans.

———. 2003a. "The Eschatology of Zechariah." In *Knowing the End from the Beginning: The Prophetic, the Apocalyptic and Their Relationships*, edited by Lester L. Grabbe and James H. Charlesworth, 74–84. New York: T&T Clark.

———. 2003b. "An Enochic Testament? Comments on George Nickelsburg's Hermeneia Commentary." In *George W. E. Nickelsburg in Perspective*, 2:373–78. Boston: Brill.

———. 2004. *Introduction to the Hebrew Bible*. Minneapolis: Fortress.

———. 2005a. *Encounters with Biblical Theology*. Minneapolis: Fortress.

———. 2005b. "The Legacy of Apocalypticism." In *Encounters with Biblical Theology*, 155–66. Minneapolis: Fortress.

———. 2007. "'Enochic Judaism' and the Sect of the Dead Sea Scrolls." In *Early Enoch Literature*, 283–99. Boston: Brill.

———. 2008. "How Distinctive Was Enochic Judaism?" *Meghillot* 5–6: 17–34.

———. 2010. *Beyond the Qumran Community: The Sectarian Movement of the Dead Sea Scrolls*. Grand Rapids: Eerdmans.

———, and Adela Yarbro Collins. 2005c. "The Book of Truth: Daniel as a Reliable Witness to Past and Future in the United States of America." In *Encounters with Biblical Theology*, edited by John Joseph Collins, 142–54. Minneapolis: Fortress.

———, and Gregory E. Sterling. 2001. *Hellenism in the Land of Israel*. Christianity and Judaism in Antiquity. Notre Dame: University of Notre Dame Press.

Conzelmann, Hans. 1960. *The Theology of St. Luke*. New York: Harper & Row.

Cook, Stephen L. 1995. *Prophecy and Apocalypticism: The Postexilic Social Setting*. Minneapolis: Fortress.

Cross, Frank Moore. 1995. *The Ancient Library of Qumran*. 3rd ed. Sheffield: Sheffield Academic Press.

Crossan, John Dominic. 1991. *The Historical Jesus: The Life of a Mediterranean Jewish Peasant*. San Francisco: HarperCollins.

———. 1994. *Jesus: A Revolutionary Biography*. San Francisco: HarperSanFrancisco.

Davies, Philip R. 2000. "Zadok, Sons of." In *Encyclopedia of the Dead Sea Scrolls*, edited by Lawrence H. Schiffman and James C. VanderKam, 1005–7. New York: Oxford University Press.

Davila, James R. 2005. "The Animal Apocalypse and Daniel." In *Enoch and Qumran Origins*, edited by Gabriele Boccaccini, J. Harold Ellens, and James A. Waddell, 35–38. Grand Rapids: Eerdmans.

De Boer, Martinus C. 1989. "Paul and Jewish Apocalyptic Eschatology." In *Apocalyptic and the New Testament*, edited by Joel Marcus and Marion L. Soards, 169–90. Sheffield: JSOT Press.

———. 1998. "Paul and Apocalyptic Eschatology." In *The Encyclopedia of Apocalypticism*, edited by John Joseph Collins, Bernard McGinn, and Stephen J. Stein, 345–79. New York: Continuum.

De Jonge, Marinus. 1953. *The Testaments of the Twelve Patriarchs: A Study of Their Text, Composition and Origin*. Assen: Van Gorcum.

Dimant, D. 1984. "Qumran Sectarian Literature." In *Jewish Writings of the Second Temple Period: Apocrypha, Pseudepigrapha, Qumran Sectarian Writings*, edited by Michael E. Stone, 483–550. Philadelphia: Fortress.

Doob Sakenfeld, Katherine. 1992. "Love (Old Testament)." In *The Anchor Bible Dictionary*, edited by David Noel Freedman, 6:375–81. New York: Doubleday.

Doty, William G. 1971. "Interpretation: Parable of the Weeds and Wheat." *Interpretation* 25 (2): 185–93.

———. 1973. *Letters in Primitive Christianity*. Philadelphia: Fortress.

Duff, Paul Brooks. 1991. "Metaphor, Motif, and Meaning: The Rhetorical Strategy behind the Image 'Led in Triumph' in 2 Corinthians 2:14." *Catholic Biblical Quarterly* 53 (1): 79–92.

Duling, Dennis C., and Norman Perrin. 1994. *The New Testament: Proclamation and Parenesis, Myth and History*. New York: Harcourt Brace.

Dunn, James D. G. 1990. *Jesus, Paul, and the Law*. Louisville: Westminster/John Knox.

———. 1991. *The Partings of the Ways: Between Christianity and Judaism and Their Significance for the Character of Christianity*. Philadelphia: Trinity Press.

Eddy, Samuel K. 1961. *The King Is Dead: Studies in the Near Eastern Resistance to Hellenism*. Lincoln: University of Nebraska Press.

Ehrman, Bart D. 1999. *Jesus: Apocalyptic Prophet of the New Millennium*. New York: Oxford University Press.

———. 2008. *The New Testament: A Historical Introduction to the Early Christian Writings*. 4th ed. New York: Oxford University Press.

Engberg-Pedersen, Troels. 2010. *Cosmology and Self in the Apostle Paul: The Material Spirit*. New York: Oxford University Press.

Evans, Craig A. 2000a. "Mark's Incipit and the Priene Calendar Inscription: From Jewish Gospel to Greco-Roman Gospel." *Journal of Greco-Roman Christianity and Judaism* 1: 67–81.

———. 2000b. "Qumran's Messiah: How Important Is He?" In *Religion in the Dead Sea Scrolls*, edited by John Joseph Collins and Robert A. Kugler, 135–49. Grand Rapids: Eerdmans.

Faierstein, Morris M. 1981. "Why Do the Scribes Say That Elijah Must Come First?" *Journal of Biblical Literature* 100 (1): 75–86.

Festinger, Leon. 1989. "When Prophecy Fails." In *Extending Psychological Frontiers: Selected Works of Leon Festinger*, 258–69. New York: Russell Sage Foundation.

———, Henry W. Riecken, and Stanley Schlachter. 1964. *When Prophecy Fails:*

A Social and Psychological Study of a Modern Group That Predicted the Destruction of the World. New York: Harper Torchbooks.

Fiorenza, Elizabeth Schüssler. 1991. Revelation: Vision of a Just World. Minneapolis: Fortress.

Fish, Stanley Eugene. 1994. Self-Consuming Artifacts: The Experience of Seventeenth-Century Literature. Pittsburgh: Duquesne University Press.

Fitzmyer, Joseph A. 1985. "More About Elijah Coming First." Journal of Biblical Literature 104 (2): 295–96.

———. 1993. Romans: A New Translation with Introduction and Commentary. New York: Doubleday.

———. 1995. The Biblical Commission's Document "The Interpretation of the Bible in the Church": Text and Commentary. Roma: Pontificio Istituto Biblico.

———. 2007. The One Who Is to Come. Grand Rapids: Eerdmans.

Forsyth, Neil. 1987. The Old Enemy: Satan and the Combat Myth. Princeton: Princeton University Press.

Frend, W. H. C. 1965. Martyrdom and Persecution in the Early Church: A Study of Conflict from the Maccabees to Donatus. Oxford: Blackwell.

Funk, Robert W. 1969. "Apocalyptic as an Historical and Theological Problem in Current New Testament Scholarship." Journal of Theology and Church 6: 175–91.

———. 1996. Honest to Jesus: Jesus for a New Millennium. San Francisco: HarperSanFrancisco.

———. 1998. The Acts of Jesus: The Search for the Authentic Deeds of Jesus. San Francisco: HarperSanFrancisco.

———, and Roy W. Hoover. 1993. The Five Gospels: The Search for the

Authentic Words of Jesus. New York: Macmillan.

Gager, John G. 1983. The Origins of Anti-Semitism: Attitudes toward Judaism in Pagan and Christian Antiquity. New York: Oxford University Press.

Gammie, John G. 1974. "Spatial and Ethical Dualism in Jewish Wisdom and Apocalyptic Literature." Journal of Biblical Literature 93 (3): 356–85.

———. 1989. Holiness in Israel. Minneapolis: Fortress.

Gärtner, Bertil. 1965. The Temple and the Community in Qumran and the New Testament. Cambridge: Cambridge University Press.

Gaventa, Beverly Roberts. 1986. From Darkness to Light: Aspects of Conversion in the New Testament. Philadelphia: Fortress.

Georgi, Dieter. 1986. The Opponents of Paul in Second Corinthians. Philadelphia: Fortress.

———. 1991. Remembering the Poor: The History of Paul's Collection for Jerusalem. Nashville: Abingdon.

Goff, Matthew. 2005. "Discerning Trajectories: 4QInstruction and the Sapiential Background of the Sayings Source Q." Journal of Biblical Literature 124 (4): 657–73.

Goldstein, J. 1981. "Jewish Acceptance and Rejection of Hellenism," in Jewish and Christian Self-Definition, edited by E. P. Sanders, 2:64–87. London: SCM.

Gombis, Timothy G. 2007. "The 'Transgressor' and the 'Curse of the Law': The Logic of Paul's Argument in Galatians 2–3." New Testament Studies 53 (1): 81–93.

Grabbe, Lester L., and Robert D. Haak. 2003. Knowing the End from the Beginning: The Prophetic, the Apocalyptic, and *Their Relationships*. New York: T&T Clark.

Gruen, Erich S. 1998. *Heritage and Hellenism: The Reinvention of Jewish Tradition*. Berkeley: University of California Press.

Gruenwald, Ithamar. 1980. *Apocalyptic and Merkavah Mysticism*. Leiden: Brill.

Gunkel, Hermann. 2006. *Creation and Chaos in the Primeval Era and the Eschaton: A Religio-Historical Study of Genesis 1 and Revelation 12*, translated by K. William Whitney Jr. Grand Rapids: Eerdmans.

Hanson, Paul. 1976a. "Apocalypse, Genre," in *The Interpreter's Dictionary of the Bible*, edited by K. Crim, *Supplement* 27–28. Nashville: Abingdon.

———. 1976b. "Apocalypticism." In *The Interpreters Dictionary of the Bible*, edited by K. Crim, *Supplement* 28–34. Nashville: Abingdon.

———. 1977. "Rebellion in Heaven, Azazel and Euhemeristic Heroes in 1 Enoch 6–11." *Journal of Biblical Literature* 96: 195–233.

Harrington, Hannah K. 2000. "The Halakah and Religion of Qumran." In *Religion in the Dead Sea Scrolls*, edited by John Joseph Collins and Robert A. Kugler, 74–89. Grand Rapids: Eerdmans.

Harris, William V. 1989. *Ancient Literacy*. Cambridge: Harvard University Press.

Hartman, Lars, and Alexander Di Lella. 1978. *The Book of Daniel*. New York: Doubleday.

Harvey, A. E. 1982. *Jesus and the Constraints of History*. Philadelphia: Westminster.

Healy, Joseph P. 1992. "Faith (Old Testament)," in *The Anchor Bible Dictionary*, edited by David Noel Freedman, 6:744–49. New York: Doubleday.

Hemer, Colin J. 1986. *The Letters to the Seven Churches of Asia in Their Local Setting*. Sheffield: JSOT Press.

Hengel, Martin. 1974. *Judaism and Hellenism: Studies in Their Encounter in Palestine during the Early Hellenistic Period*. 1st English ed. 2 vols. London: SCM.

———. 2000. "Qumran and Hellenism." In *Religion in the Dead Sea Scrolls*, edited by John Joseph Collins and Robert A. Kugler, 46–56. Grand Rapids: Eerdmans.

Hezser, Catherine. 2001. *Jewish Literacy in Roman Palestine*. Tübingen: Mohr Siebeck.

Himmelfarb, Martha. 1983. *Tours of Hell: An Apocalyptic Form in Jewish and Christian Literature*. Philadelphia: Fortress.

———. 1993. *Ascent to Heaven in Jewish and Christian Apocalypses*. New York: Oxford University Press.

———. 2007. "Temple and Priests in the *Book of the Watchers*, the *Animal Apocalypse*, and the *Apocalypse of Weeks*." In *Early Enoch Literature*, edited by Gabriele Boccaccini and John Joseph Collins, 219–35. Boston: Brill.

Hooker, Morna Dorothy. 1990. *From Adam to Christ: Essays on Paul*. Cambridge: Cambridge University Press.

Horsley, Richard A. 1985. "'Like One of the Prophets of Old': Two Types of Popular Prophets at the Time of Jesus." *Catholic Biblical Quarterly* 47: 435–63.

———. 1986. "Popular Prophetic Movements at the Time of Jesus: Their Principal Features and Social Origins." *Journal for the Study of the New Testament* 26: 3–27.

———. 1991. "Q and Jesus: Assumptions, Approaches, and Analyses." *Semeia* 55: 175–209.

———. 1993. *Jesus and the Spiral of Violence: Popular Jewish Resistance in Roman Palestine*. Minneapolis: Fortress.

———. 1997. *Paul and Empire: Religion and Power in Roman Imperial Society*. Harrisburg, PA: Trinity Press.

———. 1998. "The Kingdom of God and the Renewal of Israel: Synoptic Gospels, Jesus Movements, and Apocalypticism." In *The Encyclopedia of Apocalypticism*, edited by John Joseph Collins, Bernard McGinn, and Stephen J. Stein, 1:303–44. New York: Continuum.

———. 2009. *Covenant Economics: A Biblical Vision of Justice for All*. Louisville: Westminster John Knox.

———. 2010a. *Jesus and the Powers: Conflict, Covenant, and the Hope of the Poor*. Minneapolis: Fortress.

———. 2010b. *Revolt of the Scribes: Resistance and Apocalyptic Origins*. Minneapolis: Fortress.

———, and Jonathan A. Draper. 1999. *Whoever Hears You Hears Me: Prophets, Performance, and Tradition in Q*. Harrisburg, PA: Trinity Press.

Humphreys, W. Lee. 1973. "A Life-Style for Diaspora: A Study of the Tales of Esther and Daniel." *Journal of Biblical Literature* 92 (2): 211–23.

Hunt, Alice. 2006. *Missing Priests: The Zadokites in Tradition and History*. New York: T&T Clark.

Hurtado, Larry W. 1988. *One God, One Lord*. Philadelphia: Fortress.

Johnson Hodge, Caroline E. 2007. *If Sons, Then Heirs: A Study of Kinship and Ethnicity in the Letters of Paul*. New York: Oxford University Press.

Johnson, Luke Timothy. 1975. *Studies on the Testaments of the Twelve Patriarchs: Text and Interpretation*. Leiden: Brill.

———. 1978. *The Testaments of the Twelve Patriarchs: A Critical Edition of the Greek Text*. Leiden: Brill.

———. 1989. "The New Testament's Anti-Jewish Slander and the Conventions of Ancient Polemic." *Journal of Biblical Literature* 108 (3): 419–41.

Juel, Donald W. 1977. *Messiah and Temple: The Trial of Jesus in the Gospel of Mark*. Missoula, MT: Scholars Press.

Kampen, John. 1988. *The Hasideans and the Origin of Pharisaism: A Study on First and Second Maccabees*. Atlanta: Scholars Press.

Käsemann, Ernst. 1968. *The Testament of Jesus: A Study of the Gospel of John in the Light of Chapter 17*. Philadelphia: Fortress.

Klauck, Hans-Josef. 2001. "Do They Never Come Back? Nero Redivivus and the Apocalypse of John." *Catholic Biblical Quarterly* 63 (4): 683–98.

Klawans, Jonathan. 2000. *Impurity and Sin in Ancient Israel*. New York: Oxford University Press.

———. 2006. *Purity, Sacrifice, and the Temple: Symbolism and Supersessionism in the Study of Ancient Judaism*. New York: Oxford University Press.

Kloppenborg, John. 1987. *The Formation of Q: Trajectories in Ancient Wisdom Collections*. Philadelphia: Fortress.

Knibb, Michael. 1976. "The Exile in the Intertestamental Period." *Heythrop Journal* 17: 253–72.

Knust, Jennifer Wright. 2006. *Abandoned to Lust: Sexual Slander and Ancient Christianity*. Gender, Theory, and Religion. New York: Columbia University Press.

Koch, Klaus. 1972. *The Rediscovery of Apocalyptic: A Polemical Work on a Neglected Area of Biblical Studies and Its Damaging Effects on Theology and Philosophy*. London: SCM.

Koester, Craig R. 2008. "Roman Slave Trade and the Critique of Babylon in Revelation 18." *Catholic Biblical Quarterly* 70 (4): 766–86.

Kugler, Robert A. 2000. "Rewriting Rubrics: Sacrifice and the Religion of Qumran." In *Religion in the Dead Sea Scrolls*, edited by John Joseph Collins and Robert A. Kugler, 90–112. Grand Rapids: Eerdmans.

Kurfess, A. 1965. "Christian Sibyllines." In *New Testament Apocrypha*, edited by Wilhelm Schneemelcher, 2:703–45. Philadelphia: Westminster.

Laato, Antti. 1992. "Psalm 132 and the Development of the Jerusalemite/Israelite Royal Ideology." *Catholic Biblical Quarterly* 54 (1): 49–66.

Lakoff, George, and Mark Johnson. 1980. *Metaphors We Live By.* Chicago: University of Chicago Press.

Levine, Amy-Jill. 1988. *The Social and Ethnic Dimensions of Matthean Salvation History.* Lewiston, NY: Edwin Mellen.

———. 1999. "Anti-Judaism and the Gospel of Matthew." In *Anti-Judaism and the Gospels*, edited by William R. Farmer, 9–36. Harrisburg, PA: Trinity Press.

Lieberman, Saul. 1950. *Hellenism in Jewish Palestine.* New York: Jewish Theological Seminary.

Lincoln, Bruce. 1999. *Theorizing Myth: Narrative, Ideology, and Scholarship.* Chicago: University of Chicago Press.

Loew, Cornelius Richard. 1967. *Myth, Sacred History, and Philosophy: The Pre-Christian Religious Heritage of the West.* New York: Harcourt.

Lücke, F. 1832. *Versuch einer Vollständigen Einleitung in die Offenbarung Johannis und in die gesamte apokalyptische Literatur.* Bonn: Weber.

Luomanen, Petri. 1998. "Corpus Mixtum—an Appropriate Description of Matthew's Community." *Journal of Biblical Literature* 117 (3): 469–80.

MacRae, George W. 1978. "Heavenly Temple and Eschatology in the Letter to the Hebrews." *Semeia* 12: 179–99.

Magness, Jodi. 2002. *The Archaeology of Qumran and the Dead Sea Scrolls: Studies in the Dead Sea Scrolls and Related Literature.* Grand Rapids: Eerdmans.

———. 2004. *Debating Qumran: Collected Essays on Its Archaeology.* Leuven: Peeters.

Malchow, Bruce V. 1984. "The Messenger of the Covenant in Mal 3:1." *Journal of Biblical Literature* 103 (2): 252–55.

Malina, Bruce J. 1981. *The New Testament World: Insights from Cultural Anthropology.* Atlanta: John Knox.

———. 1995. *On the Genre and Message of Revelation: Star Visions and Sky Journeys.* Peabody, MA: Hendrickson.

Martin, Dale B. 1990. *Slavery as Salvation: The Metaphor of Slavery in Pauline Christianity.* New Haven: Yale University Press.

———. 2004. *Inventing Superstition: From the Hippocrats to the Christians.* Cambridge: Harvard University Press.

———. 2006. "Heterosexism and the Interpretation of Romans 1:18–32." In *Sex and the Single Savior: Gender and Sexuality in Biblical Interpretation*, 51–64. Louisville: Westminster John Knox.

Martin, Ralph P. 1967. *Carmen Christi: Philippians 2:5–11 in Recent Interpretation and in the Setting of Early Christian Worship.* Cambridge: Cambridge University Press.

Martyn, J. Louis. 1967. "Epistemology at the Turn of the Ages: 2 Corinthians

5:16." In *Christian History and Interpretation*, edited by John Knox, William Reuben Farmer, C. F. D. Moule, and Richard R. Niebuhr, 269–87. Cambridge: Cambridge University Press.

———. 1985. "Apocalyptic Antinomies in Paul's Letter to the Galatians." *New Testament Studies* 31 (3): 410–24.

———. 2000. "The Apocalyptic Gospel in Galatians." *Interpretation* 54 (3): 246–66.

McCutcheon, Russell T. 1999. *The Insider/Outsider Problem in the Study of Religion: A Reader*. New York: Cassell.

McGinn, Bernard. 1994. *Anti-Christ: Two Thousand Years of the Human Fascination with Evil*. San Francisco: HarperSanFrancisco.

McIver, Robert K. 1995. "The Parable of the Weeds among the Wheat (Matt. 13:24–30, 36–43) and the Relationship between the Kingdom and the Church as Portrayed in the Gospel of Matthew." *Journal of Biblical Literature* 114 (4): 643–59.

Meeks, Wayne. 1972. "The Man from Heaven in Johannine Sectarianism." *Journal of Biblical Literature* 91: 44–72.

Meier, John P. 1979. *The Vision of Matthew: Christ, Church, and Morality in the First Gospel*. New York: Paulist Press.

———. 1991. *The Roots of the Problem and the Person*. Vol. 1 of *A Marginal Jew: Rethinking the Historical Jesus*. New York: Doubleday.

———. 1994. *Mentor, Message, and Miracles*. Vol. 2 of *A Marginal Jew: Rethinking the Historical Jesus*. New York: Doubleday.

———. 2001. *Companions and Competitors*. Vol. 3 of *A Marginal Jew: Rethinking the Historical Jesus*. New York: Doubleday.

Metzger, Bruce Manning. 1971. *A Textual Commentary on the Greek New Testament*. 3rd ed. New York: United Bible Societies.

Milgrom, Jacob. 1991. *Leviticus 1–16: A New Translation with Introduction and Commentary*. New York: Doubleday.

———. 2000. *Leviticus 17–22: A New Translation with Introduction and Commentary*. New York: Doubleday.

———. 2001. *Leviticus 23–27: A New Translation with Introduction and Commentary*. New York: Doubleday.

Miller, Robert J. 2001. *The Apocalyptic Jesus: A Debate*. Santa Rosa, CA: Polebridge.

Milne, Pamela J., and John Joseph Collins. 2006. "Daniel." In *The HarperCollins Study Bible*, 1168–92. San Francisco: HarperSanFrancisco.

Mounce, Robert H. 1977. *The Book of Revelation*. Grand Rapids: Eerdmans.

Murphy, Frederick J. 1985. *The Structure and Meaning of Second Baruch*. Atlanta: Scholars Press.

———. 1986. "Sapiential Elements in the Syriac Apocalypse of Baruch." *Jewish Quarterly Review* 76 (4): 311–27.

———. 1998. *Fallen Is Babylon: The Revelation to John (Apocalypse)*. Philadelphia: Trinity Press.

———. 2002. *Early Judaism: The Exile to the Time of Jesus*. Peabody, MA: Hendrickson.

———. 2005. *An Introduction to Jesus and the Gospels*. Nashville: Abingdon.

Murphy-O'Connor, J. 1996. *Paul: A Critical Life*. New York: Clarendon.

———. 2009. *Becoming Human Together: The Pastoral Anthropology of St. Paul*. 3rd ed. Atlanta: Society of Biblical Literature.

Mussies, G. 1980. "The Greek of the Book of Revelation." In *L'apocalypse johannique et l'apocalyptique dans le Nouveau Testament*, 167–77. Louvain: University Press.

Nickelsburg, George W. E. 1998. "Enochic Wisdom: An Alternative to the Mosaic Torah?" In *Hesed Ve-Emet*, 123–32. Atlanta: Scholars Press.

———. 2000. "Apocalyptic Texts." In *Encyclopedia of the Dead Sea Scrolls*, edited by Lawrence H. Schiffman and James C. VanderKam, 1:29–34. New York: Oxford University Press.

———. 2001. *1 Enoch: A Commentary on the Book of 1 Enoch*. Hermeneia. Minneapolis: Fortress.

———. 2005a. "Response to Sarah Tanzer." In *Conflicted Boundaries in Wisdom and Apocalypticism*, edited by Lawrence M. Wills and Benjamin G. Wright, 51–54. Atlanta: Society of Biblical Literature.

———. 2005b. "Wisdom and Apocalypticism in Early Judaism: Some Points for Discussion." In *Conflicted Boundaries in Wisdom and Apocalypticism*, edited by Lawrence M. Wills and Benjamin G. Wright, 17–37. Atlanta: Society of Biblical Literature.

———2006. *Resurrection, Immortality, and Eternal Life in Intertestamental Judaism*. 2nd ed. Cambridge: Harvard University Press.

———. 2007. "Enochic Wisdom and Its Relationship to the Mosaic Torah." In *Early Enoch Literature*, 81–94. Boston: Brill.

Nickelsburg, George W. E., and James C. VanderKam. 2011. *1 Enoch 2: A Commentary on the Book of Enoch Chapters 37–82*. Hermeneia. Minneapolis: Fortress.

Nock, Arthur Darby. 1933. *Conversion: The Old and the New in Religion from Alexander the Great to Augustine of Hippo*. London: Oxford University Press.

Olson, Daniel C. 1997. "'Those Who Have Not Defiled Themselves with Women': Revelation 14:4 and the Book of Enoch." *Catholic Biblical Quarterly* 59: 492–510.

Olyan, Saul. 1993. *A Thousand Thousands Served Him: Exegesis and the Naming of Angels in Ancient Judaism*. Tübingen: Mohr Siebeck.

Patrich, Joseph. 2000. "Archeology." In *Encyclopedia of the Dead Sea Scrolls*, edited by Lawrence H. Schiffman and James C. VanderKam, 1:57–63. New York: Oxford University Press.

Patte, Daniel. 1983. *Paul's Faith and the Power of the Gospel: A Structural Introduction to the Pauline Letters*. Philadelphia: Fortress.

Patterson, Stephen J. 1993. *The Gospel of Thomas and Jesus*. Sonoma, CA: Polebridge Press.

———. 1998. *The God of Jesus: The Historical Jesus and the Search for Meaning*. Harrisburg, PA: Trinity Press.

Perrin, Norman. 1969. *What Is Redaction Criticism?* Philadelphia: Fortress.

Peters, F. E. 1971. *The Harvest of Hellenism: A History of the Near East from Alexander the Great to the Triumph of Christianity*. New York: Simon & Schuster.

Pfann, Stephen J. 2000. "Archeological Surveys." In *Encyclopedia of the Dead Sea Scrolls*, edited by Lawrence H. Schiffman and James C. VanderKam, 1:52–57. New York: Oxford University Press.

Plevnik, Joseph. 1997. *Paul and the Parousia: An Exegetical and Theological Investigation*. Peabody, MA: Hendrickson.

———. 2009. *What Are They Saying about Paul and the End Time?* New York: Paulist Press.

Poirier, John C. 2003. "Purity beyond the Temple in the Second Temple Era." *Journal of Biblical Literature* 122: 247–65.

Porter, Stanley E. 2001. "Millenarian Thought in the First-Century Church." In *Christian Millenarianism: From the Early Church to Waco*, edited by Stephen Hunt, 62–76. Bloomington, IN: Indiana University Press.

Portier-Young, Anathea. 2011. *Apocalypse against Empire: Theologies of Resistance in Early Judaism.* Grand Rapids: Eerdmans.

Potter, D. S. 1992a. "Persecution of the Early Church." In *The Anchor Bible Dictionary*, edited by David Noel Freedman, 6:231–35. New York: Doubleday.

———. 1992b. "Smyrna (Place)." In *The Anchor Bible Dictionary*, edited by David Noel Freedman, 6:73–75. New York: Doubleday.

Price, S. R. F. 1984. *Rituals and Power: The Roman Imperial Cult in Asia Minor.* Cambridge: Cambridge University Press.

Pritchard, James B. 1969. *Ancient Near Eastern Texts Relating to the Old Testament.* 3rd ed. Princeton: Princeton University Press.

Propp, Vladimir. 1968. *Morphology of the Folk Tale.* Austin: University of Texas Press.

Qimron, Elisha, and John Strugnell. 1985. "An Unpublished Halakhic Letter from Qumran." In *Biblical Archaeology Today*, 400–407. Jerusalem: Israel Exploration Society.

———. 1994. *Qumran Cave 4. V 5, Miqsat Ma'aśe Ha-Torah.* Oxford: Clarendon.

Räisänen, Heikki. 1983. *Paul and the Law.* Tübingen: J.C.B. Mohr.

Rappaport, Uriel. 1992. "Menelaus (Person)." In *The Anchor Bible Dictionary*, edited by David Noel Freedman, 4:694. New York: Doubleday.

Reed, Annette Yoshiko. 2005. *Fallen Angels and the History of Judaism and Christianity: The Reception of Enochic Literature.* Cambridge: Cambridge University Press.

Riesner, Rainer. 1992. "Essene Gate." In *The Anchor Bible Dictionary*, edited by David Noel Freedman, 2:618–19. New York: Doubleday.

Rowland, Christopher. 1982. *The Open Heaven: A Study of Apocalyptic in Judaism and Early Christianity.* New York: Crossroad.

Ruiz, Jean-Pierre. 1989. *Ezekiel in the Apocalypse: The Transformation of Prophetic Language in Revelation 16, 17–19, 10.* New York: Peter Lang.

Russell, D. S. 1964. *The Method and Message of Jewish Apocalyptic.* Philadelphia: Westminster.

Saldarini, Anthony J. 1975. "Apocalyptic and Rabbinic Literature." *Catholic Biblical Quarterly* 37 (3): 348–58.

———. 1977. "Uses of Apocalyptic in the Mishna and Tosepta." *Catholic Biblical Quarterly* 39 (3): 396–409.

———. 1979. "Apocalypses and 'Apocalyptic' in Rabbinic Literature and Mysticism." *Semeia* 14: 187–205.

Sanders, E. P. 1977. *Paul and Palestinian Judaism.* Philadelphia: Fortress.

———. 1985. *Jesus and Judaism.* Philadelphia: Fortress.

———. 1995. *The Historical Figure of Jesus.* New York: Penguin.

Schmalz, Mathew N. 1994. "When Festinger Fails: Prophecy and the Watchtower." *Religion* 24: 293–308.

Schweitzer, Albert. 1912. *Paul and His Interpreters: A Critical History*. London: A&C Black.

———. 1931. *The Mysticism of Paul the Apostle*. New York: H. Holt.

———. 2000. *The Quest of the Historical Jesus*. London: SCM.

Scullion, John J. 1992. "God (Old Testament)." In *The Anchor Bible Dictionary*, edited by David Noel Freedman, 2:1041–48. New York: Doubleday.

Segal, Alan. 1977. *Two Powers in Heaven: Early Rabbinic Reports about Christianity and Gnosticism*. Leiden: Brill.

Seow, C. L. 2003. *Daniel*. Louisville: Westminster John Knox.

Setzer, Claudia. 2005. "Does Paul Need to Be Saved?" *Biblical Interpretation* 13 (3): 289–97.

Slingerland, H. Dixon. 1977. *The Testaments of the Twelve Patriarchs: A Critical History of Research*. Missoula, MT: Scholars Press.

Smith, Dennis E. 1992. "Banquet, Messianic." In *The Anchor Bible Dictionary*, edited by David Noel Freedman, 4:788–91. New York: Doubleday.

Smith, Jonathan Z. 1975. "Wisdom and Apocalyptic." In *Religious Syncretism in Antiquity*, edited by Birger Pearson, 131–56. Missoula, MT: Scholars Press.

Smith, Mark S. 2002. *The Early History of God: Yahweh and the Other Deities in Ancient Israel*. 2nd ed. Grand Rapids: Eerdmans.

Smith, Morton. 1983. "On the History of Apokalypto and Apocalypsis." In *Apocalypticism in the Mediterranean World and the Near East*, edited by David Hellholm, 9–20. Tübingen: Mohr Siebeck.

Stendahl, Krister. 1963. "The Apostle Paul and the Introspective Conscience of the West." *Harvard Theological Review* 56 (3): 199–215.

———. 1976. *Paul among Jews and Gentiles, and Other Essays*. Philadelphia: Fortress.

———. 1993. *Final Account, or, Paul's Letter to the Romans*. Cambridge, MA: University Lutheran Church.

Stevens, Bruce A. 1987. "Why Must the Son of Man Suffer? The Divine Warrior in the Gospel of Mark." *Biblische Zeitschrift* 31 (1): 101–10.

Stone, Michael E. 1976. "Lists of Revealed Things in the Apocalyptic Literature." In *Magnalia Dei*, edited by F. M. Cross, Werner E. Lemke, and Patrick D. Miller, 414–51. Garden City, NY: Doubleday.

———. 1981. "Reactions to Destructions of the Second Temple: Theology, Perception and Conversion." *Journal for the Study of Judaism in the Persian, Hellenistic and Roman Period* 12 (2):195–204.

———. 1990. *Fourth Ezra: A Commentary on the Book of Fourth Ezra*. Minneapolis: Scholars Press.

Stout, Adelaide. 2011. "The Judicial System at Qumran." Unpublished tutorial paper, College of the Holy Cross, Worcester, MA.

Stowers, Stanley Kent. 1994. *A Rereading of Romans: Justice, Jews, and Gentiles*. New Haven, CT: Yale University Press.

Strauss, David Friedrich. 1972. *The Life of Jesus Critically Examined*. Philadelphia: Fortress.

Suter, David W. 1979. "Fallen Angel, Fallen Priest: The Problem of Family Purity in 1 Enoch 6–16." *Hebrew Union College Annual* 50: 115–35.

Swain, Joseph Ward. 1940. "The Theory of the Four Monarchies Opposition History under the Roman Empire." *Classical Philology* 35 (1): 1–21.

Talmon, Shemaryahu. 2000. "Calendars and Mishmarot." In *Encyclopedia of the Dead Sea Scrolls*, edited by Lawrence H. Schiffman and James C. VanderKam, 1:108–17. New York: Oxford University Press.

Tannehill, Robert A. 1985. "Israel in Luke-Acts: A Tragic Story." *Journal of Biblical Literature* 104: 69–85.

Tanzer, Sarah J. 2005. "Response to George Nickelsburg: 'Wisdom and Apocalypticism in Early Judaism.'" In *Conflicted Boundaries in Wisdom and Apocalypticism*, edited by Lawrence M. Wills and Benjamin G. Wright, 39–54. Atlanta: Society of Biblical Literature.

Tcherikover, Victor. 1959. *Hellenistic Civilization and the Jews*. Philadelphia: Jewish Publication Society of America.

Theissen, Gerd. 1982. *The Social Setting of Pauline Christianity: Essays on Corinth*, translated by John H. Schütz. Philadelphia: Fortress.

Thompson, Leonard. 1990. *The Book of Revelation: Apocalypse and Empire*. New York: Oxford University Press.

Throckmorton, Burton Hamilton. 1992. *Gospel Parallels: A Comparison of the Synoptic Gospels*. 5th ed. Nashville: Thomas Nelson.

Tiller, Patrick A. 1993. *A Commentary on the Animal Apocalypse of 1 Enoch*. Atlanta: Scholars Press.

Tobin, Thomas H. 1987. *The Spirituality of Paul*. Wilmington, DE: M. Glazier.

———. 2004. *Paul's Rhetoric in Its Contexts: The Argument of Romans*. Peabody, MA: Hendrickson.

Tomson, Peter J. 1990. *Paul and the Jewish Law: Halakha in the Letters of the Apostle to the Gentiles*. Minneapolis: Fortress.

Townsend, John. 1992. "Education (Greco-Roman Period)." In *The*

Anchor Bible Dictionary, edited by David Noel Freedman, 2:312–17. New York: Doubleday.

Tuckett, Christopher M. 1992. "Q (Gospel Source)." In *The Anchor Bible Dictionary*, edited by David Noel Freedman. 5:567–72. New York: Doubleday.

Tuell, Steven Shawn. 1992. *The Law of the Temple in Ezekiel 40–48*. Atlanta: Scholars Press.

Twelftree, Graham H. 1993. *Jesus the Exorcist: A Contribution to the Study of the Historical Jesus*. Tübingen: Mohr Siebeck.

Ussishkin, David. 1992. "Megiddo (Place)." In *The Anchor Bible Dictionary*, edited by David Noel Freedman, 4:666–79. New York: Doubleday.

VanderKam, James C. 1978. "Enoch Traditions in Jubilees and Other Second-Century Sources." *Society of Biblical Literature Seminar Papers* 13:229–51.

———. 1979. "The Origin, Character, and Early History of the 364-Day Calendar: A Reassessment of Jaubert's Hypotheses." *Catholic Biblical Quarterly* 41 (3): 390–411.

———. 1984. *Enoch and the Growth of an Apocalyptic Tradition*. Washington, DC: Catholic Biblical Association of America.

———. 1995. *Enoch, a Man for All Generations*. Columbia, SC: University of South Carolina Press.

———. 1998. *Calendars in the Dead Sea Scrolls: Measuring Time, The Literature of the Dead Sea Scrolls*. New York: Routledge.

———. 2000. "Apocalyptic Tradition in the Dead Sea Scrolls." In *Religion in the Dead Sea Scrolls*, edited by John Joseph Collins and Robert A. Kugler, 113–34. Grand Rapids: Eerdmans.

————, and Peter W. Flint. 2002. *The Meaning of the Dead Sea Scrolls: Their Significance for Understanding the Bible, Judaism, Jesus, and Christianity*. San Francisco: HarperSan-Francisco.

Vaux, Roland de. 1973. *Archaeology and the Dead Sea Scrolls*. London: Oxford University Press.

Vermès, Géza. 2004. *The Complete Dead Sea Scrolls in English*. Rev. ed. London: Penguin.

————, and Martin Goodman. 1989. *The Essenes: According to the Classical Sources*. Sheffield: JSOT Press.

Vielhauer, Paul. 1965. "Apocalyptic in Early Christianity, Introduction." In *New Testament Apocrypha*, edited by Wilhelm Hennecke, 2:608–41. 2 vols. Philadelphia: Westminster.

Von Rad, Gerhard, and K. C. Hanson. 2005. *From Genesis to Chronicles: Explorations in Old Testament Theology*. Minneapolis: Fortress.

Vorster, Willem S. 1992. "Gospel Genre." In *The Anchor Bible Dictionary*, edited by David Noel Freedman, 2:1077–79. New York: Doubleday.

Weber, Max, A. M. Henderson, and Talcott Parsons. 1947. *The Theory of Social and Economic Organization*. 1st American ed. New York: Oxford University Press.

Weiss, Johannes. 1971. *Jesus' Proclamation of the Kingdom of God*. Philadelphia: Fortress Press.

Westbrook, Raymond. 1992. "Punishment and Crimes (OT and ANE)." In *The Anchor Bible Dictionary*, edited by David Noel Freedman, 5:546–56. New York: Doubleday.

Willis, Wendell. 1987. *The Kingdom of God in 20th-Century Interpretation*. Peabody, MA: Hendrickson.

Wills, Lawrence. 1990. *The Jew in the Court of the Foreign King*. Minneapolis: Fortress.

————, and Benjamin G. Wright. 2005. *Conflicted Boundaries in Wisdom and Apocalypticism*. Atlanta: Society of Biblical Literature.

Wimbush, Vincent L. 1987. *Paul, the Worldly Ascetic: Response to the World and Self-Understanding According to 1 Corinthians 7*. Macon, GA: Mercer University Press.

Wright, Christopher J. H. 1992. "Jubilee, Year of." In *The Anchor Bible Dictionary*, edited by David Noel Freedman, 3:1025–29. New York: Doubleday.

Wright, N. T. 1996. *Jesus and the Victory of God*. Minneapolis: Fortress.

Yarbro Collins, Adela. 1976. *The Combat Myth in the Book of Revelation*. Missoula, MT: Scholars Press.

————. 1980. "Revelation 18: Taunt-Song or Dirge?" In *L'apocalypse johannique et l'apocalyptique dans le Nouveau Testament*, edited by J. Lambrecht, 185–204. Leuven: Leuven University Press.

————. 1984. "Numerical Symbolism in Jewish and Early Christian Apocalyptic Literature." In *Aufstieg und Niedergang der römischen Welt* no. 2.21.3, 1221–87. Berlin: de Gruyter.

————. 1986. *Early Christian Apocalypticism: Genre and Social Setting*. Semeia 36. Decatur, GA: Scholars Press.

————. 1992a. *Is Mark's Gospel a Life of Jesus? The Question of Genre*. Marquette: Marquette University Press.

————. 1992b. "Revelation, Book of." In *The Anchor Bible Dictionary*, edited by David Noel Freedman, 5:694–708. New York: Doubleday.

————. 2003. "Psalms, Philippians 2:6–11, and the Origins of Christology." *Biblical Interpretation* 11 (3/4): 361–72.

————. 2007. *Mark*. Hermeneia. Minneapolis: Fortress.

————. 2009. "Mark's Interpretation of
the Death of Jesus." *Journal of Biblical Literature* 128 (3): 545–54.

————, and John Joseph Collins. 2008.
*King and Messiah as Son of God: Di-
vine, Human, and Angelic Messianic
Figures in Biblical and Related Literature*. Grand Rapids: Eerdmans.

Glossary

abyss. An immense pit, site of punishment, fire, smoke, realm of evil cosmic beings; can be synonymous with the Pit and Sheol.

Adam Christology. Constitutive element of Paul's Christology in which Jesus, the second Adam, is the beginning and embodiment of a new humanity, part of a new creation, that overcomes the alienation between God and humanity (and the physical world) caused by Adam.

Alexander the Great. Hellenized Macedonian who conquered Greece and the Persian empire. His conquests mark the beginning of the Hellenistic period.

angel. Literally, "messenger." A being higher than a human but lower than God.

angelology. Knowledge about angels, their names, and their functions.

Animal Apocalypse. Work written in support of the Maccabean revolution, now part of the *Book of Dreams* in *1 Enoch*.

antichrist. Evil figure who appears toward the end of history and convinces many to abandon righteousness and to worship and follow him. Usually claims to be divine and fools the world through his marvelous powers.

Antiochus IV. Seleucid emperor who persecuted Judaism in 167–164 BCE.

apocalypse. A revelatory narrative in which a secret knowledge about the unseen world and the future is given to a human seer by a superhuman figure, usually either an angel or God.

Apocalypse of Abraham. Apocalypse written around the turn of the second century CE in response to the destruction of Jerusalem.

Apocalypse of Weeks. A short apocalypse divided into ten weeks; part of the Enochic *Book of Dreams.*

apocalypticism. The worldview of apocalypses.

Apocrypha. Collection of books and additions to canonical books accepted as part of the Bible by Catholics (and therefore sometimes called deuterocanonical) but not by Jews and Protestants.

ark of the covenant. Portable shrine symbolizing God's presence that accompanied Israel in the wilderness and was deposited in the Jerusalem temple.

armageddon. According to Rev. 16, the site of the great final battle between the forces of Satan and those of Christ.

Asia Minor. Modern-day Turkey.

Assumption of Moses. See *Testament of Moses.*

astral immortality. Afterlife in the company of the stars, who are thought of as angels.

Astronomical Book. Part of *1 Enoch.* Teaches the secrets of the stars and warns of human errors concerning them and the calendrical errors to which they lead.

Azazel. One of the two leaders of the angelic revolt who descends to earth in the *Book of the Watchers.* He taught a variety of illegitimate sciences, such as metalworking that led to weapon making and cosmetics.

Babylon. Capital of the empire that subjugated and subsequently destroyed Judah, Jerusalem, and its temple in the early sixth century BCE.

Babylonian exile. Removal of the Judahite community to Babylonia in 586 BCE. They were allowed to return by the Persian emperor Cyrus in 538 BCE.

Balaam's prophecy. Prophecy by the gentile prophet Balaam about Israel. The portion about a star and a scepter drew widespread messianic interpretation.

baptism. Ritual washing, which can take different forms. At the temple, at Qumran, and in Jewish daily life it is repeated in ritual circumstances for the sake of purity. John the Baptist's was a one-time affair to prepare the recipient for the coming judgment. In the Christian movement, it became an initiatory ritual uniting one to Christ's death.

Baruch. Secretary of Jeremiah; hero of the apocalypse *2 Baruch.*

Behemoth. Primordial giant land creature.

Beelzebul (also Beelzebub). One of the many names of the prince of demons.

Belial (also Beliar). One of the many names of the prince of demons.

Book of the Watchers. First book in *1 Enoch.* Tells the story of the descent of the angels to earth and the mischief they accomplish.

Cairo Geniza. Storeroom of a Cairo synagogue in which were found important ancient Jewish documents.

canon. List of books accepted as particularly authoritative. Later, the list of biblical books (canonical).

canonical. Belonging to the canon.

cherubim. A form of angel associated with guarding God, found on the ark of the covenant.

chiliasm. Belief in a thousand-year utopia on earth.

Christology. Knowledge about the person and work of Christ.

combat myth. A widely spread genre in the ancient world consisting of the following elements: A rebellious god attacks the head god, thus disrupting cosmic order. The head god is victorious, restoring order, but leaving the possibility of another rebellion, indicating the vulnerability of the cosmic and political order.

cosmogony. Creation myth.

cosmology. Knowledge of the cosmos.

cosmos. Ordered universe.

covenant. Agreement between two parties, often used as a way of conceptualizing the relationship between God and Israel and later of Christianity.

cult. Aspect of religion dealing with public worship, particularly temple, priesthood, sacrifice, hymnody, and public prayer.

Daniel. Ancient seer who is the pseudonymous author of the book of Daniel. Also the title of his apocalypse.

David. First king of the Davidic dynasty; his reign is often idealized and becomes the model for an ideal future.

day, the. Often the day of judgment; frequently qualified as "the Day of the Lord."

Day of Atonement. Major feast of the Jewish liturgical year (Lev. 16) in which the sanctuary is purified of the guilt of the inadvertent sins of the high priest and of the people.

Dead Sea Scrolls. Large collection of ancient texts discovered near the Dead Sea beginning in 1947.

demon. A superhuman figure; denizen of the unseen world. Originally, demons were not necessarily either good or bad. In apocalypses, they are bad.

desert. Uninhabited place; in Israelite and Jewish tradition, symbolic of many things, such as refuge from enemies, place of demons and wild animals, place to renew relationships with God, and so on.

Deuteronomistic History. Joshua, Judges, 1–2 Samuel, 1–2 Kings; a history of Israel from the entry into Canaan to the Babylonian exile; its judgments on history are derived from Deuteronomy.

Devil. The leader of demons; God's adversary and tempter of humanity.

diaspora. Jews living outside the homeland.

diatribe. Greek rhetorical form in which the writer or speaker interacts with an imaginary conversation partner.

Divine Warrior. God as a warrior.

Dream Visions. Part of *1 Enoch* incorporating a fragment of a book of Noah and the entire *Animal Apocalypse*.

dualism. A way of thinking of the cosmos and humanity in binary opposite terms—God (or Michael) and Satan, righteous and sinners, good angels and bad angels, and so on.

Enoch. A favorite apocalyptic seer in whose name many works were written. In Gen. 5, he is of the seventh human generation, is righteous, and after living on earth for 365 years is taken away by God. This makes him an excellent candidate to experience mysteries and come back to earth to reveal them.

1 Enoch. Collection of five originally independent works. The entire collection is apocalyptic in nature.

Enochic Judaism. Judaism as it is manifested in the Enoch literature. Some see it as different in key ways from mainstream Judaism, which emphasizes Torah and the Jerusalem temple and priesthood.

Enuma Elish. A Babylonian creation myth that incorporates the combat myth.

Epistle of Enoch. Last work in *1 Enoch*. Speaks of social injustice where the rich oppress the poor. Assures the righteous of reward and the sinners of punishment.

eschatological scenario. Description of end-time events.

eschatology. Knowledge of the end-time events:

apocalyptic. Similar to prophetic eschatology but with a greater cosmic focus and the inclusion of postmortem rewards and punishments.

prophetic. Culmination of a current historical situation, often involving punishment and restoration of Israel and punishment of its enemies.

eschaton. The culmination of history and the end of the world as we know it.

Essenes. Organized religious group spoken of by Josephus, Pliny the Elder, and Philo, and probably to be identified with the sect behind the Dead Sea Scrolls library.

Ezra. Jewish hero who brought the written Torah from Babylon to Judah in the mid-fifth century BCE. He was a Zadokite priest, a scribe expert in the Torah, and an agent of the Persian crown. Fictitious author of *4 Ezra*, in which he disputes with the angel Uriel and with God about the destruction of Jerusalem by the Babylonians, a device for addressing the destruction under Rome.

four living creatures. Four angelic creatures who carry God's throne, defend God, and appear in many throne scenes. Usually considered a kind of angel.

Fourth Ezra. Apocalypse written around the turn of the second century CE in response to the destruction of Jerusalem.

gehenna. A Jewish name for hell.

gematria. Practice of turning words and names into numbers, based on their numerical equivalents, and of deciphering such numbers.

gentile. Non-Jew.

Gog of Magog. Enemy of Israel in the great final battle of Ezek. 38–39.

hades. Greek name for the underworld.

Hasmoneans. Priestly royal dynasty that ruled Judea and the surrounding lands for much of the century stretching from the middle of the second to the middle of the first centuries BCE.

heavenly books. These are of various types, including records of human deeds, descriptions of eschatological events, lists of those to be saved.

Hellenism. Spread of Greek culture under Alexander the Great and his successors resulting in a mixture of Greek and local cultures.

Hellenistic Reform. Movement by Jewish upper class to Hellenize Jerusalem, begun in 175 BCE.

holy of holies. Innermost and holiest part of the Jerusalem temple. God's earthly dwelling place.

holy ones. Usually angels. In Paul, those in Christ.

Jaoel. Main angel in the *Apocalypse of Abraham*.

Josephus. Jewish historian who lived from 37 to around 100 CE. A Jerusalem priest who was a historian and supplies most of the information we have about first-century-CE Palestinian Judaism.

Jubilees. Apocalypse written around the middle of the second century CE; rewrites parts of Genesis and Exodus. Sometimes called "little Genesis." Emphasizes legal issues.

Jubilee year. Every fiftieth year (Lev. 25), in which debts are forgiven, Jewish slaves are freed, and property is returned to its original owner.

justification. *See* righteousness.

Leviathan. Primordial, gigantic sea creature.

living creatures (four). *See* four living creatures.

Maccabees. Priestly family that revolted against the Seleucids because of Antiochus IV's persecution of Judaism in 167 BCE. They became the Hasmonean dynasty.

Magog. *See* Gog of Magog; in Ezekiel this is the place of which Gog is prince; in other literature he becomes a person alongside Gog.

magos (magicians, magi, magoi). Specialists in mantic wisdom and astrology, associated particularly with the East and Babylonia in particular.

mantic wisdom. The science of divination.

Melchizedek. Mysterious figure who is the king and priest of non-Israelite Jerusalem, to whom Abraham paid tithes, and who is the supposed founder of a line of priests (Ps. 110). Hebrews 7 sees Jesus as a priest in Melchizedek's line, and a text from Qumran portrays Melchizedek as the end-time judge and as a figure very similar to Michael (11Q13).

messiah. One anointed with oil for a specific office or task. Usually a king, but sometimes a priest, less often a prophet.

messianic hope. Expectation of an eschatological savior figure, sometimes called a messiah explicitly, sometimes not.

millennialism (also millenarianism). Belief in a coming millennium.

millennium. Period of a thousand years; such a period that is utopian; derived from Rev. 20.

mystery. General apocalyptic word for what was hidden and is now shown to the seer; especially important for God's plans for history now revealed.

nations. The non-Israelite, non-Jewish peoples.

Nero. Roman emperor (56–68 CE) who persecuted Christians in Rome in 64 CE on the pretext that they set the great fire of Rome. After his disappearance, it was rumored that he had not died.

oracle. Direct communication from a divine being.

pantheon. Group of the highest gods.

parousia. The second coming of Jesus Christ.

Pharaoh. Egyptian king.

Pharisees. Organized religious group existing from just after the Maccabean revolt and an influential group in the formation of rabbinic Judaism after the temple's destruction in 70 CE; particularly concerned for Sabbath observance and food purity. Rivals of the Sadducees.

proto-apocalyptic. Elements from the Hebrew Bible that are not themselves apocalyptic but that contained images, patterns, and symbols that proved very useful in apocalypses.

Psalms of Solomon. Collection of eighteen psalms from the first century BCE, written in response to the taking over of Jerusalem by the Romans. Its last two psalms depict the Davidic messiah in detail.

pseudepigrapha. Writings under false names; noncanonical books that come from Second Temple Judaism beginning around the third century BCE and stretching into the second century CE.

pseudonymity. Writing under a fictitious name.

Ptolemies. Hellenistic dynasty ruling from Egypt.

Q. A sayings source that Matthew and Luke used to supplement Mark; no longer extant.

Qumran. Settlement near the northwest corner of the Dead Sea; the Dead Sea Scrolls were discovered in eleven caves near the settlement.

rapture. The taking up of the righteous so that they escape the tribulation.

realized eschatology. The transferal of things normally belonging to the end of time, like judgment or salvation, to the present.

Revelation (Book of). An apocalypse that is the final book of the Christian Bible.

righteousness. The state of being right with God.

Sadducees. Political and religious interest group in Jerusalem that was associated with the high priest. The name may derive from Zadok.

saints. *See* holy ones.

sanctuary. A holy place; synonym for the Jerusalem temple and its precincts.

Second Baruch. Apocalypse written around the turn of the second century CE in response to the destruction of Jerusalem.

seer. One who "sees" mysterious visions, particularly in an apocalypse.

Seleucids. Hellenistic dynasty ruling from Syria.

seraphim. A type of angel pictured as a winged, flaming serpent, often considered close to God.

Shemyaza. One of the two leaders of the angelic revolt in the *Book of the Watchers*.

sheol. Hebrew Bible word for the underworld. Sometimes called the Pit or the Abyss. In the Hebrew Bible, this is not a site for reward or punishment. All humans end up there in the same situation.

Sibylline Oracles. The sibyl was a female prophet known all over the ancient

Mediterranean. Jews and Christians adopted the genre of a collection of her oracles for their own purposes.

Similitudes of Enoch. First-century CE apocalypse; part of *1 Enoch.* One like a son of man is the major figure in the book. He is judge at the last judgment. He is called the messiah.

Solomon. David's son, second king of the Davidic dynasty; builder of the first Jerusalem temple; called son of God.

stars. Often heavenly, personal beings; sometimes angels.

testament. Last words of a dying patriarch or hero.

Testament of Moses (also called the *Assumption of Moses*). A testament originally written to address the crisis under Antiochus IV and then adapted to the period shortly after Herod the Great's death.

Testaments of the Twelve Patriarchs. Originally a Jewish work, now edited by Christians. Testaments for each of the Israelite patriarchs; contains ethical teaching and eschatological prediction.

theodicy. Defense of God's justice.

theogony. Creation of the gods.

theophany. An appearance of God.

throne scene. A scene featuring God's throne and God upon it. Often used to legitimate the commission and message of a prophet or seer. Becomes important in later Jewish Merkabah (chariot) mysticism.

tribulation. Time of extreme turmoil and suffering introducing the end time.

vaticinia ex eventu. Prophecies after the fact.

watcher. A type of angel, featured in the *Book of the Watchers.*

wilderness. *See* desert.

wisdom:

apocalyptic. Esoteric wisdom available only through direct revelation.

speculative. Reflection taking a more metaphysical turn, sometimes incorporating semidivine figures such as Woman Wisdom.

theological. Traditional wisdom supplemented by revelatory material such as Torah.

traditional. Insight gained from human reason exercised on observation of nature and human behavior.

wrath. God's anger at sin that takes effect through action against sinners; used especially in eschatological contexts.

Yahweh. Proper name of Israel's God.

yeşer. The evil inclination within humans.

Zadokites. Members of a prominent priestly family descended from Zadok, Solomon's high priest; particularly powerful in the postexilic period. Important group at Qumran.

Zion. Flexible term that can refer to the mountain on which the temple is built, to Jerusalem as a whole, or to the people of Israel.

Subject Index

Author Index

417

Index of Ancient Sources

69 142	4:36 146, 341	17:1 175	4:45 187
70 143	5:13 146	17:7 176	4:138 188
70–71 137, 143	5:20–6:34 146	17:8 176	5 188
71 143	5:23–30 146	17:9 176	5:1 189
72:2 133	6:35–9:25 146	17:26 176	5:1–51 189
72–82 3, 125, 132	7 154	17:31 177	5:31 189
80 133	7:12–14 256	17:49 177	5:33 189
80:8 133	7:20 147	17:51 177	5:36 189
83 126	7:44 147	18 175	5:52–110 189
83–84 133	7:118 147	18:9 178	5:107 189
83–90 133	8:36 147		5:111–78 189
85:3 89	9:3 147	**Sybilline Oracles**	5:161 190
85–90 88, 125, 133	10:16 148	1 179	5:167 190
86 89	11–13 230	1–2 179, 189	5:214 190
87 89	11:1–12:51 148	1–8 178	5:225–27 190
88 89	12:3 148	2 179, 180	5:286–433 190
89 89	12:37–38 148	2:154–73 180	5:358–60 191
89:59 90	13 236	2:271–72 180	5:421 191
89:61 90	13:1–58 148	3 181, 184, 186	5:433 191
89:73 90	13:26 149	3–5 179	5:434–531 191
90 90	13:32 149	3:1–96 181	5:435–531 189
90–104 133	13:35–38 149	3:1–97 181	11–14 178, 189
91–108 125	13:37 149	3:11 181	
91:5–7 135	13:52 149	3:19 181	**Testament of Levi**
91:9 135	14 144	3:82 182	2 193
91:9–10 136	14:1–48 149	3:97–161 182	2–5 193, 195
91:11–17 133	14:5–6 149	3:97–349 181	4 194
91:12–17 126	14:25–26 150	3:162–95 181, 183	5 194
92 135	14:45–47 150	3:192–95 183	18 195, 291
92:2 135		3:196–294 181, 183	18:5 195
92:3 134, 135	**Jubilees**	3:214 183	
92:3–5 135	1 167	3:246 183	**Testament of**
92:10 135	1:15–29 167	3:286–94 187	**Moses**
93:1–10 133	1:20 169	3:295 184	1:16–18 172
93:3–14 125	3:10 164	3:295–488 184	3 172
94:7–8 135	3:31 164, 166	3:301–13 184	3:2 110
95:3–7 136	4:5 164	3:350–488 181	4 172
96:4–8 136	4:32 164	3:419–32 184	5 173
97:8–10 135	5:19 169	3:489–91 184	6 172, 173
98:12 135	6:32–38 166	3:489–544 184	6:1 173
98:13–16 136	10 164	3:489–829 181	7 172
99:2 137	20–23 166	3:537 185	8 172, 173
100:4 135	23 167, 168, 291	3:545–656 181, 185	9 172, 173
103:1–2 135	23:26–31 168	3:606–608 186	9:7 173
104:10 137	50:12 166	3:652–66 186	10 122, 172, 173, 248,
		3:657–808 181, 185	291, 310
4 Ezra (2 Esdras)	**Psalms of Solomon**	3:686 186	10:1 173
3–14 143	1 175	3:711 186	10:5 236
3:1–5:19 144	2:26 175	3:807 186	12:4–5 174
3:7 144	17 175	3:808 186	
3:20 145		4 187, 188	

Other Works by Frederick J. Murphy

Books

The Structure and Meaning of Second Baruch. Atlanta: Scholars Press, 1985.

The Religious World of Jesus: An Introduction to Second Temple Palestinian Judaism. Nashville: Abingdon, 1991.

Pseudo-Philo: Rewriting the Bible. New York: Oxford University Press, 1993.

Fallen Is Babylon: The Revelation to John. Philadelphia: Trinity Press International, 1998.

Early Judaism: The Exile to the Time of Jesus. Peabody, MA: Hendrickson, 2002. (A substantial revision of The Religious World of Jesus.)

An Introduction to Jesus and the Gospels. Nashville: Abingdon, 2005.

Articles and Contributions to Books

"Second Baruch and the Romans." Journal of Biblical Literature 104 (1985): 663–69.

"Sapiential Elements in the Syriac Apocalypse of Baruch." Jewish Quarterly Review 76 (1986): 311–27.

"Divine Plan, Human Plan: A Structuring Theme in Pseudo-Philo." Jewish Quarterly Review 77 (1986): 5–15.

"The Temple in the Syriac Apocalypse of Baruch." Journal of Biblical Literature 106 (1987): 671–83.

"God in Pseudo-Philo." Journal for the Study of Judaism in the Persian, Hellenistic, and Roman Period 19 (1988): 1–18.

"Retelling the Bible: Idolatry in Pseudo-Philo." Journal of Biblical Literature 107 (1988): 275–87.

"The Eternal Covenant in Pseudo-Philo." Journal for the Study of the Pseudepigrapha 3 (1988): 43–57.

"Korah's Rebellion in Pseudo-Philo 16." In Of Scribes and Scrolls: Studies on the Hebrew Bible, Intertestamental Judaism, and Christian Origins, edited by Harold W. Attridge, John J. Collins, and Thomas H Tobin, SJ, 111–20. New York: University Press of America, 1990.

"The Book of Revelation." Currents in Research: Biblical Studies 2 (1994): 181–225.

"Apocalypses and Apocalypticism: The State of the Question." Currents in Research: Biblical Studies 2 (1994): 147–79.

"The Martial Option in Pseudo-Philo." Catholic Biblical Quarterly 57 (1995): 676–88.

"Seventy-Times Seven: Jesus's Teaching on Forgiveness." In Toward a Deeper Understanding of

Forgiveness: A Special Collection of Talks from the Inaugural Conference of the Center for Religion, Ethics and Culture, 73–82. Worcester, MA: College of the Holy Cross, 2001.

"The Jewishness of Matthew: Another Look." In When Judaism and Christianity Began: Essays in Memory of Anthony J. Saldarini, edited by Alan J. Avery-Peck, Daniel J. Harrington, and Jacob Neusner, 2:377–403. Boston: Brill, 2004.

Encyclopedia and Dictionary Entries

"Amen"; "angel worship"; "Baruch"; "behemoth"; "Book of Biblical Antiquities (Pseudo-Philo)"; "Cain"; "cup"; "dragon"; "Esau"; "hallelujah"; "heaven"; "heavenly Jerusalem"; "Hezekiah"; "Isaac"; "Isaiah"; "Ishmael"; "Jacob"; "Jeremiah"; "Jesse"; "Jonah"; "Joshua"; "Judah"; "Kenaz"; "Korah"; "leviathan"; "Lot"; "maranatha"; "Second Baruch"; "serpent"; "Seth"; "Solomon"; "wrath of God." In Dictionary of Judaism in the Biblical Period, edited by Jacob Neusner and William Scott Green. New York: Macmillan, 1996.

"Introduction to Apocalyptic Literature." In The New Interpreter's Bible, edited by Leander E. Keck, 7:1-16. Nashville: Abingdon, 1996.

"Pseudo-Philo." In Dictionary of Biblical Criticism, edited by John H. Hayes, 334–35. Nashville: Abingdon, 1999.

"Pseudo-Philo" and "Second Baruch." In Die Religion in Geschichte und Gegenwart, 4th ed., edited by Hanz Dieter Betz et al. Tübingen: J. C. B. Mohr, 1999.

"Second Temple Judaism." In The Blackwell Companion to Judaism, edited by Jacob Neusner and Alan J. Avery-Peck, 58–77. Oxford: Blackwell, 2000.

"Second Temple Judaism." In The Blackwell Reader in Judaism, edited by Jacob Neusner and Alan Avery-Peck, 42–59. Oxford: Blackwell, 2001.

"Pseudo-Philo, Biblical Characters in." In The Encyclopedia of Judaism, 2nd ed., edited by Jacob Neusner, Alan J. Avery-Peck, and William Green, 3:2055–6. Leiden and Boston: Brill, 2005.

"Jew/Jews" and "Palestine and Israel, terminology for." In The New Interpreter's Dictionary of the Bible, edited by Katharine Doob Sakenfeld. Nashville: Abingdon, 2009.

"Pseudo-Philo" and "faith, faithfulness." In The Eerdmans Dictionary of Early Judaism, edited by John J. Collins and Daniel Harlow. Grand Rapids: Eerdmans, 2010.

Lightning Source UK Ltd.
Milton Keynes UK
UKHW010634201020
371896UK00001B/3

9 780801 039782